THE TRANSFORMATION OF CONSUMER LAW AND POLICY IN EUROPE

This book analyses the transformation of consumer law and policy in Europe from four perspectives: first, the temporal transformation, ie, changes that can be tracked from the turn of the millennium; secondly, the substantive dimension, ie, changes in the scope of the rights and remedies provided by consumer law, as well as the underpinning values; thirdly, the institutional dimension, ie, changes in the role of national courts, national Parliaments, consumer agencies, and consumer organisations; and fourth, the procedural element, ie, the shift from individual enforcement via courts to enforcement by public regulators, consumer associations, alternative dispute resolution and the development of collective enforcement exercised by consumer agencies and/or consumer organisations.

With contributions by leading consumer law scholars from across Europe, this book is a fascinating account of how consumer law has often been shaped by national as much as European interests.

The Transformation of Consumer Law and Policy in Europe

Edited by

Hans-W Micklitz

and

Christian Twigg-Flesner

·HART·

OXFORD · LONDON · NEW YORK · NEW DELHI · SYDNEY

HART PUBLISHING

Bloomsbury Publishing Plc

Kemp House, Chawley Park, Cumnor Hill, Oxford, OX2 9PH, UK

1385 Broadway, New York, NY 10018, USA

29 Earlsfort Terrace, Dublin 2, Ireland

HART PUBLISHING, the Hart/Stag logo, BLOOMSBURY and the Diana logo are
trademarks of Bloomsbury Publishing Plc

First published in Great Britain 2023

A catalogue record for this book is available from the British Library.

A catalogue record for this book is available from the Library of Congress.

Library of Congress Control Number: 2023943195

ISBN: HB: 978-1-50996-302-7
        ePDF: 978-1-50996-304-1
        ePub: 978-1-50996-303-4

Typeset by Compuscript Ltd, Shannon

To find out more about our authors and books visit www.hartpublishing.co.uk.
Here you will find extracts, author information, details of forthcoming events
and the option to sign up for our newsletters.

PREFACE

This volume of essays is the third and final element in a project that charts the development of consumer law and policy in Europe from the end of the Second World War up to the present day (2023). This project was the brainchild of Hans-W Micklitz, who was in charge of the first two elements, but for this final element he was joined by Christian Twigg-Flesner.

The objective of this volume is to analyse the transformation of consumer law and policy in Europe since the start of this millennium. We think it is worthwhile to summarise the process we followed to arrive at this volume. First, we set out what we regarded as the broad strands of this transformation, and invited consumer law scholars from across Europe to participate. In the first instance, we asked those interested in joining us to sketch their ideas. We provided feedback to everyone and then arranged an online workshop in January 2022 to discuss ideas in more depth. We then invited contributors to flesh out their papers and arranged a hybrid workshop, held at the University of Warwick, in April 2022. After the workshop, contributors were asked to prepare full drafts of their papers in light of the workshop discussions. After another round of feedback, final versions of the papers were prepared between late 2022 and Spring 2023. These form the present volume, comprising 15 papers. Along the way, there were several other scholars who presented their ideas, but unfortunately they were not able to contribute to this volume. We are grateful for their input to the earlier phases of this project.

As editors of this volume, we are especially grateful to all the contributors who worked extremely hard to prepare papers that aligned well with the transformation focus we had taken, and who carefully responded to our feedback on draft versions of their chapters. We have learned a lot and recognised transformative themes that had not occurred to us when we embarked on this project. In finalising the papers, we benefitted hugely from the editorial work undertaken by Evgenia Ralli (Lecturer at Coventry Law School) and the thorough language reviews by Christopher Goddard (SVA Lingva Project). We thank Hart Publishing, and especially Roberta Bassi and Sinead Moloney, for their constant support of this project, which reaches beyond what editors might expect from publishing houses.

Significant financial backing for this project was provided by the *Journal of Consumer Policy*, of which we are both co-editors. We thank our fellow co-editors (Alan Mathios, Lucia Reisch and John Thøgersen) for agreeing to support this project through all these years.

Finally, academic authors know the importance of the love and encouragement of family. Their patience and occasional distractions are invaluable. Hans would like to thank Alexa, and Christian would like to thank Paul, for their patience and for their constant support, which make our lives and work so much easier.

We hope that this book will spark a conversation about (EU) consumer law and what lies ahead, between the European Commission and the Member States, together with the consumer law community.

Hans-W Micklitz
Christian Twigg-Flesner
Berlin, Florence/Coventry
May 2023

CONTENTS

LIST OF CONTRIBUTORS

Mateja Durovic is Professor of Law, King's College London.

Geraint Howells is Executive Dean, University of Galway; Visiting Professor of Commercial Law, University of Manchester.

Eleni Kaprou is Lecturer in Business Law, Queen Mary University of London.

Vanessa Mak is Professor of Civil Law, Leiden University.

Jana Vábek Markova is Accountant, Masaryk University (MUNI).

Hans-Wolfgang Micklitz is Part-time Professor of Economic Law, Law Department and the Robert Schuman Centre for Advanced Studies, European University Institute.

Emilia Mišćenić is Professor, Department of European and Private International Law, Faculty of Law, University of Rijeka.

Damjan Možina is Professor, University of Ljubljana.

Charlotte Pavillon is Professor of Private Law, University of Groningen.

Elise Poillot is Professor of Civil Law, University of Luxembourg.

Paschal Pichonnaz is Professor, University of Fribourg (Switzerland); President of the European Law Institute.

Peter Rott is Professor of Civil Law, Commercial Law and Information Law, Carl von Ossietzky University of Oldenburg.

Karin Sein is Professor of Civil Law, University of Tartu.

Markéta Selucká is Professor, Masaryk University (MUNI).

Cătălin Gabriel Stănescu is Associate Professor, University of Southern Denmark

Evelyne Terryn is Professor, KU Leuven and guest professor, UHasselt.

Christian Twigg-Flesner is Professor of Contract and Consumer Law, University of Warwick.

1

Transformation of Consumer Law and Policy in Europe

HANS-W MICKLITZ AND CHRISTIAN TWIGG-FLESNER

This book is the third and final volume in a trilogy examining the evolution of consumer law and policy in Europe.[1] The previous two volumes explored this process over a 50-year period from 1950 right up to the turn of the millennium, first by record-ing the oral history of consumer law in Europe through the voices of its fathers and mothers, and then through a more analytical approach to the making of consumer law and policy in the period after the Second World War. Over half a century, consumer policy took shape at national level and gradually resulted in the development of national consumer laws. However, as early as the mid-1970s, consumer policy caught the eye of the European Union (EU; at that time the European Economic Community). After tentative steps from 1985, the EU adopted two landmark consumer law directives in the 1990s,[2] before intensifying its legislative activity in terms both of breadth and depth early in the new millennium. The year 2000 marked a break-even point in consumer law, as well as in other areas, through the combination of three non-legally binding documents – the Lisbon Strategy 2000,[3] the Charter of Fundamental Rights 2000[4] and the White Paper on Governance in 2001.[5] The Lisbon Council introduced economic efficiency and social inclusion, the Charter enhanced the ongoing constitutionalisation of consumer rights in particular and the White Paper on Governance enlarged the tool

---

[1] See H-W Micklitz et al (eds), *The Fathers and Mothers of Consumer Law and Policy in Europe: The Foundational Years 1950–1980* (EUI, 2019); and H-W Micklitz (ed), *The Making of Consumer Law and Policy in Europe* (Hart Publishing, 2021).

[2] Council Directive 93/13/EEC of 5 April 1993 on unfair terms in consumer contracts [1993] OJ L95/29 and Directive 1999/44/EC of the European Parliament and of the Council of 25 May 1999 on certain aspects of the sale of consumer goods and associated guarantees [1999] OJ L171/12. The former is still in force at the time of writing, whereas the latter has since been replaced by Directive (EU) 2019/771 of the European Parliament and of the Council of 20 May 2019 on certain aspects concerning contracts for the sale of goods, amending Regulation (EU) 2017/2394 and Directive 2009/22/EC, and repealing Directive 1999/44/EC [2019] OJ L136/28.

[3] The Lisbon Strategy of 2000 (Lisbon European Council 23–24 March 2000, Presidency conclusions) at www.europarl.europa.eu/summits/lis1_en.htm (accessed 28 April 2023).

[4] Charter on Fundamental Rights [2000] OJ C364/1.

[5] White Paper on Governance, 25 July 2001, COM(2001) 428.

box of legal measures through governance strategies.[6] The task for this volume is to pick up the thread at the turn of the millennium, when consumer law and policy were still predominantly within the domain of national legislatures, albeit increasingly taking the shape of an EU-and-Member-States hybrid. The EU took over a much more dominant role in aligning consumer law with its overall political agenda, 'to turn the EU into the most competitive economy of the world'.[7]

The key question to be explored through the various contributions is *whether* and, more importantly, *how* consumer law and policy have been *transformed* over the first two decades or so of this millennium. Indeed, it is our starting assumption that there has been a transformation and that this transformation has taken a variety of forms. The contributions to this volume offer a rich account of the various dimensions of the transformation of consumer law and policy. But it is essential that we set out what we mean by 'transformation', why we posit that there has been a transformation of consumer law and policy, and that we also identify what seem to us to be the dominant parameters of this transformation.

We have used the term 'transformation' deliberately, because it is our contention that there has been more than merely a progressive development of consumer law and policy along a steady trajectory.[8] 'Transformation' has a variety of meanings depending on the context within which it is used.[9] However, in all these different contexts, the notion of transformation implies a (complete) change of something with regard to its form, shape, appearance, character, condition or substance – in other words, a significant departure from the established path. As we argue that consumer law and policy have undergone a transformation, we need first to set out the *drivers* behind this process, that is, what has happened to consumer law and policy in Europe to have brought about transformation.

I. Three Drivers of Transformation of Consumer Law and Policy in Europe

There are *three key drivers* of the transformation we seek to investigate in this volume: the EU's full harmonisation approach; the twin challenges of digitalisation and sustainable consumption; and, finally, crisis management through consumer law to deal with the consequences of the 2008 financial crisis as well as the Covid pandemic.

---

[6] F Cafaggi and H Muir-Watt (eds), *Making European Private Law. Governance Design* (Edward Elgar, 2008); F Cafaggi and H Muir-Watt (eds), *The Regulatory Function of European Private Law* (Edward Elgar, 2009).

[7] This is the language of the Lisbon European Council.

[8] Indeed, we might consider 'transformation' to be a variant of 'disruption' of consumer law. cf CM Christensen, *The Innovator's Dilemma* (Harvard Business Review Press, 1997) on disruption generally, and the notion of 'legal disruption' put forward in Ch Twigg-Flesner, 'The Potential of the COVID-19 Crisis to Cause Legal "Disruption" to Contracts and Contract Law' in E Hondius et al (eds), *Coronavirus and the Law in Europe* (Intersentia, 2021).

[9] The *Oxford English Dictionary* (online) lists 14 broad uses of the term in a variety of disciplines – see at www.oed.com/view/Entry/204743?redirectedFrom=transformation#eid (accessed 7 June 2023).

A. Full Harmonisation

The first driver, and the most significant factor, is the development of EU consumer law and policy in light of the Lisbon Summit, the Charter on Fundamental Rights and the White Paper on Governance. The early years of the millennium saw a significant policy shift towards full, or maximum, harmonisation, combined with an intensification of the EU's legislative programme in consumer law. The trigger for this development was the Commission-driven desire to abandon the minimum harmonisation approach that had thus far characterised much of EU consumer law and instead pursue a *full harmonisation approach*. The move from minimum harmonisation to maximum harmonisation is a true game changer, and was central to the Consumer Policy Strategy 2002–2006.[10] The EU no longer sought to create merely a common baseline for consumer protection across the Member States which had been the objective of the minimum harmonisation approach. This approach had created a basis reflecting a kind of social compromise on the degree and the level of protection against economic risks and risks to health and for the environment. In shifting to full harmonisation, the EU assumed much of the regulatory competence for consumer protection, as full harmonisation measures largely leave no room for the Member States to derogate from the EU standard in favour of a higher level of consumer protection. Admittedly, the invariable need for compromise to get sufficient agreement for the adoption of a measure has resulted in the inclusion of regulatory options for Member States on specific issues in directives that are otherwise full harmonisation measures. Many full harmonisation directives therefore do confer some leeway on the Member States to regulate particular aspects, and these aspects are thus not strictly subject to full harmonisation. Nevertheless, these permissions are often limited in scope and leave scant room for manoeuvre in an otherwise fully-harmonised field of consumer law.

At the same time as the general shift to full harmonisation, EU consumer legislation became more detailed at both a technical level (eg, precision and detail of individual provisions) and in terms of substantive scope (addressing a much wider range of issues). The effect of this is that national consumer laws have become increasingly 'Europeanised', not only through the implementation of EU legislation but also through the Charter of Fundamental Rights, which became part of the European legal order with the Lisbon Treaty in 2007. In addition, the growing importance of governance strategies in the enhanced promotion of codes of conduct and the rise of governance strategies to coordinate the enforcement of consumer law – particularly in a cross-border context – further contributed to this effect.[11] The EU now dominates consumer law and continues to expand its reach through recurring reviews of existing measures,[12] the introduction of new directives, the gradual shift from directives to directly applicable regulations and the ever stronger commitment to lay down minimum standards for the enforcement of consumer law. The last of these, in particular, goes far beyond the original intention

---

[10] [2002] OJ C137/2.

[11] F Cafaggi (ed), *Reframing Self-Regulation in European Private Law* (Kluwer Law International, 2006).

[12] See the *Acquis* Review in 2007; the REFIT fitness check in 2016; and the 'Modernisation Directive' in 2019.

of the Treaty of Rome, which left enforcement to the Member States supported by the Court of Justice of the European Union (CJEU).[13] The next move might very well be a repeat of the shift from minimum harmonisation of enforcement rules to a full harmonisation approach.

The impact of the EU on national consumer laws has (somewhat ironically) been far from uniform. Differences can be seen as between the pre-2004 Member States,[14] the 10 central and Eastern European countries that joined the EU during the big expansion of the Union in 2004,[15] with the addition of two further central European countries three years later,[16] and finally Croatia in 2013 as the most recent new Member State. Many of these 'newer' Member States did not have a national system of consumer law prior to preparing for accession to the EU, at least not in comparison to the rather sophisticated set of secondary EU rules (see the contributions by Mišćenić (chapter 11), Možina (chapter 12), Selucká and Marková (chapter 14), and Stănescu (chapter 15) in this volume).

In a simple way, one can broadly divide the pre-enlargement body of EU consumer law into general horizontal rules (contract-related rules and product liability) and rules on individual and collective enforcement. As stated earlier, this body of consumer law was adopted during the first phase of EU consumer law in the 1990s, when the minimum harmonisation approach still dominated. This body of consumer law was largely inspired by the older Member States, which were proactive from the late 1960s onwards, particularly Belgium, Denmark, France, Germany, Italy, Sweden, and the United Kingdom (UK).[17] Even then, making the most of the different forward-looking consumer laws and elevating them to the European level challenged some of the 'old' Member States with a less developed body of consumer law. This challenge was exacerbated for the post-2004 enlargement Member States, many of which were part of the former Eastern bloc that had formed after the Second World War, and which had not developed consumer laws remotely comparable to those adopted in Western democracies before the fall of the Berlin Wall in 1989.

In the new millennium, the shift to full harmonisation, officially stated as a major political aim by the European Commission, brought about major changes to all Member States, both old and more recent. This came on the heels of the European Commission's move to become the main driver of consumer law, which coincided with a decline of the welfare-state rhetoric in the old Member States. However, in the EU's constitutional structure, full harmonisation required an even tighter link of consumer law with Internal Market policy.[18] By mid-2023, the EU had almost completed the process of converting

---

[13] The CJEU did not challenge the competence of the EU to lay down requirements on the enforcement of consumer law that were claimed to be necessary to guarantee the uniform application of European Consumer Law, be it with regard to remedies or be it with regard to the establishment of regulatory agencies to monitor and survey regulated markets.

[14] Austria, Belgium, Denmark, Germany, Greece, Finland, France, Ireland, Italy, Luxembourg, Netherlands, Portugal, Spain, Sweden and the United Kingdom (until its departure in 2020).

[15] Cyprus, Czech Republic, Estonia, Hungary, Latvia, Lithuania, Malta, Poland, Slovakia and Slovenia.

[16] Bulgaria and Romania.

[17] See the contributions in Micklitz (ed), *The Making of Consumer Law and Policy* (n 1).

[18] The legal basis for most consumer law directives is Art 114 of the Treaty on the Functioning of the European Union [2016] OJ C202/1 (TFEU) and its predecessors, which concerns the establishment and functioning of the Internal Market.

all the old minimum harmonisation consumer law directives into full-harmonisation ones. A further conversion of these full-harmonisation directives into a complete set of regulations, which would be a logical next step,[19] is not impossible to imagine now.[20] Perhaps the most notable exception (at least in mid-2023) to this progressive shift is Directive 93/13/EEC on unfair contract terms.

Today, consumer policy has been almost entirely centralised in the hands of the EU. Although intended as a shared competence with the Member States, EU law is no longer merely supplementing national consumer laws but rather fully shaping the development of consumer law and policy in the Member States. Indirectly, this centralisation has strengthened the role of the European Commission in monitoring the enforcement of consumer law in the Member States and in strengthening cross-border enforcement with a single regulatory framework as well as through soft law strategies.[21] The transformation of consumer law and policy was mostly achieved by recognising consumer law as a key area of the European legal order, essential to the completion of the Internal Market, by setting a common maximum standard of protection in order to enhance economies of scale for both business and consumers.

The EU's full harmonisation mantra contrasts starkly with the reality in the Member States, as documented in the contributions to this book. This contrast is evident in respect of both older and newer Member States. Whilst this book is not meant to give an account of the current state of the interaction between European consumer law and national consumer law, this collection of 15 papers from 15 different countries on a range of topics and perspectives in consumer law demonstrates, in kaleidoscopic form, that there is not one fully harmonised European consumer law that applies throughout all the Member States. Instead, there are 27 national versions of fully harmonised European consumer laws. The old Member States, in particular those that had joined before the EU's harmonisation drive started, have often strongly resisted full harmonisation efforts where this pursues too high a level of consumer protection, and instead have sought to defend levels of protection established at national level as the maximum standard. In so far as fully harmonised EU law exceeds the prior level of protection in the old Member States, verbatim implementation became the approach for ensuring compliance with EU obligations. Indeed, even during the days of minimum harmonsation, 'gold plating' was firmly rejected by these Member States. One can see a repeat of this conflict in respect of the implementation of the minimum harmonisation rules on consumer law enforcement (see the contributions by Rott (chapter 13) and also Twigg-Flesner (chapter 16)). Perhaps one notable exception is the UK, which embraced the broad scope and full

---

[19] cf Ch Twigg-Flesner, *A Cross-Border Only Regulation for consumer transactions in the EU* (Springer, 2012).

[20] An early example of a Regulation is Regulation (EC) No 261/2004 of the European Parliament and of the Council of 11 February 2004 establishing common rules on compensation and assistance to passengers in the event of denied boarding and of cancellation or long delay of flights, and repealing Regulation (EEC) No 295/91 [2004] OJ L46/1, whereas the new General Product Safety Regulation, proposed in 2021 (COM (2021) 346 final) and adopted by the Council on 25 April 2023 at first reading, exemplifies the conversion of a Directive into a Regulation.

[21] B Hess and P Ortolani (eds), *Impediments of National Procedural Law to the Free Movement of Judgments. Luxembourg Report on European Procedural Law*, vol I (Hart, Beck, Nomos, 2019); B Hess and S Law (eds), *Implementing EU Consumer Rights by National Procedural Law. Luxembourg Report on European Procedural Law*, vol II (Hart, Beck, Nomos, 2019).

harmonisation status of the Unfair Commercial Practices Directive[22] and utilised it for major reforms to domestic consumer law (see Twigg-Flesner (chapter 16)).

Things are different in both some of the southern Member States who joined after the 'original 6' and in many of the post-2004 Member States. Here, the role of EU consumer law depended on the degree to which these Member States had already adopted consumer laws prior to their accession to the EU. In southern European countries, accession necessitated the implementation of existing EU consumer law and resulted in revisions of, and additions to, the existing bodies of national consumer law (Kaprou, chapter 10). The former communist countries that are now members of the EU (see Mišćenić (chapter 11), Možina (chapter 12), Selucká and Marková (chapter 14), and Stănescu (chapter 15)) or still candidate countries (see Durovic (chapter 9)) had to adapt their entire legal system to a market economy. The implementation of EU consumer law led to legislation transposing (fully harmonised) EU consumer law sitting alongside the remnants of pre-communist private law and retained elements of 'consumer-like' law adopted during communist times on the statute books. This situation is far more complex than that in the pre-2004 Member States, where laws giving effect to fully harmonised European consumer law interact with remaining elements of national consumer law. National law has mostly been relegated to a gap-filling rule in the increasingly dense laws based on EU harmonisation measures. Many of the contributions in this volume focusing on country-specific issues reveal a strange paradox of EU consumer law: on the one hand, EU consumer law strives to create a (mostly) harmonised set of rules in all the Member States. This has had a beneficial effect in so far as some Member States might not have grown a similarly dense consumer law had they not been driven by EU developments. In this sense, EU consumer law has pushed some Member States towards better consumer laws than might otherwise have been the case. On the other hand, the density of EU consumer law, in terms both of scope and the technical detail of its rules, has effectively imposed a straitjacket on all the Member States and thereby removed the potential for Member States to develop consumer policy and law on the basis of national concerns and interests, as well as acting as a constraint on Member States wishing to experiment with solutions to tackle new concerns such as sustainable consumption (see Terryn (chapter 8)). In this regard, close attention might be paid to the situation in the UK, now a former Member State, where first steps towards consumer law unencumbered by EU obligations are starting to appear (see Twigg-Flesner (chapter 16)).

B. Digitalisation and Sustainable Consumption

The constant call for change is not, however, confined to the EU's obsession with the maximum harmonisation approach. Further major transformations, already under

---

[22] Directive 2005/29/EC of the European Parliament and of the Council of 11 May 2005 concerning unfair business-to-consumer commercial practices in the internal market and amending Council Directive 84/450/EEC, Directives 97/7/EC, 98/27/EC and 2002/65/EC of the European Parliament and of the Council and Regulation (EC) No 2006/2004 of the European Parliament and of the Council ('Unfair Commercial Practices Directive') [2005] OJ L149/22.

way, are driven by the twin pressures of *digitalisation of consumer law* and *sustainable consumption*.

The origins of the digitalisation of consumer law reach back as far as the period around the turn of the millennium, the first step being the adoption of the Distance Selling Directive in 1997 (97/7), soon followed by the E-commerce Directive (2000/31).[23] It is important to bear these early origins in mind, especially in light of the ongoing and extensive efforts of the European Commission to develop a comprehensive digital policy and legislation for the economy and – practically – also for the society in the early 2020s. Measures already adopted include the Digital Markets Act,[24] the Digital Services Act[25] and the Data Governance Act;[26] proposals still in the legislative process as at May 2023 include the Artificial Intelligence Act,[27] the Cyber Resilience Act,[28] the Data Act[29] and the Chips Act[30] (digital sovereignty). All of these affect consumers in one way or another, yet none of these regulatory initiatives deals directly with consumer concerns.[31] Only when pressured by the European Parliament and stakeholder organisations did the European Commission launch the 'digital fairness initiative' in 2022.[32] However, this initiative will probably not lead to concrete results within the short term, as the mandate of the current Commission ends in Autumn 2024. Nevertheless, there have already been adaptations of EU consumer law to the progressive digitalisation of the economy and society. The Distance Selling Directive was replaced by the Consumer Rights Directive (2011/83/EU)[33] as long ago as 2011. A landmark development was the adoption of the Digital Content Directive (2019/770)[34] in 2019, together with the new Consumer Sales Directive (2019/771).[35] However, the European Commission seems to assume that the existing consumer law acquis is already sufficient for the effective protection of consumers against the risks of the digital world. This is apparent in the Commission's

---

[23] Directive 97/7/EC of the European Parliament and of the Council of 20 May 1997 on the protection of consumers in respect of distance contracts [1997] OJ L144/19; Directive 2000/31/EC of the European Parliament and of the Council of 8 June 2000 on certain legal aspects of information society services, in particular electronic commerce, in the Internal Market ('Directive on electronic commerce') [2001] OJ L178/1.

[24] Regulation (EU) 2022/1925 [2022] OJ L265/1.

[25] Regulation (EU) 2022/2065 [2022] OJ L277/1.

[26] Regulation (EU) 2022/868 [2022] OJ L152/1.

[27] COM (2021) 206 final.

[28] COM (2022) 454 final.

[29] COM (2022) 68 final.

[30] COM (2022) 46 final.

[31] For a first assessment, H-W Micklitz et al, *EU Consumer Protection 2.0: Structural asymmetries in digital consumer markets, A joint report from research conducted under the EUCP2.0 project* (BEUC, March 2021); for a deeper analysis, see the various position papers of BEUC on the website of the DSA, the AIA and the CRA.

[32] European Commission, *Digital fairness – fitness check on EU consumer law*, overview page, at https://ec.europa.eu/info/law/better-regulation/have-your-say/initiatives/13413-Digital-fairness-fitness-check-on-EU-consumer-law_en (accessed 28 April 2023).

[33] Directive 2011/83/EU of the European Parliament and of the Council of 25 October 2011 on consumer rights, amending Council Directive 93/13/EEC and Directive 1999/44/EC of the European Parliament and of the Council and repealing Council Directive 85/577/EEC and Directive 97/7/EC of the European Parliament and of the Council [2011] OJ L304/64.

[34] Directive (EU) 2019/770 of the European Parliament and of the Council of 20 May 2019 on certain aspects concerning contracts for the supply of digital content and digital services [2019] OJ L136/1.

[35] See n 2.

guidance on the interpretation of the Unfair Commercial Practices Directive,[36] which now includes an entire section to demonstrate how that Directive already addresses the main consumer concerns. Whether this is really the case is highly debatable.

Taking a step back, one can see that the EU's legislative policy in respect of digitalisation seems to be contradictory: on the one hand, there are the – admittedly impressive – initiatives to regulate not only the EU's digital economy, but also de facto the digital economy of all those third countries where leading digital market companies are based and which operate in the EU's Internal Market.[37] There is no counterpart to this with regard to existing consumer law and policy, which appear as static and seemingly stable. Consumer concerns have mostly had to be addressed through the interpretation and application of unfair terms legislation – thus far mostly by national courts – and, perhaps more importantly, through the gradual evolution of a consumer data protection law, where the focus has shifted from the protection of fundamental rights (privacy) to the protection of economic interests (see Sein (chapter 7)). Overall, it is clear that the Member States are not ready to take the lead in filling gaps in the existing EU consumer law but leave it to the European Commission to decide whether the consumer acquis is fit for purpose in the face of digitalisation. This is rather remarkable and demonstrates just how far the Member States seem to have surrendered their competence in the field of consumer law to the EU.

In contrast to the low-key status of the development of 'fair rules' for the digital economy, the *greening of consumer law* sits high on the political agenda of the current European Commission. However, the strong shift towards full harmonisation since the start of the millennium was in no way linked with the greening of consumer law. The European Commission did not integrate the greening of consumer law into its full harmonisation agenda. Instead, it fell to mostly academic efforts to find ways of interpreting open-textured and ambiguous provisions in the consumer acquis in such a way as to extend their reach to encompass greening/sustainable development aspects (see Terryn (chapter 8)).

The situation changed when the von der Leyen Commission took office in 2019. As at mid-2023, a number of initiatives are pending, dealing with matters such as the introduction of new information duties to enable consumers to make an informed choice in their transactional decisions, by amending the Directive 2011/83 on Consumer Rights and Directive 2005/29 on Unfair Commercial Practices, and the projected introduction of a Directive on the Right to Repair[38] (which would combine various policy instruments).[39] The latter initiative (the promotion of the right to repair) is indicative of narrow conceptual thinking that is limited to finding ways of greening the existing

---

[36] European Commission, Guidance on the interpretation and application of Directive 2005/29/EC of the European Parliament and of the Council concerning unfair business-to-consumer commercial practices in the Internal Market [2021] OJ C526/1.

[37] This is an extreme form of the 'Brussels effect'. See A Bradford, *The Brussels Effect – How the European Union Rules the World,* (Oxford University Press, 2020).

[38] Proposal for a Directive of the European Parliament and of the Council on common rules promoting the repair of goods and amending Regulation (EU) 2017/2394, Directives (EU) 2019/771 and (EU) 2020/1828 (COM (2023) 155 final).

[39] B Keirsbilck, 'Empowering Consumers to Buy Sustainable Products', *Journal of European Consumer and Markets Law* (forthcoming).

consumer acquis but which does not pursue a closer alignment between consumer law and environmental law. The right to repair is a great example of the potential such a seemingly minor remedy could usher in if its introduction were tied to the envisaged Eco-design Regulation[40] and the extensive EU rules on waste.[41] Another easy way of aligning consumer and environmental law could be to add, as a factor in the conformity requirements under the Consumer Sales Directive, the product requirements in the Eco-design Regulation.

Current initiatives are based on the identical regulatory philosophy: the policy changes pursued by the EU are not meant to be substantial – they do not seek transformation in a radical sense. All the various greening initiatives are cautiously initiating an evolutionary process, guided by the ideology of informed choice prioritising autonomy and self-determination as the key parameters of consumer law. The question arises whether consumer law in its current form is in fact part of the problem, and therefore whether much deeper measures are needed – even at risk of encroaching on the autonomy of consumers and, indeed, not only of consumers (see Terryn (chapter 8)). There is no EU legislative framework in place that comes even close to the one that will govern the digital economy in terms of extent and detail. One may rightly wonder whether and to what extent the EU's regulatory approach is based on a true recognition of the dramatic impact of the ever more visible climate change. Surely this requires a rupture in thinking, and a radical transformation of consumer law, instead of 'greenwashing' through a new but unambitious regulatory framework for a sustainable economy. One thing is sure, however: the EU, in particular the European Commission, understands that the greening of consumer law is in its hands alone, because of the situation created by the full harmonisation approach to consumer law. There is no discussion of whether sustainable consumption or the building of a sustainable economy reaches beyond the competencies of the European Commission and EU law more generally. Member States such as Belgium or France, who are currently testing new rules on the promotion of repair over replacement, will invariably run into conflict with the full harmonisation rationale and might even face infringement procedures. Clearly, something is seriously amiss if digitalisation receives all the attention whilst the planet (almost literally) burns.

C. Crisis Management and EU Consumer Law

A *third driver* of this phase could be the realisation that resilience needs to be built into consumer law for future impact-heavy events, based on the experiences of the effects of the global financial crisis in 2008, the Covid-19 pandemic since early 2020,[42] and the

---

[40] Proposal for a Regulation of the European Parliament and of the Council establishing a framework for setting ecodesign requirements for sustainable products and repealing Directive 2009/125/EC (COM(2022) 142 final).

[41] H-W Micklitz et al, *Recht auf Reparatur, Veröffentlichungen des Sachverständigenrats für Verbraucherfragen* (BRV, 2022) at www.svr-verbraucherfragen.de/wp-content/uploads/2022_SVRV_PB_Rigtht_to_Repair.pdf (accessed 28 April 2023).

[42] COVID-19- Consumer Law Research Group, 'Consumer Law and Policy Relating to Change of Circumstances Due to the COVID-19 Pandemic' (2020) 43 *Journal of Consumer Policy* 437.

latest economic crisis affecting consumers in the early 2020s caused by high inflation, high energy costs and the effects of the Russian–Ukrainian war. Despite the very different reasons behind these crises, they have in common that they all heavily affected the (economic) interests of consumers. Indeed, each of these crises mostly hit economically vulnerable consumers, and quite hard at that. In mid-2023, only two of these events have had a visible effect on consumer law – the great economic crisis of 2008 and the effects of the pandemic. The long-term effects of high inflation rates and rising interest rates will affect consumers not only in their daily lives but also, and more particularly, in their long-term economic commitments. This impact cannot yet be fully understood. However, the breadth and depth of the contributions to this book permit deeper insights into the way in which EU consumer law has been mobilised to protect economically vulnerable consumers. These insights shed light on the potential of consumer law in times of crisis, but also on its limits. The limits can only be overcome through Member State legislation to compensate for the social voids in the existing body of European consumer law.

Perhaps the most well-known and the very widely debated phenomenon is the impact of the Euro crisis in 2008/2009. The extremely low inflation rate from the start of the millennium until 2020[43] was accompanied by similarly low interest rates for mortgages and consumer loans. The great economic crisis had caused difficulties for house owners who had been speculating, alongside the banks, on steadily increasing house prices. The story of Mr Mohamed Aziz embodies the risks of hundreds of thousands of house owners in Spain and Portugal.[44] Equally affected were consumers who had taken out foreign currency loans in Swiss francs, which attracted much attention in particular in some of the new Member States that were not members of the Eurozone (see Mišćenić (chapter 11), Možina (chapter 12) and Stănescu (chapter 15)).[45] Consumer lawyers in the southern and eastern Member States discovered the potential of the preliminary reference procedure and thus broke through the resistance against using Europeanised consumer law to protect consumer debtors against the dramatic impact of rapidly increasing interest rates. It is a well-known phenomenon that each and every Member State needed a kind of wake-up call to discover the economic and political relevance of the supremacy of EU law. In the old Member States, the key conflicts concerned the tension between the economic freedoms and national laws restricting the four freedoms. In the newer Member States, Europeanised private law, consumer law, took over exactly that role. The judicial activism of the CJEU in both types of contracts, mortgages and consumer loans, was driven by a pro-consumer interpretation of Directive 93/13/EEC on Unfair Terms in particular. Member States were forced into action to take legislative measures, often triggered by judgments of the highest national courts prepared to follow the CJEU's lead. However, the constitutionalisation of private law

---

[43] Statista, *Europäische Union und Eurozone: Inflationsrate von 2001 bis 2022* at https://de.statista.com/statistik/daten/studie/156285/umfrage/entwicklung-der-inflationsrate-in-der-eu-und-der-eurozone/ (accessed 28 April 2023).

[44] Case C-415/11 *Aziz* ECLI:EU:C:2013:164.

[45] For a broader analysis of the impact in the various countries, see I Domurath and H-W Micklitz (eds), *Consumer Debt and Social Inclusion in Europe* (Ashgate, 2015); I Domurath and H-W Micklitz, 'European Integration after *Mohammed Aziz*' in J Gardner and I Ramsay (eds), *Landmark Cases in Consumer Law* (Hart Publishing, 2023) (forthcoming).

relations does not necessarily lead to the better protection of consumers. In Romania, the Constitutional Court cut back national consumer protection laws in the interest of the banks so as to reduce the economic burden (Stănescu (chapter 15)).

One immediate impact on consumers of the lockdowns during the Covid-19 pandemic concerned their travel plans and payments already made for trips that were no longer possible. The European Commission insisted that the pandemic could not be regarded as a *force majeure* event and that airlines and package tour operators had to reimburse consumers, notwithstanding the equally severe economic impact of the pandemic on businesses. It was for the CJEU to clarify legal uncertainties, although it seems that not all the Member States were prepared to follow the legal guidance from Brussels and Luxembourg.[46] Similarly, the renewed explosion of interests rates caused by rising inflation since 2022 will increase over-indebtedness if not the number of consumer insolvencies.[47] Due to the lack of EU rules on consumer insolvency, EU consumer law does not seem to be well prepared to handle the new upcoming wave of social problems that might result from the increase in financial vulnerability.

II. The Effects of the Threefold Transformation in the Institutions, Procedures and the Substance of Consumer Law and Policy in Europe

The three main drivers of the transformation of consumer law and policy throughout Europe since the turn of the millennium left a certain imprint on the national consumer law orders, mainly with regard to the leeway with which they are still formally able to operate. We now turn to the areas where this transformative effect is concretised with regard to the *substance* of consumer law, the *institutions* in charge and the *procedures* under which consumer law operates.

A. Impact on the Transformation of Substance

First, one can detect a transformation of the *substance* of consumer law in several ways, for example in the general direction of consumer policy, the notion of the consumer itself, the rights and remedies available to consumers, as well as the values that underpin consumer law and policy. We have already referred to the impact of full harmonisation, but the question remains what precisely is meant by 'full harmonisation'. Full harmonisation may be considered with regard to its legal, economic and social consequences, as well as its political instrumentalisation. One might also examine to what extent it has affected the ability of national governments to respond to crisis situations (in the absence of a clear derogation mechanism), or of the national courts to handle serious

---

[46] E Hondius et al (eds), *Coronavirus and the Law in Europe* (Intersentia, 2021).
[47] F Ferretti and D Vandone, *Personal Debt in Europe, The EU Financial Market and Consumer Insolvency* (Cambridge University Press, 2019).

consumer detriment in areas such as consumer finance, medical devices, consumer scandals (eg Dieselgate) and maybe environmental disasters.

A further aspect is the question to what extent the one-size-fits-all approach of fully harmonised consumer law can deal with the differences in the national economies and the societies not only within the EU but also within the Member States themselves, between the old centre and the new periphery, between northern, southern, eastern and western Member States. In designing this book, we have deliberately tried to cover the full range of all the different Member States, wherever they are located and whatever their particular history might be. We stress that this book does not aim to compare systematically potential differences with regard to their location or their economic strength.[48] Our aim is more modest in that we focus on the transformative effects that can be felt in many Member States. However, it is striking to see that under the ideological umbrella of full harmonisation, Member States tend mostly to defend and maintain the very specific conception of the role and function of consumer law in their countries, and thus to adjust the fully harmonised consumer law to their particular economic and social preferences. The rather widely formulated EU rules leave enough discretion to the Member States, which reduces the practical relevance of fully harmonised consumer law when it comes to individual disputes and litigation. It seems that each of the countries developed a particular consumer law identity, which resists the full harmonisation dream governing EU consumer law so vigorously defended by the European Commission, particularly when it comes to meeting the challenges of digitalisation and sustainable consumption.[49] This is especially evident in the countries that once were part of the former Yugoslavia. The old law of obligations still plays a dominant role, irrespective of whether the state has become a member of the EU or not (see Durovic (chapter 9), Mišćenić (chapter 11) and Možina (chapter 12)). In contrast, the UK, rather surprisingly, utilised the full-harmonisation approach to push through significant reforms to domestic consumer law, which helped to simplify its consumer law landscape, taking full advantage of the simplified procedure for the transposition of EU legislation provided under the now repealed European Communities Act 1972. After withdrawal, that possibility has gone, and parliamentary time needs to be found to change UK consumer law (Twigg-Flesner (chapter 16)).

A more sophisticated substantive transformation may be observed in respect of the transformation of three key consumer law concepts: the consumer image (Mak (chapter 3)), the notion of contract and tort (Sein (chapter 7)), and remedies (Pavillon (chapter 4)). There is quite a tension between the rather homogeneous European perspective and the broad range of variations resulting from the interaction of fully harmonised EU consumer law with national consumer laws, as well as from the interaction between different areas of consumer law. This is even more so when consumer law issues overlap with other fields of law – data protection law, for instance. The result might then be the emergence of a different understanding of a contract where data are the 'price', or of new remedies (Sein (chapter 7) and Pavillon (chapter 4)).

---

[48] D Kukovec, 'Law and the Periphery' (2015) 21 *European Law Journal* 406–428.
[49] H-W Micklitz, 'Editorial: The Full Harmonisation Dream' (2022) 11 *Journal of European Consumer and Markets Law* 117.

The different drivers of transformation have also reinvigorated the quest for an appropriate consumer image. For a long time, the focus of EU consumer law was on a typical (average) consumer as the yardstick for establishing the level playing field needed for the building of the Internal Market. The image of the average consumer is closely intertwined with the conviction that the consumer is a rational decision-maker who just needs to be equipped with all the information necessary for making a trans-actional decision. Indeed, the information model is the dominating regulatory tool in EU consumer law. Over time, EU law has imposed ever more sophisticated informa-tion obligations on the supplier. The information model has rightly been criticised for causing information overload, over-reliance on pre-contractual duties and the lack of appropriate remedies (Pichonnaz (chapter 5)). However, there is an additional defi-cit, which is often ignored – processing information requires capacities and skills to handle the information and to translate the information into a decision. Information is connected to education, but EU law does not know a self-standing right to educa-tion and the European Commission has not really developed educational programmes that reach beyond mere knowledge transfer. Taken seriously, consumer education could hardly be separated from the consumer image that EU consumer law aims to promote; EU consumer law equates information with knowledge about the basics of the contract, as well as the basics about the remedies. However, when it comes to making not only an informed but a responsible decision, consumer education has to go further than concerns about market participation (Poillot (chapter 6)).

Historically, the EU's average consumer image failed to recognise the many forms of consumer vulnerability, which became abundantly clear in the wake of the great economic crisis of 2008/2009. Although consumer vulnerability has been recognised up to a point, much more could be done to develop a clearer conception of it in EU consumer law. Indeed, it might be suggested that the consumer image has been instru-mentalised to prioritise the one-size-fits-all approach to realise a common level of protection over the needs of individual consumers to be protected against all sorts of economic as well as health and safety risks. This requires the normative assumption of a rather homogeneous social figure, equipped with the necessary capacities and the willingness to take rational decisions. But when one turns to the inner mechanics of the national laws, a much more sophisticated picture emerges (see Selucká and Marková (chapter 14)). The European Commission seems willing to tolerate national differences in the consumer image, as well as in the scope *sedes personae* of national consumer law. The more stable the body of EU consumer law is getting, the more room there seems to be for leeway in its concrete implementation within the Member States.[50]

However, the need for differentiation is gaining pace, including at the European level. This is the result of the pincer movement of digitalisation and the new vulner-abilities it creates, and of the new responsibilities the promotion of sustainable consumption entails. Academic research argues that the consumer in the digital econ-omy is universally, architecturally and relationally vulnerable. Digital vulnerability as a

---

[50] For a well-documented development of the CJEU's case law on the free movement of goods, see J Zglinski, *Europe's Passive Virtues: Deference to National Authorities in EU Free Movement Law* (Oxford University Press, 2020).

societal phenomenon is then translated into digital asymmetry as a legal concept.[51] The current Commission initiative on digital fairness[52] has taken up digital asymmetry as a potential trigger for reform. However, it will have to be demonstrated to what extent the EU is prepared to question the dominant paradigm that ever more information helps to overcome the information asymmetry, a paradigm that already stands on shaky ground in the non-digital economy but which does not hold up in the digital economy – neither empirically nor conceptually. The result could then be a differentiation not only in the consumer image but also in the rights and remedies granted in law. With regard to the consumer's counterparties, the development is much more advanced already. The EU's digital policy legislation differentiates between various types of business – small and medium-sized enterprises, large platforms, very large platforms – to which different rights and duties are allocated.

Elsewhere, if the need for the greening of the consumer is taken seriously then this entails the need to reinvigorate the notion of the 'citizen consumer', who has not only rights but also obligations (in this case towards society in general). The debate is mainly led by academics and has not yet reached the political level of law making (see Mak (chapter 3) and Terryn (chapter 8)).

B. Impact on the Transformation of Institutions

In respect of the *institutional* dimension, one can identify changes in the role of national courts, national parliaments, consumer agencies and consumer organisations, as well as in their interactions. These changes have been fundamental and may therefore be characterised as instances of transformation. One might suggest that the role of national governments has been reduced to that of implementing EU legislation rather than fashioning an original national consumer policy. Sometimes, that role may be instrumentalised to improve national consumer laws (Twigg-Flesner (chapter 16)). However, mostly, full harmonisation has effectively removed legislative power at the national level. The contributions in this volume underpin such an assumption, perhaps with the exception of the field of sustainable consumption where at least some Member States are ready to take innovative measures (Terryn (chapter 8)). The European Commission's eagerness to defend the full harmonisation approach undermines the potential preparedness of countries to take proactive action in fields where the EU law is not settled or is simply absent. It is arguable that national consumer policies have not merely been transformed but been displaced by a European consumer policy. This is at least true for core fields such as sale of goods, doorstep/distance selling and unfair commercial practices.

The shift of consumer law and policy away from the Member States also affects the role of consumer organisations. They have to follow the priorities and the agenda of the European Commission, which leaves little room for genuine national initiatives other than the development of enforcement mechanisms, where the minimum approach

---

[51] N Helberger et al, 'Choice Architectures in the Digital Economy: Towards a new understanding of digital vulnerability' (2022) 45 *Journal of Consumer Policy* 175.

[52] *Communication from the Commission to the European Parliament and the Council: New Consumer Agenda Strengthening consumer resilience for sustainable recovery* (COM (2020) 696 final) 13.

enables the Member States to go beyond the commonly accepted level of remedies. In enforcement, consumer organisations have an important role to play, both through lobbying and in the use of collective rights, at least in countries where consumer organisations are actively using the action for injunction or collective redress mechanisms available under the national legal regimes (Howells and Micklitz (chapter 2)).

However, the minimum harmonisation approach did not prevent the EU from initiating major changes, first and foremost in the way in which the responsibilities are shared. The agentification of EU law[53] has reached consumer law too, in regulated markets – electronic communications, energy, financial services, transport – and in the cross-border enforcement of consumer law more generally. The move from private law to public law brings administrations into a more prominent position, to the benefit of the European Commission, which may then gradually acquire competences away from national enforcement authorities and also from consumer organisations. Various contributions underpin such a trend, which is dominant in the old Member States – with the exception of Germany and Austria – but which also has a strong legacy in the former communist countries (Možina (chapter 12)).

This move triggers new responsibilities for consumer organisations. They not only have to monitor and survey possible infringements by businesses, but they also have to keep a close watch on whether national enforcement authorities are taking their responsibilities seriously. The TikTok saga demonstrates that the division of competences between national authorities and the European Commission, as well as the applicability of different EU consumer laws involving different national enforcement authorities, leads to serious enforcement gaps.[54] If such a development takes place and if consumer organisations are not properly equipped, national courts seem to be the last bulwark for defending the national identity of consumer law. The contributions to this volume demonstrate that national courts as well as the CJEU may work as consumer advocates, in particular when it comes to raising awareness of the economic impact of the great economic crisis on consumers. However, there is equally evidence that consumers may not trust in courts alone, as courts might also restrict the legislative autonomy of nation states (with regard to Romania, see Stănescu (chapter 15)).

It is important to recall that national courts operate as European courts when they decide a question of European consumer law. The dramatically increasing number of CJEU judgments in the field of consumer law pays witness to such a development, even if the references are coming from only half of the Member States and are focusing on certain fields of consumer law.[55] There is an important proviso, though. It is by no means clear whether and to what extent national courts are willing to follow the CJEU's lead, due to a lack of empirical evidence and maybe even a lack of interest in finding out

---

[53] K Verhoest, 'Agentification in Europe' in E Ongaro and S van Thiel (eds), *The Palgrave Handbook of Public Administration and Management in Europe* (Palgrave Macmillan, 2017) 327.

[54] See the BEUC website on TikTok at www.beuc.eu/tiktok, with a list of the actions, the demands and the documents; in this context, see M Cantero and H-W Micklitz, 'Too much or too little? Assessing the consumer protection cooperation (cpc) network in the protection of consumers and children on Tiktok' (BEUC, 2023) at www.beuc.eu/sites/default/files/publications/BEUC-X-2023-018_Assessing_CPC_Network_in_the_protection_of_consumers_and_children_on_TikTok-Report.pdf (accessed 28 April 2023).

[55] B Kas and H-W Micklitz, 'Judge-made private law and the European polity' in B Kas and Ch Mak (eds), *Judges in Utopia* (forthcoming in 2023).

on the part of the European Commission. Here, a more systematic analysis is needed, but this is beyond the scope of this book.

The look at institutional transformation would be incomplete without mentioning dispute settlement procedures. Over the last 20 years, the EU has succeeded in establishing a new layer for enforcing individual consumer rights. In effect, alternative dispute resolution (ADR) and online dispute resolution (ODR) are operating independently of the other institutions, but are perhaps more integral to consumer law enforcement than established court systems.[56] The move from off-line to online dispute resolution, from ADR to ODR, will promote this development, particularly in countries where courts are no true alternative due to the lengthy procedure and/or the high costs.[57] However, the ADR/ODR mechanisms do not cover collective means of dispute settlement. Collective redress claims, not least through the recently adopted Directive on Representative Actions,[58] will remain a prominent field of private collective litigation, either through consumer organisations and consumer agencies or ever more through law firms, which might utilise LegalTech developments to bundle and automate compensation claims.[59]

C. Procedural Dimension

Originally, the procedural dimension was enshrined in the formula of the 'right to be heard' – in the courts but also in administrative proceedings. Over time, the right to be heard took much more sophisticated forms – individual and collective rights, in the EU context associated with the right to judicial protection.[60] The latter is a cornerstone of the Charter of Fundamental Rights. Where consumers have invoked the Charter before the CJEU, it has mostly been in respect of a lack of judicial protection.[61] The distinction between individual versus collective rights to be enforced through public agencies or private actors, consumer organisations or law firms, is strongly intertwined with institutional transformations. This is most obvious in the increasing role of agencies. The more they are involved in consumer law enforcement, the more important it becomes whether and to what degree consumers and consumer organisations are involved in the administrative procedure, whether they can push inactive agencies into action – with or without the help and support of courts. Here, it seems that both EU law and national procedural laws suffer from procedural gaps, with a few exceptions (Howells and Micklitz (chapter 2)).

---

[56] Hess and Ortolani (eds) (n 21); Hess and Law (eds) (n 21).

[57] E van Gelder, *Consumer Online Dispute Resolution Pathways in Europe – Analysing the Standards for Access and Procedural Justice in Online Dispute Resolution Procedures* (Eleven, 2022).

[58] Directive (EU) 2020/1828 of the European Parliament and of the Council of 25 November 2020 on representative actions for the protection of the collective interests of consumers and repealing Directive 2009/22/EC [2020] OJ L409/1.

[59] M Ebers et al (eds), *Künstliche Intelligenz und Robotik* (Beck, 2020).

[60] F Cafaggi and H-W Micklitz (eds), *New Frontiers of Consumer Protection. The Interplay between Private and Public Enforcement* (Intersentia, 2009).

[61] M Safjan and D Düsterhaus, 'A Union of Effective Judicial Protection: Addressing a Multi-level Challenge through the Lens of Art 47 CFREU' (2014) 33 *Yearbook of European Law* 3.

However, not only procedural rights play a role when it comes to the right to be heard before agencies and courts: EU law demonstrates the growing reliance on private regulation. A relatively old debate concerns the participation of consumer organisations in the elaboration of technical standards. Since 2012, EU law has granted consumer organisations rights inter alia to participate via comments and opinions in the European standardisation bodies, which is tied to the fulfilment of certain minimum requirements.[62] With financial services taking the lead, the EU started to impose ever more refined due diligence obligations on banks, investment companies and, lately, large and very large online platforms. Companies have to report first and foremost on their compliance strategies to the public enforcement authorities. However, much of the confidential information is of the utmost importance for consumers, not only politically but also in case consumers intend to sue a company for non-compliance with the due diligence obligations. Via this kind of regulation, the EU has opened up a new battlefield on procedural rights. The Digital Services Act encourages very large online platforms to open the procedure on the elaboration of codes of conduct to stakeholder organisations, which, however, is not yet tantamount to a right to participate.

Finally, procedural rights are closely interlinked with the way in which information foisted upon consumers is processed, whether it is enough to submit the information in writing or whether new forms of information transmission via videos or symbols should be tested, whether information should be provided before, during or after the contract, who the addressee of the information is – the average consumer, the responsible consumer or the vulnerable consumers (Pichonnaz (chapter 5)). The debate so far remains academic and has not yet reached the level of policy making in respect of consumer law enforcement.

III. Conclusions

We started this introduction with the claim that consumer law has undergone a transformation since the turn of the millennium, and we have set out the drivers of this transformation and the various ways in which this transformation can be seen across the entirety of consumer law, at both the EU and the national levels. The contributions to this book delve into much more detail on all of the issues we have raised. The next seven chapters concentrate on particular themes in this transformative process, followed by eight chapters that focus on the transformative effects in a number of European countries, including prospective, current and past EU Member States.

The impact of full harmonisation has not at all been what the European Commission might have expected when it launched its reform drive to develop EU consumer law into a (mostly) fully harmonised field of law more than 20 years ago. It is true that Member States have slavishly transposed all these directives, and on paper it is certainly the case that consumer law has become much more harmonised. However, what really matters is not the law-in-the-books but rather the law-in-action. In many Member

---

[62] Regulation (EU) 1025/2012 on European Standardisation [2021] OJ L316/12, in particular Art 5 together with Annex III.

States, particularly post-2004 ones, consumer law lay dormant until something (the 2008 financial crisis) triggered its activation. The true transformation was the shift from disinterest or even ignorance to weaponisation in tackling significant consumer concerns. Other Member States variously resisted the impact of full harmonisation or instrumentalised it to further domestic ends. Effectively, the Member States have turned the tables on the EU: the EU's objective was to build the Internal Market and thus benefit the EU, but in the Member States, EU-derived consumer law has mostly been used to deal with national concerns.

We do not think that the story of the transformation of consumer law and policy in Europe ends here. As several of the contributions to this book show, there are both unresolved and new challenges that must be addressed. In this chapter, we have highlighted the impact of progressive digitalisation and the dramatic dangers posed by the climate emergency, both of which will push consumer law into new, and perhaps opposite, directions. This, in turn, will require a fresh look at key elements of consumer law, such as the consumer image, consumer education and the role of consumer education. One might understand these challenges as a true opportunity for consumer law to regain its role as a spearhead for legal change.

The EU is already working to address many of these challenges, but its efforts might be hampered by the mindset created by full harmonisation: a reluctance to return greater room for action to the Member States and a focus on reform initiatives that amend rather than rewrite consumer law. However, one might ask whether Member States would now be capable of acting more independently if the EU were to relax the strictures of full harmonisation. In the one country that has left the EU after several decades of membership, the UK, the release from full harmonisation has not resulted in any ground-breaking developments yet.[63] In that sense, Brexit could be an eye-opener for the Member States, in that they might see that consumer policy should not left entirely in the hands of the European Commission. The greening of consumer law provides for such an opportunity to rebalance action between the national and EU levels. One might very well question, from a doctrinal perspective, whether the current Treaty suffices to grant the EU the exclusive power to regulate sustainable consumption. In short, further transformative developments will be essential, both within and outside the EU, to meet current challenges.

---

[63] At least not as at May 2023. The consumer law aspects in the *Digital Markets, Competition and Consumers* Bill introduced into Parliament in late April 2023 are rather modest and certainly not transformative.

PART I

General Issues

2

Consumer Organisations in Europe

GERAINT HOWELLS AND HANS-W MICKLITZ

I. Introduction: The Three Stages of Transformation

This chapter argues that a significant core role of consumer organisations in Continental Europe has undergone a considerable transformation process since the early 1950s.[1] We distinguish three stages of transformation: (i) from local and regional advice centres in the post-war period to enforcement of the then rapidly developing national law; (ii) from Europeanised consumer law to coordinated enforcement at the EU level; (iii) from coordination of European consumer law enforcement to transnational enforcement promoted by legal tech. Both authors functioned as legal advisors to BEUC (*Bureau Européen des Unions de Consommat*) in attempts to hold the members of the former European Consumer Law Group together through building an infrastructure for Europe-wide collective enforcement of consumer rights.[2] In the United Kingdom (UK), consumer organisations have not followed the same route. Though they pressed for powers to act as enforcer, and even attempted this on occasion, litigation has been left to public authorities and to some extent claimant lawyers.

II. Consumer Organisations and Civil Society

Consumer organisations in Europe enjoy different national backgrounds: economically, societally, politically.[3] Consumer organisations understand themselves as part of civil

[1] We would like to thank Margit Bohle, former member of the Verbraucherinstitut, Wolfgang Bohle, former lawyer at the Verbraucherschutzverein, as well as Monique Goyens, Ursula Pachl both from BEUC.

[2] H-W Micklitz, 'The Intellectual Community of Consumer Law and Policy in the EU' in H-W Micklitz (ed), *The Marking of Consumer Law and Policy in Europe* (Bloomsbury Publishing, 2021) 63.

[3] For a first overview of the then nine Member States, see N Reich and H-W Micklitz, *Consumer Legislation in the EC Countries: A Comparative Analysis* (Van Nostrand Reinhold, 1980); and for a more recent account of the particular national context in which consumer law developed, which left a deep imprint on the role and function of consumer organisations, see the contributions in Micklitz (ed), *The Making of Consumer Law and Policy in Europe* (n 2). The European Commission has set up an up-to-date website that offers an overview of the competent ministries in charge of consumer protection, of the public agencies involved in consumer protection law and of national consumer organisations, though without any historical, economic or cultural

society. *Civil society* may have very different meanings, though. In Western democracies it may be alluded to as *democratic society*, a particular source of bottom-up democratic legitimacy;[4] whereas in the new EU Member States of Central and Eastern Europe, civil society is a *normative concept* that carries civic values,[5] while in the transnational context civil society is the *arena of collective action in the public space.*[6] All concepts take civil society as a homogeneous entity. In reality, due to politicisation, civil society mirrors the tensions between different political camps.[7] The role of the state is crucial. The state may provide funding to consumer organisations, or put representation of consumer interests into the hands of a public agency or both.

Seen through a European lens, consumer organisations belong to the political arena of collective action. Making their voice heard in the daily machinery of Brussels law-making lies in the hands of BEUC, the European umbrella organisation that unites consumer organisations from all Member States. If consumer organisations want to be heard, they must speak on behalf of 'European' consumers. The consequences become visible in the way consumer organisations behave at the European and transnational levels.

Turning back to the national level, we distinguish between East and West. In the West, consumer organisations form an integral part of democratic society. They developed, grew and transformed with changing political patterns and changing understandings of the role and function of non-governmental organisations (NGOs) in a democratic society. They go together with the move from representative democracy to participatory democracy. The call for adequate representation of consumer interests is already enshrined in the 1962 Kennedy declaration.[8] Consumer organisations are typically membership-based organisations seeking to promote the collective consumer interest. Which?, the Consumers Association in the UK, is just such an organisation. Consumer organisations vary considerably, though, in terms of how they are integrated into political decision-making, their position as financially independent institutional actors or as 'quangos' (quasi-NGOs)[9] with a public mandate, which in turn entails funding. Beyond the EU funding of BEUC, state funding of consumer organisations is absent, although nation states may fund international projects. In states such as Germany, consumer agencies (*Verbraucher Zentrale*) are funded with the express objective of representing

---

background – see at https://ec.europa.eu/info/sites/default/files/national-consumer-organisations_de_listing_en_0.pdf (accessed 6 November 2022).

[4] 'Civil society', definition and meaning in *Collins English Dictionary*. J Habermas in particular relies heavily on civil society, which could provide legitimacy to regulatory action, at least Habermas prior to the Covid crisis.

[5] In the new Member States, the wake-up call is not *Cassis de Dijon* (*Rewe-Zentrale AG v Bundesmonopolverwaltung Für Branntwein* EU:C:1979:42, Germany) or *Sunday Trading* (*Torfaen Borough Council v B & Q plc* EU:C:1989:593, UK) but references dealing with mortgages and foreign currency loans.

[6] Stamped by the definition provided for by the United Nations, 'Who we are' at www.un.org/en/civil-society/page/about-us (accessed 7 November 2022).

[7] E Grande, 'Zivilgesellschaft, politischer Konflikt und soziale Bewegungen' (2018) 31 *Forschungsjournal Soziale Bewegungen* 52, 52–60.

[8] JF Kennedy, 'Special Message to the Congress on Protecting the Consumer Interest' (Message to the Congress of the United States, 15 March 1962) at www.presidency.ucsb.edu/documents/special-message-the-congress-protecting-the-consumer-interest (accessed 6 November 2022).

[9] See at https://en.wikipedia.org/wiki/Quango (accessed 6 November 2022).

consumer interests before the courts; but these are not member-based consumer organisatons. Whether and to what extent consumer organisations can contribute to the democratisation of the EU is an open issue. The answer depends on the potential outlook of a 'more' democratic EU.[10]

What about consumer organisations in the new Member States? What kind of 'normative concept' of civil society are they carrying, and what kind of 'civic values' are enshrined that justify drawing the distinction between East and West? Civil society in a nation state is to be separated from the state. In the American understanding, civil society is the last resort of civil power. The state enjoys power in so far as civil society is ready to delegate power to governmental institutions.[11] After the fall of the Berlin Wall and the collapse of the Soviet Union, the new Member States were facing a threefold challenge: state building, market building and society building.[12] When the old Member States decided to open membership to former Soviet satellites, the EU tied full membership to, inter alia, taking over the consumer law *acquis*. The 'integration through law' paradigm[13] extended to the Eastern enlargement gave a different twist to consumer law and policy, as well as to consumer organisations in the Central and Eastern European countries. The consumer organisations are in charge of contributing to building a civil society comprising what ordoliberals call 'civil law society' (*Privatrechtsgesellschaft*).[14] The differences between East and West are documented in scholarly research on the particularities of the role and function of consumer law and policy and their advocates in the new Member States.[15]

III. Transformative Power of National Consumer Law

In Western Europe, the rise of the consumer society began in the 1960s, with an incremental delay in Eastern Europe during the communist era from the 1970s on, fully unfolding in the 1990s. Listening to President Kennedy and his description of information deficits, misleading advertising and price confusion, in addition to lack of supervision and control, this is more topical than ever, and one might wonder what exactly has changed in the intervening years, despite a plethora of new laws.[16]

---

[10] With a vast literature on the democratic deficit and potential proposals for reform of the EU, it suffices to look at the standard textbooks on EU law; for a deeper analysis, see J Dickson and P Eleftheriadis (eds), *The Philosophical Foundations of European Union Law* (Oxford University Press, 2012).

[11] U Rödel, G Frankenberg and H Dubiel, *Die Demokratische Frage: Ein Essay* (Suhrkamp Verlag, 1988).

[12] H-W Micklitz, *Rechtseinheit oder Rechtsvielfalt in Europa?: Zur Rolle und Funktion des Verbraucherrechts in den MOE-Staaten und in der EG*, vol 1 (Nomos, 1996); H-W Micklitz, 'Verbraucherschutz West versus Ost: Kompatibilisierungsmöglichkeiten in der Europäischen Gemeinschaft: Einige Vorüberlegungen' in H Heiss (ed), *Brückenschlag zwischen den Rechtskulturen des Ostseeraums* (Mohr Siebeck, 2001) 137.

[13] Initiated by Mauro Cappelletti, executed together with Monica Seccombe and JHH Weiler, published by De Gruyter between 1985 and 1988, see at www.degruyter.com/view/mvw/ITL-B (accessed 6 November 2022), with a list of all in all 7 volumes.

[14] F Böhm, 'Privatrechtsgesellschaft und Marktwirtschaft' (1966) 17 *ORDO: Jahrbuch für die Ordnung von Wirtschaft und Gesellschaft* 75, 75–151.

[15] A Wiewiórowska-Domagalska and M Grochowski, 'Consumer Law in Poland or There and Back Again' in Micklitz (ed), *The Making of Consumer Law and Policy in Europe* (n 2) 193.

[16] JF Kennedy, 'Special Message to the Congress on Protecting the Consumer Interest' (15 March 1962) at www.jfklibrary.org/asset-viewer/archives/JFKPOF/037/JFKPOF-037-028 (accessed 6 November 2022).

The 1950s and 1960s were the founding years of consumer organisations: the Danish *Forbrugerrådet* (Danish Consumer Council) in 1947; the German *Arbeitsgemeinschaft der Verbraucherverbände* (AGV – consortium of consumer associations)[17] in 1953 and the *Verbraucherzentralen* (VZen – consumer advice centres) in the late 1950s; the Dutch *Consumentenbond* in 1953; and the UK Consumers' Association in 1957. Their aim was to guide the consumer through the rapidly growing consumer society via individual help and price comparison. In some countries, such as Italy and Greece, the consumer movement is more diverse, with many small interest groups that may be designated as consumer organisations, although in Italy *Altro consumer* is the largest – founded in 1973 and now with 346,000 members. The second major pillar of consumer work results from comparative testing of quality and prices. *Que Choisir* and *Which?* were founded in 1957, *Stiftung Warentest* in 1964. Testing institutions should provide the consumer with independent information on products and follow-up services.

Subsequent to President Kennedy's consumer message, the Western democracies adopted consumer policy programmes in the 1960s and 1970s, with the EU following in 1976 and 1981. These programmes breathe the spirit of the social welfare state, the state accepting responsibility for protecting the consumer as the weaker party in the economy. Consumer rights rhetoric sets the tone for the transformation of political programmes into legislative action. This closely mirrors the action taken, in the shape of protection against unsafe products, cars, drugs and technical (electrical) devices, ensuring that the consumer receives the necessary information from the supplier prior to the contract, protection against misleading (and unfair) advertising and sales promotion, adequate remedies against unsafe and defective products, and remedies against unfair standard terms, misleading advertising and door-to-door selling.[18] The wave of legal acts led to legalisation and the juridification of consumer policy. Consumer organisations across Europe became involved first in individual and then later in collective enforcement.

Individual consumers were now seeking professional advice in individual litigation. The consumer organisations had to hire competent lawyers who could provide help in totally new fields of law. Institutionally speaking, consumer organisations turned into a major source of knowledge on consumer problems. They organised regular office hours, developed standard letters and occasionally drafted letters of complaint against companies. Scholarly attention turned to 'access to justice'[19] – that is, the scope for consumers to defend their rights, first against the seller company under complaints procedures and subsequently in alternative dispute settlement procedures and the courts. Consumer organisations were well aware that those who joined them formed a minority. Member States commissioned various studies on access to justice; the EU organised a conference in Montpellier, which triggered the founding of the European Consumer Law Group.[20]

---

[17] The German phrase is difficult to translate. The AGV was an umbrella organisation for associations working in the field of consumer law; for details, see N Reich and H-W Micklitz, *Consumer Legislation in the Federal Republic of Germany: A Study* (Van Nostrand Reinhold, 1981).

[18] In the late 1970s, the European Commission asked Norbert Reich to evaluate consumer protection law in the then nine Member States, published with van Nostrand Reynolds: Reich and Micklitz (n 3).

[19] M Cappelletti, *Access to Justice* (Giuffrè Editore/Sijthoff/Noordhoff, 1978).

[20] U Reifner and M Volkmer, *Neue Formen der Verbraucherrechtsberatung* (Campus Verlag, 1988).

In collective enforcement, the USA set the tone for the rest of the world through adding the US class action to consumer protection in 1964.[21] None of the Member States was ready to follow the USA – at least not at that time. Legislators introduced cease-and-desist orders – first in the field of advertising, later in control of standard terms – but stayed away from collective redress.[22] The political debate turned on the question of who should be granted standing to sue – a public agency and/or consumer organisations – and, if consumer organisations, in what kind of institutional and procedural settings? Already in the 1970s, Member States were divided. These differences have survived all institutional changes in consumer organisations.

A. Consumer Organisations in Germany

The UK and Germany mirror perfectly well the two camps: in the UK, collective enforcement was put into the hands of the then Office of Fair Trading (OFT), established in 1973 (the predecessor of the Competition and Markets Authority (CMA)); and in Germany, collective enforcement for misleading advertising was delegated to consumer organisations in 1964 and for standard terms in 1977. There was no NGO 'and' state: it was an 'either ... or' choice.

The implications for the institutional design of consumer organisations in Germany were huge.[23] The AGV – the political arm of German consumer organisations – and the advice centres in the different German *Länder* – the practical arm – founded the *Verbraucherschutzverein* (VSV) in 1965 as the new legal branch. The VSV was mandated to sue advertisers, calling for cease-and-desist orders. There was no precedent. The legal staff had to learn from scratch how to handle their new powers. They had to decide on the cases they wanted to bring to court, they had to set political priorities, and they had to gain the necessary skills and professionalise in leading litigation in the collective interest of consumers. The VSV might have borrowed from the long-standing experience of the *Zentrale zur Bekämpfung des Unlauteren Wettbewerbs*, the Central Office for Combating Unfair Competition.[24] As early as 1896, the German legislator mandated 'associations for the promotion of industrial business interests'[25] to control misleading advertising. But unlike a self-financed business organisation, state-induced consumer law enforcement required public funding.

---

[21] JF Handler, *Social Movements and the Legal System: A Theory of Law Reform and Social Change* (Academic Press, 1978).

[22] The German Government was discussing the introduction of collective compensation schemes for misleading and unfair advertising in the late 1970s, though without result: H-W Micklitz, 'Kollektiver Schadensersatzanspruch im UWG: Scheitern oder Neubeginn' in H-W Micklitz (ed), *Rechtseinheit oder Rechtsvielfalt in Europa?: Rolle und Funktion des Verbraucherrechts in der EG und den MOE-Staaten* (Nomos, 1996) 383.

[23] On the history of the *Verbraucherverbandsklage*, see A Halfmeier, '50 Jahre Verbraucherverbandsklage Möglichkeiten und Grenzen Kollektiver Rechtsschutzinstrumente: Bilanz und Handlungsbedarf' (Bundesverband der Verbraucherzentralen und Verbraucherverbände Verbraucherzentrale Bundesverband eV, September 2015) at www.vzbv.de/sites/default/files/downloads/Gutachten-50_Jahre_Verbandsklage-vzbv-2015.pdf (accessed 6 November 2022).

[24] See at www.wettbewerbszentrale.de/de/home/ (accessed 6 November 2022).

[25] See Halfmeier (n 23).

When it came to deciding who should enforce the German *Gesetz zur Regelung des Rechts der Allgemeinen Geschäftsbedingungen* (Standard Terms Act), adopted in 1976, the German legislature relied on the long-established practice and tradition of private law enforcement in the control of unfair and misleading commercial practices. All associations that legitimately defended the collective consumer interest were granted standing: business organisations, chambers of commerce and consumer organisations. The VSV received public funds to hire two lawyers to supervise and monitor the tens of thousands of standard consumer contract terms. The *Verbraucherinstitut* (VI – Consumer Institute) was established by the *Stiftung Warentest* and the AGV in 1978. Its purpose was not only to educate consumer advice centre staff, but also to act as disseminators of knowledge about consumer rights – not limited to but including the growing field of consumer protection laws.

Adoption of the Standard Terms Act broke new legal and political ground. The two lawyers had to fill an empty regulatory space. They had to learn on the job and translate their newly gained experience into an educational programme to the benefit of all the other consumer lawyers in the Federal Republic. The VI organised training seminars and covered participants' travel and accommodation costs. The action for injunction established in advertising law served as a source of inspiration for the control of standard terms. The consumer advice centres of the German *Länder* provided the VSV with copies of standard terms. Prior to the digital economy, consumer organisations faced difficulties in accessing standard terms. Lack of political guidance on what to do left much discretion in the hands of the VSV in terms of how to professionalise its activities. The two lawyers started to collect standard terms of leading German companies – Lufthansa, TUI, Mercedes – in order to initiate litigation against those same companies. German companies were not prepared to be confronted with consumer organisations with the power to drag them before the courts. The Standard Terms Act, much more than legal standing in advertising, put an end to the image of consumer protection and consumer organisations as the grubby children of society. They had an active role to play in German law and politics.[26]

B. Private Associations and Public Authorities in the UK

The origins of the consumer movement in the UK were rather different from those in Germany, which perhaps explains why litigation has been and remains a less prominent feature of its operation. Dorothy Goodman first proposed establishing a consumer organisation modelled on the US Consumer's Union, because she found that no assistance was given to young couples making their first large-scale purchases.[27] The early days of the Consumers' Association (CA) were marked by a lively amateur approach; indeed, the Molony Report criticised it as a self-perpetuating oligarchy,[28] which forced

---

[26] W Bohle and H-W Micklitz, 'Erfahrungen mit dem AGB-Gesetz im nichtkaufmännischen Bereich: Eine Zwischenbilanz nach 6 Jahren' (1983) 28 *Betrieds Berater Zeitschrift fur Recht und Wirtschaft* 1.

[27] M Hilton, *Consumerism in 20th Century Britain* (Cambridge University Press, 2003) 194.

[28] *Final Report of Committee on Consumer Protection* (Cmnd 1781, 1962) 122, cited in Hilton (n 27) 225.

it to adopt more democratic structures. During the 1960s it also reached out to local communities to establish local consumer groups organised under the banner of the National Federation of Consumer Groups. There were 91 local groups in 1965, but at around the turn of the millenium their funding was withdrawn from both the CA and government and they have now ceased to function – at least on anything like the previous scale – with Plymouth being the last active group. The National Consumer Federation seeks to maintain an independent platform for the consumer voice.

The early members of the consumer movment linked into prior political discourse such as within the think tank Political and Economic Planning (PEP), a prominent member of which, Michael Young, had slipped a commitment on consumer protection into the Labour manifesto of 1949. Which? has become a powerful lobbying force. Moreover, its disavowal of open party politics has helped it push a consumer agenda that can appear to be non-partisan. It has achieved success through reliance on technical objectivity in its testing and high-quality journalism in its magazines

Doubtless, many of the CA's more than half a million members only use it for practical reasons to make use of the test results and guides. Its membership consists predominantly of middle-class professionals.[29] They may not see consumerism as having a political agenda, but the organisation has obtained from them the capacity to represent the consumer voice. Council members may be more engaged with the consumer policy agenda as a broader political force than its membership or even some of its paid workforce who are engaged in testing and journalism. One of its founders, Michael Young, certainly had a view that consumerism was part of the social democratic state, and when later he was Chair of the National Consumer Council, his establishment of the Consumer Congress was envisioned as making the consumer voice heard, much as the Trade Unions and Confederation of British Industry used their congresses to represent worker and employer interests.[30] Many of the CA's professional workers focus on comparative testing and producing the magazine to provide information and be informed by a philosophy of promoting choice. This inevitably means the concerns of affluent (member) consumers are frequently to the fore. However, this has not prevented the CA from running several campaigns with a wider agenda. It has also tackled the wider consumer agenda through a variety of alternative strategies.

In 1963, the CA established the Research Institute for Consumer Affairs (RICA). The period from the 1970s onwards has seen major consumer law reforms and Which? has been engaged in law-reform discussions – led in this regard for many years by its legal officer, David Tench, who was an influential voice on consumer reform in the UK and Europe. In recent times the CA has focused on individual issues, which have allowed it to raise its profile and develop consumer policy without having to be aligned with partisan politics or even an overall philosophy.

The Association also campaigned successfully for legal power to seek injunctions, but has not invoked that power, preferring to leave legal action to the regulators. It has on several occasions used its power to make super complaints to regulators that have led to investigations of sections of the economy, such as that regarding safeguards for push

---

[29] Hilton (n 27) 212.
[30] ibid 287–88.

payments in 2016. It has tended to use the rhetoric of the market to seek out a better deal for consumers. It did use its power to bring a consumer class action in the competition context relating to the pricing of football shirts, but that was not too successful as few consumers had the motivation to join an action for small gains, especially as the retailers also made alternative offers to those affected.

Through its memberships of BEUC and especially Consumers International (CI, formerly the IOCU, the International Organisation of Consumers' Unions), the CA has been able indirectly to support a broader view of the consumer as citizen. Beyond the philosophical divide between those who see the movement simply about individual consumer empowerment and others having a broader social democratic image of what consumers can achieve, more practical tensions are derived from the need for Which? to be profitable. It has sometimes been criticised for using forceful promotional marketing for its services. Its attempts to take on the car industry by becoming a supplier (Carbusters) or marketing its own credit card have proved too difficult to maintain at both a practical and a philosophical level.

Alongside membership-based consumer organisations, there has also been government-sponsored consumer representation in the UK. This dates back to the First World War, which gave rise to problems with food supply relating to rationing and the shortage of supplies. This led to a working-class consumer movement under the War Emergency: Workers' National Committee (WEC). This in turn caused the Government to establish a Consumer Council within the Food Ministry (1918–21). This had only an advisory role, and many believed it was established to drag the radical WEC into government bureaucracy where its views could be diluted by more traditional stakeholders. However, it did serve to foster the first recognisably distinctive consumer policy. Consumer representation in the food sector continued through the Food Council established in 1925, and despite not being very effective, it was only suspended when war broke out in 1939. Additionally, a Consumer Committee of the Agricultural Marketing Boards was established in the 1930s. However, the consumer voice was not strong, with producer and worker interests being to the fore.[31]

Labour's attempt in 1930 to pass a Consumer Council Bill failed, but during this time there was a nascent appreciation that consumerism should expand beyond being merely concerned with providing the necessities. Much of the concern in the first half of the twentieth century was about anti-trust abuses and profiteering, which prevented the working class from having a living wage due to the price of food and also shortages in the supply chain.

After the Second World War, industries were nationalised and Consumer Councils were established that were linked to them. Examples of these include the Domestic Coal Consumers' Council, 14 Electricity and Consultative Councils and 12 Gas Consultative Councils (one for each region), a Central Transport Users' Consultative Committee with 11 area Transport Users' Consultative Committees, and a Consumer Council for the oil industry. This structure was criticised for lack of expertise on the part of consumer representatives, who often had limited connections to consumer concerns and in any event had few powers to influence industry.

---

[31] ibid 117–24.

The year 1963 saw the establishment of a Consumer Council. This was a relatively innocuous, poorly funded body with a deliberately conservative membership that was barred from comparative testing, dealing with individual complaints or launching prosecutions.[32] Instead, its brief was to research, lobby for reform and educate consumers. It therefore followed the tradition of accepting that the market was essentially functioning well and just needed to be enhanced by empowered consumers, even stating that the most telling pressure came from the 'informed and competent consumer'.[33] Yet the Council's staff did begin to engage in broader debates that saw consumerism as part of social policy, and its last Chairman, Lord Donaldson, acknowledged that it was not enough to focus on the individual consumer and that 'Someday someone will have to invent a new, publicly financed body to promote and protect the consumer interest'.[34] The Consumer Council was axed by Edward Heath in 1970 as part of a cost-cutting exercise, though it is also conjectured that he was opposed to Des Wilson, of Shelter, becoming its next Director. Its abolition produced such a public outcry that Whincup argues this 'led to a much more fundamental shift ... than if the axe had been spared'.[35]

In 1973, the Conservative Government established the OFT, and in 1975 the Labour Government established the National Consumer Council (NCC), with separate councils for Scotland and Wales. The NCC was assigned the explicit role of looking after disadvantaged consumers – those whom the CA could perhaps not always afford to prioritise – and its remit took a very broad view of consumer protection, including access to public services such as council tenants' rights and NHS patients' rights.[36] The NCC had been seen by Labour as an important plank it its 'third way' politics, but it was merged with Energywatch and Postwatch to form Consumer Focus, which was renamed Consumer Futures in 2013 and eventually abolished in 2014. Citizens Advice currently deals with consumer issues and has a Consumer and Public Services policy research team. The motivation for these changes seemed to be mainly money-saving.

The regulated industries have a patchwork of consumer input. OFGEM works to protect consumer interests in the gas and electricity markets, with OFWAT filling the same role in the water market; non-executive directors can be seen as having a role to play in protecting the consumer interest. Water companies have a Customer Challenge Group to ensure service works in the interest of consumers. In telecommunications, OFCOM has a Communications Consumer Panel and an Advisory Committee on Older and Disabled People. The Financial Consumer Authority operates a Consumer Panel. After the Second World War, a Central Transport Consultative Committee (CTCC) and a network of regional Transport Users' Consultative Committees were established, later being replaced by new bodies with extended powers. The Railways Act 1993 abolished this structure and replaced it with the Rail Users' Consultative Committee (RUCC)

---

[32] ibid 228–41.

[33] ibid 235.

[34] ibid 239.

[35] M Whincup, *Consumer Legilsation in the United Kingdon and Republic of Ireland* (Van Nostrand Reinhold, 1980), cited in Hilton (n 27) 7.

[36] Hilton (n 27) 279–97.

network, comprising the Central Rail Users' Consultative Committee (CRUCC) and eight regional committees (the Rail Passengers' Council and Rail Passengers' Committees). This became Passenger Focus in 2006, which was extended to cover buses as well as rail in 2018. In 2014 the remit was extended so as to cover road users too, the body being renamed Transport Focus.

The OFT had been the main government department dealing with consumer law affairs. It came under criticism for being ineffective, but this was mostly directed at its competion law work, for it enjoyed a good reputation amongst consumer advocates. The OFT certainly took its role of enforcement against unfair terms seriously. It tackled problematic sectors by issuing guidance and also published reports of unfair terms it challenged. Axing the OFT might also have been linked to attempts to save resources, but is seems doubtful that that goal was achieved, as many of its functions were simply moved to the CMA. There was also an attempt to enhance the central coordination of local trading standards officers. These local authority officers are responsible for enforcement on the ground. Some coordination is achieved through the home authority principle, under which businesses operating across the country deal with one authority to reduce the risk of conflicting practices. In order to enhance enforcement across boundaries, especially in priority areas, the National Trading Standards Board was established.

C. Consumer Organisations in Communist Eastern European Countries

Many former communist countries experienced a timid rise of the consumer society in the 1970s. Their legal orders were built on a distinction between the law on B2B relations (the different state-run companies), the law on B2C relations – what is called consumer law in Western terms – and the law on C2C relations – the law among socialist citizens.[37] Socialist citizens began to complain about substandard quality and called for Western products. The transformation of the communist economy required currencies. The countries took action on two levels: (i) setting production quality standards; and (ii) introducing rights and remedies for citizens.

The German Democratic Republic (GDR) might serve as an example.[38] In the 1970s, Ikea decided to involve the former GDR in furniture production. Difficulties in meeting Western quality standards led to rules on measurement and technical specifications and to a split market – the top quality went to export, the 'rest' to GDR citizens.

---

[37] Norbert Reich built his argument on the socialist experience: N Reich, 'Zivilrechtstheorie, Sozialwissenschaft und Verbraucherschutz' (1974) 7 *Zeitschrift für Rechtspolitik* 187; for a deeper analysis, see H-W Micklitz, 'Person, Civil Status and Private Law' in H-W Micklitz, S Grundmann and M Renner, *New Private Law Theory: A Pluralist Approach* (Cambridge University Press, 2021) 341.

[38] The following results from research undertaken by H-W Micklitz/ Ch Rößler/ Th Roethe, *Irreführende/ unlautere Werbung und kollektiver Schadensersatz – Eine Pilotstudie im Land Brandenburg*, Manuscript, 1993, on file with the author, as well as Thomas Roethe, *Zum Konsumentenschutz in den MOE Ländern – Transition und Rechtsvielfalt* as well as H-W Micklitz, *Kollektiver Schadensersatzanspruch im UWG – Scheitern oder Neubeginn*, both in Micklitz (ed), *Rechtseinheit ofer Rechtsvielfalt in Europa* (n 22), pp 205–240 und 383–414; on the GDR in particular, see Ths Roethe, *Arbeiten wie bei Honecker, leben wie bei Kohl: Ein Plädoyer für das Ende der Schonfrist* (Eichborn Verlag, 1999) which integrates the empirical evidence collected.

The GDR Government reacted through adoption of the *Zivilgesetzbuch*[39] in 1975, which was celebrated by leftist scholars as a more 'social version' of the West German *Bürgerliches Gesetzbuch*. Citizens of the GDR were entitled to express their discontent through the so-called *Eingabe* (complaint) – a rather informal remedy addressed to the political authorities, in the end to the head of state.[40] German unification put an end to the legal regime of the GDR.

A communist state allows no space for civil society organisations and consumer organisations. The 'consumer' interest lay in the hands of the Communist Party. After unification, the West German model was copy-pasted '*tel quel*' to the former GDR, without further ado and without taking into consideration the communist legacy and the *Eingabe* system – which was deeply anchored in the people's mindset. The West German consumer advice centres served as a blueprint.

IV. Transformative Power of EU Consumer Law

The decline of the social welfare state in the Western democracies provided space for the EU to re-design consumer law as a means to complete the Internal Market. 'Protection' in consumer law gradually vanished and was replaced by the concept of consumer law.[41] The 1985 Sutherland Report[42] underpins the regulatory philosophy and ideology of consumer law and policy in the EU up to today. Consumer law and policy turned into a means to an end and lost its status as a self-standing policy. That said, the base is said to be a high level of protection in line with Article 114(3) TFEU.[43]

In the aftermath of the Single European Act, the EU successfully implemented the programmes of action of 1976 and 1981, due to the introduction of majority voting. The dense set of rules developed over the ensuing decades looks like an infant European Consumer Code, comprising rules on regulating the modalities of contract conclusion, general rules on the control of unfair commercial practices and standard terms, as well as rules on sales contracts, travel contracts, time-share contracts, consumer credit, product liability, on collective enforcement of unfair standard terms and unfair commercial practices, and on individual enforcement through ADR and ODR and, lately, through collective redress. The Brussels I Regulation and the Rome I and II Regulations define common standards on jurisdiction and on the applicable law for individual and collective enforcement.[44]

---

[39] See at www.ra-morgenstern.de/Morgenstern/ZGB-DDR.pdf (accessed 6 November 2022).

[40] I Markovits, *Gerechtigkeit in Lüritz: Eine ostdeutsche Rechtsgeschichte*, 2nd edn (CH Beck, 2014).

[41] H-W Micklitz, 'The Expulsion of the Concept of Protection from the Consumer Law and the Return of Social Elements in the Civil Law: A Bittersweet Polemic' (2012) 35 *Journal of Consumer Policy* 283.

[42] P Sutherland, *The Internal Market after 1992: Meeting the Challenge: Report presented to the Commission by the High Level Group on the Functioning of the Internal Market (commonly called the Sutherland Report)* (1992) SEC (92) 2044 final.

[43] The Commission, in its proposals envisaged in paragraph 1 concerning health, safety, environmental protection and consumer protection, will take as a base a high level of protection, taking account in particular of any new development based on scientific facts. Within their respective powers, the European Parliament and the Council will also seek to achieve this objective; see with regard to the competences Stephen Weatherill *Contract Law of the Internal Market* (Intersentia, 2016).

[44] S Weatherill, *EU Consumer Law and Policy*, 2nd edn (Edward Elgar, 2005); S Weatherill, *Contract Law of the Internal Market* (Intersentia, 2016); N Reich et al (eds), *European Consumer Law*, 2nd edn (Intersentia,

Homogenisation of the consumer market not only increased choice to the benefit of all consumers, but also meant that the types of consumer problems were common throughout Europe. The Diesel Scandal has affected all consumers who bought a diesel car from VW – not only Europe-wide but worldwide. Contrary to the position in the 1990s, the European Commission tilted the balance between public and private enforcement to the benefit of public enforcement. By focusing on transborder problems, the Commission avoided competence questions. The primary addressees of Regulation 2006/2004 on cooperation in transborder enforcement[45] are public authorities. The revised Regulation enlarges their competences and grants residual powers to the European Commission.[46] Even countries such as Austria and Germany had to complement private enforcement through public enforcement authorities, at least in the transborder context.

A. Private Collective Enforcement in Germany

In the year 2000, the institutional landscape of consumer organisations in Germany changed considerably. Under massive pressure from the Ministry of Economy, the AGV – the political arm – along with the *Verbraucherschutzverein* – the legal arm – and the *Verbraucherinstitut* – the educational arm – were merged into the *Bundesverband Verbraucherzentrale Bundesverband* (VZBV). The reasons behind the state-pressured merger were manifold. The Ministry intended to put an end to overlapping competences, to have one single addressee and to overcome internal competition over state subsidy. The potential effect on Brussels was an intended side-effect.[47]

Legal competencies were allocated to the respective policy fields around which the VZBV organised its work. The VZBV takes care of German consumer interests through its Brussels bureau[48] and membership within BEUC. The revised statutes make clear that the VZBV represents consumer interests at the national, European and international level, and if necessary enforces the consumer interest through collective action, nationally and internationally. The VZBV does not claim to be legitimated to enforce the collective interests of European consumers.[49]

2014); G Howells, Ch Twigg-Flesner and Th Wilhelmsson, *Rethinking European Consumer Law* (Routledge, 2017).

[45] Originally OJ L 364, 9.12.2004, 1–11, now repealed and replaced through Reg 2394/2017 OJ L 345, 27.12.2017, 1–26.

[46] H-W Micklitz and P Rott, 'Verbraucherrecht' in M Dauses and M Ludwigs (eds), *Handbuch des EU Wirtschaftsrecht*, 57th edn (Beck, 2022) 885.

[47] One of the authors, Hans Micklitz, was personally involved in the merger as he was consulted by the consumer organisations – the *Verbraucherschutzverein* – and by the Ministry of Economics, more concretely Max Wiest.

[48] See at www.vzbv.de/en (accessed 6 November 2022).

[49] See at www.vzbv.de/sites/default/files/downloads/2020/07/06/vzbv_satzung_2020.pdf (accessed 6 November 2022); see § 2 Zweck: 'Der Verein verfolgt den Zweck, gemeinsam mit den Verbraucherzentralen und Verbänden, die seine Mitglieder sind, Verbraucherinteressen wahrzunehmen, den Verbraucherschutz zu fördern, die Stellung des Verbrauchers in der sozialen Marktwirtschaft zu stärken und zur Verwirklichung einer nachhaltigen Entwicklung beizutragen; nsbesondere indem er (a) in der Öffentlichkeit und gegenüber Gesetzgebung, Verwaltung, Justiz, Unternehmen und Wirtschaftsverbänden auf nationaler, europäischer und internationaler Ebene – auch durch Zusammenarbeit mit anderen Verbänden – die Interessen und Rechte der Verbraucher unter Berücksichtigung des Allgemeinwohls vertritt, … (e) Verbraucherrechte, erforderlichenfalls auch durch Anrufung der Gerichte und Nutzung der gesetzlich geregelten Verbandsklagebefugnisse, sowohl

In order to understand how the VZBV sees its role in transborder collective enforcement, one needs to go back to the 1990s. German consumers were spammed with so-called sweepstakes from companies located in France. In a Franco-German conflict, the question arose whether French consumer organisations should and could defend the interests of German consumers and/or whether German consumer organisations had legal standing to sue a French company in order to protect German consumers against French sweepstakes. The EU Commission sponsored a test case,[50] which demonstrated the need for mutual recognition of legal standing, which was later realised in Directive 98/27. The litigation showed the overwhelming difficulties in determining the competent jurisdiction and choice of the applicable law. To date, the mutual recognition of standing has been the only step so far. Neither the Brussels Regulation nor the Rome I and Rome II Regulations deal with the particularities of the collective dimension of consumer law enforcement, as their focus is on cross-border litigation between two individuals.[51] The then VSV perceived the whole exercise as a defeat and was not ready to engage in a similar exercise, even after adoption of Directive 98/27[52] and the three Regulations on private international law.

In response, German consumer organisations developed two different strategies. The first is to sue a company that is operating worldwide. The initial experience resulted from an action for an injunction against Lufthansa and the International Air Transport Association (IATA) rules.[53] One of Lufthansa's – rejected – defence lines was that IATA rules do not come under the jurisdiction of German courts. In trying to protect German consumers against unfair terms of internationally operating companies, the VZBV indirectly represents the interest of all potentially affected European consumers. However, the EU consumer *acquis* does not provide for mutual recognition of judgments in the field of consumer law. The second strategy is built on the preliminary reference procedure. Through this approach, German and Austrian consumer organisations managed to raise consumer protection standards in the EU.[54]

Not least due to the growing importance of public enforcement authorities in transborder cooperation, the German Government and political parties are advocating for the establishment of a consumer agency side by side with consumer organisations. A possible candidate is the German Cartel Office.[55] The recently adopted Directive

national als auch international durchsetzt, insbesondere indem er Verstöße gegen verbraucherschützende Vorschriften nach dem Unterlassungsklagengesetz, dem Gesetz gegen den unlauteren Wettbewerb, dem Recht der Allgemeinen Geschäftsbedingungen und verbraucherrelevanten Datenschutzvorschriften verfolgt sowie sonstige Vorschriften im Interesse der Verbraucher durchsetzt'.

[50] H-W Micklitz, 'Cross-Border Consumer Conflicts: A French-German Experience' (1993) 16 *Journal of Consumer Policy* 411.

[51] See N Reich, 'Cross Border Consumer Protection' in Reich et al (eds) (n 43) 285.

[52] Directive 98/27 on Injunctions, OJ L 166, 11.6.1998, p 51–55, Brussels Regulation on jurisdiction, recognition and enforcement OJ L 351, 20.12.2012, p 1–32; Rome I Regulation on contract 593/2008 OJ L 177, 4.7.2008, p 6–16, Rome II Regulation 864/2007 on tort OJ L 199, 31.7.2007, p 40–49.

[53] BGH NJW 1983, 1322; F Bultmann, *30 Jahre Praxis der AGB-Verbandsklage: Gutachten im Auftrag der Verbraucherzentrale Bundesverband* (Verbraucherzentrale Bundesverband eV, 2008) at www.vzbv.de/sites/default/files/downloads/gutachten_30_jahre_verbandsklage_vzbv_2008.pdf (accessed 6 November 2022); Halfmeier (n 23).

[54] Case C-92/11 *RWE Vertrieb AG v Verbraucherzentrale Nordrhein-Westfalen eV* ECLI:EU:C:2013:180; N Reich, '"I Want My Money Back": Problems, Successes and Failures in the Price Regulation of the Gas Supply Market by Civil Law Remedies in Germany' (2015) EUI Department of Law Research Paper 2015/05.

[55] See the contributions in H Schulte-Nölke and Bundesministerium der Justiz und für Verbraucherschutz (eds), *Neue Wege zur Durchsetzung des Verbraucherrechts* (Springer, 2017).

2020/1828 on representative actions[56] enables national governments to closely monitor private collective enforcement through consumer organisations. Germany tightened the grip on consumer organisations.[57]

B. Private and Public Collective Enforcement in the UK

Public authorities have played an important role in consumer protection and have often liaised with consumer groups. The OFT, established in 1973, had both consumer protection and competition functions. Its abolition and replacement with the CMA in 2013 was part of an overhaul that sought both to streamline enforcement and to make it more effective by combining the OFT and the Competition Commission. The OFT had a long and proud history in the consumer protection sector, though it had only limited resources. Enforcement action is now even more problematic. The CMA has a role, as does the National Trading Standards Board, but it has only limited resources. An earlier proposal to establish a Consumer Advocate to bring consumer claims has not been followed up.

The OFT took some important test cases on unfair terms to the courts. Even though it finally lost overall, these cases did provide some useful clarifications of the law. For instance in *First National Bank*,[58] the concept of good faith was explained; and in *Abbey National*,[59] although the bank charges were not held to be subject to review, industry practice changed, with charges being reduced, and subsequent legislation introduced a requirement of prominency before price and core terms were excluded from review.[60] The unfair commercial practices case of *Ashbourne*[61] highlighted that behavioural economics may be taken into account when judging unfairness. In this case, overoptisimism about using gyms was relevant when assessing the fairness of long minimum membership terms.

The OFT also sought to use European law, namely the Injunctions Directive,[62] to bring an action in the Belgian courts in relation to a company that was targeting UK consumers with misleading prize draw promotions.[63] Although the OFT eventually won the case, this was an unfortunate experience with lengthy court procedures and complex legal issues, making it unlikely that the OFT would embark on such litigation again. However, it prompted a change in strategy, with the Consumer Protection Cooperation Regulation[64] promoting the probably more practical approach of encouraging action by agencies in the state where the business is located.

---

[56] OJ L 406, 3.12.2020, p 17–25.

[57] Micklitz and Rott (n 46) no 871–74, according to Directive 1828/2018, Art 4 III lit a).

[58] *Director General of Fair Trading v First National Bank plc*, [2001] UKHL 52.

[59] *Office of Fair Trading v Abbey National plc and Others* [2009] UKSC 6.

[60] Consumer Rights Act 2015, s 64.

[61] *The Office of Fair Trading v Ashbourne Management Services Ltd and Others* [2011] EWHC 1237 (Ch).

[62] Directive 98/27/EC of the European Parliament and of the Council of 19 May 1998 on injuctions for the protection of consumers' interests [1998] OJ L166/51.

[63] *Office of Fair Trading v Duchesne* (Cour d'Appel, Brussels, 8 December 2005).

[64] Regulation (EC) No 2006/2004 of the European Parliament and of the Council of 27 October on cooperation between national authorities responsible for the ebforcement of consumer protection laws [2004] OJ L364/1.

Consumer organsations themselves have not played a major role in litigation. Which? is a member organisation, and there has always been a tension between the technocratic arm that favours scientific work and testing in order to provide advice to consumers who join and subscribe to the organisation's magazine so that they can navigate the marketplace, on the one hand, and, on the other, those with wider political aspirations who see consumers in a structurally weak position needing law reform to support them. Whilst Which? has at times moved into the law reform debates, it has by and large stayed removed from taking a role in litigation. One exception was the football shirts case, but its bad experience there has only made it more nervous of entering the litigation arena. It is noticeable that, at the European level, Which? has engaged with transnational issues affecting consumers but has not joined in legal actions. It has tended to look to the regulator to resolve collective consumer issues. Indeed, the super-complaints procedure has legitimated this role, as it allows Which? to force the regulator to investigate potential consumer abuses.

Collective actions are left in the hands of private lawyers. Product liability collective actions had been brought by claimant firms taking advantage of legal-aid funding. However, this source of funding has disappeared. Much criticism had arisen from the payment of large sums of money to lawyers in relation to claims that sometimes never even reach court. Recently, a new wave of consumer litigation has been fuelled by competition law. The development is being fueled by US law firm establishing themselves in London and encouraging such claims. An important recent example involved Mastercard.[65]

C. Collective Enforcement in the New Member States

New Member States joined the EU in 2004 (Cyprus, the Czech Republic, Estonia, Hungary, Latvia, Lithuania, Malta, Poland, Slovakia, Slovenia), in 2006 (Bulgaria and Romania) and in 2013 (Croatia). In 1993, the old Member States decided in the Copenhagen Council[66] to tie membership of the EU to democratisation under the Western European meaning, namely 'institutional stability of democratic institutions, rule of law and human rights'. The PHARE programme[67] turned out to be of crucial importance for the promotion of consumer law in the former communist states. The Centre de Droit de la Consommation (CDC) in Louvain-la-Neuve, headed by Thierry Bourgoignie, received considerable funding from the programme to organise adaptation of local laws to the European *acquis* through knowledge building.

One might understand the Copenhagen Council as a form of ordoliberal thinking, in that the market order should be embedded into competition law and civil society should be built through private law order. Joining the EU implies taking on EU competition law,

---

[65] *Merricks v Mastercard* [2021] CAT 28.

[66] European Council, 'Conclusions of the Presidency' (21–22 June 1993) at www.consilium.europa.eu/media/21225/72921.pdf, 12 (accessed 6 November 2022), 'Membership requires that the candidate country has achieved stability of institutions guaranteeing democracy, the rule of law, human rights and respect for and protection of minorities, the existence of a functioning market economy as well as the capacity to cope with competitive pressure and market forces within the Union.'

[67] See at www.europarl.europa.eu/enlargement/briefings/33a1_en.htm.

but for the second limb the EU could not offer a model that reached beyond piecemeal rules on non-discrimination, labour and consumer law. The candidate states reinvigorated their former private law regimes, which had been abolished by or complemented by communist ideologies, and they took on the EU's private law *acquis*. Looking back, the EU did not take the missing private law society seriously enough. It relied on self-generating forces in the new Member States and the imposition of EU consumer law to accompany market building.

For 10 years the CDC was a spider in the web. The European Commission financed consultancies following an identical approach: the existing laws – civil law rules, administrative rules of all kinds – were screened against the respective EU consumer law directives and regulations so as to identify gaps and propose regulatory action. Consumer law experts from the old Member States were writing their reports and getting together at conferences and workshops in the candidate states. The CDC produced a series of working papers, which have unfortunately not all been made publicly available.[68] The EU rules on collective enforcement provided very limited incentives for promoting consumer organisations. By 2000, the new Member States had overwhelmingly tailored the enforcement system to the needs of public authorities, with consumer organisations enjoying legal standing only in Slovenia and the Czech Republic.[69]

The formation of consumer organisations in the new Member States turned into a painful process, as yet still incomplete. The CDC made efforts to integrate into the various conferences in the candidate states not only academics, but also existing or emerging consumer organisations and consumer authorities. However, building and promoting consumer organisations did not form part of the PHARE programme. Only after these states became full members did the European Commission start three different strategies to promote consumer organisations. First, through cooperation between BEUC/ICRT (International Consumer Research and Testing) in the testing of products and,[70] second, through providing funds to BEUC via an operational grant, which allowed BEUC to unfold different strategies, partly co-financed by the richer Western organisations. BEUC engaged consultants between 2011 and 2016 to map and evaluate consumer organisations so as to decide on the most appropriate candidates for membership. Thenceforth, BEUC has differentiated between full members and affiliate members. Currently, not all Central and Eastern European consumer organisations have been granted full membership.[71] BEUC supports capacity building through reduction of the annual fee, reimbursement of travel and accommodation costs for official BEUC meetings and free access to BEUC's internal documentation centre, and gives one member of the new Member States a voice in the Executive.[72] In 2015,

---

[68] Our work as part of this project was published, see G Howells and H-W Micklitz, *Report on Consumer Sales and Associated Guarantees in Ten CEECS* (Consumer Institutions and Consumer Policy Programme, Louvain-la-Neuve, Centre de Droit de la Consommation, 1999).

[69] H-W Micklitz et al, *Verbraucherschutz durch Unterlassungsklagen, Rechtliche und Praktische Umsetzung der Richtlinie Unterlassungsklagen 98/27/EG in den Mitgliedstaaten* (Band (Volume) 17 VIEW Schriftenreihe (Nomos 2017)).

[70] See at www.international-testing.org/ (accessed 6 November 2022).

[71] BEUC, 'Membership Development' at www.beuc.eu/membership-development (accessed 6 November 2022).

[72] BEUC, 'BEUC Statutes' (14 May 2020) at www.beuc.eu/publications/2020_beuc_statutes_en.pdf (accessed 6 November 2022).

Which? established a fund for underfinanced consumer organisations so as to support their work. In a third strategy, the European Commission is funding legal educational training of all consumer organisations in both East and West via programmes such as TRACE, Consumer Champion and Consumer Pro.[73]

So far, the situation of consumer organisations in the new Member States remains unstable, with the exceptions of Slovenia and the Czech Republic, where consumer organisations have managed to develop a business model. The others are suffering from a lack of financial support from their governments, and in Hungary and Poland from general distrust of civil society.

V. Transborder and International Law Enforcement

The analysis would be incomplete without looking into further trends. This more prospective outlook allows us not only a look into possible developments at the EU level, but also to place the role and function of consumer organisations into the much broader transnational environment. Digitisation of the economy and society enables modes of transnational cooperation that would have been unthinkable 20 years ago.

However, one important difference exists between the role and place of consumer organisations in the European and in the transnational legal environment. Through Regulation 2017/2394,[74] the EU developed administrative space where national consumer agencies are legally empowered to exchange and request information and even take coordinated action. The transnational counterpart, ICPEN (International Consumer Protection Enforcement Network) established by the OECD, is built around voluntary cooperation between its members.[75] However, civil society organisations, such as consumer organisations, enjoy a strategic advantage in occupying the public area. In contrast to states, they are not bound by the constraints of international public law.

A. Coordination of Collective Enforcement in the EU

After the dissolution of the European Consumer Law Group, BEUC raised funds from the European Commission to strengthen cross-border enforcement through cooperation among consumer organisations and consumer law experts. Both authors served as legal advisors for more than a decade in the first Consumer Law Enforcement Forum (CLEF) and later in the Consumer Justice Enforcement Forum (COJEF I and COJEF II).[76] These projects created guidelines to help enhance the ability of consumer

---

[73] See at https://ec.europa.eu/chafea/consumers/information-education/consumer-champion/index_en.htm (accessed 6 November 2022).

[74] Regulation (EU) 2017/2394 of the European Parliament and of the Council of 12 December 2017 on cooperation between national authorities responsible for the enforcement of consumer protection laws and repealing Regulation (EC) No 2006/2004 [2017] OJ L345/1.

[75] See at https://icpen.org/protecting-consumers-worldwide (accessed 6 November 2022).

[76] Consumer Law Enforcement Forum Project, 'Guidelines for Consumer Organisations on Enforcement and Collective Redress' (September 2009) prepared by G Howells and H-W Micklitz, at www.mpo.cz/

organisations to utilise rights and looked at practical cases to see what lessons could be learned. From 2016 onwards, BEUC received funds again via an 'operational grant' to continue work. BEUC selects and monitors national enforcement projects and produces reports on matters such as the Diesel Scandal, on enforcement gaps in the General Data Protection Regulation[77] and control deficits in the cybersecurity of digitised toys.[78]

Some evidence suggests that consumer organisations can engage in dispute resolution, but this has mainly been at the national level and remains problematic.[79] The overall experience gained in the new millennium may be condensed into a rather simple message: consumer organisations from all over the EU are extremely reluctant to engage in transborder enforcement, due to the complexity of the legal issues, namely jurisdiction, legal standing and the applicable law, the high costs involved and limited benefits for 'their consumers'. The only way to motivate national consumer organisations to take action was via coordination around crucial consumer problems identified EU-wide. Thereby, they created a new type of collective action, coordinated action. There have been examples of consumer organisations taking parallel action against companies seen as having bad practices. The most significant case is perhaps that of Apple,[80] where there were concerns about whether consumers were being misled about the value for the guarantee being offered. In that case, even the European Commission was energised to seek to encourage Member States to draw their enforcement authority's attention to the problem. However, these parallel actions do not have force beyond the national jurisdiction.

B. Centralisation of Enforcement within the EU

The EU is trying to centralise law enforcement through building European agencies. Thinking along that line, the European Commission might try to complement transborder cooperation through promotion of an EU Consumer Protection Agency. Regulation 2017/2394 already grants the European Commission residual powers.

---

assets/dokumenty/40585/45442/550298/priloha001.pdf (accessed 6 November 2022); Consumer Justice Enforcement Forum, 'Guidelines for enforcement on consumer rights' (2013) prepared with the support of G Howells and H-W Micklitz; Consumer Justice Enforcement Forum II, 'Enforcement of Consumer Rights: Strategies and Recommendations' (May 2016) prepared with the support of E Terryn, G Howells and H-W Micklitz, at www.beuc.eu/publications/beuc-x-2016-051_cojef_ii-enforcement_of_consumer_rights. pdf (accessed 6 November 2022).

[77] Regulation (EU) 2016/679 of the European Parliamnet and of the Council of 27 April 2016 on the protection of natural persons with regard to the processing of personal data and on the free movement of such data, and repealing Directive 95/46/EC (General Data Protection Regulation) [2016] OJ L119/1.

[78] BEUC, 'Volkswagen Dieselgate Four Years Down the Road: An overview of enforcement actions and policy' (2019) at www.beuc.eu/publications/beuc-x-2019-050_report_-_four_years_after_the_dieselgate_ scandal.pdf (accessed 6 November 2022); BEUC, 'The Long and Winding Road: Two years of the GDPR: A cross-border data protection enforcement case from a consumer perspective' (2020) at www.beuc.eu/ publications/beuc-x-2020-074_two_years_of_the_gdpr_a_cross-border_data_protection_enforcement_ case_from_a_consumer_perspective.pdf (accessed 6 November 2022).

[79] BEUC, 'Stepping Up the Enforcement of Consumer Protection Rules' (2020) at www.beuc.eu/sites/ default/files/publications/beuc-x-2020-083_enforcement_mapping_report.pdf (accessed 6 November 2022).

[80] M Durovic, 'The Apple Case: The Commencement of Pan-European Battle against Unfair. Commercial Practices' (2013) 9(3) *European Review of Contract Law* 253.

Similar developments may be observed in Directive 1828/2018 on representative actions. Article 4 III lays down minimum requirements for consumer organisations in cross-border collective redress. These aim at exercising control over collective litigation. Member States must review at least every five years whether the notified national consumer organisations meet the requirements. In Germany this is required every two years. The Commission, Member States and the defendant company may challenge compliance. The tightened grip on civil society organisations will certainly not enhance cross-border litigation. However, the Regulation paves the way for the establishment of consumer organisations with members from more than one Member State, which may be designated as qualified entities and initiate collective action. The obvious institution to take on this role seems to be BEUC, which could enforce consumer law Europe-wide. As an umbrella organisation, BEUC would need the support of its members, that is, the national consumer organisations.

C. Transnationalisation of Enforcement Beyond the EU

National consumer organisations as well as BEUC are members of Consumers International (CI). The Europeanisation of consumer problems, consumer law and consumer law enforcement has strengthened the role of BEUC in the international environment. In order to coordinate their activities, BEUC, ICRT, ANEC (the European Association for the Coordination of Consumer Representation in Standardisation) and CI have concluded a Memorandum of Agreement that allocates the tasks between the different consumer organisations so as to avoid overlap and conflict. Roughly speaking, the tasks are divided along the line of institutions, with BEUC and ANEC addressing European institutions, and CI and ICRT addressing international institutions. However, the international institutions are mainly involved in policymaking. In terms of law enforcement, they seek to influence outcomes through campaigns. Whereas BEUC is to the fore in promoting the organisation of transborder enforcement in the EU, CI seems to operate much more at the policy level. To date this has been done by BEUC through member organisations, but in the future it may be able to bring actions itself under the Directive on representative actions. The key difficulty seems to be much more about coordination between the consumer organisations than the new legal framework.

A more coordinated and effective enforcement of consumer law through consumer organisations and consumer agencies may increase the so-called 'Brussels effect'. It should be recalled that EU consumer law is perhaps not ideal, but it is certainly the most developed consumer law, initiated and adopted by a supranational organisation. Therefore, even today we can observe the strong impact of EU consumer law in, for example, Africa, Asia and South America, not necessarily directly through cooperation between the EU and these countries or regions, but through the old colonial powers, which have still left deep traces in the national legal systems.[81] Many

---

[81] H-W Micklitz, T Naude and Ch Twigg-Flesner (eds), 'Special Issue on Consumer Law and Policy in Africa' (2018) 41 *Journal of Consumer Policy* 303; M Barata et al, 'An Introduction to the Issue on South America' (2022) 45 *Journal of Consumer Policy* 1; G Howells et al (eds), *Consumer Protection in Asia: Past Present Future* (Cambridge University Press, 2022).

countries in Africa, South America or Asia have taken up UK or Spanish consumer law, which in fact is by and large EU consumer law. Perhaps the most prominent field in which the Brussels effect of judgments of the Court can be traced is the area of data protection, which is ever more strongly turned into consumer data protection law, as demonstrated through the involvement of consumer organisations, for example, in *Weltimmo*,[82] *Fan Page*,[83] *Fashion*,[84] *Facebook*[85] and *Schrems I-III*.[86]

VI. Outlook – The Need for Consumer Organisations to Embrace the Digital Age and Act at Both the Local and International Level

This chapter has tried to demonstrate how consumer organisations have transformed over the post-war decades and how crucial their involvement is for the enforcement of consumer law. It has equally demonstrated that one of the greatest barriers to enforcement of consumer law is 'enforcement nationalism'. The consumer society has led to a world in which consumers suffer from the same problems but where national solutions can differ considerably. Enforcement authorities, whether public or private, do not respond adequately to the universal character of consumer problems. They seek to protect 'their stakeholders', which means the *national* collectivity of consumers. If other consumers and other countries benefit from national enforcement strategies, all well and good; but there is no enforcement strategy aiming at the protection of consumers across Europe or in a particular region of the world. Evidence for this deficiency is abundant. It might suffice to look at Dieselgate and how car manufacturers benefited from enforcement nationalism. This is not to say that enforcement should and must be centralised in the hands of European or even international organisations. However, enormous potential exists for coordinating enforcement strategies, which is only enhanced in the digital age.

Enforcing consumer law needs resources; and enforcing consumer law through consumer organisations needs nation states that are ready to provide adequate funding for the task. It seems that only Austria and Germany, as well as the Nordic countries, are ready to take the necessary steps: the first because consumer organisations function as a kind of outsourced executive branch of the competent ministries; the second because they have a strong and long-lasting commitment to protecting the collective interests of consumers far beyond the average. If nation states are not ready to provide the funding, they should at the very least grant consumer organisations standing to push public

---

[82] Case C-230/14 *Weltimmo sro v Nemzeti Adatvédelmi és Információszabadság Hatóság* ECLI:EU:C:2015:639.
[83] Case C-210/16 *Unabhängiges Landeszentrum für Datenschutz Schleswig-Holstein v Wirtschaftsakademie Schleswig-Holstein GmbH* ECLI:EU:C:2018:388.
[84] Case C-40/17 *Fashion ID GmbH and Co KG v Verbraucherzentrale NRW eV* ECLI:EU:C:2019:629.
[85] Case C-319/20 *Meta Platforms Ireland Limited v Bundesverband der Verbraucherzentralen und Verbraucherverbände – Verbraucherzentrale Bundesverband eV* ECLI:EU:C:2022:322.
[86] Case C-362/14 *Maximillian Schrems v Data Protection Commissioner* ECLI:EU:C:2015:650; Case C-498/16 *Maximilian Schrems v Facebook Ireland Limited* ECLI:EU:C:2018:37; Case C-311/18 *Data Protection Commissioner v Facebook Ireland Limited and Maximillian Schrems* ECLI:EU:C:2020:559.

agencies into action. The UK super-complaint procedure still works as a model that should be taken over by other nation states, if not by the EU.

The key role that consumer organisations can play in enforcement standing side by side with public agencies is well documented and easy to legitimate. However, outside the field of law enforcement, the future of consumer organisations seems less settled. Absent state funding for whatever reason, consumer organisations are dependent on self-financing strategies, on membership fees or on sponsorship from industry. The average age of subscribers to *Which?* has risen from 60 to 70 years in the last decade. Is this paradigmatic for membership-based consumer organisations? Not necessarily, as *Altro Consumo* demonstrates, because it has raised its membership in particular through all sorts of collective redress strategies. Historically, consumer organisations provided independent information and advice to consumers who were seeking orientation in the consumer society. The Internet has taken over large parts of such activities. Users are expecting that access to information will be free, and the same is true at least as regards basic advice. The younger generation seems to require new strategies. They hesitate to subscribe as a member to a consumer organsation. UFC-Que Choisir Association des Consommateurs de France (UFC) developed an app on cosmetics, which turned out to be an enormous success. In return for free access, UFC successfully asked for a donation. Digitisation is transforming the economy – and society. What exactly this means for civil society in whatever shade is far from clear. However, the challenge to established NGOs is visible and requires an institutional response. Consumer organisations need to connect locally – but also join up regionally and internationally – to the global challenges facing consumers in globalised and digital markets.

3

How Can Consumer Interests be Protected When Consumer Identities are Increasingly Diffuse?

VANESSA MAK*

I. Introduction

Consumer laws emerged in the United States (US) and Europe in the 1960s and 1970s in response to an upscaling of production and the perceived weakness of consumers in negotiating and assessing the quality of goods and services offered.[1] Regulation took the form of specific rules on contractual rights and tort liability, applicable to 'business-to-consumer relationships' (B2C relationships) in which the consumer was broadly defined as a natural person not acting in the course of a business or profession. In substance, regulation focused on information rights for consumers, which should help them assess the quality of goods and services offered.

While that framework served consumer protection goals well, the complexities of modern consumer markets may demand greater differentiation between types of consumers.[2] The one-size-fits-all model of consumer law no longer seems appropriate. In modern consumer markets, consumers have simultaneously become more vulnerable and more active, in particular under the influence of the rapid emergence of digital consumer markets and platformisation. I will expand upon these developments below. In terms of setting the scene for questions of transformation, it can be helpful, by way of example, to think of young people who have discovered that buying and re-selling limited edition shoes or vintage clothes can be quite a lucrative side-activity for individuals who are otherwise not active as traders.[3] Should they be subject to contract

---

* The research agenda presented in this chapter will be the subject of a Vici project (2022–27), funded by the Netherlands Organisation for Scientific Research (NWO).

[1] I Ramsay, *Consumer Law and Policy: Text and Materials on Regulating Consumer Markets* (Hart Publishing, 2012) 41 ff.

[2] V Mak, *Legal Pluralism in European Contract Law* (Oxford University Press, 2020) 119 ff; H-W Micklitz, *Brauchen Konsumenten und Unternehmen eine neue Architektur des Verbraucherrechts?: Gutachten A zum 69. Deutschen Juristentag* (CH Beck, 2012).

[3] For examples, see the online platforms Kickzswap and Vinted.

and tort rules applicable to consumer-to-consumer (C2C) relations, or do they constitute a new category of 'prosumers'?[4]

Digitalisation is but one influence on consumer markets. The same consumer who is buying or selling things on online platforms is called upon to make choices that contribute to sustainable consumption. In this respect, consumer identities are expanded to include not only their economic role as market actors but also their position as consumer-citizens with a responsibility to adjust their choices and behaviour in the light of societal objectives and values.[5]

By retaining one consumer image in regulation, which considers the consumer as a weaker party in relation to businesses and aids her by providing information, European consumer law has become unable to keep up with the demands that digitalisation, platformisation and sustainability place on consumer markets. This contribution will consider in what respects a transformation of the consumer image can lead to better-fitting regulation and policies. That is not to say that the old consumer image and the information paradigm in European consumer law should be abolished. Instead, the question is what alternatives can be identified, and whether they can be implemented into EU law and national private laws in such a way that consumer law becomes able to address the needs of modern markets. That question has come to the fore in other research too, for example in behavioural studies that have shown that consumers often do not read information or are hindered from properly understanding it due to cognitive limitations.[6] Also, advances in the capabilities of data-driven technologies have given rise to studies on the personalisation of consumer law.[7] Still, no viable alternative has emerged that can replace the information-based approach in consumer law. Existing solutions often take the form of amendments to the information paradigm, whilst acknowledging that a larger overhaul of consumer law may be needed.[8] However, such a reform would require

---

[4] The term 'prosumer' was coined by Alvin Toffler in 1980. See A Toffler, *The Third Wave* (Bantam Books, 1980) 280. Economic scholarship has in recent years put forward that the consumer concept should be revised, partly to take into account household production and other aspects of prosumer behaviour. See M-B Piorkowsky, 'Alfred Marshalls Konsumenten sind Prosumenten' in M-B Piorkowsky and K Kollmann (eds), *Vergessene und verkannte Vordenker für eine Kritische Konsumtheorie* (Springer, 2019) 21; M-B Piorkowsky, 'Ansätze für ein neues Haushaltverständnis in der ökonomischen Grund- und Allgemeinbildung' in C Müller et al (eds), *Bildung zur Sozialen Marktwirtschaft* (De Gruyter, 2014) 254, 264–66.

[5] cp V Mak and E Terryn, 'Circular Economy and Consumer Protection: The Consumer as a Citizen and the Limits of Empowerment through Consumer Law' (2020) 43 *Journal of Consumer Policy* 227.

[6] P Hacker, *Verhaltensökonomik und Normativität. Die Grenzen des Informationsmodells im Privatrecht und seine Alternativen* (Mohr Siebeck, 2017); F Gómez Pomar and M Artigot Golobardes, 'Rational Choice and Behavioural Approaches to Consumer Issues' in H-W Micklitz, A-L Sibony and F Esposito (eds), *Research Methods in Consumer Law: A Handbook* (Edward Elgar, 2018) 119; JA Luzak, 'Who Calls the Tune? Stocktaking of Behavioural Consumer Protection in Europe' in H-W Micklitz, A-L Sibony and F Esposito (eds), *Research Methods in Consumer Law: A Handbook* (Edward Elgar, 2018) 239; K Purnhagen, 'More Reality in the CJEU's Interpretation of the Average Consumer Benchmark – Also More Behavioural Science in Unfair Commercial Practices?' (2017) 8 *European Journal of Risk Regulation* 437.

[7] O Ben-Shahar and A Porat, *Personalized Law. Different Rules for Different People* (Oxford University Press, 2021); C Busch and A De Franceschi (eds), *Algorithmic Regulation and Personalized Law* (Bloomsbury Publishing, 2020).

[8] For a recent analysis of the information paradigm, see M Narciso, 'Reviewing the Information Paradigm. The Role of Online Reviews in the Regulation of Information in EU Consumer Law' (PhD dissertation, Maastricht University, 2022).

a more thorough examination and would need to be designed and evaluated carefully. This contribution aims to provide a starting point for the reform that is being sought.

The structure of this contribution is as follows. Section II will elaborate on the changes in consumer markets that have triggered a desire for transformation of the consumer image. These triggers, relating to digitalisation and sustainability, are universal in the sense that they affect market places around the world. Arguably, however, the transformation of consumer law can start with a European-focused approach, as regulation in this region is in some ways more advanced than other regions in its dealing with digital markets and sustainability. Section III will elaborate on this point. Section IV then turns to three specific images of the consumer that can be used as ideal types for a further examination of the ways in which a new consumer image can be constructed. These are ideal types and, as will be seen, some overlap between them is unavoidable. They nevertheless provide a starting point for a systematic unpacking of the consumer image in the light of digitalisation, platformisation and sustainability. Section V veers back to the overarching perspective and asks how the insights from the studies of the three ideal types can inform a new perspective on the consumer image in European consumer law. It posits that a transformation of the consumer image will have to take account of the historical development of consumer images in EU law, as well as regulatory techniques that help find the right balance between over- and under-protection of certain consumer groups. On an institutional level, the ways in which lawmakers at different levels of regulation – including EU law, national laws and private regulation – can integrate new perspectives on consumer law and policy require attention. Section VI concludes by briefly summarising what the main challenges are and how they will be addressed. The outlook for the future is optimistic: European consumer law has matured from a one-size-fits-all model focused on B2C relations to a legal framework that encapsulates the values of EU law and that can be a building block for a new architecture for consumer law in digital markets and in relation to sustainability. The time is now right for engaging in a thorough examination of existing rules of consumer law, including those laid down in national contract and tort laws. The aim will be to design rules that are tailored to the new vulnerabilities and opportunities arising for consumers in digital markets, and to unlock the capacities of consumers to contribute to more sustainable consumption.

This chapter therefore proposes a fundamental reassessment of the consumer image. It is triggered by the observation that the consumer concept that has been central to European consumer law since its inception – of the consumer as a weaker party vis-à-vis a business, who through information can be placed in a more equal position – is no longer fitting. The influences of digitalisation and sustainability on consumer markets, as described above, require a reassessment of vulnerabilities of, as well as new opportunities for, consumers. That reassessment could well result in new conceptions of 'the consumer' in regulation and policy making. In other words, a 'transformation of the consumer'. The outcomes however, are to be determined. The next sections will make a start.

II. Triggers for Transformation of the Consumer Image

The need for transformation of the consumer image is triggered by three developments in consumer markets: digitalisation; platformisation; and the pursuit of sustainability. These three topics are central themes of the European Commission's consumer agenda 2020–25 and also influence consumer policies at the national level of EU Member States, as well as globally.

Digitalisation in consumer markets denotes the emergence of markets for digital goods and services, such as e-books, apps, music, videos and streaming services.[9] Consumers in these markets are not only weaker in relation to businesses due to a lack of bargaining power or a lack of information on the quality of products, as they are in markets for physical goods, but they are also vulnerable to exploitation, as they are subjected to sophisticated and opaque techniques seeking to manipulate their purchasing decisions.[10] In this context, the existing information-orientated approach of consumer laws may no longer suffice.[11]

Platformisation concerns the rise of online platforms, such as Amazon and Airbnb, which facilitate the sale of goods and services between traders and consumers. On these platforms, products are offered by professional as well as non-professional traders. This means that consumers, that is natural persons not acting in the course of a business or profession, can move to the supply side of the market and become so-called 'prosumers' (conflating the concepts of 'consumer' and 'producer').[12] While peer-to-peer sales are not a new phenomenon and are regulated by the general rules of contract and tort law, platformisation upsets the balance that existing laws have struck between the interests of traders, buyers and third parties. Online platform operators are seldom held liable for harm suffered by consumers buying from prosumers (or other traders) through a platform. Yet platform operators can have a meaningful role in safeguarding the quality of goods and services offered on their platform. Legislators are grappling with the question how to regulate platform responsibilities, as seen, for example, in the EU's proposal for a Digital Services Act (DSA).[13] That also demands a reappraisal of prosumer responsibilities.[14]

---

[9] Specific regulation was introduced in Directive (EU) 2019/770 of the European Parliament and of the Council of 20 May 2019 on certain aspects concerning contracts for the supply of digital content and digital services (Digital Content Directive) [2019] OJ L136/1.

[10] eg. algorithmic manipulation through targeted advertising; cp G Wagner and H Eidenmüller, 'Down by Algorithms? Siphoning Rents, Exploiting Biases, and Shaping Preferences: Regulating the Dark Side of Personalized Transactions' (2019) 86 *The University of Chicago Law Review* 581.

[11] For a more detailed analysis see section IV.A.

[12] cf Toffler (n 4).

[13] European Commission, 'Proposal for a Regulation of the European Parliament and of the Council on a Single Market for Digital Services (Digital Services Act) and amending Directive 2000/31/EC' COM (2020) 825 final. For commentaries, see C Cauffman and C Goanta, 'A New Order: The Digital Services Act and Consumer Protection' (2021) 12 *European Journal of Risk Regulation* 758; C Busch and V Mak, 'Putting the Digital Services Act in Context' (2021) 10 *Journal of European Consumer and Market Law* 109. The DSA proposal was published together with a proposal for a Digital Markets Act (DMA): European Commission, 'Proposal for a Regulation of the European Parliament and of the Council on contestable and fair markets in the digital sector (Digital Markets Act)' COM (2020) 842 final. On that proposal, see R Podszun, P Bongartz and S Langenstein, 'The Digital Markets Act: Moving from Competition Law to Regulation for Large Gatekeepers' (2021) 10 *Journal of European Consumer and Market Law* 60; R Podszun, 'The Digital Markets Act: What's in it for Consumers?' (2022) 11 *Journal of European Consumer and Market Law* 1.

[14] For a more detailed analysis see section IV.B.

The pursuit of sustainability is a third trigger for a re-conceptualisation of the consumer concept. The main question in this context is what role can be expected of consumers besides governments and the private sector in pursuing sustainable consumption. Sustainable consumption has become an important societal goal and is part of the UN Sustainable Development Goals (goal number 12).[15] Consumers themselves are part of the strategy adopted by governments and policy makers to achieve more sustainable approaches to consumption. For consumer law, this demands a re-evaluation of the consumer protection-orientated approach adopted in B2C relationships. Should consumers not share the responsibility to make sustainable choices, as consumer citizens, and how can that be achieved? This aspect of the transformation of 'the consumer' stands apart from digital markets. However, it provides a vital step in the construction of a consumer concept that takes account of the complexities of modern consumer markets. Whereas the other questions so far highlighted focus on market-driven vulnerabilities of consumers,[16] the issue of consumer citizenship in relation to sustainable consumption highlights the role of consumer law beyond market regulation, in the pursuit of societal goals. Consumer markets are increasingly influenced by such goals.[17] Furthermore, this perspective highlights that consumer concepts should not only be adjusted to weaknesses following from growing asymmetries in digital consumer markets, but should also take account of responsibilities that rest on consumers as citizens.

These trends form the starting point of a deconstruction of the consumer concept, revealing divergences from the one-size-fits-all model of existing consumer laws. The challenge is to reconstruct consumer laws along the lines of a contextual approach to consumer protection, meaning that consumer concepts in regulation are tailored to the identities and behaviour of consumers in markets changed by digitalisation, platformisation and sustainability goals. I will elaborate on the way in which these questions can be approached in section IV of this chapter.

III. Focus on Europe

The challenge of how to regulate consumer markets in our day and age is of course a question that affects legislators and policy makers globally. There is a case to be made, however, for taking Europe as a starting point.

Europe can be a focal point for the transformation of consumer law due to the EU's unique position in the regulation of consumer markets. The EU stands apart from other large consumer markets by its openness to global competitors (in contrast to China, which gives preference to local businesses) and the willingness to regulate for the sake

---

[15] UN Sustainable Development Goals, see UN, 'Do you know all 17 SDGs?' at sdgs.un.org/goals (accessed 26 October 2022).
[16] cp European Commission, 'Understanding Consumer Vulnerability in the EU's Key Markets' (January 2016) at ec.europa.eu/info/publications/understanding-consumer-vulnerability-eus-key-markets_en (accessed 26 October 2022). See also P Siciliani, C Riefa and H Gamper, *Consumer Theories of Harm* (Hart Publishing, 2019).
[17] cf Consolidated Version of the Treaty on European Union [2008] OJ C115/13, Arts 2 and 3. See also Mak and Terryn (n 5).

of fair competition, responsible use of data and consumer protection (in contrast to the more reluctant stance of the US to regulation). It is in many cases a frontrunner, as exemplified by the 2016 General Data Protection Regulation (GDPR),[18] the 2020 proposal for the DSA, and a highly developed set of consumer legislation and case law. However, the EU is not in the lead on every topic, and note will be taken of regulatory solutions adopted earlier in other legal systems. In relation to sustainability, for example, a large number of US States have already adopted rules on reparability of products.[19]

The framework of EU law also provides a solid basis for developing a contextualised approach to consumer concepts. Due to the shared competence of the EU legislator and the legislators of the EU Member States, European consumer law is made up of a mixture of EU and national laws. An implication of this is that a balance always needs to be struck between harmonisation and the maintenance of diversity. The challenge that European consumer law is faced with, nonetheless, is a much greater degree of contextualisation than currently exists. Recent years have seen EU consumer laws converge towards a concept of the 'average consumer' as someone who is 'reasonably well-informed, and reasonably observant and circumspect'.[20] An exception to this highly capable consumer is made for those who are vulnerable due to 'mental or physical disability, age or credulity'.[21] Also in some cases national laws maintain general rules of contract or tort that protect consumers, depending on the circumstances of each case. The rise of digital and platform markets, and the call for sustainable consumption, demands a new contextualisation. Greater account will have to be taken of structural factors that give rise to new vulnerabilities, and of situational factors that characterise different forms and degrees of consumer vulnerability.[22]

The reassessment of the consumer image and consequent adaptations of existing rules and policies will affect a number of EU instruments. In the EU, consumer protection rules applicable to the digital market are laid down primarily in directives that are generally applicable to consumer contracts and/or relations, such as the Unfair Contract Terms Directive (UCTD),[23] the Consumer Rights Directive (CRD),[24] and the UCPD. Some rules are derived from the Digital Content Directive and the GDPR. Further, for

---

[18] Regulation (EU) 2016/679 of the European Parliament and of the Council of 27 April 2016 on the protection of natural persons with regard to the processing of personal data and on the free movement of such data, and repealing Directive 95/46/EC (General Data Protection Regulation) [2016] OJ L119/1.

[19] E Terryn, 'A Right to Repair? Towards Sustainable Remedies in Consumer Law' (2019) 27 *European Review of Private Law* 851.

[20] See inter alia Case C-210/96 *Gut Springenheide GmbH and Rudolf Tusky v Oberkreisdirektor des Kreises Steinfurt – Amt für Lebensmittelüberwachung* ECLI:EU:C:1998:369, [1998] ECR I-4657; Case C-26/13 *Árpád Kásler and Hajnalka Káslerné Rábai v OTP Jelzálogbank Zrt* ECLI:EU:C:2014:282; Case C-51/17 *OTP Bank and OTP Faktoring v Teréz Ilyés and Emil Kiss* ECLI:EU:C:2018:750; MBM Loos, 'Transparency Under the UCTD: Could You Please Explain what these Terms are Supposed to Mean?: Case note to CJEU, C-51/17 OTP Bank and OTP Faktoring' (2020) 9 *Journal of European Consumer and Market Law* 25.

[21] Directive 2005/29/EC of the European Parliament and of the Council of 11 May 2005 concerning unfair business-to-consumer commercial practices in the internal market (Unfair Commercial Practices Directive) [2005] OJ L149/22 (UCPD), Art 5(3).

[22] See section V.

[23] Council Directive 1993/13 of 5 April 1993 on unfair terms in consumer contracts [1993] OJ L95/29.

[24] Directive 2011/83/EU of the European Parliament and of the Council of 25 October 2011 on consumer rights [2011] OJ L304/64.

sustainability, the policing of information based on the CRD and the UCPD is complemented by specific rules on consumer rights following, for example, from the Consumer Sales Directive (CSD).[25] The analysis of the UCPD, the UCTD and the CRD is central to the reconstruction of the consumer image. These three Directives have a core position in the regulation of fairness and transparency in EU consumer law.[26] The question is whether they achieve enough.

IV. Re-imagining the Consumer

The deconstruction and reconstruction of a consumer image in European consumer law is in some ways daunting, as so much of consumer law and policy has been built around this one notion of the consumer as a weaker party in relation to businesses. Any adjustment of the prevailing consumer image will have repercussions in the rules that apply to B2C relations as well as adjoining rules of private law, for example the rules that apply to C2C relations. Adjustments to the consumer image will also affect the ways in which law is used as an instrument to steer consumer behaviour. The benchmark that is chosen is important. Is it the 'average consumer' who is reasonably informed, and reasonably observant and circumspect, and who has until now been the primary point of reference for EU consumer law and policy? Or is there room for a shift towards a more encompassing perspective, taking account of the consumer who is vulnerable due to socio-demographic characteristics, behavourial characteristics, personal situation or market environment?[27]

The bigger questions cannot be answered without considering smaller, more focused areas of research. In order to get a firmer grasp on the topic, a number of case studies can highlight which changes are affecting consumer markets. In this respect, the three trends previously identified – digitalisation, platformisation and the pursuit of sustainability – give direction as to what should be the leading questions in this enquiry. I will examine here how each of these trends may be developed further into a research agenda that is able to support a reconstruction of the consumer image in European consumer law.

A. The Digital Consumer

The consumer of goods and services in the digital market is dealing with suppliers who know many things about her preferences and may exploit that knowledge. Sales platforms such as Amazon, Bol.com, or Rakuten France gather information on consumer preferences and use that information to optimise the way in which products are

---

[25] Directive (EU) 2019/771 of the European Parliament and of the Council of 20 May 2019 on certain aspects concerning contracts for the sale of goods [2019] OJ L136/28.

[26] cf Siciliani, Riefa and Gamper (n 16); J Luzak and M Junuzovic, 'Blurred Lines: Between Formal and Substantive Transparency in Consumer Credit Contracts' (2019) 8 *Journal of European Consumer and Market Law* 97.

[27] cf European Commission (n 16) 383.

marketed on their websites. Social media platforms like Facebook similarly gather data on user preference and use this information for a range of purposes, including targeted advertising, where ads appear on a user's timeline based on her 'likes' and clicks on the website.[28]

Businesses therefore use data-driven technologies to learn how consumers behave and to influence their purchasing decisions. They often do this without the consumers' knowledge or understanding.[29] Such practices create a 'digital asymmetry', a term denoting the structural imbalance between tech-providers and consumers, due to consumers' structural and universal inability to fully understand the digital architecture.[30]

In terms of reassessment of the consumer image, this observation leads to a first hypothesis, namely: digital asymmetry requires a re-conceptualisation of consumer vulnerability in digital markets, combined with tailored rules for protection of digital consumers. One angle allowing a further examination of the topic can be a study on the use of profiling by businesses, focusing on the creation of personalised 'persuasion profiles'. Persuasion profiles may be defined as 'collections of estimates of the expected effects of different influence principles for a specific individual. Hence, an individual's persuasion profile indicates which influence principles are expected to be most effective.'[31]

Notably, profiling is only one aspect of the ways in which businesses use technology to manipulate consumer behaviour in digital markets. It is often accompanied by the use of user interface design choices that coerce, steer or deceive users into making unintended and potentially harmful decisions ('dark patterns'),[32] or personalised pricing, differentiating prices and marketing conditions depending on a user's personal characteristics.[33] Profiling can be taken as a starting point for examination of the consumer image in digital markets, since it constitutes the core aspect of digital asymmetry; the point where businesses gain their structurally stronger market position

---

[28] Consumer law and data protection coincide here, although a balance still has to be found with regard to free speech, content moderation and protection against misleading advertising. See, eg, C Goanta and S Mulders, '"Move Fast and Break Things": Unfair Commercial Practices and Consent on Social Media' (2019) 8 *Journal of European Consumer and Market Law* 136.

[29] eg by running A/B experiments on websites.

[30] N Helberger et al, *EU Consumer Protection 2.0. Structural Asymmetries in Digital Consumer Markets* (BEUC Report, March 2021) at beuc.eu/publications/beuc-x-2021-018_eu_consumer_protection.0_0.pdf (accessed 26 October 2022); A Jablonowska et al, 'Consumer Law and Artificial Intelligence. Challenges to the EU Consumer Law and Policy Stemming from the Business' Use of Artificial Intelligence' (2018) EUI Working Paper LAW 2018/11 at cadmus.eui.eu/handle/1814/57484 (accessed 26 October 2022); S Zuboff, *The Age of Surveillance Capitalism* (PublicAffairs, 2019).

[31] M Kaptein et al, 'Personalizing Persuasive Technologies: Explicit and Implicit Personalization Using Persuasion Profiles' (2015) 77 *International Journal of Human-Computer Studies* 38, 39–40; Helberger et al (n 30) 6. See also J Chester, 'Cookie Wars: How New Data Profiling and Targeting Techniques Threaten Citizens and Consumers in the "Big Data" Era' in S Gutwirth et al (eds), *European Data Protection: In Good Health?* (Springer, 2012) 53.

[32] SS Chivukula et al, 'Nothing Comes Before Profit: *Asshole Design* in the Wild' in *Proceedings of the 2019 CHI Conference on Human Factors in Computing Systems Extended Abstracts (CHI'19 Extended Abstracts)*, 4–9 May 2019, Glasgow (ACM, 2019) 1.

[33] M Bourreau and A De Streel, 'The Regulation of Personalised Pricing in the Digital Era' (25 September 2020) Note for the OECD, DAF/COMP/WD(2018)150 at one.oecd.org/document/DAF/COMP/WD(2018)150/en/pdf (accessed 25 October 2022).

vis-à-vis consumers. The results from such a study can then be related to mechanisms that increase digital asymmetry, such as dark patterns and personalised pricing.

The concept of digital asymmetry provides a hook for the development of a consumer image tailored to the digital market. The trade-off that needs to be made is whether such a consumer image can do better than the existing framework of European consumer law. How does digital asymmetry differ from existing concepts of consumer weakness and vulnerability in European consumer law? And if European consumer law is to protect consumers from exploitation due to digital asymmetry, which rules in current regulation offer protection and what amendments are needed? The initial steps have been taken through a reassessment of the UCPD in the light of digital asymmetry.[34] It could be that regulation needs to go further. One key characteristic of digital asymmetry is that business models in digital markets have become so opaque that traders themselves cannot provide information on how exactly the digital architecture is constructed, and what that entails for the way in which consumer data are gathered, processed and shared with third parties. Even if they were able to provide information on the workings of the digital architecture, the degree of complexity could well be so great that even the reasonably well-informed average consumer of EU law would have difficulty understanding it. In that light, European consumer law can at least provide a basis for reassessing the balance of fairness between tech companies and their users.[35]

B. The Prosumer

The consumer in platform markets has other characteristics, or so it seems at first glance. In online platform markets consumers have become active on the supply side, for example selling t-shirts or toys from their bedrooms through online platforms like marktplaats.nl or Amazon.com. This type of consumer has already been referred to as a consumer turned 'prosumer'.[36] Further distinctions could potentially be made within this concept. For example, one might distinguish between consumers who produce the goods they sell (eg through 3D printing) and consumers who only buy goods and sell them on. In terms of presenting the research problem, however, it suffices for now to realise that the position of prosumers on online platforms is subject to several risks.

Depending on whether the prosumer qualifies as a professional trader,[37] prosumer–consumer contracts are governed by consumer law or by general contract law. Neither regime seems to be quite fitting for prosumers in the platform economy. A number of problems have already been identified in the literature on online platforms, most recently in the debate following the publication of the DSA proposal.

---

[34] Helberger et al (n 30) 46 ff.

[35] cf C Goanta, 'European Consumer Law: The Hero of Our Times' (2021) 10 *Journal of European Consumer and Market Law* 177.

[36] See section I. For an examination in the legal domain, see also I Brown and CT Marsden, *Regulating Code: Good Governance and Better Regulation in the Information Age* (MIT Press, 2013) 183 ff.

[37] For guidance, see Case C-105/17 *Evelina Kamenova v Okrazhna prokuratura – Varna* ECLI:EU:C:2018:808 (*Kamenova*) para 38.

First, prosumers may be exposed to liability towards consumer-buyers contracting with them, for example if goods are defective and cause harm to the consumer or if information concerning the product characteristics is misleading. Under existing regulation, the prosumer will often be solely liable. Platform operators cannot be held liable, in most cases, because they are not party to the contract between prosumer and consumer-buyer and therefore not responsible for unsatisfactory performance. Product liability under the EU's Product Liability Directive cannot be directed to platforms if they are not the producer, importer or distributor of the goods.[38] Further, most platforms benefit from the 'host exemption' of the E-commerce Directive,[39] holding that hosts are not liable for illegal information posted by users unless they were alerted to it and failed to remove it. In consequence, prosumers, whether professional traders or not, will often bear the burden of liability. As the weaker party in relation to the platform, plus the one less sizeable and less likely to provide an adequate remedy to the consumer, one may wonder whether this outcome is justifiable.[40]

Second, platform operators often bind external traders to strict performance targets through contractual standard terms. Non-compliance leads to warnings and eventually denial of access to the platform. Regulation (EU) 2019/1150 on fairness in platform-to-business relationships goes some way towards protecting small traders.[41] However, this Regulation applies only to professional traders on online platforms, not to non-professional prosumers.

In terms of reassessment of the consumer image, these observations lead to a second hypothesis, namely: the regulation of private law relationships in the platform economy requires the introduction of a 'prosumer' category and rules tailored to it. Should this idea be followed through, the consequence may be that rules will be designed that in certain circumstances hold platform operators jointly and severally liable for harm caused by prosumers to consumers. What will need to be examined is in what circumstances this should be the case, taking account of existing legal frameworks for third-party liability in contract and tort.

In order to redesign the legal framework, it will be helpful to have a better picture of what characterises prosumers. Do we need to see them as a separate category, or can we place them within existing categories of 'traders' and 'consumers' in European consumer law? This question is unresolved, in part because the characteristics of

---

[38] Council Directive 1985/374/EEC of 25 July 1985 on the approximation of the laws, regulations and administrative provisions of the Member States concerning liability for defective products [1985] OJ L210/29. This Directive is under review and a proposal for a new Directive on Liability for defective products was presented by the European Commission at the end of September 2022 (COM (2022) 495 final). Directive 2001/95/EC of the European Parliament and of the Council of 3 December 2001 on general product safety [2001] OJ L11/4 was also reviewed, and the new General Product Safety Regulation (proposed in 2021 (COM (2021) 346 final)) was adopted by the Council on 25 April 2023.

[39] Directive 2000/31/EC of the European Parliament and of the Council of 8 June 2000 on certain legal aspects of information society services, in particular electronic commerce, in the Internal Market ('Directive on electronic commerce) [2000] OJ L178/1.

[40] C Busch, 'Rethinking Product Liability Rules for Online Marketplaces: A Comparative Perspective' (2021) European Legal Studies Institute Osnabrück, Research Paper Series No 21-01 at dx.doi.org/10.2139/ssrn.3897602 (accessed 25 October 2022).

[41] Regulation (EU) 2019/1150 of the European Parliament and of the Council of 20 June 2019 on promoting fairness and transparency for business users of online intermediation services [2019] OJ L186/57.

'trader' and 'consumer' concepts in EU law and the national laws of the Member States are not uniformly established. The Court of Justice of the European Union (CJEU) provided some guidance in the *Kamenova* case, concerning the definition of the 'trader' in the Unfair Commercial Practices Directive.[42] The list of characteristics provided by the Court sets out when a natural person selling products through an online platform should be considered a trader. It takes into account, inter alia, whether the sale takes place in an organised manner, whether the seller has specific expertise with regard to the products offered, whether the seller has a legal status allowing her to engage in commercial activities (eg registration with a chamber of commerce), whether the seller is subject to value-added tax, and whether the seller regularly purchases new or secondhand goods in order to resell them.[43] This list is not exhaustive, however, and Member States may maintain their own assessment criteria alongside the guidance given by the CJEU.

The development of a legal framework that befits 'prosumers' in the platform market is therefore still in its infancy. For its further development, it could be helpful to identify in what respects prosumers require protection as a weaker party and in what respects they are more self-reliant compared to other consumers. To this end, findings from behavioural studies on consumer decision making in online market places and studies on active (versus passive) consumers may provide a starting point for further analysis. Research has shown that consumer behaviour is influenced by biases and heuristics, which means that the information-based approach, which is prevalent in existing consumer law, is often not effective in steering consumers towards rational, informed choices.[44] Further, differences have been seen in the ways in which active consumers and passive consumers operate in consumer markets. This ranges from the ways in which they process information[45] to the personality traits and market conditions that trigger consumers to complain and hold businesses account-able for unfair practices[46] or to behave in a sustainable manner.[47] Prosumers are likely to have more characteristics of active than of passive consumers. If this is confirmed, it is still a question whether prosumers' behaviour and cognitive limitations in decision-making processes differ from those of other consumers. Therefore, further research, for example in the form of an empirical study of prosumers on online platforms, may be warranted.

The outcomes of the suggested analyses can form the basis for assessing whether a new category of 'prosumers' should be introduced into EU consumer law and/or the laws of the Member States. By means of synthesis one might ask: (i) what liability

---

[42] *Kamenova* (n 37). See also C Twigg-Flesner, 'Bad Hand? The "New Deal" for EU Consumers' (2018) 15 *Zeitschrift für das Privatrecht der Europäischen Union* 166.

[43] *Kamenova* (n 37) para 38.

[44] O Ben-Shahar and CE Schneider, *More Than You Wanted to Know. The Failure of Mandated Disclosure* (Princeton University Press, 2014).

[45] J Luzak, 'Online Disclosure Rules of the Consumer Rights Directive: Protecting Passive or Active Consumers?' (2015) 4 *Journal of European Consumer and Market Law* 79.

[46] YA Arbel and R Shapira, 'Theory of the Nudnik: The Future of Consumer Activism and What We Can Do to Stop It' (2020) 73 *Vanderbilt Law Review* 929.

[47] M Maciaszcyk and M Kocot, 'Behavior of Online Prosumers in Organic Product Market as Determinant of Sustainable Consumption' (2021) 13 *Sustainability* 1157.

rules for misleading information or dangerous products currently apply to prosumers in the EU, depending on professional or non-professional status; (ii) whether liability should be divided differently amongst platforms and prosumers; and (iii) whether the introduction of a 'prosumer' category would be required for achieving that aim. The usual challenge of combining behavioural studies and law applies here, namely that the translation of behavioural findings to legal rules always requires normative choices. A discursive approach, discussing how available alternatives fit within the doctrinal framework of existing laws and with policy objectives, can help identify what options for regulation are available and how they can contribute to achieving a balance between the interests of prosumers, platforms and consumers. At the same time, an analysis of the position of prosumers on online platforms can contribute to theory-building in private law. Seeing that contract and tort law are based on the autonomy of parties, an analysis of this kind contributes to determining (i) what degree of autonomy can be expected from prosumers; and (ii) when the autonomy of platform operators should be curtailed for the sake of prosumer protection.[48]

The development of a prosumer image for platform regulation could also benefit from comparisons with other areas in which consumers have moved to the supply-side of the market. Most notable is the rise of the prosumer in energy markets, where consumers increasingly generate their own household electricity through solar panels. The position of these types of prosumers in regulation is still under development.[49] Interestingly, not only their legal position in the consumer energy market is subject to evaluation, but also their position as contributors to sustainability goals in society. In that respect, the prosumer concept coincides with the third notion of the consumer presented here, the consumer-citizen.

C. The Consumer-Citizen

The third aspect of a reassessment of the consumer image is triggered by a changing perspective on what society expects of consumers. The consumer concept historically developed as an instrument for the protection of individuals in markets, that is, in an economic context where they were regarded as weaker parties vis-à-vis businesses. In this day and age, that image is changing. Consumers are regarded as individuals who not only operate in a market, but who are also part of the pursuit of societal goals.

One of the most urgent societal goals involving consumer action is sustainability. The pursuit of sustainable consumption in the light of climate change is high on the

---

[48] Autonomy is defined as the capacity for self-development through free choice, noting that this freedom can be restricted if it curtails another party's autonomy. cp H Dagan, 'Autonomy, Pluralism and Contract Law Theory' (2013) 76 *Law and Contemporary Problems* 19.

[49] See, eg, A Butenko and K Cseres, 'The Regulatory Consumer: Prosumer-Driven Local Energy Production Initiatives' (2015) Amsterdam Centre for European Law and Governance Research Paper 3/2015 at www.uu.nl/sites/default/files/ucwosl-cve_20160311-the_regulatory_consumer_prosumer-driven_local_energy_production_initiatives-butenko-cseres.pdf (accessed 25 October 2022); K Cseres, 'Consumer Social Responsibility in Dutch Law. A Case Study on the Role of Consumers in the Energy Transition' (2019) 12 *Erasmus Law Review* 94; S Milciuviene et al, 'The Role of Renewable Energy Prosumers in Implementing Energy Justice Theory' (2019) 11 *Sustainability* 5286.

national, European and global agenda.[50] Although measures focus on the supply side, consumers can play an active role in the pursuit of sustainability.[51] However, rules of consumer law often clash with environmental protection goals.[52] The European legislator has started a process of integration of consumer and environmental policies (fitting with Article 11 TEU),[53] but experiences in the drafting process of the new CSD suggest that while lip service is paid to sustainability (eg recital 32 of the Directive), it has not been integrated as a policy objective in the rules of the new CSD.[54]

The reconstruction of a consumer image for European consumer law therefore also requires examination of the question of which consumer concept fits with the pursuit of sustainability goals through consumer law. An angle that may be useful here is that of the consumer citizen, meaning the consumer as an active participant in the pursuit of social policies.[55] Notably, the consumer in this context may also be conceptualised from the viewpoint of vulnerability, as climate change poses a threat to the vulnerable of the future, the 'future generations' acknowledged in climate litigation such as the *Urgenda* case.[56] While that vulnerability is acknowledged, the reassessment of the consumer image proposed here focuses on how regulation can engage today's consumers in the pursuit of sustainability, and therefore a re-conceptualisation of the consumer as a consumer citizen.

This leads to a third hypothesis: consumers may have to give up some protection if that leads to more sustainable outcomes.[57] For example, if goods are defective and consumers have a choice of remedy for non-conformity, where they can choose either repair or replacement, they may have to opt for the more sustainable remedy.[58] One aspect of reassessing the consumer image in the light of sustainability, therefore, is that the hierarchy of remedies in consumer sales law requires a reboot. The challenge in that respect is to determine how consumer law can be tailored to the pursuit of sustainability whilst maintaining consumer protection. Preliminary studies suggest that the new CSD leaves room for EU Member States to regulate remedies for non-conforming goods in ways that promote sustainable use and recycling. Member States can maintain remedies

---

[50] Besides the EU Green Deal and the UN Sustainable Development Goals, see, eg, at the national level Netherlands, 'Circular Economy 2050' www.government.nl/topics/circular-economy/circular-dutch-economy-by-2050#:~:text=2050A%20waste%2Dfree%20economy,and%20raw%20materials%20are%20reused (accessed 25 October 2022).

[51] J Karsten and LA Reisch, 'Sustainability Policy and the Law' (2008) 4 *German Policy Studies* 45. See also Mak and Terryn (n 5).

[52] C Kye, 'Environmental Law and the Consumer in the European Union' (1995) 7 *Journal of Environmental Law* 31; Mak and Terryn (n 5); H-W Micklitz, 'Squaring the Circle? Reconciling Consumer Law and the Circular Economy' (2019) 8 *Journal of European Consumer and Market Law* 229.

[53] Treaty on European Union (TEU) [2012] OJ C326/13.

[54] See E Van Gool and A Michel, 'The New Consumer Sales Directive 2019/771 and Sustainable Consumption: A Critical Analysis' (2021) 10 *Journal of European Consumer and Market Law* 136.

[55] S McGregor, 'Keynote: Consumer citizenship: A pathway to sustainable development' (International Conference on Developing Consumer Citizenship, Hamar, Norway, April 2002); SA de Vries, H de Waele and M-P Granger (eds), *Civil Rights and EU Citizenship: Challenges at the Crossroads of the European, National and Private Spheres* (Edward Elgar, 2018).

[56] M Grochowski, 'Does European Contract Law Need a New Concept of Vulnerability?' (2021) 10 *Journal of European Consumer and Market Law* 133. See also Hoge Raad, ECLI:NL:HR:2019:2006 (*Urgenda*).

[57] cp A Halfmeier, 'Abschied vom Konsumschutzrecht' (2022) *Zeitschrift für Wirtschafts- und Verbraucherrecht* 3.

[58] cp Mak and Terryn (n 5).

for 'hidden defects' beyond the legal guarantee period, maintain favourable conditions for the consumer's right to withhold payment until sellers have fulfilled their obligations, and determine when the legal guarantee period is suspended or interrupted.[59] However, the new CSD also contains a rule that makes the remedy of termination of contract and return of the price more readily available than before, thereby undermining the position of repair and replacement as primary remedies in the hierarchy (Article 13(4) CSD). Furthermore, the Directive could have done more to promote the sale of secondhand goods and the recycling of goods, backed up with consumer protection through quality control and information rights.[60]

With regard to sustainable consumption, it is important to realise that consumer law cannot by itself do all the work. The rules of consumer law constitute only one part of the policy mix used by legislators to encourage sustainable consumption. For consumers to make the right choices, it is important to understand the psychology of sustainable consumerism and the ways in which it can be stimulated through information and marketing.[61] Also, regulators and policy makers should ensure that the supply side of the market provides sustainable options for consumers.[62]

V. Reconstructing the Consumer Image in EU Law

Bringing together the lines set out in section IV, the following step is to develop an overarching perspective on the contextual use of consumer concepts in law. That requires developing a normative perspective on the way in which the consumer should be conceptualised in the light of, using shorthand,[63] new *vulnerabilities* arising from digitalisation, new ways of *empowerment* for prosumers due to platformisation and new *responsibilities* as a consumer citizen in the pursuit of sustainable consumption. These three elements – vulnerability, empowerment and responsibility – have characterised European consumer law since its inception.[64] However, the changes in market structures in the digital economy, with an opaque architecture for data protection, product safety, and contractual rights and liability, require a re-balancing that goes beyond individual B2C relationships. Information rights cannot sufficiently address the structural asymmetry between tech-firms and consumers, nor can existing contract and tort laws address the structural imbalance between prosumers and platform operators.

---

[59] Van Gool and Michel (n 54) 143.

[60] ibid 147–48. cp also E Terryn and E Van Gool, 'The Role of European Consumer Regulation in Shaping the Environmental Impact of E-Commerce' (2021) 10 *Journal of European Consumer and Market Law* 89.

[61] L Steg, 'Environmental Psychology and Sustainable Consumption' in L Reisch and J Thogersen (eds), *Handbook of Research in Sustainable Consumption* (Edward Elgar, 2015) 70.

[62] Mak and Terryn (n 5) 229–30.

[63] The picture is of course more complex, as the above analysis has shown. Moreover, the term 'empowerment' is often regarded as part of regulators' rhetoric to support consumer regulation based on the notion of a rational consumer, which, as was also seen, is not in line with the findings from behavioural studies on consumers' cognitive limitations.

[64] D Leczykiewicz and S Weatherill, 'The Images of the Consumer in EU Law' in D Leczykiewicz and S Weatherill (eds), *The Images of the Consumer in EU Law. Legislation, Free Movement and Competition Law* (Hart Publishing, 2016) 1.

The position of the consumer citizen is likewise not structurally embedded in existing consumer and environmental regulation and policies, where the focus is still primarily on information and labelling.

Besides being subject to structural factors, consumer vulnerability is situational, 'meaning that a consumer can be vulnerable in one situation but not in others, and that some consumers may be more vulnerable than others'.[65] Situational factors are sometimes integrated into consumer laws, for example in Article 5(3) UCPD, which distinguishes consumers who are vulnerable due to age or mental or physical infirmity. Nevertheless, such rules are exceptions, and moreover they also are limited in their differentiation. Age, for example, is not always a distinguishing factor, as some children are more aware of marketing manipulation than others.[66]

The common denominator in these contexts is consumer laws' lack of attention to structural and situational factors. Although the European Commission has recognised such factors, alongside individual characteristics, as part of policy making in EU consumer law – referring to '[a] consumer, who, as a result of socio-demographic characteristics, behavourial characteristics, personal situation, or market environment' is vulnerable[67] – the way in which they should be integrated into consumer law requires further development.

It is submitted that the architecture of a new approach to consumer concepts can be built on three connected foundational parts: (i) a study of 'consumer identities' in European private law, examining how they have been embedded in EU law's consumer concepts over time and how they might evolve in the future (section V.A); (ii) a study of regulatory theories that can support choices that lawmakers face between the use of categories and personalisation (section V.B); and (iii) a study of lawmaking processes in European consumer law, taking account of the legal pluralist constellation within which rules are made 'beyond the state' (section V.C).[68]

A. Consumer Identities in European Private Law

How has the differentiation in consumer identities been embedded in consumer concepts in European consumer law, and what can we learn from this for future regulation? This question provides a building block alongside the three perspectives set out in section IV for the development of a new conception of 'the consumer' in European private law. It requires an examination of contract and tort as the main areas of harmonisation of EU consumer law.

Two strands of enquiry may be followed. First, a start may be made by examining the development of consumer identities in EU law since the inception of EU consumer

---

[65] European Commission, 'Understanding Consumer Vulnerability in the EU's Key Markets: Factsheet' (February 2016) 2 at ec.europa.eu/info/sites/default/files/consumer-vulnerability-factsheet_en.pdf (accessed 25 October 2022).

[66] S van der Hof et al, 'The Child's Right to Protection against Economic Exploitation in the Digital World' (2020) 28 *The International Journal of Children's Rights* 833.

[67] European Commission (n 16) 383.

[68] For a study of legal pluralism in European consumer markets, see V Mak, *Legal Pluralism in European Contract Law* (Oxford University Press, 2020).

law. The year 1975 may be taken as a starting point, as the first consumer programme at the European level was adopted then. The consumer concept at that time was influenced by national policies of social justice. It developed towards the 'average consumer' as a *homo economicus* as part of the EU's internal market programme after the Single European Act 1985. In recent years it has adopted a differentiated stance in which social justice considerations have led to consumer protection beyond economic interests (eg, to manage the repercussions of the 2008 financial crisis on consumer mortgages).[69] The adoption of the EU's Digital Single Market Agenda and the EU Green Deal can perhaps be seen as the start of a new phase.[70] A more comprehensive picture may be obtained by charting how consumer identities have been perceived in literature and policy documents on European consumer law, including EU internal market law, EU harmonised consumer law and selected national laws.

Second, complementary to the first part, an analysis may be made of the way in which consumer identities have been translated into consumer concepts in EU consumer law and national consumer laws, focusing on contract and tort law. Such an analysis should include the development of consumer concepts in legislation, case law and literature on European consumer law, including EU internal market law, EU harmonised consumer law and national laws of the Member States.

B. Regulatory Choices: Between Categories and Personalisation

What we need, furthermore, is a theoretical framework that can provide guidance for regulatory choices between categorical and contextualised consumer protection. While the claim made at the outset of this chapter challenges the existing one-size-fits-all model of consumer law, it also recognises that something may be lost if that model is replaced by a contextual approach. The advantage of a categorical model is that the net of consumer protection is cast widely: every natural person not acting in the course of a business or profession benefits from it. Over-regulation is an accepted consequence of this approach. What do we lose if we let go of it?

Regulatory theories can provide a framework for developing a more structured view on the alternatives that could be considered besides the existing model of European consumer law. One such framework may be provided by the decision theory framework developed by Hacker for consumer law.[71] That framework provides a tool for regulatory choices in circumstances of uncertainty, for example where the characteristics and behaviour of a group (such as consumers) differentiate considerably. It narrows the scope for normative regulatory choices by comparing what rules would be adopted if

---

[69] H-W Micklitz, *The Politics of Justice in European Private Law. Social Justice, Access Justice, Societal Justice* (Cambridge University Press, 2018) 316 ff.

[70] Micklitz (n 52); Helberger et al (n 30).

[71] P Hacker, *Verhaltensökonomik und Normativität. Die Grenzen des Informationsmodells im Privatrecht und seine Alternativen* (Mohr Siebeck, 2017); P Hacker, 'Regulating Under Uncertainty about Rationality: From Decision Theory to Machine Learning and Complexity Theory' in S Grundmann and P Hacker (eds), *Theories of Choice. The Social Science and the Law of Decision Making* (Oxford University Press, 2021).

(i) most people act rationally, or (ii) most people act in boundedly rational ways. These two sides of the spectrum circumscribe the space within which normative choices can be made by regulators. The key normative choice lies in the criteria used to rank the different outcomes.[72]

The normative criteria for ranking alternative regulatory options can be developed through a political philosophical analysis, building on scholarly work on the foundations of European private law. While European private law is based on liberal political ideologies, it may be argued that there is an overlapping consensus on the categorical protection of weaker parties.[73] That finding may be used as the basis for a discursive approach, through which arguments in support of and against the rules identified at step one may first be mapped and then weighed against each other. The theory may also be tested against the findings from studies on specific areas of consumer law (section IV) and on the development of consumer concepts in EU law (section V.A).

C. The Transformation of the Consumer: Reconstruction of EU Consumer Laws along Contextualised Lines

The lines of enquiry come together in the final question: should European consumer laws be reconstructed along contextualised lines and, if so, how? What limitations to this approach should be taken into account in the multi-level regulatory framework of the EU? The research question is normative in nature and asks an overarching and fundamental question for lawmaking in European consumer law: considering that consumer laws are created at the EU level, the national level and through other sources (eg private regulation, standardisation), is it desirable to replace the one-size-fits-all approach to consumers with a contextualised approach? An attempt at answering this question may be made by examining the consequences for lawmaking that a turn towards a contextualised consumer in European consumer law concept will have.

The theoretical grounding for such a reassessment is dependent on the perspective that one takes with regard to lawmaking in European private law. Lawmaking in European private law occurs at different levels of regulation, including the national, the European and the international level, as well as private lawmaking through contracting and standardisation. Earlier studies have examined how lawmakers at these different levels interact. In European consumer law, the following models have been identified: (i) top-down harmonisation; (ii) regulatory competition; and (iii) legal pluralism, meaning the co-existence of legal norms without a formal hierarchy, with variations in 'strong' and 'ordered' legal pluralism.[74]

---

[72] Hacker, 'Regulating Under Uncertainty about Rationality' (n 71); A Rapoport, *Decision Theory and Decision Behaviour*, 2nd edn (Palgrave Macmillan, 1998).

[73] J Rawls, *Justice as Fairness. A Restatement* (Harvard University Press, 2001); MW Hesselink, *Justifying Contract in Europe: Political Philosophies of European Contract Law* (Oxford University Press, 2021); H Muir Watt, 'Conflicts of Law Unbounded: The Case for a Legal-Pluralist Revival' (2016) 7 *Transnational Legal Theory* 313; Mak (n 68) ch 3.

[74] JM Smits, 'Plurality of Sources in European Private Law, or: How to Live with Legal Diversity?' in R Brownsword et al (eds), *The Foundations of European Private Law* (Hart Publishing, 2011) 323; MW Hesselink, 'How Many Systems of Private Law are there in Europe? On Plural Legal Sources, Multiple

The legal pluralist model has gained acceptance in recent years, a process coinciding with a slow-down in top-down harmonisation by the EU legislator.[75] The proposal for a DSA package in December 2020 does not seem to have changed this outlook. Although the proposed legislation may again give a boost to regulation at the EU level, in its current design it relies heavily on voluntary monitoring by platform operators.[76] Only very large online platforms ('gatekeepers', a presumed status for platforms having more than 45 million monthly active end users and more than 10,000 yearly active business users in the EU) are subject to stricter regulation, focusing on controlling the market power that they gain through data aggregation.[77]

Taking this legal framework as a starting point, the introduction of a contextualised approach to consumer protection in European consumer laws will require analysis along several axes. First, the debate of 'who makes rules and at what level of regulation' will have to be re-visited.[78] Which lawmaking actors are active in developing European consumer laws? Besides the EU legislator and national legislators, the scope of the enquiry will also increasingly need to include private actors who develop their own rules of engagement. Important categories of private regulators in the digital market are tech-firms such as Facebook and Apple, which determine on what terms consumers can obtain their digital content and services; and online platforms such as Amazon and Airbnb, which bind users to their standard terms and conditions and codes of conduct. While they are obliged to comply with rules of EU and national consumer laws, they have a large amount of freedom in contract law to set their terms. Their position as private lawmakers is reinforced by the absence of effective oversight and enforcement mechanisms for these contractual terms.[79] This means that private actors will be considered not just as the subjects of EU and national consumer laws, but also as lawmaking actors that define which rules apply in consumer markets, which conforms to the legal pluralist perspectives mentioned above. Private actors can in this respect contribute to the development of consumer law in digital markets and platform markets, and they can be facilitators or innovators of sustainable consumption.

As an aside, the autonomy of tech-firms and online platforms as lawmaking actors in consumer markets may be viewed with scepticism, as many of these firms' practices push the boundaries of values that are central to the EU legal order. Transparency, fairness, and in particular the balance between free speech and information control are thorny issues on which platforms such as Facebook (or now: Meta) have been called out. With a focus on online marketplaces, the enquiry proposed here is primarily concerned with economic interests. It only tangentially engages with questions of free speech and the dissemination of information. In that light, it is relevant to note that the rules created

---

Identities and the Unity of Law' in L Niglia (ed), *Pluralism and European Private Law* (Hart Publishing, 2013) 199; R Michaels, 'Of Islands and the Ocean: The Two Rationalities of European Private Law' in R Brownsword et al (eds), *The Foundations of European Private Law* (Hart Publishing, 2011) 139; Micklitz (n 69).

[75] Micklitz (n 69) 35–38, 191; Mak (n 68) 109.

[76] Busch and Mak (n 13).

[77] European Commission, Digital Market Act proposal (n 13) Art 3.

[78] On multilevel governance in EU regulation, see L Hooghe and G Marks, *Multi-Level Governance and European Integration* (Rowman and Littlefield Publishers, 2001).

[79] Mak (n 68) ch 9.

by private regulators have proved not inherently to favour business interests over those of consumers. On online marketplaces that connect traders and consumers, such as Amazon, the pursuit of high levels of customer satisfaction effectively results in high levels of consumer protection. The trade-off is that third-party traders who offer their products through the platform are bound by strict terms and conditions.[80] Moreover, the regulatory power of online platforms is curbed by the interaction with other lawmakers. Even if the legislator is slow in taking action, alternative mechanisms exist that moderate autonomous lawmaking action. Standardisation is an important one, as well as the creation of model laws or optional instruments. Also, online dispute resolution (ODR) can function as a regulatory instrument that places checks and balances on the practices of online platforms.[81]

Besides the institutional framework, a reassessment of substantive rules will be required. If the consumer image is adapted to the needs of digital markets and sustainability, should European consumer laws be amended, introducing a contextualised approach? If so, which instruments should be amended and how? This question goes to the heart of the existing EU consumer *acquis* and touches upon rules laid down in the UCPD, CRD, CSD and UCTD. Amendments of these directives could already result in a better fit with the position of consumers in digital markets, and facilitate their role as consumer citizens in relation to sustainability. It could also be that additional regulation is desirable at the EU level and/or the national level.

On a fundamental level, the reassessment of substantive rules also requires an answer to the question whether EU consumer law applies horizontally to all transactions or whether it should differentiate. More specifically, should lawmakers at the EU level strive for a horizontal approach in the way that, for example, rules on unfair terms apply to all consumer contracts (UCTD), or should consumer laws differentiate between sectors (eg energy, telecommunication, digital services)? There is no easy answer to this question. Historically, some parts of EU consumer law have developed from an overarching horizontal approach. Instruments concerning transparency and fairness in contract law, such as the UCTD and the UCPD, apply to almost all consumer contracts. The UCPD even extends beyond that and applies to all B2C relationships, regardless of whether they are contractual or non-contractual in nature. At the same time, the piecemeal development of EU consumer law has also resulted in sector-specific regulation, for example in the energy market and the telecom market. The division of regulatory competences over various directorates within the European Commission may be partly to blame for the sometimes uncoordinated approach to consumer regulation at the EU level, as well as the failure to connect consumer law to related fields, such as labour law or environmental protection.[82] Notably, legislators at the national level are subject to similar organisational constraints. The reassessment of consumer law proposed here, however, can provide a stepping stone towards a more holistic approach to consumer

---

[80] cf ibid ch 7.

[81] For an analysis of the operation of these instruments in platform markets, see ibid 203 ff.

[82] SA de Vries, 'General Reflections on the Exercise of Economic Rights by EU Citizens' in SA de Vries et al (eds), *EU Citizens' Economic Rights in Action. Re-thinking Legal and Factual Barriers in the Internal Market* (Edward Elgar, 2018) 2, 11.

law. Connections can be made to similar discussions in labour law, where the notion of the 'worker' has been subject to debate in recent years, in particular in the light of the rise of the gig economy.[83] Connections can also be made to other concepts that coincide with or are similar to the consumer image, such as the 'author' in copyright law or the 'client' in financial services regulation. Such an approach can lead to a broader reassessment of notions of vulnerability and responsibility in EU and national private laws.

VI. Conclusions and Outlook

An assessment or re-imaging of the consumer can be a starting point for a modernisation of consumer law in the light of digitalisation, platformisation and sustainability. Consumer law scholars have for a longer time been searching for alternatives to the one-size-fits-all model of consumer law that regards the consumer as a weaker party in relation to businesses but in reality pays little heed to vulnerabilities. Also, the information paradigm that permeates consumer law has been challenged and chafed at, though not displaced, by studies on behaviour, cognitive limitations and nudging. Still, there has been no significant move forward, and as a result the regulation of consumer markets has fallen behind. Regulators and policy makers around the world are debating the rise of tech-giants and the risks they pose to users, as well as the challenges of climate change and the need for sustainable consumption. Regulatory action is not forthcoming, however, or only at a very slow pace.

In this contribution, I have set out a research agenda focusing on three key aspects in which the regulation of consumer markets could be improved. They concern new vulnerabilities affecting digital consumers, new opportunities for 'prosumers' operating on the supply side of consumer markets through online platforms, and a call for consumers as citizens to contribute to sustainable consumption. Each of these contexts requires a reassessment of the consumer image and, subsequently, a reassessment of the existing rules applying to businesses, consumers and other actors in these markets. Arguably, other aspects than these three could have been selected for further study – but perhaps these can be explored in other projects. Questions of re-imaging could, for example, be applied to the 'worker' concept in labour law, the 'author' in copyright law or the 'client' in financial services law.

The three areas selected for a reassessment of the consumer image provide input for an overarching analysis of the consumer image in European consumer law. As suggested here, lines of enquiry can focus on the historical and future development of the consumer image in EU law; the spectrum along which regulatory choices can be made, ranging from categorised protection to personalised approaches; and the institutional context within which consumer regulation is embedded. Europe may be of particular interest for such an analysis. It provides a framework for regulation that, even if it gives space to private actors to set their own rules, curbs that power by maintaining

---

[83] J Prassl, *Humans As a Service* (Oxford University Press, 2018).

correcting mechanisms in regulation and alternatives such as standardisation. Those active in the European consumer market will moreover have to comply with the values of EU law as laid down in the Treaties.

The idea of 'transformation of the consumer image' provides a starting point for an overhaul of consumer law. By re-imaging, or re-imagining, the consumer we may make a start with designing rules that can answer the challenges of digitalisation, platformisation and sustainable consumption.

4

Effective Judicial Protection, Private Enforcement and the Reshaping of Substantive Remedies

CHARLOTTE PAVILLON

I. Introduction: Transformation of the Substance

A. Of Remedies and Remedial Autonomy

Since the start of the millennium, consumer law, under the influence of EU law, has been undergoing a series of temporal, substantive, institutional and procedural transformations. This chapter portrays the second dimension of transformation. At its heart lies the transformation of *substantive remedies* as part of the evolution of enforcement of European consumer law by means of private law. While Member States have been moving towards more public enforcement of consumer law (a procedural transformation),[1] the Court of Justice of the European Union (CJEU) has kept an eye on effective protection of the *individual* consumer, more specifically on the consumer who, during the financial crisis, has been sued for non-payment. The procedural framework firmly set by the CJEU is largely based on the principle of effective judicial protection. This, in particular, holds true for the *ex officio* application of EU consumer law. The CJEU has ruled that a procedural remedy must be designed in an efficient way that empowers national courts to assess compliance with mandatory EU consumer law of their own motion.

Within this procedural setting, Member States have made (sometimes drastic) choices as regards the substantive remedies available to both the consumer and the professional party under national private law. The *ex officio* application of EU consumer law has led to the creation of hard-and-fast rules that courts can apply effortlessly in default cases, whereas the effectiveness principle has limited the remedies available

---

[1] Thanks to Regulation (EU) 2017/2394 of the European Parliament and of the Council of 12 December 2017 on cooperation between national authorities responsible for the enforcement of consumer protection laws and repealing Regulation (EC) No 2006/2004 (the CPC Regulation) [2017] OJ L 345/1.

to the professional party. By strengthening the procedural position and remedies of the individual consumer who appears before a civil court, the CJEU has increasingly emphasised the deterrent potential of private law remedies. This recent consolidation of private enforcement has deeply impacted the design of new remedies available to the consumer at the national level, their dissuasive nature being put forward.

Based on Article 47 of the Charter of Fundamental Rights of the European Union (CFR)[2] and Article 19 of the Treaty on European Union (TEU),[3] national Member States must lay down remedies to ensure effective enforcement of individual rights derived from EU law. In addition to 'European remedies' laid down in EU legislation, Member States should devise effective remedies for breaches of EU law. The remedial autonomy of Member States refers to the leeway given to Member States to create remedies *under national law* that guarantee effective enforcement of EU law in national courts. However, the remedial autonomy of Member States is subjected to boundaries: like procedures, remedies have to meet the *Rewe* principles of effectiveness and equivalence.[4] The effectiveness principle aims to guarantee the effective application of substantive EU law. This principle has been distinguished from the principle of effective judicial protection of an individual's rights under EU law, which has mainly influenced the shaping of national procedural remedies warranting the justiciability of EU rights and access to a court.[5] The latter principle greatly contributes to the first principle by enhancing substantive protection of consumers, namely by effectuating substantive remedies for breaches of EU consumer law. The effectiveness of remedies is also strongly tied to the need for deterrent sanctions, in order to prevent future breaches of EU consumer law. Last but not least, national remedies that enforce EU consumer rights are subject to the proportionality principle, which entails that 'measures provided for under national legislation must not exceed the limits of what is appropriate and necessary in order to attain the objectives legitimately pursued by the legislation in question'.[6]

National courts are held to interpret national law, including national remedies, in so far as possible to achieve the results envisaged by a directive while respecting the above principle. This interpretation has in many cases been clarified by means of preliminary referrals to the CJEU. In recent years, an intensive vertical dialogue between national courts and the CJEU has changed the national approach to remedies available to consumers. The term 'remedy' encompasses *both* a procedural and a substantive dimension: whereas the term 'procedural remedy' indicates the existence of means of recourse to which the consumer has access in order to press their claim, 'substantive remedy' refers to the intended outcome of the process and characterises the redress and relief to which the consumer is entitled, that is, a claim right or cause of action such as nullification of unfair terms or termination of a contract. Vanessa Mak distinguishes between substantive remedies and their enforcement through the courts. She points to the fact that the term 'remedies' is not used consistently in the literature and that it may,

---

[2] Charter of Fundamental Rights of the European Union [2012] OJ C326/391.
[3] Treaty on European Union (consolidated version 2016) [2016] OJ C202/13.
[4] Case 33/76 *Rewe-Zentralfinanz* ECLI:EU:C:1976:188, [1976] ECR 1989.
[5] S Prechal and R Widdershoven, 'Redefining the Relationship between "Rewe-Effectiveness" and Effective Judicial Protection' (2011) 4 *Review of European Administrative Law* 31.
[6] Case C-418/11 *Texdata Software* ECLI:EU:C:2013:588, para 52.

depending on the context, refer to either category. A substantive remedy may refer to a 'legal response to a wrong, for example a breach of contract, reflecting substantive rights for the aggrieved party to obtain the performance that he contracted for or a (monetary) equivalent of it'.[7] However, the term is also used in a stricter sense, namely as a means of enforcing substantive rights. In her book on protection of the performance interest, Mak lays the emphasis on the broader approach of substantive remedies as the substantive rights whose enforcement is sought.[8]

This chapter opts for the latter approach. It focuses on the evolution at the *national* level of *substantive* remedies for breaches of EU consumer law. This so-called hybridisation approach combines old and new solutions at the national level,[9] that is, remedies under national law, to the requirements of effective and equivalent protection under EU law.[10] This approach has been adopted in the field of consumer law in so far as secondary legislation allows leeway to Member States to opt for (hybrid) solutions under national private law in the case of an infringement of the implementing legislation. Consumer directives do not always provide for specific (European) remedies: most information duties in the Consumer Rights Directive (CRD)[11] are not linked to a remedy. And even when they do, they often fail to detail the exact scope or modalities of a remedy (for instance, what are the consequences of non-bindingness of an unfair term/when would a replacement claim be deemed disproportionate?). Most consumer protection directives (including the Unfair Commercial Practices Directive (UCPD)[12]) oblige Member States to devise remedies but leave it to the Member States to decide what remedies are proportionate and effective. Hybridisation entails that remedies take up both national and European elements, leading to 'diversified rules at the national level that conform to certain EU-wide, judge-made standards'.[13]

B. Chapter Outline

This chapter depicts two developments that have formed new and changed existing remedies available both to consumers and to professional parties. The starting point of the substantive transformation depicted in this chapter is that since the year 2000,

---

[7] V Mak, *Performance-oriented Remedies in European Sale of Goods Law* (Bloomsbury Publishing, 2009) 51.

[8] ibid.

[9] N Reich, 'Horizontal liability in EC law: Hybridisation of remedies for the compensation in case of breaches of EC rights' (2007) 44 *CMLR* 705.

[10] cf D Leczykiewicz, 'Compensatory Remedies in EU law: The Relationship between EU Law and National Law' in P Giliker (ed), *Research Handbook on EU Tort Law* (Edward Elgar Publishing, 2017).

[11] Directive 2011/83/EU of the European Parliament and of the Council of 25 October 2011 on consumer rights, amending Council Directive 93/13/EEC and Directive 1999/44/EC of the European Parliament and of the Council and repealing Council Directive 85/577/EEC and Directive 97/7/EC of the European Parliament and of the Council [2011] OJ L304/64.

[12] Directive 2005/29/EC of the European Parliament and of the Council of 11 May 2005 concerning unfair business-to-consumer commercial practices in the internal market and amending Council Directive 84/450/EEC, Directives 97/7/EC, 98/27/EC and 2002/65/EC of the European Parliament and of the Council and Regulation (EC) No 2006/2004 of the European Parliament and of the Council [2005] OJ L149/22.

[13] A van Duin, *Justice for Both: Effective Judicial Protection under Article 47 of the EU Charter of Fundamental Rights and the Unfair Contract Terms Directive* (PhD Thesis, University of Amsterdam, 2020) 208.

a growing body of case law has been focusing on the effective procedural protection of consumers. Changes in the procedural remedies available to the consumer have led to a new approach to substantive remedies in many Member States since both types of remedies are closely intertwined.[14] National substantive remedies for breaches of EU consumer law have been reshaped and upgraded as a result of the interpretation the CJEU has given to the *Rewe* principles of effectiveness and equivalence, and to the European requirement for effective, proportionate and deterrent sanctions. While means of private enforcement definitely require substantive remedies,[15] they also give shape to those remedies.[16] A full understanding of substantive rights and remedies requires their contextualisation within a procedural framework. The interdependence between the procedural and substantive protection of consumers, more specifically the transformative effect of the procedural on the substantive, lies at the core of this chapter.

The transformation process is twofold. First, it entails the creation of one-size-fits-all, swiftly applicable, consumer-friendly remedies. Second, it concerns the further sharpening of remedies and their gradual transformation into genuine sanctions, boosting enforcement of consumer law by means of private law, as it has been carefully (re)awakened by the *New Deal*. Section II deals with the first aspect of transformation of remedies. It delves into CJEU case law on effective judicial consumer protection, wherein the emphasis is put on individual protection and redress, and assesses the influence of this case law on the shaping of substantive remedies under national law. Section III explores the second aspect of transformation of remedies. It analyses how those remedies have been 'revamped' by EU case law pertaining to the need for effective *and deterrent* civil law remedies and sanctions, wherein the accent is put on preventing further breaches of consumer law. Finally, some conclusions are drawn in section IV on how case law-induced transformation of private law remedies relates to the already much-discussed institutional transformation of enforcement.

II. Transformation of Substantive Remedies to Ensure Effective Judicial Protection

A. The Need for Effective Remedies

According to the principle of cooperation laid down in Article 4 TEU, Member States must take the necessary measures to ensure fulfilment of the obligations under the Treaty, and in particular, national courts must provide appropriate judicial protection

---

[14] C Leone and A van Duin, 'The Real (New) Deal: Levelling the Odds for Consumer-Litigants: On the Need for a Modernisation, Part II' (2019) 27 *European Review of Private Law* 1227, 1227–50.

[15] Due to (previous) lack of individual remedies in the UCPD, the Court ran into the limits of the *ex officio* review obligation: Case C-109/17 *Bankia v Marí Mereno* ECLI:EU:C:2018:735; cf Leone and Van Duin (n 14) 1243–44.

[16] Th O Main, 'The Procedural Foundation of Substantive Law' (2009–2010) 87 *Washington University Law Review* 801, 802.

of rights that EU law confers on individuals. Effective judicial protection of consumer rights is enshrined in Article 47 CFR, which requires – among other things – an effective *remedy* for infringements of EU (consumer) rights. Van Duin has established that Article 47 CFR fulfils a transformative function where it originates a debate about the 'design of procedures in consumer cases': an example is the Spanish mortgage enforcement regime, where judicial control of unfair terms is now possible – also on appeal – as a result of a 'trialogue' between the Spanish civil courts, the CJEU and the Spanish legislature.[17]

The transformative function of Article 47 CFR defined as 'enhanced effectiveness'[18] touches upon the right to effective remedies, *both* procedural/judicial *and* substantive. Whereas the CJEU, in its case law, appears to focus on the first type of remedies, namely a means of recourse giving access to a court – for instance, the *Aziz* ruling[19] led to the creation of a new remedy in the procedural sphere *at national level* (the introduction of unfair terms as an opposition ground in mortgage enforcement proceedings)[20] – an effective judicial/procedural remedy will generally culminate in obtaining a *substantive* remedy.[21] Such a substantive remedy may be seen as the end point of an 'effective procedural path' and is determined by its factual and legal context.[22] Enhanced effectiveness hinges on the availability or creation of substantive remedies at national level.

National remedies ought to be developed to secure enforcement of obligations that are of concern to individuals.[23] This approach is particularly relevant where consumer directives do not confer an explicit right upon consumers to obtain redress. This had been the case with the UCPD, until harmonisation of remedies was achieved by the Omnibus Directive.[24] At the time the UCPD was implemented into national law, the Belgian Government had already undertaken to fill this 'void' by creating a civil law remedy for unfair commercial practices, entitling the consumer to keep the product, in the shape of the good delivered or service provided, free of charge.[25] A Belgian judge

---

[17] Van Duin (n 13) 101. According to Van Duin, Art 47 CFR itself does not, in the case law of the CJEU, constitute a *direct source* of new remedies but solely serves to underpin the need for effective procedures enabling consumers to enforce their rights.

[18] ibid 206–07.

[19] Case C-415/11 *Mohamed Aziz v Caixa d'Estalvis de Catalunya, Tarragona i Manresa (Catalunyacaixa)* ECLI:EU:C:2013:164.

[20] The *Aziz* ruling can be seen as an example of 'hidden constitutionalisation', as the CJEU does not explicitly refer to the CFR. H-W Micklitz, 'Unfair Contract Terms – Public Interest Litigation before European Courts: Case C-415/11 Mohamed Aziz' in V Colaert and E Terryn (eds), *Landmark Cases of EU Consumer Law – in Honour of Jules Stuyck* (Intersentia, 2013) 649; Van Duin (n 13) 90.

[21] Case C-483/16 *Zsolt Sziber v ERSTE Bank Hungary Zrt* ECLI:EU:C:2018:367 (the substantive remedy being restitution of amounts unduly paid).

[22] Van Duin (n 13) 88.

[23] Case C-237/07 *Dieter Janecek v Freistaat Bayern* ECLI:EU:C:2008:447.

[24] Directive (EU) 2019/2161 of the European Parliament and of the Council of 27 November 2019 amending Council Directive 93/13/EEC and Directives 98/6/EC, 2005/29/EC and 2011/83/EU of the European Parliament and of the Council as regards the better enforcement and modernisation of Union consumer protection rules [2019] OJ L328/7 (cf the new Art 11a UCPD).

[25] Arts VI.38, VI.94 under 1° and VI.99 Wetboek van economisch recht (Belgian Code of Economic Law). This remedy is discussed by T de Graaf, 'Consequences of nullifying an agreement on account of personalised pricing. A Dutch and Belgian perspective on the consequences of consumers exercising nullification and price reduction rights in cases of online personalised pricing infringing upon the EU Unfair Commercial Practices

may only exercise this discretionary power if a certain threshold has been met: it needs to be established that the contract would never have been concluded without the unfair commercial practice.[26] A similar remedy, based on Article 27 CRD, is available to the consumer in the case of inertia selling. In Belgium, it equally applies to a situation where the consumer has actively sought to buy a good but has been misled about its main characteristics.

The Dutch legislator had considered introducing the same remedy when implementing the UCPD into Dutch civil law. The Belgian remedy was discussed in the Dutch Parliament, but the Dutch Minister of Justice dismissed the remedy as being too 'punitive'.[27] The Minister nevertheless commissioned a report on the effectiveness of the remedy in Belgium.[28] Since the reporters were not able to prove the effectiveness of the Belgian remedy due to a lack of jurisprudence, the Dutch legislator chose not to implement a similar remedy in Dutch law. It finally opted for a remedy consisting of nullification of a contract concluded under the influence of an unfair commercial practice.[29] If such a nullification right is exercised by the consumer then the entire agreement is nullified, and therefore is considered null and void with retroactive effect as of the moment it was concluded.[30] As a result, performances rendered are considered to have lacked a legal basis *ab initio* and each party can (in theory) demand restitution of whatever it has performed for the other party.[31]

B. New Judge-made Straightforward Remedies

A remarkable feature of EU case law in the field of consumer law is the CJEU's active and far-reaching intervention in the domestic procedural legal order. Since the start of the new millennium,[32] the Court has repeatedly stressed the active role of national civil courts in applying EU consumer law of their own motion. The transformative impact of this line of jurisprudence touches upon different topics, some of which (the impact on procedural law, judicial dialogue and coordination) have been extensively discussed in the literature.[33] It is well known that case law on *ex officio* application of consumer law has transformed individual court-based enforcement, making this type of enforcement all the more relevant, for instance in payment orders and default proceedings. However,

---

Directive (UCPD) and whether they are effective, proportionate and dissuasive' (2019) 5 *Journal of European Consumer and Market Law* 1051, 1051–73.

[26] Verslag Commissie Bedrijfsleven, Parl St Kamer, 2006-07, DOC 51, 2983/004, 9. However, other authors have argued that a causal link between unfair commercial practice and the conclusion of the contract suffices: R Steennot and P Geerts, 'De implementatie van de richtlijn oneerlijke handelspraktijken in België en Nederland' (2011) 3 *Tijdschrift voor Privaatrecht* 747, 754–56.

[27] Parliamentary papers II 2011/2012, 32320, no 3 and Parliamentary papers II 2011/2012, 30928, no 17.

[28] See P Geerts et al, *Oneerlijke handelspraktijken: praktijkervaringen in België met de sanctie van artikel 41 WMPC* (Boom Juridische uitgevers, 2011) 72–77.

[29] Art 6:193j para 3 Dutch Civil Code (DCC).

[30] Art 3:53 DCC.

[31] Art 6:203 DCC.

[32] Joined Cases C-240/98 to C-244/98 *Océano Grupo Editorial SA v Roció Murciano Quintero (C-240/98) and Salvat Editores SA v José M. Sánchez Alcón Prades (C-241/98), José Luis Copano Badillo (C-242/98), Mohammed Berroane (C-243/98) and Emilio Viñas Feliú (C-244/98)* ECLI:EU:C:2000:346, [2000] ECR I-04941, para 26.

[33] A Beka, *The Active Role of Courts in Consumer Litigation* (Intersentia, 2020).

less attention has been drawn by the impact of the *ex officio* powers of national courts on substantive law. Since procedural and substantive remedies are closely intertwined, *ex officio* enforcement has clearly also produced 'substantive' effects, some of which have been given more thought than others.[34]

A transformation induced by *ex officio* enforcement that has not often been dealt with is that this 'automatic' application of consumer law (Unfair Contract Terms Directive (UCTD),[35] CRD, Consumer Credit Directive (CCD)[36]) has triggered a more *abstract* and *formal* approach by civil courts to national private law concepts such as harm/prejudice[37] or fair dealing, thus closing the gap between private and public enforcement.[38] *Ex officio* application of consumer law has also prompted the introduction of judge-made 'one-size-fits-all' contractual remedies at the national level.[39] A recent example from the Netherlands is the civil sanctions applied to breaches of informational duties laid down in the CRD. Clear-cut European substantive remedies are still lacking as far as concerns most informational duties emanating from the CRD.[40] Enforcement of these professional duties depends to a large extent on the availability of effective national remedies and on the Member States' willingness to draft new ones.

Following a ruling by the Dutch Supreme Court in November 2021,[41] lower courts have reached a common agreement[42] that in default cases the price to be paid by a consumer will be partially nullified where the professional party has breached a material information duty laid down in the CRD. The breach needs to be sufficiently serious, but nullification does not require a causal relationship between the missing information and the consumer's decision to enter into the agreement. Courts may opt for a price reduction of 50 or 25 per cent, dependent on there being more than three sufficiently serious

---

[34] At the heart of the *ex officio* duties of national courts lies the image of a consumer who is ignorant of their legal rights or deterred from enforcing them on account of the costs that judicial proceedings would involve. The question how this image relates to the 'average consumer' who is key to internal market integration has been extensively debated. cf D Leczykiewicz and S Weatherill (eds), *The Images of the Consumer in EU Law: Legislation, Free Movement and Competition Law* (Hart Publishing, 2016).

[35] Council Directive 93/13/EEC of 5 April 1993 on unfair terms in consumer contracts [1993] OJ L95/29.

[36] Directive 2008/48/EC of the European Parliament and of the Council of 23 April 2008 on credit agreements for consumers and repealing Council Directive 87/102/EEC [2008] OJ L133/66.

[37] cf H Jacquemin and E de Duve, 'L'information précontractuelle et contractuelle des consommateurs' in Ch Verdure, *Contrats et protection des consommateurs* (Anthemis, 2016) 44.

[38] The *erga omnes* effect of a finding of unfairness in individual contracts follows from Case C-472/10 *Nemzeti Fogyasztóvédelmi Hatóság v Invitel Távközlési Zrt* ECLI:EU:C:2012:242.

[39] Procedural rules have improved the justiciability of consumer rights. The Dutch Supreme Court ruled that courts can find *ex officio* that 'all-in telephone subscriptions' that have been sold to consumers may be partially nullified if no separate price for the phone has been determined by the parties: Dutch Supreme Court, 12 February 2016, *Lindorff/Nazier* ECLI:NL:HR:2016:236. This approach fits in nicely with the new Directive (EU) 2020/1828 of the European Parliament and of the Council of 25 November 2020 on representative actions for the protection of the collective interests of consumers and repealing Directive 2009/22/EC (the Collective Redress Directive), [2020] OJ L 409/1.

[40] Exceptions being the duty to inform about the price (nullity) and the right of withdrawal.

[41] Dutch Supreme Court, 12 November 2021, *Arvato* ECLI:NL:HR:2021:1677. In this ruling, the highest Dutch court ruled that lower courts must of their own motion assess the breach of informational duties by (online) sellers and service providers and apply the remedies available under Dutch law: C Pavillon and L Tigelaar, 'The ex officio enforcement of information duties of the Consumer Rights Directive by Dutch courts' (2022) 6 *Journal of European Consumer and Market Law* 228.

[42] *Richtlijn Sanctiemodel essentiële informatieplichten* (15 December 2021) at www.rechtspraak.nl/ SiteCollectionDocuments/richtlijn-sanctiemodel-essenti%C3%ABle-informatieplichten-v15122021.pdf (accessed 2 November 2022).

breaches of the law, regardless of the actual harm suffered by the consumer. Strikingly, the partial nullity of the price departs from national restitution laws and from earlier jurisprudence[43] but is deemed to be in line with the principle of effectiveness. The agreement reached by the courts amounts to creation of a hybrid ready-made (substantive) remedy that has the advantage of being easily applicable in default cases. It also avoids complicated restitution issues. An interesting parallel may be drawn between this clear-cut 'user-friendly' remedy and fixed flight-delay compensation under the Denied Boarding Regulation.[44]

C. Private Law Remedies Available to a Professional Party

The CJEU case law on effective judicial protection has also directly transformed the remedies available to the infringing professional party under national law. In the field of unfair contract terms, EU case law has considerably limited the possibility for an infringer of consumer law (such as a user of unfair contract terms) to invoke national remedies, even when consumers themselves are breaching a contract (a breach that triggered application of the unfair term). For instance, the *Aziz* judgment ruled that certain provisions of Spanish mortgage law did not comply with the UCTD.[45] As a result of this judgment, enforcement of securities against consumer borrowers has become more difficult.

The *Dexia Netherlands* ruling of 27 January 2021 forbids a professional party from claiming damages under national (supplementary) contract law after a penalty clause has been deemed unfair and removed from the contract.[46] The CJEU held that

> provisions of Directive 93/13 must be interpreted as meaning that a seller or supplier which has imposed on a consumer a term declared unfair and, consequently, void by the national court cannot claim the statutory compensation provided for by a supplementary provision of national law which would have been applicable in the absence of that term where the contract is capable of continuing in existence without that term.[47]

Allowing a national court to apply default national rules on damages – as was the case in the Netherlands[48] and in many other Member States[49] – undermines the objective of

---

[43] cf Opinion issued by A-G Wissink ECLI:NL:PHR:2020:466, para 4.37.

[44] Regulation (EC) No 261/2004 of the European Parliament and of the Council of 11 February 2004 establishing common rules on compensation and assistance to passengers in the event of denied boarding and of cancellation or long delay of flights, and repealing Regulation (EEC) No 295/91 [2004] OJ L46/1.

[45] *Aziz* (n 19).

[46] Joined Cases C-229/19 and C-289/19 *Dexia Netherlands v XXX and Z* ECLI:EU:C:2021:68; Case C-625/21 *VB v Gupfinger Einrichtungsstudio GmbH* ECLI:EU:C:2022:971. In Case C-395/21 *DV (Honoraires d'avocat – Principe du tarif horaire)* ECLI:EU:C:2023:14, the Court interpreted Arts 6(1) and 7(1) UCTD 'as not precluding the national court, where a contract for the provision of legal services concluded between a lawyer and a consumer is not capable of continuing in existence after a term, found to be unfair, which sets the price of the services on the basis of an hourly rate has been removed and those services have already been provided, from restoring the situation in which the consumer would have been in the absence of that term, even if, as a result, the seller or supplier does not receive any remuneration for the services provided'.

[47] *Dexia Netherlands* (n 46) para 67.

[48] Dutch Supreme Court, 21 April 2017, *Tijhuis/Dexia* ECLI:NL:HR:2017:773.

[49] M Storme and J Werbrouck, 'Invloed van het Europees recht op het Belgisch contractenrecht en (in) consistentie van dat laatste met het eerste' (2022) 16 *Nederlands Tijdschrift voor Burgerlijk Recht* 120, 125 write about 'a break with traditional, Belgian contract law'.

the UCTD. This case law – which is accurately applied by national courts[50] – limits the professional party's right to an effective remedy and may lead to unjust enrichment of a consumer. This perspective remains underexposed, even though different authors have raised this concern.[51] The question then arises as to what extent a breach of consumer law justifies such a far-reaching impairment of the other (professional) party's fundamental right to effectuate their rights.

Under national sales law, a seller may claim restitution of a good or compensation for its use after a contract is rescinded. When rescission of the contract results from the consumer's invocation of their withdrawal rights under the CRD, such claims are subject to limitations set by the CJEU. Under paragraph 357 of the German Civil Code (*Bürgerliches Gesetzburch*, BGB), a seller may claim compensation for the value of the use of consumer goods delivered. In view of this conflict, the Amtsgericht Lahr referred the preliminary question whether the BGB provision is compatible with the Distance Selling Directive[52] and more specifically the right of withdrawal. In its *Messner* ruling,[53] the CJEU found that a seller's right to claim compensation for the value of the use of consumer goods acquired under a distance contract might dissuade a consumer from effectively exercising their right of withdrawal. The conflicting provision in the BGB would therefore need to be put aside. An exception was made for the situation where the consumer had 'made use of those goods in a manner incompatible with the principles of civil law, such as those of good faith or unjust enrichment'. Article 14(2) CRD elaborates on the costs a consumer should bear in the event of not having been informed about their right of withdrawal.

In the *Quelle* ruling,[54] the seller had already been denied the right to claim compensation under §346 BGB for the value of the use of a replaced defective good. This provision indeed conflicts with Article 3(2) of the Consumer Sale and Guarantee Directive 1999/44 (CSD),[55] which requires that the replacement be made 'free of charge'. Charging the consumer for use of the defective product would deter the consumer from exercising their right to require that the good be brought into conformity with the contract under Article 3(2) CSD. Article 14(4) of the new Consumer Sales Directive[56] has in the meanwhile codified the *Quelle* ruling.[57]

Rescission of a contract leads to restitution of what passed under the rescinded contract while taking into consideration the rules on unjust enrichment. Do national

---

[50] cf Belgian Supreme Court, 9 October 2020, C.19.0631. N, Feka nv, ECLI:BE:CASS:2020:ARR.20201009. 1N.1.

[51] Van Duin (n 13) 197; M Storme, 'On the Usefulness of Default Rules and Disproportionate Sanctions in Consumer Law' (2021) 3 *European Review of Private Law* 399, 399–402.

[52] Directive 97/7/EC of the European Parliament and of the Council of 20 May 1997 on the protection of consumers in respect of distance contracts [1997] OJ L144/19.

[53] Case C-489/07 *Pia Messner v Firma Stefan Krüger* ECLI:EU:C:2009:502.

[54] Case C-404/06 *Quelle AG v Bundesverband der Verbraucherzentralen und Verbraucherverbände* ECLI:EU:C:2008:231, [2008] ECR I-2685.

[55] Directive 1999/44/EC of the European Parliament and of the Council of 25 May 1999 on certain aspects of the sale of consumer goods and associated guarantees [1999] OJ L171/12.

[56] Directive (EU) 2019/771 of the European Parliament and of the Council of 20 May 2019 on certain aspects concerning contracts for the sale of goods, amending Regulation (EU) 2017/2394 and Directive 2009/22/EC, and repealing Directive 1999/44/EC [2019] OJ L136/28.

[57] 'The consumer shall not be liable to pay for normal use made of the replaced goods during the period prior to their replacement.'

rules on restitution and compensation fully apply when a contract is rescinded in the case of non-conformity of goods with the contract, or does effective protection of the consumer warrant their entitlement to a full refund? Even though the CJEU has clarified that Member States may, in the case of rescission of an agreement on account of a defect, provide that any reimbursement to the consumer may be reduced to take account of the use of the goods that the consumer has enjoyed since they were delivered,[58] the national approach to remedies of rescission and nullification is somehow impacted by the *Quelle* and *Messner* cases. Moreover, among legitimate reasons why, in the case of rescission, no compensation should be awarded to the seller for use of the good is that the seller is being rewarded for having failed to replace or repair the defective good within a reasonable period of time and without significant inconvenience to the consumer.[59] As will be discussed in the next section, the decision by some national courts to deny the seller compensation for use of a good has been guided both by the principle of effectiveness *and* by the principle of dissuasiveness. Rejection of a seller's claim depends on how much emphasis is put on the dissuasive effect of the remedy invoked by the consumer in comparison to the proportionality principle when balancing the consumer's and the seller's interests.[60]

III. Transformation of Remedies into Effective and Deterrent Sanctions

A. Civil Courts as 'Enforcement Bodies'

Article 11a UCPD, as introduced by the Omnibus Directive, requires Member States to devise some specific contractual remedies for victims of unfair commercial practices. The addition of contract law remedies to the UCPD is illustrative of the fact that enforcement is not solely a matter of public law. Some Member States rely heavily on public law enforcement and do/did not equip consumers with effective remedies in the case of an unfair/misleading commercial practice. This lack of civil law remedies has hindered enforcement of the UCPD following the Dieselgate scandal. The ensuing *New Deal for consumers* contains both new remedies for unfair commercial practices[61] and a collective redress procedure.[62] However, the *New Deal* is viewed mainly as a booster of public enforcement[63] but it has regrettably failed to harmonise procedural rules.[64] The Omnibus Directive expands on the roles and tools of administrative bodies

---

[58] In accordance with recital 15 CSD (see paras 38–39). Detailed arrangements whereby rescission of the contract is effected may be laid down in national law.

[59] De Graaf (n 25) 1051–73.

[60] ibid para 4.1.

[61] On 11 April 2018, the European Commission adopted a 'Proposal for a directive on better enforcement and modernisation of EU consumer protection rules' COM/2018/0185 final, the first pillar of the *New Deal*.

[62] The second pillar of the New Deal is the Collective Redress Directive(n 39).

[63] C Scott, 'Consumer law, Enforcement and a New Deal for Consumers' (2019) 27 *European Review of Private Law* 1279.

[64] Leone and Van Duin (n 14).

but largely ignores the transformative effect of private enforcement, which has been spurred by the case law of the CJEU on *ex officio* enforcement and reinvigorated by the collective redress initiative. The interaction between means of private enforcement and substantive remedies has been given little consideration in the *New Deal*.[65]

The empowerment of civil courts as enforcers of EU consumer law next to public supervisory bodies[66] is mainly due to EU case law on (*ex officio*) remedies and sanctions.[67] The growing case law on deterrent civil sanctions for breaches of consumer law in individual cases has largely added to this role.[68] Since the early 2010s, the Court has continuously stressed the need for civil courts to apply remedies that are effective in terms both of compensating the consumer and discouraging the infringer from disobeying the law. As far as unfair contract terms are concerned, non-deterrent remedies were banned altogether.[69] This is where remedies evolve into sanctions in the sense of the *Van Colson* ruling.[70] They become what the French call a '*peine privée*'.[71]

'Sanctioning' breaches of consumer law is no longer only part of the administrative enforcement toolkit. In several Member States it has, in the meantime, integrated the private enforcement toolkit. In the case law pertaining to effective, proportionate and dissuasive 'sanctions' for breaches of the CCD, it becomes clear that such sanctions also belong in the realm of private law. In some cases, civil penalties such as forfeiture of entitlement to contractual interest already existed prior to transposition of the CCD. After these remedies were used to transpose the Directive, the Court emphasised and reinforced their deterrent effects. In *Le Crédit Lyonnais*, the CJEU assessed whether the civil penalty under French law for a creditor's breach of its pre-contractual obligation to assess a borrower's creditworthiness was compatible with the CCD.[72] This penalty, laid down in the *Code de la consommation*, leads to the deeming of the credit granted as interest-free and free of charges. As such, it was interpreted restrictively by the

---

[65] One notable exception being the firm advice in the recital of the Collective Redress Directive(n 39) paras 10 and 47 to avoid imposition of punitive damages on the infringer. According to the recital, it 'should only be possible to bring a representative action for redress measures under this Directive where Union or national law provides for substantive rights' under civil law such 'as the right to compensation for damage, contract termination, reimbursement, replacement, repair or price reduction as appropriate and as available under Union or national law'. That said, the recital does not elaborate on the interrelationship between collective redress and individual remedies, nor does the Directive. Interesting questions are whether a collective redress scheme can and should allow for full compensation at the individual level and how overcompensation – which would amount to punitive damages – can be prevented.

[66] T Nowak and M Glavina, 'National courts as regulatory agencies and the application of EU law' (2020) 43 *Journal of European Integration* 739, 739–53.

[67] cf Case C-618/10 *Banco Español de Crédito, SA v Joaquín Calderón Camino* ECLI:EU:C:2012:349; Case C-26/13 *Árpád Kásler and Hajnalka Káslerné Rábai v OTP Jelzálogbank Zrt* ECLI:EU:C:2014:282; Joined Cases C-70/17 and C-179/17 *Abanca Corporación Bancaria SA v Alberto García Salamanca Santos and Bankia SA v Alfonso Antonio Lau Mendoza and Verónica Yuliana Rodríguez Ramírez* ECLI:EU:C:2019:250; Case C-118/17 *Zsuzsanna Dunai v ERSTE Bank Hungary Zrt* ECLI:EU:C:2019:207.

[68] Most recently *Dexia Netherlands* (n 46); *Gupfinger* (n 46); *Honoraires d'avocat* (n 46).

[69] *Dexia Netherlands* (n 46); *Gupfinger* (n 46); *Honoraires d'avocat* (n 46); *Banco Espanol de Crédito* (n 67).

[70] Case 14/83 *Sabine von Colson and Elisabeth Kamann v Land Nordrhein-Westfalen* ECLI:EU:C:1984:153, [1984] ECR 1891 marked the development of a new and important general requirement of EU law, namely that sanctions for breaches of EU rules must be effective, proportionate and dissuasive.

[71] N Douche-Doyette, *La sanction de la violation du droit de la consommation dans les contrats de consommation* at https://hal.univ-lorraine.fr/tel-01749257/document (PhD Thesis, Université de Lorraine, 2012).

[72] Case C-565/12 *LCL Le Crédit Lyonnais SA v Fesih Kalhan* ECLI:EU:C:2014:190.

Cour de cassation, which only applied the penalty to the contractual interest but not to the statutory rate. According to the CJEU, 'if the penalty of forfeiture of entitlement to interest is weakened, or even entirely undermined, by reason of the fact that the application of interest at the increased statutory rate is liable to offset the effects of such a penalty, it necessarily follows that that penalty is not genuinely dissuasive'.[73]

Although the referring court's questions relate, in the *Ultimo Portfolio Investment* case,[74] solely to the penalty resulting from the combination of Articles 24 and 138c of the Polish Code of minor offences, it is apparent from the written observations submitted to the Court, subject to confirmation by the referring court, that Polish law provides for a number of other penalties, *including civil penalties*, which the national courts may impose in the event of failure to comply with the obligation to check a consumer's creditworthiness. Private enforcement by civil courts comes into play where public enforcement does not suffice. In the field of EU competition law, the Court has explicitly acknowledged the deterrent function of damages as a complement to public enforcement. This was stressed by Advocate General Wahl in his Opinion in *Skanska*.[75] However, the complementary role of private enforcement has only been implicitly recognised in the case law on unfair contract terms and consumer credit contracts, remaining somehow underexposed.

B. The Rise of (New) Regulatory Contract Law Remedies

Private law remedies are not only about *restoring* rights, but also about enforcing them and preventing future breaches of EU law.[76] Exploitation of remedies for regulatory goals such as prevention[77] is becoming very clear in the jurisprudence on unfair contract terms. This approach to substantive remedies forms part of the paradigm shift towards regulatory private law.[78] The fundamental purpose of remedies in contract law is not to punish the breaching party but – if possible – to put the consumer in the position in which they would have been had there been no breach. The case law of the EU has changed this classic approach to national private law remedies by conferring on them a regulatory dimension, sometimes even transforming them into genuine 'sanctions'. The CJEU, by stressing the dissuasive effect of European directives, has spurred creation of new 'deterrent remedies' at the national level: compensatory or restitutive remedies for the consumer that may amount to overcompensation and/or unjustified enrichment since the consumer does not need to prove that they incurred damage. No proportionality test is involved either.

---

[73] ibid.

[74] Case C-303/20 *Ultimo Portfolio Investment SA v KM* ECLI:EU:C:2021:479.

[75] Opinion issued by AG Wahl in Case C-724/17 *Vantaan kaupunki v Skanska Industrial Solutions Oy and Others* ECLI:EU:C:2019:204.

[76] C Pavillon, 'Private Enforcement as a Deterrence Tool: A Blind Spot in the Omnibus-directive' (2019) 27 *European Review of Private Law* 1297, 1297–1328.

[77] G Bellantuono, 'Contract Law and Regulation' in P Monateri (ed), *Handbook of Comparative Contract Law* (Elgar Publishing, 2017) 111.

[78] H-W Micklitz, 'The Visible Hand of European Regulatory Private Law – The Transformation of European Private Law from Autonomy to Functionalism in Competition and Regulation' (2009) 28 *Yearbook of European Law* 3, 27.

The Belgian remedy available to victims of unfair commercial practices is an example of such a 'deterrent remedy'.[79] The Dutch courts have also been keen on viewing remedies as sanctions and to deviate from the national law of restitution after a contract is nullified because of breach of an information duty. The Dutch Supreme Court held that an 'all-in telephone subscription', including telecommunication services and a 'free' mobile phone, could be qualified as a consumer credit contract and that this contract might be partially nullified if no separate price for the phone was determined by the parties and if the consumer was not informed about this separate price, since the CCD mandates that this information is to be given.[80] The provider is then obliged to refund to the consumer the amounts it received for the phone. The consumer must return the phone but is in principle not obliged to pay compensation for enjoyment or use of the phone. By opting for this remedy, the Court went further than simply restoring the consumer's rights and served the general consumer interest of preventing further infringements of the CCD.

Recently a Dutch sub-district court applied a 'deterrent remedy' in a case where a distance-selling contract was deemed in breach of the Dutch provision implementing Article 8(2) CRD.[81] The contract was partially nullified, in the sense that the consumer was not obliged to pay the purchase price whereas the trader was still obliged to perform.[82]

Transposition of European directives and their interpretation by the CJEU have led Member States to devise new, hybrid remedies that meet the European requirements of effectiveness, proportionality and deterrence (the so-called 'triad').[83] Those remedies do not always fit into the existing national private legal order. The whole relationship between (pre-empting national private law) remedies and sanctions has become blurred in recent European and national jurisprudence (in France, Belgium and the Netherlands, for instance). In the Netherlands, the imposition by civil courts of private sanctions in consumer cases recently even made the news.[84] The focus on the deterrent aspect of private law remedies has met with criticism in the light of the proportionality

---

[79] R Steennot, 'The Belgian Civil Remedy in Case of an Unfair Commercial Practice Towards a Consumer: an effective, proportionate and dissuasive sanction?' in D Pavelkova, J Strouhal and M Pasekova (eds), *Business and Economics Series* (WSEAS Press, 2012) 17.

[80] Dutch Supreme Court, 12 February, *Lindorff/Nazier* ECLI:NL:HR:2016:236.

[81] 'The trader shall ensure that the consumer, when placing his order, explicitly acknowledges that the order implies an obligation to pay. If placing an order entails activating a button or a similar function, the button or similar function shall be labelled in an easily legible manner only with the words 'order with obligation to pay' or a corresponding unambiguous formulation indicating that placing the order entails an obligation to pay the trader. If the trader has not complied with this subparagraph, the consumer shall not be bound by the contract or order.'

[82] See the decisions of the sub-district court of Haarlem (North-Holland): ECLI:NL:RBNHO:2022:5035; ECLI:NL:RBNHO:2022:5029; ECLI:NL:RBNHO:2022:5030.

[83] cf the new Art 8b UCTD and the existing Art 24 CRD. F Cafaggi and P Iamiceli, 'The Principles of Effectiveness, Proportionality and Dissuasiveness in the Enforcement of EU Consumer Law: The Impact of a Triad on the Choice of Civil Remedies and Administrative Sanctions' (2017) 25 *European Review of Private Law* 575, 575–618.

[84] Because it misled the consumer about the price to pay for its services, a sewerage firm from Soest had to repay the whole amount, plus interest and costs, to the consumer, even though the sewers were flowing smoothly again: ECLI:NL:RBMNE:2021:5843. This court decision was picked up by one of the major newspapers in the Netherlands: A Prins, 'Klusjesman doet zijn werk, maar dan komt de rekening: "2660 euro: dat gaat helemaal nergens over"' *AD* (8 January 2022).

requirement. Research has shown that balancing the three principles of effectiveness, proportionality and dissuasiveness is a highly delicate act.[85] Civil courts face the difficult challenge of tying national contractual remedies to the obligation to warrant effective application of an ever-expanding body of consumer rules.

Uncertainty is rife regarding the principle of proportionality. The case law on the UCTD has so far largely ignored the proportionality principle. So far as can be seen, *Kušionová* is the only case where the CJEU assesses Article 7 UCTD in relation to the triad.[86] An interesting question is whether the proportionality principle should pertain to public interests other than consumer protection, such as sustainability goals. Could a remedy spurring the circular economy be considered more proportionate than a remedy that impacts the environment (provided it is equally effective)? Could consumers then be 'forced' to accept reparation instead of replacement, or a price reduction instead of rescission?[87] It appears that EU private law remedies are not yet seen as instrumental to achieving sustainability goals. Much criticism has focused on the new Consumer Sales Directive for not addressing the hierarchy between remedies for non-conformity in light of the transition to a circular economy. This new take on remedies is a clear example of a potential future transformative process.[88]

C. The Search for EU Guidance

The European legislator has not yet fully acknowledged the civil courts' need for guidance when fulfilling their new-found role as *enforcers* of consumer law. The Omnibus Directive provides very little guidance for national civil courts that have to give shape to 'deterrent remedies' in accordance with EU case law.[89] The criteria laid down in the Directive (in Articles 1(5), 3 and 4)[90] have clearly been drafted for public enforcement purposes and would need to be somewhat geared towards a civil procedure in order to be useful for civil courts. In the meantime, civil courts and legislators both have much leeway to flesh out and apply the principles in conformity with national prerogatives.

In recent years, civil courts have been actively seeking definitions and guidance on how to interpret and apply the principles underlying remedies and sanctions for breaches of consumer rights, at both the national and European levels. In order to

---

[85] Cafaggi and Iamiceli (n 83) 575–618.

[86] Case C-34/13 *Monika Kušionová v SMART Capital*, as ECLI:EU:C:2014:2189 para 62.

[87] K Kryla-Cudna, 'Sales Contracts and the Circular Economy' (2020) 28 *European Review of Private Law* 1207, 1210.

[88] M Grochowski, 'European Consumer Law after the New Deal: A Tryptich' (2020) 1 *Yearbook of European Law* 387, 387–422.

[89] It contains guidelines for national enforcement bodies but largely ignores the enforcement tasks of civil courts.

[90] These articles entail the obligation for Member States to ensure that, when deciding whether to impose an administrative penalty and its level, the administrative authorities or courts shall give due regard to the following criteria, where relevant: the nature, gravity and duration or temporal effects of the infringement; the number of consumers affected, including those in other Member State(s); any action taken by the trader to mitigate or remedy the damage suffered by consumers; where appropriate, the intentional or negligent character of the infringement; any previous infringements by the trader; the financial benefits gained or losses avoided by the trader due to the infringement; any other aggravating or mitigating factor applicable to the circumstances of the case.

obtain advice on the proportionality or deterrent effect of sanctions, they regularly turn to the highest national courts or refer to the CJEU for a preliminary ruling.[91] Recent case law indicates that the fairly vague and general triad provision in Article 23 CCD requires a holistic or rather 'contextual' interpretation. The CJEU ruled that in interpreting Article 23 CCD, national courts must take into account not only the special national provisions adopted to transpose the Directive but also the other provisions of the relevant law that should be interpreted in the light of the workings and objectives of the Directive.[92] Indeed, transposition does not necessarily require legislative action. The *Ultimo Portfolio Investment* judgment offers some useful insights into how to interpret the triad and adds to earlier case law on the proportionality of sanctions for breaches of the rules implementing the CCD (such as *Le Crédit Lyonnais*[93] and *Home Credit Slovakia*[94]). This contextual approach would equally fit the new provision on the triad in the UCTD (Article 8b).

IV. How Substantive Transformation Relates to Institutional Transformation

In recent years the EU legislator has somehow steered away from its conventional approach, whereby the Union provides rights while remedies are established separately in the Member States.[95] Before the turn of the twenty-first century, consumer directives already provided for European remedies. This was the case for the (later repealed) Doorstep Selling Directive,[96] the Distance Selling Directive,[97] the UCTD and the CSD. Recent *maximum* harmonising directives have expanded existing remedies and added new remedies. The emphasis on the enforceability of consumer rights and the need for sufficient relief for the consumers concerned has triggered amendments to existing directives. The CRD has extended the cooling-off period and has implemented EU case law interpreting existing remedies to the benefit of consumers.[98] In the aftermath of Dieselgate, the Omnibus Directive has created a right to individual contractual remedies for consumers harmed by unfair commercial practices. The Digital Content Directive

---

[91] *Le Crédit Lyonnais* (n 72); Case C-42/15 *Home Credit Slovakia* ECLI:EU:C:2016:431; Joined Cases C-349/18 to C-351/18 *Nationale Maatschappij der Belgische Spoorwegen (NMBS) v Mbutuku Kanyeba and Others* ECLI:EU:C:2019:936; Joined Cases C-96/16 and C-94/17 *Banco Santander SA v Mahamadou Demba and Mercedes Godoy Bonet and Rafael Ramón Escobedo Cortés v Banco de Sabadell SA* ECLI:EU:C:2018:643; Case C-829/18 *Crédit Logement SA v OE* (removed from the registers) ECLI:EU:C:2019:552; *Dexia Netherlands* (n 46); *Ultimo Portfolio Investment SA* (n 58); *Gupfinger* (n 46); Case *Honoraires d'avocat* (n 46) para 27.

[92] *Ultimo Portfolio Investment* (n 74); *Crédit logement* (n 91).

[93] *Le Crédit Lyonnais* (n 72). If the ability of the consumer to take an informed decision is involved, the forfeiture sanction is proportionate.

[94] *Home Credit Slovakia* (n 91).

[95] Cafaggi and Iamiceli (n 83) 576–80.

[96] Directive 85/577/EEC of 20 December 1985 to protect the consumer in respect of contracts negotiated away from business premises [1985] OJ L372/31.

[97] Directive 97/7/EC (n 52).

[98] cf *Pia Messner* (n 53); Case C-511/08 *Handelsgesellschaft Heinrich Heine GmbH v Verbraucherzentrale Nordrhein-Westfalen e V* ECLI:EU:C:2010:189, [2010] ECR I-3047.

has introduced new remedies for lack of conformity of digital content.[99] This proliferation of EU consumer law remedies laid down in maximum directives arguably reduces the room for national remedies and often distorts national systems of remedies.[100]

As demonstrated in this chapter, the case law of the CJEU has had a major impact on how Member States give substance to their remaining remedial autonomy. In different Member States, substantive remedies have undergone a noticeable transformation under the influence of recent EU case law regarding (i) effective judicial protection of the consumer and (ii) the need for effective and deterrent civil law sanctions. It goes without saying that the vertical dialogue with the CJEU has induced Member States to booster private enforcement *in individual cases* at the national level.

To some extent, this case law – more specifically the *ex officio* duties of civil courts and the emphasis on deterrent sanctions – has also led to disruption of the national system of (contractual) remedies. For instance, the '*effet utile*' of consumer protection directives and the obligation of civil courts to apply protection rules of their own motion have seriously impaired the effectuation of the rights of the infringing professional party. These disruptions are admittedly not entirely due to a decrease in remedial autonomy. Even though the autonomy of Member States to opt for a certain remedy is bound by the requirements of effectiveness, proportionality and deterrent effect, the openness of those principles still leaves Member States some leeway for devising remedies that fit the national protection culture. However, if we look at the broader picture, we are witnessing a fundamental change in the role of civil courts as *enforcers* of consumer law in individual cases. In the case of the Dutch price reduction remedy, although it has been the autonomous choice of the Supreme Court to set aside the causation requirement and restitution obligations, this choice was made so as to enable a large-scale *ex officio* application of the remedy by lower courts.

The substantive transformation discussed in this chapter largely stems from a new conception of the role of civil judges, which in turn forms part of a broader institutional transformation entailing the reinvention of judicial enforcement in the face of the rise of administrative enforcement. Cafaggi asserts that authority-driven administrative protection has not arisen at the expense of but rather as a complement to party-driven judicial protection.[101] However, with 'super protective' remedies slowly turning into sanctions, both enforcement mechanisms sometimes overlap and even compete with each other,[102] requiring more coordination between supervisory entities and civil courts.[103]

---

[99] Directive (EU) 2019/770 of the European Parliament and of the Council of 20 May 2019 on certain aspects concerning contracts for the supply of digital content and digital services [2019] OJ L136/1.

[100] This development is illustrative of a shift from a separation model to a substitution model: O Cherednychenko, 'Islands and the Ocean: Three Models of the Relationship between EU Market Regulation and National Private Law' (2021) 84 *MLR* 1294, 1317.

[101] F Cafaggi, 'The Great Transformation. Administrative and Judicial Enforcement in Consumer Protection: a Remedial Perspective' (2009) 21 *Loyola Consumer Law Review* 496.

[102] cf F Cafaggi, 'Judicial and Administrative Protection Intertwined – The Right to an Effective, Proportionate, and Dissuasive remedy' in B Kas and C Mak (eds), *Civil Courts and the European Polity: The Constitutional Role of Private Law Adjudication in Europe* (Bloomsbury Publishing, 2023), 175.

[103] As is suggested by recital 14 of the Omnibus Directive, 'Member States could lay down the appropriate coordination mechanisms for actions at national level regarding individual redress and penalties.'

5

Information Duties

PASCAL PICHONNAZ

I. Introduction: The Rise of the Information Model

This chapter deals with the transformation of information duties. While in the 1960s and 1970s the effectiveness or usefulness of the information model was intensely debated, at least in the literature, it then became widespread in terms of implementation, in particular as a pre-contractual information model. The European Union (EU) lawmaker first adopted this approach indiscriminately. Only later was it recognised that a more refined approach was needed. The rise of digitalisation, as well as more recent results of behavioural sciences, again put into question the actual information model. This leads to a transformed information model, which might enhance the goals that it aims to achieve and ensure better enforcement of consumer rights.

As long ago as 1973, in his seminal contribution on regulation of information duties in consumer transactions, William Whitford analysed the purpose and effect of information duties in consumer transactions.[1] Despite the raising of regulations of information duties, scholars in the 1960s and 1970s were debating whether disclosure was useless, and whether these pre-contractual information duties had any impact either on consumer behaviour or on the substance of transactions.[2] Whitford's view was that pre-contractual disclosure regulations had less impact on consumer behaviours than post-contractual disclosure regulations, which made the latter more attractive.[3] In anticipation of the behavioural law and economics approach,[4] Whitford asserted that post-contractual disclosure regulations were more likely to cause behavioural changes in consumers than were pre-contractual disclosure regulations. This was explicable, so he asserted, because of fewer considerations conflicting with a desire to maximise contractual gain, but above all because it was easier to be sure that most consumers would be interested in information when it was given. Moreover, the cost of information would then be passed on to buyers, which, according to Whitford, made

---

[1] WC Whitford, 'The Functions of Disclosure Regulation in Consumer Transactions' (1973) 2 *Wisconsin Law Review* 400.

[2] See references ibid 403.

[3] ibid 466–69.

[4] ibid 460–61.

sense when dealing with post-contractual information. In contrast, for pre-contractual information, the paradox was that if the aim was to impact consumer behaviour and potentially induce the consumer not to conclude a given contract, the cost of that pre-contractual information would be borne by those who either did not care about that information and concluded a contract or had (other) incentives to conclude the contract despite the pre-contractual information.[5]

These reflections did not prevent the creation of a huge wave of information duties in EU legislation to implement an information model aiming at indirect consumer protection.[6] Many recent trends show both the limitations of such an information model and the need to transform it. Behavioural economics has shown the theoretical and practical limits of any impact of pre-contractual information on consumer behaviour,[7] but has also unearthed new ways of incentivising (nudging) consumers towards more protective behaviours.[8]

However, in order to avoid throwing out the baby with the bathwater, information duties should certainly not be dropped all of a sudden but should potentially be transformed so as to make them more effective with regard to a better-defined aim. To show this transformation process of information duties, this chapter will first define the current normative information model and its goals (section II), before going on to address the limits of information duties (section III) and focus on how to shift the paradigm of the information model (section IV) by looking at why, when and how to give information on contractual parties. The chapter will end by assessing whether withdrawal or post-contractual help could be more effective in addressing the goals set (section V).

---

[5] ibid.

[6] On information duties in European contract law, see Research Group on Existing EC Private Law (Acquis Group) (ed), *Contract II: General Provisions, Delivery of Goods, Package Travel and Payment Services* (Sellier, European Law Publishers, 2009) 7–9 (section 2, Arts 2:201–2:208), including commentaries by Ch Twigg-Flesner and Th Wilhelmsson, ibid 115–48; Study Group on a European Civil Code and Research Group on EC Private Law (Acquis Group), *Principles, Definitions and Model Rules of European Private Law: Draft Common Frame of Reference (DCFR)*, Outline edn (Sellier, European Law Publishers, 2009) Arts II.-3:101–II.-3:108, in particular Art II.–3:103, and the commentary at 212–18; R Schulze and F Zoll, *European Contract Law*, 3rd edn (Beck, Hart and Nomos, 2021) 122, paras 32–48. For a general overview of pre-contractual information duties in the Common European Sales Law, see J Delvoie and St Reniers, 'Pre-contractual Information in the Proposal for a Common European Sales Law' in I Claeys and R Feltkamp (eds), *The Draft Common European Sales Law: Towards an Alternative Sales Law?* (Intersentia, 2013) 43, 49.

[7] See, for an overview, eg, J Baron and T Wilkinson-Ryan, 'Conceptual Foundations: A Bird's-Eye View' in J Teitelbaum and K Zeiler (eds), *Research Handbook on Behavioural Law and Economics* (Edward Elgar, 2018) 25; A-L Sibony and G Helleringer, 'EU Consumer Protection and Behavioural Sciences: Revolution or Reform?' in A Alemanno and A-L Sibony (eds), *Nudge and the Law: A European Perspective* (Bloomsbury, 2015) 209; O Bar-Gill, *Seduction by Contract, Law, Economics, and Psychology in Consumer Markets* (Oxford University Press, 2012); O Bar-Gill, 'Consumer Transactions' in E Zamir and D Teichman (eds), *The Oxford Handbook of Behavioural Economics and the Law* (Oxford University Press, 2014) 465; E Zamir and D Teichman, *Behavioural Law and Economics* (Oxford University Press, 2018) 281.

[8] eg, A Alemanno and A Spina, 'Nudging Legally: On the Checks and Balances of Behavioural Regulation' (2014) 12 *International Journal of Constitutional Law* 429; A Alemanno and A-L Sibony (eds), *Nudge and the Law: A European Perspective* (Bloomsbury Publishing, 2015); C Sunstein, 'Nudges that Fail' (2017) 1 *Behavioural Public Policy* 4; D Hummel and A Maedche, 'How Effective is Nudging? A Quantitative Review on the Effect Sizes and Limits of Empirical Nudging Studies' (2019) 80 *Journal of Behavioral and Experimental Economics* 47; M Santos Silva, 'Nudging and Other Behaviourally Based Policies as Enablers for Environmental Sustainability' (2022) 11 *Laws* 9.

II. The Normative Information Model and its Goals

A. Information as Triggering a Behavioural Change or Shifting the Risk on to a Party that did not Change its Behaviour

As early as in the Roman markets of the third century BC, sellers had to inform their potential buyers of any hidden defects in some of the goods they wished to sell.[9] The primary aim was then not to change a potential buyer's intent to buy goods but to shift the risk of a defect on to the buyer. Clearly, those who declined to buy those goods might have done so thanks to this information. Others buying the goods would have done so in full cognisance and could not complain when the information was accurate. They could potentially take measures to prevent the occurrence of the risk, or deal with the declared risk of the defect.

This idea of a behavioural change triggered by information and a shift of risk linked to some potential defect is still valid today, as shown by some scholars several years ago.[10]

B. Information should Rebalance the Structural Imbalance

During the twentieth century, information duties grew tremendously, not only in consumer law but also in other fields such as commercial law. In this latter area, the most important trigger was probably the approach taken by merger and acquisition (M&A) transactions,[11] which followed the common law tradition, imposing multiple so-called representations ('Representations and Warranties') on the seller of a (target) company. Indeed, given that in English common law misrepresentation by silence is not possible,[12] the only way to stop sellers from hiding important (detrimental) facts is to

---

[9] D. 21.1.1 (Ulp. 1 ed aed cur): '[E]ademque omnia, cum ea mancipia venibunt, palam recte pronuncianto.' ['[A]nd similarly, any [defect], with which *mancipia* were sold, should be openly manifested.']; also Aulu-Gelle, *Noctes Atticae*, 4,2,1 ('Titulus servorum singulorum scriptus sit curato ita, ut intelligi recte possit, quid morbi vitiive cuique sit, quis fugitivus errove sit noxave solutus non sit.' ['The title of each slave should be written in such a way that one can understand correctly which ones are affected by illnesses or vices, which ones are fugitives or vagabonds or still under a risk of being delivered to a third party as *noxa*.']); W Ernst, *Handbuch des Römischen Privatrechts* (Mohr Siebeck, 2022) 2199, § 79 Klagen aus Kauf (actio empti, actio venditi), no 314; P Pichonnaz, *Les fondements romains du droit privé*, 2nd edn (Schulthess Verlag, 2020) no 2345.

[10] For such an idea, see esp K Riesenhuber, 'Party Autonomy and Information in the Sales Directive' in S Grundmann et al (eds), *Party Autonomy and the Role of Information in the Internal Market* (De Gruyter, 2001) 348; C Twigg-Flesner, 'Information Disclosure about the Quality of Goods: Duty or Encouragement?' in G Howells, A Janssen and R Schultze (eds), *Information Rights and Obligations* (Ashgate, 2005) 135.

[11] CA Hill, BJM Quinn and StD Sollomon, *Mergers and Acquisitions, Law, Theory, and Practice* (West Publishing, 2019) 372–403; R Tschäni, H-J Diem and M Wolf (eds), *M&A-Transaktionen nach Schweizer Recht*, 3rd edn (Schulthess Verlag, 2021) 209–15 (paras 420–31); O Duys and K Henrich, in W Hölters (ed), *Handbuch Unternehmenskauf*, 8th edn (Verlag Dr Otto Schmidt, 2015) ch 16, paras 16.108–16.116.

[12] See *Keates v Lord Cadogan* (1851) 10 CB 591; *Bradford Third Equitable Benefit Building Society v Borders* [1941] 2 All ER 205, 211; A Burrows, *A Casebook on Contract*, 6th edn (Bloomsbury Publishing, 2018) 629; J Beatson, A Burrows and J Cartwright, *Anson's Law of Contract*, 30th edn (Oxford University Press, 2016) 320; E McKendrick, *Contract Law*, 7th edn (Oxford University Press, 2016) 583, 585, 587; E Peel, *Treitel: The Law of Contract*, 14th edn (Sweet & Maxwell, 2015) para 9–019.

force them to disclose a long list of 'representations' of facts and to warrant or promise the accuracy of those facts. Any breach of those representations and warranties triggers different consequences, such as acceleration of all claims or the right to terminate the contract at will.[13] Such drafting perspectives also affected M&A transactions under civil law, even if fraud by silence is possible in civil law systems, especially in the case of breach of a duty to disclose based on the principle of good faith.[14]

A typical feature of representations in M&A transactions is that information is asymmetric, that is one party (the seller) has all the information about the entity sold, whereas the buyer has only very limited access to information before the deal is closed. This structural imbalance could partly be changed by the buyer's requirement that the seller discloses some non-obvious features of the entity sold. If the latter refuses to make those disclosures ('representations'), that stance often becomes a 'deal breaker', given that it is a sign of potential bad faith by the seller. These duties to disclose also aim at regulating the consequences of post-contractual defects or breaches by the seller. The focus is on what matters to the buyer; the seller gives information on facts that in turn the buyer may invoke in the event of post-contractual disputes. They do not directly aim at inducing the buyer not to buy the targeted company; on the contrary, they aim at reassuring the buyer that they have all the information, rebalancing the structural imbalance in the post-contractual phase. In that sense, these information duties follow the pattern suggested by Whitford of (more effective) post-contractual duties.

Indeed, M&A pre-contractual information is not necessarily triggered by statutory requirements, as is the case with consumer law. However, information duties in consumer law were triggered by a similar concern. With mass production, professionals became – even more than before – contractual parties benefiting from holding a lot of information on their products and on the typical behaviour of their potential buyers. At the same time, they sometimes enjoyed a dominant position, as one of a few providing specific goods, allowing them to impose specific conditions on goods sold or services provided, including by standardising contractual terms.

This structural imbalance between a professional – as a repeat player potentially enjoying a dominant position – and a consumer – not having all the information about goods or services offered – was tackled in two ways:

1.   On the one hand, abuse of a dominant position was addressed by competition law.[15] This did not change the fact that consumers might have been trapped into contracts by dominant competitors but, at least indirectly, it forced those dominant competitors not to abuse their position, including when drafting their standard terms or applying commercial practices.[16] Indirectly, consumers were better protected.

---

[13] CA Hill, BJM Quinn and St D Sollomon, *Mergers and Acquisitions, Law, Theory, and Practice* (West Publishing, 2019) 425 ('Notwithstanding anything in this Agreement to the contrary, this Agreement may be terminated and abandoned *at any time prior to the Effective Time*, … whether before or after the adoption of this Agreement by stockholders of the Company … [there follows a list of situations]').

[14] On the duty to disclose under civil law, see *DCFR* (n 6) Art II.–3:101, and the commentary in the *DCFR* (n 6) 200–05.

[15] Consolidated version of the Treaty on Functioning of the European Union [2012] OJ C326/49 [TFEU], Art 102 (ex Art 82 Treaty establishing the European Community [TEC] [2002] OJ C325/33).

[16] ibid Art 102(2) (ex Art 82 TEC), 'Such abuse may, in particular, consist in: (a) directly or indirectly imposing unfair purchase or selling prices or other unfair trading conditions; … (d) making the conclusion

2. On the other hand, information duties were gradually put into place in an attempt to rebalance the relationship between the professional provider and the consumer. The underlying idea was that a well-informed consumer might play a role in the market, especially in not concluding contracts with professionals offering bad goods or services for sale, or who would not behave properly. This is linked to the 'change of behaviour' paradigm.

The idea was also that the market might gradually become more transparent thanks to the provision of more information to consumers, which would 'sanitise' the market. Bad players would be ousted thanks to greater market transparency. This would then again enable consumers to act in the most economically efficient way. As we have seen, this normative perspective on information duties was challenged by some scholars, who considered that it would be advisable, and more effective, to replace the normative model ('what consumers ought to know') with a more predictive model ('what consumers need to know'), based on a more practical analysis.[17]

C. Enhancing Market Transparency and Fair Competition

A more indirect way to change behaviours is to enhance market transparency. From the outset, market transparency was meant to ensure better functioning of the market, thus indirectly ensuring that better products and services were available, since bad products and services would be known as such and not bought or contracted for. This information model therefore has only an indirect impact on protecting consumers.

In his famous 'Special Message to the Congress on Protecting the Consumer Interest' of 15 March 1962, President John F Kennedy specifically mentioned the recurring ignorance of consumers due to mass advertising and lack of information; with that in mind, he declared that the Federal Government would meet its responsibility to consumers in the exercise of their rights, among other things by recognising their 'right to be informed, to be protected against fraudulent, deceitful, or grossly misleading information, advertising, labelling, or other practices, and to be given the facts … need[ed] to make an informed choice'.[18] As stated at the time, 'Government can help consumers to help themselves by developing and making available reliable information.' A paternalistic twist was clearly evident in this approach.

Similar ideas triggered Council Resolution of 14 April 1975 on a preliminary programme of the European Economic Community for a consumer protection and information policy.[19] This information policy aimed at taking both measures on a

---

of contracts subject to acceptance by the other parties of supplementary obligations which, by their nature or according to commercial usage, have no connection with the subject of such contracts.'

[17] Whitford (n 1) 423.

[18] JF Kennedy, 'Special Message to the Congress on Protecting the Consumer Interest' (Message to the Congress of the United States, 15 March 1962) at www.presidency.ucsb.edu/documents/special-message-the-congress-protecting-the-consumer-interest (accessed 18 January 2023).

[19] Council Resolution of 14 April 1975 on a preliminary programme of the European Economic Community for a consumer protection and information policy [1975] OJ C92/1 at eur-lex.europa.eu/legal-content/EN/TXT/?uri=CELEX%3A31975Y0425%2801%29&qid=1642436955094 (accessed 18 January 2023); S Weatherill, *EU Consumer Law and Policy*, 2nd edn (Edward Elgar Publishing, 2005) 6.

macrolevel – with suitable information to the public on misleading behaviours, on enhancing information about products to enhance safety and proper protection of health, and to ensure economic rights – as well as measures having an effect on a microlevel, with information duties to be implemented in specific contracts.

By now, the trend of the normative information model has come to form the core of EU legislation as regards consumer law. As partly shown by the work of the Acquis Group,[20] information duties cover both pre-contractual duties and post-contractual duties, and in some instances even information duties during performance. For example, information duties during performance exist in Article 8(3)(a) of the Directive on certain aspects concerning contracts for the supply of digital content and digital services (Digital Content Directive (DCD)),[21] which provides:

> Where the consumer fails to install, within a reasonable time, updates supplied by the trader in accordance with paragraph 2, the trader shall not be liable for any lack of conformity resulting solely from the lack of the relevant update, provided that:
> (a)   the trader informed the consumer about the availability of the update and the consequences of the failure of the consumer to install it …[22]

Furthermore, Article 19(1)(c) and (d) DCD, linked to recital 76, imposes on the seller a duty to inform about modification of the digital content of a contract.

As a concretisation of the principle of good faith, these principles were developed in accordance with two main features:

1.   The less accessible a good or a service is before conclusion of a contract, the higher the level of information should be. This principle is similar to concerns raised for M&A transactions. The risk of deceit and misrepresentation is higher if the consumer has no access to the goods or services in advance. As for M&A transactions, though, this information only makes sense if there is a genuine way to sanction any breach of such information.
2.   The more informed a consumer is, the more transparent the market and the safer the transaction will be. Once consumers are well-informed, they should be able to rationally decide what to do and thus play their role as market equalisers.

The myth of a transparent market and of rationally behaving consumers has been like a mantra over the years. However, little empirical research has confirmed that position. For example, a report of 2021 by the German Council of Experts for Consumer Issues (*Sachverständigenrat für Verbraucherfragen* (SVRV)) rather shows the contrary. This Report demonstrates empirically how little impact information has on consumers, at least in the digital world.[23] On the one hand, digital literacy is not a common

---

[20] Research Group on the Existing EC Private Law (n 6); T Wilhelmsson, G Howells and H-W Micklitz, 'European Consumer Law' in M Bussani and F Werro (eds), *European Private Law: A Handbook*, vol I (Carolina Academic Press et al, 2009) 245, 270–73; Schulze and Zoll (n 6) 109–12.

[21] Directive (EU) 2019/770 of the European Parliament and of the Council of 20 May 2019 on certain aspects concerning contracts for the supply of digital content and digital services [2019] OJ L136/1.

[22] On this see, eg, D Staudenmeyer, 'Die Richtlinien zu den digitalen Verträgen' [2019] *ZEuP* 663; see also Sachverständigenrat für Verbraucherfragen (SVRV) (ed), *Gutachten zur Lage der Verbraucherinnen und Verbraucher 2021* (Sachverständigenrat für Verbraucherfragen, 2021) 379.

[23] For much information, see Sachverständigenrat für Verbraucherfragen (n 22) 393–99 and proposals 399–402.

good amongst consumers but varies considerably, according to different criteria.[24] On the other hand, information does not necessarily reach the consumer at the right moment, in the appropriate form and in the appropriate content, as shown in section IV. Reflection is therefore needed as to the limits of information duties and potential transformation thereof.

III. The Limits of Information Duties

Information duties have shown their limits in recent years. This is linked both to the issue of defining who the 'average consumer' is (section III.A) and the result of different approaches to the information model (section III.B).

A. Information for the 'Average Consumer'

To achieve its goal, information is necessarily targeted at a specific person or a specific group of persons. In consumer law, this targeted group is the so-called 'average consumer', a consumer who is 'reasonably well informed and reasonably observant and circumspect to a high level of protection',[25] as underlined by recital 4 of the then Directive 2011/83/EU.[26] This notion has slightly evolved over the years, having a direct effect on the ambit of information provided and to be provided. Behind the evolution of the concept, however, also stands the evolution of the understanding of the role of information and some findings of behavioural research that have shown that the average consumer standard is largely at odds with empirical evidence.[27]

One of the most recent Directives – and above all a central one for consumer protection, namely Directive 2019/771/EU on certain aspects concerning contracts for the

---

[24] ibid 281–302.

[25] Established case law since Case C-210/96 *Gut Springerheide* ECLI:EU:C:1998:369, para 31, and even more recently Case C-179/21 *Victorinox* ECLI:EU:C:2022:353, para 41 (emphasis added): 'In those circumstances, the weighing up of a high level of consumer protection and the competitiveness of enterprises, as set out in recital 4 of Directive 2011/83, must lead to the conclusion that the trader is required to provide the consumer with pre-contractual information on the manufacturer's commercial guarantee only where the legitimate interest of the average consumer, *who is reasonably well informed and reasonably observant and circumspect*, to a high level of protection must prevail in the light of his or her decision whether or not to enter into a contractual relationship with that trader.' See also Case C-249/21 *Fuhrmann-2* ECLI:EU:C:2022:269, para 33.

[26] Directive 2011/83/EU of the European Parliament and of the Council of 25 October 2011 on consumer rights, amending Council Directive 93/13/EEC and Directive 1999/44/EC of the European Parliament and of the Council and repealing Council Directive 85/577/EEC and Directive 97/7/EC of the European Parliament and of the Council [2011] OJ L304/64 ('Consumer Rights Directive' (CRD)).

[27] Sibony and Helleringer (n 7) 214; K Purnhagen and E Van Herpen, 'Can Bonus Packs Mislead Consumers? A Demonstration of How Behavioural Consumer Research Can Inform Unfair Commercial Practices Law on the Example of the ECJ's Mars Judgment' (2017) 40 *Journal of Consumer Policy* 217 (with an experiment based on Case C-470/93 *Verein gegen Unwesen in Handel und Gewerbe Köln eV v Mars GmbH* ECLI:EU:C:1995:224, [1995] ECR I-1923).

sale of goods (Sale of Goods Directive (SGD))[28] – defines the consumer as follows in Article 2(2):

> 'consumer' means any natural person who, in relation to contracts covered by this Directive, is acting for purposes which are outside that person's trade, business, craft or profession …

This has to be read in conjunction with Article 169(2) TFEU, which provides that the Union is to contribute to the attainment of a high level of consumer protection in the context of completion of the internal market.[29]

As such, the definition does not describe very clearly what type of consumer is envisaged. It underlines, however, that consumers form a central component of the European internal market. A high level of consumer protection is linked to completion of the internal market (Article 169 TFEU). However, because of the principle of conferral (Article 5(2) TEU[30]), the strategy of the EU cannot be a full-scale strategy, as would be the case in domestic law.[31]

According to the area of law, or the type of strategy, consumers have not always been seen in the same way.

i. Homo Economicus

In some areas, such as unfair competition law, informing consumers should ensure more transparent functioning of the market. Well-informed consumers are supposed to play their role as market players, to maintain functioning and fair competition between providers of goods and services.[32] For example, the consumer as market actor gained importance recently with the Proposal for a Regulation establishing a framework for setting ecodesign requirements for sustainable products.[33] Recital 26 indicates that

> the availability of a product passport should significantly enhance end-to-end traceability of a product throughout its value chain. Among other things, the product passport should help consumers make informed choices by improving their access to product information relevant to them …

and recital 38 sets the goal by stating as follows:

> To drive consumers towards more sustainable choices, labels should … provide information allowing for the effective comparison of products.

The consumer as an efficient market player, and even inducer of changes, might be a new tendency.

---

[28] Directive (EU) 2019/771 of the European Parliament and of the Council of 20 May 2019 on certain aspects concerning contracts for the sale of goods, amending Regulation (EU) 2017/2394 and Directive 2009/22/EC, and repealing Directive 1999/44/EC [2019] OJ L136/28.

[29] Directive (EU) 2019/771 of the European Parliament and of the Council of 20 May 2019 on certain aspects concerning contracts for the sale of goods, amending Regulation (EU) 2017/2394 and Directive 2009/22/EC, and repealing Directive 1999/44/EC [2019] OJ L136/28 (SGD), recital 2.

[30] Treaty on European Union [2012] OJ C326/01.

[31] D Leczykiewicz and S Weatherill, 'The Images of the Consumer in EU Law' in D Leczykiewicz and S Weatherill (eds), *The Images of the Consumer in EU Law* (Hart Publishing, 2016) 1.

[32] ibid 5.

[33] European Commission, 'Proposal for a Regulation of the European Parliament and of the Council establishing a framework for setting ecodesign requirements for sustainable products and repealing Directive 2009/125/EC' COM (2022) 142 final.

ii. *The Vulnerable Consumer and the Empowered Consumer*

A vulnerable consumer that has to be empowered was the image that guided the first consumer-orientated directives in the EU.[34] Consumers may be especially vulnerable in some sectors, such as competition law, energy law[35] or financial law.[36] Consumers may not all be similarly vulnerable, though. Some may be more vulnerable than others, whether due to specific vulnerabilities, such as physical disability or intellectual disability, or situations of extreme need or poverty.[37] The model has not come to an end, but it is also not necessarily the primary aspect.

To find the optimal balance between consumers as efficiency triggers and individuals in need of protection is not an easy task. This is even more true with the rise of behavioural economics, where consumer autonomy is important, on the presumption that consumers are not necessarily vulnerable but indeed may be 'confident consumers'[38] or even very active consumers.

When vulnerable consumers are well protected, they may become empowered consumers.[39] They are then supposed to be fully autonomous, active actors on the market. For example, this trend is evident with the Unfair Contract Terms Directive (UCTD[40]). Many cases in the CJEU have underlined the importance of substantive transparency, first and foremost with non-negotiated clauses. To illustrate, the well-known *Andriucic* case mentions that

> the requirement of transparency of contractual terms ... cannot be reduced merely to their being formally and grammatically intelligible, but that must be understood in a broad sense.[41]

This means that the transparency requirement has to be viewed as

> requiring also that the contract should set out transparently the specific functioning of the mechanism to which the relevant term relates and the relationship between that mechanism and that provided for by other contractual terms, so that that consumer is in a position to evaluate, on the basis of clear, intelligible criteria, the economic consequences for him which derive from it.[42]

The transparency requirement is therefore a substantive one, which implies that the other party, the consumer, is able to understand the legal and economic consequences of those terms. This necessarily implies envisaging a consumer with a certain level of maturity and understanding. This approach also has an impact on the 'average consumer' model.

---

[34] See for an excellent overview, see S Freedman, 'A Short History of Consumer Policy in the EU' in Leczykiewicz and Weatherill (eds) (n 31) 447.

[35] Leczykiewicz and Weatherill (n 31) 8.

[36] I Ramsay, 'Changing Policy Paradigms of EU Consumer Credit and Debt Regulation' in Leczykiewicz and Weatherill (eds) (n 31) 159.

[37] See for others N Reich, 'Vulnerable Consumers in EU Law' in Leczykiewicz and Weatherill (eds) (n 31) 139.

[38] See for this notion Ch Twigg-Flesner, 'The Importance of Law and Harmonisation for the EU's Confident Consumer' in Leczykiewicz and Weatherill (eds) (n 31) 183.

[39] On this, see especially S Weatherill, 'Empowerment is not the only Fruit' in Leczykiewicz and Weatherill (eds) (n 31) 203.

[40] Council Directive 93/13/EEC of 5 April 1993 on unfair terms in consumer contracts [1993] OJ L95/29.

[41] Case C-186/16 *Andriucic* ECLI:EU:C:2017:703, para 44.

[42] ibid para 45.

iii. Prosumer: Consumer as Producer

Protection of consumers stops when consumers turn into prosumers, a mixed role between consumer and producer.[43] However, prosumers remain market actors, and their fluid position may have an impact on the way in which information should be treated and disseminated.

As a result of this very brief overview, it already becomes clear that the 'average consumer' is multi-faceted and not always an 'average' consumer at all. Moreover, sometimes the balance leans more towards protection, at others more towards efficiency or empowerment. This certainly has a direct impact on the various features of information duties, as will be seen below.

B. Some Drawbacks of the Information Model

European consumer law has been shaped from the outset predominantly under the paradigm of the information model, and this still largely applies today,[44] not least because it is in line with the wording of Article 169 TFEU.[45] The information model may be summarised as follows: giving enough information to the consumer reduces the asymmetries of information between consumers and professionals, which in turn enables the empowering of consumers – making them efficient market actors – or protecting them. All three aims may seem to be achieved, at least partially, by the information model. However, some authors have denounced consumer law and its 'cornucopia of mandatory information requirements'.[46]

The information model has shown limits and drawbacks.[47] We will look at a couple of them here.

i. Information is Often Totally Disregarded or At Least not Processed Thoroughly

This has been shown by the Eurobarometer linked to the GDPR,[48] whose data have been collected through surveys showing that 37 per cent of people interviewed did not read

---

[43] On the notion of prosumer, see among others H Heiss and LD Loacker (eds), *Grundfragen des Konsumentenrechts* (Schulthess Verlag, 2020) 31–45; C Meller-Hannich, *Wandel der Verbraucherrollen: Das Recht der Verbraucher und Prosumer in der Sharing Economy* (Duncker & Humblot, 2019) 116–25.

[44] St Grundmann, 'Targeted Consumer Protection' in Leczykiewicz and Weatherill (eds) (n 29) 234.

[45] Reich (n 37) 147.

[46] O Bar-Gill and O Ben-Shahar, 'Regulatory Techniques in Consumer Protection: A Critique of European Consumer Contract Law' (2013) 50 *CML Rev* 109, esp 113.

[47] See, eg, the empirical analysis by SVRV (n 22) 399–402.; see also the quite critical view of the EU as being too protective of consumers in G Howells, 'Europe's (Lack of) Vision on Consumer Protection' in Leczykiewicz and Weatherill (eds) (n 29) 442; H Unberath and A Johnston, 'The Double-Headed approach of the ECJ Concerning Consumer Protection' (2007) 44 *CML Rev* 1237.

[48] GK Ebner, *Die Informationspflichten Der DS-GVO – Eine Kritische Analyse* (Nomos, 2022) 102; European Commission, 'Special Eurobarometer 487a: The General Data Protection Regulation' (March 2019) 47. A similar result arises from the data about reading about data protection on Facebook: 78% of the people interviewed admitted that they had only skimmed the provisions or not read them at all, see R Rothmann

the data protection information at all, and about half read it only partially, though this is also valid for other fields.[49]

ii. Information is Often not Sufficient to Protect Consumers, Given the Impossibility to Negotiate

When contracts are concluded on a take-it-or-leave it basis, information cannot really empower consumers. This has been blatant in relation to standard terms and conditions; one could see this as a reason why the CJEU developed the substantive transparency requirement in relation to the UCTD. In *Andriucic* and in all cases of consumer credits in Swiss francs,[50] the substantive requirement of transparency required service providers not only to communicate information that was formally and grammatically intelligible, but also to ensure that its content could be understood in a broad sense.

iii. Complex Information is Disregarded

Behavioural sciences have shown that the more complex information is, the more likely it will be disregarded by the addressee.[51] Consumers simplify decisions, for example by ignoring insignificant-looking price dimensions and taking mental shortcuts,[52] also called heuristic;[53] this means that when prices are complex, and in particular when they are two-dimensional rather than one-dimensional, consumers experience problems in choosing the right price.[54] As a result, professionals may have an interest in displaying multidimensional prices, or multidimensional information, to reduce the impact of adverse information.[55] Complexity is already created by the fact that some information may need to be coordinated or put together to give the full picture.

---

and B Buchner, 'Der typische Facebook-Nutzer zwischen Recht und Realität' (2018) 42 *Datenschutz und Datensicherheit* 342, 344 with references. On the no-reading tendency, see, eg, I Ayres and A Schwartz, 'The No-Reading Problem in Consumer Contract Law' (2015) 66 *Stanford Law Review* 545.

[49] Zamir and Teichman (n 7) 302–04; see, for an attempt to justify a view against such a position, S Segger-Piening, 'No Need to Read: "Self-Enforcing" Pre-Contractual Consumer Information in European and German Law' in K Mathis and A Tor (eds), *Consumer Law and Economics* (Springer, 2021) 89.

[50] For the most recent, see cases originating from Slovenia, Case C-405/21 *FV v Nova Kreditna Banka Maribor dd* ECLI:EU:C:2022:793; from Poland, Joined Cases C-80/21 to C-82/21 *EK, SK v DBP* (C-80/21) and *BS, WS v M* (C-81/21) and *BS, ŁS v M* (C-82/21) ECLI:EU:C:2022:646; Case C-19/20 *Bank BPH* EU:C:2021:341; Case C-260/18 *Dziubak* EU:C:2019:819; from Hungary, Case C-932/19 *OTP Jelzálogbank and Others* EU:C:2021:673 ('foreign currency'); from Romania, Case C-186/16 *Andriucic* ECLI:EU:C:2017:703; from Hungary, Case C-186/16 *Andriucic* ECLI:EU:C:2017:703; Case C-26/13 *Kásler and Káslerné Rábai* EU:C:2014:282. See also S Cámara Lapuente, 'Control of Price Related Terms in Standard Form Contracts in the European Union: The Innovative Role of the CJEU's Case-Law' in YM Atamer and P Pichonnaz (eds), *Control of Price Related Terms in Standard Form Contracts* (Springer International Publishing, 2019) 81.

[51] Bar-Gill, *Seduction by Contract* (n 7); Bar-Gill, 'Consumer Transactions' (n 7) 465–90; Zamir and Teichman (n 7) 281–324; see also YM Atamer and P Pichonnaz, 'Control of Price Related Terms in Standard Form Contracts, General Report' in Atamer and Pichonnaz (eds) (n 50) 3, esp 5 ff.

[52] Sibony and Helleringer (n 7) 213.

[53] The term 'heuristic' was invented by the mathematician George Polya (1945), who thought of heuristics as a weak method, something that helps in solving a problem. It is a rule that can be applied easily when we are stuck on a problem; see Baron and Wilkinson-Ryan (n 7) esp 26 ff.

[54] O Bar-Gill, 'The Law, Economics And Psychology of Subprime Mortgage Contracts' (2009) 94 *Cornell Law Review* 1073, esp 1120; Baron and Wilkinson-Ryan (n 7) 36 ff (hyperbolic discounting).

[55] Bar-Gill (n 54) 1120; Atamer and Pichonnaz (n 51) 5 ff.

iv. *Text is More Difficult to Process than Images*

The success story of social media based on pictures might at least support such a perspective. Eco-labelling and eco-design also tend to support the idea that pictograms might be more effective than text.[56] This is why pictograms are used increasingly often; they offer a useful short-cut to information, but might also have heuristic biases, given that they reduce information to a single picture. During the Covid-19 pandemic, the authorities used pictograms to ensure quick and effective communication of basic information. This worked well and to some extent transformed the understanding of how information should be communicated.

v. *Information as Nudges*

Behavioural economics has also shown that information may be presented in such a way that it may even nudge the consumer's behaviour into making certain decisions, despite some adverse information. This leads of course to the well-known tension between consumer protection and consumer autonomy of will.[57]

vi. *Information does not Necessarily Trigger Rational Decisions*

Findings from the behavioural sciences have also shown that consumers act based on imperfect rationality due to systematic biases,[58] and that even rational apathy may lead consumers not to choose the best solution in the market.[59] This is a widespread phenomenon, not caused only by exceptional situations. Furthermore, it can only be avoided in a limited way by information given before or at the time of concluding the contract.

Individuals tend to be over-optimistic about their future, as pointed out by cognitive studies and social psychology.[60] Accordingly, consumers are also inclined to be optimistic about adverse results, even if they receive information about them. It has to be

---

[56] Regulation (EC) No 66/2010 of the European Parliament and of the Council of 25 November 2009 on the EU Ecolabel [2009] OJ L27/1; Directive 2009/125/EE of the European Parliament and of the Council of 21 October 2009 establishing a framework for the setting of ecodesign requirements for energy-related products [2009] OJ L285/10; on 30 March 2022 the EU Commission published a Proposal for a Regulation establishing a framework for setting ecodesign requirements for sustainable products and repealing Directive 2009/125/EC (COM(2022) 142 final), especially Arts 14 and 15 on 'labels'.

[57] See, eg, R Thaler and C Sunstein, *Nudge* (Yale University Press, 2008); A Scholes, 'Behavioural Economics and the Autonomous Consumer' (2012) 14 *Cambridge Yearbook on European Legal Studies* 297; Sibony and Helleringer (n 7) 7.

[58] Baron and Wilkinson-Ryan (n 7) 36 ff (hyperbolic discounting).

[59] Bar-Gill, 'Consumer Transactions' (n 7) 465–90; Zamir and Teichman (n 7) 281–324; see also Atamer and Pichonnaz (n 51) 5 ff.

[60] Bar-Gill (n 54) 1120; MG Faure and HA Luth, 'Behavioural Economics in Unfair Contract Terms, Cautions and Considerations' (2011) 34 *Journal of Consumer Policy* 337, 344; H Luth, *Behavioural Economics in Consumer Policy: the Economic Analysis of Standard Terms in Consumer Contracts Revisited* (Intersentia, 2010) 48–55 (on information overload, risk perception, self-serving biases, status-quo biases, framing, anchoring and bounded willpower); K Mathis and AD Steffen, 'From Rational Choice to Behavioural Economics, Theoretical Foundations, Empirical Findings and Legal Implications' in K Mathis (ed), *European Perspectives on Behavioural Law and Economics* (Springer, 2015) 40; Zamir and Teichman (n 7) 61–64.

understood that consumers tend to be myopic – they overvalue the short-term benefits of a transaction at the expense of the future drawbacks (hyperbolic discounting).[61] This type of bias leads, for example, to the choice of mortgage-loan contracts with escalating payments, given the fact that myopic borrowers place excessive weight on initial low payments and insufficient weight on future high payments.[62]

These various drawbacks of the informational model may call for answers and for transformation, as we shall see in section IV. However, some answers have already been partially given in a change from the information model towards a more 'protective model' for vulnerable consumers,[63] such as in the credit and mortgage area;[64] some in justifying the 'information model' through a self-enforcing approach.[65] I believe that more can and should be done.

IV. A Transformed 'Information Model'

The 'information model' should evolve and transform itself thanks to better under-standings of its drawbacks, but also thanks to new technologies and opportunities (section IV.A). Indeed, this remains in line with the wording of Article 169(1) TFEU,[66] which provides, inter alia:

> In order to promote the interests of consumers and to ensure a high level of consumer protec-tion, the Union shall contribute ... to promoting [consumers'] right to information ... in order to safeguard their interests.

Information without sanctions in the event of breach is not effective, which is why the issue of appropriate sanctions will also briefly be addressed in section IV.B.

A. New Features for Information

The information model should not be abandoned but should be transformed.

i. Pre-contractual Information

Institutionally, it is probably almost impossible to abandon the numerous pre-contractual information requirements, given the way the information model has transformed and infused all areas of EU private law. The CRD[67] has more than 20 information require-ments. Similarly, the DCD and the SGD, to mention just a couple of directives, are full

---

[61] Bar-Gill (n 54) 1120; Sibony and Helleringer (n 7) 213.
[62] YM Atamer, 'Why Judicial Control of Price Terms in Consumer Contracts Might Not Always Be the Right Answer – Insights from Behavioural Law and Economics' (2017) 80 *MLR* 624, 631; Bar-Gill (n 54) 1120; Atamer and Pichonnaz (n 51) 3, 5 ff.
[63] See especially Twigg-Flesner (n 38) 187–90.
[64] For a convincing analysis of the history, and drawbacks, see Ramsay (n 36) 159–82, esp 178–81.
[65] Segger-Piening (n 49) 89 ff.
[66] Reich (n 37) 147.
[67] CRD (n 26).

of information requirements. And this cornucopia of information duties[68] is indeed read by some consumers.[69] But, more importantly, there is a growing public awareness about the usual content of this information. So even if, due to cognitive biases, consumers do not read it, or more often do not act rationally based on the information they obtain, the mere existence of these information requirements creates a general pre-understanding about the content of the information.

Given the absence of a clear link between the pre-contractual information given to a specific party and the behaviour triggered by it, in concluding or not concluding a specific contract, the main reason for continuing to insist on pre-contractual liability has to be found on the provider's side. The provider has to identify some key factors and make them available. Those factors that are in line with the provider's interest would be communicated in any case; those that are linked to a shift of some risks on to the consumer have to be mentioned in order to be valid. This triggers two possible results:

1. *Self-regulation.* If providers shift too many risks on to consumers, whom they have to inform thereof, they may well limit themselves and – in some sense – self-regulate themselves.
2. *A path to some remedies.* If providers try not to inform potential consumers about some of the more extreme shifts of risks then, in the event of problems, these shifts may be considered as unfair and be treated as ineffective, or may trigger a right to withdraw or similar remedy. This means that pre-contractual information should concentrate on the key factors consisting of a shift of risks compared to the risk existing under the default rules.

In a nutshell, from a macro-level perspective, information duties have historically also been the preferred option in enforcing a proportionality approach that would favour information over intervention. It might indeed be better to inform the consumer about some important features of goods than prevent them from being sold. Now that the *Cassis de Dijon* principle has fully expanded,[70] this macro feature of information has transformed and is no longer really central.

ii. New Timing for Information

Whitford's proposal to give information when it is needed (section I) seemed difficult to implement in the 1970s, in the absence of adequate technology. Nowadays, however, digitalisation of the economy enables the giving of information at a post-conclusion moment, more specifically when this information is needed.

Therefore, all information that would be needed for a party when a breach of obligations or modification of the contract occurs should automatically be given at that moment. This information will be important for the post-breach or at least

---

[68] Bar-Gill and Ben-Shahar (n 46) 109 ff, esp 113.

[69] See, eg, the analysis done for the European Commission, 'Special Eurobarometer 487a' (n 48) 2, 16: 'The majority (60%) read privacy statements on the Internet – although they are more likely to do so partially (47%) than fully (13%).'

[70] Case C-120/78 *Rewe-Zentral AG v Bundesmonopolverwaltung für Branntwein* ('*Cassis de Dijon*') ECLI:EU:C:1979:42.

post-conclusion moment in helping consumers, or any other party, to determine their behaviour. Where a breach occurs, consumers will be much more interested in information related to the breach. If that information was not supposed to induce the consumer not to conclude a specific contract, at least the information should be given at that later stage, spontaneously and effectively.

Indeed, one problem is not only a shift of some risks on to the consumer (which should still be dealt with by pre-contractual information) but also a tendency to render enforcement of any right more cumbersome for consumers. It would, however, be of central importance to help the consumer as much as possible by informing them about all the rights and possibilities at that stage of the contractual relationship.

This happens to some extent with information in the case of flight cancellations. Companies give passengers adequate information on paper, or more often now by way of digital bot, to help them in dealing with their rights. Thanks to digital possibilities, requests are forwarded to companies in appropriate forms. At the very least, information about any right is, or should be, provided, with appropriate links to facilitate enforcement.

The new paradigm should comprise 'duties to inform when information is needed' in a way that is effective and enables rapid and easy enforcement of those rights.

iii. Transforming Towards a More Granular System

If information is given at the right moment, it should also be designed to fit the specific needs of a given consumer. This calls for a transformation of the content of information towards more granular information,[71] as has been applied, for example, in financial law, as mentioned by Ian Ramsay.[72] More vulnerable consumers may need more information, when a group of consumers as such is more vulnerable, or information may need to be presented in a different way when a specific consumer is a vulnerable consumer.[73] Creating categories is not an easy task, but this is not sufficient to justify refusal to try to implement such an approach.

For post-conclusion information, granularity does not mean that information has to be adapted to any single consumer; but according to the area, post-conclusion information should be given in the quantity and quality needed for that area. Granularity is then based on objective criteria.

For specific vulnerable consumers (see above), the use of some specific media may be imposed on sellers and service providers to apply the non-discrimination feature to information duties as well.

iv. Selecting More Appropriate Formats

As pictures might sometimes communicate more efficiently and effectively than text, one may wonder to what extent some information should also be given through pictures.

---

[71] See, eg, C Busch and A De Franceschi (eds), *Algorithmic Regulation and Personalized Law: A Handbook* (Publishing, 2020) ch 1.
[72] Ramsay (n 36) 159–82, esp 174.
[73] ibid 173.

For pre-contractual information, this might in particular be the case for information duties that are aimed at protecting consumers or at least nudging their choices. Eco-labelling is one good example of nudging the consumer towards more environmentally friendly devices (see section III.B.iv). However, pictures on cigarette packaging do not seem to be very effective, which is an indication of the limits of a paternalistic approach.

Pre-contractual information aimed at informing consumers about the shift of risk could also be given with pictograms. For example, a 'no-liability for slight negligence' clause or automatic renewal of a contract in the absence of appropriate cancellation could be expressed in pictograms. The Claudette algorithm driven by artificial intelligence (AI) and machine learning to identify unfair terms (in red), potentially unfair terms (in orange), and other items of standard terms and conditions is a step in that direction too.[74]

For post-contractual information, one might envisage chatbots and appropriate links automatically generated and sent to consumers. This is the case in some areas, while in others much remains to be done.

v. *What About Appropriate Intermediaries?*

Some authors have suggested avoiding the hurdle of having pre-contractual information provided to the consumer directly; instead, there should be public or private intermediaries that the consumer could use to get information, or more specifically the best price on the market or the most appropriate product or service in light of the consumer's own data.[75] By centralising producers' information, these online platforms could make matches for consumers. This has been put in place in some retail banks[76] or for insurance, with insurance intermediaries paid by the insurers.

This proposal may seem interesting at first sight, as information is given only to the intermediaries, which then make informed choices for consumers. The nudging or inducement effect might therefore be more effective. However, apart from potential GDPR issues, this approach triggers the de-empowerment of consumers. Consumers are no longer in the driving seat but are supposed to follow 'advice' by a 'fully informed' intermediary. The remedy then becomes more dangerous than the actual situation. Indeed, the cornucopia of information requirements would not be reduced, with the result that the burden on producers will remain, but information will be sent to

---

[74] See claudette.eui.eu/demo (accessed 20 January 2023); M Lippi et al, 'CLAUDETTE: an automated detector of potentially unfair clauses in online terms of service' (2019) 27 *Artificial Intelligence Law* 117; F Ruggeri et al, 'Detecting and explaining unfairness in consumer contracts through memory networks' (2022) 30 *Artificial Intelligence Law* 59; for its use in the field of the GDPR, see the study report by G Contissa, 'CLAUDETTE meets GDPR Automating the Evaluation of Privacy Policies using Artificial Intelligence' (2018) at beuc.eu/sites/default/files/publications/beuc-x-2018-066_claudette_meets_gdpr_report.pdf (accessed 20 January 2023); 130.136.9.51/claudette GDPR/ (accessed 20 January 2023).

[75] Bar-Gill, *Seduction by Contract* (n 7) 242; Bar-Gill, 'Consumer transactions' (n 7) 482–83; see also Atamer (n 62) 647 f.

[76] Atamer (n 60) 651, citing the Competition and Markets Authority, *Retail Banking Market Investigation: Final Report* (2016) 441–61 at assets.publishing.service.gov.uk/media/57ac9667e5274a0f6c00007a/retail-banking-market-investigation-full-final-report.pdf (accessed 20 January 2023).

intermediaries. Fully in charge, those intermediaries will be agents for consumers. The decision to conclude or not to conclude a specific contract would seem tailor-made but would be fully in the hands of intermediaries, which consumers will have no other choice than to follow. It will be central to determine who owns or influences those intermediaries. This also presupposes that all consumers in a given sector would have intermediaries. This seems to be not only difficult to imagine, but also not favouring empowered consumers and freedom in the market.

B. Specific Challenges with Online Platforms, DLT and Autonomous Contracting

Online platforms, smart contracts concluded or encapsulated in distributed ledger technology (DLT), such as blockchain, and autonomous contacting may present some further challenges as to information requirements. We deal briefly with each of these points in this subsection.

i. *Information and Online Platforms*

Regulation (EU) 2019/1150[77] (also called the P2B Regulation) applies to businesses that use online platforms to offer their goods or services to consumers. The information required aims not only at protecting consumers, but also at ensuring a fair, transparent and predictable business environment, including, in Article 3(1)(d), by imposing duties on providers to inform consumers 'on any additional distribution channels and potential affiliate programmes through which providers of online intermediation services might market goods and services offered by business users', or to give information on the functioning and effectiveness of the internal complaint-handling system (Article 11(4)) and other duties.[78]

The difficulty with online platforms is that these are not necessarily parties to contracts with consumers. The Digital Services Act (DSA)[79] has added further information duties, including those linked to terms and conditions (Article 15 DSA). Thus, very large online platforms or search engines (within the meaning of Article 33 DSA) must publish their terms and conditions in the official languages of all the Member States in which they offer their services (Article 14(6) DSA). Again, these duties to inform go beyond the informing of sole contractual partners and aim at broader information, to fulfil the two aims mentioned above, have larger information to empower the parties, and ensure fair competition through a more transparent market.

---

[77] Regulation (EU) 2019/1150 of the European Parliament and of the Council of 20 June 2019 on promoting fairness and transparency for business users of online intermediation services [2019] OJ L186/57.

[78] ibid Art 3(1)(d) and (e): '(d) include information on any additional distribution channels and potential affiliate programmes through which providers of online intermediation services might market goods and services offered by business users; (e) include general information regarding the effects of the terms and conditions on the ownership and control of intellectual property rights of business users'; see also European Law Institute Model Rules on Platform (2019) Art 4 on the transparency of rankings.

[79] Regulation (EU) 2022/2065 of the European Parliament and of the Council of 19 October 2022 on a single market for digital services and amending Directive 2000/31/EC (Digital Services Act) [2022] OJ L277/1.

When notifying any proposed changes to their terms and conditions, providers of online intermediation services must notify business users about this on 'a durable medium' (Article 3(2) P2B Regulation). This has to be done in the same format as for information on restriction, suspension and termination pursuant to Article 4 P2B Regulation. Article 2(13) P2B Regulation defines 'durable medium' as

> any instrument which enables business users to store information addressed personally to them in a way accessible for future reference and for a period of time adequate for the purposes of the information and allows the unchanged reproduction of the information stored.

In line with the UCTD, this requirement should enable business users in effect to review the information at a later stage (recital 18); this may, however, prove to be quite challenging when most of the information is digitalised. For example, should this be in pdf format and should it be downloadable? Or would it be enough to have this information on the website (with a permanent link)?

The ELI (European Law Institute) Model Rules on Online Platforms use the same term in Article 12(1)(a), but the problem remains the same, given that there is no definition of a 'durable medium'. The portability of reviews (Article 7 ELI Model Rules) has an indirect impact on how to organise the durable medium, and therefore may call for some further transformation of information in the case of online platforms.

ii. Distributed Ledger Technology and its Effect on the Transformation of Information Duties

In the *Content Services* decision,[80] which deals with Directive 97/7/EC,[81] the Court interpreted the notion of 'durable medium' in Article 5(1) of the Directive by reference to Article 2(f) of Directive 2002/65/EC, concerning distance marketing of consumer financial services,[82] and to Article 2(10) CRD.[83] The Court stated:

> It follows that a durable medium, within the meaning of Article 5(1) of Directive 97/7, must ensure that the consumer, in a similar way to paper form, is in possession of the information referred to in that provision to enable him to exercise his rights where necessary.[84]

And further:

> Where a medium allows the consumer to store the information which has been addressed to him personally, ensures that its content is not altered, and that the information is accessible for an adequate period, and gives consumers the possibility to reproduce it unchanged, that medium must be regarded as 'durable' within the meaning of that provision.[85]

---

[80] Case C-49/11 *Content Services Ltd v Bundesarbeitskammer* ECLI:EU:C:2012:419.

[81] Directive 97/7/EC of the European Parliament and of the Council of 20 May 1997 on the protection of consumers in respect of distance contracts [1977] OJ L144/19.

[82] Directive 2002/65/EC of the European Parliament and of the Council of 23 September 2002 concerning the distance marketing of consumer financial services and amending Council Directive 90/619/EEC and Directives 97/7/EC and 98/27/EC [2002] OJ L271/16 (Distance Marketing Directive).

[83] *Content Services* (n 80) paras 8–11 and paras 38–44.

[84] ibid para 42.

[85] ibid para 43.

As such, a link to a website was considered as not being sufficient, given that nothing indicated that the website to which the link connected

> allows that consumer to store information which is personally addressed to him in such a way that he can access it and reproduce it unchanged during an adequate period without the seller being able to amend the content unilaterally.[86]

Therefore, it could not be considered a 'durable medium'.

In the *Tiketa* decision of 24 February 2022,[87] the CJEU had again to analyse the meaning of the requirement for 'information [to] be provided in plain and intelligible language and on a durable medium' in accordance with Articles 2(10) and 8(7) CRD. The Court considered that the information given to a consumer who actively accepts standard terms and conditions by ticking the box provided for that purpose is sufficient to consider that the information is given, but not that it has been confirmed on a 'durable medium'.[88]

This line of decisions creates a particular challenge for smart contracts concluded on DLT or in relation to DLT. Any information given to the consumer must respect the requirement of being confirmed via a 'durable medium' in accordance with the *Tiketa* decision. On the one hand, the individual blocks of a blockchain cannot be changed, but conclusion of a contract imposes on the provider the duty to 'provide the consumer with confirmation of the contract on a durable medium'. This means determining a way to reach that consumer, via adequate means, and in a plain and intelligible way, which is not the case if the provider keeps the information only in a machine-readable format.

One way to deal with that difficulty could be to have some information in a framework agreement that would be sent to the consumer on conclusion of the contract. It remains the case that most of the information would then have to be provided in a technical way that fulfils the requirements of Article 2(10) CRD.

The ELI Principles on Blockchain Technology, Smart Contracts and Consumer Protection, approved by the ELI Council on 5 July 2022 and by the ELI Membership on 8 September 2022, restate the requirement for information to be provided on a durable medium (Principle 16(d)). The commentary underlines that 'the information must always be available on a durable medium in natural language to allow any consumer to read and understand what the information contains', but then reduces the need for a 'durable medium' by stating as follows:

> [A]s Smart Contracts, given their algorithmic nature, will most likely only be used in a setting of mass and standardised transactions, otherwise the time and effort of coding such contracts do not seem worthwhile, consumers not only are in need of a durable medium on which the contractual terms and conditions are stored (ie ex post, after the contract has been concluded), but also need to know in advance (ex ante, before the conclusion of a legally binding contract) what the Smart Contract implies. Publication in natural language on the user's website will then give a consumer the easiest access to information about what the Smart Contract implies. The sanction here is that, if such information is not given as indicated, the consumer can withdraw from the legally binding agreement or, in the case of a non-communicated update, can terminate the agreement.

---

[86] ibid para 46.
[87] Case C-536/20 *'Tiketa' UAB v MŠ, other party: 'Baltic Music' VšJ* ECLI:EU:C:2022:112.
[88] ibid paras 50–53.

This again brings us back to the effectiveness of information given at time of conclusion of a contract compared to post-contractual information. Evidently, new technologies call even more for a real transformation of the information model.

iii. Automated Contracting: A Need to Transform the Information Model

Smart fridges do not read, but people buying such fridges may be presumed to do so. The issue is therefore to determine how to adapt information so that it reaches the user/owner of an intelligent fridge at a time before any contractual commitments arising out of a/an (automated) transaction concluded between a fridge and a third party.

It is certainly important to give some information before and on conclusion of the sales contract when the consumer buys the fridge. However, it is also fundamental that some further information is given at the time of conclusion of these automated contracts.

One could imagine warnings – for example, with six or 12 hours' advance notice – about concluding a contract and the potential consequences. Such a warning could, for instance, be sent on a smartphone or another device and would need to be acknowledged.

Apart from the timing challenge, one is faced with further difficulties underlined by behavioural sciences. Will this system not lead to an overflow of information, especially if someone has several of these devices? Should these warnings need to be read or just acknowledged? There is a risk of putting too much of a burden on the consumer in asking for information to be read if this is considerable. The result would then be cognitive disregard. Again, post-contractual information might be more efficient than pre-contractual information, which therefore clearly calls for a more in-depth transformation of the information model.

iv. Towards a Three-Level Model

In light of what has been said so far, it might be useful to consider transforming the information model towards a three-level model, which might operate as follows:

- *The first level* could be provided by pictograms, giving initial, almost intuitive, information. This would help the consumer gain a pre-understanding either of risk allocation or of fundamental features of the contract. It will not necessarily trigger a rational decision, as we have seen, but it may nudge the consumer towards certain behaviour.

- *The second level* would be a series of overall pieces of information that would be provided to everyone, and which would principally be provided at the pre-contractual stage. The aim is similar, but this information, based on the information model, would be important to trigger risk allocation in the event of absence of given information.

- *The third – and potentially the most important – level* would be composed of more detailed and personalised information, to be given at the moment when the information is needed and in a way that would ensure efficient enforcement of any consumer rights.

One would then have to integrate the various points mentioned previously, as to the medium, the timing and the specifics of some situations, to get a full picture of the transformed model.

V. The Right to Withdraw as a Possible Remedy to Enforce Information Duties

Duties without remedies for breach are not very effective. Information without remedies would be provided only if it were in the interest of those required to provide it. However, if information duties meet the well-understood interests of providers of goods or services then there is little need for legislation to cover such information duties, given that providers or other actors will pass this information to consumers anyway.

Clearly, what is tackled by the 'information model' is the need for information that would normally not be given freely by providers. This implies a need for one or several remedies. This is true for pre-contractual information in a three-level model. Post-conclusion information may call for diverse remedies, such as a regime of adverse inferences or the like.

Pre-contractual information failure – and therefore the most common remedy in EU law – has been sanctioned by a right to withdraw as long as the information needed has not been given to the consumer.[89] In earlier directives, the right to withdraw would not lapse as long as the information was not given. The CJEU went as far as to accept the idea that a consumer might withdraw from a contract even after performance, while then fixing a time limit within which to do so.[90]

The right of withdrawal may be a way to put some pressure on the provider of goods or services to comply with information requirements. If the deal is a valuable deal, it would be best to give the information as soon as possible, to enable the right to withdraw to lapse early enough.

The advantage of the right to withdraw is also that it is a self-enforcement remedy. There is no need to go to court to enforce it; a mere declaration may suffice. It also enables the consumer to decide whether they want to maintain the contractual relationship or not; the remedy is therefore flexible, even if the information has not been provided.

However, the remedy is not fully satisfactory, for at least three reasons:

1. *It is an all-or-nothing remedy.* If the aim of the information to be given to consumers were to enable them to negotiate differently, the absence of the information would only give them the choice between withdrawal or keeping the contract 'as is'. This may be suboptimal, especially when there was a way to negotiate in the first instance – that is, had the information been given on time. As already mentioned, though, consumer contracts may often be concluded on a take-it-or-leave-it basis.

---

[89] It can be found in: Directive 2013/36/EU of the European Parliament and of the Council of 26 June 2013 on access to the activity of credit institutions and the prudential supervision of credit institutions and investment firms, amending Directive 2002/87/EC and repealing Directives 2006/48/EC and 2006/49/EC [2013] OJ L176/338, Art 9; Directive 2008/122/EC of the European Parliament and of the Council of 14 January 2009 on the protection of consumers in respect of certain aspects of timeshare, long-term holiday product, resale and exchange contracts [2009] OJ L33/10, Art 6; Directive 2008/48/EC of the European Parliament and of the Council of 23 April 2008 on credit agreements for consumers and repealing Council Directive 87/102/EEC [2008] OJ L133/66 (Consumer Credit Directive), Art 14; Distance Marketing Directive (n 82) Art 6; Directive 2014/17/EU of the European Parliament and of the Council of 4 February 2014 on credit agreements for consumers relating to residential immovable property and amending Directives 2008/48/EC and 2013/36/EU and Regulation (EU) No 1093/2010 [2014] OJ L60/34, Art 14(6). See also for an overview, Schulze and Zoll (n 6) 157–72, paras 118–49.

[90] Case C-412/06 *Annelore Hamilton v Volksbank Filder eG* ECLI:EU:C:2008:215.

2. *It is a remedy that does not per se support sustainability.* For contracts for the sale of goods, withdrawal from the contract is not necessarily a sustainable solution. The goods are returned to the seller, and often either refurbished or destroyed, which creates a waste of goods that would be or could be apt for sale. This means that the seller should have duties attached to the right of withdrawal, imposing on it the further duty to resell the goods in the most effective and sustainable way. The right to withdraw should therefore be attached to a duty for the seller not to throw the goods away but refurbish them before resale.

3. *Restitution of services in the case of withdrawal is challenging.* As it appears, for example, from Directive 2008/48/EC,[91] withdrawal of credit may create some difficulties as regards making restitution for enrichment of consumers having benefited from a loan during a certain period without any contractual basis. Is there then a right to claim disgorgement of unjustified consumer enrichment, or should the absence of interest be a contractual sanction for lack of information? The EU legislator has opted for the former in Article 14(3)(b) of the Consumer Credit Directive, given that the consumer must repay not only the capital but also 'interest accrued', 'calculated on the basis of the agreed borrowing rate'.[92] There is no such thing as a free lunch, but the obligation to repay capital and accrued interest 'no later than 30 calendar days after despatch by the consumer to the creditor of notification of withdrawal' may indeed prove very difficult. However, in the context of the penalties that Member States must introduce, in accordance with Article 23 of the Consumer Credit Directive, the absence of certain obligatory information in a credit agreement may result in loss of borrowing interest. Nevertheless, the penalties must be proportionate, which means that the severity of any penalties must be commensurate with the seriousness of the infringements for which they are imposed, in particular by ensuring a genuinely deterrent effect while respecting the general principle of proportionality.[93] As explained by Advocate General Hogan, breach of the duty to inform seems less serious than other breaches (for instance, absence of a creditworthiness test), which therefore cannot justify total loss of interest.[94]

---

[91] Consumer Credit Directive (n 89).

[92] Art 14(3)(b) reads as follows: 'If the consumer exercises his right of withdrawal, he shall … (b) pay to the creditor the capital and the interest accrued thereon from the date the credit was drawn down until the date the capital is repaid, without any undue delay and no later than 30 calendar days after the dispatch by him to the creditor of notification of the withdrawal. The interest shall be calculated on the basis of the agreed borrowing rate. The creditor shall not be entitled to any other compensation from the consumer in the event of withdrawal, except compensation for any non-returnable charges paid by the creditor to any public administrative body.'

[93] See on this Joined Cases C-33/20, C-155/20 and C-187/20 *UK v Volkswagen Bank GmbH* (C-33/20) and *RT, SV, BC v Volkswagen Bank GmbH, Skoda Bank, subsidiary of Volkswagen Bank GmbH* (C-155/20) and *JL, DT v BMW Bank GmbH, Volkswagen Bank GmbH* (C-187/20) ECLI:EU:C:2021:629, AG Hogan, para 123; see also Case C-42/15 *Home Credit Slovakia* EU:C:2016:842, para 63.

[94] *Volkswagen Bank* (n 93), AC Hogan, para 124, 'From this point of view, it should be noted that, on the one hand, interest on a loan does not merely remunerate the management of the loan, but also compensates, where appropriate, for the loss of monetary value. On the other hand, the omission of any of the information referred to in Article 10 of Directive 2008/48 already leads to an extension of the withdrawal period. Consequently, as regards information relating not to the content of the contract, but merely to the legal environment of the contract – as is the case with information relating to out-of-court procedures – the omission of the latter

These aspects were not dealt with in the *Volkswagen Bank* case of 9 September 2021.[95]

For other services, it might well be difficult to find an equitable solution in the event of withdrawal. For example, Article 8(2) of Directive 2008/122/EC on timeshares provides that '[w]here the consumer exercises the right of withdrawal, the consumer shall neither bear any cost nor be liable for any value corresponding to the service which may have been performed before withdrawal'.

This means that if services have already been provided, there will be no 'restitution' or compensation in money.

This may lead one to envisage or devise other enforcement mechanisms. One possibility would be to use adverse inferences, through fictions. If the lender would not give information about interest rates, or the cost of currency exchange, these costs would be inferred as being the market rates. This also reflects what Advocate General Hogan asserts as to late-payment interest rates.[96]

The same could be true for services that would have been used: market rate, if any, might apply. This has been done in mergers and acquisitions, where representations and warranties or the disclosure letter always allow for negative inferences to be drawn for what has not been disclosed. The solution might be close to withdrawal with flexible rules on restitution.

VI. Conclusions: Features of a Transformed Information Model

It might be time to devise a transformed information model. It is argued that there should be more post-contractual information, more granular information that would be adapted to the consumer group. More granular or personalised information would also ensure better protection for specifically vulnerable consumers. This may also enable more automatic enforcement of consumer rights thanks to recourse to AI. In such a case, the need might no longer arise for a self-remedy such as the right to withdraw.

---

from the contract does not appear to justify the *complete* loss of that interest. (See, judgment of 9 November 2016, *Home Credit Slovakia* (C-42/15, EU:C:2016:842, paragraph 72)). Such an omission is much less serious than, eg, the absence of an assessment of the applicant's creditworthiness (See, judgment of 27 March 2014, *LCL Le Crédit Lyonnais* (C-565/12, EU:C:2014:190, paragraph 45 et seq.)) or a failure to mention the APR or certain information concerning the cost of the loan for the consumer. (See, judgment of 9 November 2016, *Home Credit Slovakia* (C-42/15, EU:C:2016:842, paragraph 70)). In my view, the Member States have a certain discretion in this regard and may provide that failure to provide certain items of unrelated to the obligations of the parties is to be compensated by the award of liquidated damages.'
[95] Case C-33/20 *Volkswagen Bank* ECLI:EU:C:2021:736.
[96] *Volkswagen Bank* (n 93) AG Hogan, para 125, 'Similarly, in those cases where the default interest rate applicable at the time of conclusion of the contract in the form of a specific figure – as referred to in question 1 – has not been expressly indicated, then in so far as such an item of information does not concern the cost of the credit itself, but rather one of potential delay, it seems to me also more in accordance with the principle of proportionality that such omission would be remedied by precluding the creditor from claiming the interest for late payment provided for in the contract (and not the interest on the loan), including, if necessary, the award of damages.'

In transforming its information model, the EU legislator should keep to the idea that information has the aim of empowering consumers in overcoming vulnerability, but that it should also induce some choices that ensure that consumers are efficient market players for the overall benefit of a better-functioning market. However, the actual information model suffers from serious drawbacks that should not be neglected; these are mostly linked to the fact that consumer behaviours may not fulfil the expectations of the legislator, given the reality unearthed by the behavioural sciences.

A post-contractual information model might therefore be more effective in many respects than a pre-contractual information model. Transformation of the information model towards a post-contractual information regime may, for example, enhance enforcement of rights and ultimately lead to the better functioning of the market. Again, this does not mean that the pre-contractual information model should be fully abandoned. It keeps its validity if rightly transformed. For example, some information, given by the use of pictograms, might be more suitable at the pre-contractual phase, supporting the principal aim of giving a quick but efficient understanding of why a contract might be risky or indicating when risks are shifted on to the consumer. Pre-contractual information duties should therefore be transformed into a new approach, which could be the three-level information model. New technologies also call for a different approach as to the issue of providing information on 'durable means', as we have seen. Distributed ledger technology or automated contracting may justify a different regime, with pre-contractual warnings, and then post-contractual information, all targeted at the specific problem.

As explained, the three-level information model consists of giving information in the first stage through pictograms; these are supposed to focus on the risk of concluding the contract or on the shift of some risks on to the consumer. The second stage would ensure that some general information is given at a later time, when needed for performing some aspects of the contract. The third, and most important, stage consists of more granular information, to be given when and where needed, and employing a medium that allows for efficient enforcement. This three-level model or three-step process of information would be an effective way to give information. Transformation of the information model might take into account the drawbacks of the actual normative model of information and ensure better fulfilment of the aim of information. New technologies certainly allow transformation of the model and ensure that it makes sense. All concerned should therefore benefit from it.

6

Consumer Education in the EU

ELISE POILLOT

I. Introduction

Why does consumer education matter in the first place? Because since the twentieth century, consumers have been commonly portrayed as agents 'capable of ensuring and enhancing economic growth and political democracy'.[1] Educating consumers forms part of the process of making them become such agents by providing them with the resources to make informed choices, that is, decisions made after considering options based on adequate and accurate information. Subsequently and unsurprisingly, consumer education illustrates, as does consumer law and policy, the tension between the different approaches to consumption. The reason for that tension hinges on the differing objectives one may assign to consumer education. In other words: what should consumers be educated to do? Should consumers be educated in such a way as to make the best choices for the market to function as efficiently as possible? Or should they be educated to be critical towards the consumption options they are offered so as to allow for a change in how economic growth and political democracy are conceived? This is a difficult question to answer. To do so, one needs first to examine the conceptual elements of consumer education. The objective of educating consumers very much depends on the conception of who consumers are and their role in (post-modern) society. Understanding this role is therefore a prerequisite for any analysis of what consumer education has been, or what it could or should be.

Before turning our attention to what consumer education in the European Union (EU) has been in the past and why it has not taken on as transformative a role as it might have done, a review must be conducted of the various conceptions on the figures and roles of consumers, as well as of the role assigned to consumer education in the EU. As a matter of fact, the conceptual elements of consumer education are found at the very core of the possible reasons why consumer education as such has not spurred a transformation of consumer policy and law. This does not mean that consumer education cannot play such a role. Indeed, the ultimate objective of this chapter is to demonstrate that, with a new perspective, consumer education can play a highly relevant role in

---

[1] N Olsen, 'Consumer imaginaries, political visions and the ordering of modern society' in H-W Micklitz (ed), *The Making of Consumer Law and Policy in Europe* (Bloomsbury Publishing, 2021) 283.

the process of transforming EU consumer law and policy. Section II of this chapter will therefore explore the conceptual elements of consumer education as they stand. Section III will analyse the current context of consumer education within the EU, pointing out its weaknesses. Section IV will examine why consumer education has not led to any transformation of EU consumer law and policy but has rather emphasised a misunderstanding of the role that consumer information can play. Finally, section V will call for transformation of EU consumer law and policy through a new approach to consumer education. Section VI concludes.

II. The Conceptual Elements of Consumer Education

When thinking about consumer education in the EU, two questions need to be tackled: Who is meant to be educated – in other words, whom are we talking about when we refer to consumers? And how was consumer education conceived in the context of building and developing the EU? Interestingly, the various forms of defining the social-political figures of consumers in support of theories of smooth and efficient functioning of the market may differ but, in the end, they all assign the same destiny to consumers: to be informed so as to make the right choice. Only under this condition will they be what they are meant to be: the key actors and the cornerstone of the market. Policy and legislation in the EU define/represent consumers with elements from various scholarly imaginings of what a consumer is. These interpretations were conceived 'to give meaning and coherence to our economic practices and decisions' and to 'order modern society according to [various] political visions'.[2] Therefore, it is not surprising that, in the EU, consumer education was originally twinned as a concept with that of consumer information. Consumers may differ according to time and context, but invariably they appear destined to being informed before being educated.

A. The Consumer as a Socio-Political Figure: Many Faces, One Destiny

The following developments draw on the history of the economic and political 'consumer imaginaries' as presented by Niklas Olsen in his enlightening contribution to the book on *The Making of Consumer Law and Policy in Europe* edited by Hans Micklitz (2021). In his paper, Olsen presents the main figures of consumers as they have been theorised to support various systemic political and economic doctrines related to the development of market economies. All of them correspond to some moment in EU legal history. Having them in mind is crucial to understanding why consumer education was born as an avatar of consumer information.

The journey through many faces of 'consumer imaginaries' starts with the figure of the 'weak consumer', an individual who is 'vulnerable, susceptible and in need of state protection from a malfunctioning marketplace and manipulative advertising'.[3]

---

[2] ibid 277.
[3] ibid 284.

The New Deal reformers depict the 'citizen consumer' who needs to have their rights secured in the face of unsafe products, unfair pricing and misleading advertising. This vision of consumers justifies a 'socially embedded managed capitalism and regulatory framework'; from vulnerable, however, the consumer becomes powerful, with a 'regulatory system protecting its needs and promoting its capacities'.[4] This conceptual approach of the consumer had a considerable influence on the European integration project in the early 1970s.[5] However, the figure of the weak consumer was subject to some criticism, mainly because it put too much emphasis on regulation and did not place enough on the fact that consumers were 'naturally sovereign in the marketplace'.[6] Unsurprisingly, further elaborations by scholars all tended to decrease the role of regulation and to promote the consumer as a key agent exercising free will on the market. From weak, the consumer became liberated, sovereign and marketised.

Born in Germany, the liberated consumer was a concept strongly supported by Ludwig Erhard, who served as Minister of Economics from 1949 to 1963. These consumers are persons exercising their free will in the market. They were presented as 'the symbol of democratic citizen responsible for rebuilding the German economy and society' and regarded as 'part of the theory of ordoliberalism: a strong state guaranteeing competition and the rule of law'.[7] Liberated by that context, they were therefore able to exercise free choice. Consumers were free to consume and perceived as those who would judge 'over good and evil in the economy, over the useful and the useless'.[8] Free choice in terms of consumption was held to be one of the 'inviolable freedoms of human beings' and hence described as the cornerstone of democracy. According to Erhard,[9] there was no democracy without freedom of consumer choice. Very interestingly, in Erhard's view, rather than being educated, consumers needed to be assisted by being extensively informed in order to make the right choices in the marketplace. The theory of the liberated consumer is said to have 'played a key role in the attempt to create, uphold, and reinforce a single European market space from the 1980s onwards, when the European Commission dispensed with its earlier social outlook in favour of a focus on markets, competition, efficiency, and consumer choice'.[10]

The sovereign consumer is the circumspect, responsible person who comes to a decision based on informed choices. As recounted by Niklas Olsen, this type of consumer was 'invented by Ludwig von Mises in the early twentieth century' and 'given

---

[4] ibid 285.

[5] J Davies, *The European Consumer Citizen in Law and Policy* (Palgrave Macmillan, 2011) 22–27.

[6] Olsen (n 1) 287.

[7] ibid 288. 'Ordoliberalism refers to an ideal economic system that would be more orderly than the laissez-faire economy advocated by classical liberals.' It is characterised by two distinctive features: 'a prominent and positive role for the state in upholding the liberal economic order and the importance of the 'social question' due to the need to embed economic activity in a sound society'. G Schnyder and M Siems, 'The Ordoliberal Variety of Neoliberalism' in S Konzelmann and M Fovargue-Davies (eds), *Banking Systems in the Crisis: The Faces of Liberal Capitalism* (Routledge, 2013) 251.

[8] L Erhard, 'Die Prinzipien der deutschen Wirtschaftspolitik (Auszüge aus einem vortrag vor der Deutsch-Belgish-Luxemburgischen Handelskammer am 31 Mai 1954 in Antwerpen)' (2005) 104 *Orienterierung zur Wirstchafts-und Gessellschaftspolitik* 13, 17.

[9] L Erhard, 'Zur Kritik an den neuen Ordnung (Rundfunksprache, 6 August 1948)' in L Erhard (ed), *Gedanken aus fünf Jahrzehnten. Reden und Schriften* (ECON Verlag, 1988) 133.

[10] Olsen (n 1) 290.

new features and energies in the 1970s American deregulation movement, founded by business groups, free-market think tanks and conservative politicians, who aimed to roll back the regulatory state'.[11] These consumers are rational and utility-maximising agents, and again are described as a 'key drivers of capitalism and of liberal democracy'.[12] Interestingly, this new vision of consumers, strongly supported and then popularised by scholars from the Chicago School of Economics, at the time appealed to left-wing intellectuals in North America and Europe. This is probably related to the fact that this vision emphasises the 'individual consumer's capacity for rationality and autonomy',[13] turning them into fully fledged individuals rather than weak individuals at the mercy of supposedly inefficient and repressive federal agencies or legislatures. Frank Trentmann supports the view that the internal market agenda of the Commission is partly based on the figure of the sovereign consumer. According to him, 'the consumer would be the locomotive; choice and competition the fuel. A new European citizen was born: the "market citizen".[14] In other words, 'choice would empower consumers'.[15] The concept of 'sovereign consumer' seduced the EU institutions, and principally the EU Commission, which, 'in constructing the internal market in the 1980s. The sovereign consumer is also a well-known figure in the case law of the Court of Justice of the EU (CJEU). As pointed out by Comparato, 'the sociological model of a rational and well-informed consumer was epitomised' in the *Gut Springenheide* case of the CJEU,[16] in which the Court decided that

> in order to determine whether a statement intended to promote sales ... is liable to mislead the purchaser ... the national court must take into account the presumed expectations which it evokes in an average consumer who is reasonably well-informed and reasonably observant and circumspect.[17]

A category derived from that of the sovereign consumer was further developed by other scholars from the Chicago School of Economics: the efficient consumer. This vision is deeply rooted in the belief of the scholars who conceptualised the figure of the sovereign consumer that efficiency is the key value of economic activity and that antitrust policies should be based on that assumption. Monopolies of larger corporations were therefore not to be treated as hindering the development of the market but rather as making it more efficient and subsequently more given to contributing to 'consumer welfare', the cornerstone of the newly developed theory. In Robert Bork's influential book, *The Antitrust Paradox*, consumers are conceived of as the people who should rule, 'with the sole purpose of creating efficiency, without regard to what others saw as basic economic, social, and political rights of individual consumers'.[18]

---

[11] ibid.

[12] ibid.

[13] ibid 294.

[14] F Trentmann, *How We Became a World of Consumers, from the Fifteenth Century to the Twenty-First* (Harper Collins, 2016) 559.

[15] ibid 559–60.

[16] Case C-84/44 *Gut Springenheide GmbH v Rudolf Tusky* ECLI:EU:C:1998:369.

[17] G Comparato, *The Financialisation of the Citizen: Social and Financial Inclusion through European Private Law* (Hart Publishing, 2020) 169.

[18] Olsen (n 1) 297.

The theory of the efficient consumer thus dissociated consumption and democracy, placing economic concerns above all. This dissociation of economics and democracy somehow challenges the foundations of the EU. Predictably, that approach had no real impact on the EU legal system. The theory of the efficient consumer probably pushes too much towards deregulation to match EU ideology. That said, it has been argued that this vision of market efficiency as a tool to promote consumer welfare could appeal to EU institutions, leading them to realign 'competition and consumer law with economic thinking on efficiency and welfare that informs American antitrust theory'.[19]

The marketised consumer is the last imaginary presented by Niklas Olsen. Another avatar of the consuming individual and a symbol of centre-left political forces in the 1990s, the concept emerged from an 'analysis that reframed the traditional understanding of the relation between the state, the individual, and the market in mainstream economics'[20] by elevating 'consumer sovereignty into the only norm according to which societal well-being can be measured',[21] reworking 'the ideal of traditional political democracy by interpreting it through market metaphors'[22] and questioning 'the role of the state as a collective decision-maker and social planner'.[23] The marketised consumer was instrumental in reforming the public sector. The concept derives from a theory developed by Anthony Downs to re-conceptualise democracy. According to Downs, the democratic political system would be improved if it were to become a marketplace dominated by individual interests. With the perception of the contemporary democratic system as an 'un-democratic enterprise run by a new ruling class, in the shape of public employees in control of the public sector, against the interest of the majority of the population',[24] an adjustment of the system based on the choice of the population – sovereign consumers – would allow them to subject 'the functions of the public sector to their demands',[25] turning 'the welfare state into a more efficient and democratic society'.[26] This theory, praised and implemented by centre-left governments in search of a 'third way' between laissez-faire capitalism and the faltering welfare state, led to privatisation and the marketisation of public administration. This trend is not by any means unknown in the EU context, as it is perfectly in line with, for example, the liberalisation of energy markets promoted and executed by the EU.

As different as they are, all the theories presented have a common trend: consumers – whatever the level of regulatory protection they are granted – are seen to play a key role in the marketplace and contribute to the development of the market as long as they act as informed consumers. Consumer information is therefore of the essence in any democratic liberal society.

---

[19] ibid 298.
[20] ibid 300.
[21] ibid.
[22] ibid.
[23] ibid.
[24] ibid.
[25] ibid.
[26] ibid 303.

Where there is no state but only a market, as was the case for the EEC and is probably still the case for the EU, the consumer is the new citizen. It is therefore not surprising that all consumer imaginaries are somehow related to how consumers have been politically instrumentalised by the EU. As a market in search of democratic and political legitimacy, the EEC and then the EU could not but allocate a pivotal role to consumers and rely on theories that reconciled consumption and democracy. If freedom of consumer choice stands at the heart of the concept of democracy, then the single market can be considered an expression of democracy. Informed consumers become the paradigm of EU citizens and consumer information the cornerstone of the EU democratic system. Asymmetrical information is also perceived as a factor of weakness. This appears very clearly in the case law of the Court. In many judgments, and more specifically those regarding interpretation of the Unfair Contract Terms Directive (UCTD),[27] the Court recalled that EU consumer legislation is based 'on the idea that the consumer is in a weak position vis-à-vis the seller or supplier, as regards both his bargaining power and his level of knowledge'.[28]

The action taken by the EEC and then the EU institutions to educate consumers perfectly reflect this ideological orientation. Education comes with, but after, information. However, before turning our attention to this sequence, one last thing should be said about the many consumer imaginaries that have been presented. Much criticism may be levelled against them. As the focus of this chapter is on consumer education, we will not address the controversies and debates around these conceptualisations of the consumer. Nevertheless, one of these criticisms needs to be contemplated: the absence of consideration of consumers' 'bounded rationality' in terms of their choices. In fact, it is now well known that 'when individuals make decisions, their rationality is limited by various deficiencies, including irrationality'.[29]

In order to exploit this trait of limited rationality, a new technique has emerged, that of nudging. Consumers can be subtly pushed towards and encouraged to change their behaviour against their own will.[30] To do so, be it for political or marketing purposes (sometimes for a combination of both), consumers' cognitive boundaries, biases or habits are used to serve a particular rationality. The boundaries between nudging and manipulation are tight, especially in an ever more digitalised world, where personal data allow for an in-depth knowledge of people's behaviour. Could the nudged – not to say manipulated – individual be the contemporary imaginary of the consumer? Such a pessimistic perspective renders the discussion about education of consumers even more topical and necessary, since EU consumers were born to be informed. The EU constitutional framework perfectly reflects that vision.

---

[27] Council Directive 93/13/EEC of 5 April 1993 on unfair terms in consumer contracts [1993] OJ L95/29.

[28] See, eg the *Oceano Grupo* case, the first judgment related to the active role of courts (ex officio power) in the field of unfair contract terms, Joined Cases C-240/98 to C-244/98 *Océano Grupo Editorial SA v Roció Murciano Quintero* (C-240/98) *and Salvat Editores SA v José M Sánchez Alcón Prades* (C-241/98), *José Luis Copano Badillo* (C-242/98), *Mohammed Berroane* (C-243/98) *and Emilio Viñas Feliú* (C-244/98) ECLI:EU:C:2000:346, [2000] ECR I-04941, para 25.

[29] Olsen (n 1) 300.

[30] On nudging, see K Yeung, 'Hypernudge': Big Data as a Mode of Regulation by Design' (2017) 20 *Information, Communication & Society* 118.

B. Consumer Education Policy in the EU: No Self-Standing Right to Education

Consumer education can certainly not be described as the dark side of consumer legislation in the EU. In the short history of the EU, consumer education featured among the basic rights proclaimed by the first action taken by the Union – at that time still the EEC – in the field of consumer policy: the Council Resolution of 14 April 1975 on a preliminary programme of the European Economic Community for a consumer protection and information policy.[31] Its content was heavily influenced by the special message addressed to the US Congress on 19 March 1962[32] by President John Fitzgerald Kennedy on protecting the consumer interest, in which he exposed four basic rights: the right to safety, the right to be informed, the right to choose and the right to be heard. However, consumer education seems to be a distinctive feature of the EEC policy. Even if no reference is made to that right in Kennedy's address, the preliminary programme mentions it as one of the five basic consumer rights it proclaims: the right to protection of health and safety; the right to protection of economic interests; the right of redress; the right to information and education; and the right to representation (the right to be heard). The preliminary programme has been depicted as the 'inauguration'[33] of a 'soft law' policy trend that gave rise to 'initiatives of significance in the gradual development of a political atmosphere conducive to recognition of the distinctive function that may be performed by consumer policy'.[34]

From the very beginning, it is worth observing that the right to education is not a self-standing right. Education comes along with information. Interestingly, the concept of education did not give rise to in-depth reflection at the EU level. The same could probably be said concerning information, but looking at the socio-political figure as it stands in the history of the EU, the objective of information is rather clearer. It is about having consumers make the right economic choice. Information therefore covers the elements that are necessary to compare offers on the market. Information is a mere factual concept, so as a consequence, providing information does not consist of a transfer of knowledge. This is reflected in EU legislation. The content of information to be delivered to consumers is about facts but not knowledge. The example of chapter II of the Consumer Rights Directive[35] is illustrative of that approach. This chapter comprises a single article (Article 5) regarding 'Information requirements for contracts other than

---

[31] Council Resolution of 14 April 1975 on a preliminary programme of the European Economic Community for a consumer protection and information policy [1975] OJ C92/01.

[32] See at jfklibrary.org/asset-viewer/archives/JFKWHA/1962/JFKWHA-080-003/JFKWHA-080-003 (accessed 26 December 2022).

[33] S Weatherill, *EU Consumer Law and Policy* (Edward Elgar Publishing, 2014) 6.

[34] ibid. The 1975 Resolution on a preliminary programme was followed in 1981 by the Council Resolution of 19 May 1981 on a second programme of the EEC for a consumer protection and information policy [1981] OJ C133/1, based on the same essential premises as those that underlie the first Resolution.

[35] Directive 2011/83/EU of the European Parliament and of the Council of 25 October 2011 on consumer rights [1981] OJ L304/64 ('Consumer Rights Directive').

distance or off-premises contracts'. These requirements are about 'the main character-istics of the goods or services'; 'the identity of the trader, such as his trading name, the geographical address at which he is established and his telephone number'; 'the total price of the goods or services inclusive of taxes, or where the nature of the goods or services is such that the price cannot reasonably be calculated in advance', and so on. The legislature takes the view that consumers should be informed. They should not have to look for these facts. It is much more difficult to understand the content that is to constitute education. Education notably aims to empower people by giving them the means to gain ability, skills and knowledge, and to hold critical views. Its objective is not limited to economic purposes. Looking at what was done by the European institu-tions in the field of consumer education, one cannot claim that those purposes were ignored. However, they were strongly limited by how consumers were instrumentalised to play a key role in establishing the internal and then the single market. Consumers were educated to drive the functioning of the single market, not to be able to challenge the central organising role of the market.

Remarkably, when these five rights were eventually given a constitutional mean-ing when being formally integrated into the EU treaties, the right to (consumer) education was at first forgotten. Article 129(a) of the Maastricht Treaty,[36] which marked a turning point in the development of EU consumer policy by including for the first time a separate title in an EU treaty for consumer protection, only referred to the right to information. Only with the Treaty of Amsterdam[37] did the right to (consumer) education come to constitutional life. The Amsterdam Treaty not only renumbered Article 129(a), allowing for intervention by the EU legisla-ture in the field of consumer protection not tied to the objective of developing the single market, it also amended its content. The right to education as a supplement to the right to information, as well as the right to representation (transformed into the right for consumers to organise themselves), was introduced into the Treaty (Article 153).[38] Article 169, as it stands in the consolidated version of the Treaty on the Functioning of the European Union[39] (TFEU), is, from that viewpoint, an identi-cal copy of Article 153. This elevation of rights to a 'constitutional' level reflects the considerable influence of the five consumer rights proclaimed in the Resolution on the preliminary programme.[40] However, not all the rights proclaimed had the same impact. Consumer education, which remains in the shadow of consumer informa-tion, was an exception because it was said to be considered 'to come too clearly into the realm of national competences on consumer protection policies'.[41] Furthermore,

---

[36] Treaty on European Union [1992] OJ C191/1.

[37] Treaty of Amsterdam amending the Treaty on European Union, the Treaties establishing the European Communities and certain related acts [1997] OJ C340/05.

[38] It is to be noted that the right of redress disappeared during the process of integration of consumer rights in the treaties due to the general scope of that right. It is not specific to consumers but rather appears as a general principle of EU law, today encapsulated in Art 47 of the Charter of Fundamental Rights of the European Union [2012] OJ C326/02.

[39] Treaty on the Functioning of the European Union of 13 December 2007 – consolidated version [2016] OJ C202/47.

[40] L Krämer, 'The origins of consumer law and policy at EU level' in Micklitz (ed) (n 1) 25.

[41] ibid.

education has always been a competence of the Member States. Sitting on the fence of a poorly legally based competence of the Community (even after the Maastricht Treaty, consumer protection remained a shared competence) and full competence of the Member States, that of education, the right to consumer education was from the very beginning not likely to have a bright future. Indeed, all rights received concrete application in EU legislation,[42] with the exception of consumer education. And when the European institutions dealt with consumer education, not much guidance was given by the EEC to the Member States on how to implement it. The preliminary programme of 1975[43] – which is the very first document referring to consumer education – broadly refers to 'the practical expression' that will be given to this right by the Community, which will pursue 'a comprehensive information policy based on surveys, comparative studies, publications, and conferences organised in close cooperation with Member States'.

Twinned with the right to information since its introduction into EU consumer policy, the right to education was never promoted as a self-standing right. On the contrary, the right to information entered the EU Treaty as such, before being re-complemented with the right to education after the redrafting of the Maastricht Treaty by the Treaty of Amsterdam.[44] This omission may only have been a procedural mistake. It probably reflects the 'political unconsciousness' of the EU. Looking at EU legislation, it is clear that, while information policy gave rise to intensive legislative production, consumer education policy was not a priority. This could of course be the consequence of the institutional domestic dimension of consumer education, since the competence of education remains with the Member States. But even in such a context, the European institutions could have done much more, involving higher education in the process and starting to re-think how education could be more prominent and less twinned with information.[45]

Unsurprisingly, the right to education gave rise to limited action from EU institutions, all starting at the end of the 1990s, mostly consisting in programmes and framework or follow-up of activities conducted at the domestic level through reports. The last report on such action was issued in 1989. It is predictably dedicated to action conducted at the national level that covers education in primary and secondary schools, which is reported without critical views on how it could be improved and coordinated at the European level.[46] Born ill-equipped as a 'complementary right', does the right to education have the capacity to transform consumer law and policy, or will it only lead to a dead end?

---

[42] Here are some examples of the concretisation of the other rights: Council Directive 85/374/EEC of 25 July 1985 on the approximation of the laws, regulations and administrative provisions of the Member States concerning liability for defective products [1985] OJ L210/29; UCTD (n 27); Directive (EU) 2020/1828 of the European Parliament and of the Council of 25 November 2020 on representative actions for the protection of the collective interests of consumers and repealing Directive 2009/22/EC [2020] OJ L409/1.

[43] Council Resolution (n 31).

[44] Treaty on European Union (n 36), Art 129(b), and Treaty of Amsterdam (n 36), Art 152.

[45] See the proposals for this 'infeducation' action in section V.B.

[46] European Commission, 'Report by the commission on consumer education in primary and secondary schools' COM (89) 17 final.

III. Consumer Education: A Dead-End Street?

A. The Search for a Definition of the Right to (Consumer) Education

The right to consumer education has not been formally defined since it is not a self-standing right and has always been treated as a right to be implemented by the Member States in the first place. It therefore follows that the few definitions given of this right put the emphasis on information. A rather illustrative way of how the European institutions conceive consumer education was expressed by the Commission in a 1992 Memo. In this document, the Commission states that the right to information and education of consumers means that they should be able to make an informed choice by

> being put in a position to assess the features and price of the goods and services offered to them in order to be able to make a rational choice of which to buy; properly informed about the most efficient and safe way to use products and services; aware of the procedures to follow to obtain redress

but that

> supplying information is [however] not sufficient: consumer policy must also try to ensure that consumers have the necessary skills to seek out, understand and integrate available information into their buying decisions in order to become discriminating consumers, capable of making an informed choice and conscious of their rights and responsibilities.[47]

Consumer education is not exactly a new topic. In 1941, in a monograph entitled *The Status and Future of Consumer Education*, two American scholars, De Brum and Harmon Wilson, observed that consumer education had been given attention since the 1930s. During this period consumers became increasingly conscious of problems facing them, and as a result many 'consumer organisations took an interest in consumer education.'[48] The authors also noted that it was natural that 'any general consciousness among individuals would cause some influence on education. Out of this natural situation has developed the movement of consumer education in the schools.'[49] But if the movement had developed, no clear meaning had emerged of what consumer education actually involved. At the time, 'there [were] probably as many different definitions of consumer education as there [were] people who [were] interested in this field.'[50] The two scholars did not give a precise definition of the topic but proposed objectives that they believed could be agreed on. These objectives were expressed in terms of 'development'. The first was 'development of general socio-economic understanding', as consumers need to be alert to the problems and needs of our economic society. The second was 'development of procedures and principles', meaning that consumers 'must

---

[47] European Commission, 'Consumer Policy in the European Community: An Overview' (1992) MEMO/92/68.
[48] J De Brum and W Harmon Wilson, *The Status and Future of Consumer Education* (Southwestern Publishing Co, 1941) 7.
[49] ibid 8.
[50] ibid.

know and understand the various ways and means of satisfying [their] needs and wants'. If they cannot be experts 'in selecting every particular item [they] should acquire some awareness of the problems and procedures involved'.[51] The third and last consisted of 'development of specific choice making', the problem of choice making involving:

> (a) making a decision as to the spending of money for one commodity or service rather than another, or (b) selecting a particular brand or source of goods and services after determining the particular commodity or service for which the money is to be spent.[52]

The situation has certainly evolved since the 1940s, as consumer education has become a global issue, even arousing the interest of the Organisation for Economic Cooperation and Development (OECD), which published a book on it.[53] Today, more sophisticated definitions of consumer education are available. According to a Report drawn up in 1986 regarding a draft resolution concerning consumer education in primary and secondary schools,[54]

> consumer education is about the development of critical awareness and knowledge needed for making wise and intelligent choices about the proper use of goods and services in both the private and public sectors in our society. It is essential to people of all ages, but it is particularly important for children and young persons.[55]

The Report recalls that, in a Council of Europe Working Party in 1971, the need for consumer education was expressed in the following terms:

> [W]hat we can and should do is to make sure that tomorrow's citizens are furnished with the basic details of knowledge and appreciation which will enable them to exercise their freedom of choice and their personal and collective responsibilities in the light of the different options and manifold problems which will face them as consumers not only in today's but also in tomorrow's society.[56]

In *Promoting Consumer Education*, the following definition of consumer education, reproducing that of Wells and Atherton, is proposed by the OECD, that is

> a process of gaining skills, knowledge and understanding needed by individuals in a consumer society such that they can make full use of consumer opportunities presented in today's complex marketplace.[57]

Knowing that much action on consumer education is inspired by or performed by the OECD, it can be assumed that this definition, combined with the one indirectly reported in the memo of 1992, fleshes out what consumer education is. To this author's knowledge, and since 1992, if many references have been made to the need for consumer

---

[51] ibid 10.
[52] ibid.
[53] OECD, *Promoting Consumer Education. Trends, Policies and Good Practices* (OECD, 2009).
[54] H McMahon (Rapporteur), 'Report drawn up on behalf of the Committee on Youth, Culture, Education, Information and Sport on the proposal from the Commission of the European Communities to the Council (Doc C2-91/85 – COM (85) 369 final) for a draft resolution concerning consumer education in primary and secondary schools' (Report No A2-232/85) at aei.pitt.edu/49169/1/A9078.pdf (accessed 26 December 2022).
[55] ibid 9.
[56] ibid.
[57] OECD (n 53) 9, quoting J Wells and M Atherton, 'Consumer Education: Learning for Life' (1998) 21 *Consumer* 15, 21.

education by the many European 'soft documents' dealing with this topic, no definition either of the concept of consumer education or of the right to education and information was formulated. Despite this, coming to the conclusion that consumer education is a dead-end street would not reflect reality, as concrete action taken in this field by EU institutions will show.

B. Concrete Action in the Field of Consumer Education

In 1977, a Report on a preliminary programme was published.[58] It referred to the establishment of 'a special service' – not named – enabling 'special attention to be given to consumer education' and mentioning 'visits paid to the Member States to get a first-hand view of what was being done in each of them' and collection of 'a great deal of material to provide an early assessment of the differing needs within the Community'.[59] This confirms that consumer education was left to the competence of the Member States, and consequently was mostly implemented at the national level. Most activities organised in the different Member States concerned school pupils[60] and sometimes young adults.[61] All activities reported also mostly consisted of educating consumers to make informed choices. The title of the education programme for school pupils in Germany, 'Keep your eyes open when buying shoes', was illustrative of this trend. Not only did it confirm that the ideology of liberated and sovereign consumers strongly impacted EU consumer policy, it also illustrated the meaning of 'consumer education' as perceived by the Member States. This approach was further reinforced by the second programme of the EEC for a consumer protection and information policy of 1981, establishing, as a priority measure in this area, the continuance of the wide-ranging exchange of views on national experience and joint considerations of the aims and methods of consumer education in schools. In the view of the EEC institutions, concrete action in the field of consumer education clearly must be performed at the level of school curricula (at both primary and secondary levels). The reason for this approach lies in the fact that 'consumer education [must] be performed during the period of compulsory education'.

As President Kennedy stated in his special message to Congress (see section II.B), 'all of us are consumers'. Having in mind that consumers are held to be key agents of EU 'market citizenship', the broader the target of people to be educated, the more efficient the EU will be as a capital market democracy.

That vision was explicitly stated in the Report drawn up in 1986 regarding a draft resolution concerning consumer education in primary and secondary schools,[62] which expressed the need to enable consumers to exercise their freedom of choice and emphasised the necessity to target more specifically children and young persons in that

[58] Commission of the European Communities, 'Consumer protection and information policy' (1977) Report No 1 at aei.pitt.edu/3101/1/3101.pdf (accessed 9 August 2022).
[59] ibid 18.
[60] ibid 38–45; eg, as in Denmark, France, Germany, Italy, Luxembourg and the Netherlands.
[61] ibid 42; this was the case in Ireland.
[62] McMahon (n 54).

regard. The Report also recalled that, in a Council of Europe Working Party in 1971, the need for consumer education was expressed in the following terms:

> Consumer education is part of a life-long process which is relevant so long as individuals are faced with choices of their own – like what to spend their money or their leisure on, which shops to buy from, what sort of transport to use and which educational courses to follow. As they become old enough to look after themselves young people will also need to know how to manage their money properly and reach important decisions on matters like where to live and what professional services they should use. They will need to learn to cope with various difficulties they might face as consumers, such as being unemployed, getting into debt or becoming homeless and to know what are the appropriate agencies and persons to turn to for help and advice.[63]

Beyond putting strong emphasis on information, this statement also perfectly illustrates how EU institutions build the concept of consumer education on the consumer imaginaries previously presented. The subsequently adopted Resolution of 1986 endorsed the notion that consumer education policy was to take the form of introducing consumer education 'into primary and secondary education in accordance with appropriate procedures'.[64] The text also emphasised that this curriculum would need to be reflected upon and established by the Member States in the first place because of the 'diversity of national and regional education systems in the Member States in regard to the curricula … as well as differences in economic, legal and social structures within the Community', otherwise 'it would be impossible to devise a detailed Community curriculum for consumer education'.[65] However, the Resolution offered some guidance as to what measures should be taken at Member-State level. The Council took the view that consumer education should not 'require treatment as a separate subject' in the curriculum: it had to be 'set in the context of teaching about those aspects of contemporary society which affect the rights and responsibilities of consumers', namely 'the operation of market forces', 'the role of consumers in the economy', 'an awareness of environmental questions', 'attitude to advertising', 'attitude to the mass media' and 'use of leisure time'.[66] It is worth stressing that this Resolution seems to be one of the first documents officially expressing the need to take environmental questions into account when educating consumers.

The Resolution also referred to measures to be taken at Community level. Facilitation of views on what had been achieved in terms of education at the national level, already mentioned in previous documents, was of course among them, as was organisation of the training of teachers in charge of educating consumer pupils. More interesting still, the Resolution envisaged, for the first time, 'the inclusion of consumer affairs in higher education'.[67] Beyond the traditional 'education of school pupils at national level to become informed consumers', the Resolution was a rather ambitious document, calling for information on their rights to be divulged and acknowledging that higher education could play a role in educating consumers. This materialised into several projects

---

[63] ibid 9.
[64] Resolution of the Council and the Ministers for Education, meeting within the Council, of 9 June 1986, on consumer education in primary and secondary schools [1986] OJ C184/21.
[65] ibid 22.
[66] ibid.
[67] ibid.

monitored and sometimes partially managed at the European level and for which the Commission invested over €30 million in a range of consumer schemes to develop consumer education.[68]

In December 2003, the Commission launched the DOLCETA ('Developing On-Line Consumer Education and Training for Adults'), subsequently known as the 'Consumer Education Online' project. This was a comprehensive, Europe-wide project aimed at educating consumers. For eight years, experts in the Member States gradually developed eight extensive modules covering areas such as consumer law, financial literacy, sustainable consumption and product safety. The aim of the project was to raise EU citizens' awareness of their consumer rights. The project not only targeted the general public, but it also provided information and materials for lecturers, teachers and non-profit organisations. The project was not adjudged sustainable, since its evaluation concluded that the resource established was 'outdated in its delivery mode, in a static, albeit online format, which also limited its accessibility to the target groups of vulnerable people'.[69] Therefore, although its content was considered 'useful and broadly relevant, it was recommended that the mode of delivery should be reconsidered'.[70] Its content was re-used for another example of consumer education action initiated at the EU level in 1995 but implemented at the domestic level: 'Europa Diary', a multilingual paper-based diary, targeted at students aged 15–18, with a focus on consumer affairs. As reported by Brennan et al, it was 'accompanied by structured teacher resources and lesson plans' and 'was distributed to over four million students in more than 27000 schools'.[71] The evaluation further concluded 'that both actions may duplicate national resources in some Member States, and that they are not responsive enough to policy developments in relation to the frequency of updating'.[72] The last edition of the Europa Diary is dated 2011–12. It has now been transformed into the 'consumer classroom', that is, a

> multilingual pan-European community website for teachers [bringing] together an extensive library on consumer education from across the EU and provides interactive and collaborative tools to help prepare and share lessons with students as well as with other teachers.[73]

Another project supported by the Commission was TRACE (Training for Consumer Empowerment), a scheme delivering focused training, advice and support to consumers on both national and cross-border consumer issues. Its goal was to have courses planned to build capacity within national consumer organisations and encourage

---

[68] As detailed in ICF GHK, *Empowered Consumers and Growth: Literature Review – Final Report* (May 2012) at assets.publishing.service.gov.uk/government/uploads/system/uploads/attachment_data/file/34743/12-977-empowered-consumers-and-growth-literature-review.pdf (accessed 24 August 2022).

[69] C Brennan et al, 'Consumer Education and Empowerment in Europe: Recent Developments in Policy and Practice' (2017) 4(2) *International Journal of Consumer Studies* 147, 153.

[70] ibid.

[71] ibid 148. The diaries are still available on the website of the Publications Office of the European Union at op.europa.eu/en/publication-detail/-/publication/441bb7af-bcfb-44e9-9d4c-01841614cc15 (accessed 27 December 2022).

[72] Commission staff working document, 'Accompanying the document report from the commission to the European Parliament and the Council on the evaluation of the Union's finances on the results achieved' SWD/2012/0383 final.

[73] In accordance with the definition of the programme on the webpage dedicated to it, at ec.europa.eu/chafea/consumers/information-education/consumer-classroom/index_en.htm (accessed 23 August 2022).

transfer of best practice between Member States, raising skills and capacity. The ultimate objective of the project was to better position national organisations to help cross-border consumers. The project was seen as relevant, although some weaknesses were pointed out, such as the time involved and the language barrier, as the course was taught only in English. A follow-up on that initiative seems to have been implemented through the Consumer PRO project, presented as 'a capacity-building project aimed at making consumer organisations and other actors in consumer policy better equipped to protect consumers in their respective countries'.[74] This was an initiative of the European Commission under the European Consumer Programme that started in July 2019 and implementation of which has been entrusted to BEUC, which acts as the umbrella group for national consumer groups. Another example of action taken was the establishment of a 'European Integrated Master Programme', launched in 2008 in 10 Member States, the objective of which was 'to develop research and teaching in consumer affairs in EU higher education institutions, creating consumer "professionals" who then move into the labour market and work in organisations that champion EU consumers'.[75] The programmes were multi-national and interdisciplinary. Funding ended in 2011, each course consortium being 'expected to sustain their programme with alternative options'.[76] The evaluation conducted on the 'European Integrated Master Programme' project highlighted 'a potential employment generation impact', but also suggested that 'at the European scale the overall impact for the European consumer marketplace is likely to be limited and localised'.[77] Of the 10 established programmes, only one was repeated after the end of the funding.[78] More interestingly, the financial sector received special attention in terms of consumer education.

C. The Right to 'Sector-Based Consumer Education': Financial Education

A turning point in consumer education was the Euro crisis and the role therein of over-indebted consumers, a crisis that threatened the stability of the Union and the Eurozone countries. 'Societal problems resulting from [such crisis were] brought before European courts which then had to engage in social engineering'.[79] Subsequently, EU institutions suddenly understood that over-indebtedness of consumers was a problem, especially since, according to the dominant ideology, consumers were the key agents of a European democratic liberal society. Private indebtedness is the promise of

---

[74] As described on the website of Bureau Européen de l'Union des Consommateurs (BEUC) at beuc.eu/consumer-pro-boosting-professionals-consumer-protection (accessed 24 August 2022).

[75] ICF GHK (n 68) 45.

[76] Brennan et al (n 69) 152.

[77] ibid.

[78] MSc in Consumer Science, offered by the School of Management of the Technical University of Munich. Interestingly, it seems that this programme does not currently offer classes on consumer law. See at mgt.tum.de/programs/master-in-consumer-science (accessed 24 of August 2022).

[79] H-W Micklitz, 'Unfair Contract Terms – Public Interest Litigation before European Courts Case C-415/11 Mohamed Aziz' in V Colaert and E Terryn (eds), *Landmark Cases of EU Consumer Law – in Honour of Jules Stuyck* (Intersentia, 2013) 639.

growth. Indebtedness allows for 'citizens to fully participate in society and fulfil their economic role as consumers, increasing the demand for products and services'.[80] When consumers cannot play the crucial role assigned to them, a 'dramatic and still ongoing institutional crisis' is the result.[81] In 2007, the Commission released a Communication on Financial Education[82] aimed at determining a strategy in that field. The context in which financial education gained momentum in the EU appears to be very similar to that of the harmonisation policy in the field of EU consumer law. Rather than having a general policy in the field, sector-based approaches would be privileged. In other words, a 'we will cross that bridge when we come to it' strategy. Special attention would be given to a specific field of consumer education whenever problems arose. In 2007, consumer education took the route of a sector-based policy. Unfortunately, it appears that the changes implemented mainly concern form and not substance. In its Communication, the Commission takes the view that financial education lies in the field of competence of the Member States as it relates to education. Action taken will therefore only 'support, supplement and monitor the policy pursued by the Member States in this field'.[83] This official confirmation that consumer education belongs within the competence of the Member States could be discussed.[84] However, at this stage of the chapter, it need only be stressed that even when particular attention is dedicated to consumer education for contextual reasons, the philosophy of the educational approach does not really differ from what had previously been promoted. Indeed, the Communication suggests that financial education be implemented in the school education curriculum and promoted at all stages of life on a continuous basis. The 11-page document details, for the first time, the vision of the Commission in the field of (sector-based) consumer education. It requires 'financial education programmes to be carefully targeted to meet the specific needs of citizens' and that 'financial education schemes should include general tools to raise awareness of the need to improve understanding of financial issues and risks'.[85] It also presents some new orientations as to what can be done in the field of consumer education, such as 'establishment of schemes including general tools to raise awareness of the need to improve understanding of financial issues and risks'.[86] The Communication insists on the necessity for arranging and delivering 'training of teachers'.[87] It should also be noted that the document acknowledges the complementary nature of education in quite a precise manner, by stating that 'financial education is a complement to measures aiming to ensure the appropriate provision of information, protection and advice to consumers'.[88]

---

[80] Comparato (n 17) 1.

[81] ibid.

[82] European Commission, 'Financial Education' COM (2007) 808 final 7 at eur-lex.europa.eu/LexUriServ/LexUriServ.do?uri=COM:2007:0808:FIN:EN:PDF (accessed 19 August 2022).

[83] ibid 2. Undoubtedly, the reference to supplementary action by the EU Commission can be perceived as a way to allow for more action from the EU Commission. But to supplement, you need to demonstrate that what was achieved at the national level was not sufficient. This would, however, require that coordination be put in place at the EU level and that the actions of Member States be regularly assessed by the EU.

[84] See section V of this chapter, 'The Call for Transformation'.

[85] European Commission (n 82) 8.

[86] ibid.

[87] ibid 9.

[88] ibid 2.

Unlike general consumer education, (consumer) financial education certainly became a priority of the EU institutions. This even led to the establishment of an expert group on financial education.[89] Beyond producing several reports on the topic, the group was also successful in convincing the European Commission to 'insert a declaration on the importance of financial education in the conclusions of the G20': 'this reference did indeed, eventually, appear in the G20 High Level Principles on Financial Consumer Protection 2011'.[90] The Principles acknowledge that 'financial consumer protection should be reinforced and integrated with other financial inclusion and financial education policies. This contributes to strengthening financial stability'.[91] Much action has been taken in that field, including at the European level.[92] The reason for this intense activity may also lie in the fact that financial education has, under the von der Leyen Presidency of the EU Commission, been entrusted to the Directorate General for Financial Stability, Financial Services and Capital Markets Union. Besides, the shadow of another sub-prime crisis was an excellent incentive to develop tools and programmes. It is also worth stressing that financial literacy was a problem tackled at a level broader than simply in Europe: the OECD was a key player in much of the action taken in this field.[93]

The last relevant document in the field of financial education is a joint document from the Commission and International Network on Financial Education of the OECD (INFE) on a Financial Competence Framework for Adults in the EU.[94] This framework is 'not intended as a curriculum, rather as a conceptual basis on which to build a variety of financial education policies and measures'.[95] It provides a set of outcome-based competences that can be used to 'support the development, implementation and update of national financial literacy strategies', 'support the design of financial education programmes and the development of financial education learning materials and tools' and 'facilitate the assessment of financial literacy levels and the evaluation of financial literacy initiatives'.[96] The document sets out the awareness, knowledge and understanding, skills and behaviour, confidence motivation and attitudes consumers should have for various topics (for example, money and currencies, mortgages). It only determines objectives; it is then for the intended users of the framework (policymakers and practitioners, according to its authors) to create 'their own policies and programmes', with the document recommending that it be used in that manner rather than as a curriculum and stressing that its content can 'easily be adapted to address the needs of specific life

---

[89] Commission Decision 2008/365/EC of 30 April 2008 setting up a group of experts on financial education [2008] OJ L125/36.

[90] Comparato (n 17) 173.

[91] G20 High Level Principles on Financial Consumer Protection (October 2011) 4 at oecd.org/daf/fin/financial-markets/48892010.pdf (accessed 21 August 2022).

[92] For an overview of these actions see finance.ec.europa.eu/consumer-finance-and-payments/financial-literacy_fr#about (accessed 21 August 2022).

[93] The OECD also published a handbook on financial literacy, OECD, *Improving Financial Literacy: Analysis of Issues and Policy* (OECD, 2005).

[94] European Union and OECD, 'Financial Competence Framework for Adults in the European Union' (2022) at oecd.org/daf/fin/financial-education/financial-competence-framework-for-adults-in-the-European-Union.pdf (accessed 21 August 2022).

[95] ibid 6.

[96] ibid.

situations or target groups'.[97] The document will probably offer appreciable support to the entities who will oversee financial education. But its weakness lies in the fact, clearly stated in the document, that its success

> will depend on the ability to build a common understanding and generate willingness from the Member States and stakeholders to use the framework in order to inform and contribute to financial literacy policies and initiatives.[98]

In his book *The Financialisation of the Citizen*, published in 2018, Comparato formulates criticisms specifically addressed to financial education. Not only do they still apply to the 'Financial Competence Framework for Adults in the European Union' but they can also be directed towards consumer education at a more general level. Indeed, like 'consumer education', 'financial education appears to be a quite general and vague label under which extremely different education strategies are conceived, so that describing a sole model of financial education is currently impossible'.[99] Since no European strategy exists 'in Europe, and even within the different regions of the same countries, a great variety of forms and schemes enabled at the various levels to promote financial literacy can be detected'.[100] This is also true for general consumer education, as appears from the reports of the EU Commission.[101] Similarly to what is done in financial education, programmes are provided by different entities – consumer organisations, public administration, research centres and even sometimes by the private sector[102] – with the risk, in the last specific case, of 'unfairness in business practices if the programmes are employed by the provider to promote its own services to a particularly vulnerable group of people'.[103] And because a strong emphasis is put on school education, which is today subject to budget cuts in many Member States in terms of public education, entrusting consumer education to schools may not prove to be as efficient as one might wish.

From a conceptual standpoint, it has also been observed that the continuous references in financial education

> to the need to teach the consumer about the financial products he or she will purchase and how to manage money, appear as the behaviourist re-edition of the trust in the information paradigm ... by the macro-economic concern of achieving financial stability, rather than the regulation of the products to be purchased by that consumer.[104]

In the end, although financial education certainly demonstrates that consumer education is a topic of interest for the EU institutions, rather than opening new horizons for consumer education, the Communication on financial education confirms the limits of consumer education at the EU level and, subsequently, its lack of capacity to transform consumer education and, in turn, consumer policy. It is now clear that action

[97] ibid.
[98] ibid 7.
[99] Comparato (n 17).
[100] ibid.
[101] See Commission of the European Communities (n 54); European Commission, 'Report by the commission on consumer education in primary and secondary schools' COM (89) 17 final.
[102] Commission of the European Communities (n 54); European Commission (n 101).
[103] Comparato (n 17) 176.
[104] ibid.

will be taken at the domestic level, since consumer education is presented as falling within the competence of the Member States in the field of education. No global action is therefore to be expected at the EU level. This is regrettable since, without any general coordination and general strategy defined at the EU level, that approach may be criticised. This lack of coordination at the EU level cannot guarantee that consumer education policy is pursued at all or promoted within the Union.

In 2018, the Commission issued its Communication on a 'New Deal for consumers',[105] a vast marketing communication plan on consumer protection, that unfortunately seems to confirm that attention given to consumer education as a general matter of policy was scarce. Only one paragraph of the 17-page document is dedicated to consumer education. It states, in very broad terms, that

> [t]he Commission has committed to continue its efforts in consumer education, as only knowledgeable consumers can use their rights effectively. The scope of current success- ful consumer education projects such as the Consumer Classroom could be widened by influencing the behaviour of other target groups, with a particular focus on vulnerable consumers ...[106]

thus confirming its lack of ambition in that field. Borrowing its title from the highly ambitious series of programmes, public work projects and regulations enacted by President Franklin Roosevelt, the New Deal for Consumers was promoted through a major communication plan. In the field of consumer education, it confirmed the Commission's lack of vision and its incapacity to understand that consumer education could have been a means to transform and improve consumer policy and law.

IV. The 'Non-Transformation' of Consumer Policy and Law Through Consumer Education

A. The Missed Opportunity for a General Policy on Consumer Education

Sector-based education is a useful approach, as it allows the specifics of the various sectors of consumption to be tackled and issues encountered by groups who require specific attention and special means of education (so-called vulnerable consumers) to be addressed, not to mention its capacity to deal with the different cultural backgrounds of European consumers. However, at the same time, sector-based education cannot exist without a solid general policy for consumer education, in much the same way as regulation for specific contracts can only be built upon general contract law.

General coordination at the level of the Directorate General in charge of consumer affairs is even more desirable, as the Commission is about to develop a sector-based approach to consumer education probably leading to the transferral of implementation

---

[105] European Commission, 'Communication from the Commission to the European Parliament, the Council and the European Economic and Social Committee: A New Deal for Consumers' COM (2018) 183 final.
[106] ibid 14.

of planned projects to Directorates General other than the one in charge of consumer affairs. This has already happened in the field of financial education. The New Consumer Agenda of 2020 is also illustrative of this new approach. While focus is put on digital education, since 'digital transformation requires consumers to have strong digital literacy and digital competences that should be promoted by education and training in a lifelong learning perspective as highlighted by the Digital Education Action Plan 2021–2027',[107] the Agenda tackles the issue of consumer education only in a very vague manner. 'Action 18' of the Agenda provides for development of 'a strategic approach to improving consumer awareness and education, addressing also the needs of different groups, on the basis inter alia of equality and non-discrimination approaches',[108] without providing any further detail.

The Consumer Agenda's absence of vision is highly regrettable given the current context of political and environmental instability. In an Opinion issued in 1996, the Economic and Social Committee had already expressed its concerns about the EU Commission's lack of ambition in the field of consumer education.[109] Recalling that 'consumer protection in an open, wide-reaching market like the single market increasingly depends on basic education',[110] the Committee noted that

> since the schools consumer training pilot project launched in Denmark in 1978 (referred to in the second Commission programme) and completed in 1984, there have been no further integrated Community-level school training projects, although the final project report recommended that serious thought be given to repeating similar programmes.[111]

The Committee also stressed that consumer education should 'accompany individuals throughout their school and university education',[112] echoing the Council Resolution of 1986 as to the involvement of higher education, a wish that has not as yet given rise to any reflection or proposal. The Opinion also refers to the 'specific consumer law programmes that should be tailored for legal practitioners (judges, lawyers, university professors) or representatives of consumer organisations, information centres, social centres, etc' and that should comprise 'on-going training courses, specific consumer law modules within university courses, specialist publications, data banks', considering that the Commission did not give 'sufficient prominence' to possible initiatives of this kind. [113]

Since then, several of these issues have been tackled, notably through concrete action undertaken by the EU Commission in the first decade of this century.[114] It would probably be an exaggeration to depict consumer education as a dead-end street; the real picture of what has been attempted in that field could only be presented after

---

[107] European Commission, 'Communication from the Commission to the European Parliament and the Council New Consumer Agenda: Strengthening consumer resilience for sustainable recovery' COM (2020) 696 final 19.

[108] ibid.

[109] Opinion on the 'Single market and consumer protection: opportunities and obstacles' (96/C 39/12) [1996] OJ C39/35 (accessed 27 December 2022).

[110] ibid para 4.4.1.

[111] ibid para 4.4.2.

[112] ibid para 4.4.3.

[113] ibid para 4.4.3.

[114] See below.

having studied all the action undertaken at the national level. Nevertheless, doubts can be expressed as to the efficacy of what has been done.[115] No general conclusions were drawn from the various educational activities at the domestic level and no European coordination was ever established regarding this topic. Not only did this approach not allow for a change in the policy related to consumer education, but it also seems that it did not lead to a rethink of the use of information in the field of consumer protection, despite the strong connection between the two rights. Information not only precedes education, it also took over education.

B. 'Information Takes it All (Education is Standing Small)'

While the development of consumer education was almost exclusively left to the Member States, the 'EU has been exceptionally active in the consumer protection field', since 'almost all the areas of consumer law (from advertising and marketing through contract and tort law rules to enforcement and redress) have been touched by EU law'.[116] These extremely productive interventions by the EU legislature have undoubtedly provided European consumers with strong protection of their rights. Consumer information has been assigned an extensive role in the legislative policy of the EU for several reasons. First, and as extensively developed in this chapter, because information is of the essence of all the imaginaries of consumer figures: an informed consumer will play their role as the market's key agent. Second, because

> information is an appealing strategy for the EU as it makes less formal demands on producers to change their basic product designs which may be based on national traditions and regulations. Instead, many consumer concerns can be addressed by providing information.[117]

Besides, while a legal policy based on information duties is extremely simple to implement – provided that an agreement has been reached at the level of the Council – establishing a consumer education policy involves a cost for the EU. Privileging an information-based policy rather than an education-based one is therefore rather tempting. All these reasons could explain why no real reflection was conducted on how in practice to connect the right to information with the right to education, even though these two rights are two sides of the same coin.

In the end, the EU produced more and more information-based legislation, while action taken at Member-State level was apparently focusing on informing consumers as to their rights or enabling them to make rational choices by comparing products and services rather than on educating them to process the information legally required to be disclosed to them. The absence of coordination of educational consumer programmes at the EU level did not allow re-connection of information and education. At some point, it was realised that 'consumers have limited ability to understand and process information' and that 'this is not just an issue for those with literacy, numeracy

---

[115] This project did not allow for an in-depth study of the efficacy of the performance of the programmes conducted in the different Member States but the topic would be worthy of a research project.

[116] G Howells, Ch Twigg-Flesner and Th Wilhelmsson, *Rethinking EU Consumer Law* (Routledge, 2018) 1.

[117] ibid 33.

or financial skills deficits'.[118] Indeed, all consumers have limited ability to handle and process information, not to mention that – assuming they can handle and process the information – the process may not lead them to make a rational choice because of their 'bounded rationality'. The EU has been said to have engaged 'at a theoretical level with behavioural economics',[119] with relative success in tackling the issue of processing information because putting behavioural economics into practice is not easy. To this author's knowledge, there is, in contrast, no evidence of any theoretical reflection on how to combine consumer information with consumer education having been engaged with at the EU level. Yet education is certainly a way to facilitate the processing of information.

The financial field, which was of special interest for educational matters, could have given the opportunity to the EU institutions to reflect on the effectiveness of consumer information policies. The issue of 'financial literacy' was critically analysed by the academic community. It was wisely pointed out by some scholars that 'the movement known under the slogan financial literacy [that] tries to implement financial education in school curricula, offer Internet resources, leaflets and permanent education in which private households can learn how their financial needs and income can match the requirements of financial services' was not an encouraging experience.[120] It is well known that 'people want only advice without education' and advice is difficult to target directly towards people 'at a time that would still be helpful'.[121] Reifner and Herwig therefore propose a 'focus more generally on all forms of information that reach the consumer before financial services are contracted'.[122] The decisions of the CJEU in the field of unfair terms in consumer mortgage credit contracts confirms this need. The Luxembourg Court imposed 'substantive transparency' as to complex contractual terms.[123] The context of unfair terms in such contracts presents the specific interest of combining a general consumer law issue (that of unfair terms in consumer contracts) with a problem related to the specific regulation of mortgage credits. In this situation, the heavy load of information to be disclosed to consumers is already provided for by the law.[124] In that context, it can hardly be considered that consumers are not informed. But mortgage credits require more than information because of their complexity. Examples of that complexity are loans denominated in foreign currency or loans with 'floor clauses' limiting the variation of interest rates. To give an example, in *Andriciuc v Banca Românească SA*,[125] the Court held:

> [A] term under which the loan must be repaid in the same foreign currency as that in which it was contracted must be understood by the consumer both at the formal and grammatical

---

[118] ibid.

[119] ibid.

[120] U Reifner and I Herwig, 'Consumer Education and Information Rights in Financial Services' (2003) 12 *Information and Communication Technology Law* 125, 126.

[121] ibid.

[122] ibid.

[123] Case C-26/13 *Árpád Kásler and Hajnalka Káslerné Rábai v OTP Jelzálogbank Zrt* ECLI:EU:C:2014:282, para 75; Case C-96/14 *Jean-Claude Van Hove v CNP Assurances SA* ECLI:EU:C:2015:262, para 50.

[124] See Directive 2014/17/EU of the European Parliament and of the Council of 4 February 2014 on credit agreements for consumers relating to residential immovable property and amending Directives 2008/48/EC and 2013/36/EU and Regulation (EU) No 1093/2010 [2014] OJ L60/34, Art 11.

[125] Case C-186/16 *Ruxandra Paula Andriciuc and others v Banca Românească SA* ECLI:EU:C:2017:703, para 51.

level, and also in terms of its actual effects, so that the average consumer, who is reasonably well informed and reasonably observant and circumspect, would be aware both of the possibility of a rise or fall in the value of the foreign currency in which the loan was taken out, and would also be able to assess the potentially significant economic consequences of such a term with regard to his financial obligations.

In other words, the fact that you were provided with information on the basis of a legal requirement does not mean that you are sufficiently informed to make a well-informed choice. In *Francisco Gutiérrez Naranjo v Cajasur Banco SAU*,[126] where the CJEU had to deal with the consequences of a temporal limitation on the effects of the invalidity of 'floor clauses' included in mortgage loan contracts, the Court insisted on the need for adequacy of the information supplied to the consumer concerning the extent, both legal and economic, of the consumer's contractual commitment. This is what substantive transparency is about, and it requires much more than mere information from the trader. The number of cases referred to the Luxembourg Court regarding unfair terms in mortgage loans demonstrates that this is a systemic problem that should be addressed at the legislative level for the sake of consumer interests and legal certainty. The most efficient approach would be to prohibit complex loans of these types. This would probably be too drastic and not politically feasible. Besides, the financial creativity of credit institutions should not be underestimated: other complex mortgage loans would flourish. This is where information and education should be combined. The requirement laid down by the CJEU goes beyond information. Traders are required to explain complex loan mechanisms. This is an educational exercise that takes time and requires pedagogical competences. Assuming this could be done in written form, there will always be doubt as to whether consumers really become aware of the information disclosed, raising probatory issues for traders, as it is well established case law that the burden of proof would be on them.[127] Yet, as we shall see, techniques are available that combine informative and educational goals that could resolve these issues, as well as the issue of consumers' full awareness of their commitments.

Efforts were made at the EU level to improve the form and content of information. The requirement of substantive information, put forward by the CJEU in its case law, was already under discussion within the EU Commission. As previously noted (see section III.A), a Memo dating from 1992 clearly stated that

> supplying information is not sufficient: consumer policy must also try to ensure that consumers have the necessary skills to seek out, understand and integrate available information into their buying decisions in order to become discriminating consumers, capable of making an informed choice and conscious of their rights and responsibilities.[128]

In other words, educating consumers means providing them with the tools to process and interpret the information they are given, so that they are able to form their own

---

[126] Joined Cases C-154/15 and C-307/15 *Francisco Gutiérrez Naranjo v Cajasur Banco SAU, Ana María Palacios Martínez v Banco Bilbao Vizcaya Argentaria SA (BBVA), Banco Popular Español SA v Emilio Irles López and Teresa Torres Andreu* ECLI:EU:C:2016:980; Case C-308/15 *Banco Popular Español SA v Emilio Irles López and Teresa Torres Andreu* ECLI:EU:C:2016:980.

[127] Case C-449/13 *CA Consumer Finance SA v Ingrid Bakkaus and others* ECLI:EU:C:2014:2464.

[128] European Commission (n 47).

opinions upon which they will base their transactional decisions. The statement even goes one step beyond by considering that an informed decision should also be a responsible decision, bringing into the frame of action considered the issue of responsible consumer citizens. However, in the same Memo the action considered by the EU Commission as likely to develop consumer information and education mostly consisted of supporting comparative studies on prices and product tests, in rendering information more readable by using labelling, in 'establishing centres in trans-frontier regions … with the aim of providing specialist information and advice to consumers undertaking cross-frontier transactions'.[129] No real transformation of the duty to inform was proposed, though.

Looking back at what has already been done, 'delegating' education to Member States while focusing on information duties at the EU level appears to have been a failure. Yet the new challenges faced by consumers require a new approach to the rights to information and to education. With the digital era, new risks have emerged: cross-border purchases are increasing, with the risk of facing even more difficult enforcement of consumer rights. While the digital risk of misuse of personal data has been partially addressed by the General Data Protection Regulation,[130] nevertheless consumer law also has a part to play in this field.[131] Information and education should have in important role in addressing these new challenges. But the capacity to address them in an effective manner will depend on the ability of policymakers to rethink their role in the EU context. In other words, an unfulfilled need for transformation still exists.

V. The Call for Transformation

Looking at how European consumer education has evolved since it was proclaimed a right – first by Council Resolution of 14 April 1975 as a preliminary programme of the European Economic Community for consumer protection and information policy and then by the Treaty of Amsterdam – it can be seen that, while some progress has been made and some lessons have been learned, the room for improvement is vast and some lessons remain unlearned. In this section some suggestions will be made on how to improve what has already been achieved and how to give a new impetus to consumer education.

A. Lessons Learned

Among the lessons learned from the development of consumer education in the EU is the need for a change in the narrative of consumer education.

---

[129] ibid.

[130] Regulation (EU) 2016/679 of the European Parliament and of the Council of 27 April 2016 on the protection of natural persons with regard to the processing of personal data and on the free movement of such data, and repealing Directive 95/46/EC [2016] OJ L119/1.

[131] See E Poillot, 'La protection des données personnelles par le droit européen de la consommation' in M Combet (ed), *Le droit de la consommation au XXIe siècle. Etat des lieux et perspectives* (Larcier, 2022) 301.

i. Changing the Narrative of Consumer Education

From 1975 until now, developments of consumer education as they appear with regard to the ample literature on the topic, whether it be of 'soft law' or of an academic nature, clearly reveal that a new 'consumer imaginary' has emerged: that of the 'new citizen consumer'. European education, following a global trend,[132]

> has moved conceptually from strictly focusing on consumers in the household and in the marketplace to issues involving consumer usage of the global natural resources, citizenship and leadership, solidarity and sustainability, and a more global view of consumption and its impact from micro-environments to macro-environments.[133]

The 'new citizen consumer' shares some features with the 'citizen consumer' imaginary promoted by the New Deal reformers, as they represent a 'socially embedded managed capitalism and regulatory framework'[134] and add a new dimension to the concept: that of sustainability. The new citizen consumer is the symbol of environmental concerns, and this new imaginary should be the driver not only for consumer education but also for policymaking and legislative action. Having this concept at the heart of EU consumer policy would allow us to answer the question with which we started this chapter: For what purpose should consumers be educated? They should be educated to become 'new citizen consumers'. They should be educated to be critical as regards the choices they are making when they consume. This is a sine qua non for a change in how economic growth and political democracy are conceived.

Let us be absolutely clear. It will take time for such a change of narrative, one that requires a radical change of approach to consumption to materialise at the political level. And it does not come without risks, either. We may not like the outcome if people do not think as we, academics, believe they should think. However, the environment has now become a critical issue to address. Environmental concerns are already embedded in EU policies and are slowly infusing consumer legislation. A political reorientation is under way and consumer education will contribute to it. The goal to be achieved is to have consumers resisting mass consumption. In *Consumed*, Barber observes that 'if those who are consumed are to be instrumental in resisting consumption, however, they will in the long term still require large scale social reinforcement to succeed'.[135] As populism is becoming one of the driving political ideologies in Europe, any attempt to change the narrative of people who have been educated to be mass consumers to promote economic growth and contribute to the smooth functioning of the market will not succeed if merely a soft transition from mass consumption to a more environmentally friendly way of living is attempted. To quote Barber again,

> changes will come from the inside out but also from the outside in, much as successful therapy does. It will require action by reengaged citizens as well as by resisting consumers. The restoration of a health pluralism in which human values are multiple and material consumption

---

[132] See OECD (n 53).
[133] EB Goldsmith and S Piscopo, 'Advances in Consumer Education: European initiatives' (2014) 38(1) *International Journal of Consumer Studies* 52, 52.
[134] Olsen (n 1) 285.
[135] BR Barber, *Consumed: How Markets Corrupt Children, Infantilize Adults, and Swallow Citizens Whole* (WW Norton & Company, 2007) 260.

but one in a cornucopia of human behaviors will in fact quite precisely require a social therapy that treats our defining civic schizophrenia – a civic therapy that restores the balance between private and public, giving our public civic selves renewed sovereignty over our private consumer selves and putting the fates of citizens ahead of the fate of the markets.[136]

The challenge for the EU, born as a market and built upon the development of that market, will be critical, as

this involves both a restoration of capitalism to its primary role as an efficient and productive way of meeting real economic needs, from supply (or push) back to demand (or pull), and a restoration of the democratic public as sovereign regulator of our plural life worlds – of which the market place is just one among equals.[137]

Establishing a general policy in the field of consumer education would permit reconsideration of the conceptual elements of consumer education. It would be an opportunity to proclaim a change of paradigm as to the figure of the consumer and to clearly state that the European vision of consumption is to promote responsible living through better life choices. It would subsequently allow for substitution of the figure of the informed consumer who efficiently contributes to the smooth functioning of the market and economic growth with that of the consumer citizen who 'makes selective and reflected lifestyle choices and is capable of challenging traditional ways of viewing and managing social and economic relationships'.[138] This would also permit the explicit acknowledgement, as already wished by some legal scholars, that EU consumer law 'has a social welfare function'.[139] This may of course not be politically appealing, as it calls for a reorientation of the single market policy. On the other hand, the 'consumer citizen responsible for their choices' is a figure already mentioned in the EU's vast 'non normative production' (for example, reports, communications) in the field of consumer education. Many of these documents express the wish to build on a series of core values promoting responsible living through better life choices.

Promoting a vision of consumer education as a way to achieve responsible living – through applying various skills so that a reorganisation of present priorities takes place in tandem with a redefining of human relationships, as well as an improvement in the interaction between scientific knowledge and societal well-being and in how societies manage economic, social and ecological challenges – requires vocal proclamation. This will not happen without a clear statement from the EU institutions that this is an overarching goal for consumer education in the twenty-first century that applies to any consumption sector. The principles of such a policy should be defined at the level of the Directorate General in charge of consumer affairs. Even though consumer protection is a matter that, as provided by Article 12 TFEU, 'shall be taken into account in defining and implementing other Union policies and activities', the impulse for its implementation must be given by this Directorate.

---

[136] ibid 261.
[137] ibid.
[138] WV Thoresen, 'Consumer Citizenship Education – Guidelines' (2005) 1 *Higher Education: The Consumer Citizenship Network* (including translated versions in other languages) 12 at tuningacademy.org/wp-content/uploads/2014/02/CCN-Learning-Teaching-Guidelines-vol-1final-21-09-05-_2_.pdf (accessed 23 August 2022).
[139] Howells, Twigg-Flesner and Wilhelmsson (n 116) 3.

Consumer education is an important issue that has been insufficiently dealt with by the European institutions. This does not mean that national approaches should be abandoned. On the contrary, they should probably be reinforced given the variable geometry of the EU consumer landscape and the necessity to consider cultural diversity. But domestic action requires more coordination, since 'it was recognised that consumer education practices and policies in Europe suffered from fragmentation'.[140] Acknowledging the need for a change of narrative is not sufficient. The vision and the implementation of consumer education also need to be revised.

ii. Rethinking Consumer Education

In its 2009 report, *Promoting Consumer Education. Trends, Policies and Good Practices*, the OECD identified and pointed out the key issues and the challenges of consumer education. Unsurprisingly, a 'lack of overall strategies' is the report's first concern.[141] The report – which considered national experiences in the field of consumer education – notes that 'most countries do not have an overall consumer education strategy'. The same observation holds for the EU, and there is a clear need to define one. That is not for this contribution to do. However, based on the analysis conducted in the previous sections and those presented in the OECD report, some suggestions may be made.

I suggest that this strategy should be built on a common approach to consumer education at the EU level. The 'vague label' – to recall the words of Comparato[142] – needs to be given content. Since 2009, as we have seen in this chapter, the situation has not really changed. The first action to be taken would therefore be to address the lack of coherence in consumer education initiatives. Due to the legal framework, the competence of Member States in this field and the absence of a general policy in consumer education, the European picture looks more like a cubist work – analysed, broken up and reassembled in abstract form instead of being depicted from a single viewpoint – than an impressionist one, as is often the case in the field of EU consumer law and policy.

One possible way forward for an overall EU consumer strategy would be to draft guidelines establishing the goals and structure of the strategy as well as its targets. An in-depth analysis of initiatives conducted at the Member-State level in the preceding five years would be a first step. It would permit those concerned to determine what the common features of these initiatives are and what could constitute a common ground for an EU strategy, which should of course be built upon the concept of the citizen consumer.

Guidelines reflecting the philosophy of the EU consumer education strategy should also be developed. These should address the objectives, the structure and the targets of consumer education. Among the objectives of a common strategy for education must be the development of critical thinking towards consumption choices and lifestyles. Consumer education should no longer be about consumers as key agents of the functioning of the market but about enabling them to become the key players, driving a turn

---

[140] Goldsmith and Piscopo (n 133) 52.
[141] OECD (n 53) 39.
[142] Comparato (n 17) 175.

toward sustainability based upon a widespread understanding of the risks of hyper-consumerism. Building on, *mutatis mutandis*, the theory of submissive consumers developed by Schelsky, Geblen and Freyer, and exposed by Olsen in his paper[143] – who argued that mass consumption involved degradation of culture and loss of political freedom, and that the freedom of choice offered by modern consumerism 'drained individuals of their personality, destroyed their social relations, and alienated them from authentic modes of existence'[144] – it becomes urgent to equip students and citizens with critical thinking as to what being a consumer is. This is not only a task for consumer lawyers and consumer policymakers; it is a political choice that should be embraced by all EU institutions, which would in turn be able to promote this vision on a global level. Consumer education should contribute to establishing 'new forms of global civic governance'.[145]

The guidelines on consumer education should also be of help in structuring consumer education as it 'takes many forms and takes place in many different settings, from formal courses in schools or universities to informal experience in families, communities and workplaces'.[146] Structuring consumer education will again be about analysing what has already been done, relying on what is already proposed at the EU level. It is about structuring the national *acquis* in the field, defining what the roles of the different institutions or entities involved can be and building upon what has already been successfully realised at the EU level. In this regard, the work achieved by the Citizen Consumer Network and more specifically their Citizen Consumer Education Guidelines are still relatively unknown, at least to law lecturers and legal scholars.[147] Bringing academia and legal scholars into the game is an absolute necessity, especially because GAFAM (namely, Google, Apple, Facebook, Amazon and Microsoft) are ready to invest in education (and already have).[148] Yet academia and legal scholars have been mostly absent, with some exceptions such as the 'Clinicity' project conducted by the University of Luxembourg, where masters students informed high-school students about their rights and the risks of concluding contracts online. This project adopted a train-the-trainer technique, also known as 'cascade training', and was not only about informing young people as to their rights but also about developing the critical skills of masters students[149] towards consumer law and consumer policies. Developed in the frame of a consumer legal clinic, it demonstrates the potential of such programmes for educating consumers. Clinics bring together practitioners, lecturers, researchers and students, as do Consumer Law Chairs.[150] They are a formidable tool to promote a

---

[143] Olsen (n 1) 286.

[144] ibid.

[145] Barber (n 135) 339.

[146] OECD (n 53) 11.

[147] Thoresen (n 138).

[148] See Meta Diversity, a training programme by Facebook at diversity.fb.com/initiative/facebook-university/ (accessed 27 December 2022). TikTok is also investing in the educational field – see seller-sg.tiktok.com/university/home?tab=policy_center#:~:text=TikTok%20Shop%20Seller%20University%20is,Policy%20Center (accessed 27 December 2022).

[149] See the video on the project at youtube.com/watch?v=P71uUaUm2Ko (accessed 1 September 2022).

[150] The Chaire en droit de la consommation of Paris Cergy University is a good example of a chair sponsored by different types of stakeholders, all having diverging interests in the field of consumer law: see at chairedroit-delaconsommation.cyu.fr/ (accessed 1 September 2022).

new vision of consumer law and policy. They allow for cooperative schemes – praised by the OECD report – to be put in place. For example, the Luxembourg law clinic brings together the Luxembourg consumer organisation (Union Luxembourgeoise des Consommateurs), the Luxembourg Bar Association and the University of Luxembourg. A psychologist and a judge are also involved in the programme.[151] Beyond the cooperation established, the clinic educates everyone involved in the programme, as it is also a forum for discussion on consumer law. It further develops the concept of training professionals in the field of consumer law already implemented by the BEUC,[152] as well as that of the training of trainers. The Luxembourg Clinic is a member of the European Network for Clinical Legal Education. Its staff participate in train-the-trainer sessions organised by this network.[153]

A targeted approach to consumer education has already materialised. This needs to be developed further. A sector-based strategy for consumer education has emerged and seems to be the way forward. As revealed by this analysis, consumer financial literacy has been considered a priority. Digital literacy should also be taken seriously. Remarkably, the 'Digital Education Action Plan', which has been adopted in view of 'resetting education and training for the digital age', contains no reference to consumer education. The topic is indirectly tackled since the Commission acknowledges the necessity to educate people in order to provide them with 'basic digital skills' that 'should become part of the core transferable skills that everyone should have to be able to develop personally; engage in society as an active citizen; use public services; and exercise basic rights' and stresses that a 'sound understanding of the digital world should be part of the formal and non-formal education provided in every education and training institution. Essential public services are increasingly delivered through e-government, making basic digital skills indispensable for everyday life'.[154] E-commerce also forms part of consumers' daily life. Special emphasis should therefore be placed on digital education for consumers. Lack of digital skills can lead consumers to enter into contractual relationships without being aware of it or through being manipulated. Paraphrasing what Tocqueville said about the impact that the power of public opinion could have on democracy, one could say that the use of data by traders in the context of electronic commerce leads to a situation where 'the body is left free but the mind is enslaved'.[155] Consumers are at risk of losing their freedom of consent. Informed consumers will make no free choices. They will be taken where they are required to go, whether through truly invasive techniques of manipulation, sludge practices or nudging. Sludge practices render a process more difficult than it should be in order to arrive at an outcome that is not in the best interests of the consumer.[156] The practice of nudging, as explained by a website presenting different methods of nudging to businesses, allows a seller or service provider 'to

---

[151] For more on the Consumer Law Clinic, see at wwwen.uni.lu/studies/fdef/master_in_european_business_law_ll_m/clinique_du_droit (accessed 1 September 2022).
[152] See section III.B.
[153] See at encle.org/ (accessed 1 September 2022).
[154] European Commission, 'Communication from the Commission to the European Parliament, the Council and the European Economic and Social Committee, Digital Education Action Plan. Resetting education and training for the digital age' COM (2020) 624 final 9.
[155] A de Tocqueville, *Democracy in America* (Vintage Books, 1990) 264.
[156] See at behavioraleconomics.com/resources/mini-encyclopedia-of-be/sludge/ (accessed 22 October 2022).

gently push your customers towards the action you want using subtle cues' instead of hitting them 'over the head with your call to action'.[157] What can be done by marketing techniques can be undone by education, when education equips people with critical thinking and a basic knowledge of marketing techniques. Digital education of consumers was rapidly evoked by the new Consumer Agenda of 2020, where it is observed that 'children and minors are particularly exposed to misleading or aggressive commercial practices online' and that 'it is important to invest more in lifelong consumer education and awareness raising, for people at all stages of life from school onwards'.[158] In this document, the EU Commission also indicates a plan 'to develop a strategic approach to improving consumer awareness and education, addressing also the needs of different groups, on the basis inter alia of equality and non-discrimination approaches'.[159] It cannot be disputed that certain categories of consumers are more vulnerable than others; however, in digital markets, 'consumer vulnerability is not simply a vantage point from which to assess some consumers' lack of ability to activate their awareness of persuasion'; on the contrary, 'in digital marketplaces, most if not all consumers are potentially vulnerable'. Consequently,

> instead of singling out certain groups of consumers, digital vulnerability describes a universal state of defencelessness and susceptibility to (the exploitation of) power imbalances that are the result of increasing automation of commerce, data-based consumer-seller relations and the very architecture of digital marketplaces.[160]

In short, a strong need exists for sector-based education in the digital field. We can only hope that as much effort will be put into this sector as has been the case in the financial one.

B. Lessons Still to be Learned: Rethinking Consumer Information Through 'Infeducation'

Under the EU legal framework, education comes with information. As revealed in this analysis, the twinning of the two rights has had a string of impacts on the right to education, but no real reflection was given to how to connect the right to information with the right to education in practice. While information can be educational, the difference between information and education is the level of engagement. An example showcasing this difference of level is that of mortgage loans. A requirement for substantive transparency has emerged out of the consolidated case law of the CJEU. In the notice providing guidance on interpreting and applying Directive 93/13 on unfair contract terms, the EU Commission observes that sellers or suppliers are now required by the CJEU 'to provide certain information or explanations prior to the conclusion of the contract'.[161]

---

[157] See at enginess.io/insights/nudge-digital-marketing (accessed 1 September 2022).
[158] European Commission (n 107) 17.
[159] ibid 19.
[160] N Helberger et al, *EU Consumer Protection 2.0.* (BEUC, 2021) 5.
[161] Commission notice – Guidance on the interpretation and application of Council Directive 93/13/EEC on unfair terms in consumer contracts [2019] OJ C323/4, 27.

By imposing this burden on traders, the Court indirectly acknowledges the failure of the system based on the assumption that a well-informed consumer will make the best commercial transaction. Information duties being the cornerstone of consumer protection under EU law, this failure hinders efficient protection of those who can probably be depicted as the best protected consumers in the world.

Many authors have addressed the issue of the failure of mere information. Many of these advocate for reviewing the system through a multidisciplinary lens.[162] I would like to propose here a new approach, namely that of 'infeducation'. This approach aims to deliver content to consumers based on a message that informs and educates them at the same time, as I believe raw information is of no use to consumers. 'Infeducation' takes the form of audio and verbal communication (such as videos, podcasts). Complex information would be delivered by video, where the consumer would be put 'in a position to evaluate, on the basis of clear, intelligible criteria, the economic consequences for him' that derive from the transaction, as required by the case law of the Luxembourg Court.[163] Such a system would help alleviate the burden now put on traders in complex contracts and more specifically in the field of consumer credit (mortgage loans, loans in foreign currency). The influence of alternative sources and content of information has long been recognised as impacting perceptions and behaviour.[164] Yet they seem to have been used only as marketing techniques to influence consumers. It is therefore suggested that they be used as vehicles for consumer information and education. Videos, for instance, allow complex messages to be conveyed in a clear and comprehensible manner and are accessible to audiences of most kinds, while reading and processing written information can reduce the impact of the message conveyed, some groups of consumers experiencing difficulty in reading and processing certain information.

Taking the example of foreign currency loans: these became a major problem in the EU, leading national judges to refer numerous preliminary requests to the CJEU, which now requires traders to employ a pedagogical approach to the information duties imposed on them. A video, approved at the EU level, explaining the complexity of the percentage rate mechanism could lead to a less problematic situation for consumers and to the bringing of fewer actions before the courts. It would also guarantee equal treatment of consumers, since they would be informed through a unique channel by a video that would have been made by professionals from different fields (such as lawyers, pedagogues, economists, psychologists, market researchers). The video would not only inform people but also educate them, since its objective, beyond that of disclosing the required information, would be to explain the consequences of the commercial agreement and to warn the consumer against irrational choices. The video – which consumers would be required to watch, with the possibility to do so on different types of devices[165] – should of course be complemented by an analysis of the financial situation of the consumers concerned.

---

[162] See, inter alia, Pichonnaz in ch 5 of this volume.

[163] *Kásler and Rábai* (n 123) para 75; *Van Hove* (n 123) para 50.

[164] GT Tonsor and Ch A Wolf, 'Effect of Video Information on Consumers: Milk Production Attributes' (2012) 94 *American Journal of Agricultural Economics* 503, 503–08.

[165] Computers at home, smartphones and of course devices made available by traders on their premises. For distance watching, technology would allow verification that the 'infeducation' system has been used by consumers. Electronic signatures could also be requested for in-premises attendance.

Many benefits attach to adopting a similar system:

- It guarantees clear and transparent information of consumers, as its content would be previously approved by a public entity.
- It overcomes the barrier that written information can present to certain groups of consumers by helping them to better understand and process information.
- It allows them to take a critical approach to what they are about to commit to by also warning them orally as to the consequences of a pending commercial transaction.

Consumers always cross bridges when they come to them. This kind of approach to education also allows for tackling the problem of people not willing or not having the time to be educated. This is where information and education should be combined. Finally, I believe that imposing this system on traders may also benefit them. They are now required to explain complex contracts and legal technicalities. This is not an easy task, and it takes time and requires pedagogical competences. It also means that traders must invest in training for their employees. This system would alleviate the costs of information put on traders. Clearly, the burden of proof that information has been disclosed should remain with the trader. But in such a context, technology, and more specifically the blockchain, would prove very helpful for traders.

'Infeducation' may be the way forward. We live in a complex world, leading to an increasing need to protect vulnerable people. However, rethinking consumer information should not be done on sector-based grounds. It requires a global vision. As a general concept, it should also be embedded and developed into a general policy at the EU level.

The highly protective design of EU consumer law has proved to be a disappointment in terms of its effects, since enforcement of consumer rights remains a major issue in the EU. Education can form part of the solution. Successful education reforms require good policy design, strong political commitment and effective implementation capacity. Resources are a key issue – indeed, without being overly pessimistic, we have doubts as to the capacity of many Member States to allocate a budget for consumer education. Financial support from the EU in that field is a sine qua non for its success.

VI. Concluding Remarks: No Illusory Promise of Consumer Empowerment

Information and education serve different purposes and have different economics. Information aims to inform, inspire and act as a reference. Education, on the other hand, aims to empower and transform. This requires a partnership between student and teacher that involves hands-on guidance and support. Information and education have been tightly connected under the EU legal framework. Consequently, information and education have often been treated as a 'whole package', which must be implemented in its entirety. But if we take away the learning environments and the teachers, we shall be left with nothing more than a glorified informed consumer, who will be able neither to make the best individual choices nor become an actor in a changing world or a driver for new policymaking and legislative action. Combining information and education will be one of the key challenges of the coming decades. In the latest communications from the EU Commission, and more specifically the New Deal for Consumers, the concept of empowerment is worshipped and somehow sold as a marketing argument to convince us that, in the context of a fast-changing world, the EU will provide consumers with the tools to address the challenges of a new and evolving marketplace. If empowerment is only about consumers' being informed and overloaded by a critical mass of pieces of information, or if the information disclosed to them only aims to allow them to be key agents of a smoothly functioning single market, they will not be empowered. If we want to transform consumer protection in the EU, empowerment should not have as an objective the functioning of the market but rather the emancipation of consumers from the market. This is the direction that both information and education should take. In this regard, the role of legal academics will be crucial because, as rightly observed by Leo Tolstoy, 'Everyone thinks of changing Humanity, but no one thinks of changing himself.'[166]

---

[166] Leo Tolstoy, *Some Social Remedies: Three Methods of Reform* (1900) at archive.org/stream/pamphlet-stransl00tolsgoog/pamphletstransl00tolsgoog_djvu.txt (accessed 2 September 2022).

7

The Growing Interplay of Consumer and Data Protection Law

KARIN SEIN

I. Introduction

This chapter examines the growing interplay of consumer law with data protection law since the millennium, and especially during the last decade. It argues that an important transformation of consumer law has occurred since then: consumer law has become increasingly intertwined with and complemented by data protection law. The growing reliance on the availability of personal data in online trade has led consumer law to utilise data protection law in order to compensate for the digital consumer vulnerability: using information that is obtained by bypassing data protection rules enables traders to manipulate our ability to exercise free will in the digital environment. This chapter will subject this tendency to scrutiny, explore the growing role and function of data protection law in modern consumer law, and look at their interactions and interdependencies.

The chapter starts (in section II) with the description of the situation at the millennium, when both areas of law – although largely harmonised at the EU level – were still developing somewhat independently from each other, and describes the beginning of the debates about their complementary use. In the following sections, it is shown that both areas of law have now become intermingled to a great extent, starting with the data protection and consumer law standards, and ending with the possibilities for their collective enforcement. The chapter further argues that digitalisation and the increasing reliance on the availability of personal data in online trade have changed the understanding of what exactly consumer law is in its contemporary meaning. This argument is based on the descriptions of several legal areas where the connection points between data protection and consumer law have become especially evident: information obligations and transparency (section III); protecting consumers against unfair digital marketing practices (section IV); the roles of privacy by design and by default as contractual standards (section V); collective redress (section VI); and data contract law (section VII). The analysis in these sections concentrates mainly on these developments at the European level, adding specific examples from certain Member States.

As this transformation is largely induced by digitalisation, section VIII illustrates the experiences and understanding of privacy, as well as the use of data protection law for protecting consumers, in Estonia – a small but digitally advanced Member State. It shows that the transformative developments described at the European level do not necessarily match the reality in all Member States, and that the role of data protection law in consumer protection may vary depending on the perception of privacy in the particular society.

II. State of the Affairs at the Millennium

Originally, data protection law aimed at protecting citizens – the data subjects – against surveillance and other privacy breaches vis-à-vis the state. Data protection and consumer law had different purposes: data protection as public law sought to guarantee that the processing of personal data occurred lawfully, fairly and transparently; whereas consumer law aimed at ensuring that consumers were not taken advantage of unfairly when engaging in economic transactions.[1] Correspondingly, data protection and consumer law developed independently from each other in the 1990s and 2000s, whether on the legislative, judicial or academic level.

Over the last decade, however, we have observed that protecting people's privacy not only against the state but with respect to private enterprises has become increasingly important. This has gained additional gravity with the emergence of the digital economy, and, more recently, with the development of big tech, machine learning and artificial intelligence. The common denominator for this innovation-driven industry is its dependence on the availability of (personal) data. Traders collect, use and sell personal data that they receive from or about consumers, either to personalise their products or to make use of automated decision making, dynamic pricing or even price discrimination.[2] Gathering vast amounts of personal data from or about consumers enables traders to take unfair advantage of those who are making their consumption decisions. Prominent examples are profiling,[3] tracking[4] and selling data for advertising purposes that threaten our privacy, but data breaches may also lead to identity theft, potentially creating financial harm to the consumer.

As the phenomenon of consumer protection via data protection has gained importance with the development of digital consumer markets, the legal debate around it has intensified, especially in the current decade. Already in 2010, it was argued in the

---

[1] N Helberger et al, 'The Perfect Match?: A Closer Look at the Relationship between EU Consumer Law and Data Protection Law' (2017) 5 *CML Rev* 1427, 1431.

[2] On price discrimination, see Fr Zuiderveen Borgesius and J Poort, 'Online price discrimination and EU data privacy law' (2017) 40 *Journal of Consumer Policy* 347, 347 ff; N Helberger et al, *EU Consumer Protection 2.0: Structural asymmetries in digital consumer markets* (Brussels, 2021) 92 ff.

[3] Consumer profiles can, for example, be used to personalise prices or to decide whether a consumer can obtain credit.

[4] Prominent examples are Google's and Apple's advertising identifiers, which enable the traders to track phone users, combine information about their online and mobile behaviour, and provide personalised advertising. Privacy enforcement NGO Noyb recently launched actions against such practices.

legal literature that effective consumer protection requires effective data protection regulation: 'the protection of consumers' personal data is an integral part of consumer protection'.[5] In the German judicial practice, starting from 2013, courts used unfair term rules and attacked a considerable number of privacy policy clauses of big-tech enterprises on the ground of lack of transparency.[6] In 2014, the European Data Protection Supervisor initiated a debate on the interplay between data protection, competition law and consumer protection in the context of big data, and claimed that 'consumers are also data subjects, whose welfare may be at risk where freedom of choice and control over one's own personal information is restricted by a dominant undertaking'.[7] Kerber argued in 2016 that in addition to protecting the safety and economic interests of consumers, European consumer law also has the objective of protecting the privacy of consumers as their fundamental right.[8] A year later, Helberger and others pointed out that 'consumer law and data protection law can usefully complement each other and that a new "data consumer law" is emerging'.[9] Scholars increasingly point out that data protection and consumer law share partially similar problems and aims, policy arguments, concepts (such as individual autonomy) and solutions,[10] and plead for a holistic view of data protection and consumer protection, as well as of competition law.[11] This debate has only intensified since the adoption of the General Data Protection Regulation (GDPR)[12] in 2016 and the Digital Content Directive (DCD)[13] in 2019, and will surely carry on, not least as related to the newly adopted rules on data sharing in the Data Governance Act (DGA).[14]

---

[5] D Svantesson and R Clarke, 'A best practice model for e-consumer protection' (2010) 26 *Computer Law & Security Review* 32.

[6] P Rott, 'Data protection law as consumer law – How consumer organisations can contribute to the enforcement of data protection law' (2017) 6 *European Consumer and Market Law* 113, 114–16.

[7] European Data Protection Supervisor, 'Privacy and competitiveness in the age of big data: The interplay between data protection, competition law and consumer protection in the Digital Economy' (Preliminary Opinion, March 2014) 31.

[8] W Kerber, 'Digital markets, data, and privacy: competition law, consumer law and data protection' (2016) 11 *GRUR International* 643.

[9] Helberger et al (n 1) 1427 ff.

[10] However, Svantesson also warns about the potential clashes of data protection law with consumer protection law. DJ Svantesson, 'Enter the quagmire – the complicated relationship between data protection law and consumer protection law' (2018) 34 *Computer Law & Security Review* 28, 30–31.

[11] D Clifford, I Graef and P Valcke, 'Pre-formulated Declarations of Data Subject Consent – Citizen-Consumer Empowerment and the Alignment of Data, Consumer and Competition Law Protections' (2019) 20 *German Law Journal* 679; Kerber (n 8) 647; see also Ph Hacker, 'Manipulation by Algorithms. Exploring the Triangle of Unfair Commercial Practice, Data Protection, and Privacy Law' (2021) *European Law Journal* 1; Kl Wiedemann, 'Data Protection and Competition Law Enforcement in the Digital Economy: Why a Coherent and Consistent Approach is Necessary' (2021) 52 *International Review of Intellectual Property and Competition Law* 915, 915–33.

[12] Regulation (EU) 2016/679 of the European Parliament and of the Council on the protection of natural persons with regard to the processing of personal data and on the free movement of such data, and repealing Directive 95/46/EC (General Data Protection Regulation) [2016] OJ L119/1.

[13] Directive (EU) 2019/770 of the European Parliament and of the Council on certain aspects concerning contracts for the supply of digital content and digital services [2019] OJ L136/1.

[14] Regulation (EU) 2022/868 of the European Parliament and of the Council on European data governance and amending Regulation (EU) 2018/1724 (Data Governance Act) [2022] OJ L152/1. See a critical review of the proposal by G Spindler, 'Schritte zur europaweiten Datenwirtschaft – der Vorschlag einer Verordnung zur europäischen Data Governance' (2021) 37 *Computer und Recht* 98, 98 ff.

III. Information Obligations and Transparency

When describing the complementary use of data protection and consumer law, it should first be pointed out that they both rely heavily upon the information and transparency paradigm to mitigate information asymmetries and enable individuals to make informed decisions such as giving consent for data processing or concluding a credit contract. The aim of the information obligations is to compensate for the information asymmetry: consumers, as well as data subjects, are considered weaker parties, inter alia due to the lack of information that prevents them from making rational choices.[15] Therefore, both the GDPR as well as different consumer law directives contain long lists of circumstances about which the data subject or consumer must be informed. Despite the differences in transparency standards, the underlying idea of the information paradigm remains the same – as does the problem of information overload.

The information paradigm has been criticised extensively and rightfully as ineffective for different reasons.[16] Indeed, when looking at the Estonian practice, most of the case law is not about breaching information obligations, be it under consumer or data protection law. And even if one were to oblige traders to inform consumers about the value of the personal data they are giving to the trader as a counter-performance, this obligation would be impossible to comply with in practice, as the value of personal data can only be approximated but not determined with sufficient precision.[17]

In certain situations, however, information obligations can still play a role: although the information overload does not necessarily lead to the making of better decisions by the consumers, their breach can lead to sanctions. Helberger and others argue that the 'true added benefit of consumer law to inform consumers about personal data use could be in the extra level of flexibility and attention to the individual context that consumer law affords'.[18] More precisely, not informing consumers about, for example, online price personalisation or personal data sharing may constitute not only a breach of the data protection law but also an infringement of consumer law: it could be considered an unfair commercial practice.[19] This would open up the possibility of applying the remedies and sanctions under unfair commercial practices law. Moreover, consumer protection authorities (and not only data protection authorities) may step in to sanction these breaches. Hence, data protection law has become an additional enabler of consumer law, as the breach of the information and transparency obligations of the data protection law may be targeted by consumer protection entities and consumer law sanctions.

---

[15] A Kozios, 'Paying with Data: A Study on EU Consumer Law and the Protection of Personal Data' (PhD Thesis, Uppsala Universitetet, 2022) 165.

[16] See, eg, O Ben-Shahar and CE Schneider, *More Than You Wanted to Know: The Failure of Mandated Disclosure* (Princeton University Press, 2014).

[17] Ph Hacker, 'Regulating the Economic Impact of Data as Counter-Performance: From the Illegality Doctrine to the Unfair Contract Terms Directive' in S Lohsse, R Schulze and D Staudenmayer (eds), *Data as Counter-Performance: Contract Law 2.0?* (Hart/Nomos, 2020) 47, 48.

[18] Helberger et al (n 1) 1439.

[19] ibid 1440–41.

IV. Data-driven Marketing Strategies and Fairness Paradigm of the Unfair Commercial Practices Directive

The data-intense practices so far described make consumers vulnerable to advertising and other commercial practices influencing their transactional decisions: in the modern digital economy, digital service providers design their digital environments in a way that is optimised for searching, identifying and targeting consumers' exploitable weaknesses and personal biases.[20] Using information that is obtained by bypassing data protection rules enables traders to constantly manipulate our ability to exercise free will in the digital environment.

This is where data protection meets unfair commercial practices regulation. In principle, data exploitation may be qualified as commercial practice under the Unfair Commercial Practices Directive (UCPD).[21] Article 2(k) UCPD defines a 'transactional decision' as any decision taken by a consumer concerning whether, how and on what terms to purchase, make payment in whole or in part for, retain or dispose of a product, or exercise a contractual right in relation to the product, whether the consumer decides to act or to refrain from acting. It is argued – and also confirmed by several German courts – that certain data-related decisions, such as whether to consent to process personal data, are also transactional decisions within the meaning of the UCPD so that its prohibitions on misleading advertising and aggressive practices would be applicable.[22] Consequently, in certain situations, breach of data protection law could be sanctioned by unfair commercial practices regulation, that is, consumer law.

A specific area where both consumer law and data protection law are trying to cooperate in protecting consumers against manipulative practices aimed at distorting consumers' free will is the fight against the so-called 'dark patterns'. Dark patterns are specific techniques used online with the purpose of influencing consumers' behaviour, for example to lead them to consent to the collection of personal data and consequently to share more personal information than they intended, or tricking the user to accept overpriced or recurring offers. Dark patterns include, for instance, repeatedly showing pop-ups or misleading designs of the webpage or consent options. Although it is argued that the unfair commercial practices law is uniquely qualified and better positioned than the data protection regime to fight them, it is also admitted that the problem in practice is the poor enforcement of consumer law.[23] As the use of dark patterns may also violate data protection law, especially the rules on the data minimisation principle, free consent and transparency,[24] this opens the possibility to resort to more effective sanctions under

---

[20] Helberger et al (n 2) 3.

[21] ibid 63.

[22] ibid 20–21. However, qualifying algorithmic manipulation as misleading or aggressive practices under the UCPD is hindered by several obstacles. Hacker (n 11) 9 ff.

[23] MR Leiser and MM Caruana, 'Dark Patterns: Light to be Found in Europe's Consumer Protection Regime' (2021) 6 *European Consumer and Market Law* 237, 252.

[24] EDPB, Guidelines 3/2022 on dark patterns in social media platform interfaces: How to recognise and avoid them' (March 2022) 2–3; see also D Clifford, 'Citizen-Consumers in a Personalised Galaxy: Emotion Influenced Decision-Making, a True Path to the Dark Side?' in L Edwards, Sch Burkhard and E Harbinja (eds), *Future Law: Emerging Technology, Regulation and Ethics* (Cambridge University Press, 2020) 20.

the data protection legislation. In addition to the existing consumer and data protection rules, the newly adopted Digital Services Act[25] contains a specific prohibition on the use of dark patterns – although limited to providers of online platforms. Article 25 of the Act prohibits these providers to

> design, organise or operate their online interfaces in a way that deceives or manipulates the recipients of their service or in a way that otherwise materially distorts or impairs the ability of the recipients of their service to make free and informed decisions.

Again, we see that while having an origin in unfair commercial practices law, the specific regulation is limited to the online world and, more specifically, to certain digital economy players.[26]

Apart from dark patterns, we also find an interaction of consumer law and data protection in the argument that there may be a breach of unfair commercial practices law if the trader advertises its app as being 'free' but fails to inform consumers that it tracks and uses the consumer's personal data.[27] While an Italian court has found such practices to be misleading,[28] a lower-instance court from Germany has considered Facebook's similar advertising practices to be legitimate.[29] Even if one might criticise the court's argumentation, the question of causality between such advertising and the consumer's transactional decision remains: would consumers, with their growing awareness about the value of their personal data, indeed refrain from getting a Facebook account even if it were not advertised as being free? Similarly, consumers would not be helped much by declaring as unfair any standard terms referring to the free provision of a digital service, when in fact consumers' personal data are being processed:[30] this would not have any positive contract law effect. This shows that the consumer law rules may have limits when trying to stop certain unfair data-related practices.

Under the UCPD, the concepts of average and vulnerable consumers play a key role in assessing the fairness of commercial practices. Digital markets have, however, shifted the understanding of who can be considered vulnerable: through data analytics, profiling and targeted advertising, it is easier than ever to exploit consumers' vulnerabilities. Helberger and others suggest identifying new groups of vulnerable consumers, such as

> particularly active online users who leave a correspondingly large data footprint, 'quantified self' consumers who use smart devices to track their own behaviour, or those that are particularly perceptible [sic] to digital market manipulation.[31]

---

[25] Regulation (EU) 2022/2065 of the European Parliament and of the Council on a Single Market For Digital Services and amending Directive 2000/31/EC (Digital Services Act) [2022] OJ L277/1.

[26] See the critique by Busch and Mak on the failure to distinguish between online platforms that may be qualified as information society services and those that may not (and hence keeping the online-offline division) in the Digital Markets Act. Ch Busch and V Mak, 'Putting the Digital Services Act in Context' (2021) 10 *European Consumer and Market Law* 110.

[27] Helberger et al (n 1) 1443.

[28] M Kulesza, 'Italian court says Facebook isn't free' *In Principle* (13 February 2020).

[29] Decision of Kammergericht Berlin, 20 December 2019, 5 U 9/18.

[30] As suggested by M Loos and J Luzak, *Update the Unfair Contract Terms Directive for digital services* (Study requested by the JURI committee, 2021) 21.

[31] Helberger et al (n 1) 1458.

It is even argued that due to the increasing automation of commerce, datafied consumer-seller relations, where every consumer has a persuasion profile, the knowledge gap on digitalisation and the very architecture of digital marketplaces, most if not all consumers are potentially vulnerable in digital marketplaces, although the concept of vulnerability should be replaced by the one of digital asymmetry.[32] Even if one were to find these suggestions to be going rather too far, at least in some respects, it cannot be denied that the digital economy based upon data-intensive market practices poses challenges that cannot be solved by consumer law alone but need complementary assistance from data protection law.[33]

V. Privacy by Design and by Default as Contractual Standards

Data protection law could also provide an additional benchmark to assess the fairness of consumer contract conditions. For instance, Helberger and others have argued that a contract might be considered unfair if it were to breach the data protection law's data minimisation principle, or security or privacy by design and privacy by default requirements.[34] Moreover, principles of privacy by default and by design may serve as contractual standards, thus the trader's not respecting them could lead to a breach of contract. This approach was suggested by Wendehorst[35] as well as by the European Law Institute,[36] and has already found its way into the DCD,[37] hence becoming a mandatory provision of European consumer contract law. The application of privacy by design and by default rules – data protection rules by origin – has a consequence that if a digital product does not comply with these requirements, consumers are not only able to exercise their rights under data protection law but they can also terminate the contract, return the product and demand their money back. Interestingly, privacy by design and by default requirements do not qualify as contractual standards under the new Sale of Goods Directive,[38] at least there is no reference to them in the recitals,[39] but the same conclusion could be reached under the general fitness-for-purpose test

---

[32] Helberger et al (n 3) 5, 11, 46, 51. It should not be reduced to information asymmetry, however, as providing more information cannot correct this asymmetry.

[33] In this sense also, see Durovic and Lech: consumer law needs to be supported by other fields of EU law, such as competition law and data protection law. M Durovic and Fr Lech, 'A Consumer Law Perspective on the Commercialization of Data' (2021) 5 *European Review of Private Law* 728.

[34] Helberger et al (n 1) 1451.

[35] Ch Wendehorst, *Sale of Goods and Supply of Digital Content – Two Worlds Apart?* (Study Commissioned by the Policy Department for Citizen's Rights and Constitutional Affairs at the Request of the JURI Committee, 2016) 14–15.

[36] European Law Institute, *Statement on the European Commission's Proposed Directive on the Supply of Digital Content to Consumers* (ELI, 2016) 23–24.

[37] See recital 48 DCD.

[38] Directive (EU) 2019/771 of the European Parliament and of the Council on certain aspects concerning contracts for the sale of goods, amending Regulation (EU) 2017/2394 and Directive 2009/22/EC, and repealing Directive 1999/44/EC [2019] OJ L136/28.

[39] K Sein and G Spindler, 'The new Directive on Contracts for Supply of Digital Content and Digital Services – Conformity Criteria, Remedies and Modifications – Part 2' (2019) 15 *European Review of Contract Law* 372.

in Article 7(1) of the Directive.[40] Consequently, data protection concepts of privacy by design and by default regulated in Article 25 of the GDPR may afford consumers contractual remedies and enable them to return, for example, spying home appliances as defective products.

This development once again highlights a connection point between the data protection and consumer protection laws, as well as the added value of data protection law to the European consumer law: the concepts originally developed for the protection of privacy now serve the purpose of establishing standards of contractual conformity. In other words, data protection and consumer law complement each other not only on the sanctions side but also when establishing fair standards for contractual performance. As the concepts of privacy by design and by default – although technology-neutral in principle – are mostly relevant for the digital environment, it further illustrates that this transformation is driven by digitalisation.

VI. Collective Redress

The constant development of collaboration between data protection and consumer protection law has been especially evident in the field of collective enforcement. Whereas the 2009 Injunctions Directive[41] afforded consumer protection entities legal standing in cross-border injunction proceedings, it did not solve the question of whether these entities might also pursue data protection breaches. This remained subject to the national law and – apart from the application of unfair terms rules to privacy policies – was mostly rejected by the German courts until the German legislation was changed in 2016.[42] Since then, the German and other consumer associations have pursued several important lawsuits against big online trade and social media enterprises, some of which have eventually ended up in the Court of Justice of the European Union (CJEU): *Weltimmo*,[43] *Facebook Fan-Page*[44] as well as *Fashion ID*.[45] In the last of these cases, in 2019, the CJEU clarified that the Data Protection Directive[46] indeed allows national legislation to grant legal standing to a consumer association to initiate legal proceedings against a person who has allegedly breached EU data protection law.

Moreover, just recently, the CJEU has confirmed that the full harmonisation approach of the GDPR still allows for a national regulation entitling competitors and national consumer protection associations to file injunction claims for data protection infringements based on the infringement of the prohibition of unfair commercial

---

[40] Helberger and others have proposed to reach the same result under Art 6(5) of the Consumer Rights Directive (CRD). See Helberger et al (n 1) 1440.

[41] Directive 2009/22/EC of the European Parliament and of the Council on injunctions for the protection of consumers' interests [2009] OJ L110/30.

[42] Rott (n 6) 116.

[43] Case C-230/14 *Weltimmo sro v Nemzeti Adatvédelmi és Információszabadság Hatóság* ECLI:EU:C:2015:639.

[44] Case C-210/16 *Facebook Fan pages* ECLI:EU:C:2018:388.

[45] Case C-40/17 *Fashion ID GmbH & Co KG v Verbraucherzentrale NRW eV* ECLI:EU:C:2019:629.

[46] Directive 95/46/EC of the European Parliament and of the Council on the protection of individuals with regard to the processing of personal data and on the free movement of such data [1995] OJ L281/31.

practices, a breach of a consumer protection law or the prohibition of the use of invalid general terms and conditions. This was clarified in the *Facebook Ireland* case,[47] following a preliminary reference from the German Federal Court. The issue is of practical relevance, as the GDPR does not specify a collective redress procedure, leaving that within the competence of the Member States.[48] The Court of Justice stressed, inter alia, that infringement of the consumer protection rules may be related to or give rise to the infringement of the rules on the protection of personal data of the consumers,[49] acknowledging thereby the interrelationship of these two fields of law. In any case, the issue of consumer protection entities' legitimation to pursue data protection breaches has now found a European-wide legislative solution in the new Representative Actions Directive[50] of 2020. Starting from mid-2023, this Directive obliges the Member States to nominate qualified entities who are entitled to bring not only domestic but also cross-border representative actions and whose legal standing should be recognised in the other Member States. Annex I to the Representative Actions Directive defines the instrument's scope by listing the EU law acts for which representative actions should be possible, and this list also contains data protection legislation, including the e-Privacy Directive.[51] Moreover, Member States must foresee at least one collective compensatory enforcement mechanism: the qualified entities should be entitled not only to file injunctions, but also to claim compensation on behalf of the consumers/data subjects. Here, the transformation of consumer law is visible in the new tools available to the consumer protection entities: they are now entitled by law to pursue data protection infringements.

The importance of collective redress is increasingly evident in cases of non-material damage claims, where opponents have warned of the creation of a major litigation industry.[52] The controversial issue of non-material damage claims for data protection breaches has received clarification from the decision of the CJEU,[53] after the Austrian Supreme Court asked whether a claim for damages under Article 82 GDPR requires the claimant to have suffered specific damage, or whether a violation of GDPR is sufficient to qualify for the award. The Court further inquired whether the threshold for non-material damage requires that the infringement has consequences of a certain degree or weight that extend beyond anger or annoyance caused by the said infringement.[54]

---

[47] Case C-319/20 *Facebook Ireland Limited* ECLI:EU:C:2022:322.

[48] Estonia, for example, currently does not foresee any possibility of compensatory collective redress, either for consumer law or for data protection breaches.

[49] *Facebook Ireland Limited* (n 47) paras 66, 78.

[50] Directive (EU) 2020/1828 of the European Parliament and of the Council on representative actions for the protection of the collective interests of consumers and repealing Directive 2009/22/EC [2020] OJ L409/1.

[51] Directive 2002/58/EC of the European Parliament and of the Council concerning the processing of personal data and the protection of privacy in the electronic communications sector (Directive on privacy and electronic communications) [2008] OJ L201/37.

[52] See on that and related legal issues, BP Paal and I Kritzer, 'Geltendmachung von DS-GVO-Ansprüchen als Geschäftsmodell' (2022) 34 *Neue Juristische Wochenschrift* 2438.

[53] Case C-300/21 *Österreichische Post AG* ECLI:EU:C:2023:370.

[54] Request for a preliminary ruling from the Austrian Supreme Court (OGH) Case C-300/21, 12 May 2021. Displaying a similar tendency, the German Federal Constitutional Court ruled that a lower court should have asked for a preliminary ruling from the CJEU – and not have decided itself that the threshold for compensation had not been reached – see decision of the German Constitutional Court (BVerfG) 14 January 2021, 1 BvR 2853/19. Interestingly, the case was only about the unlawful sending of one advertising e-mail. See also D Flint, 'Does Non-material Damage under GDPR Need to Be Material or Is That Immaterial?' (2021) 3 *European Business Law* 159, 159–61.

The CJEU held that there is no threshold of seriousness for non-material damage but, on the other hand, a mere infringement of the GDPR is not sufficient in itself to entitle the data subject to compensation.[55]

From the Estonian point of view, it will be interesting to see the reaction of the Estonian Government to *Österreichische Post AG* decision. Notably, the Estonian Supreme Court has taken the position that it may be enough for the state to compensate for immaterial damage inflicted by the illegal publication of sensitive health data from its registry (in the given case, social security documents about the disability of a minor were accessible on the Internet) simply by apologising and acknowledging that there has been a data protection violation.[56] Therefore, following a recent huge leak, where a hacker was able to download the passport photos of more than 300,000 Estonian citizens from the state database, the Estonian Data Protection Authority has admitted that it is not likely that compensation will be obtainable for non-material damage from the state for this infringement.[57] As the CJEU came to the conclusion that there is no considerable threshold for non-material damage claims under the GDPR, not only businesses but also (e-)governments would be under considerable pressure to invest in proper data privacy measures, and the collaboration between consumer and data protection law could lead to better privacy for citizens.

The data protection and consumer protection authorities complement each other not only in collective redress, but also when applying administrative fines for data protection breaches. A recent example of cooperation between consumer and data protection authorities comes from Norway, where the Norwegian Data Protection Authority issued an advance notification of a 100 million NOK (€9,600,000) fine to the dating app Grindr, because of a legal complaint filed by the Norwegian Consumer Council.[58] Some months later, the Norwegian Data Protection Authority imposed an administrative fine of NOK 65,000,000 – approximately €6.5 million – for not complying with the GDPR rules on consent.[59]

These cases show that data protection law is playing a growing role in the collective enforcement of consumer interests, be it via the cooperation of data protection and consumer protection authorities or the possibility to file claims for immaterial damage under the GDPR, which surely has the potential to have a preventive effect on traders

---

[55] *Österreichische Post AG* (n 53).

[56] At least in situations where the data leak was not extensive. See the decision of the Estonian Supreme Court (Riigikohus) 6 January 2021, 3-19-1207. In the Estonian legal literature, it has been suggested that not every violation of GDPR (eg where the data controller does not inform the data subject quickly enough about the processing of his or her personal data) should entitle the data subject to claim for non-material damage. By contrast, in cases where violation of data protection rules amounts to a breach of personality rights (eg publishing confidential data), the existence of the non-material harm should be presumed and compensated for. K Sein, M Mikiver and P Krõõt Tupay, 'Pilguheit andmesubjekti õiguskaitsevahenditele uues isikuandmete kaitse üldmääruses' (2018) 2 *Juridica* 112.

[57] Kr Kontro, 'Fotode lekkimise eest hüvitise saamine on vähetõenäoline' *ERR* (30 July 2021) at www.err.ee/1608293655/fotode-lekkimise-eest-huvitise-saamine-on-vahetoenaoline (accessed 18 August 2022).

[58] Forbrukerradet, 'Historic victory for privacy as dating app receives gigantic fine' (26 January 2021) at www.forbrukerradet.no/news-in-english/historic-victory-for-privacy-as-dating-app-receives-gigantic-fine/?fbclid=IwAR1VP537PxtAjxeUgtSLAOg7Xr7nSaGvt-PJjAGUEukV4RD5klSQ83qUpGg (accessed 18 August 2022).

[59] Datatilsynet, 'Administrative fine – Grindr LLC' at www.datatilsynet.no/contentassets/8ad827efefcb489ab1c7ba129609edb5/administrative-fine---grindr-llc.pdf (accessed 18 August 2022).

abusing or simply not caring about consumers' personal data. Again, the examples illustrating this development stem mainly from the digital world – although they are by no means limited to that.

VII. Data Contract Law

A. Ongoing Debate about Data-as-Counter-performance

The intermingling of data protection with consumer law is further illustrated by the development of the so-called data contract law. Personal data are an essential commodity in the modern digital economy. It has become common knowledge that many digital services are offered not in exchange for a monetary payment but in exchange for the provision of personal data, which can later be used for profiling, targeted advertising or training artificial intelligence, amongst other things. Previously, such 'free' services without monetary payment were not subject to European consumer law: neither the Consumer Rights Directive[60] nor other consumer contract law directives were applicable to data-paid contracts. This changed with the adoption of the DCD, which applies irrespective of whether the consumer pays for the digital content or digital service with money (a price) or by providing his or her personal data.[61]

This principle has been described as 'a ground-breaking step' and as entering into 'uncharted territory',[62] and is often referred to as the concept of data-as-counter-performance. There is already an abundant amount of literature on how to combine this concept with the data protection rules, especially the prohibition on tying clauses under Article 7(4) GDPR.[63] Yet it must be stressed that talking about data as counter-performance in the context of the DCD is not exactly correct, as Article 3(1) DCD only guarantees that consumers who have provided data and not money for the services are entitled to the same level of protection, that is, that the contractual quality standards are the same and that they can use the same contractual remedies.[64] By contrast, the Directive does not regulate whether providing personal data should be seen as a counter-performance in the true sense, that is, whether there is a synallagmatic connection between the trader's obligation to provide a digital service and the consumer's obligation to provide his or her personal data. Questions such as whether the trader is entitled to terminate the contract if the consumer does not provide the personal data

---

[60] Directive 2011/83/EU of the European Parliament and of the Council on consumer rights, amending Council Directive 93/13/EEC and Directive 1999/44/EC of the European Parliament and of the Council and repealing Council Directive 85/577/EEC and Directive 97/7/EC of the European Parliament and of the Council [2011] OJ L304/64.

[61] Art 3(1) DCD.

[62] R Schulze and D Staudenmayer, *EU Digital Law* (Nomos, 2020) 61.

[63] Art 7(4) GDPR provides 'When assessing whether consent is freely given, utmost account shall be taken of whether, *inter alia*, the performance of a contract, including the provision of a service, is conditional on consent to the processing of personal data that is not necessary for the performance of that contract.'

[64] Schulze and Staudenmayer (n 61) 73. See also recitals 12, 24 and 40 DCD, leaving the questions of the contract formation and validity, as well as the contractual consequences of withdrawal of consent, to the national law.

that he has promised (eg if he or she withdraws consent) are not covered by the DCD and are subject to national law. In Estonia, for example, withdrawal of consent may entitle the trader to terminate the contract, if withdrawal of consent can be considered a 'valid reason' in that particular contract.[65] The DCD regulates neither whether consumers can be required by contract law to provide the promised personal data, nor whether they would be liable for failing to do so or for providing false or low-quality data. Thus, it is within the discretion of the Member States to stipulate, for example, that withdrawal of consent should not entitle the trader to claim damages or apply contractual penalties. Moreover, the DCD does not foresee that data subjects should be able to sell their personal data, nor whether such a contract might be invalid: all these questions depend upon national contract law doctrines.[66] Of course, this brings with it a certain level of legal fragmentation and potential hurdles to the data economy, but on the other side it enables the Member States to enact more 'data consumer protection'.

When speaking about the data contract law, one must also bear in mind that the European Data Protection Board, as well as the European Data Protection Supervisor, is strongly opposing the concept of data as counter-performance and commercialisation of personal data as such. In his often-cited opinion on the DCD, the European Data Protection Supervisor compared the selling of personal data to the sale of human organs.[67] In its guidelines on consent, the European Data Protection Board stated that the GDPR 'ensures that the processing of personal data for which consent is sought cannot directly or indirectly become the counter-performance of a contract'.[68] The CJEU did not use the opportunity to elaborate upon the data-as-counter-performance concept and legitimacy of personal data processing in the case of 'free' digital services in the *Planet49* case, although Advocate General Szpunar suggested that in these cases, the use of personal data for advertising purposes should be considered legitimate under Article 6(1)(b) GDPR, as being necessary for the performance of the contract.[69] That issue, as well as the famous conflict between the concept of data-as-counter-performance and the prohibition of bundling clauses in Article 7(4) GDPR, should be resolved in the new Facebook case, initiated by Max Schrems and brought to the CJEU by the Austrian Supreme Court.[70] Various solutions to overcome this conflict have been suggested in the legal literature,[71] and the future possibilities for commercialisation of personal data largely depend upon the outcome of this case. The question is fundamental: should personal data be legally considered a tradable asset, that is, are consumers as data subjects entitled to dispose of their personal data; and if so, then under what conditions, and what concepts could be used to guarantee that they achieve a fair price for their data?

---

[65] See para 62^{18} of the Estonian Law of Obligations Act.

[66] Art 3(1) DCD.

[67] European Data Protection Supervisor, 'Opinion 4/2017 on the Proposal for a Directive on certain aspects concerning contracts for the supply of digital content' (2017) 5.

[68] EDPB Guidelines 05/2020 on consent under Regulation 2016/679 para 26.

[69] Case C-673/17 *Planet49 GmbH* EU:C:2019:246, Opinion of AG Szpunar, para 99.

[70] Preliminary reference from the Austrian Supreme Court C-446/21, 20 July 2021.

[71] C Langhanke and M Schmidt-Kessel, 'Consumer Data as Consideration' (2015) 4 *European Consumer and Market Law* 218, 218 ff; A Sattler, 'Personenbezogene Daten als Leistungsgegenstand' (2017) 72 *Juristenzeitung* 1036, 1036ff; A Metzger et al, 'Data-Related Aspects of the Digital Content Directive' (2018) 9 *Journal of Intellectual Property, Information Technology and Electronic Commerce Law* 93, 93 ff.

Despite the outcome of the *Facebook* case, the data-as-counter-performance approach of the DCD has led to European consumer law's being more generally applicable to 'free', that is data-paid, services. For example, soon after the adoption of the DCD, the Omnibus Directive[72] brought data-paid consumer contracts within the scope of the amended CRD.[73] This is further evidence of the transformation of consumer law: the data protection concerns, and the practices of personal data commercialisation, have brought about the extension of the scope of the European consumer contract law rules to data-paid digital services.

Treating personal data as counter-performance poses a further question as to whether it excludes the possibility of subjecting consent clauses to unfairness control. Article 4(2) of the Unfair Contract Terms Directive[74] (UCTD) excludes assessment of unfairness as 'to the adequacy of the price and remuneration, on the one hand, as against the services or goods supplies in exchange, on the other, in so far as these terms are in plain intelligible language', that is, the core terms of the contract. In other words, if we treat the provision of a consumer's personal data as remuneration, can we then still apply the substantive fairness test, that is assess whether this remuneration is too high or low for a particular service under the UCTD?[75] Indeed, as Clifford and others observe, it would appear odd, given the aim of pre-formulated declarations of consent.[76] In this context, it is convincingly argued that recital 42 of the GDPR explicitly mentions that privacy policies may not contain clauses that are unfair in the sense of the UCTD (hence, implying that the UCTD is applicable); and from an economic perspective too, we should still apply the UCTD to declarations of consent because the ignorance of privacy policies by the consumers weakens competition on the market.[77] Furthermore, recital 42 of the GDPR calls for 'parallel, concurrent, but substantively distinct, fairness assessments, thus reflecting the differences vis-à-vis the Charter foundations of the respective frameworks'.[78] In any event, an unfairness test is available if the data are not provided as counter-performance, and terms violating the data minimisation principle of Article 5 GDPR could be considered unfair.[79] Consequently, data protection principles may also be used as standards for the assessment of unfairness of contract terms, and thereby offer supplementary protection for the consumers. And vice versa: the unfair terms rules help to protect the data subjects. This interplay once again

---

[72] Directive (EU) 2019/2161 of the European Parliament and of the Council amending Council Directive 93/13/EEC and Directives 98/6/EC, 2005/29/EC and 2011/83/EU of the European Parliament and of the Council as regards the better enforcement and modernisation of Union consumer protection rules [2019] OJ L328/7.

[73] See Art 3(1a) of the amended CRD.

[74] Council Directive 93/13/EEC on unfair terms in consumer contracts [1993] OJ L95/29.

[75] cf Helberger et al (n 1) 1452–53. They report German and Norwegian practices where different data-related clauses of big-tech companies have been declared unfair, and argue that as the provision of personal data is not considered 'price' under the DCD then it is possible to apply the unfairness test to such clauses.

[76] Clifford, Graef and Valcke (n 11) 697.

[77] Hacker (n 17) 63, 64. Furthermore, the unfairness test should be applied to contractual clauses where traders try to bypass the need for obtaining consent by obliging themselves to provide personalised advertising, thus relying upon Art 6(1)(b) GDPR as the legal basis for data processing. Ch Wendehorst and Fr Graf von Westphalen, 'Das Verhältnis zwischen Datenschutz-Grundverordnung und AGB-Recht' (2016) 52 *Neue Juristische Wochenschrift* 3747, 3750.

[78] Clifford et al (n 11) 690.

[79] Loos and Luzak (n 30) 35.

illustrates the transformation of consumer law, as being increasingly intertwined with the data protection law, and that these two legal areas support each other. It also shows the importance and 'weight' of consumer law, as it has a direct effect on data protection instruments such as privacy policies or pre-formulated consents.

B. Data Intermediaries and the Shift from Protecting the Data Subjects to the Creation of the European Data Economy

The question of the interaction between data protection and consumer law is especially evident in the digital economy where data originating from consumers – be it given voluntarily or collected by tracking or other means – form a critical resource. For the big-tech and artificial intelligence industry, consumer data are crucial for fostering innovation, including in areas of public (and consumer) interest such as better health-care. This is reflected in the European Commission's aims to achieve a well-functioning European Data Economy, foster data sharing, and provide innovative companies with better access to data.[80] We must keep in mind the dual role of the European data protection law: its aim is not only to protect individuals' privacy, but also to secure the free movement of personal data.[81]

The aim of free movement of personal data in the EU is coming more and more into focus, especially after the adoption of the DGA as well as publication of the proposal for the European Data Act.[82] One of the aims of the new DGA is to encourage wider re-use of data held by the public sector bodies, including personal data. The Data Act, in turn, seeks to enable consumers to access the data on their connected devices and share this data for the aftermarket, or to use it for getting a better price or access to data-driven services.[83] Following the trends in the European consumer protection legislation, the internal market considerations are playing a gradually ascending role in the European data legislation, with a clear tendency to favour consumer data moneti-sation: this means less data protection and more protection for consumers' monetary interests,[84] that is the economic value of their data.

The vital problem – how to transfer personal data from consumers to traders while respecting their privacy – is now sought to be resolved by the institution of data inter-mediaries as neutral persons between data users and data subjects. The DGA sees data intermediaries as tools for empowering data subjects, creating trust and mini-mising privacy risks, but at the same time as a means to incentivise personal data sharing. Another issue is whether the public law requirements foreseen for the data

---

[80] See, eg Commission, 'Towards a Thriving Data-driven Economy' (Communication) COM (2014) 442 final.

[81] See Art 1(1) GDPR. The dual purpose of the European data protection law is also stressed by Svantesson (n 10) 29.

[82] European Commission, 'Proposal for a Regulation of the European Parliament and of the Council on harmonised rules on fair access to and use of data (Data Act)' COM (2022) 68 final.

[83] See ibid Art 5 and recital 13.

[84] Durovic and Lech require a respective paradigm shift in EU consumer law and more protection for the 'the proprietary interest and economic preferences of consumers in their own personal data'. Durovic and Lech (n 33) 708.

intermediaries are appropriate for guaranteeing their neutrality and compliance.[85] One might also wonder what the objective conformity standards of a data intermediary service as a digital service would be under Article 8 DCD, and whether consumer contract law would be suitable to define the fairness criteria of a digital service aimed at protecting privacy (and data monetising) interests of the consumers.

The aim of the European legislator to create a European Data Economy will eventually result in nudging consumers to monetise their personal data. Should the use of data intermediaries be a success story, it will also mean a shift in the academic discussions, concentrating them around the question of how to guarantee consumers a fair price for their personal data. Further, it would also mean that consumer law is influencing – and even reducing – the data protection standards as we witness the consumerisation of data protection law: the shift from the protection of the fundamental right to the protection of economic interests.

VIII. Data Protection Law Complementing Consumer Law – The Estonian Experiences

The preceding analysis mainly illustrated the growing interplay of data protection and consumer law at the European level and showed that this transformation was largely driven by digitalisation. We now turn to analysing whether these European developments are correspondingly reflected in Estonia, one of the most digitally advanced Member States, and examine the role of data protection law in the protection of consumers in Estonia.

When asked about the function of data protection law in enhancing the interests of consumers in Estonia, it must first be stressed that, for historical and societal reasons, data protection has never played such a prominent role as it has, for example, in Germany. This is surely a paradox, as both Germany and Estonia have experienced a totalitarian past: in Estonia, totalitarianism was associated with foreign occupation powers and not our 'own' state; the trust in the public structures and state institutions is relatively high in Estonia.[86] The rather modest importance of privacy has several other possible reasons, among them the wide accessibility of public online services starting from the early 2000s and the idea of an open information society.[87] Estonia's advanced e-state and public digital services, based upon the once-only principle,[88]

---

[85] Critical on the public law requirements set for the data intermediaries by the DGA, as such requirements would be contraproductive in developing functioning data intermediaries models, see L Specht-Riemenschneider et al, 'Die Datentreuhand: Ein Beitrag zur Modellbildung und rechtlichen Strukturierung zwecks Identifizierung der Regulierungserfordernisse für Datentreuhandmodelle' (2021) 6 *MMR-Beilage* 25.

[86] This seems to resemble the situation in Nordic countries, where citizens have relatively high levels of trust in the state and public authorities. Th Wilhelmsson, 'The Emergence of Nordic Consumer Law and a Nordic Consumer Law Community and Its Impact on Nordic Legal Unity' in H Micklitz (ed), *The Making of Consumer Law and Policy in Europe* (Hart Publishing, 2021) 179.

[87] For a critical overview, see P Krõõt Tupay, 'Estonia, the Digital Nation: Reflections on a Digital Citizen's Rights in the European Union' (2020) 6 *European Data Protection Law Review* 294, 294–300.

[88] The once-only principle (OOP) means that the state is not allowed to ask citizens for the same information twice. The EU will also launch an OOP Initiative in 2023.

are very much appreciated by the citizens as they make communication with the state considerably quicker and easier.

Second, Estonian people value transparency as public access to information and to online public services helped to combat corruption after gaining re-independence.[89] The Public Information Act adopted in 2000 provided guarantees of access to information, its ideology being largely influenced by the Swedish legislation[90] with its extensive transparency policy. The Estonian Data Protection Authority (*Andmekaitse Inspektsioon*) was entrusted with responsibility for implementing the Act; thus, the Scandinavian transparency policy initially obliged the Data Protection Authority to guarantee access to and not protection of data. Even though Estonia used the legislation of Germanic countries as a blueprint for creating its own new legal acts, the Scandinavian transparency culture is still probably one of the reasons why data protection does not enjoy the same value for citizens in Estonia as it does in Germany.[91] To give a practical example, Estonia has a German type of *Grundbuch*, but it is publicly accessible online for everyone without a valid reason being required.

The limited importance of data protection in Estonia is also largely the result of the national Data Protection Authority's being heavily underfinanced and having a severe lack of resources. Moreover, its previous director has declared that the Authority does not primarily aim at sanctioning enterprises but rather sees its role as cooperation and consulting data controllers on privacy issues: prevention instead of sanctions.[92] Indeed, Estonia has not applied considerable penalties for data protection breaches,[93] but this trend might be changing given that the Estonian Data Protection Authority recently threatened a gas station that used video and audio surveillance on its premises with a fine of €25,000 and forced it to stop those illegal practices.[94] Public awareness about the importance of privacy seems to be increasing as well.

All in all, it can be concluded that data protection law does not play a major role in protecting consumer interests in Estonian practice. Whereas the previous director of the Estonian Data Protection Authority, Viljar Peep, has acknowledged that in the digital

---

[89] V Kalnins, *Process-tracing Study Report on Estonia* (Hertie School of Governance, 2015) 23 at www.korruptsioon.ee/sites/www.korruptsioon.ee/files/elfinder/dokumendid/d3.3-estonia_process-tracing-report-kalnins1.pdf (accessed 18 August 2022).

[90] The orientation towards the Swedish model is evident from the explanatory memorandum of the Estonian Public Information Act adopted in 2000. In addition to Swedish law, US, UK, Irish and Finnish laws were also used as comparisons. Avaliku teabe seaduse eelnõu 462 SE I seletuskiri 22 ff. On the Estonian understanding of open society, see also P Krõõt Tupay and M Mikiver, 'Der estnische E-Staat – Zukunftsweisendes Vorbild oder befremdlicher Einzelgänger?' (2015) 1 *Osteuropa Recht* 6.

[91] For example, Estonia is one of the few democratic countries where the criminal sentence registry, as well as information about a person's membership of a political party, is publicly accessible.

[92] V Peep, 'Andmekaitseõigusest andmekaitseasutuse pilguga' (2018) 2 *Juridica* 116, 123. Only wilful, repetitive and serious data protection breaches deserve sanctioning in his opinion. He justifies this position by reference to the study by C Hodges, *Law and Corporate Behaviour: Integrating Theory of Regulation, Enforcement, Compliance and Ethics* (Hart Publishing, 2015).

[93] Since the GDPR came into force, the Estonian Data Protection Authority has applied moderate penalties only in 4–12 cases per year. Andmekaitseinspektsioon, *Aastaraamat 2020* at www.aastaraamat.aki.ee (accessed 18 August 2022).

[94] Olerex, 'Inspektsioon sundis Olerexi lõpetama vestluste salvestamise tanklates' *ERR* (21 December 2021) at www.err.ee/1608442712/inspektsioon-sundis-olerexi-lopetama-vestluste-salvestamise-tanklates (accessed 18 August 2022).

markets, data protection and consumer protection are intertwined, making supervision and enforcement by different regulators complicated,[95] there has been limited discussion about consumer vulnerability in digital markets or data-intense business models in the legal literature or in media.[96] The Estonian Consumer Protection Authority has also not intervened, either under consumer law or under data protection law.

Moreover, Estonian consumers are not particularly concerned about their personal data, at least not in commercial relationships. In a large-scale survey of Estonians' approach to the right to privacy as a human right and everyday technologies in 2014, 41 per cent of respondents were of the opinion that concerns about data protection were exaggerated and 74 per cent agreed with the statement that 'they have nothing to hide'.[97] As Estonia is a peripheral Member State, Estonian consumers are more worried about getting access to products and services available to consumers in the other EU Member States: it is no coincidence that it was Andrus Ansip, the former Estonian Prime Minister and ex-Commissioner for the Digital Single Market, who initiated the Geoblocking[98] and Portability[99] Regulations. And even in the 2019 Eurobarometer study on Europeans' attitude toward cyber security, Estonians were just as concerned about whether they can inspect goods received or ask a real person for advice as they were about the possibility of misuse of their personal data.[100] Therefore, Estonian consumers would benefit from pan-European coordinated enforcement of infringements, as the national authorities lack the necessary resources and there is limited public demand for stricter action.

In court practice, data protection law does not play a role in protecting consumer rights either, with the sole exception of publication of the names of debtors by debt-collection companies. This extensive, stigmatising and uncontrolled practice was criticised in the legal literature already in 2004.[101] And, as has been the case with the general consumer law, the leading role in using data protection law for consumer interests was taken not by the national supervisory authority but by the Estonian Supreme Court,[102] which has used data protection rules to protect indebted consumers against

---

[95] Peep (n 90) 116, 118.

[96] Exceptions are, eg, M Mikiver, 'Kes on tarbija kliendiandmete peremees? Otseturustus krediidiasutuste näitel' (2015) 4 *Juridica* 262; and, more recently, A Daniel, 'Isikuandmete töötlemine nõusoleku alusel. Elisa, Telia ja Tele2 üld- ja andmekaitsetingimuste näide' (2019) 8 *Juridica* 589, 589–602, who shows that in many cases, consents obtained by Estonian telecom operators do not comply with the GDPR requirements.

[97] Estonian Institute of Human Rights, 'The Right to Privacy as a Human Right and Everyday Technologies' (2014) 48–49 at www.eihr.ee/en/privacy-as-a-human-right-and-everyday-technologies (accessed 18 August 2022).

[98] Regulation (EU) 2018/302 of the European Parliament and of the Council on addressing unjustified geo-blocking and other forms of discrimination based on customers' nationality, place of residence or place of establishment within the internal market and amending Regulations (EC) No 2006/2004 and (EU) 2017/2394 and Directive 2009/22/EC [2018] OJ L60I/1.

[99] Regulation (EU) 2017/1128 of the European Parliament and of the Council on cross-border portability of online content services in the internal market [2017] OJ L168/1.

[100] Special Eurobarometer 499: Cyber security, Factsheet Estonia. October 2019.

[101] I Pilving, 'Sugupuud müügiks ja roolijoodikud häbiposti? Isikuandmetega seonduvad piirangud avaliku teabe avaldamisel' (2004) 2 *Juridica* 75, 75ff.

[102] This interesting phenomenon could be associated with the fact that in contrast to most Eastern European countries, Estonia replaced the old communist judiciary at least partially at the beginning of the 1990s. Moreover, already in the 2000s, the first young judges who had studied abroad (mostly in Germany), and who had participated in drafting the new legislation while working in the Ministry of Justice, were appointed as judges in the Supreme Court.

debt-recovery companies that were publicly reporting their (partially non-existing or prescribed) debts.[103] One might therefore say that data protection rules have mainly been used for additional consumer protection in the case of consumer credit and other traditional consumer contracts and – despite Estonia's being a very digital society – not in modern digital transactions.

This might change if the Estonian Government, which is constantly aiming at being a pioneer of digitisation, moves forward with setting up the so-called 'Consent Service'. Namely, Estonia, with its interconnected public registries and a rather relaxed attitude to potential privacy issues, is considering fostering a data-driven economy by allowing data subjects to give access to their personal data (including health data) in these registries to private sector players.[104] The necessary digital environment is already available and the draft law regulating the legal aspects of the service has been out since November 2021. Moreover, the first pilot project, enabling the transfer õof tax authority data to an Estonian credit institution for the purpose of checking a consumer's creditworthiness, commenced in December 2021, even before the law has been adopted.

The Consent Service allows data subjects to tick a box in a governmental digital environment and thereby give consent for access to their personal data in public registries by a business (eg an insurance or a marketing company, or a private-sector medical services provider).[105] Creating such an innovative digital Consent Service raises questions about possible privacy and discrimination risks, especially as far as the re-use of sensitive personal data (health data) is concerned. What if a later deterioration in health leads to the loss of your insurance coverage? Is consent to share your medical data in an e-health portal with an insurance company, given in exchange for a lower insurance premium or cheaper service, even valid under Article 7 GDPR? Can you just sell your personal data, including health data, for money, and should indebted consumers use it as a means to cover their debts? Should a government create a public service that indirectly sets incentives for citizens to sell their personal data, and should it encourage businesses to require more personal data? These questions are not new but become crucial given the potential amount of personal data that could be easily transferred from different public databases to the private sector via such a public service.

IX. Conclusions

Over the last decade, we have observed a transformation of consumer law: it has become increasingly intertwined with and complemented by data protection law. These areas of law share partly similar problems and aims, policy arguments, concepts and solutions. The increasing reliance on the availability of personal data in online trade

---

[103] See the Estonian Supreme Court decisions 3-3-1-70-11, 2-17-1026 and 3-2-1-80-13.
[104] Estonian Information System Authority, Consent Service at www.ria.ee/en/state-information-system/consent-service.html (accessed 18 August 2022).
[105] Riigi Infosüsteemi Amet, Aastaraamat 2020 (2020) 26 at www.ria.ee/sites/default/files/ria_aastaraamat_2020_48lk_est_veeb.pdf (accessed 18 August 2022).

has made consumer law utilise data protection law to compensate for digital consumer vulnerability. We can therefore see that digitalisation has changed the understanding of what exactly consumer law is in its contemporary meaning. Data protection law can act as an additional enabler of consumer law: for example, the breach of information and transparency obligations of data protection law may be targeted by consumer law sanctions. Moreover, consumer protection authorities (and not only data protection authorities) may step in to sanction these breaches. And vice versa: a digital economy based upon data-intensive market practices poses challenges that cannot be resolved by consumer law alone but that need complementary aid from data protection law. For example, data protection principles can be relied upon when establishing fair standards for contractual performance.

The impact of data protection law on consumer protection is clearly more evident in the digital world. However, it would be premature to claim that online consumer law is somehow functionally different from offline consumer law and therefore leading to a split within consumer law. True, consumer law has somewhat different challenges in the online environment, and this has very much to do with the growing commercialisation of personal data, as certain business models are only to be found in the digital economy. Yet the underlying idea of protecting the consumer as a weaker party remains at the core of both online as well as offline consumer law. And while data protection surely plays a major role in protecting the interests of digital consumers/ data subjects, privacy rules can still have an important role in protecting consumers in the offline world, as the Estonian experience with abusive debt collection practices (stigmatising defaulting consumers in an offline environment) shows.

In my view, it would be equally premature to argue that data protection law is making consumer law obsolete or poses a vital threat to it. The discussion in Germany of whether the GDPR precludes consumer associations from pursuing data protection breaches under consumer law rules has been brought to an end by the CJEU in the *Facebook Ireland* case, and the whole issue will become obsolete with the transposition of the Representative Actions Directive. In the *Facebook Fan-page* and *Fashion ID* cases, which have been offered as examples of clashes between data protection and consumer law, the CJEU resolved the issues by using a wide interpretation of the concept of the controller, and did not stress the exclusivity of data protection law nor exclude the possibility of imposing liability via application of consumer law.[106] The possibility of applying the unfair terms rules to data subjects' consent is *expressis verbis* foreseen in the recitals of the GDPR, and the UCPD is used to tackle data protection breaches in practice. Following these tendencies, one could perhaps rather claim that consumer law is influencing – and even reducing – the data protection standards, as we are able to witness the consumerisation of data protection law. The aim of the European legislator to create a European Data Economy will eventually result in nudging consumers to monetise their personal data, and will concentrate the discussions on the question of how to guarantee a fair price for personal data.

---

[106] It is therefore hard to support the position of Svantesson that 'the right of data protection holds a higher position in the hierarchy of rights than does consumer protection' and that 'where consumer protection law imposes duties that go beyond what is catered for under the balance struck in data protection law, consumer protection law has, at least prima facie, overstepped its mandate': Svantesson (n 10) 32–34.

The Estonian experiences illustrate how an aspiration to create innovative digital public services may leave data protection concerns somewhat backstage. Moreover, those digital citizens who are accustomed to enjoying the bureaucracy-free nature of such services are not necessarily aware of or concerned about the protection of their personal data. This has also a historic reason, as Scandinavian-modelled transparency helped to combat corruption after Estonia regained independence at the beginning of the 1990s. Correspondingly, a somewhat relaxed approach to privacy, be it online or offline, is noticeable, and hence the debate about using data protection rules for the protection of consumer interests is only in its infancy. Data protection rules have mainly been used for additional consumer protection in the case of traditional consumer credit contracts and – despite Estonia's being a very digital society – not in modern digital transactions. It is therefore fair to say that the growing interplay of data and consumer protection taking place at the European level is not yet reflected in all Member States.

The interaction and intertwinement of data protection and consumer law show that although data protection rules are not directly aimed at consumers, they are not irrelevant to consumer protection: privacy rules are often protecting the individuals who are acting in their consumer capacity. This is particularly obvious in the online environment: the use of modern technology poses major challenges to consumer-citizen autonomy. The dilemma of private autonomy and the human rights nature of data protection culminates in the discussions over the concept of data-as-counter-performance: it has yet to be seen and heard to predict how it will be possible to reconcile the aim of protecting the interest of consumers to get a fair economic value for their personal data, the wish to facilitate a European data economy and the need to guarantee the right of privacy as a fundamental right.

8

Can Consumer Law Become Sustainable?

EVELYNE TERRYN*

> The significant problems we face cannot be solved at the same level
> of thinking we were at when creating them.
>
> Albert Einstein

I. Introduction

The major challenges for our society, our planet and our species – sustainability and digitisation – are also the major challenges for today's consumer law. Both the green transition and the digital transition put into question what has been regarded by many as a fundamental characteristic of European consumer law: individual autonomy and self-determination, in other words the right to make one's own choices in the market. Today's European consumer law focuses on economic rights and on enabling individual choices, with limited attention to externalities or planetary boundaries. We are currently overshooting those boundaries and risk ecological collapse accompanied by social instability – and consumer law is currently part of the problem.

Consumption choices play an important role in overshooting these boundaries. They have a major impact on global emissions: they are responsible for two-thirds of global greenhouse gas (GhG) emissions.[1] Consumption choices impact not only global emissions, but also biodiversity, land use, water use and availability of resources in general. The flipside of this enormous impact is that changes in consumption choices can also have a major positive effect: such changes have the potential to bring down global

---

* This chapter is current as at December 2022.

[1] D Ivanova et al, 'Quantifying the Potential for Climate Change Mitigation of Consumption Options' (2020) 15 *Environmental Research Letters* 9; See also E Van Gool, '"Climate-washing": B2C communicatie in de klimaatcrisis beoordeeld in het licht van de oneerlijke handelspraktijken, soft law en nieuwe wetgeving' 2023 *Droit de la consommation – Consumentenrecht* 3.

emissions by 40 to 70 per cent by 2050.[2] Water use could be reduced by 50 per cent merely by shifts in dietary patterns,[3] and land use by up to 80 per cent.[4] Furthermore, if we realise that 90 per cent of material used for every person in the EU is wasted to landfill and the air after one-time use,[5] it is clear that there is an enormous potential for changes in the way we consume. What is more, there is not only a need to transform consumption patterns and choices fundamentally – but transformation is also urgent.[6] The decline in biodiversity is only accelerating,[7] and if we want to keep the aim of 1.5°C global warming somewhat within reach, global emissions should already be reduced by almost 45 per cent (compared to 2010) by 2030.[8]

The central thesis in this chapter is that consumer law in its current form is part of the problem instead of part of the solution, and that a fundamental transformation is urgently necessary to make consumer law contribute to sustainability in general and to more sustainable consumption in particular. For consumer law to remain relevant, there is no other option than to become sustainable and to support sustainable consumption and production, as well as to support and enable different, more circular business models. Ideally, consumer law contributes to the creation of a 'safe and just operating space for humanity', in which ecological limits and social goals are balanced (cf Raworth's Doughnut Model[9]).

In section II, this chapter will analyse the role and importance of private autonomy and self-determination in current consumer law (as part of a broader problem of unsustainable private law) and the unsustainable consequences which that entails. Section III will then move on to assess the transformation that is necessary to make consumer law more sustainable. It will also be argued that, given the urgency and the many uncertainties in terms of the optimal regulatory mix to achieve more sustainable consumption, there should be room for national experimentation.

---

[2] Intergovernmental Panel on Climate Change (IPCC), 'Climate Change 2022: Mitigation of Climate Change' (2022) Working Group III: Contribution to the Sixth Assessment Report 2022 at report.ipcc.ch/ar6wg3/pdf/IPCC_AR6_WGIII_PressConferenceSlides.pdf (accessed 22 February 2022).

[3] L Aleksandrowicz et al, 'The Impacts of Dietary Change on Greenhouse Gas Emissions, Land Use, Water Use, and Health: A Systematic Review' (2016) 11 *PLoS ONE* (3 November 2016) doi: 10.1371/journal.pone.0165797.

[4] ibid.

[5] Data for 2014 EU 28, see A Mayer et al, 'Measuring Progress towards a Circular Economy: A Monitoring Framework for Economy-wide Material Loop Closing in the EU28' (2018) 23 *Journal of Industrial Ecology* 62.

[6] Ivanova et al (n 1); M Martin et al, 'Ten New Insights in Climate Science 2022' (2022) 5 *Global Sustainability* 1, 12–13.

[7] The global rate of species extinction is at least tens to hundreds of times higher that it has averaged over the past 10 million years, see IPBES, 'Global assessment report on biodiversity and ecosystem services of the Intergovernmental Science-Policy Platform on Biodiversity and Ecosystem Services' (2019) at https://ipbes.net/global-assessment (accessed 22 February 2023).

[8] See IPCC, 'Summary for policy makers' in V Masson-Delmotte, *Global Warming of 1.5°C: An IPCC Special Report on the Impacts of Global Warming of 1.5°C above Pre-Industrial Levels and Related Global Greenhouse Gas Emission Pathways, in the Context of Strengthening the Global Response to the Threat of Climate Change, Sustainable Development, and Efforts to Eradicate Poverty* (Cambridge University Press, 2018) 3, 12, point C.1.

[9] K Raworth, *Doughnut Economics: Seven Ways to Think Like a 21st Century Economist* (Penguin, 2017).

II. Consumer Law as a Silo with Private Autonomy as a Driving Force – Part of the Larger Problem of Unsustainable Private Law

A. The Emergence of Consumer Law in Parallel with an Unsustainable Consumption Society

Historically, the emergence of consumer law can be linked to the development of a consumer society. Howells, Ramsay and Wilhelmsson call consumer law 'the reflection of the consumer society in the legal sphere': the need for legal rules to protect those who consume was indeed felt more urgently 'when consumption, above the level of what people need just to survive, [became] an important aspect of life in society'.[10] The trend to attach increasing importance to consumption had been ongoing for several centuries,[11] but increasing affluence, the changing nature of the way business is conducted and the massification of consumption – all contributed to adoption of a body of consumer protection rules, mainly from the 1950s onwards.[12]

Consumer protection law in Europe first emerged at national level,[13] in each Member State with its own specifics and nuances. President Kennedy's oft-cited special message to the US Congress in 1962, proclaiming the basic rights of consumers, certainly gave impetus to the rapid growth of consumer legislation from the 1960s and 1970s onwards.[14] Then, from the 1970s on, European institutions started to develop an interest in consumer protection and the first consumer protection programmes followed.[15] The first consumer programme explicitly refers to changed market circumstances, the increased abundance and complexity of goods and services; to the fact that 'the consumer, in the past usually an individual purchaser in a small local market, has become merely a unit in a mass market' and is 'no longer able to properly fulfil the role of a balancing factor'.[16] The first binding instruments, adopted in the 1980s, were mostly minimum harmonisation instruments. From 2000 onwards, the shift to maximum harmonisation in European consumer protection instruments reduced the scope for a national consumer (protection) policy and even abolished it within the harmonised scope (see also section III.B.ii).

---

[10] G Howells, I Ramsay and Th Wilhelmsson, 'Consumer Law in its International Dimension' in G Howells and Th Wilhelmsson (eds), *Handbook of Research in International Consumer Law*, 2nd edn (Edward Elgar Publishing, 2018) 4.

[11] See in general F Trentmann, *Empire of Things: How We Became a World of Consumers, from the Fifteenth Century to the Twenty-First* (HarperCollins, 2016).

[12] Howells, Ramsay and Wilhelmsson (n 10) 4–6.

[13] See in detail on the emergence of consumer law in the EU, H-W Micklitz et al (eds), *The Fathers and Mothers of Consumer Law and Policy in Europe: The Foundational Years 1950–1980* (2019) EUI at https://cadmus.eui.eu/handle/1814/63766 (accessed 22 February 2023).

[14] E Hondius, 'Preface' ibid 10.

[15] Council Resolution of 14 April 1975 on a preliminary programme of the European Economic Community for a consumer protection and information policy [1975] OJ C92/1; Council Resolution of 19 May 1981 on a second programme of the European Economic Community for a consumer protection and information policy [1981] OJ C133/1; see in more detail, L Krämer, 'European Commission' in Micklitz et al (eds) (n 13) 23, 26.

[16] Council Resolution of 14 April 1975 (n 15) 3.

Whereas originally the protection of a weaker consumer was central in many national regimes, the focus in European consumer law came to be on the rational consumer whose right to self-determination (private autonomy) in the market must be guaranteed.[17] This right to self-determination can be understood as the right to make choices in the (internal) market according to one's own preferences,[18] thereby furthering the realisation of the internal market.[19]

This focus on self-determination presupposes a consumer capable of making choices and enjoying the widest possible options to choose from. This individualistic view and focus on private autonomy is not limited to consumer law. It can be linked to a broader focus on private autonomy in private law in general and in contract law specifically, described by De Page as

> [t]he power of individual wills to regulate themselves all the terms and conditions of their commitments, to decide alone, and without legal supervision, the subject matter and scope of their agreements, in brief, to give their contracts the content and object which they consider appropriate and which they are free to choose in complete freedom, guided solely by their own interests and under the sole guarantee of their validly exchanged reciprocal consents.[20]

Thus, EU consumer law could be described as the guardian of the economic rights of the non-professional player in the (internal) market. Private autonomy and contractual freedom should in principle suffice to protect these economic rights and to guarantee a bargain in accordance with one's own preferences. However, consumer law acknowledges that the preconditions for such a bargain might be absent, especially due to information asymmetry between professional and non-professional players.[21] Information was and is therefore used as the main corrective mechanism in EU consumer law;[22] further-reaching intervention – such as by regulating the content of contracts – implies greater intrusion into private autonomy and is therefore only a subsidiary protection mechanism.[23]

---

[17] See also H-W Micklitz, 'Squaring the Circle? Reconciling Consumer Law and the Circular Economy' (2019) 8 *Journal of European Consumer and Market Law* 229, pointing out that the protective element faded into the background when the EU took over consumer policy in the aftermath of the Single European Act [1987] OJ L169/1.

[18] See, on the omnipresent risk of manipulation of such interests and preferences, C Sunstein, 'Fifty Shades of Manipulation' (2016) 213 *Journal of Marketing Behavior* 32.

[19] Most EU consumer legislation indeed tends to be based on internal market justifications, see Howells, Ramsay and Wilhelmsson (n 10) 9. See also the legal basis used for most directives, Art 114 of the Treaty on the Functioning of the European Union (TFEU, Consolidated version of the Treaty on European Union [2012] OJ C326/13) rather than Art 169 TFEU.

[20] H De Page and R Dekkers, *Traité élémentaire de droit civil, T. II., Les obligations (première part)* (Bruylant, 1964) 437. See also Bourgoignie, linking the individual approach to consumer law to a contractualist approach to a society based on the free choice of consumers whether or not to fulfil their needs and on equality of contractual partners, T Bourgoignie, *Éléments pour une théorie du droit de la consommation: au regard des développements du droit belge et du droit de la Communauté économique européenne* (Librairie Générale de Droit et de Jurisprudence, 1988) 35.

[21] U Mattei and A Quarta, *The Turning Point in Private Law* (Elgar Edward Publishing, 2019) 95.

[22] See, eg, on the information paradigm that plays a central role in EU consumer policy, N Reich and H-W Micklitz, 'Economic Law, Consumer Interests and EU Integration' in N Reich et al (eds), *European Consumer Law* (Intersentia, 2014) 1, 21; S Weatherill, *EU Consumer Law and Policy* (Edward Elgar Publishing, 2013) ch 4.

[23] In this sense, J Drexl, *Die wirtschaftliche Selbstbestimmung des Verbrauchers* (Mohr Siebeck, 1998).

Consumer law in recent decades seems to have neatly inscribed itself in what Habermas called the 'colonisation of the lifeworld',[24] in an instrumental and commodity logic, and has reduced the human/citizen to a consumer with only economic rights. Moreover, the market in which this citizen-consumer makes choices has often been narrowed down to a linear relationship with a direct contract partner, in which the consumer plays a passive role. Pitlo has called this 'the invention of the consumer', a legal fiction of an economic agent, endowed with a system of preferences and a capacity to choose.[25]

Plenty of examples illustrate this narrow view. These examples emerge not only from the legal instruments themselves, but also from the way these instruments are interpreted, as will be illustrated in section III.A. Thus the Consumer Rights Directive – which, inter alia, regulates distance contracts – focuses on the relationship between trader and consumer, stating:

> The harmonisation of certain aspects of consumer distance and off-premises contracts is necessary for the promotion of a real consumer internal market striking the right balance between a high level of consumer protection and he competitiveness of enterprises, while ensuring respect for the principle of subsidiarity.[26]

The only interests in the balance are those of consumers, on the one hand, and, on the other, the competitiveness of enterprises. The Directive itself seems to leave limited scope for other interests to be taken into account.[27] The Unfair Consumer Practices Directive (UCPD) seems even clearer: its aim is to harmonise national (trade practices) legislation that protects the economic interests of consumers.[28] The Directive does 'not cover national rules intended to protect interests which are not of an economic nature'.[29]

Consumer law furthermore not only focuses on the citizen-consumer with only economic rights, but also sees that same citizen-consumer in a passive role. Consumer law has clearly been developed with the then (and still) dominant make-use-dispose industry in mind.[30] The consumer is considered as the final stage and the passive link in

---

[24] See on Habermas' theory, inter alia, F Silva, 'Colonization of the Lifeworld' in A Allen and E Mendieta (eds), *The Cambridge Habermas Lexicon* (29 March 2019) doi:10.1017/9781316771303.012, 36.

[25] L Pinto, *L'invention du consommateur: Sur la légitimité du marché* (Presses Universitaires de France, 2018) 202.

[26] Directive 2011/83/EU of the European Parliament and of the Council of 25 October 2011 on consumer rights, amending Council Directive 93/13/EEC and Directive 1999/44/EC of the European Parliament and of the Council and repealing Council Directive 85/577/EEC and Directive 97/7/EC of the European Parliament and of the Council [2011] OJ L304/64, recital 4.

[27] See – already 30 years ago – for criticism on the (lack of) interrelation between consumer policy and environmental policy, L Krämer, 'On the Interrelation between Consumer and Environmental Policies in the European Community' (1993) 16 *Journal of Consumer Policy* 455.

[28] Directive 2005/29/EC of the European Parliament and of the Council of 11 May 2005 concerning unfair business-to-consumer commercial practices in the internal market and amending Council Directive 84/450/EEC, Directives 97/7/EC, 98/27/EC and 2002/65/EC of the European Parliament and of the Council and Regulation (EC) No 2006/2004 of the European Parliament and of the Council ('Unfair Commercial Practices Directive') (UCPD) [2005] OJ L149/22, Art 1.

[29] See UCDP Guidance 2021, point 1.1.1 at https://ec.europa.eu/info/sites/default/files/c_2021_9320_1_ucpd-guidance_en.pdf (accessed 22 February 2023).

[30] See also E Van Gool, *Product Liability in Circular, Collaborative and Functional Economy: A Comparative and Economic Study of Liability for Alternative Consumer Good Distribution and Production Methods* (PhD dissertation, Katholieke Universiteit Leuven, forthcoming 2023).

a process of 'consumption' or even destruction[31] of a good or service after a short period of exclusive and often non-intensive use.[32] This is clear from the personal scope of application of consumer law that is limited to B2C transactions – with professionals on the one side and passive non-professionals on the other. Industrialisation and the massification of production also reduced the role of the consumer to a passive one. Van Gool rightly points out that consumer law is not well adapted to the taking up of a more active role by the consumer (once more). He points out that – as was the case before industrialisation and mass consumption – in recent more sustainable business models, consumers also often do take up additional and more active roles. They resell their goods instead of discarding them; potentially after they have repaired or refurbished them, they may even be involved in production (for instance, of electricity) or share/borrow/lease their goods.[33] Current consumer law struggles with the qualification of consumers/prosumers engaging in a more active role. Consumer law has problems in qualifying such active consumers and hardly provides any protection where consumers leave the traditional linear buy-use-discard model.[34]

Consumer law has thus provided an extreme simplification of reality and abstracted consumption and consumer transactions from the underlying ecosystem, which is highly problematic, as is discussed in section II.B.

B. The Dangers of Consumer Law Operating in Isolation

For some decades this extreme simplification of reality seemed to work: consumer law could limit itself to merely weighing the interests of individual consumers and traders and thus try to find a 'balance'. This focus on economic rights and on the individual interests of consumers allowed consumer law to operate 'in splendid isolation' from what precedes consumption – such as the working conditions and environmental conditions in which goods are produced and transported – and in 'splendid isolation' from what comes after consumption or after the exercise of a consumer right. Consumers do not need to see how their clothes or meat are produced – nor what happens after withdrawal or if goods are thrown 'away' after use. They are 'freed from the guilt' of remembering the work and natural resources that went into their products.[35] 'The traces of production' are removed from the product.[36] After all, to deal with these aspects, other branches of law exist: social law, international law, environmental law, waste regulation …

Consumer law in particular and private law in general deal primarily with individual interests and individual consumer satisfaction, seemingly leaving little room

---

[31] cf also the Latin '*consumere*' (to use up).

[32] V Packard, *The Waste Makers* (McKay, 1960) 306; Van Gool (n 30).

[33] Think of systems such as Peerby (peer-to-peer borrowing facilitated by a platform) at www.peerby.com.

[34] See, on the lack of protection in the event that consumers choose 'product as a service', B Keirsbilck, E Terryn and E Van Gool, 'Consumentenbescherming bij 'servitization' en product-dienst-systemen (PSS)' (2019) 56 *Tijdschrift voor Privaatrecht* 817.

[35] Th Wilhelmsson, 'Consumer Law and the Environment: From Consumer to Citizen' (1998) 21 *Journal of Consumer Policy* 45, 48.

[36] ibid; F Jameson, *Postmodernism or the Cultural Logic of Late Capitalism* (Verso, 1991).

for other and collective interests.[37] Systemic concern for labour exploitation, for the environment, animal welfare ..., is left out of (current) consumer law.[38]

A brief look at the (extensive) information requirements of the Consumer Rights Directive provides sufficient illustration. Information that allows consumers to determine the ecological impact of the good or service they are acquiring is mostly missing.[39] The Directive does require information to be provided on the 'main characteristics' of a good or service and on delivery and the time of delivery. However, that is not sufficient to allow a consumer buying online to determine the ecological impact of their purchase.[40] This also requires information on means of transport used, 'last mile' delivery, packaging, whether or not deliveries are split and the like. An explicit obligation to inform the consumer about the expected lifetime or repairability of goods (including the availability of spare parts) is also currently lacking at the EU level,[41] although this might change as a result of one of the new legislative proposals discussed in section III.B.

More fundamentally, consumers have stopped seeing how every product used or consumed ultimately comes from nature, and how consumption forms part of and impacts a system that is closed, finite and fragile.[42] Not only consumption, but also consumer law and private law more generally have been detached and abstracted from the underlying, fragile ecosystem.[43] In the (sub)urban existence where most (Western) consumers live, it is particularly easy to forget that our comfortable lives are inextricably linked to the health and vitality of natural habitats, Seibert argues.[44]

Unfortunately, the rather dramatic consequences of this silo thinking and of the artificial divide between culture and nature are now becoming clear, even in Europe. Van Reybrouck has called our behaviour the colonisation of the future:[45]

> Colonialism is not just something of the past. We are today colonising the future. And today we are occupying future decades with the same brutality and recklessness with which other continents and continents were taken in previous centuries. As if there were nothing there in the future, as if there were no one living there, as if it were ours. As if we can just go our own way. We can exploit it, exhaust it, use it. We can rob our children and grandchildren in it and even restrict their freedom or condition their health.[46]

---

[37] See, with regard to private law, V Ulfbeck and O Hansen, 'Sustainability Clauses in an Unsustainable Contract Law?' (2020) 16 *European Review of Contract Law* 182, 182–205.

[38] See Mattei and Quarta (n 21) 95.

[39] See in more detail E Terryn and E Van Gool, 'The Role of European Consumer Contract Law in Shaping the Environmental Impact of E-commerce' (2021) 10 *Journal of European Consumer and Market Law* 89.

[40] ibid.

[41] Unless current information obligations are interpreted extensively, see E Van Gool, 'De nieuwe richtlijn consumentenkoop en duurzame consumptie' in I Claeys and E Terryn (eds), *Nieuw recht inzake koop & digitale inhoud en diensten* (Intersentia, 2020) 331; T Brönneke, 'Premature Obsolescence: Suggestions for Legislative Counter-Measures in German and European Sales & Consumer Law' (2017) *Journal of European Environmental and Planning Law* 368.

[42] See D Attenborough, *A Life on our Planet* (Ebury Publishing, 2020), who describes how the first trip to the Moon mainly revealed the fragility and finite nature of Earth.

[43] N Graham, 'Teaching Private Law in a Climate Crisis' (2021) 3 *The University of Queensland Law Journal* 403.

[44] M Seibert, 'Systems Thinking and How It Can Help Build a Sustainable World: A Beginning Conversation' (2018) *The Solutions Journal* at mahb.stanford.edu/blog/systems-thinking-can-help-build-sustainable-world-beginning-conversation (accessed 1 February 2023).

[45] D Van Reybrouck, *De kolonisatie van de toekomst* (De Bezige Bij, 2022) 15.

[46] ibid 16 (own translation).

That 'future' is furthermore much closer than some might have expected.[47] We are experiencing wildfires,[48] droughts and flooding in unprecedented forms. We are already facing adaptation limits.[49] Adaptation and the required changes will only become more radical and difficult as we approach 1.5°C or even 2°C of mean global warming.[50]

As mentioned, consumption choices make a difference in this process. They are responsible for two-thirds of global GhG emissions[51] whereas – as mentioned – changes in demand for goods and services can reduce global emissions by 40 to 70 per cent by 2050.[52] And although it is also clear that changes in individual consumption behaviour will not be sufficient, systems thinking implies that consumption (and consumer law) is also tackled. A consumer law (and private law more generally) that focuses exclusively on individual interests and fails to see how consumption is inextricably part of a larger system is simply not tenable.[53] Silo thinking is indeed not without danger:

> The great ecological issues of our time have to do in one way or another with our failure to see things in their entirety. That failure occurs when minds are taught to think in boxes and not taught to transcend those boxes or to question overly much how they fit with other boxes.[54]

III. Towards a Sustainable Consumer Law?

A shift in thinking and transformation seems to have been occurring over recent years – a shift that is accelerating. The lack of interrelation between consumer law and environmental law was already under criticism decades ago,[55] and legal research has tried to propose ways to reconcile consumer law (or private law more generally) and (ecological) sustainability and to 'recalibrate' consumer law. Some contributions focus on specific aspects such as e-commerce,[56] remedies in sales contracts,[57] repair[58] and planned

---

[47] ibid.

[48] In increasing numbers, see Martin et al (n 6) 4; IPCC, 'Climate Change 2022: Impacts, Adaptation and Vulnerabilities' (2022) Working Group II: Contribution to the Sixth Assessment Report 2022 11, ch 18 at www.iau-hesd.net/sites/default/files/documents/ipcc_ar6_wgii_summaryforpolicymakers.pdf? (accessed 1 March 2023); M Jones et al, 'Global and Regional Trends and Drivers of Fire under Climate Change' (2022) 60 *Reviews of Geophysics* 1, 1–76.

[49] Martin et al (n 6) 4; IPCC, 'Climate Change 2022: Impacts, Adaptation and Vulnerabilities' (n 48) ch 18.

[50] Martin et al (n 6) 4.

[51] Ivanova et al (n 1); Van Gool (n 1).

[52] IPCC 'Climate Change 2022: Mitigation of Climate Change' (n 2).

[53] See also Graham (n 43) 403; see especially Mattei and Quarta (n 21) 170.

[54] D Orr, *Earth in Mind: On Education, Environment and the Human Prospect* (Island Press, 2004) 94–95.

[55] Wilhelmsson (n 35) 45–70; K Tonner, 'Consumer Protection and Environmental Protection: Contradictions and Suggested Steps Towards Integration' (2000) 23 *Journal of Consumer Policy* 63, 63–78. Both authors also formulate suggestions to reconcile consumer law and environmental protection.

[56] H-W Micklitz et al, *Onlinehandel im Spannungsfeld von Verbraucherschutz und Nachhaltigkeit* (English trans: *E-commerce and the Tradeoff between Consumer Protection and Sustainability*) (Publications of the Advisory Council for Consumer Affairs (Sachverständigenrat für Verbraucherfragen, SVRV), 2020) 52; Terryn and Van Gool (n 39).

[57] E Van Gool and A Michel, 'The New Consumer Sales Directive 2019/771 and Sustainable Consumption: A Critical Analysis' (2021) 10 *Journal of European Consumer and Market Law* 136.

[58] H-W Micklitz et al, 'Recht auf Reparatur: Publications of the Advisory Council for Consumer Affairs' (Sachverständigenrat für Verbraucherfragen, 2022) 68 at https://reuse-verein.org/fileadmin/user_upload/documents/Berichte/SVRV_Policy-Brief_Recht-auf-Reparatur_2022.pdf (accessed 13 June 2023); E Kieninger, 'Recht auf Reparatur ("Right to Repair") und Europäisches Vertragsrecht' (2020) *Zeitschrift für Europäisches*

obsolescence.[59] Other contributions have been taking a more general approach.[60] Consumer organisations are also increasingly paying attention to (ecological) sustainability. Actions and position papers are adopted pleading for clearer information on more sustainable choices:[61] against greenwashing,[62] against planned obsolescence[63] and for a right to repair, albeit at times somewhat hesitant when more sustainability implies less consumer choice.[64]

As far as concerns new EU legislation, quite a number of initiatives are on the table. However, this chapter argues that more could already be done, as there are missed opportunities in the interpretation of the consumer *acquis*. With regard to reform of consumer law, the proposals do not seem sufficient: a more fundamental transformation seems needed. Moreover, given the urgency and the many uncertainties about the optimal regulatory mix to achieve more sustainable consumption, it is argued that there should be room for national experimentation.

A. Current Consumer Law – A More Sustainable Interpretation of the Consumer Acquis

European consumer law could already be interpreted (more) sustainably by both the Court of Justice of the European Union (CJEU) and national courts than is currently

---

Privatrecht 264, 264–78; E Terryn, 'A Right to Repair? Towards Sustainable Remedies in Consumer Law' (1 August 2019) *European Review of Private Law* 851.

[59] A Michel, *Premature Obsolescence: In Search of an Improved Legal Framework* (PhD dissertation, Katholieke Universiteit Leuven, 2022) 573.

[60] See, eg, I Back and EM Kieninger, 'Ökologische Analyse des Zivilrechts' (2021) 22 *JuristenZeitung* 1088, 1088–98; A Halfmeier, 'Nachhaltiges privatrecht' (2016) 5 *Archiv für die civilistische Praxis* 717; CMDS Pavillon, 'Herijking van consumentencontractenrecht: duurzaamheid als nieuw ijkpunt?' in CMDS Pavillon and WH van Boom, *Privaatrechtelijke bescherming herijkt* (Uitgebracht voor de Vereniging voor Burgerlijk Recht, 2021) 11.

[61] See, eg, BEUC, 'Position paper: Proposal on Empowering Consumers for the Green Transition' (2022) BEUC-X-2022-105 at BEUC-X-2022-105_Empowering_consumers_for_the_green_transition.pdf (accessed 23 February 2023); BEUC, 'Durable and repairable products: Changes needed for a successful path towards the green transition' (2021) BEUC-X-2021-061 at www.beuc.eu/sites/default/files/publications/ beuc-x-2021-061_durable_and_repairable_products_beuc_position_paper.pdf (accessed 23 February 2023); BEUC and ANEC, 'Making more sustainable products the new normal. Consumer recommendations for a meaningful EU Sustainable Product Initiative' (2021) BEUC-X-2021-075 at www.beuc.eu/sites/default/ files/publications/beuc-x-2021-075_making_more_sustainable_products_the_new_normal.pdf (accessed 23 February 2023).

[62] See, eg BEUC, 'Getting rid of green washing: Restoring consumer confidence in green claims' (2020) BEUC-X-2020-116 at www.beuc.eu/sites/default/files/publications/beuc-x-2020-116_getting_rid_of_green_washing. pdf (accessed 23 February 2023).

[63] See, eg the action brought by UFC *Que choisir* against Nintendo in September 2020, 'Nintendo Switch: L'UFC-Que Choisir dénonce l'obsolescence programmée des manettes Joy-Con' *Que choisir* (22 February 2020) at www.quechoisir.org/nos-combats-switch-nintendo-l-ufc-que-choisir-denonce-l- obsolescence-programmee-des-manettes-joy-cons-n72823/ (accessed 23 February 2023), and the Europe-wide complaint launched by BEUC in January 2022 against Nintendo for premature obsolescence, BEUC, 'Press Release: BEUC launches Europe-wide complaint against Nintendo for premature obsolescence' (2021) BEUC-PR-2021-002 at www.beuc.eu/sites/default/files/publications/beuc-pr-2021-002_beuc_launches_europe- wide_complaint_against_nintendo_for_premature_obsolescence.pdf (accessed 23 February 2023).

[64] See, eg, the position paper on the right to repair, where BEUC pleads in favour of maintaining the right of the consumer to choose between repair and replacement, BEUC, 'Sustainable consumption of goods –

the case.[65] The current balancing exercise – mainly limited to weighing the interests of traders against the interests of consumers – confirms the prevalence of silo thinking and leads to problematic outcomes, as the *Slewo* case illustrates.[66]

Slewo concerned the right of withdrawal in distance contracts and, more specifically, the exception to the right of withdrawal for 'sealed goods which are not suitable for return due to health protection or hygiene reasons and were unsealed after delivery'.[67] The CJEU held that that exception did not apply to mattresses from which the protective film had been removed by the consumer. According to the Court, this did not make the mattress definitely unsuitable for being used or sold again. The existence of a market for second-hand mattresses and the fact that the same mattress is used by multiple guests in a hotel were invoked to sustain this argument; in addition, the analogy was drawn with a garment: garments can also come into contact with the human body when tried on and may be returned.[68] The Court reached this decision taking account 'not only of the wording of that provision but also its context and the objective pursued by the rules of which it forms part'.[69] Due regard was paid to the aim of consumer protection,[70] and that aim was balanced against the competitiveness of enterprises, as followed from recital 4 of the Consumer Rights Directive. Environmental concerns – depreciation of the good, the impact on resources and the like – were not taken into account, although this could have tilted the balance, as argued below.

At national level, the cases in which replacement of a defective good with a refurbished good was deemed prohibited under the Consumer Sales Directive may be referred to.[71] Environmental/sustainable development arguments were not taken into account at all in these cases, although this could arguably have tilted the balance and led to a different interpretation. The question is then of course whether EU law allows a more sustainable interpretation of consumer law. This first requires the availability of some room for interpretation – cf the maxim *interpretatio cessat in claris* – as changing the meaning of a clear and precise EU law provision would be contrary to the principles of legal certainty and the principle of inter-institutional balance (cf Article 13(2) TEU).[72]

Promoting the right to repair and reuse: Accompanying paper to BEUC response to the public consultation' (2022) BEUC-X-2022-034 4 at beuc-x-2022-034_public_consultation_on_right_to_repair.pdf (accessed 23 February 2023).

[65] See in general on the methods of interpretation in EU Law, N Fennelly, 'Legal Interpretation at the European Court of Justice' (1996) 20 *Fordham International Law Journal* 656; J Bengoetxea, N MacCormick and L Moral Soriano, 'Integration and Integrity in the Legal Reasoning of the European Court of Justice' in G de Búrca and JHH Weiler (eds), *The European Court of Justice, Collected Courses of the Academy of European Law* (Oxford University Press, 2001) 43; M Poiares Maduro, 'Interpreting European Law: Judicial Adjudication in the Context of Constitutional Pluralism' (2007) 1 *European Journal of Legal Studies* 1; G Conway, *The Limits of Legal Reasoning and the European Court of Justice* (Cambridge University Press, 2012).

[66] Case C-681/1727 *Slewo* ECLI:EU:C:2019:255.

[67] Consumer Rights Directive (n 26) Art 16(e).

[68] *Slewo* (n 66) paras 42–45.

[69] ibid para 31, with reference to Case C-485/17 *Verbraucherzentrale Berlin* ECLI:EU:C:2018:642, para 27 and Case C-332/17 *Starman* ECLI:EU:C:2018:721, para 23.

[70] Consumer Rights Directive (n 26) Art 1(32), read in the light of recitals 3, 4 and 7 TFEU and Charter of Fundamental Rights of the European Union (CFEU) [2016] OJ C202/389, Art 169 and Art 38.

[71] See, eg, Court of Amsterdam of 18 April 2017, ECLI:NL:RBAMS:2017:2519, the consumer is entitled to a new replacement good in the event of a lack of conformity. The different impact on resource use and waste generation of a replacement by a refurbished good instead of a new good was not taken into consideration.

[72] Consolidated version of the Treaty on European Union [2016] OJ C202/53; K Lenaerts and JA Gutiérrez-Fons, 'To Say What the Law of the EU Is: Methods of Interpretation and the European Court

However, many provisions in consumer law are open to different interpretations in one or more languages, or are open-textured. The different methods of interpretation applied by the EU courts in such cases do allow sustainability objectives to be taken into account when interpreting both Treaty provisions and secondary legislation. Both the 'contextual' method and the 'teleological' method play an important role in the interpretation of EU law (and they are often interlinked).[73] Contextual interpretation implies that a provision of EU law is placed in its context and interpreted in the light of the provisions of EU law as a whole, 'regard being had to the objectives thereof and to its state of evolution at the date on which the provision in question is to be applied'.[74] Environmental protection definitely belongs to the normative system within which EU laws (and national implementing provisions) are to be interpreted, and indeed this is one of the objectives of the EU.

Article 37 of the Charter is also relevant in this regard. It requires a high level of environmental protection and improvement of the quality of the environment to be integrated into the policies of the Union and ensured in accordance with the principle of sustainable development.[75] Both primary[76] and secondary EU law[77] must be interpreted in light of the Charter. Furthermore, sustainable development, a high level of protection and improvement of the quality of the environment are also clear objectives of the EU, as stems from Article 3(3) TEU[78] and Article 11 TFEU,[79] on which Article 37 of the Charter is (amongst others) based. In *ADBHU*, the Court held that environmental protection is one of the essential objectives of the EU.[80]

---

of Justice' (2013) EUI Working Papers, AEL 2013/9 7 at https://cadmus.eui.eu/bitstream/handle/1814/28339/AEL_2013_09_DL.pdf?sequence=1&isAllowed=y (accessed 23 February 2023).

[73] ibid 25.

[74] cf Case C-283/81 *CILFIT v Ministero della Sanità* ECLI:EU:C:1982:335, [1982] ECR 3415, para 20 (with regard to the role of a national judge when interpreting EU law).

[75] The explanations – which shall be given due regard by the Courts of the Union and the Member States (cf CFEU (n 70) Art 52) – furthermore clarify that 'The principles set out in this Article [37] have been based on Articles 2, 6 and 174 of the EC Treaty, which have now been replaced by Article 3(3) of the Treaty on European Union and Articles 11 and 191 of the Treaty on the Functioning of the European Union. It also draws on the provisions of some national constitutions.'

[76] With this proviso, namely, that an interpretation of the Treaties in light of the Charter cannot amount to a modification via judicial interpretation; see K Lenaerts and JA Guttiérez-Fons, 'The Place of the Charter in the EU Constitutional Edifice' in St Peers et al, *The EU Charter of Fundamental Rights. A Commentary* (Bloomsbury Publishing, 2014) 1572.

[77] ibid 1575.

[78] Art 3(3) TEU provides:

> The Union shall establish an internal market. It shall work for the sustainable development of Europe based on balanced economic growth and price stability, a highly competitive social market economy, aiming at full employment and social progress, and a high level of protection and improvement of the quality of the environment. It shall promote scientific and technological advance.
>
> It shall combat social exclusion and discrimination, and shall promote social justice and protection, equality between women and men, solidarity between generations and protection of the rights of the child.
>
> It shall promote economic, social and territorial cohesion, and solidarity among Member States.
>
> It shall respect its rich cultural and linguistic diversity, and shall ensure that Europe's cultural heritage is safeguarded and enhanced.

[79] Art 11 TFEU provides 'Environmental protection requirements must be integrated into the definition and implementation of the Union's policies and activities, in particular with a view to promoting sustainable development.'

[80] Case C-240/83 *Procureur de la République v Association de défense des brûleurs d'huiles usagées (ADBHU)* ECLI:EU:C:1985:59, para 13.

A much greater role should in any event be accorded to the integration obligation set out in Article 11 TFEU.[81] This requires integration of the 'environmental protection requirements' in Union policies and activities 'in particular with a view to promoting sustainable development'.[82] This did not happen in the aforementioned CJEU case, in which the Court only considers the objectives that are explicitly mentioned in applicable secondary legislation. The broader objectives of EU law are not taken into consideration, nor is any attempt made to balance the interests of consumers and traders with environmental protection requirements. Wasmeier pointed out earlier that this is contrary to what Article 11 TFEU requires:

> An analysis of the teleology of a certain provision must relate to the whole context, and not only to a single element taken in isolation. Consequently, not only the effet utile for a specific purpose (for instance, free movement of goods or harmonisation of tax rates), but also the effect on the environment must be taken into account.[83]

Taking Article 11 TFEU seriously requires the Court to focus

> to a greater extent and also ex officio … on what the objective of sustainable development and the reference thereto in Article 11 TFEU entails with regard to a duty to integrate environmental protection in all EU law areas – also in areas where environmental concerns traditionally have not been even considered.[84]

The integration obligation entails that environmental protection requirements be taken into account whenever Union law is applied and interpreted,[85] so that EU 'law should basically be interpreted in a way that renders it consistent with environmental protection requirements'.[86]

In this regard it is also interesting to see that the Explanatory Memorandum to the latest proposal to revise both the UCPD and the Consumer Rights Directive (see section III.B)[87] now explicitly mentions that the proposal respects not only Article 38 (a high level of consumer protection) and Article 16 (freedom to conduct a business), but also Article 37 of the Charter (a high level of environmental protection). Although the *travaux préparatoires* play a more limited role compared to the other methods of

---

[81] B Sjafjell and A Wiesbrock (eds), *The Greening of European Business under EU Law: Taking Article 11 TFEU Seriously* (Routledge, 2015); M Wasmeier, 'The Integration of Environmental Protection as a General Rule for Interpreting Community Law' (2001) 38 *CML Rev* 159.

[82] See B Sjafjell, 'The Environmental Integration Principle: A Necessary Step Towards Policy Coherence for Sustainability' in F Ippolito, M Eugenia Bartolino and M Condinanzi (eds), *The EU and the Proliferation of Integration Principles under the Lisbon Treaty* (Routledge, 2019) ch 6.

[83] Wasmeier (n 81) 166.

[84] See Sjafjell (n 82) 114; in a similar sense J Nowag, 'The Sky is the Limit: On the Drafting of Article 11 TFEU's Integration Obligations and its Intended Reach' in B Sjåfjell and A Wiesbrock, *The Greening of European Business under EU Law: Taking Article 11 TFEU Seriously* (Routledge, 2015) ch 2.

[85] Nowag (n 84).

[86] AM Weidemann, *Die Bedeutung der Querschnittsklauseln für die Kompetenzen innerhalb der Europäischen Gemeinschaft: Eine Untersuchung aus deutscher Sicht* (Lang, 2009) 161–62; Wasmeier (n 81) 159, 'in the interpretation of Community legislation, preference should be given to the interpretation that renders the relevant provision consistent with the principle of integration, ie with environmental protection requirements'.

[87] European Commission, 'Proposal for a directive amending Directives 2005/29/EC and 2011/83/EU as regards empowering consumers for the green transition through better protection against unfair practices and better information' COM (2022) 143 final.

interpretation,[88] such an explicit reference can only provide additional arguments for an environmentally friendly interpretation.

Such ecological interpretation or an interpretation in accordance with Article 11 TFEU could indeed have tilted the balance in the previous cases, with *Slewo* as the most clear-cut of these.[89] If environmental protection requirements had been taken into account in the balancing exercise, the balance in *Slewo* should have tipped in the direction of no right of withdrawal. If a good can no longer be sold as new after withdrawal then not only the cost for traders (that is eventually passed on to all their consumers) is high, but also the ecological impact of withdrawal. The limited benefit of maintaining such a right of withdrawal for the consumer – consisting concretely in the possibility to test a mattress without protective film – does not outweigh the disadvantage that it renders the mattress a second-hand good and leads to its depreciation. Refusing the right to withdraw to a consumer who removed the protective film does not deprive them of the right to test the good – only of the right to test the good without its protective film. That might create a small inconvenience, but it is hard to see how this outweighs the environmental impact due to depreciation of the good.

A sustainable (re)interpretation of consumer law can of course only be a small part of the solution[90] – in the first place because this already presupposes that provisions are open to interpretation[91] – but is nevertheless a step that also needs to be taken in order for consumer law to become part of the solution instead of part of the problem. However, legislative action will also be necessary – a step that is considered in sections III.B and III.C.

B. Initiatives at EU Level

Legislative action in order to make consumer law more sustainable is definitely being considered and the green transition is now high on the EU agenda. The first circular economy action plan was adopted in 2015,[92] followed in 2020 by a new circular economy action plan[93] as one of the main building blocks of the European Green Deal.[94] This plan comprises several legislative proposals and other initiatives to establish a strong and coherent product policy framework that should make 'sustainable products, services and business models the norm and transform consumption patterns so that

---

[88] Lenaerts and Gutiérrez-Fons (n 72) 24, who point to a tendency towards the increasing importance of the *travaux préparatoires*, albeit their lesser importance compared with other methods of interpretation (including contextual and teleological interpretation).

[89] *Slewo* (n 66).

[90] cf similarly Mattei and Quarta, who have pleaded for a transformation of private law, including contract law. They plead for a transformation of contractual justice into systemic ecological justice, which is necessary to take into account the needs both of future generations and of non-human species. Mattei and Quarta (n 21) 109.

[91] cf *interpretatio cessat in claris*.

[92] European Commission, 'Communication: Closing the Loop – An EU Action Plan for the Circular Economy' COM (2015) 614.

[93] European Commission, 'Communication: A New Circular Economy Action Plan for a Cleaner and More Competitive Europe' COM (2020) 98 final.

[94] European Commission, 'Communication: The European Green Deal' COM (2019) 640 final.

no waste is produced in the first place'.[95] Several initiatives are relevant for consumer law. Furthermore, the New Consumer Agenda of 2020 fits into and complements both the Green Deal and the Circular Economy Action Plan. That agenda also identifies the green transition as one of the key priorities. The list following is not exhaustive, but some of the main initiatives merit mentioning as they indicate the direction in which EU consumer law is transforming. Moreover, the initiatives, which cover all phases in the life of a consumer product, also illustrate that life-cycle thinking is taking greater prominence at EU level:

- At the *design/production stage*, there is first and foremost the Sustainable Products Initiative.[96] This proposed regulation aims to replace the Ecodesign Directive,[97] which focuses on energy-related products, and proposes a framework for the adoption of implementing regulations that should make new products placed on the EU market more sustainable. The scope of application of the original Ecodesign Directive would be substantially broadened so as to encompass a broader range of products (beyond energy-related products). It would also include additional criteria on durability, reusability, repairability and recyclability, and no longer mainly focus on energy efficiency.[98] This Initiative also introduces a 'digital product passport' that should help consumers make informed choices, and enable economic operators and other actors in the value chain (such as repair services or recycling centres) to process a product sustainably.[99]

- At the *marketing/pre-contractual stage*, there is the Initiative on strengthening the role of consumers in the green transition.[100] This Initiative aims to stimulate and allow the consumer to play a role in the transition to a more sustainable economy, mainly through changes in information requirements. The proposed changes (for instance, to the Consumer Rights Directive and the UCPD) should ensure that consumers receive reliable information on environmental characteristics, such as lifespan; a commercial guarantee of durability; and repair options. Additional black-listed practices are considered in the UCPD to tackle greenwashing and some specific forms of product obsolescence. A minimum set of requirements is considered for sustainability logos and claims. The Initiative on 'substantiating green claims' aims to provide an additional tool in the fight against greenwashing.[101] This Initiative could lead to EU legislation that requires companies making environmental claims

[95] cf European Commission (n 93) 3.
[96] European Commission, 'Proposal for a Regulation of the European Parliament and of the Council establishing a framework for the establishment of Ecodesign requirements for sustainable products and repealing Directive 2009/125/EC' COM (2022) 142 final ('SPI').
[97] Directive 2009/125/EC of the European Parliament and of the Council of 21 October 2009 establishing a framework for the setting of ecodesign requirements for energy-related products (recast) [2009] OJ L285/10.
[98] See, for more detailed comments, B Keirsbilck and E Terryn, 'Duurzaamheid en consumentenrecht' in G Croissant and A Van Hoe (eds), *Recht en duurzaamheid* (Larcier, 2022) 433.
[99] SPI (n 96) recital 26 and Art 8(3).
[100] See European Commission, 'Proposal for a directive amending Directives 2005/29/EC and 2011/83/EU as regards empowering consumers for the green transition through better protection against unfair practices and better information' (n 87).
[101] See at https://ec.europa.eu/info/law/better-regulation/have-your-say/initiatives/12511-Environmental-performance-of-products-businesses-substantiating-claims_en (accessed 3 February 2023).

to substantiate them via the Environmental Footprint methods. When Product Environmental Footprint Category Rules or Organisation Environmental Footprint Sector Rules have been adopted, green claims should be substantiated on that basis. When no such rules exist, claims could be substantiated via a study compliant with the PEF/OEF method.[102]

- At the *use stage*, the Initiative on Sustainable Consumption of Goods – promoting repair and reuse[103] – aims to introduce a 'right to repair' and to stimulate consumers to buy more second-hand and refurbished goods. Different options were formulated for public consultation, including a revision of the quite recently adopted Consumer Sales Directive that indeed failed to make use of its full potential to stimulate more sustainable consumption.[104] The Commission will also look into the potential role of (commercial) guarantees with regard to repair and longer lifespan when revising the 2019 Consumer Sales Directive.[105]

- At the *end-of-life stage*, the Commission wants to propose new waste reduction aims for specific waste streams when revising the Waste Framework Directive.[106] The Commission has also announced that it will propose harmonised EU extended producer responsibility rules for textiles with eco-modulation of fees, as part of the forthcoming revision of the Waste Framework Directive in 2023.[107]

These proposals are undoubtedly a step in the right direction. They can contribute to keeping resources and materials longer in the economy. They do introduce (some) attention to the ecological impact of consumption into consumer law. A 'right to repair' can prolong the lifespan of goods, as do stricter rules on premature obsolescence; a digital product passport attaches 'the traces of production' to the product; further changes in ecodesign regulation can ensure that only more sustainable products have access to the market and this for a far wider range of products. Moreover – the effect of ecodesign regulation should not be underestimated, as such regulation has been shown to have an extraterritorial effect as mandatory product design requirements are taken up in jurisdictions outside the EU (cf the so-called 'Brussels effect'[108]).

However, there are two major problems. First, national sustainable consumption initiatives that often go beyond the EU proposals mentioned are currently also being

---

[102] cf European Commission, 'Call for Evidence for an Impact Assessment: Sustainable consumption of goods – promoting repair and reuse' (2022) Ref Ares(2022)175084 3, option 3. The PEF/OEF is a multi-criteria measure of the environmental performance of a good or service or a goods/services-providing organisation from a life-cycle perspective.

[103] See at https://ec.europa.eu/info/law/better-regulation/have-your-say/initiatives/13150-Sustainable-consumption-of-goods-promoting-repair-and-reuse_en.

[104] See especially Van Gool and Michel (n 57) 136–48; Directive (EU) 2019/771 of the European Parliament and of the Council of 20 May 2019 on certain aspects concerning contracts for the sale of goods, amending Regulation (EU) 2017/2394 and Directive 2009/22/EC, and repealing Directive 1999/44/EC [2019] OJ L136/28.

[105] Consumer Sales Directive (n 104).

[106] See in more detail Keirsbilck and Terryn (n 98); Directive 2008/98/EC of the European Parliament and of the Council of 19 November 2008 on waste and repealing certain Directives [2008] OJ L312/3.

[107] European Commission, 'Communication: EU Strategy for Sustainable and Circular Textiles' COM (2022) 141 final.

[108] See, for a thorough analysis, A Bradford, *The Brussels Effect – How the European Union Rules the World* (Oxford University Press, 2020).

adopted. Additional EU measures that continue to opt for maximum harmonisation risk curbing much-needed room for national experiments (see section III.C.i). Second, the starting point of the EU initiatives is still about fulfilling individual desires and ensuring the right to self-determination, albeit in a market with slightly more sustainable products and services. A more fundamental transformation or shift in thinking has not yet occurred (see section III.C.ii).

C. Initiatives at National Level

A similar proliferation of national initiatives on sustainable consumption is ongoing.[109] France can probably be considered a forerunner in this regard.[110] For example, the French 'Loi Hamon' had already introduced information requirements on the availability of spare parts in 2014,[111] and a prohibition on planned obsolescence in 2015.[112] Additional information requirements on the environmental characteristics of products were introduced in 2020 by the *Loi anti-gaspillage et à l'économie circulaire* (AGEC),[113] as well as a repairability score.[114] The *Loi portant lutte contre le dérèglement climatique et renforcement de la résilience face à ses effets* of 2021 added (among other things) a ban on advertising for fossil fuels,[115] as well as specific conditions for use of the term 'CO2-neutral'.[116] Extended producer responsibility for textiles was already introduced in 2007.[117]

---

[109] This subsection is based on earlier work by E Terryn and EV Irambona, 'Duurzame consumptie en maximum harmonisatie: water en vuur?' in A Janssen (ed), *Schuring tussen duurzaamheid en het Europees Economisch recht en het Europees Privaatrecht* (Kluwer, forthcoming 2023).

[110] See more extensively Michel (n 59) paras 467 et seq.

[111] See Code de la Consommation, Art L 111-4, inserted by Loi no 2014-344 du 17 mars 2014 relative à la consommation, JORF no 0065 du 18 mars 2014 5400 ('Loi Hamon'); Décret no 2014–1482 du 9 Décembre 2014 relatif aux obligations d'information et de fourniture concernant les pièces détachées indispensables à l'utilisation d'un bien, JORF no 0286 du 11 décembre 2014 20707.

[112] Loi no 2015-992 du 17 août 2015 relative à la transition énergétique pour la croissance verte, JORF no 0189 du 18 août 2015; the relevant provision was changed in 2021. See Code de la Consommation, Art L 441-2: 'Est interdite la pratique de l'obsolescence programmée qui se définit par le recours à des techniques, y compris logicielles, par lesquelles le responsable de la mise sur le marché d'un produit vise à en réduire délibérément la durée de vie pour en augmenter le taux de remplacement.'

[113] Loi no 2020-105 du 10 février 2020 relative à la lutte contre le gaspillage et à l'économie circulaire, JORF no 0035 du 11 février 2020 (AGEC), inserting a new Art L 541-9-1 in the Code de l'Environnement; Décret no 2022-748 du 29 avril 2022 relatif à l'information du consommateur sur les qualités et caractéristiques environnementales des produits générateurs de déchets, JORF no 0101 du 30 avril 2022.

[114] Code de l'Environnement, Art L 541-9-2.

[115] Code de l'Environnement, Art L 229-61 provides 'Est interdite la publicité relative à la commercialisation ou faisant la promotion des énergies fossiles. Un décret en Conseil d'Etat précise la liste des énergies fossiles concernées et les règles applicables aux énergies renouvelables incorporées aux énergies fossiles. N'entrent pas dans le champ de l'interdiction les carburants dont le contenu en énergie renouvelable est réputé supérieur ou égal à 50 %.'

[116] Loi no 2021–1104 du 22 août 2021 portant lutte contre le dérèglement climatique et renforcement de la résilience face à ses effets, Art 12; Décret no 2022-539 du 13 avril 2022 relatif à la compensation carbone et aux allégations de neutralité carbone dans la publicité, JORF no 0088 du 14 avril 2022.

[117] Code de l'Environnement, Arts L 541-10 et seq. The obligations were reinforced by the AGEC (n 113).

Sustainable consumption is also attracting attention in Germany, mainly in policy programmes[118] and studies commissioned by the Government[119] but somewhat less through specific legislation.[120] Similar observations can be made for the Netherlands, where a governmental programme was developed to make the economy circular by 2050.[121] Belgium also has a proposal pending to tackle planned obsolescence,[122] as well as a proposal to introduce a repairability and durability score.[123] A minimum score would even be needed to enter the Belgian market.[124] In addition, a proposal was introduced in September 2022 for a prohibition on advertising for fossil fuel.[125]

This enumeration of measures is certainly not exhaustive but provokes two observations relevant for this chapter. First, similar problems in terms of sustainability are sometimes tackled in various ways at national level, which can provide relevant insights on the pros and cons of a specific approach.[126] Second, the conformity of many of these initiatives with EU law may be questioned, as the scope for a national sustainable

---

[118] Bundesministerium für Ernährung und Landwirtschaft (BMUB), 'Nationales Programm für nachhaltigen Konsum – Gesellschaftlicher Wandel durch einen nachhaltigen Lebensstil' (2019) 335; BMUB, 'German Resource Efficiency Programme II – Programme for the sustainable use and conservation of natural resources' (2016); BMUB, 'Deutsches Ressourceneffizienzprogramm III 2020–2023 – Programm zur nachhaltigen Nutzung und zum Schutz der natürlichen Ressourcen' (2020) at www.bmu.de/download/deutsches-ressourceneffizienzprogramm-progress-iii (accessed 23 February 2023).

[119] S Schlacke, K Tonner and E Gawel, 'Stärkung eines nachhaltigen Konsums im Bereich Produktnutzung durch Anpassungen im Zivil- und öffentlichen Recht' (2015) Umweltbundesamt Study; S Prakash et al, 'Einfluss der Nutzungsdauer von Produkten auf ihre Umweltwirkung – Schaffung einer Informationsgrundlage und Entwicklung von Strategien gegen "Obsoleszenz"' (2016) Umweltbundesamt Study; F Keimeyer et al, 'Weiterentwicklung von Strategien gegen Obsoleszenz einschließlich rechtlicher Instrumente – Abschlussbericht' (2020) Umweltbundesamt Study; see also Micklitz et al (n 58) 68.

[120] Some proposals were formulated to regulate planned obsolescence, but were ultimately not adopted; see Michel (n 59) paras 76 et seq and: Antrag vom 17.04.2013 zum Ressourcenschutz durch Vorgabe einer Mindestnutzungsdauer für technische Produkte, BT-Drucks. 17/13096; Antrag vom 12.06.2013 zum Geplanten Verschleiß stoppen und die Langlebigkeit von Produkten sichern, BT-Drucks. 17/13917; Antrag vom 14.07.2016 zum Längere Lebensdauer für technische Geräte, BT-Drucks. 18/9179; Antrag vom 09.01.2020 'Elektroschrott – Wertstoffkreisläufe schließen', BT-Drucks. 19/16412; Antrag vom 09.01.2020 'Elektroschrott reduzieren – Recht auf Reparatur', BT-Drucks. 19/16419; Antrag vom 13.04.2021 'Elektro- und Elektronikgeräte effizienter nutzen – Langlebigkeit, Reparatur, Sammlung und Recycling verbessern', BT-Drucks. 19/28429; Antrag vom 05.04.2022 'Rohstoffversorgung sicherer machen – Stoffkreisläufe schließen', BT-Drucks. 20/1338.

[121] See at www.rijksoverheid.nl/onderwerpen/circulaire-economie/nederland-circulair-in-2050 (accessed 23 February 2023). Extended producer responsibility for the textile sector will be introduced in 2023, see Ontwerp besluit uitgebreide producentenverantwoordelijkheid textiel at www.rijksoverheid.nl/documenten/besluiten/2022/04/21/bijlage-2-ontwerpbesluit-uitgebreide-producentenverantwoordelijkheid-textiel (accessed 23 February 2023).

[122] Proposition de loi visant à lutter contre l'obsolescence programmée et à soutenir l'économie de la réparation, *Doc parl*, Ch, 2019, 19 juillet 2019, no 0193/001; Proposition de loi modifiant le Code civil et le Code de droit économique, visant à lutter contre l'obsolescence programmée et l'obsolescence prématurée et à augmenter les possibilités de réparation, *Doc parl*, Ch, 2019–2020, 19 novembre 2019, no 0771/001; Proposition de loi visant à lutter contre l'obsolescence organisée et à soutenir l'économie circulaire, *Doc parl*, Ch, 2019–2020, 7 janvier 2020, no 0914/001.

[123] Projet de loi relatif à l'introduction d'un indice de réparabilité et de longévité et à la diffusion de l'information sur la durée de la compatibilité logicielle des produits (2022) at https://ec.europa.eu/growth/tools-databases/tris/fr/search/?trisaction=search.detail&year=2022&num=634 (accessed 23 February 2023).

[124] ibid Art 6.

[125] Wetsvoorstel tot instelling van een verbod op reclame voor fossiele energie, *Parl St* Kamer 2021–22, no 2874/001.

[126] A good example is combatting the destruction of new goods, see H Roberts et al, 'Product Destruction: Exploring Unsustainable Production-Consumption Systems and Appropriate Policy Responses' (2023) 35

consumption policy is limited. It is striking that in Belgium, several draft parliamentary resolutions are also pending, calling the EU to action, for example to make the right of withdrawal more sustainable and to ban fossil fuel advertising.[127]

i. Conformity with EU Law? Limited Room for a National Sustainable Consumption Policy

National sustainable consumption measures indeed risk being contrary to EU law.[128] In the absence of EU harmonisation, such national measures need to comply with the provisions on free movement.[129] However, measures hindering free movement of goods may be justified not only for reasons of consumer protection but also for environmental reasons,[130] provided the proportionality test is met.[131] Since *Keck*,[132] advertising restrictions enjoy a somewhat different regime:[133] they are considered as selling arrangements, which are in principle only assessed under Article 34 TFEU if they have a greater effect on imported goods than on domestic goods and thus prevent market access.[134]

Moreover, for technical regulations – such as the national repairability score initiatives – the 'TRIS'[135] notification procedure[136] needs to be complied with. Notification is followed by a status quo period of three months to allow the Commission and Member

---

Sustainable Production and Consumption 300. We see different approaches in different Member States. For instance, France has a ban on the destruction of unsold goods, Germany a transparency and due diligence obligation, Belgium adapted VAT legislation when goods are given away: ibid 303.

[127] eg Voorstel van Resolutie betreffende de reclame als hefboom voor het bereiken van de klimaatambities, *Parl St* Kamer 2021–22, no 2878/001; see also Voorstel van Resolutie betreffende de evolutie naar een duurzaam en evenwichtig herroepingsrecht in het kader van e-commerce, *Parl St* Kamer 2021–22, no 2355/001.

[128] See for an in-depth analysis, Terryn and Irambona (n 109).

[129] See especially N De Sadeleer, 'Environmental Measures as an Obstacle to Free Movement of Goods in the Internal Market' in C Dalhammar, E Maitre-Ekern and C Bugge (eds), *Preventing Environmental Damage from Products* (Cambridge University Press, 2018) 125–50.

[130] Consumer protection, eg Case C-120/78 *Cassis de Dijon* ECLI:EU:C:1979:42; Environmental protection, eg Case C-240/83 *ADBHU* (n 80); Case C-302/86 *Danish bottles* ECLI:EU:C:1988:42.

[131] Case C-161/09 *Kakavetsos-Fragkopoulos* ECLI:EU:C:2011:110, para 39.

[132] Joined Cases C-267/91 and C-268/91 *Keck* ECLI:EU:C:1993:905, [1993] ECR I-06097.

[133] See also Commission Notice Guide on Articles 34–36 of the Treaty on the Functioning of the European Union (TFEU) (Text with EEA relevance) 2021/C 100/03 [2021] OJ C100/38.

[134] See, eg Case C-412/93 *Leclerc-Siplec* ECLI:EU:C:1995:26; Joined Cases C-34/95, C-35/95 and C-36/95 *Konsumentombudsmannen (KO) v De Agostini (Svenska) Förlag AB (C-34/95) and TV-Shop i Sverige AB* (C-35/95 and C-36/95) ECLI:EU:C:1997:344, [1997] ECR I-03843. See in detail D Kraft, 'Advertising Restrictions and the Free Movement of Goods – The Case Law of the ECJ' (2007) 18 *European Business Law Review* 517; D Doukas, 'Untying the Market Access Knot: Advertising Restrictions and the Free Movement of Goods and Services' (2007) 9 *The Cambridge Yearbook of European Legal Studies* 177.

[135] Technical Regulation Information System.

[136] Currently regulated by Directive (EU) 2015/1535 of the European Parliament and of the Council of 9 September 2015 laying down a procedure for the provision of information in the field of technical regulations and rules on information society services (codification) [2015] OJ L241/1 (Single Market Transparency Directive). The procedure was established in 1983 by Council Directive 83/189/EEC of 28 March 1983 laying down a procedure for the provision of information in the field of technical standards and regulations [1983] OJ L109/8. Later codified by Directive 98/34/EC of the European Parliament and of the Council of 22 June 1998 laying down a procedure for the provision of information in the field of technical standards and regulations [1998] OJ L204/37 and amended by Directive 98/48/EC of the European Parliament and of the Council of 20 July 1998 amending Directive 98/34/EC laying down a procedure for the provision of information in the field of technical standards and regulations [1998] OJ L217/18 (mainly to extend its application to information society services).

States to examine the draft legislation. If the Commission issues a detailed opinion based on a potential infringement of EU law, the initial standstill period is extended by several months.[137] Both the French and Belgian draft repairability score initiatives were notified.[138] The French legislation did not lead to a detailed opinion; however, the Belgian draft was considered to infringe several ecodesign implementing regulations[139] as well as potentially Article 34 TFEU, leading to an extension of the standstill period.

Once a harmonisation measure has been adopted, further-reaching national measures are only possible if the instrument has a safeguard clause, or on the basis of the derogation mechanism of Article 114(4) and (5) TFEU. The latter option has rightfully been mentioned by some authors as creating some potential for national sustainable consumption measures,[140] but the conditions for maintaining existing further-reaching provisions or for imposing new further-reaching provisions are strict,[141] and they are strictly interpreted by the CJEU[142] and the European Commission.[143] Especially for adoption of new (stricter) provisions, the conditions of 'new scientific evidence relating to the protection of the environment ... on grounds of a problem *specific* to that Member State arising after the adoption of the harmonisation measure' seem hard to fulfil for new national sustainable consumption initiatives.[144] Such national sustainable consumption initiatives will often be designed to resolve an EU-wide problem, which is exactly what this derogation does not allow for.[145]

Given the strict conditions for successfully invoking the derogation clause of Article 114 TFEU, all hope is then vested in the harmonisation instrument itself, which might – even in the case of maximum harmonisation – contain safeguard clauses. The directly relevant consumer protection directives are maximum harmonisation

---

[137] Single Market Transparency Directive (n 136) Art 6(2).

[138] Notification reference French legislation: 2020/468/F; notification reference Belgian legislation: 2022/0634/B, 2022/0635/B, 2022/0636/B, 2022/0637/B.

[139] Commission Regulation (EU) 2019/2023 of 1 October 2019 laying down ecodesign requirements for household washing machines and household washer-dryers pursuant to Directive 2009/125/EC of the European Parliament and of the Council, amending Commission Regulation (EC) No 1275/2008 and repealing Commission Regulation (EU) No 1015/2010 [2019] OJ L315/285; Commission Regulation (EU) 2019/2022 of 1 October 2019 laying down ecodesign requirements for household dishwashers pursuant to Directive 2009/125/EC of the European Parliament and of the Council amending Commission Regulation (EC) No 1275/2008 and repealing Commission Regulation (EU) No 1016/2010 [2019] OJ L315/267; Commission Regulation (EU) 2019/2021 of 1 October 2019 laying down ecodesign requirements for electronic displays pursuant to Directive 2009/125/EC of the European Parliament and of the Council, amending Commission Regulation (EC) No 1275/2008 and repealing Commission Regulation (EC) No 642/2009 [2019] OJ L315/241; European Commission, Communication of the Commission – TRIS/(2022) 04493 2 at https://ec.europa.eu/growth/tools-databases/tris/fr/search/?trisaction=search.detail&year=2022&num=634 (accessed 1 March 2023).

[140] CMDS Pavillon, 'Herijking van het consumentencontractenrecht: Duurzaamheid als nieuw ijkpunt?' in CMDS Pavillon and WH van Boom (eds), *Privaatrechtelijke bescherming herijkt* (Uitgeverij Paris, 2021) 54; Micklitz (n 17) 336–37.

[141] See N de Sadeleer, 'Procedures for derogations from the principle of approximation of laws under article 95 of the EC Treaty' (2003) 40 *CML Rev* 889. The procedure has also not often been used.

[142] See, eg Case C-3/00 *Denmark v Commissie* ECLI:EU:C:2003:167, para 54.

[143] European Commission, 'Communication from the Commission concerning Article 95 (paragraphs 4, 5 and 6) of the Treaty establishing the European Community' COM (2002) 760 final, para 10 at https://data.consilium.europa.eu/doc/document/ST-5110-2003-INIT/en/pdf (accessed 23 February 2023).

[144] Art 114(5) TFEU (emphasis added). See also de Sadeleer (n 141); I Maletic, *The Law and Policy of Harmonization in Europe's Internal Market* (Edward Elgar, 2013).

[145] de Sadeleer (n 141) 900.

directives, with limited exceptions to the maximum harmonisation character and definitely no general safeguard clause for national measures that aim to go beyond the level of sustainability chosen in the Directive. They leave limited scope for a national sustainable consumption policy. For example, the Consumer Sales Directive leaves some room for longer national guarantee periods, but it does not allow a change to the hierarchy of remedies.[146] The Consumer Rights Directive does not allow Member States to make the right of withdrawal more sustainable, for example by creating additional exceptions or by limiting the right of the consumer to handle the goods during the period for withdrawal.[147] In our opinion, the latter Directive also opposes information instruments, such as the repairability score that France introduced and that Belgium wants to introduce.[148]

A bit more leeway seems to be available for national bans on certain forms of advertising or stricter national rules on 'carbon-neutral' claims. Indeed, the UCPD only harmonises national rules concerning commercial practices that protect consumers' economic interests or that have a double aim (protection of both the economic interests of consumers and other interests).[149] To the extent that (national) courts accept that the French ban on fossil-fuel advertising is indeed adopted solely to protect environmental interests,[150] it could be in conformity with the Directive.[151] The ban then still needs to pass the free-movement test, provided it hinders access to the market more for foreign products. Even if it were to be considered a barrier to trade, it might still be justified for reasons of environmental protection. Zglinksi argues that an evolution in time can be seen in the case law of the CJEU, which seems to give more room to Member States to maintain national measures that impede free movement.[152] De Sadeleer's analysis – specifically

---

[146] See critical comment on the Directive's (lack of) contribution to sustainable consumption in Van Gool and Michel (n 57) 136–47.

[147] See E Terryn and E Van Gool, 'The Role of European Consumer Regulation in Shaping the Environmental Impact of E-Commerce' (2021) 10 *Journal of European Consumer and Market Law* 89.

[148] Terryn and Irambona (n 109). Additional information requirements can only be imposed in respect of contracts concluded on business premises (Consumer Rights Directive (n 26) Art 5(4)). National information requirements that also apply to distance and off-premises contracts are contrary to the Directive.

[149] UCPD (n 28) Art 1; Commission Notice – Guidance on the interpretation and application of Directive 2005/29/EC of the European Parliament and of the Council concerning unfair business-to-consumer commercial practices in the internal market [2021] OJ C526/1.

[150] The process preceding the adoption of and the Explanatory Memorandum to the *Loi contre le dérèglement climatique* – which introduced the aforementioned French ban on advertising fossil fuels and regulation of the term 'CO2-neutral' – indeed indicates that environmental protection was envisaged. This law is part of a democratic pilot project with a dual objective: more participatory democracy and just ecological transition (Exposé de motifs Projet de loi no 3875 portant lutte contre le dérèglement climatique et renforcement de la résilience face à ses effets). Consumer protection is not mentioned as an objective. The Explanatory Memorandum also shows that the intention of the law – where the measures concern consumption – is to change consumption behaviour and to encourage less consumption. The fact that these advertising regulations were included in the Code de l'Environnement (before the Code de la Consommation) could also be used as an argument to confirm the (exclusive) environmental objective. The environmental objective is also explicitly reflected in the text of the law (see Art 1).

[151] Interestingly, the Belgian proposal refers not only to environmental protection aims, but also to consumer protection purposes, Wetsvoorstel tot instelling van een verbod op reclame voor fossiele energie (n 125) 8 and 9, fn 6. This implies that it could be considered contrary to the UCPD to the extent that the draft act pursues a double aim.

[152] J Zglinski, *Europe's Passive Virtues: Deference to National Authorities in EU Free Movement Law* (Oxford University Press, 2020), based on an analysis of case law on free movement between 1974 and 2013.

about invoking environmental protection as a justification – is similar. Although there is certainly no absolute coherence in the case law of the CJEU, he at least sees a tendency towards a more balanced outcome and a less strict interpretation of justifications.[153] This more flexible attitude is also logical in view of changes to the European treaties, which do reflect a better balance between sustainable development and the internal market, including explicit reference to sustainable development in Article 3(3) TEU.[154]

ii. Need for National Experiments and Regulatory Sandboxes for Sustainable Consumption

The limited scope for a national sustainable consumption policy is regrettable. The choice for maximum harmonisation in consumer law has already been criticised in the past, and that choice has become even more problematic given the urgent need to promote more sustainable consumption.

The arguments pro maximum harmonisation in consumer law are well known.[155] Companies would no longer have to take into account divergent legislation within the harmonised field and cross-border trading would become easier. Transaction fees would be reduced. For consumers, the advantage of a single set of rules within the EU is highlighted: this would give them confidence in cross-border purchases, which in turn contributes to realisation of the internal market. Furthermore, maximum harmonisation would significantly improve legal certainty, for both consumers and traders.[156] But these arguments have all been met with criticism.[157]

For example, there is no convincing empirical evidence that maximum harmonisation would be needed to encourage consumers to make cross-border purchases.[158] Additionally, the reduction in transaction costs following harmonisation of consumer contract law (not of technical requirements) can also be questioned: harmonisation also entails transaction costs.[159] Furthermore, in private law it is an illusion that, after harmonisation, companies only have 'one set of rules'[160] to take into account when

---

[153] de Sadeleer (n 129) refers to a number of more recent judgments where the Court accepted justification for restrictive measures on environmental grounds.

[154] ibid 137–38.

[155] See, eg European Commission, 'Green Paper on the Review of the Consumer Acquis' COM (2006) 744; see Consumer Rights Directive (n 26) recital 7.

[156] Consumer Rights Directive (n 26) recital 7.

[157] See Th Wilhelmsson, 'The Abuse of the Confident Consumer as a Justification for EC Consumer Law' (2004) 27 *Journal of Consumer Policy* 317; E Terryn, *Bedenktijden in het consumentenrecht* (Intersentia, 2005) 68–80; M Faure, 'Towards a Maximum Harmonization of Consumer Contract Law?' (2008) 15 *Maastricht Journal of European and Comparative Law* 433; R Van den Bergh, 'The Uneasy Case for Harmonizing Consumer Law' in K Heine and W Kerber (eds), *Zentralität unde Dezenrtalität von Regulierung in Europa* (Lucius & Lucius, 2007) 184.

[158] See the analysis of the 'Qualitative study on cross-border shopping in 28 European countries' (May 2004) in E Terryn, *Bedenktijden in het consumentenrecht* (Intersentia, 2005) 70; see also the studies cited by Faure (n 157); and very convincingly, Th Wilhelmsson, 'The Abuse of the 'Confident Consumer' as a Justification for EC Consumer Law' (2004) 27 *Journal of Consumer Policy* 317, 328–29.

[159] See Faure (n 157) 439–41.

[160] cf European Commission, 'Proposal for a Directive of the European Parliament and of the Council on consumer rights' COM (2008) 614, recital 8.

drafting contracts. Harmonisation is always limited to the scope of the directive in question and attempts at a more comprehensive harmonisation of private law have been unsuccessful.[161] Demarcation problems remain unavoidable[162] and there will always be a complex interaction with national (private) law, even with maximum harmonisation. A recent and EU-wide analysis of implementation of the maximum harmonisation Directives 2019/770[163] and 2019/771[164] on digital content and services and consumer sales confirms this very clearly.[165] The variation in transposition is very large, as is the fragmentation and increased complexity of national law. Micklitz rightly speaks of the 'full harmonisation dream'.[166]

The advantages of maximum harmonisation in consumer law are therefore questionable.[167] The disadvantages much less so. Responding nationally (and quickly) to changed circumstances or problematic situations is no longer possible after maximum harmonisation, only the (rather long and cumbersome) European procedure allows regulatory changes.[168] Maximum harmonisation leaves no room to take differences in national expectations and/or different needs of consumers into account.[169] Micklitz furthermore points to the disadvantage that maximum harmonisation reduces Member States and their administrations to implementation machines that preferably literally copy the provisions of the directive and no longer think 'out of the EU box'. In the longer term, he fears an impact on the knowledge and competences of national administrations.[170]

---

[161] eg the Consumer Rights Directive (n 26) was given much more limited scope than the original proposal (n 160, which also sought to regulate purchase and unlawful terms); European Commission, 'Proposal for a Regulation of the European Parliament and of the Council on a Common European Sales Law' COM (2011) 635 final, 284(COD), also failed.

[162] See, eg, the numerous preliminary references on the compatibility of national measures with the UCPD and its precise scope, including Case C-126/11 *Inno v Unie van Zelfstandige Ondernemers vzw (UNIZO) and others* ECLI:EU:C:2011:851; Case C-304/08 *Plus Warenhandelsgesellschaft* ECLI:EU:C:2010:12; Case C-13/15 *Cdiscount* ECLI:EU:C:2015:560; Case C-343/12 *Euronics* ECLI:EU:C:2013:154, para 31; Case C-288/10 *Wamo* ECLI:EU:C:2011:443, para 40.

[163] Directive (EU) 2019/770 of the European Parliament and of the Council of 20 May 2019 on certain aspects concerning contracts for the supply of digital content and digital services [2019] OJ L136/1.

[164] Consumer Sales Directive (n 104).

[165] See H-W Micklitz, 'The Full Harmonization Dream' (2022) 11 *Journal of European Consumer and Market Law* 117. The national reports are be published in A De Franceschi and R Schulze (eds), *Harmonizing Digital Contract Law, The Impact of EU Directives 2019/770 and 2019/771 and the Regulation of Online Platforms* (Nomos, 2023).

[166] Micklitz (n 165) 117.

[167] Note that the criticism applies mainly to consumer contract law and commercial practices; the barriers for companies that wish to engage in cross-border trade are much greater in terms of technical requirements (which include technical specifications under the Single Market Transparency Directive (n 136) that determine the required characteristics of a product but also 'other requirements' that 'significantly affect the composition, the nature or marketing of the product') for which the notification procedure described above has been elaborated.

[168] The recent addition of another exception to the maximum harmonisation nature of the UCPD, to allow Member States to permit certain sales practices in the context of unsolicited visits or excursions, illustrates this need to be able to respond nationally to problematic situations. See UCPD (n 28) Art 3(5)(e), (6), as replaced by Directive (EU) 2019/2161 of 27 November 2019 amending Council Directive 93/13/EEC and Directives 98/6/EC, 2005/29/EC and 2011/83/EU of the European Parliament and of the Council as regards better enforcement and modernisation of consumer protection rules in the Union [2019] OJ L328/7. See also Directive 2019/2161, recital 54.

[169] See also in this regard the example mentioned in the preceding footnote.

[170] Micklitz (n 165) 120.

Maximum harmonisation also means that the level of protection is determined at European level. The average consumer is the benchmark there, so that offering more protection to the weaker consumer becomes impossible.[171] Maximum harmonisation further implies that the level of sustainability is determined at European level. Not only can weaker consumers therefore no longer receive additional protection at national level, but the same is also the case for the environment. This is all the more problematic now that the existing consumer directives by no means stimulate sustainable consumption.[172] Maximum harmonisation leaves no room for national experiments and entails the danger of 'fixing the goal posts'.[173] However, in the relatively new domain of sustainable consumption, room for experimentation seems more than necessary given the uncertainties as to the best legislative approach to stimulate more sustainable consumption. National legislative experiments have inspired the European legislator in the past,[174] and it is clear that recent European proposals on sustainable consumption are also using national legislation as a source of inspiration.[175]

What 'one-size-fits-all' maximum harmonisation entails simply does not match with sustainable consumption.[176] One of the recommendations of Micklitz et al in their recent study on the 'right to repair' is to enable national regulatory 'sandboxes'.[177] This could indeed provide the necessary space for national experiments.

Regulatory sandboxes are concrete frameworks that provide a structured context for experimentation and enable testing in a real-world environment of innovative technologies, products, services or approaches for a limited time and in a limited part of a sector.[178] The experiments are conducted under regulatory supervision, thus ensuring that appropriate safeguards are in place.[179] Regulatory sandboxes also make it possible to provide a framework within which economic operators can operate without being bound by existing – and sometimes strict – legal provisions. This technique is currently mainly used in the field of digitisation.[180] The UK has been at the forefront of

---

[171] See critically MW Hesselink, 'EU Private Law Injustices' (2022) 41 *Yearbook of European Law* 1, 22–3.

[172] See, eg for criticism of the Consumer Rights Directive, Terryn and Van Gool (n 146); for criticism of the (new) Consumer Sales Directive, Van Gool and Michel (n 57) 136–47.

[173] G Howells, 'European Consumer Law – the Minimal and Maximal Harmonisation Debate and Pro Independent Consumer Law Competence', in St Grundmann and J Stuyck (eds), *An Academic Green Paper on European Contract Law* (Kluwer, 2002) 75.

[174] eg for unlawful clauses, where the German and Scandinavian examples were used, and for consumer credit, where the English example inspired, see Th Wilhelmsson, 'Private law in the EU – Harmonized Fragmented Europeanisation' (2002) 78 *European Review of Private Law* 91, 93.

[175] See, eg reference to existing initiatives in several Member States, European Commission, 'Proposal for a Regulation establishing a framework for setting ecodesign requirements for sustainable products and repealing Directive 2009/125/EC where the Commission takes the initiative to prevent the destruction of new goods' COM (2022) 142 final, recital 46.

[176] Micklitz et al (n 57) 72.

[177] ibid.

[178] Council Conclusions on Regulatory Sandboxes and Experimentation Clauses as tools for an innovation-friendly, future-proof and resilient regulatory framework that masters disruptive challenges in the digital age, [2020] OJ C447/01.

[179] ibid.

[180] S Ranchordás, 'Experimental Lawmaking in the EU: Regulatory Sandboxes' (2021) University of Groningen Faculty of Law Research Paper Series No 12/2021 3 at https://deliverypdf.ssrn.com/delivery.php?ID=7031021 18110006022104000116097110064063039030001048013074088003010087095081097073094048055006126041126113096111125099067127029057017032014011085105029102105123099004073055050090870270690 0510311708900401411508410510703108412710311302411910103109910600 2&EXT=pdf&INDEX=TRUE

the introduction of regulatory sandboxes in the financial sector,[181] but they are also used outside the UK and outside the financial sector. For example, in Germany, the transport sector in such a framework is investigating whether self-driving minibuses can be safely used for passenger transport.[182] The Netherlands allows experimentation (and deviation from existing regulations) with new models for sustainable energy supply.[183]

At EU level, the need for regulatory sandboxes was mainly raised with regard to new (and digital) technologies.[184] The European Commission's proposal for a Regulation on artificial intelligence now effectively includes an 'experimental provision' that allows the creation of regulatory sandboxes by Member States: controlled environments to test innovative technologies for a limited time on the basis of a testing plan agreed with the competent authorities.[185]

Regulatory sandboxes could be used to pursue sustainability goals within consumer law too.[186] Sustainable development also requires continued innovation and, more than ever, an interdisciplinary approach, so that such a regulatory sandbox can offer opportunities to explore new techniques.[187] There is uncertainty about the effect of a number of (proposed) measures on sustainable consumption, the range of potential measures is large, there is the risk of path dependency in regulation,[188] all aspects that ideally require a regulator to be able to make adjustments quickly – which is exactly what such a regulatory test environment allows for.[189] Explicit 'experimental provisions' would be needed at EU level, allowing Member States to derogate from the maximum harmonisation character of EU instruments within the framework of these regulatory sandboxes. Allowing Member States to set up regulatory sandboxes entails a risk of fragmentation of the internal market, but a lesser risk than completely abandoning maximum harmonisation.[190] European supervision of the design and implementation of national

---

(accessed 23 February 2023); Financial Conduct Authority, 'Regulatory Sandboxes' at www.fca.org.uk/publication/research/regulatory-sandbox.pdf (accessed 23 February 2023); Terryn and Irambona (n 109).

[181] Ranchordás (n 180); Financial Conduct Authority (n 180).

[182] Federal Ministry for Economic Affairs and Energy, 'Making Space for Innovation: Handbook for regulatory sandboxes' (July 2019) 11 at www.bmwk.de/Redaktion/EN/Publikationen/Digitale-Welt/handbook-regulatory-sandboxes.pdf?__blob=publicationFile&v=2 (accessed 23 February 2023).

[183] See Besluit Experimenten Decentrale Duurzame Elektriciteitsopwekking – BWBR0036385 at https://wetten.overheid.nl/BWBR0036385/2015-04-01 (accessed 23 February 2023); JF Koenders and SL Pipping, 'Het Besluit experimenten decentrale duurzame elektriciteitsopwekking doorgelicht' (2016) 4 *Nederlands Tijdschrift voor Energierecht* 115. For a similar initiative in the UK, see OFGEM, 'Insights from Running the Regulatory Sandbox' (23 October 2018) at www.ofgem.gov.uk/publications-and-updates/insights-running-regulatory-sandbox (accessed 23 February 2023).

[184] Council Conclusions on Regulatory sandboxes and experimentation clauses as tools for an innovation-friendly, future-proof and resilient regulatory framework that masters disruptive challenges in the digital age (Brussels, 16 November 2020) 13026/20 BETREG 27 at https://data.consilium.europa.eu/doc/document/ST-13026–2020-INIT/en/pdf (accessed 23 February 2023).

[185] European Commission, 'Proposal for a Regulation of the European Parliament and of the Council laying down harmonised rules on artificial intelligence (artificial intelligence act) and amending certain union legislative acts' COM (2021) 206 final, Art 53.

[186] See in more detail Terryn and Irambona (n 109).

[187] See D Bauknecht et al, 'Exploring the Pathways: Regulatory Experiments for Sustainable Development – An Interdisciplinary Approach' (2020) 9 *Journal of Governance and Regulation* 2 at www.econstor.eu/bitstream/10419/208382/1/1683885708.pdf (accessed 23 February 2023).

[188] ibid.

[189] In the same sense Micklitz et al (n 57) 55.

[190] Terryn and Irambona (n 109).

regulatory sandboxes could further limit that risk and contribute to rapid development of a European framework for successful national initiatives.

D. Need for a More Fundamental Transformation of Consumer Law

A second major criticism of the initiatives mentioned is that they still take fulfilment of individual desires and ensuring the right to self-determination as a starting point, albeit in a market with slightly more (ecologically) sustainable products and services.[191] Mont and Dalhammar's earlier criticism – that (EU) consumer policy very seldom addresses how total consumption may be decreased and mainly supports 'greener' consumption – still stands.[192] Many of the initiatives mentioned indeed focus on consuming better alternatives of the same goods and services, such as eco-labelled, energy-efficient or more easily repairable goods. What is also missing in the proposals mentioned is attention to the social aspect of sustainable consumption. There is limited attention to ensuring access to essential goods or services; nor do the proposed additional information requirements focus on working conditions or effects on producers. Moreover, there is limited focus on shifting consumption to alternative, less impactful ways of using goods or services, for instance from buying to sharing or pay per use; from private to public transport; from meat to plant-based food.[193] Furthermore, while the potential of alternative business models (sharing, leasing, product as service) is recognised at EU level,[194] at the same time concrete proposals to regulate service contracts in order to ensure their circularity or to ensure a similar level of protection as for sales contracts are still missing. And the most radical, but arguably the most efficient shift to bringing consumption and planet once more into balance[195] – namely, reducing consumption to sufficient consumption – is hardly mentioned. The question in any event remains whether the aforesaid proposals will indeed suffice to bring consumption back into line with what the Earth can effectively support. Unfortunately, it is not tenable to think only in terms of individual needs. The Brundlandt definition of sustainable is also receiving some criticism, because it is strongly based on needs that are potentially infinite and as it is less framed in terms of the finite nature of resources.[196] Rovers reformulates the definition as follows:

---

[191] If one were to classify the EU proposals on Hopwood's scheme (B Hopwood, M Mellor and G O'Brien, 'Mapping the Views on Sustainable Development' (2005) 13 *Sustainable Development* 38), they could rather be classified in the status quo/weak reform part of the scheme. B Hopwood et al, 'Developing a Framework for Mapping Sustainable Design Activities' in D Durling et al (eds), *Design and Complexity – DRS International Conference 2010* (Montreal, Canada, 7–9 July) at https://dl.designresearchsociety.org/drs-conference-papers/drs2010/researchpapers/33 (accessed 23 February 2023).

[192] O Mont and C Dalhammar, 'Sustainable Consumption: At the Cross-Road of Environmental and Consumer Policies' (2005) 8 *International Journal of Sustainable Development* 258.

[193] C Dalhammar, 'Reconstituting the Consumer in EU Law and Policy: Towards a More Multi-dimensional Approach' (ACES conference, UVA Amsterdam, August 2022).

[194] European Commission, 'Maak de cirkel rond – Een EU-actieplan voor de circulaire economie' COM (2015) 614 final 8, 'innovatieve vormen van consumptie kunnen ook de ontwikkeling van een circulaire economie ondersteunen, bv. [...] het afnemen van diensten in plaats van producten [...]'.

[195] See, eg, J Hickl, *Less is More* (Penguin, 2021) 336.

[196] 'Brundlandt rapport', UN World Commission on Environment and Development, 'Our Common Future, Chapter 2: Towards Sustainable Development' A/42/427 at www.un-documents.net/ocf-02.htm (accessed

Sustainable development is the management of our resources in closed cycles, with the sun as the main source and resources evenly distributed so that needs can be met to the maximum extent possible, in a way that can be sustained for the long future.[197]

Restoring a balance requires taking the finite character of the system into account and taking the finite nature of resources as a starting point. After all, this – in combination with the technical possibilities – determines the extent to which needs can be met equitably.

A more thorough 'sustainability due diligence' of consumer law seems long overdue and the introduction of systems thinking in consumer law is more than necessary.[198] A (more) sustainable consumer law demands that it be reconnected with the 'whole' and underlying ecosystems, that abstract thinking in which the impact of consumer transactions is neglected be abandoned, and that consumer law be no longer considered as an institution that can be separated from its impact.[199] A transformation is not yet on the table, along with the aforementioned proposals, in which consumption (and consumer law) is rethought in terms of available (finite) resources and in terms of what is available to each citizen of those resources within the framework of a sustainable and regenerative resource management, rather than in terms of individual desires. That will require more drastic measures than additional information obligations or an adjustment of remedies or guarantee periods. A recalibration of consumer law (and private law alone) will unfortunately not suffice.[200]

Solutions closer to such a fundamental shift – such as an individual tradable carbon-budget ('carbon wallet'),[201] or imposing higher prices for those wishing to consume more than a set base quantity,[202] or introducing 'consumption corridors'[203] – currently tend to be proposed by academics rather than by policymakers. But here, too, we might be overtaken by reality faster than we considered possible.[204] Biber seems right in

---

23 February 2023): 'Sustainable development is development that meets the needs of the present without compromising the ability of future generations to meet their own needs.'

[197] R Rovers, 'Not People, But Resources: Brundlandt 2.0' (27 November 2016) at ronaldrovers.com/not-people-but-resources-brundtland-2-0/ (accessed 23 February 2023).

[198] See in the same sense, eg Pavillon (n 60) 13–104; V Mak and E Terryn, 'Circular Economy and Consumer Protection: The Consumer as a Citizen and the Limits of Empowerment Through Consumer Law' (2020) 43 *Journal of Consumer Policy* 227; Micklitz (n 17) 229–37.

[199] cf similarly for contract law in general, Mattei and Quarta (n 21) 10.

[200] See, eg, sceptical about the impact of measures that aim to change consumer/citizen behaviour, S Barr, A Gilg and G Shaw, 'Citizens, consumers and sustainability: (Re)Framing environmental practice in an age of climate change' (2011) 21 *Global Environmental Change* 1224. See also Pavillon (n 60), who distinguishes between partial and full recalibration of consumer law.

[201] See, eg, recently F Fuso Nerini et al, 'Personal carbon allowances revisited' (2021) 4 *Nature Sustainability* 1025; see also recent TNO-research that found only limited support for a personal tradable carbon budget, TNO, 'Draagvlak voor leefstijlbeleid tegen klimaatverandering' (Survey 2021) at tno.nl/nl/over-tno/nieuws/2021/6/draagvlak-systeem-emissies-consumenten/ (accessed 23 February 2023).

[202] See J Bouwens (professor of accounting) pleading for a progressively increasing energy price, at nrc.nl/nieuws/2022/08/24/energie-oplossing-voor-naderende-energiecrisis-prijsdifferentiatie-a4139690 (accessed 23 February 2023).

[203] With a lower limit on consumption that guarantees access to basic needs, but also with an upper limit, see R Defila and A Di Giulio, 'The Concept of "Consumption Corridors" Meets Society: How an Idea for Fundamental Changes in Consumption is Received' (2020) 43 *Journal of Consumer Policy* 315.

[204] See, however, the political agreement of 18 December 2022, to further expand the ETS system, eg also to road transport and buildings by 2027 – European Parliament, 'Revision of the EU Emissions

concluding that '[n]o matter which strategy we adopt and no matter which specific legal approach we use, the dramatic increase in human impairments to global systems will trigger an increase in government intrusion in individual lives and decision-making'.[205]

In such a transformed consumption landscape, consumer law will more than ever have a role to play in also assuring socially sustainable consumption, in protecting the weaker and weakest consumers and ensuring their access to a 'fair share' of sustainably managed resources.[206] In this transformed consumer law, in addition to the initiatives mentioned, additional protection will be needed in alternative business models that lead to more efficient use of goods (share models, rental models), and solutions will be needed for consumers taking up a more active role.[207]

Finally, a more sustainable consumer law may still include a role for protecting the consumer's (and citizen's) right of self-determination, but again, this will require fundamental recalibration and attention to all the implications of consumption behaviour. Self-determination and private autonomy have never been completely without limitations,[208] but in a sustainable consumer law this is only tenable if an intra- and inter-generational element is added. Self-determination then becomes the right to make one's own (consumption) choices, as long as these choices do not impede others' opportunities for a good life[209] and do not interfere with sustainable and regenerative management of resources. Not only does 'others' then refer to both current and future generations,[210] but also other species and biodiversity require far more attention.[211] That this can lead to a reduction in consumption and also to a reduction in consumer rights, or at least to different rights, is inevitable.

Trading System' 2021/0211(COD); European Parliament, 'Press Release: Climate change: Deal on a more ambitious Emissions Trading System (ETS)' (18 December 2022) at www.europarl.europa.eu/news/en/press-room/20221212IPR64527/climate-change-deal-on-a-more-ambitious-emissions-trading-system-ets (accessed 1 March 2023).

[205] E Biber, 'Law in the Anthropocene Epoch' (2017) 106 *Georgetown Law Journal* 5.

[206] H-W Micklitz, 'The Law of the Labour and Consumer Market Society' in H-W Micklitz, *The Politics of Justice in European Private Law* (Cambridge University Press, 2018) 316, 318–19 for references to the limited number of European instruments that already pay attention to the access problem of vulnerable consumers, including Directive 2003/54/EC concerning common rules for the internal market in electricity [2003] OJ L176/37. See also Hesselink (n 171) 23 for a similar plea.

[207] See for proposals, B Keirsbilck, E Terryn and E Van Gool, 'Consumentenbescherming bij servitisation en product-dienst systemen (PDS)' (2019) 56 *Tijdschrift voor Privaatrecht* 817, 817 ff; H Slachmuylders et al, 'Duurzaam ondernemen en het recht: circulaire bedrijfsmodellen – juridische knelpunten' in M Beyens (ed), *De rol van de bedrijfsjurist in de duurzame ontwikkeling van de onderneming/Le rôle du juriste d'entreprise dans le développement durable*, 1st edn (Larcier, 2021) 7.

[208] See also Halfmeier (n 60) 717–62.

[209] A Di Giulio and D Fuchs, 'Sustainable Consumption Corridors: Concept, Objections, and Responses' (2014) 23 *GAIA – Ecological Perspectives for Science and Society* 184, 184–92; R Defila and A Di Giulio, 'The Concept of "Consumption Corridors" Meets Society: How an Idea for Fundamental Changes in Consumption is Received' (2020) 43 *Journal of Consumer Policy* 315, 315–44.

[210] See also, with regard to the German climate act (reference to the intergenerational aspect) German Bundesverfassungsgericht, decision of 24 March 2021, 1 BvR 2656/18, 1 BvR 288/20, 1 BvR 96/20, 1 BvR 78/20.

[211] M Seibert, 'Systems Thinking and How It Can Help Build a Sustainable World: A Beginning Conversation' *MAHB* (8 November 2018) at mahb.stanford.edu/blog/systems-thinking-can-help-build-sustainable-world-beginning-conversation/ (accessed 23 February 2023).

IV. Conclusion

European consumer law has been transformed over the last decades to a set of rules that primarily protect the economic interests of the consumer as a market player and a participant in the internal market. Ever-increasing consumption and lack of attention to externalities comes with a huge impact on the environment and on climate change, with a risk of ecological collapse and social instability. This focus on self-determination and individual consumer choice fails to take into account the negative impacts of consumption, notwithstanding that consumption plays a major role in the current overshooting of the planetary boundaries.

At both European and national levels, a shift in thinking seems to have been occurring over recent years, and an important number of initiatives are currently being undertaken to make consumer law more sustainable. It is argued that more is possible and necessary. First, it is already possible to interpret consumer law more sustainably, by taking not only the interests of traders and consumers into account but also environmental and sustainable development requirements. As far as legislative initiatives are concerned, it is argued that EU initiatives should not exclude further national experimentation. Given the urgency and the many uncertainties as to the optimal regulatory mix to achieve sustainable consumption, room should be available for this. Experimentation clauses allowing for national regulatory sandboxes can also be used to pursue sustainability goals within consumer law.

Finally, it is argued that the proposals that are currently on the table at EU level – although steps in the right direction – do not go far enough. They still take fulfilment of individual desires and ensuring the right to self-determination as a starting point, albeit in a market with more (ecologically) sustainable products and services. The focus lies on consuming more ecological alternatives of the same goods and services, not on reducing consumption or switching to alternative, less impactful ways to use goods or services. What is also missing in the proposals mentioned is attention to the social aspect of sustainable consumption. There is limited attention to ensuring access to essential goods or services; and to working conditions or effects on producers. A more systemic and holistic approach to consumer law is needed, taking into account the social, economic and environmental impacts of consumption. A more sustainable consumer law may still protect the right to self-determination, but only if an intra- and inter-generational element is added. Self-determination then becomes the right to make one's own (consumption) choices, as long as these choices do not impede others' opportunities for a good life and do not interfere with sustainable and regenerative management of resources. That this can lead to a reduction in consumption and also to a reduction in consumer rights, or at least to different rights, is inevitable.

PART II

Country-Specific Issues

9

Serbia: From Nothing to Something?

MATEJA DUROVIC

I. Introduction

This chapter examines the transformation of consumer law in Serbia, a candidate state for EU membership, as something that was imposed by the European Union (EU) as a condition for Serbia's progress in its ongoing EU integration process. The main argument that this chapter attempts to make is that the transformation of consumer law in Serbia has been very much top-down, and that the practical relevance of consumer law has only slowly, from a non-existent concept, started to develop, manifest and improve the position of the Serbian consumer.

Moreover, this chapter tries to clarify and critically examine the transformation of consumer law in Serbia in the last two decades, in order to set up some suggestions for reform that Serbian consumer law should follow in order to improve the legal landscape of consumer protection. At the end of the day, the main conclusion of the chapter seems to be that it would be unfair to say that the levels of consumer protection have not improved in the last 20 years in Serbia. Still, more efforts should be invested to reach the levels required by the European system of consumer protection, so that the Serbian consumer will be better protected and feel more confident while acting on the market.

II. Consumer Law as a New Concept

The Republic of Serbia is a country in South-Eastern Europe, whose private law developed under the influence of diverse legal systems: French, German, Swiss, Austrian and Italian private laws. Serbia was one of the first European countries to have its own modern, progressive Civil Code, adopted in 1844,[1] but the concept of consumer law has arrived only recently.

Even in 2022, consumer law was still seen as a rather new legal discipline in the Republic of Serbia. In the previous two decades, Serbian consumer law primarily

---

[1] S Avramović, 'Mixture of legal identities: Case of the Dutch (1838) and the Serbian Civil Code (1844)' (2018) 66 *Anali Pravnog fakulteta u Beogradu* 13, 19.

developed as a result of Serbian efforts to join the EU.[2] The mandatory requirements for EU membership include an obligation requiring full alignment of the national laws of a candidate state with EU law, and the rules on consumer protection have traditionally represented an important part of EU law.[3] As an opening remark, this explanation of the reason behind the development of consumer law in Serbia is of essential importance. It demonstrates that the idea about the existence of specific rules aimed at protecting consumers as weaker players on the market in their relationship with traders did not develop over the years organically or as a goal of national policymakers.

On the contrary, the idea of consumer law was something that was imposed on Serbia from outside, the meaning and application of which have never been properly understood.[4] This is a major issue, as a lack of proper understanding – not only of the concepts of consumer law, but also of the reasons behind the development of consumer law and its main goals – has eventually contributed to insufficient practical application of consumer law in Serbia and resulted in so many changes to the legislative framework for consumer protection in Serbia. However, this is something that it not exclusive to the Serbian example but an experience shared, to a large extent, with all of the jurisdictions of the Western Balkans.[5] Albania, Montenegro and all other jurisdictions of the region have all been struggling to establish a more effective system of consumer protection as a pre-condition for their progress towards EU integration.[6]

III. Development of Consumer Law in Serbia

Prior to adoption of the first consumer-specific legislation in the early 2000s, the main source of rules regulating consumer transactions was the general, old Law of Obligations of the Socialist Federal Republic of Yugoslavia.[7] From 1978, the Law of Obligations was the principal source of contract law and tort law rules in Yugoslavia, and eventually of Serbia as one of the newly formed countries after the dissolution of Yugoslavia. Even today, after all the economic, societal and political transformations that have taken place in Serbia in the last 45 years, this Law still applies, although with some minor subsequent amendments.

Despite being a rather modern and progressive piece of legislation for the time of its adoption, and despite Serbia's then being a country based on socialist ideology, as proved by its longevity, the Law of Obligations has not recognised the concept of the consumer as a weaker party in a contractual relationship with a strong trader.

---

[2] C Riefa and M Durovic. 'Serbian Consumer Law: Out with the Old, In with the New' (2015) 22 *Maastricht Journal of European and Comparative Law* 862, 862–78.

[3] J Stuyck and M Durovic, 'External Dimension of EU Consumer Law' in M Cremona and H-W Micklitz (eds), *External Dimension of EU Private Law* (Oxford University Press, 2016) 212–35.

[4] M Durovic and N Lazarevic, 'Towards the European Union: The Serbian Law on Consumer Protection and the Position of the Serbian Consumer' (2014) 3 *Journal of European Consumer and Market Law* 17, 17–25.

[5] Y Svetiev, 'How Consumer Law Travels' (2013) 36 *Journal of Consumer Policy* 209.

[6] See M Karanikic et al, *Modernising Consumer Law* (Nomos, 2012) 9–162.

[7] Zakon o obligacionim odnosima (English trans: The Law of Obligations) published in the Official Gazette of the Socialist Federal Republic of Yugoslavia (SFRY) Nos 29/78, 39/85, 45/89; Official Gazette of the Federal Republic of Yugoslavia (FRY) No 31/93.

The concept of consumer protection, in the modern sense, and a special legal regime for consumer transactions in the Law of Obligations 1978 is today still non-existent. Additionally, the most important global legal instrument in the field of consumer protection – the UN Guidelines on Consumer Protection adopted in 1985, with its changes in 1999 and 2015[8] – has never been mentioned or used as an inspiration for developing Serbian consumer law, although the Guidelines have influenced so many other legal systems.[9]

In October 2000, democratic changes took place in Serbia that also meant expression of a strong political intention to join the EU as part of the enlargement process. A new chapter was opened in the country's foreign policy. One must not forget that the goal of common European consumer policy is not only achievement of a high level of consumer protection, but also strengthening of the internal market through abolition of the differences in consumer law regimes through harmonisation of law.[10] This is why countries wishing to join EU also have to align their national rules.

In the EU accession process, alignment with the consumer *acquis* is a part of the so-called Negotiation Chapter 28 that deals with two topics: health and consumer protection. The European Commission continually reminded Serbia of its obligation to secure application of consumer law. Still today, diverse EU and Member States' national funding is used to support work on this Negotiation Chapter (eg IPA projects, GIZ, US aid).

As a result of Serbian efforts to join the EU, the first Law on Consumer Protection was adopted in 2002,[11] being replaced in 2005 with the second Law on Consumer Protection.[12] Due to their narrow scope, lack of alignment with European values and almost no effect in practice, these two Laws do not deserve to draw any attention but for the fact that they brought into being, for the first time in the history of Serbia, a separate, consumer protection-focused piece of legislation and thus introduced this concept into the Serbian legal system. This is what is most important about these two pieces of legislation; their application in practice remained minor.

Likewise, since the very beginning of the development of its rules on consumer law, Serbia's policy decision was to opt for regulation of consumer protection in a separate piece of legislation rather than amending the existing general private law legislation (namely, the Law of Obligations).[13] Again, this policy choice is not surprising, as consumer law has been seen as something imposed from outside, from abroad, unlike

---

[8] UN Guidelines for Consumer Protection at unctad.org/system/files/official-document/ditccplp-misc2016d1_en.pdf (accessed 3 September 2022).

[9] M Durovic and H-W Micklitz, *Internationalisation of Consumer Law: A Game Changer* (Springer, 2017).

[10] See, eg Directive 2005/29/EC of the European Parliament and of the Council of 11 May 2005 concerning unfair business-to-consumer commercial practices in the internal market and amending Council Directive 84/450/EEC, Directives 97/7/EC, 98/27/EC and 2002/65/EC of the European Parliament and of the Council and Regulation (EC) No 2006/2004 of the European Parliament and of the Council ('Unfair Commercial Practices Directive') (UCPD) [2005] OJ L149/22, Art 1.

[11] Zakon o zaštiti potrošača (English trans: Law on Consumer Protection) published in the Official Gazette of the Federal Republic of Yugoslavia No 37/02.

[12] Zakon o zaštiti potrošača (English trans: Law on Consumer Protection) published in the Official Gazette of the Republic of Serbia No 45/05.

[13] H-W Micklitz, 'Do Consumers and Businesses Need a New Architecture of Consumer Law – A Thought Provoking Impulse' (2013) 32 *Yearbook of European Law* 266.

the Law of Obligations, which is considered to be the pearl and pride of Serbian legal tradition, not to be disturbed by any foreign element.

Interestingly, in the same period Serbia adopted its new Constitution (2006), which has one article that gives the right to be protected as a consumer a constitutional dimension, something highly innovative in Serbia as the right to be protected as a consumer is one of the new generation of human rights.[14] The article points out that 'The Republic of Serbia protects consumers. Actions against the health, safety and privacy of consumers, as well as all dishonest actions on the market, are especially prohibited.'[15] Still, and sadly, this article is almost never referred to either by law enforcers or by the Serbian courts, or in publications on consumer law issues, unlike the Court of Justice of the European Union (CJEU), which extensively refers to a similar provision of the Charter while deciding on consumer law matters.[16] Likewise, it does not seem that consumers are aware of this constitutionally guaranteed right on which they can rely.

In terms of the legislative framework, the first significant Serbian Law on Consumer Protection was adopted only in 2010, as a result of group work by foreign and domestic legal experts.[17] It may be observed that adoption of this law was a consequence of conclusion of the Stabilisation and Association Agreement (SAA) that Serbia signed with the EU in 2008. The SAA contains a provision that requires all of the candidate states to have aligned their national laws with EU law, so the obligation to harmonise consumer law became an obligation established on the basis of an international treaty.[18] Adoption of the new law in 2010 was something highly innovative, having for the first time introduced into the Serbian legal system fundamental elements of EU consumer law that had not existed in the previous two pieces of legislation.

The topics covered in the 2010 Law included an extensive set of rules on unfair commercial practices, unfair contract terms, the sale of consumer goods, information requirements, the right of withdrawal and collective redress. Some of these rules had already been an integral part of the two previous legal frameworks for consumer protection for some years, but the 2010 Law demonstrated for the first time a high level of alignment with the consumer *acquis*.[19] However, this Law was never properly applied in practice due to issues with effective enforcement and a lack of strong political will and push to have these standards applied.[20]

---

[14] I Benohr, *EU Consumer Law and Human Rights* (Oxford University Press, 2013) 46.

[15] Constitution of the Republic of Serbia 2006, Art 90.

[16] Charter of Fundamental Rights of the European Union [2012] OJ C326/391, Art 38.

[17] Official Gazette of the Republic of Serbia No 73/2010.

[18] Stabilisation and Association Agreement between the European Communities and their Member States of the one part, and the Republic of Serbia, of the other part [2013] OJ L278/16, Art 78 foresees cooperation between the contracting parties in harmonising consumer protection standards in Serbia with those of the EU, and places this obligation in the context of successful functioning of the market economy and administrative capacities to ensure market surveillance and law enforcement in this area. In addition, the same provision clarifies the obligation to harmonise consumer protection legislation in Serbia with EU law, achieving effective legal protection.

[19] For an overview of the EU Consumer Law, see G Howells, C Twigg-Flesner and T Wilhelmsson, *Rethinking EU Consumer Law* (Routledge, 2018).

[20] M Durovic and N Lazarevic, 'Towards the European Union: The Serbian Law on Consumer Protection and the Position of the Serbian Consumer' (2014) 3 *Journal of European Consumer and Market Law* 17, 17–25.

In order to improve enforcement mechanisms, the next Law on Consumer Protection was already adopted in 2014.[21] The main reason behind the legislative change was to transform the enforcement process – which, according to the Law of 2010, had relied more on the courts – to a more administrative-focused enforcement. Even so, the mechanisms offered by the Law of 2014 again turned out to be insufficiently effective and the enforcement mechanisms were inadequate. The outcome was that a high level of discrepancy between consumer law in the books and consumer law in practice has remained and further actions were required.[22] In the meantime, in 2019, Serbia adopted its new five-year Consumer Protection Strategy covering the period from 2019 to 2024.[23] This Strategy focuses on the need to enhance consumer protection and strengthen the institutional framework and capacities of the bodies in charge of enforcing consumer law, but not much has changed during the years that have passed since its adoption in terms of real improvement of consumer protection in Serbia. The major outcome of the Strategy has been adoption of the new, fifth Law on Consumer Protection.

After adoption of the Strategy, discussion started on the need to adopt a new Law on Consumer Protection. Eventually, in September 2021, Serbia passed the new Law on Consumer Protection, which is currently in force.[24] With its 196 articles, it is a very long and detailed piece of legislation. The main innovations it has introduced are in relation to strengthening and enhancing state enforcement mechanisms, as well as giving more importance to out-of-court consumer dispute resolution mechanisms.[25] Still, in many situations when EU law has left open that possibility, Serbia has not benefited from the minimum harmonisation character of certain rules and has provided a higher level of protection than envisaged by European legislation.[26] Likewise, in the case of European rules where maximum harmonisation is required, Serbia hardly went beyond what is written in the text of the Directive, in order to address issues not covered by the text of European legislation, which has been a missed opportunity to set up an adequate national consumer protection mechanism.[27]

The 2021 Law on Consumer Protection is already the fifth piece of specialised legislation on consumer protection adopted in Serbia in a period of less than two decades. The focus of the changes was always on enforcement, as the aim was to adopt a system best suited to the needs and particularities of the Serbian market, society, economy and legal system. The push for all these five changes came from the EU, in particular through its assessment of Serbian consumer law, which has demonstrated a lack of alignment with EU consumer law. The Serbian Ministry of Trade, as the competent body for consumer protection, initiated all of these changes, but to some extent

---

[21] Official Gazette of the Republic of Serbia Nos 62/14, 6/16 and 44/18.

[22] D Protić, 'Consumer Protection in Serbia: What are Some Possible Directions for Progress?: A Public Policy Discussion Document with Options for Possible Solutions' (2020) European Policy Centre at cep.org.rs/wp-content/uploads/2020/07/Consumer-protection-in-Serbia.pdf (accessed 13 December 2022).

[23] See at pravno-informacioni-sistem.rs/SlGlasnikPortal/eli/rep/sgrs/vlada/strategija/2019/93/1 (accessed 13 December 2022).

[24] Zakon o zaštiti potrošača (English trans: Law on Consumer Protection) 2021 published in the Official Gazette of the Republic of Serbia No 88/21.

[25] ibid ch XIII.

[26] eg, Council Directive 93/13/EEC of 5 April 1993 on unfair terms in consumer contracts [1993] OJ L95/29, Art 8.

[27] eg, UCPD (n 10) Art 4.

several national and international legal experts were involved, primarily through foreign funding coming from the European Commission or the German Government, though the role of the experts in the legislative process was limited. Likewise, participation by other stakeholders, such as consumer organisations, was limited, in some cases, surprisingly, due to their lack of expertise in the field of consumer protection.

It is important to note that in recent years it has been suggested that the Serbian Law of Obligations might be replaced by a new, more general Serbian Civil Code, something seen as part of a revival of Serbia's old legal legacy, bearing in mind that Serbia was among the first European countries to have a modern Civil Code, adopted in 1844.[28] However, a recently published draft of the Serbian Civil Code also ignores the existence of specific rules on consumer protection, making almost no reference to consumer law and a specific consumer protection regime.[29]

IV. Consumer Problems in Serbia

In Serbia, consumers are faced with several diverse consumer law problems.[30] For example, one of the major complaints is in relation to lack of conformity of shoes (because they wear out quickly, or they do not have characteristics as initially advertised or claimed). The travel sector is another industry sector where Serbian consumers are faced with numerous problems: trips are cancelled at the last minute without any justified reason; guests are put in hotels that materially differ from what was advertised; extra fees are imposed on consumers – fees not mentioned at the moment of conclusion of the contract – and the like. That is why the 2021 Law on Consumer Protection pays special attention to this and grants a number of competences to tourism inspectors.

In addition, a number of problems have arisen in connection with services of general economic interest. This is primarily to do with services provided by public utility companies and telecommunications companies, which aggravates the severity of these violations. Moreover, it can reasonably be expected that these violations will be significantly more frequent than suggested by the volume of proceedings actually conducted (a total of 16 cases in the five years from 2017), especially in areas where service providers enjoy monopoly positions in the market, such as utilities. A significant contributor to unfair contractual provisions are regulations on the manner and conditions of provision of utility services by local governments, as well as sectoral regulations laying down the conditions for provision of services to end users (such as energy and telecommunications services), which are not always adequately harmonised with prescribed consumer rights and in practice often prevail over those rights.[31] It is important to note that all of the major companies in charge of supplying electricity, water and telecommunication services are owned by the state.

---

[28] M Durovic, 'Serbian Contract Law: Its Development and the New Serbian Civil Code' (2011) 7 *European Review of Contract Law* 65, 65–77.
[29] Draft of Civil Code of the Republic of Serbia at mpravde.gov.rs/files/NACRT.pdf (accessed 13 December 2022).
[30] See at mtt.gov.rs/tekst/sr/2306/zastita-potrosaca.php (accessed 13 December 2022).
[31] Protić (n 22).

However, consumer credit contracts have probably been the biggest consumer law problem in practice. One of these is the issue with consumer contracts concluded in Swiss francs, with consumers severely negatively affected when, as a result of the global economic crisis, the rate of exchange between the Swiss franc and the euro (EUR) and the Serbian dinar (RSD) soared.[32] In that sense, there is a huge similarity with the EU Member States in Eastern and South-Eastern Europe, as in this part of the world there has been a general problem with consumer credit agreements affecting so many consumers – and Serbia is no exception.[33] Serbia solved this problem by adopting a new Law on Conversion of Consumer Credits Stipulated in Swiss Francs, with the attempt to protect consumers the result of a strong push by society.[34]

In addition, over the past few years, a large number of lawsuits have appeared, brought by consumers – beneficiaries of loans granted by banks, especially housing loans – against the banks for the purpose of recovering part of the monies paid by the consumers in the name of processing loan costs or calculating interest. The catalyst for the increase in the number of these lawsuits was the 2018 Opinion of the Supreme Court of Serbia in connection with a large number of cases in banking disputes, in which it was asked to rule on the nullity of provisions of a credit agreement that allow the bank to charge the borrower for the costs of processing and releasing the loan in an exchange rate, at a percentage in relation to the value of the loan.[35]

This legal position established that the bank has the quoted right only if the bank's offer contained clear and unambiguous information on the costs of the loan. Based specifically on the express requirement that the bank's offer must contain clear and unambiguous data on the calculation of loan costs, a large number of lawsuits followed, demanding reimbursement of loan processing costs, asserting that this condition was not fulfilled at the time of conclusion of the contract. As no special classification of these cases is foreseen according to court registers, and in practice the details on the cases involving the dispute are not completely uniform in the records, it is not possible to obtain precise information on the number of these cases. However, estimates from the Association of Serbian Banks indicate that between 220,000 and 250,000 lawsuits of this type are currently active, and that the number of individual users who appear as claimants in these lawsuits is between 50,000 and 80,000.[36]

Under the pressure of a large influx of similar lawsuits, which created an enormous burden on the regular work of the courts, as well as other issues that were open to the

---

[32] European Parliament, 'Unfair Terms in Swiss Franc Loans: Overview of European Court of Justice Case Law' (2021) Briefing, European Parliamentary Research Service at europarl.europa.eu/RegData/etudes/BRIE/2021/689361/EPRS_BRI(2021)689361_EN.pdf (accessed 13 December 2022).

[33] E Miscenic, 'Currency Clauses in CHF Credit Agreements: A "Small Wheel" in the Swiss Loans' Mechanism' (2020) 6 *Journal of European Consumer and Market Law* 226, 226–35.

[34] Law on Conversion of Consumer Credits Stipulated in Swiss Francs Sl glasnik RS, No 31/2019.

[35] Legal Opinion of the Supreme Court of Serbia of 22 May 2018, 'Pravni stav o dozvoljenosti ugovaranja troškova kredita' at vk.sud.rs/sites/default/files/attachments/%D0%9F%D1%80%D0%B0%D0%B2%D0%BD%D0%B8%20%D1%81%D1%82%D0%B0%D0%B2%D0%B0%20%D0%BE%20%D1%82%D1%80%D0%BE%D1%88%D0%BA%D0%BE%D0%B2%D0%B8%D0%BC%D0%B0%20%D0%BA%D1%80%D0%B5%D0%B4%D0%B8%D1%82%D0%B0.pdf (accessed 19 December 2022).

[36] N Kovacevic, 'Masovni sporovi – rešenje (masovnih problema) ili (masovni) problem?' (2021) at otvorenavratapravosudja.rs/teme/ostalo/masovni-sporovi-resenje-masovnih-problema-ili-masovni-problem (accessed 13 December 2022).

professional and general public regarding these cases, the Supreme Court of Cassation recently intervened again, by means of an 'amendment' to the 2018 legal Opinion. The amendment consists of a note that the bank need not separately prove the structure and amount of costs included in the total amount of loan costs detailed in the offer that the loan beneficiary accepted by concluding the loan agreement.[37]

The issue with this type of agreement and the legal Opinion of the Supreme Court of Serbia that affected legal certainty has not yet been resolved but is still ongoing. Moreover, many consumer law issues have been the result of irresponsible lending.[38] Generally speaking, in terms of consumer credits, a major issue has been about transparency requirements and the validity of several clauses in consumer credit agreements.

This again is something not unique to Serbia; it is all too present in the Western Balkans and throughout the whole of Eastern Europe, something also addressed by the CJEU in its case law.[39] Still, in the case of Serbia, consumer credit is also discussed in the context of its alignment with the Law of Obligations and in particular its good faith clause,[40] rather than trying to resolve these issues on the basis of consumer law rules. In that sense, it may be observed that the story with consumer credit agreements represents a crucially important moment for the transformation of consumer law in Serbia, as it has shown Serbian consumers the potential power that consumer law may have in reality. This has clearly been achieved due to the broad publicity that these cases have enjoyed in Serbia, followed by their legal scrutiny.

V. Transformation of Consumer Education and Consumer Rights Awareness

The aspect of consumer awareness of the existence and meaning of consumer rights when actively consuming is probably the area where there has been the greatest progress during the development of consumer law in Serbia. Consumers are now more vocal and try harder to fight for their rights. Of great help in terms of better education for consumers about the existence and content of consumer rights have been numerous consumer education campaigns, supported primarily by diverse EU or EU Member States' funds. The idea has been to educate consumers about the existence and content of their rights. and also to teach consumers what they are expected to do in the event that their rights are infringed.

Furthermore, one of the most popular – as well as the oldest – daily newspapers in Serbia, *Politika*, now publishes, on a weekly basis, two full pages dedicated exclusively to diverse consumer law issues with which Serbian consumers are faced, as well as

---

[37] Legal Opinion of the Supreme Court of Serbia of 16 September 2021, 'Pravni stav o dozvoljenosti ugovaranja troškova kredita' at vk.sud.rs/sites/default/files/attachments/PRAVNI%20STAV%20O%20 DOZVOLJENOSTI%20UGOVARANJA%20TROŠKOVA%20KREDITA.pdf (accessed 19 December 2022).

[38] OO Cherednychenko and JM Meindertsma, 'Irresponsible Lending in the Post-Crisis Era: Is the EU Consumer Credit Directive Fit for Its Purpose?' (2019) 42 *Journal of Consumer Policy* 483, 483–519.

[39] Case C-453/10 *Jana Pereničová and Vladislav Perenič v SOS financ spol sro* ECLI:EU:C:2012:144.

[40] Law of Obligations 1978 (n 7) Art 12.

informing the public about developments in other jurisdictions, with the focus on the EU.[41] Every year, 15 March, as World Consumer Day, is celebrated with many activities and strong media coverage, the aim of which is to increase consumers' awareness of their rights, but also to encourage traders to comply with consumer law.

Nevertheless, a marked lack of willingness remains, on the part of traders, to act on consumer complaints regarding products purchased. Some categories of traders, such as state-owned companies (for example, in charge of electrical energy supply) or some companies that represent foreign investment, seem to be – at least unofficially – more exempted from alignment with consumer law, although EU law is clear that a trader's ownership model has no effect on the binding force of consumer legislation.[42]

In spite of two decades of continuous development of the framework for consumer protection and improvement of consumer law awareness among consumers, in the legal world there is still a noticeable struggle to properly accept and understand consumer law. At the level of university education and law schools, consumer law modules are very scarce, if they exist at all. Unlike in the case of some other jurisdictions, such as the UK, consumer law is not studied as part of the module on contract/obligations law. In addition, no proper, in-depth monograph on consumer law nor even a commentary on consumer legislation has been written in Serbia, despite the clear need for such a publication. Consumer law is not part of the rather extensive requirements for the official state-run bar exams either, which are required before joining any of the bars and becoming a judge in Serbia. In their submissions to the courts, lawyers seem reluctant to refer to specific consumer law legislation, preferring, in the case of consumer law disputes, still to rely on the rules of the old Law of Obligations – rules with which they are familiar.

VI. Transformation of Enforcement Mechanisms

Consumers always need access to justice when their rights are infringed.[43] Securing efficient and proper enforcement has remained the biggest challenge for consumer law and policy on a global level.[44] It may be said that consumer law in a country is only as good as its system of enforcement. In its judgment in *Alassini*, the CJEU confirmed a mandatory obligation of Member States to secure the consumer's right to effective protection and access to justice.[45] The legal design of enforcement mechanisms in the EU varies, however, and may be placed into two main categories: countries relying on the courts; and countries relying on the administrative authorities. Like all other Western Balkan countries, Serbia has been struggling with the proper design of consumer law enforcement mechanisms.[46] The aim of improving enforcement was the main reason behind all

---

[41] See at politika.rs/sr/tags/articles/2069/potrosaci (accessed 13 December 2022).
[42] Case C-92/11 *RWE Vertrieb AG v Verbraucherzentrale Nordrhein-Westfalen eV* ECLI:EU:C:2013:180.
[43] S Wrbka, *European Consumer Access to Justice* (Cambridge University Press, 2014).
[44] H-W Micklitz and G Saumier (eds), *Enforcement and Effectiveness of Consumer Law* (Springer, 2018).
[45] Joined Cases C-317/08 to C-320/08 *Rosalba Alassini and others v Telecom It Spa and others* ECLI:EU:C:2010:146, [2010] ECR I-02213, para 61.
[46] Y Svetiev, 'How Consumer Law Travels' (2013) 36 *Journal of Consumer Policy* 209, 228.

three of the latest legislative changes in Serbia. The eternal dilemma has been whether to opt for reliance on the courts or on the administrative authorities as the principal authorities in charge of enforcement.

The outcome of all the numerous legislative attempts to improve consumer protection in Serbia was, however, that whatever rules could be applied in practice were unsatisfactory, leaving consumers with little redress in cases where protection should have been available.[47] Collective enforcement, a very powerful tool for the protection of consumers, although broadly envisaged by the Law on Consumer Protection, has been insufficiently used in practice.[48]

Indeed, since 2016 and so far, precisely 25 cases of collective redress of consumers have ended successfully, according to the official statistics of the Serbian Ministry of Trade.[49] Most of these cases have been brought against providers of mobile phone and Internet services, and against water supply companies, and have dealt with diverse forms of unfair contract terms, such as provisions that enable unilateral changes of prices, and unfair commercial practices, such as those that sanction misleading omissions, where traders failed to provide all relevant information to the consumer in their marketing messages. Still, the potential of consumer law has not yet been fully used. Moreover, Serbia has not yet transposed the provisions of the latest European developments in the field.[50]

VII.   Judicial Enforcement

The problem with enforcement by the courts in Serbia is that proceedings have traditionally been very long and time-consuming, although in that respect there has been some improvement, primarily as a result of the case law of the European Court of Human Rights in connection with the European Convention on Human Rights, which guarantees the right to a fair trial and the right to an effective legal remedy.[51] Another improvement has been the abolition of any kind of court fee for consumer law disputes, which is an important step forward. In attempts to support consumer access to the courts, for any consumer dispute the value of which is below RSD 500,000 (a bit more than EUR 4,200), all judicial fees have been abolished.[52]

This is undoubtedly a great development, but one must not forget that court proceedings in Serbia still typically last for many years. Again, the very long duration of proceedings is something that substantially undermines the protection to the consumer

---

[47] M Karanikic Miric, 'Understanding the Enforcement Malfunction of Consumer Legislation in Serbia' (2013) 36 *Journal of Consumer Policy* 231, 231–46.

[48] Law on Consumer Protection 2021 (n 24) ch XIV.

[49] See at mtt.gov.rs/informacije/zastita-potrosaca/resenje-o-povredi-kolektivnoginteresa-potrosaca/ (accessed 1 September 2022).

[50] Directive (EU) 2020/1828 of the European Parliament and of the Council of 25 November 2020 on representative actions for the protection of the collective interests of consumers and repealing Directive 2009/22/EC [2020] OJ L409/1.

[51] Convention for the Protection of Human Rights and Fundamental Freedoms (European Convention on Human Rights, as amended) (ECHR), Arts 6 and 13.

[52] Law on Consumer Protection 2021 (n 24) Art 148.

offered by the courts. In order to address this issue, the new Law on Consumer Protection has imposed an obligation on the courts to record every consumer lawsuit and to submit data on the number of consumer disputes, rulings and the average duration of consumer disputes to the Ministry in charge of justice, on the prescribed form, by 31 March of the current year.[53] However, to this day, evidence or a list of consumer law cases decided by the courts in Serbia is missing.

Bearing in mind that consumer law cases are of low value, many consumers cannot be bothered to pursue their rights before the courts. Moreover, some judges seem to be reluctant to attend any of the consumer law training sessions, still judging consumer law disputes on the basis of the old Law of Obligations of 1978 that contains no consumer law-specific rules. Despite all these deficiencies, enforcement of most consumer contract-related issues still remains within the competence of the Serbian courts, these primarily involving the rules on unfair contract terms, as only the courts are allowed to decide on the validity and terms of contracts. However, as we have seen, the courts seem to be reluctant to apply the rules on unfair contract terms. As a result, although in the EU the rules on unfair contract terms afford extremely powerful protection to the consumer, especially after the development of very fruitful case law of the CJEU in this field, Serbia has seen very few cases decided on this legal ground.[54]

While examining the Serbian rules on consumer protection, as well as how they are interpreted and applied in practice, it is possible to observe that there is hardly any reference to or codification of the outcome of the case law of the CJEU. Although Serbia as a candidate state is obliged to follow case-law developments, that connection is clearly missing. It should not be forgotten that the CJEU in Luxembourg is the only judicial institution entitled to provide autonomous interpretation of EU law, including the rules on consumer protection. All this deserves attention and further work on improvement. Judges need more education and training on consumer law.

One might argue that the reason for the omission to follow CJEU case law is the consequence of the fact that these decisions are not published in the Serbian language, as Serbia is still not an EU Member State. However, that argument fails, as the judgments of the Court are published in Croatian, a language very similar to Serbian, which enables all judges and other interested parties to understand case law without any problem.

VIII. Administrative Enforcement

Administrative enforcement seems to be a better option for Serbia, as it is more efficient and also more inclined to accept the consumer *acquis* method of reasoning. In that sense, the role of trade and other relevant market inspectors has to be praised, as they have tried really hard to secure better enforcement of consumer law. Under the latest

---

[53] ibid.
[54] EH Hondius, 'Unfair Contract Terms and the Consumer: ECJ Case Law, Foreign Literature, and Their Impact on Dutch Law' (2016) 24 *European Review of Private Law* 457, 457–72.

Law on Consumer Protection (2021), two types of inspectors are in charge of enforcing consumer law: market inspectors and tourist inspectors.[55] For most breaches in relation to the sale of goods and provision of services, both market inspectors and tourist inspectors have powers to address any breach of consumer law in the area of tourism, where an increasing number of problems have arisen in recent years in relation to travel services: package travel, hotel reservations, and so on.

The Ministry in charge of consumer protection has always been the Ministry of Trade. A step forward, some years ago, was establishment of a separate Assistant Minister at the head of a department exclusively in charge of consumer law. However, for diverse reasons, such as financial constraints and the prohibition on employment of new civil servants, this department remains under-staffed and is thus limited in its activities. The maximum fine that can be issued is not that high: RSD 2,000,000 (roughly EUR 17,000) – this is something that should be increased in the future.[56] If fines for breach of consumer law are not sufficiently high, some traders may have more economic incentive to breach consumer law and pay the fines, as this would be a cheaper option for them than fully complying with consumer law.

Still, as enforcement of the rules on unfair commercial practices is within the competence of this Ministry, it is possible to observe a positive development and an increasing number of cases. In that sense, it may be said that consumers in Serbia benefit more (much more) from the system of protection secured through the rules on unfair commercial practices than from the rules on unfair contract terms that are supposed to be enforced by the courts. The sanctioning of breaches of consumer law – which are subject to inspection supervision, administrative procedures for the protection of the collective interest of consumers – and misdemeanour procedures – which are supported by administrative measures or the possible sanctioning of traders – by their nature cannot ensure sufficient protection of individual consumer rights and interests but rather work to influence traders' behaviours. For their individual rights, consumers have to rely once again on inadequate protection by the courts. Likewise, the studies that need to be carried out by the Ministry on how the Serbian consumer really behaves while on the market are missing, and these would benefit better enhancement of consumer law enforcement.[57]

The Ministry of Trade is also in charge of the ambitious idea of developing a National Register of Consumer Complaints, which is still ongoing.[58] Consumers have the right to file a consumer complaint with the Ministry of Trade, reporting a violation of a regulated right. In addition, announced as one of the special novelties introduced by the new Law on Consumer Protection is a new register, to be kept by the agency in charge of regulation of telecommunication services. All those consumers who do not want to be harassed by traders who offer them various products on the phone will be able to apply to register their details in this registry. Traders could be fined if they call consumers whose numbers have been entered on the register. This provision, although

---

[55] Law on Consumer Protection 2021 (n 24) Art 181.

[56] ibid Art 187.

[57] AL Sibony, 'Can EU consumer law benefit from behavioural insights? An analysis of the unfair Commercial Practices Directive' (2014) 22 *European Review of Private Law* 901.

[58] See at zapotrosace.gov.rs/ (accessed 13 December 2022).

one might argue that it is fine from the perspective of consumer protection, might be questionable from the perspective of the rules on unfair commercial practices and their maximum harmonisation character. Although this practice may resemble one of those blacklisted by the UCPD, it is not the same as the one listed in the blacklist in Annex I to the Directive.

IX. Transformation of Alternative Methods for Resolving Consumer Disputes

Certain other methods for resolving consumer disputes represent an excellent alternative to a state-backed enforcement mechanism, but only if they are aligned with the strict requirement for secure protection of the consumer as the weaker party.[59] In recent years, Serbia has witnessed the development of diverse forms of alternative resolution of consumer disputes. All of the recent Serbian Laws on Consumer Protection supported the idea of constructing an adequate legal framework, with the aim of diminishing pressure on the courts. Traders have to inform the consumer about the existence and models of out-of-court methods of dispute resolution before a consumer contract has been concluded. Mediation seems to be the most successful model in Serbia, and there has been a substantial step forward in that direction as an increasing number of disputes are resolved in this manner.

The Serbian Law on Consumer Protection has also established the National Council for Consumer Protection. This Council has a consultative role and is formed by law by the Government.[60] It consists of representatives of state institutions, scholars and organisations working on consumer protection policy. The Council serves to create a unified consumer protection policy in the Republic of Serbia, so its tasks are: to propose measures and activities to improve consumer protection policy; to prepare overall analyses that will indicate the shortcomings of the system; to participate in drafting the Consumer Protection Strategy; and to inform the public and report to the Government on all issues relevant to this area. Unfortunately, the practical importance and effects of the existence of this body are much less than their potential.

X. Transformation of the Consumer Movement

Consumer organisations represent one of the pillars of an efficient system for enforcement of consumer law in all of the EU Member States.[61] Serbia's problem is not the lack of a consumer movement but rather the lack of a sufficiently educated, trained

---

[59] A Biard, 'Monitoring Consumer ADR Quality in the EU: A Critical Perspective' (2018) 26 *European Review of Private Law* 171, 171–95.

[60] See at pravno-informacioni-sistem.rs/SlGlasnikPortal/eli/rep/sgrs/vlada/odluka/2021/9/4 (accessed 13 December 2022).

[61] Consolidated version of the Treaty on the Functioning of the European Union [2012] OJ C326/47, Art 169(1).

and supported consumer movement. Likewise, consumer organisations require more visibility and awareness among the general public.

The development of consumer law in Serbia has led to the establishment of numerous consumer organisations in the country. As a result, today, more than 100 consumer organisations exist in Serbia, of which 26 are recognised in that capacity by the Ministry of Trade, which, as already noted, is in charge of consumer protection.[62] The reason behind this boom in the establishment of consumer organisations was (at least partially) the fact that many saw the establishment of a consumer organisation as an excellent business opportunity, due to the funding opportunities available from the government budget and the various EU and EU Member State grant opportunities that have opened up since the early 2000s. In other words, the prevailing motivation was not to help society and the Serbian consumer, but the means to run a business and secure a personal income.

Accordingly, the presence of a high number of consumer organisations in Serbia must not be read as a sign of developed Serbian consumer law and policy. In reality, most of these consumer organisations have remained rather small, with very few people involved, and somewhat inactive, lacking more training and skills. None of the consumer organisations from Serbia is a member of BEUC – the European Consumer Organisation.[63] For improving the overall level of consumer protection in Serbia, what is certainly needed is further strengthening of the consumer movement, not quantitatively but qualitatively. The number of consumer organisations should decrease, and those selected to remain should be appropriately prepared to address consumer law challenges and help, for example, with collective redress, which was introduced as a legal mechanism for the first time under the previous Serbian Law on Consumer Protection but almost never applied in practice.[64]

XI. (Lack of) Adaptation of Consumer Law and Policy to the Digital Age

The Fourth Industrial Revolution and the process of digitalisation, as accelerated by the global Covid-19 pandemic, have brought substantial challenges to all areas of law worldwide, including consumer law and policy.[65] Serbia is no exception in that respect. The development of new technologies, such as smart contracts, online platforms or artificial intelligence, has introduced new risks to consumers, and consumer law rules need to be adapted in order to secure a high level of consumer protection in the digital age.[66] Accordingly, the EU is trying to keep pace with rapid

---

[62] See at 195.222.96.203/evidentirana-udruzenja.php (accessed 5 September 2022).
[63] The European Consumer Organisation at beuc.eu (accessed 13 December 2022).
[64] B Babovic, 'Legislative changes in the field of consumer collective redress' (2014) 2 *Anali Pravnog fakultetat u Beogradu* 215, 219.
[65] R Brownsword, *Law, Technology and Society: Re-imagining the Regulatory Environment* (Routledge, 2019).
[66] G Howells, 'Protecting Consumer Protection Values in the Fourth Industrial Revolution' (2020) 43 *Journal of Consumer Policy* 145, 145–75.

technological changes and secure proper evolution of its consumer protection mechanisms.[67]

However, as of late 2022, Serbian consumer legislation contains no rules specifically designed to protect consumers on the digital market. Interestingly, although the new Law on Consumer Protection was drafted and adopted as recently as in late 2021, it does not incorporate nor even mention any digital aspects of consumer protection. This is surprising, not only because consumers in Serbia are exposed to these new risks like consumers all over the world, but also because in 2019, the EU itself adopted its new Directive 2019/2161/EU on modernisation and better enforcement of EU consumer law,[68] which represents the first step towards adapting existing EU consumer law to the digital era.[69] The deadline for transposition of this Directive passed in December 2021, yet a debate on incorporating it into the Serbian legal system has so far not even started.

Similarly, the rules of the new 'twin' directives on the supply of digital content and digital services (Directive 2019/770/EU)[70] and on contracts for the sale of goods (Directive 2019/771/EU)[71] have not been addressed at all. The incorporation of all these rules is something that the EU expects from Serbia, but most importantly it is something that is of essential importance for all consumers in Serbia, who are increasingly being exposed to the legal issues that digitalisation brings. It is such a pity that the chance to develop these rules was missed in 2021 when the new Law on Consumer Protection was being prepared. The reason behind this lack of action was possibly that there was no EU pressure on Serbia to follow these steps, which leads us back to the observation at beginning of this chapter, namely, that the approach to consumer law in Serbia is as something being imposed from the outside rather than being organically developed.

From an enforcement perspective, the digital age also requires more coordination among the authorities in charge of competition law, data protection law and consumer law, which is very important, for example, from the perspective of commercialisation of consumer data, where consumer personal data are being harvested and sold on by traders.[72] In Serbia today, three totally different authorities are in charge of these three fields of law: for competition law, there is a separate Agency for Protection of Competition; for data protection, there is a Data Protection Authority; and for consumer law, as noted previously, the Ministry of Trade is in charge. There is hardly any institutional design that secures adequate communication, exchange of information and coordination

---

[67] M Durovic, 'Adaptation of Consumer Law to the Digital Age: The Case of the New European Directive 2019/2161 on Modernisation and Better Enforcement of Consumer Law' (2020) 68 *Belgrade Law Review* 120, 120–35.

[68] Directive (EU) 2019/2161 of the European Parliament and of the Council of 27 November 2019 amending Council Directive 93/13/EEC and Directives 98/6/EC, 2005/29/EC and 2011/83/EU of the European Parliament and of the Council as regards the better enforcement and modernisation of Union consumer protection rules [2019] OJ L328/7.

[69] M Grochowski, 'European Consumer Law after the New Deal: A Tryptich' (2020) 39 *Yearbook of European Law* 387, 387–422.

[70] Directive (EU) 2019/770 of the European Parliament and of the Council of 20 May 2019 on certain aspects concerning contracts for the supply of digital content and digital services [2019] OJ L136/1.

[71] Directive (EU) 2019/771 of the European Parliament and of the Council of 20 May 2019 on certain aspects concerning contracts for the sale of goods, amending Regulation (EU) 2017/2394 and Directive 2009/22/EC, and repealing Directive 1999/44/EC [2019] OJ L136/28.

[72] M Durovic and F Lech, 'A Consumer Law Perspective on the Commercialization of Data' (2021) 29 *European Review of Private Law* 701, 701–32.

among them. Moreover, the digitalisation of the market also requires development of diverse forms for the resolution of consumer disputes that would fit the digital age.[73] Serbia has not progressed much in that respect. In that sense, it may be concluded that more efforts are certainly needed in that direction to secure protection of the Serbian consumer in the digital age.

Similarly to the case of digitalisation, the current and ongoing issue of sustainability at the European level, and how to make consumer law more sustainable, is something that has not yet entered the discourse of Serbian consumer law and policy.[74] For example, the right to have goods replaced in the event of lack of conformity is still an equal choice option for the consumer as the right to have them repaired under the 2021 Law on Consumer Protection.[75]

However, consumers themselves are becoming increasingly interested in the issue of sustainability, especially in the context of energy efficiency. This is the result not only of consumer education, but also and primarily of the rising inflation phenomenon, which anticipates a future financial crisis in Serbia (as well as in the rest of Europe) that will open up a number of new consumer law cases. One must not forget how the previous 2008 global financial crisis affected consumers in the EU, and the response of EU consumer law and the fruitful CJEU case law that has developed as a result of it.[76]

XII. Concluding Observations

All in all, it may be concluded that Serbian consumer law has undergone a huge process of transformation in the last 20 years: from a non-existent concept into being established and recognised as a separate branch of law that positively affects the everyday life of every Serbian consumer. Nevertheless, consumer law still seems to be something innovative that did not manage to fully penetrate the logic and basis of the Serbian legal system and its stakeholders. However, it would be unfair – and, most importantly, untrue – to say that Serbian consumers are not better protected in 2022 than they were in 2002: some progress is certainly noticeable, as during this period consumer law has transformed from nothing into something that consumers have heard of and that, in some cases, they can rely on to help them resolve their consumer law problems.

More efforts have yet to be made to improve the general framework of consumer protection and diminish the gap between consumer law in the books and consumer law in action. Where further transformation is particularly needed is the mindset of judges, legal practitioners and policymakers, who need to understand what consumer protection means in practice and the entire set of principles on the basis of which consumer

---

[73] P Cortes, *The Law on Consumer Redress* (Cambridge University Press, 2017).

[74] E Terryn, 'A Right to Repair? Towards Sustainable Remedies in Consumer Law' (2019) 27 *European Review of Private Law* 851, 851–73.

[75] Law on Consumer Protection 2021 (n 24) Art 51.

[76] eg, Case C-415/11 *Mohamed Aziz v Caixa d'Estalvis de Catalunya, Tarragona i Manresa (Catalunyacaixa)* ECLI:EU:C:2013:164.

law has developed, as well as strengthening the entire institutional mechanism in charge of consumer law. Consumer law cases in Serbia have to be decided on the basis of consumer law, not on the basis of the general Law of Obligations.

Moreover, Serbian consumers themselves are already more aware of the existence and meaning of their consumer rights and are increasingly attempting to fight for their rights. That is a great achievement, and probably represents the aspect where the greatest progress has been made. In contrast to this, the consumer movement itself, although increasingly present, is not much help in enhancing consumer protection; it needs to be strengthened and reformed, while more training and a better regulatory framework are needed to ensure the quality of work of consumer organisations and to decrease their number. Last, but not least, what needs to be improved is the adaptation of consumer law to the challenges brought about by digitalisation of the market and all the threats (and opportunities) that the new technologies are bringing to the Serbian consumer. In that sense, Serbia has so far missed implementing all the recent European developments in the field – a failure that must be corrected in the (near) future.

10

Greece: A Tale of Two Acts

I. Introduction

This chapter examines the role European Union (EU) law played in transforming consumer law in Greece. Greece joined the EU in the 1981 enlargement and has been, by and large, a pro-European country, even when shaken to its core by the 2008 financial crisis.

The timeline of the analysis begins in the 1990s, when the main Greek consumer legislation was enacted, and follows developments from the millennium to the financial crisis and until today. It seeks to demonstrate that EU consumer law directives have had a positive effect on national law and played a key role in establishing consumer protection as a separate hybrid area of law and increasing the level of protection for consumers. It also raises the point that the success of EU consumer law goes beyond a simple top-down construction and one-size-fits-all approach and requires an adjustment to the needs of the particular Member State, in this case Greece.

Greek consumer law preceded EU consumer law but does not have a long tradition in Greece, and it is safe to say that the vast majority of Greek consumer law today is EU consumer law. Consumer protection is not a key priority for the Greek legislator, nor did it need to be with a robust framework provided by EU consumer law. Still, Greece has introduced legislation to protect consumers for specific issues, such as most notably in the years of the financial crisis, N.3869/2010 on overindebted households.[1] The enforcement system has also been transformed by EU law, offering resources to enforcement authorities and access to a network of European authorities. Indeed, EU law has had a transformative effect on Greek consumer law, but that does not tell the whole story. Greece has its own national priorities and traditions, which often do not align with those of EU consumer law. When there is such a misalignment, legal provisions tend to be under-utilised and do not produce their intended transformative effect.

---

[1] N.3869/2010 published in the *Official Government Gazette of the Hellenic Republic* (ΦΕΚ Α′) No 130/3.8.2010.

To demonstrate this phenomenon, this chapter focuses on the effect of two main directives, namely, the Unfair Contract Terms Directive (UCTD) and the Unfair Commercial Practices Directive (UCPD).[2] This choice was made as these two directives are important developments in EU consumer law. They offer a useful contrast in the Greek context, as the first has generated greater interest and has been more relevant on a practical level than the second. This chapter examines the legislative framework as well as relevant case law.

Section II introduces the Greek consumer law system, covering substantive law and enforcement; section III covers unfair terms, including both substantive law and case law on consumer credit; while section IV focuses on unfair commercial practices, covering development of consumer standards and case law. Finally, section V concludes.

II. Characteristics of the Greek Legal System

Before going on to examine unfair terms and practices, a brief introduction to the Greek consumer protection system is in order.

A. Legislative Framework

The first Greek law on consumer protection was N.1961/91, which transposed Directive 85/374/EEC on liability for defective products into Greek law.[3] All key consumer law areas were regulated by N.1961/91, from quality requirements and health and safety of the consumer to misleading advertising, unfair terms and distance contracts, as well as provisions on consumer organisations.[4] The provisions of N.1961/91 on unfair terms and unfair practices are examined in sections III and IV in further detail.

Only a couple years later, in 1994, a new consumer law was introduced to transpose the UCTD into Greek law, and N.1961/91 was repealed, in spite of the two laws sharing very similar content and structure. Aleksandridou points out the example of Germany incorporating consumer provisions into its unfair competition law (*Gesetz gegen den unlauteren Wettbewerb*, UWG) and questions whether Greece actually needed a separate consumer protection law.[5] Schinas suggests that there is a lack of trust from EU bodies relating to how faithfully Greece transposes EU law, which in turn

---

[2] Council Directive 93/13/EEC of 5 April 1993 on unfair terms in consumer contracts [1993] OJ L95/29; Directive 2005/29/EC of the European Parliament and of the Council of 11 May 2005 concerning unfair business-to-consumer commercial practices in the internal market and amending Council Directive 84/450/EEC, Directives 97/7/EC, 98/27/EC and 2002/65/EC of the European Parliament and of the Council and Regulation (EC) No 2006/2004 of the European Parliament and of the Council [2005] OJ L149/22.

[3] Council Directive 85/374/EEC of 25 July 1985 on the approximation of the laws, regulations and administrative provisions of the Member States concerning liability for defective products [1985] OJ L210/29.

[4] See N.1961/91 Για την προστασία του καταναλωτή και άλλες διατάξεις (English trans: For Consumer Protection and other Provisions) published in the *Official Government Gazette of the Hellenic Republic* (ΦΕΚ Α') No 132/1991.

[5] Ε Αλεξανδρίδου, 'Η οδηγία για τις αθέμιτες εμπορικές πρακτικές' (English trans: 'Unfair Commercial Practices Directive') (2005) 6 *ΔΕΕ* 639, 641.

has a negative effect on the relationship between Greek law and EU law.[6] So perhaps Greece thought that introducing a new law would be easier than convincing the EU that Greek law offers equivalent protection.

The law introduced in 1994 was N.2251/94, which has turned out to be much longer-lasting than the previous one as it continues to be the main consumer law statute in Greece.[7] Since its introduction, N.2251/94 has been revised multiple times, adding provisions via ministerial decrees, including the UCTD. The way EU consumer law directives have been transposed into Greek law has been criticised in the literature, as no effort was made to codify the legislation or organise it in a systematic way.[8] Thus N.2251/94 became a fragmented, far-reaching law that became difficult for traders and consumers to follow.[9]

This phenomenon indicated the underlying tension between the EU and the national legislator, as EU consumer law is transposed, often in a hurry, to fulfil an obligation without proper reflection on the role the legislation is to play in the national legal system and how it would best be integrated, something that might contribute to the lack of visibility that sometimes accompanies consumer legislation.

The codification of N.2251/94 came only after a recommendation by the Organisation for Economic Cooperation and Development, as part of the obligations deriving from the Memorandum of Understanding that Greece signed with the EU to harmonise legislation with the needs of electronic commerce.[10] The much-needed codification of N.2251/94 took place in 2018 with Ministerial Decree 5338/2018.[11] Unless otherwise specified, that codification is the version of N.2251/94 used in this chapter. The codification helped to simplify the legislation and removed inconsistencies, especially regarding the definitions of 'consumer' and 'trader'.[12]

In short, on a substantive level, the EU has played a key role in transforming Greek consumer law. While the seed was there with N.1961/91 covering key consumer law areas and offering a level of protection very similar to that of EU law at the time, it is clear that EU law became the driving force behind consumer law that kept adding and updating provisions on various areas. It is thanks to EU consumer law that N.2251/94 is now a framework law for consumer protection in Greece. It is not possible to know how Greek consumer law would have developed without the influence of EU law, but it

---

[6] Ι Σχινάς, 'Ιδέες και κατευθύνσεις του N.2251/94' (English trans: 'Ideas and directions of N.2251/94') [1998] *Digesta Law Review* 1 at digestaonline.gr/index.php/12-1998/334-1998-sxinas (accessed 13 November 2022).

[7] N.2251/94 Προστασία των καταναλωτών (English trans: Consumer Protection) published in the *Official Government Gazette of the Hellenic Republic* (ΦΕΚ Α') Νο 191/16.11.94.

[8] Δελούκα- Ιγγλέση, *Δίκαιο του Καταναλωτή Ενωσιακό και Ελληνικό* (English trans: European Community's and Greek Consumer Protection Law) (Εκδόσεις Σάκκουλα, 2014) 26–27.

[9] Ε Φιλιπποπούλου, 'Η νομοθετική μεταρρύθμιση στο δίκαιο καταναλωτή με τον νόμο 4512/2018 λόγω των νέων αναγκών που δημιουργεί το ηλεκτρονικό εμπόριο' (English trans: 'The Legal Reform of consumer protection law through the law of 4512/2018 due to the new needs created by e-commerce') (2019) 2 *ΔΙΤΕ* 153, 155.

[10] ibid 153.

[11] Υπουργική απόφαση (English trans: Ministerial Decree) Νο 5338/2018 Κωδικοποίηση του ν. 2251/1994 (Α΄ 191) «Προστασία των Καταναλωτών» σε ενιαίο κείμενο» (English trans: Consolidated Consumer Protection Law of N.2251/1994) published in the *Official Government Gazette of the Hellenic Republic* (ΦΕΚ Β') Νο 40/17.01.2018.

[12] Φιλιπποπούλου (n 8) 156.

is safe to say that it would be less extensive, given that consumer protection is not a top priority for the Greek legislator. However, as will also be seen in section II.B, although having legislation in place is indispensable, it is nevertheless not sufficient on its own to ensure the effective protection of consumers: enforcement has an important role to play in the success of the system.

B. Enforcement System

Beyond the legislative framework, it is useful to briefly examine the Greek enforcement system for consumer protection. The main public authority responsible for enforcement of consumer law in Greece is the General Secretariat for Consumer Protection, which was founded by law in 1997.[13] The most recent iteration, following a restructuring of the ministries, was set out in 2017, making the Secretariat a branch of the Ministry for Growth and Investment.[14] The function of the General Secretariat has been indirectly influenced by EU consumer law, as it has seen its remit expand, along with the scope of EU consumer law, to include more topics, such as e-commerce. Still, the enforcement priorities of the General Secretariat are inevitably dictated primarily by national concerns, such as regulation of debt collection companies, rather than EU priorities, such as the digital market or sustainable consumption.

The General Secretariat for Consumer Protection is responsible for consumer education and maintains a phone line for consumer complaints. However, no data on consumer complaints are made publicly available. The General Secretariat can investigate consumer complaints and, via the issuing of ministerial decrees, has the power to: order cessation of infringement by the trader; issue fines ranging from €1,500–1,000,000; and order temporary closure of a business from three months to one year if more than three fines have been issued.[15]

The second public body in charge of consumer protection is the Consumer Ombudsman, an independent authority founded by law in 2004, under the supervision of the Minister for Growth.[16] The Consumer Ombudsman is an extra-judicial dispute resolution body that receives consumer complaints and can mediate between traders and consumers.

In terms of enforcement, the Consumer Ombudsman is certainly an example of the transformative effect that EU consumer law has had in Greece. Unlike the General Secretariat for Consumer Protection, which forms part of the Ministry, the Consumer Ombudsman largely owes its existence to EU law. It is a body whose mission is based on alternative dispute resolution (ADR) as championed in EU law.[17] Its connection

---

[13] Π.Δ. (English trans: Presidential Executive Order) 197/1997 published in the *Official Government Gazette of the Hellenic Republic* (ΦΕΚ Αʹ) No 156/1997).

[14] Π.Δ. (English trans: Presidential Executive Order) 147/2017 published in the *Official Government Gazette of the Hellenic Republic* (ΦΕΚ Αʹ) No 192/13.02.2017.

[15] N.2251/94 (n 11) Art 13 a.2.

[16] N.3297/2004 published in the *Official Government Gazette of the Hellenic Republic* (ΦΕΚ Αʹ) No 259/23.12.2004.

[17] ibid Art 1.

with EU consumer law is also shown by the fact that it is the designated Greek office of the European Consumer Centre.[18]

The Consumer Ombudsman also engages scientific personnel with specialist knowledge in the field of consumer law, and is probably the only authority whose charter requires such expertise.[19] Mediation is not particularly popular in Greece, but the Consumer Ombudsman has been successful in establishing itself as an inextricable part of consumer law enforcement and gaining the trust of consumers. However, the impact of the Consumer Ombudsman has limits, as it does not have the power to punish traders, while the naming and shaming technique adopted by the authority has a limited impact in Greece, where few consumers are aware of these announcements. Unlike the General Secretariat for Consumer Protection, the Consumer Ombudsman publishes an annual report containing information on its handling of complaints, organised by sector, and its policy papers.[20] Still, the Consumer Ombudsman is an example of how a European concept can be successful within the Greek framework and offer valuable support to consumers.

There are also several sectoral authorities dealing with consumer protection within their remit, including the National Telecommunications and Post Commission, the Regulatory Authority for Energy and others.[21] These sectoral authorities cooperate with the horizontal ones, namely, the General Secretariat and the Consumer Ombudsman.

Finally, collective action is an important aspect of private enforcement of consumer law in Greece. Greek consumer organisations – those that have over 500 members and have been inscribed in the register for consumer organisations for more than a year, or when illegal behaviour has harmed at least 30 consumers – are able to bring a collective action to request an injunction or damages, amongst other things. Collective actions have played a crucial role in the enforcement of unfair terms, as examined in section III.

The EU Injunctions Directive in particular has provided the regulatory framework that has facilitated consumer organisations in bringing collective actions.[22] Greek law has also played an important part in strengthening collective action. According to Article 10 paragraph 20 of N.2251/94, an irrevocable decision on a collective action is applicable against everyone, even if they were not parties to the trial. This provision has been heavily criticised in the literature, and the prevailing view is that it should be interpreted restrictively so as not to conflict with the general rules in Greek law on res judicata. This means that individual consumers can invoke the injunction order for violation, such as where there is an unfair term, but it is ultimately not binding on the court.

---

[18] See at eccgreece.gr/el/european-consumer-centres-network-el/jurisdiction-and-procedure-greek-european-consumer-centre_el/ (accessed August 2022).

[19] N.3297/2004 (n 15) Art 2.

[20] For the annual reports of the Greek Consumer Ombudsman, see at synigoroskatanaloti.gr/stk_YReports.html (accessed August 2022).

[21] For a more thorough review of the sectoral authorities and the Greek enforcement system in general, see A Douga and V Koumpli, 'Enforcement and Effectiveness of Consumer Law in Greece' in H-W Micklitz and G Saumier (eds), *Enforcement and Effectiveness of Consumer Law* (Springer, 2018) 307.

[22] Directive 2009/22/EC of the European Parliament and of the Council of 23 April 2009 on injunctions for the protection of consumers' interests [2009] OJ L110/30.

However, it is possible to extend the res judicata principle to all traders via the mechanism of Article 10 paragraph 1 of N.2251/94. According to that provision, the Minister for Growth, invoking reasons of public welfare, may issue a decision (which is a law of the state), extending the res judicata of an irrevocable injunction order to all traders.

Extending the effect of the decision is a powerful tool for ensuring compliance by traders and for protecting consumers, and it is highly effective in most cases. However, there have been reported incidents when traders would include a term found to be unfair but with minor changes. This meant there was a need for another collective action against the 'new' term. Business associations did not identify any particular negative effects as a result of this extension of res judicata. That could be explained by the fact there have not been so many ministerial decrees extending res judicata.

Enforcement authorities as well as consumer organisations are called upon to enforce EU consumer law and, in some cases, such as the Consumer Ombudsman, are the embodiment of EU consumer law values, as ADR bodies are not common in Greece. The EU's consumer law has provided all enforcement agencies with a framework in which to operate and has given access to a network of other authorities with which they would not otherwise be in contact. Nevertheless, it is important to keep in mind that these organisations and authorities operate in the Greek market, and their activities reflect national consumer issues that may not necessarily align with EU consumer law priorities. For example, especially during the financial crisis, all the aforementioned bodies focused their activities on supporting overindebted consumers.

III. Unfair Contract Terms

Unfair contract terms are an area of great practical importance in Greek consumer law. The first time they were regulated in Greece was with the short-lived N.1961/91. The unfair terms provisions of N.1961/91 were quite like those of the UCTD, including a general clause on fairness of terms, which required terms to be clear, precise and expressed in plain language that could be understood by the average consumer.[23] It also included rules for interpreting terms, as well as a list of unfair terms.[24] Unfair terms were not binding on the consumer, although the contract would continue to stand.[25]

The UCTD was transposed into Greek law with N.2251/94 for protection of consumers. As previously mentioned, N.2251/94 is the main Greek consumer protection statute and covers different areas. It takes advantage of the minimum harmonisation character of the UCTD and goes beyond it in some areas.[26]

In particular, the grey list of unfair terms in the UCTD is a blacklist of practices in N.2251/94. The Greek legislator has also made use of the possibility to add terms to

---

[23] N.1961/91 (n 4), Art 22.
[24] ibid Arts 24, 25.
[25] ibid Art 26.
[26] UCTD (n 2) Art 8.

the list. While the UCTD includes only 17 terms on the list, the blacklist of N.2251/94 includes 32 terms.[27] The terms added by the Greek legislator tend to be quite specific and drawn from practice. They include terms that place an undue financial burden on the consumer and terms that limit the legal rights of the consumer – for example by reversing the burden of proof, or mandatory international arbitration clauses.[28] The list of unfair terms is not exhaustive and it is possible to add new terms via the issue of a ministerial decree, which – as we have seen in section II.B – in Greece enjoys the force of law. This power is reserved for the Minister for Growth, who can extend to all traders the effect of a final decision declaring a term to be unfair, provided that such an action would be 'of broader public interest for the smooth functioning of the market and protection of consumers'.[29]

The inclusion of additional terms and the decision to make the list a blacklist shows the preference of the Greek legislator for greater legal certainty. An extensive blacklist facilitates the work of enforcement agencies, as well as private enforcement by consumer organisations and individual consumers. Similarly, Greek case law on unfair terms praises the advantages of the blacklist in terms of legal certainty.[30] Over-reliance on the blacklist may mean that proving the unfairness of terms that are not included in the list may be more difficult, yet Greek case law specifies that it is possible to bring an action using both the general clause and the blacklist.[31]

Another difference of Greek law compared to the UCTD is extension of the scope beyond consumers to include very small enterprises. The following criteria need to be cumulatively fulfilled:

1. The term has not been the subject of individual negotiation.
2. One of the contractual parties fulfils the criteria in the law for a very small enterprise.
3. The very small enterprise is the final recipient of the product or service.[32]

This enlargement of the scope is well-suited to the Greek market, which is made up mostly of very small, small and medium-size enterprises, which often do not have the expertise and resources assumed in business-to-business transactions.

It is clear that the UCTD has provided a more extensive and detailed framework for unfair terms than was previously available in Greece, and has transformed the regulatory landscape by assisting in the creation of consumer law as a distinct area of law. It is also fortuitous that the UCTD fits in well with the existing Greek legal system with its detailed Civil Code and law of obligations. The minimum harmonisation aspect of the UCTD has allowed for greater flexibility, and Greece has made use of that to bring the UCTD closer to the Greek approach, such as the need for greater legal certainty, thus striking a fair balance.

---

[27] N.2251/94 (n 10) Art 2.7.
[28] ibid κε, κστ, κζ, λα.
[29] ibid Art 10.21.
[30] See, eg, ΕφΑθ 5101/2011, NoB 2011, 2139; ΕφΑθ 2386/2006, ΧρΙΔ 2007, 613, as quoted in Γ Δέλλιος, *Γενικοί Όροι Συναλλαγών*, 2nd edn (English trans: *General terms and conditions*) (Εκδόσεις Σάκκουλα, 2013) 294, fn 823.
[31] Δέλλιος (n 30) 295.
[32] N.2251/94 (n 11) Art 2.9.

A. Case Law on Unfair Terms

The success of the UCTD in Greece may also be seen in the growing body of case law on the subject. However, it took several years for judges' attitudes – in terms of control of fairness of terms – to change. According to Karakostas, judges were hesitant to control contractual terms before the introduction of N.1961/91, a phenomenon that continued even after the introduction of N.2251/94 and until the end of the 1990s.[33] Judges would prefer to adhere to the notion of contractual freedom and would prefer a restrictive interpretation to an examination of the imbalance of power between trader and consumer.[34] Indeed, the attitudes of the judiciary have played a significant part in the impact that unfair terms legislation has had in Greece.

i. Consumer Credit Case Law

The first major Greek case on unfair terms came about only in 2000, concerning the unfairness of a term in a credit-card contract stating that for cash withdrawals consumers would be charged a fee of 3 per cent of the amount withdrawn, a decision also upheld by the Supreme Court of Greece, *Areios Pagos*.[35] This was the start of a long string of cases on unfair terms in banking contracts. The banking sector has generated a lot of case law, something that may be attributed to the high value and long duration of banking contracts, which make it more likely that consumers will seek judicial protection. Consumer organisations have played an important role in bringing collective actions and have been very active, especially in the 2000s. It is not possible to include all relevant case law here, but this section will cover a selection of cases. Some other examples of credit-card contracts include terms for processing consumers' personal data, which were also in breach of data protection rules,[36] and terms on charges to consumers for verifying the amount owed, for maintaining an account with a low available balance, and notifying consumers of changes in terms and conditions only via leaflets in bank branches.[37]

There have also been several cases on unfair terms in mortgages, for example a term according to which interest rates were calculated on the basis of 360 days a year or where the consumer was liable to pay damages to the bank in the event of early repayment.[38] Other cases focused on terms on how to calculate the maximum amount of interest rates that can legally be demanded.[39]

When the 2008 financial crisis started severely affecting the Greek mortgage market, one might have expected that unfair terms regulation would become more relevant, as was

---

[33] Ι Καράκωστας, 'Σημείωση στην ΕφΑθ 6291/2000 – Νομολογιακή απαρχή του κοινοτικού ελέγχου καταχρηστικών ΓΟΣ επί τραπεζικών συμβάσεων' (English trans: 'Note to ΕφΑθ 6291/2000 – Judicial Interpretation of the EC's Control of Abusive Terms and Conditions in Banking Contracts') (2000) 11 *ΔΕΕ* 1122, 1122.

[34] ibid.

[35] ΕφΑθ 6291/2000, ΑΠ 1219/2001.

[36] ΑΠ 147/2004.

[37] ΑΠ 652/2010.

[38] ΑΠ 430/2005.

[39] ΑΠ 912/2011.

the case in Spain, which sent the Court of Justice of the European Union (CJEU) a high number of preliminary references on unfair terms. The same course was not followed in Greece, even though the two countries faced similar issues. In fact, successful cases on unfair terms declined during the crisis. In their book on unfair terms in banking during the crisis, Koukoulis and Pantelidou argue that before the crisis an 'anti-bank' sentiment dominated and judges were more willing to protect consumers.[40] However, during the crisis, the climate was reversed and cases would often be dismissed as too vague, the principle of transparency being applied in a superficial manner.[41] This reflected fears among judges that consumers would cease to fulfil their financial obligations to banks, thus contributing to the potential collapse of the banking system.[42]

The case law on consumer credit in Greece has always been a David v Goliath battle, with consumer organisations and consumer groups taking on banks as major credit institutions. While the judiciary was more willing to examine the unfairness of terms after the millennium, that changed with the financial crisis, when protection of the banking system took priority. This phenomenon did not allow for completion of the transformation of unfair terms law in Greece. Instead, it revealed that national attitudes can present obstacles to transformation and to the empowerment of consumers as envisioned by EU consumer law.

ii. Swiss Franc Loans

There is a notable exception to this reluctance to utilise unfair terms legislation during the crisis, namely the case of Swiss franc (CHF) loans. These loans not only generated Greek case law, but also became the first preliminary reference that Greek courts sent to the CJEU on consumer protection law. Loans in Swiss francs have become a prominent social and economic issue in many EU Member States, such as Poland, Croatia, Romania and Hungary.[43] Greece, unlike other affected states such as Romania and Croatia – which introduced conversion laws to protect debtors – did not take legislative action on the issue.[44] This inaction made the issue more pressing and mobilised affected consumers to organise and file collective actions.[45] This led to an array of judgments on the issue, published from 2013 onwards.[46]

---

[40] ΑΝ Κουκούλης και Κ Παντελίδου, *Οι καταχρηστικοί ΓΟΣ στις τραπεζικές συμβάσεις υπό το πρίσμα της οικονομικής κρίσης* (English trans: *Abusive General Terms and Conditions in Banking Contracts in the Light of Economic Crisis*) (Νομική Βιβλιοθήκη, 2021) 157.

[41] ibid.

[42] ibid 158.

[43] See, eg R Vassileva, 'Monetary Appreciation and Foreign Currency Mortgages: Lessons from the 2015 Swiss Franc Surge' (2020) 28 *European Review of Private Law* 173.

[44] European Parliament, 'Unfair Terms in Swiss Franc loans-Overview of European Court of Justice Case Law' (March 2021) European Parliamentary Research Service Briefing a europarl.europa.eu/thinktank/en/document/EPRS_BRI(2021)689361 (accessed August 2022).

[45] See, eg, the Association of Swiss Franc Lenders, an ad-hoc association for lobbying, sharing news and pursuing legal action on the issue, at daneia-chf.gr/archiki.html (accessed August 2022).

[46] See, eg, ΠΠρΞάνθης 23/2014, which decided that the term stating that the amount payable should be decided according to the exchange rate on the day of payment was unfair and the exchange rate on the date of conclusion of the credit agreement should be used instead; ΠολΠρωτΑθ 334/2016, which decided that the conversion terms were not transparent and that the bank engaged in misleading practices by failing to inform consumers about the risks involved in such credit agreements.

In 2019, the Swiss francs loan issue seemed to be resolved by the ΟλΑΠ 4/2019 judgment of *Areios Pagos* in plenary meeting, where it decided that terms that reflect mandatory statutory or regulatory provisions are outside the scope of the UCTD and are therefore not assessed for their fairness.[47] The term in question was that debtors had to fulfil their obligations either in Swiss francs or in euros, according to the exchange rate at the time of payment. This judgment seemed to close the path to debtors in terms of pursuing further legal action.[48] The stance of *Areios Pagos* is consistent with what was mentioned earlier in section III.A about unfair terms during the crisis, namely, that Greek judges were hesitant to use the tools provided by EU legislators, such as – notably – the UCTD.[49] However, this was not the end of the legal debate on Swiss franc loans in Greece.

One year later, in 2020, The First Instance Court of Athens issued a judgment that questioned the *Areios Pagos* decision, arguing that the exception of Article 1(2) UCTD on which it was based was never transposed into Greek law, and decided to refer questions to the CJEU. This was the first preliminary reference from Greece on consumer law, and one of very few in general, showcasing its importance, at least for the Greek legal order. In *Trapeza Peiraios*, the CJEU clarified its position on the transposition of Article 1(2) UCTD.[50] Four questions were referred, which were:

1. As part of minimum harmonisation, is it possible for Member States not to transpose Article 1(2) UCTD to allow the fairness assessment of contractual terms that reflect mandatory statutory or regulatory provisions?
2. Can it be considered (as argued by *Areios Pagos*) that Article 1(2) has been indirectly transposed by Articles 3(1) and 4(1) UCTD?
3. Do Articles 3(1) and 4(1) UCTD include the Article 1(2) UCTD exception?
4. Is the assessment of a term in a credit agreement that reflects regulatory provisions of national law within the scope of the Directive if it has not been the subject of individual negotiation?[51]

The Court recognised that Article 1(2) UCTD should be interpreted narrowly as it introduces an exception from the scope of the UCTD and the term in question does repeat Article 291 of the Greek Civil Code.[52] It was decided that the Article 1(2) exception had not been indirectly transposed into Greek law. Still, the Court stated that non-transposition cannot alter the scope of application of the Directive, which must remain the same in all Member States.[53] As the Court recognised in its judgment, there were two sides in this debate: on the one hand, the referring court and the claimants, arguing that non-transposition of Article 1(2) UCTD in the national legal order reflected

---

[47] ΟλΑΠ 4/2019.

[48] Χ Χασάπης, 'Το πρώτο προδικαστικό ερώτημα προς το Δικαστήριο της ΕΕ για τα δάνεια σε ελβετικό φράγκο- Ενημερωτικό σημέιωμα με αφορμή την υπ'αριθμόν 1599/2020 ΠΠρΑθ' (English trans: 'The First Preliminary Reference to the CJEU for the Swiss Franc loans – Informative note on the basis of No 1599/2020 ΠΠρΑθ') (2020) 5 *Συνήγορος* 64, 66.

[49] See n 40.

[50] Case C-243/20 *DP, SG v Trapeza Peiraios* ECLI:EU:C:2021:1045.

[51] ibid para 23.

[52] ibid para 38.

[53] ibid para 45.

the desire of the Greek legislator, albeit silent, to provide a higher level of protection to consumers than that provided by the UCTD; while, on the other hand, the bank and the Greek Government argued otherwise.[54] Ultimately, the CJEU stated that it is possible for Member States to extend the protection granted by the UCTD to instances that fall outside its scope if that is not incompatible with the aims of the Directive but is compatible with Article 8 UCTD.[55] However, that does not seem to be the case with current Greek law, as it does not have an express provision extending the scope of the UCTD to terms caught by Article 1(2) UCTD.

This decision seems to conclude the legal saga of the issue of Swiss franc loans in Greece. Consumers are not able to seek judicial protection on the basis of the UCTD, and the Greek state does not seem willing to introduce legislation that would protect them. This case also tells another tale, of how the UCTD empowered Greek consumers and consumer organisations to enforce their rights in court, even if this particular decision did not turn out to be in the consumers' favour. It also reveals the attitudes of the Greek state and a number of its judiciary towards EU law, who tend to see this issue as an internal one, best handled by Greek law and decisions not taken in a vacuum but also with the potential economic consequences in mind.

iii. Other Sectors (Telecommunications, Energy, Insurance)

Beyond the banking sector, unfair terms have also been relevant in other sectors, most notably in insurance and telecommunications.[56] In the insurance sector, one of the terms declared unfair was allowing the insurer to unilaterally alter the premium, according to its own judgment, at the date of renewal of the contract.[57] Another example is that of a term stating that if there is a big difference between the declared age of the insured and their real age, the contract is automatically void.[58] Similarly, in the telecommunications sector, a term that allowed a company to unilaterally change the price list without pre-determined criteria was found to be unfair.[59] These early cases showcase the impact of unfair terms legislation as one that empowered consumers to enforce their rights and strike out terms that were clearly unfair. The number of cases coming from other sectors was reduced during the crisis, perhaps reflecting shifts in priorities, with consumer law not being one of them. Ultimately, consumer law is designed to respond to the needs of the market.

One of the latest important developments for unfair terms is in the field of energy, reflecting the impact of rising energy prices and the impact of the energy crisis on consumers. A 2022 Greek law announced the temporary suspension of use of a term adjusting energy prices, tying them to wholesale prices, as a measure for tackling the financial consequences of the crisis.[60] This kind of term has been criticised in the

---

[54] ibid para 52.

[55] ibid para 62.

[56] Α Βάρκα-Αδάμη και Ν Παππά, *Εισαγωγή στο Δίκαιο Προστασίας Καταναλωτή* (English trans: *Introduction to Consumer Protection Law*) (Νομική Βιβλιοθήκη, 2010) 48.

[57] ΑΠ 1030/2001.

[58] ΕφΑΘ 1448/98.

[59] ΠΠΡΑΘ 2438/97.

[60] N.4951/2022 published in the *Official Government Gazette of the Hellenic Republic* (ΦΕΚ Α') No 129/04.07.2022, Art 138.

literature, with academics arguing that the very existence of this legal provision on suspension is an indirect admission of the unfair character of the term and the fact that the term lacks transparency.[61] This issue may be decided in court, as in 2022 a collective action was brought against the public energy provider, DEI, for its term on adjusting the price of the commission charged to consumers in contracts for the supply of electricity.[62]

The examples from these sectors echo developments in the field of consumer credit, where unfair terms legislation became a tool utilised by the consumer movement to take on powerful companies. Similarly to consumer credit, shifting national priorities and a tendency to protect the industry have also led to a lower number of cases, However, as indicated by case law brought to tackle the energy crisis, that may be changing.

IV. Unfair Commercial Practices

Before the introduction of a specialised law for consumer protection, there was a view that unfair practices could be covered by the law on unfair competition, N. 147/1914, especially Articles 1 and 3. However, when the first law for consumer protection N.1961/91 was enacted, any discussion on the necessity for separate consumer protection law was abandoned.[63] Nevertheless, unfair competition and unfair practices law remain closely connected, and sometimes even at odds with each other. For example, in a 2011 case, a taxi union brought an unfair competition case against a nightclub that provided free transportation for its clients by mini-bus, advertising the service on its premises.[64] The practice was found to breach unfair competition laws, although it does not contravene unfair practices law as a free service promoting the products of the trader.[65] This leads to the undesirable result that a practice is found to be fair or unfair, depending on whether the action is filed by a trader or a consumer.[66]

The first Greek consumer protection law, N.1961/91, also included provisions relevant to unfair practices, but limited to misleading and unfair advertising.[67] The provisions on unfair advertising represent a departure from the focus of the

---

[61] Γ Μεντής, 'Η αναστολή της ρήτρας αναπροσαρμογής της τιμής ηλεκτρικής ενέργειας – Τα βασικά στοιχεία της νέας ρύθμισης (άρθρο 138 του Ν.4951/2022) και η ένταξή της στο ισχύον σύστημα του ιδιωτικού δικαίου – η ρήτρα φεύγει η αδιαφάνεια αυξάνεται' (English trans: 'Suspension of the Electricity Price Adjustment Clause – The Basic Elements of the New Regulation (Article 138 of Law 4951/2022) and its Integration into the Current System of Private Law – The Clause Goes Away, Lack of Transparency Increases) (2022) 7 *ΕφΑΔΠολΔ* 787, 787–93; Γ Δέλλιος, 'Έλεγχος κύρους των ρητρών αναπροσαρμογής του τιμήματος σε συμβάσεις προμήθειας ηλεκτρικής ενέργειας' (English trans: 'Checking the Validity of Price Adjustment Clauses in Electricity Supply Contracts') [2022] *NoB* 1003, 1003 ff.

[62] See at ekpizo.gr/οι-δράσεις-μας/ενέργεια-συλλογικέςομαδικές-αγωγές/κατατέθηκε-η-πρώτη-συλλογική-αγωγή-κατά-της-δεη (accessed August 2022).

[63] Αλεξανδρίδου (n 5) 639.

[64] ΜΠρΑγρ 738/2011.

[65] Π Καλαμπούκα-Γιαννοπούλου, 'Νομολογιακά δεδομένα επί αθέμιτων εμπορικών πρακτικών' (English trans: 'Case law on unfair commercial practices') (2014) 5 *ΔΕΕ* 479, 485.

[66] ibid.

[67] N.1961/91 (n 4) Arts 18 and 20.

UCPD on the economic behaviour of the consumer and also regulate the moral aspect of advertisements. In particular, they forbade advertisements that used national symbols/issues, that took advantage of the prejudices of consumers, that were damaging to children or that discriminated against social groups.[68] However, after N.1961/91 was repealed, no provisions on moral advertising were retained. Still, there is a legacy of this early law in the weight placed on advertising to children, as seen in section IV.A.i.

The UCPD was transposed into Greek law by N.3587/2007, which amended N.2251/1994, bringing significant changes to it as the main piece of Greek consumer legislation. The UCPD presented a real transformation of Greek consumer law, as there was a much broader concept of what an unfair practice is and it had a wider scope of application. It is doubtful whether the Greek legislator would ever have introduced provisions of a level equivalent to the UCPD. It was also the first time that aggressive commercial practices were regulated in Greek consumer law. As the UCPD is a maximum harmonisation directive, there was little to no room for adapting the Directive to national concerns or priorities, as has been the case in connection with unfair terms.

An example of the resulting divergence may be seen in the definition of a 'consumer', as the general definition employed by N.2251/94 before the addition of unfair practices was much broader than that under the UCPD. In particular, it stated that a consumer is

> every natural or legal person or unions of entities without a legal personality who constitute the target group of products or services offered in the market and who use products or services being their end user. A consumer is also: aa) every target group of promotional activities, bb) every physical or legal entity who gives a guarantee in favour of the consumer on condition that they do not act in the context of their professional or business activity.[69]

In order to avoid expanding the scope of application of consumer law to the extent that it would include even large companies, there had been a coordinated effort in the case law and in the literature to limit and qualify this general concept mostly via the use of Article 281 of the Greek Civil Code on abuse of a right.[70] Fortunately, following codification of N.2251/94, this issue has been resolved.

A. Case Law

Unlike unfair terms examined in section III.A, there is little case law on unfair practices. The reasons behind this are unclear. It could be attributed to a lack of familiarity with the provisions, or perhaps issues of unfair practices are being dealt with using unfair competition rules. It could also be an issue of enforcement, as public enforcement could be taking the lead in the case of unfair practices, with consumers filing complaints with the General Secretariat for Consumer Protection or with the

---

[68] ibid Art 20.
[69] N.2251/94 (n 7) Art 1, para 4(a).
[70] For a thorough review of the debate, see Ε Περράκης 'Άρθρο 1 N.2251/94' (English trans: 'Article 1 of Law 2251/94') in Ε Αλεξανδρίδου (ed), *Δίκαιο Προστασίας Καταναλωτή: Ελληνικό- Κοινοτικό* (English trans: *Consumer Protection Law: Greek-European Community* (Νομική Βιβλιοθήκη, 2008) 51.

Consumer Ombudsman rather than going to court. Additionally, consumer organisations, which were instrumental in bringing cases for unfair terms, are less active in the
field of unfair practices. It is not easy to identify the reason behind this, but it could be
due to a lack of perceived benefits for individual consumers or the outcome of overall
lower awareness of provisions for seemingly all stakeholders.

For issues relating to advertisements, there is the Council for Control of Communication (Συμβούλιο Ελέγχου Επικοινωνίας (ΣΕΕ) – SEE), a non-profit organisation
founded in 2003 by the Union of Advertising Companies and the Hellenic Advertisers
Association, which enforces the Greek code of conduct for advertisements and
communication.[71] The SEE's function is regulated by law, and it is very active in issuing
decisions and helping regulate the advertising market.[72]

i. Consumer Standards

This subsection will cover a selection of case law on unfair practices, focusing on the
interpretation of consumer standards and financial services. The UCPD adopts as its
legal standard the average consumer, which is found in Article 9 N.2251/94.[73] The Greek
legislator did not incorporate the definition of the average consumer found in recital
18 of the UCPD, but nevertheless the definition applies. The level of education and
relevant expertise of the average consumer is taken into account in assessing a practice.
In a case concerning excessive mobile phone data usage charges, the court considered
the fact that the consumer was a computer engineer in assessing whether he had taken
reasonable measures to avoid the charges.[74] If a more sophisticated consumer could
not avoid the charges then the average mobile phone user could not have either.[75] In
an unfair competition and consumer law case between two companies selling medical
scanners, featuring an advertisement in a specialised magazine about scanners, the
court stated that the magazine's target audience had specialised knowledge and would
accept the claims made in the advertisement without investigating them further.[76] This
shows that the average consumer standard may also be a higher standard, depending
on the audience at which the practice is targeted, following the UCPD.[77]

Greek law also prioritises the protection of children as vulnerable consumers.
There is a provision forbidding the broadcasting of advertisements aimed at children
between 7am and 10pm.[78] That provision was found not to contravene EU law or
the Greek Constitution, as it is necessary to avoid exposing children to advertising

---

[71] See at see.gr (accessed August 2022).
[72] For a list of the decisions of SEE, see at see.gr/αποφάσεις/ (accessed August 2022).
[73] N.2251/94 (n 11) Art 9.
[74] ΕιρΑθ 1488/2013.
[75] ibid.
[76] ΕφΑθ 2130/2013.
[77] See UCPD (n 2) Art 5.3. 'Commercial practices which are likely to materially distort the economic
behaviour only of a clearly identifiable group of consumers who are particularly vulnerable to the practice
or the underlying product because of their mental or physical infirmity, age or credulity in a way which the
trader could reasonably be expected to foresee, shall be assessed from the perspective of the average member
of that group.'
[78] N.2328/1995 published in the *Official Government Gazette of the Hellenic Republic* (ΦΕΚ Α')
No 159/03.08.95, Art 14.8.

targeting them.[79] In another case, a toy company argued that its TV advertisement for a philosophy board game was not addressed to children below the age of 14 as it required advanced knowledge; a claim that was rejected by the court, which stated that children up to the age of 14 may possess that knowledge.[80] The General Secretariat for Consumer Protection also operates a Commission for Protection of the Mental Health of Underage Consumers, which can issue opinions on withdrawing products that may be harmful to under-age consumers and locate commercial practices that may present a threat to under-age consumers.[81]

ii. Banking and New Technologies

There have been some recent cases against banks concerning unfair practices as regards the digital services they provide. These serve as an example of how unfair practices are employed in today's market. These cases are appeals against decisions of the Minister for Growth to administer fines to traders. This strengthens the argument that unfair practices law is primarily enforced by public authorities, in this case the General Secretariat for Consumer Protection. There is an interest in strengthening public enforcement. In 2020, a new unit for control of the market was founded, aimed at protecting consumers from illegal goods and services, among other things, and which has extended powers to conduct controls and administer fines.[82]

In an administrative appeal court case, a bank appealed the decision of the Minister for Growth to administer a fine for breaching the misleading commercial practices provisions, following a consumer complaint.[83] The consumer claimed that on its website and in promotional material, the bank had advertised its mobile banking service as being offered free of charge. However, when the consumer performed a bank transfer using the mobile banking app, they were charged a commission.[84] The bank claimed that downloading the app was free but that transactions were subject to a charge, and that that was common knowledge.[85] Still, the appeal was rejected and the bank was found to be engaging in a misleading practice by presenting a service as being free of charge when that was not the case.[86]

In another instance, a bank offered a service called 'alpha alerts', by which consumers would receive an SMS alert on their mobile phones after every transaction using their bank card. Consumers would be charged for these SMSs. As consumers had not requested the service, which was simply added on and could not easily be deleted from the service even after requesting the bank to do so, the practice was found to be aggressive and, in particular, the blacklisted practice of inertia selling.[87]

---

[79] ΠολΠρΑθ 523/2000.
[80] ΕφΑθ 5760/2001.
[81] For more information, see at mindev.gov.gr/προστασία-του-καταναλωτη/#1626415699433-da275d1e-5671 (accessed August 2022).
[82] For more information, see at mindev.gov.gr/dimea/ (accessed August 2022).
[83] ΔΕφΑθ 1191/2021.
[84] ibid.
[85] ibid.
[86] ibid.
[87] Ν.2251/94 (n 11) Art 9στ (κι).

What these cases have in common, apart from being appeals against administrative fines, is that they cite CJEU case law and reveal a very thorough knowledge and understanding of EU law. This is hopeful, and shows that the apparent paucity of case law does not mean that Greek judges do not closely follow developments at the EU level.

Overall, it is clear that EU consumer law has brought about a positive transformation in the field of unfair practices by providing a broader, more detailed and ambitious framework than was previously in place in Greece. That legal framework may still not be being used to its full potential, despite being in place for decades, but it has certainly aided in increasing protection for consumers. It is not easy to decipher the reasons why the unfair practices provisions have been less utilised than, say, unfair contract terms. As the Greek market becomes increasingly digitalised and is catching up with developments at the EU level, unfair practices may become more relevant and their impact in transforming Greek consumer law more profound.

V. Conclusion

This chapter has examined the transformation wrought in the Greek system by EU consumer law directives. It has shown how the main consumer law legislation, N.2251/94, came to be in order to implement EU law directives, and how constant amendments to that law resulted in confusion and legal uncertainty until its recent codification.

The chapter has examined the profound impact the UCTD has had in Greece as it has become a valuable tool for consumers and consumer organisations to enforce their rights, especially in consumer credit. It has also highlighted the way in which unfair contract terms were interpreted in a more restrictive manner during the financial crisis, so as not to allow destabilisation of the financial system. It has further shown how the minimum harmonisation aspect of the UCTD allowed the Greek legislator to increase the legal certainty of unfair terms legislation and expand its scope.

In contrast to that, unfair commercial practices appear to be an uneasy addition to the Greek legal order, and one that does not seem to be well understood by consumers and which does not produce the same amount of case law. The UCPD has certainly provided a far-reaching and high level of protection in Greece, but its enforcement is in practice reserved for public authorities.

In conclusion, EU consumer law has had a positive effect on Greek consumer law and has certainly offered a substantive consumer law framework that is more extensive, more modern and more ambitious than the Greek legislator was likely to provide, and as such has presented a big improvement. Still, it has been shown that simply having the legislative framework in place is not enough; without the cooperation of all stakeholders the transformation cannot be complete. While EU law has taken root in Greece by helping to empower consumers and improve enforcement, it has found its limits when coming up against national considerations for protection of the financial system and the Greek market more broadly. It is important to recognise the importance of Member States in tailoring measures to the needs of their legal system and market. This will allow for a transformation that is more adaptable and more successful.

11

Croatia: Something from Nothing

EMILIA MIŠĆENIĆ

I. Introduction: The Three Phases of Transformation of Croatian Consumer Law

This chapter addresses the main phases of transformation of consumer law in Croatia, as well as its different aspects and dimensions. Although transformation, as a general concept, is in principle concerned with changes that occur in different areas such as the economy, politics, society and the like,[1] the focus of this chapter is legal transformation. Particular attention is paid to certain dimensions of transformation, such as the substantive or procedural dimension affecting the substance and content of consumer protection rules and their enforcement in Croatia's legal system. However, in order to offer a more systematic overview of the legal transformation of Croatian consumer law, the chapter emphasises its temporal aspect and divides the transformation into three main phases. These phases may roughly be divided into:

1. creating consumer law in Croatia (the first phase);
2. the first attempts at enforcing consumer law during the first consumer collective redress proceedings (the second phase); and
3. entering the current phase, concerned with strengthening consumer law enforcement (the third phase).

Temporal transformation, combined with other procedural and substantive dimensions of legal transformation, is used to demonstrate how everything has been transformed in this segment of Croatia's legislation, and that where there was almost nothing, today there is something with respect to consumer law and consumer protection.

Over the past several decades, these various dimensions of legal transformation have shaped Croatian consumer law as it is today. The latter was also, however, very much affected by other aspects of transformation, such as the societal, the political and the economic. The legal transformation of consumer law can therefore not be

---

[1] The *Cambridge Dictionary* describes 'transformation' as 'a complete change in the appearance or character of something or someone', see at dictionary.cambridge.org/dictionary/english/transformation (accessed 4 May 2022).

observed in isolation from the political and economic changes that have shaped the Croatian legal context. Although this is not a novelty per se, and it also happens in all other legal systems, the transformation of consumer law in Croatia has been strongly affected by a shift from one legal regime to another and the changes that occurred in the economic system.[2]

As a relatively young European Union (EU) Member State with post-communist roots and emerging from a former socialist regime, Croatia has gone through a variety of political and economic transformations. After the dissolution of the Socialist Federal Republic of Yugoslavia (SFRY),[3] Croatia became an independent state, went through a transition period, and eventually joined the EU as the latest Member State in 2013.[4] The latter process was initiated in 1999 with the Stabilisation and Association Process for the countries of South-Eastern Europe[5] and the signing of the Stabilisation and Association Agreement between the Republic of Croatia and the European Communities and their Member States (SAA) on 29 October 2001.[6]

These were only some of the major political, economic and legal changes and challenges in Croatia's system and society, which formed the soil in which the consumer *acquis* was about to be planted. However, this 'new' transformation was accompanied by many difficulties and leftovers from the 'old' regime. As a country with no developed market economy, Croatia faced the challenges of transformation into a capitalist society, development of fair market competition and consumer protection.[7] Once it had been accepted as an EU candidate country, and with the beginning of the accession negotiations, Croatia entered the second phase of the transformation, which was focused on harmonising its legal framework and rules with the *acquis*. The legal transformation, in the form of approximation of law, introduced changes to the Croatian legal framework, which had not known the concept, meaning or rules of consumer protection.[8]

The aim of this chapter is therefore to analyse how the legal transformation, through alignment with the *acquis*, affected Croatian consumer law, and to emphasise

---

[2] On different components affecting the association process in CEEC countries, see F Cafaggi et al, 'Europeanization of Private Law in Central and Eastern Europe Countries (CEECs): Preliminary Findings and Research Agenda' (2010) EUI Working Paper 15/2010 1 ff; see also K Cseres, 'Instrumentalization of Consumer Law in Central and Eastern Europe for Populist Politics: A Citizen-Consumer Perspective; (2022) Amsterdam Law School Research Paper No 19 2.

[3] Constitutional Decision on Sovereignty and Independence of the Republic of Croatia, Official Gazette (OG) No 31/91; Decision of the Croatian Parliament on severing all state-building bonds with the states forming the Yugoslav Federation, OG No 53/91. See S Fabijanić Gagro and B Vukas, 'The Path of the Former Yugoslav Countries to the European Union: From Integration to Disintegration and Back' (2012) 2 *Maastricht Journal of European and Comparative Law* 300, 300–16.

[4] Treaty between Member States of the European Union and the Republic of Croatia concerning the Accession of the Republic of Croatia to the European Union [2012] OJ L112, in force from 1 July 2013.

[5] European Commission, 'Communication from the Commission to the Council and the European Parliament of 26 May 1999 on the stabilisation and association process for countries of South-Eastern Europe' COM (1999) 235 final.

[6] The Act on Confirmation of the Stabilisation and Association Agreement between the Republic of Croatia and the European Communities and their Member States, OG IA Nos 14/01, 15/01, 14/02, 1/05, 7/05, 9/05 and 11/06. The SAA entered into force on 1 February 2005.

[7] S Rodin, 'Croatian Accession to the European Union: The Transformation of the Legal System' in K Ott (ed), *Croatian Accession to the European Union*, vol 1: *Economic and Legal Challenges* (SSOAR, 2003) 223.

[8] E Miscenic, 'Croatian Consumer Protection Law: From Legal Approximation to Legal Fragmentation (Part I)' (2018) 22 *Studia Iuridica Toruniensia* 189.

its main transformative aspects and challenges. From the introduction of the first Consumer Protection Act (CPA) in 2003[9] until adoption of the recent fourth CPA in 2022,[10] Croatian consumer law experienced many – though at the same time not too many – 'effective' transformations. By observing multiple dimensions of legal transformation, such as procedural, substantive or institutional, the author draws the conclusion that consumer law is still lacking the main component – effective protection of consumer rights and effective enforcement. Nonetheless, there are cases in which the substantive dimension of legal transformation – in the form of legislative changes or amendments to laws – has affected the effectiveness of consumer protection and resulted in an increase in consumer awareness and initiation of individual and collective legal actions.

The most relevant example demonstrating the strong interconnection between the different dimensions of transformation is undoubtedly Croatian case law on consumer credit agreements denominated or expressed in Swiss francs (CHF). The case law on consumer credit agreements, concluded by simultaneous use of unfair commercial practices and unfair contractual terms, contributed significantly to the discussion on legal transformation. The chapter therefore analyses to what extent changes introduced by the relevant case law have contributed to further development of institutional, substantive and procedural dimensions of Croatian consumer law. Before presenting this legal transformation, which occurred in the form of numerous legislative amendments and the first consumer collective redress proceedings, section II offers some insight into the first phase of transformation – the evolution of Croatian consumer law.

II. The Evolution of Consumer Law in Croatia

For the purpose of analysing legal transformation and its different dimensions in Croatia's legal order, this section first describes the background and evolution of Croatian consumer law. The evolution of consumer law in Croatia started with the SAA signed on 29 October 2001.[11] Article 69 SAA introduced the so-called harmonisation clause, requiring approximation of Croatia's law to the *acquis*, with emphasis on the 'fundamental elements of the internal market *acquis*'.

Therefore, the focus of attention at an early stage included EU consumer directives as approximation measures that follow the objective of the internal market. In addition to general provisions on the approximation of laws in Article 69 SAA, Article 74 SAA contained special requirements concerning consumer protection. Under this article, Croatia was obliged to align its legislation with the EU consumer *acquis* and ensure active development of consumer protection policy, along with effective enforcement of consumer law.

This put pressure on the Croatian authorities to come up with quick results in an area of law that was underdeveloped and not recognised as a special field of law within Croatia's

---

[9] Consumer Protection Act, OG No 96/03.
[10] Consumer Protection Act, OG No 19/22, in force from 28 May 2022.
[11] The SAA (n 6) entered into force on 1 February 2005.

legal system.[12] Previously, as part of the SFRY, Croatia followed the planned economy system, where consumer protection was not recognised as such. The Yugoslav legal system contained some legal rules, though these were of general application and offered incidental benefit and protection to consumers like any other party to a contract.[13] These rules, which were not systematically regulated, were later imported into the new Croatian legal framework, as well as into those of other former Yugoslav countries.

An important legal Act containing provisions relevant to consumers was the Obligations Act (OA) of 1978.[14] This Act on the law of obligations contained rules on product liability, invalid general terms and conditions, instalment sales contracts, sales contracts and guarantees, amongst others.[15] Due to a monistic approach, the rules covered all obligation relationships, including commercial contracts, so that the term 'consumer' was not mentioned as such. Taking everything into consideration, the extent of legal transformation that was required to align the legal framework with the requirements of the *acquis* can only be imagined.

In the years that followed, the focus of attention was thus initially on the substantive dimension of transformation, which demanded a complete change of Croatia's regulatory framework in order to introduce the new consumer protection rules and policy. During the initial stage of harmonisation, Croatia's legislator decided to protect the OA from structural changes that would result from alignment with the *acquis*. Therefore, a substantive legal transformation, in the form of amending the OA rules, was not intended. However, this approach was soon abandoned precisely due to the need for approximation with the EU consumer *acquis* and transposition of EU consumer directives.[16] Once the first CPA had been adopted in 2003, the former OA of 1978 was replaced by the new OA in 2005, in order to align legislation with several EU consumer directives.[17]

The result of this approach was the substantive legal transformation of the OA rules, which were supposed to be protected from changes. This was also the beginning of the legal fragmentation of Croatian consumer law. The CPA 2003 was aligned with eight – and the OA 2005 with four – EU consumer directives, the rules of which often overlapped or differed with respect to the content and scope of application.[18] In 2007, the CPA 2003 was replaced by a new CPA, transposing the Unfair Commercial Practices Directive (2005/29/EC), the Injunction Directive (98/27/EC) and the Distance

---

[12] E Čikara, 'Die Angleichung des Verbraucherschutzrechts in der Europäischen Gemeinschaft: Unter besonderer Berücksichtigung des Verbraucherschutzrechtes in der Republik Kroatien' (2007) 28 *Collected papers of the Law Faculty of the University of Rijeka* 1067.

[13] T Josipović, 'Anpassung des kroatischen Zivilrechts an europäische Standars' in R Welser (ed), *Privatrechtsentwicklung in Zentral- und Osteuropa* (Manz Verlag, 2008) 141.

[14] Obligations Act, OG SFRJ 29/78, 39/85, 46/85, 45/89 and 57/89. OA was transposed into the Croatian legal framework in 1991. See the Act on the Transposition of the Obligations Act, OG No 53/91; Obligations Act, OG Nos 53/91, 73/91, 111/93, 3/94, 107/95, 7/96, 91/96, 112/99 and 88/01.

[15] Z Čadjenović et al, *EU Consumer Contract Law, Civil Law Forum for South East Europe – Collection of studies and analyses* (Jugoslovenski pregled, 2010).

[16] T Josipović, 'Das Konsumentenschutzgesetz – Beginn der Europäisierung des kroatischen Vertragsrechts' in St Grundmann and M Schauer (eds), *The Architecture of European Codes and Contract Law* (Kluwer Law International, 2006) 145.

[17] CPA 2003 (n 9). The OA 1978 (n 14) was repealed by the new OA enacted in 2005, OG Nos 35/05.

[18] E Mišćenić, 'Consumer Protection Law' in T Josipović (ed), *Introduction to the Law of Croatia* (Kluwer Law International, 2014) 279.

Marketing of Financial Services Directive (2002/65/EC).[19] After amending the OA in 2008,[20] the European Commission confirmed 'a good level of legal alignment' in Croatian consumer law.[21] However, in reality the transformation presented was far from 'good' and there were failures within its substantive dimension, which later had detrimental consequences on enforcement of Croatian consumer law.

After joining the EU in 2013, Croatia continued to approximate its laws to the newly adopted EU consumer directives. In 2014, the new CPA was adopted and aligned with the Consumer Rights Directive (2011/83/EU).[22] However, even in 2009, the legislator started to transpose some EU directives into special legal acts by referring to the CPA and the OA as acts relevant for consumer protection and obligation relationships.[23] Eventually, this process resulted in a sea of legal acts relevant for consumer protection, which are difficult to comprehend or apply in practice. Instead of choosing one or another familiar approach of transposing EU consumer directives into domestic laws, Croatia's legislator has chosen the third route of combining the integrative approach with implementation in the CPA and many other special consumer protection acts.

In addition to the CPA and the OA, the consumer in Croatia is protected by the Consumer Credit Act, the Mortgage Consumer Credit Act, the Payment System Act, the E-Commerce Act, the Insurance Act, the Electronic Communications Act, the Alternative Consumer Dispute Resolution Act, the General Product Safety Act and many others.[24] The famous Twin Directives (2019/770 and 2019/771)[25] were recently transposed as two separate legal acts. The newly introduced EU rules on the conformity

---

[19] Consumer Protection Act, OG Nos 79/07, 125/07, 75/09, 79/09, 89/09, 133/09, 78/12 and 56/13. The three other Directives transposed by the CPA 2007 were: Directive 2005/29/EC of the European Parliament and of the Council of 11 May 2005 concerning unfair business-to-consumer commercial practices in the internal market and amending Council Directive 84/450/EEC, Directives 97/7/EC, 98/27/EC and 2002/65/EC of the European Parliament and of the Council and Regulation (EC) No 2006/2004 of the European Parliament and of the Council [2005] OJ L149/22; Directive 98/27/EC of the European Parliament and of the Council of 19 May 1998 on injunctions for the protection of consumers' interests [1998] OJ L166/51; Directive 2002/65/EC of the European Parliament and of the Council of 23 September 2002 concerning the distance marketing of consumer financial services and amending Council Directive 90/619/EEC and Directives 97/7/EC and 98/27/EC [2002] OJ L 271/16.

[20] OG No 41/08.

[21] Commission of the European Communities, Croatia 2008 Progress Report, SEC(2008) 2694, final 36.

[22] Consumer Protection Act, OG Nos 41/14, 110/15 and 14/19. The CPA 2014 transposed Directive 2011/83/EU of the European Parliament and of the Council of 25 October 2011 on consumer rights, amending Council Directive 93/13/EEC and Directive 1999/44/EC of the European Parliament and of the Council and repealing Council Directive 85/577/EEC and Directive 97/7/EC of the European Parliament and of the Council [2011] OJ L304/64.

[23] The first example of this was the General Product Safety Act, OG Nos 30/09, 139/10, 14/14 and 32/19, adopted in 2009 and aligned with Council Directive 87/357/EEC of 25 June 1987 on the approximation of the laws of the Member States concerning products which, appearing to be other than they are, endanger the health or safety of consumers [1987] OJ L192/49 and Directive 2001/95/EC of the European Parliament and of the Council of 3 December 2001 on general product safety [2002] OJ L11/4.

[24] Consumer Credit Act, OG Nos 75/09, 112/12, 143/13, 147/13, 9/15, 78/15, 102/15, 52/16 and 128/22; Mortgage Consumer Credit Act, OG No 101/17 and 128/22; Payment System Act, OG Nos 66/18 and 114/22; E-Commerce Act, OG Nos 173/03, 67/08, 36/09, 130/11, 30/14 and 32/19; Insurance Act, OG Nos 30/15, 112/18, 63/20, 133/20 and 151/22; Electronic Communications Act, OG No 76/22; Alternative Consumer Dispute Resolution Act, OG Nos 121/16 and 32/19; General Product Safety Act, OG Nos 30/09, 139/10, 14/14 and 32/19. See E Miscenic, 'Croatian Consumer Protection Law: From Legal Approximation to Legal Fragmentation (Part II)' (2018) 23 *Studia Iuridica Toruniensia* 191, 191 ff.

[25] Directive (EU) 2019/770 of the European Parliament and of the Council of 20 May 2019 on certain aspects concerning contracts for the supply of digital content and digital services [2019] OJ L136/1; Directive (EU) 2019/771 of the European Parliament and of the Council of 20 May 2019 on certain aspects concerning

of goods and guarantees entered the OA rules on material defects of things, while rules on supply of digital content and digital services entered the newly adopted Digital Content and Digital Services Act.[26] In May 2022, the fourth CPA entered into force[27] because of alignment with the Omnibus Directive (2019/2161),[28] as well as with some of the rules of the Twin Directives.[29]

Having presented the evolution of Croatian consumer law in general, section III now depicts how the particular dimensions of legal transformation were influenced by different legislative choices during the first phase of evolution and how some of these choices affected enforcement of consumer law in Croatia.

III. The Transformative Aspects of Approximation of Croatian Consumer Law

The evolution of consumer law that occurred during the first phase of legal transformation resulted in creation of a new field of law within Croatia's legal system. However, the extensive substantive legal transformation of Croatian consumer law was followed by a variety of complex issues affecting all the other dimensions of legal transformation. The overall change introduced by the substantive dimension of legal transformation impacted institutional capacities, which were not ready for change and lacked knowledge and experience in the area of consumer law.[30]

On the other hand, this had an adverse effect on the procedural dimension and enforcement of consumer law. The newly introduced consumer law and its extensive rules, which differed from the familiar domestic legal rules, were not welcomed by enforcement bodies and other competent authorities. It was believed that these new pieces of EU legislation adversely affected the existing civil law rules and created unnecessary legal fragmentation, which in turn impacted enforcement and legal certainty.[31]

For a long time after adoption of the first CPA in 2003, the courts and other enforcement bodies simply ignored the existing legislation on consumer protection.[32] Despite

---

contracts for the sale of goods, amending Regulation (EU) 2017/2394 and Directive 2009/22/EC, and repealing Directive 1999/44/EC [2019] OJ L136/28.

[26] Obligations Act, OG Nos 35/05, 41/08, 125/11, 78/15, 29/18 and 126/21, in force from 1 January 2022; Act on certain aspects concerning contracts for the supply of digital content and digital services, OG No 110/21. See A De Franceschi and R Schulze (eds), *Harmonizing Digital Contract Law – The Impact of the EU Directives 2019/770 and 2019/771* (CH Beck, Hart, Nomos, 2023).

[27] CPA 2022 (n 10).

[28] Directive (EU) 2019/2161 of the European Parliament and of the Council of 27 November 2019 amending Council Directive 93/13/EEC and Directives 98/6/EC, 2005/29/EC and 2011/83/EU of the European Parliament and of the Council as regards the better enforcement and modernisation of Union consumer protection rules [2019] OJ L328/7.

[29] Directives (EU) 2019/770 and 2019/771 (n 25).

[30] A similar situation happened both in Serbia and Slovenia – see chs 9 and 12 of this volume, respectively.

[31] E Miscenic, 'Legal Risks in Development of EU Consumer Protection Law' in E Miscenic and A Raccah (eds), *Legal Risks in EU Law: Interdisciplinary Studies on Legal Risk Management and Better Regulation in Europe* (Springer International Publishing, 2016) 153.

[32] On similar experience of the other Western Balkan countries, see H-W Micklitz and M Durovic, 'The Law of the Western Balkan Countries in the Mirror of Consumer Law' in M Karanikic, H-W Micklitz and N Reich (eds), *Modernising Consumer Law, The Experience of the Western Balkan* (Nomos, 2012) 9.

the principle of *iura novit curia*, according to which the courts know the law, the courts were dealing with consumer disputes as ordinary civil law cases and resolving them by applying the familiar civil law provisions of the OA. Therefore, although the substantive dimension of legal transformation occurred in order to satisfy the requirements of alignment with the *acquis*, Croatian consumer law was in reality a dead letter due to undeveloped institutional and procedural dimensions. Even though the laws on consumer protection were in place, they were not sufficiently observed in practice and there was a significant lack of case law.[33]

Legal scholars offered different justifications for this treatment of consumer law. Josipović argued that poor enforcement could have been attributed to consumer fatigue and unwillingness to initiate proceedings, as well as to general ignorance of consumer law.[34] Nonetheless, other important reasons stand behind the reluctance to apply and enforce the newly introduced consumer law, which can be directly connected to the different dimensions of legal transformation.

First, the transposition of EU consumer law occurred very quickly, in order to satisfy the requirements of the *acquis* and make political progress in the accession negotiations. Political and institutional pressure – demanding immediate results and closure of accession negotiations chapters – was high and did not leave much time or space for thorough elaboration of the transposition process. Croatia's legislator opted for the so-called 'copy-paste' technique, and pursued this by literally transposing EU consumer directives into newly adopted or amended laws.[35]

This created discrepancies in the substantive dimension of legal transformation through introduction of new and unfamiliar EU concepts alongside concepts familiar from the original domestic laws. At times, the legislator combined this technique with integration and adaptation of EU legal concepts to those existing in domestic law. For instance, the legal term 'credit agreement' from the former Consumer Credit Directive (CCD) (87/102/EEC)[36] was translated in the CPAs 2003 and 2007 as 'consumer loan'. However, here too, the substantive dimension of legal transformation was affected, since the EU legal term was narrowed down to 'loans', despite the much broader substantive meaning under the Directive. Moreover, it caused misinterpretation of the EU concept at the national level, which was incorrectly understood as equivalent to the civil law concept of loan agreement under the OA.[37]

The literal transposition of EU consumer directives into the CPA, the OA and other laws was also undermined by the poor quality of translation of the corpus of the *acquis*,

---

[33] E Miscenic, 'Unfair Contract Terms in the Contract Law, Country Report for Croatia' in *Civil Law Forum for South East Europe-Collection of Studies and Analyses* (SEELS Network, 2012) 195.

[34] T Josipović, 'Enforcement Activity in Consumer Protection Regulation in Croatia' (2013) 36 *Journal of Consumer Policy* 307.

[35] Critically, A Łazowski and St Blockmans, 'Between Dream and Reality: Challenges to the Legal Rapprochement of the Western Balkans' in R Petrov and P Van Elsuwege (eds), *Legislative Approximation and Application of EU Law in the Eastern Neighbourhood of the European Union: Towards a Common Regulatory Space?* (Routledge, 2014) 108.

[36] Council Directive 87/102/EEC of 22 December 1986 for the approximation of the laws, regulations and administrative provisions of the Member States concerning consumer credit [1987] OJ L42/48.

[37] E Cikara, *Gegenwart und Zukunft der Verbraucherkreditverträge in der EU und in Kroatien, Die Umsetzung der Richtlinie 87/102/EWG und Richtlinie 2008/48/EG in das deutsche, österreichische und kroatische Verbraucherkreditrecht* (LIT Verlag, 2010) 372–73.

as well as by the incoherence of EU legal terms and the definitions contained within the directives. This resulted in translation and transposition of the basic consumer right of withdrawal within the same and different legal acts as the right of cancellation, retraction, termination, unilateral termination of the contract and the like.[38] This terminological inconsistency led to substantive incongruence, since the meaning and the legal consequences of EU legal terms on the right of withdrawal were often incorrectly equated with those of the civil law right to terminate a contract, which, differently from the EU concept, is not free of charge.[39] Over the years, most of these inconsistencies have been eliminated, but some of them remain. For instance, the CPAs of 2014 and 2022 describe the right of withdrawal as 'the right to unilaterally terminate the contract', while the very same right is translated as 'the right of withdrawal' in the Consumer Credit Act and the Mortgage Consumer Credit Act.[40]

Another key aspect affecting multiple dimensions of legal transformation during the first phase of the evolution of Croatian consumer law was the inconsistency existing between various consumer rules of different national laws. Little to no effort has been invested in achieving coherence between the CPA, the OA and other consumer protection legislation. These laws defined the consumer and other legal concepts in an inconsistent manner. Different definitions have resulted in diverging case law that has sometimes protected persons who are not consumers and denied protection to those who clearly are consumers. In one of the older cases, a craftswoman signing a business contract was qualified as a consumer, while the contract signed within the business premises of a trader's intermediary was qualified as an off-premises contract.[41] Misunderstanding of the main concepts of consumer law was a direct consequence of legal fragmentation and of inconsistency among consumer protection rules transposed in different legal acts. As a result, the issues created within the substantive dimension of legal transformation of Croatian consumer law affected its procedural dimension, namely enforcement of consumer law.

This argument can be strengthened by other legislative examples. For instance, the Unfair Contract Terms Directive (UCTD)[42] was transposed 'almost' literally into the CPA, while some of its provisions were integrated into existing rules of the OA on the invalidity of general terms and conditions. For years, this double-track system confused courts and other authorities, which resolved consumer disputes relying only on the OA provisions. Some important substantive differences in legal regulation of the two acts contributed to this choice. Even today, the CPA's unfairness test differs from the OA invalidity test, while some of the UCTD rules, such as the grey list of unfair contractual terms, are missing from the OA.[43]

---

[38] S Šarčević and E Čikara, 'European vs National Terminology in Croatian Legislation Transposing EU Directives' in S Šarčević (ed), *Legal Language in Action: Translation, Terminology, Drafting and Procedural Issues* (Nakladni zavod Globus, 2009) 193, 204–06.

[39] By analogy, see Case C-489/07 *Messner* ECLI:EU:C:2009:502, para 23.

[40] See Consumer Credit Act and Mortgage Consumer Credit Act (n 24). See also E Mišćenić, 'Legal Translation vs Legal Certainty in EU Law' in E Miscenic and A Raccah (eds), *Legal Risks in EU Law: Interdisciplinary Studies on Legal Risk Management and Better Regulation in Europe* (Springer International Publishing, 2016) 99.

[41] Judgment of the High Administrative Court of the Republic of Croatia, Us-3781/2011-4 of 28 February 2012.

[42] Council Directive 93/13/EEC of 5 April 1993 on unfair terms in consumer contracts [1993] OJ L95/29.

[43] Miscenic (n 33) 195.

Another example of issues occurring within the substantive dimension of the legal transformation of Croatian consumer law are the rules on the conformity of goods and commercial guarantees. When transposing the former Consumer Sales Directive (99/44/EC)[44] into the OA, the legislator widened the scope of its provisions to all obligation relationships, while keeping some applicable to B2C relationships. The introduction of consumer provisions and definition of the 'consumer contract' was quite a novelty and a significant departure from the OA provisions, which originally protected consumers in the same way as any other party to an obligation relationship. However, subsequent amendments introduced by the Consumer Rights Directive (2011/83/EU)[45] were transposed elsewhere, namely into the CPA, which now contains some of the rules on sale of goods, such as those on passing of risk and delivery, including definitions of 'consumer sale of goods' and 'warranty'.[46] This double set of legal rules was kept even after alignment with the Consumer Sales Directive (2019/771).[47]

Taking into consideration the issues presented regarding the substantive dimension of the legal transformation of Croatian consumer law, one can deduce why difficulties have arisen in enforcement of consumer law. Most likely these could have been avoided, had there been institutional capacities competent enough to avoid the above-presented difficulties created during the process of alignment with the *acquis*. Institutional and substantive weaknesses in the legal transformation of consumer law have had a direct impact on the procedural dimension and the enforcement of consumer law. As explained, for quite a long time, enforcement bodies avoided applying the newly introduced consumer protection rules.

The 'real' transformation of enforcement of consumer law began almost 10 years after the introduction of the first CPA in 2003. This was triggered by severe economic consequences experienced by tens of thousands of Croatian consumers in the aftermath of the global financial crisis.[48] Affected by financial difficulties and repayment of debts in Croatian kuna/Swiss franc (HRK/CHF) and Swiss franc credit agreements, consumers started to initiate court proceeding. These events led to the second most important phase of the legal transformation of Croatian consumer law, with an emphasis on procedural aspects and enforcement of consumer law.[49]

IV. Croatian Case Law Related to Swiss Franc Consumer Credit Agreements: A Wake-up Call for Consumer Protection

The change that was the main driver of transformation of Croatian consumer law began during the debt crisis caused by the HRK/CHF and Swiss franc consumer credit

---

[44] Directive 1999/44/EC of the European Parliament and of the Council of 25 May 1999 on certain aspects of the sale of consumer goods and associated guarantees [1999] OJ L171/12.

[45] Directive 2011/83/EU (n 22).

[46] E Mišćenić, 'Croatia' in De Franceschi and Schulze (eds) (n 26) 127.

[47] Directive (EU) 2019/771 (n 25).

[48] M Baretić and S Petrović, 'Enforcement and Effectiveness of Consumer Law in Croatia' in H-W Micklitz and G Saumier (eds), *Enforcement and Effectiveness of Consumer Law* (Springer, 2018) 203.

[49] E Mišćenić and V Tomljenović, 'National Report (Croatia)' in B Hess and St Law (eds), *Implementing EU Consumer Rights by National Procedural Law* (Beck/Hart/Nomos, 2019).

agreements. While the first phase of the transformation was related to the creation and evolution of the new field of consumer law, the second phase was concerned with enforcement of consumer law. The first real incentive to achieve consistent interpretation, application and enforcement of consumer law was the first consumer collective redress proceedings related to credit agreements denominated or indexed in Swiss francs.[50]

These contracts were offered on Croatia's market from 2003 to 2009, and featured violations of the newly introduced consumer law, which had been harmonised with the former CCD, the former Misleading Advertising Directive,[51] the Unfair Commercial Practices Directive[52] and the UCTD. Case law confirmed the use of misleading advertising and other unfair commercial practices, as well as violations of consumer credit and banking rules on pre-contractual and contractual information requirements, assessment of creditworthiness and so on. Additionally, credit agreements were concluded with the simultaneous use of two contractual terms related to essential elements of the contract, namely the so-called currency clause and the variable interest rate.[53] Both contractual terms were undetermined and subject to unilateral change by the contractor and therefore unfair.

However, it was not until the aftermath of the global financial crisis that Croatian consumers became aware of the economic and legal consequences of the financial, exchange rate and interest risks to which they were exposed.[54] During that period, credit instalments increased between 50 per cent and 80 per cent compared to the agreed initial amount – and in some cases even more. Due to inability to repay their debt – owed predominantly to foreign commercial banks – thousands of Croatian consumers ended up in debt, bankrupt or even homeless.[55] In 2016, the Constitutional Court found that the debt crisis caused by the HRK/CHF and Swiss franc credit agreements had led to 'grave social conditions that hundreds of thousands of Croatian citizens live in'.[56]

---

[50] Legal scholars have written extensively on foreign currency loans in SEE countries: M Durovic, 'Mišćenić, Emilia, Silvija Petrić. 2020. Nepoštenost valutne klauzule u CHF i HRK/CHF kreditima (Unfairness of Currency Clause in CHF and HRK/CHF Loans). Zagreb: Narodne novine, 355' (2022) 1 *Annals of the Faculty of Law in Belgrade* 355, 355–58; M Radović, 'Legality of the Currency Clause after Entry into Force of the Law on Conversion' (2021) 69 *Annals of the Faculty of Law Belgrade* 192; R Vassileva, 'Monetary Appreciation and Foreign Currency Mortgages: Lessons from the 2015 Swiss Franc Surge' (2020) 28 *European Review of Private Law* 173; D Možina, *Kreditne pogodbe v švicarskih franak* (GV Založba, 2018); J Fazekas, 'The Consumer Credit Crisis and Unfair Terms Regulation – Before and After Kásler' (2017) 3 *Journal of European Consumer and Market Law* 99; M Józon, 'Unfair Contract Terms Law in Europe in Times of Crisis: Substantive Justice Lost in the Paradise of Proceduralisation of Contract' (2017) 3 *Journal of European Consumer and Market Law* 157, 157–66; P Tereszkiewicz, 'Fremdwährungskredite als Frage des Verbraucherschutzes Eine Zwischenbilanz' in B Heiderhoff and R Schulze (eds) *Verbraucherrecht und Verbraucherverhalten* (Nomos, 2016) 83; P Tereszkiewicz, 'Neutral Third-Party Counselling as Nudge Toward Safer Financial Products? The Case of Risky Mortgage Loan Contracts' in M Klaus and T Avishalom (eds), *Nudging – Possibilities, Limitations and Applications in European Law and Economics* (Springer, 2016) 170.

[51] Council Directive 84/450/EEC of 10 September 1984 concerning misleading and comparative advertising [1984] OJ L250/17.

[52] Directive 2005/29/EC of the European Parliament and Council of 11 May 2005 concerning unfair business-to-consumer commercial practices in the internal market [2005] OJ L149/22.

[53] E Mišćenić, 'Currency Clauses in CHF Credit Agreements: A 'Small Wheel' in the Swiss Loans' Mechanism' (2020) 6 *Journal of European Consumer and Market Law* 226, 226–35.

[54] E Miscenic, 'Foreign Currency Loans in Croatia' in MJ Golecki and P Tereszkiewicz (eds), *Protecting Financial Consumers in Europe: Comparative Perspectives and Policy Choices* (Brill, 2023) 123.

[55] P Poretti, 'Debt Collection Practices under Croatian Enforcement Law – Is there a way out for over-indebted consumers?' (2018) 6 *Journal of European Consumer and Market Law* 263.

[56] Decision of the Constitutional Court of the Republic of Croatia of 13 December 2016, U-I-392/2011 et al, 84.

The Croatian National Bank estimated that around 75,000 consumers concluded these high-risk credit agreements.[57]

The unfair manner in which the credit agreements were concluded on the Croatian market affected society as a whole. However, at the same time, it also prompted a genuine transformation of consumer law. Croatian consumer law was transformed from a dead letter into a real tool for protection of consumer rights. Consumer associations recognised the importance of consumer law, and in 2012 initiated the first collective redress proceedings against the use of unfair contractual terms in consumer credit agreements. In addition, both substantive and institutional transformation occurred, as the competent national authorities became more aware of their role and duties in consumer protection. Different legislative amendments – aimed at increasing transparency and strengthening information requirements in consumer credit law – contributed to the legal transformation of Croatian consumer law.[58]

The rest of this section of the chapter therefore focuses on analysis of the two most important aspects driving the development of Croatian consumer law and its transformation during the second phase. Section IV.A, on unfairness and transparency, shows how multiple dimensions of legal transformation, particularly procedural transformation, were affected by the first consumer collective redress proceedings. Section IV.B, on the conversion of consumer credits, is an example of legal transformation occurring at all levels: institutional, procedural and, above all, substantive.

A. Unfairness and Transparency

An extensive and highly controversial debate on the unfairness and transparency of disputed contractual terms began in 2012, when the Croatian Union of Consumer Protection Associations – Potrošač – invoked the unfairness of variable interest rates and currency clauses used in HRK/CHF and Swiss franc credit agreements in the first consumer collective redress proceedings.[59] National case law reveals that the main discussion was about transparency and different treatment of the two contractual terms.

To start with, the ordinary civil courts classified both the disputed contractual terms under the exclusion transposed from Article 4(2) UCTD. According to the corresponding provision of the CPAs of 2003 and 2007, assessment of the fairness of contractual terms on the subject of the contract and the price is not permitted if these terms are plain, easily intelligible and easily noticeable.[60]

Substantive changes in the wording and content of the national provisions, made during the transposition of Article 4(2) UCTD, had a huge impact on interpretation and eventually determined the outcome of the proceedings.[61] By ignoring the interpretation

---

[57] Croatian National Bank Report from 2015 on Issues of Citizens Indebtedness in CHF loans.

[58] T Josipović and H Ernst, 'Recent Crisis-Motivated Reforms in Croatian Private Law' (2015) 13 *European Lawyer Journal* 78, 78 ff.

[59] E Miscenic, 'Croatian Case "Franak": Effective or "Defective" Protection of Consumer Rights?' (2016) V *Harmonius Journal of Legal and Social Studies in South East Europe* 184, 184 ff.

[60] CPA 2003 (n 9) Art 84; CPA 2007 (n 19) Art 99.

[61] According to Art 4(2) UCTD, 'Assessment of the unfair nature of the terms shall relate neither to the definition of the main subject matter of the contract nor to the adequacy of the price and remuneration, on

of the Court of Justice of the European Union (CJEU) of the first category of terms related to the 'main subject matter of the contract' and of the 'adequacy of the price and remuneration', the Croatian courts concluded that the currency clause fell under the 'subject of the contract' and the variable interest rate under the notion of 'price'.[62]

The clear distinction drawn by CJEU case law between credit agreements denominated in the foreign currency, such as in *Kásler and Káslerné Rábai*,[63] and loans denominated and to be repaid in foreign currency, as in *Andriciuc and Others*,[64] had not drawn the Croatian courts' attention. Had it done so, and had the Croatian courts observed CJEU case law, the legal discourse would have been significantly different. The exclusion does not apply to contractual terms related to a 'mechanism for amending the prices of the services provided to the consumer',[65] such as variable interest rate, or to terms that 'merely determine the conversion rate of the foreign currency in which the loan agreement is denominated',[66] such as currency clauses.[67] Thus the substantive issues created during the first phase of consumer law transformation changed the outcome of the proceedings and affected the second phase of transformation, namely, enforcement of consumer law.

Disregard of the duty of consistent interpretation and CJEU case law related to autonomous and uniform interpretation of legal concepts arising under Article 4(2) UCTD[68] reflected on the transformation of Croatian consumer law and its procedural dimension. Once the first category of terms was incorrectly interpreted as encompassing disputed contractual terms, transparency requirements became the focus of attention. However, once again the Croatian courts neglected settled CJEU case law interpreting the UCTD wording: 'plain and intelligible language'.[69]

Moreover, in one of its rulings of 2015, the Supreme Court explicitly rejected application of the transparency requirements from *Kásler and Káslerné Rábai* because of factual differences between the Hungarian and Croatian cases.[70] By following the reasoning of the High Commercial Court,[71] the Supreme Court treated disputed contractual terms

---

the one hand, as against the services or goods supplies in exchange, on the other, in so far as these terms are in plain intelligible language.' See E Miscenic, 'Uniform Interpretation of Article 4(2) of UCT Directive in the Context of Consumer Credit Agreements: Is it possible?' (2018) 3 *Revue du droit de l'Union européenne* 127, 127–59.

[62] Judgment of the High Commercial Court of the Republic of Croatia of 14 June 2018, 43 Pž-6632/2017-10, 50: 'The term binding the credit principal to the Swiss franc is a term on the contract subject.'; 58: 'The essential elements of a credit contract are definitely the subject and the price, and interest is price'.

[63] Case C-26/13 *Kásler and Káslerné Rábai* ECLI:EU:C:2014:282.

[64] Case C-186/16 *Andriciuc and Others* ECLI:EU:C:2017:703, paras 39–41. See also Case C-609/19 *BNP Paribas Personal Finance* ECLI:EU:C:2021:469, para 33; Case C-51/17 *OTP Bank and OTP Faktoring* ECLI:EU:C:2018:750, para 68; Case C-118/17 *Dunai* ECLI:EU:C:2019:207, para 48.

[65] Case C-143/13 *Matei* ECLI:EU:C:2015:127, para 56; Case C-472/10 *Invitel* ECLI:EU:C:2012:242, para 23.

[66] *Kásler and Káslerné Rábai* (n 63) para 58.

[67] Commission Notice, Guidance on the interpretation and application of Council Directive 93/13/EEC on unfair terms in consumer contracts [2019] OJ C323/04, 24.

[68] Case C-143/13 *Matei* ECLI:EU:C:2015:127, para 50, 'must normally be given an autonomous and uniform interpretation throughout the European Union'.

[69] M Junuzović, 'Transparency of (Pre-)Contractual Information in Consumer Credit Agreements: Is Consistency the Missing Key?' (2018) 14 *Croatian Yearbook of European Law and Policy* 70, 70–98.

[70] Judgment and order of the Supreme Court of the Republic of Croatia of 9 April 2015, Revt-249/14-2, 22.

[71] Judgment and order of the High Commercial Court of the Republic of Croatia of 13 June 2014, Pž-7129/13-4, 50 and 53.

differently and found the variable interest rate to be 'absolutely unintelligible to an average consumer'.[72] The variable interest rate was unintelligible due to highly complex terminology understandable only to banking professionals.

On the other hand, the currency clause 'institute is absolutely recognised and accepted in our society and [it] has been applied for years, including to legal transactions such as credit contracts that natural persons conclude with banks'.[73] The Supreme Court found claims of the unintelligibility of currency clauses to be unacceptable and concluded that 'on the contrary, this contractual term was very well known to consumers, including all the legal consequences that it produces'.[74] Instead of observing the duty of consistent interpretation and the UCTD's 'substantive transparency requirements', the Croatian courts transformed the meaning of the wording 'plain and intelligible language'. Moreover, when interpreting national provisions transposing Article 4(2) UCTD, the courts neglected the higher standard of consumer protection introduced that required contractual terms to be 'plain, easily intelligible, and easily noticeable' (Article 84 CPA 2003; Article 99 CPA 2007). As opposed to CJEU case law, the Supreme Court incorrectly relied on the argument of general acceptance and familiarity of the concept to consumers.[75] According to CJEU settled case law, the transparency requirement

> is to be understood as requiring not only that the relevant term should be grammatically intelligible to the consumer, but also that the contract should set out transparently the specific functioning of the mechanism … and the relationship between that mechanism and that provided for by other contractual terms … , so that that consumer is in a position to evaluate, on the basis of clear, intelligible criteria, the economic consequences for him which derive from it.[76]

The Supreme Court argued that

> full-age, adult and averagely circumspect persons cannot expect that the circumstances in society, in particular economic ones, will remain unchanged after a long period of time, which undoubtedly affects the value and the exchange rate of the national kuna, as well as other currencies in the world, such as EUR, Swiss franc, Japanese yen, US dollar etc.[77]

This ruling therefore interfered with both the procedural and the substantive dimension of consumer law and affected some of its important aspects, such as the meaning of transparency requirements, information duties and the image of the average consumer, who should be 'reasonably well informed'.[78] In this case, the information duty was reversed on

---

[72] Judgment and order of the Supreme Court (n 70) 33.
[73] ibid 18.
[74] ibid.
[75] ibid 19.
[76] *Kásler and Káslerné Rábai* (n 63) para 75; *Invitel* (n 65) paras 24, 26 and 28; Case C-92/11 *RWE Vertrieb* ECLI:EU:C:2013:180, para 49; Case C-96/14 *Van Hove* ECLI:EU:C:2015:262, para 51; Case C-348/14 *Bucura* ECLI:EU:C:2015:447, para 55; *Andriciuc and Others* (n 64) paras 44 and 45; Case C-119/17 *Lupean and Lupean* ECLI:EU:C:2018:103, para 32; *BNP Paribas Personal Finance* (n 64) para 42. See also R Mańko, 'Unfair terms in Swiss franc loans: Overview of European Court of Justice Case Law' (March 2021) *European Parliamentary Research Service* 1, 1–12.
[77] Judgment and order of the Supreme Court (n 70) 19.
[78] D Leczykiewicz and S Weatherill (eds), *The Images of the Consumer in EU Law: Legislation, Free Movement and Competition Law* (Hart Publishing, 2016).

to consumers, who were expected to be familiar with the risks and mechanisms arising under complex HRK/CHF and Swiss franc credit agreements, and to inform themselves.[79]

This method of transformation of Croatian consumer law did not go unnoticed. In 2017, the European Commission commented that the 'Croatian courts, including the Supreme Court still do not see themselves as European courts.'[80] A year earlier, in 2016, the Constitutional Court ordered a renewal of the collective redress proceedings with respect to the part of the Supreme Court ruling on the transparency of currency clauses.[81] According to the Constitutional Court,

> the Supreme Court used different interpretations of the notion of the intelligibility of the disputed contractual terms on the currency clause, on the one hand, and contractual terms on variable interest rates that depend on the unilateral decision of the banks, on the other hand.[82]

The lack of argumentation and decisional justification, accompanied by disregard for CJEU case law, represented a violation of the right to a fair trial. By following the instructions of the Constitutional Court, in 2017 the Supreme Court ordered the High Commercial Court to reassess the fairness of currency clauses.[83] In 2018, the High Commercial Court reversed the previous rulings and established that a violation of transparency requirements caused the unfairness of currency clauses:

> [T]he unintelligibility of contractual terms binding the principal to Swiss francs ... is a serious cause of significant imbalance between contractual parties' right and obligations to the detriment of the consumer.[84]

A year later, the Supreme Court confirmed that finding,[85] and in 2021 the consumer collective redress finally got closure in a decision by the Constitutional Court reaffirming the non-transparency and unfairness of disputed contractual terms.[86]

In terms of transformation, what we have witnessed is a transformation within the transformation of Croatian consumer law and of the procedural dimension in particular. During the renewed trial, the collective redress proceedings experienced a complete change with respect to assessment of the transparency and unfairness of currency

---

[79] On different interpretations of the role of transparency, see F Esposito and M Grochowski, 'The Consumer Benchmark, Vulnerability, and the Contract Terms Transparency: A Plea for Reconsideration' (2022) 18 *European Review of Contract Law* 1, 1–31; B Schmitz and Ch Pavillon, 'Measuring Transparency in Consumer Contracts: The Usefulness of Readability Formulas Empirically Assessed' (2020) 5 *Journal of European Consumer and Market Law* 191; V Mak, *Legal Pluralism in European Contract Law* (Oxford University Press, 2020) 144–46.

[80] European Commission, An evaluation study of national procedural laws and practices in terms of their impact on the free circulation of judgments and on the equivalence and effectiveness of the procedural protection of consumers under EU consumer law, Strand 2 Procedural Protection of Consumers, JUST/2014/RCON/PR/CIVI/0082, 2017, 61.

[81] Decision of the Constitutional Court of the Republic of Croatia of 13 December 2016, U-III-2521/2015 et al.
[82] ibid 20.

[83] Order of the Supreme Court of the Republic of Croatia of 3 October 2017, Revt-575/16-5.

[84] Judgment of the High Commercial Court of the Republic of Croatia of 14 June 2018, 43 Pž-6632/2017-10, 53 and 62.

[85] Judgment and order of the Supreme Court of the Republic of Croatia of 3 September 2019, Rev-2221/2018-11, 24.

[86] Decision and order of the Constitutional Court of the Republic of Croatia of 3 February 2021, U-III-4150-2019 et al, 103. See T Josipović, 'Kroatische Verbraucher vs Kredite in CHF – ein Drama in fünf Akten ohne Schlussakt' (2020) 6 *Osteuropa Recht* 4, 4–33.

clauses, therefore resulting in a reversal of the outcome in one of the most significant consumer cases in Croatia. However, this time, enforcement of Croatian consumer law had transformed for the better, benefiting both consumers and the *acquis*.

Confirmation of these conclusions came more recently in the form of the decision of the European Court of Human Rights (ECtHR) in *OTP Banka dd and others v Croatia*.[87] In this case, the ECtHR ruled on several complaints by five different banks as applicants, who submitted applications against Croatia due to 'alleged unfairness of civil proceedings before commercial courts concerning a collective consumer dispute'. The Court found complaints related to alleged violation of Article 6(1) of the European Convention on Human Rights inadmissible and confirmed that 'there is nothing to suggest that the domestic courts lacked impartiality or that the proceedings were otherwise unfair'.[88]

B. Transformation by Conversion

The transformation presented of Croatian consumer law in the course of the collective redress proceedings related to the HRK/CHF and Swiss franc consumer credit agreements was not the end but rather the beginning of the transformation process. Issues related to loans triggered the transformation of Croatian consumer law at all levels, and had a significant impact on its institutional, procedural and substantive dimensions. Although a detailed analysis would exceed the limits of this chapter, it is worth noting how different dimensions merged and affected one another.

As the awareness of Croatian consumers increased, the number of individual proceedings against credit institutions began to grow, therefore contributing to the evolution of the procedural dimension. In turn, this improved institutional awareness of the importance and role of existing consumer law. Changes began to occur with respect to consumer associations and other competent bodies, which became more involved in pursuing the goal of consumer protection. This is not surprising, taking into consideration the overall impact on Croatia's society of the debt crisis caused by high-risk loans.[89] There was a need for a more systematic legal solution, and Croatia's legislator intervened on several occasions in order to strengthen the transparency and information requirements related to consumer credit.

These events combined led to another transformation of Croatian consumer law, this time from the substantive point of view, but nevertheless triggered by developments at the procedural and institutional levels. After 2012, Croatia's legislator introduced several amendments to the Consumer Credit Act (CCA) and the Credit Institutions Act (CIA), and increased transparency in regard to interest rates, the annual percentage rate of charge (APRC), and pre-contractual and contractual information duties.[90]

---

[87] *OTP Banka dd and others v Croatia* App nos 38541/21, 39015/21, 39063/21, 39167/21 and 41145/21 (ECtHR, 8 November 2022).

[88] ibid para 16.

[89] P Rodik, 'The Impact of the Swiss Franc Loans Crisis on Croatian Households' in SM Değirmencioğlu and C Walker (eds), *Social and Psychological Dimensions of Personal Debt and the Debt Industry* (Palgrave Macmillan, 2015) 61.

[90] Amendments to the Consumer Credit Act in 2012 and 2013 (OG Nos 112/12, 143/13, 147/13), and to the Credit Institutions Act (OG No 54/13) in 2013.

The legislative interventions related to the APRC were invoked in the *Horžić* case,[91] where the CJEU found that the amendments introduced were not the result of approximation and therefore were not precluded by the Consumer Credit Directive (2008/48/EC).[92]

However, once the Swiss National Bank announced in 2015 that it would no longer hold the minimum exchange rate of the Swiss franc in relation to the euro (EUR),[93] Croatia's legislator intervened directly in HRK/CHF and Swiss franc credit agreements. First, it fixed the Swiss franc exchange rate in relation to the Croatian kuna;[94] and several months later, in September 2015, it adopted the so-called Conversion Act(s). These acts, which were another amendment to the CCA and the CIA,[95] enabled consumers to convert HRK/CHF and Swiss franc contracts into HRK/EUR and euro contracts.[96] In doing so, Croatia's legislator enabled the transformation, though this time of consumer credit contracts. The conversion was an extraordinary and one-time measure that enabled consumers who opted to do so to convert their high-risk credit contracts, but with retroactive effect, from the moment of contract conclusion.

The micro transformation presented had macro effects on Croatia's society and consumer law. The unexpected development of the substantive dimension of consumer law resulted in significant changes and movement at the institutional and procedural levels. The case that had once been limited to Croatian society and the Croatian state had now crossed the border and become a European and international legal, economic and – above all – political issue.[97]

The legislator affirmed that the amendments were in line with the UCTD and settled CJEU case law. The aim was to benefit both contractual parties by preserving the validity of the disputed contracts and restoring 'the legal and factual situation that the consumer would have been in had those unfair terms not existed'.[98] Nonetheless, the European Commission initiated infringement proceedings under Article 258 of the Treaty on the Functioning of the European Union (TFEU)[99] and sent a formal notice of violation of the free movement of capital and freedom of establishment.[100]

---

[91] Joined Cases C-511/15 and C-512/15 *Renata Horžić and Siniša Pušić v Privredna banka Zagreb and Božo Prka* ECLI:EU:C:2016:787, para 36.

[92] Directive 2008/48/EC of the European Parliament and Council of 23 April 2008 on credit agreements for consumers and repealing Council Directive 87/102/EEC [2008] OJ L133/66.

[93] Swiss National Bank, 'Swiss National Bank discontinues minimum exchange rate and lowers interest rate to -0.75%' (Press release, Zurich, 15 January 2015).

[94] Act on Amendments to the Consumer Credit Act, OG No 9/15 and Act on Amendments to the Credit Institutions Act, OG No 19/15 fixed the Swiss franc exchange rate to 6.39 HRK for 1 CHF. On the similar Hungarian solution, see Fazekas (n 50).

[95] Act on Amendments to the Consumer Credit Act, OG No 102/15; Act on Amendments to the Credit Institutions Act, OG No 102/15.

[96] Chapter IV.a CCA entitled 'Conversion of credits denominated in CHF' and denominated in kunas with currency clause in CHF' (Arts 19.a–19.i); Chapter XXVIII.a CIA entitled 'Conversion of credits denominated in CHF and denominated in kunas with currency clause in CHF' (Arts 357.a–357.i).

[97] European Commission, Macroeconomic Imbalances, Country Report – Croatia 2015, June 2015, 59–60.

[98] Case C-483/16 *Sziber* ECLI:EU:C:2018:367, para 55; Case C-118/17 *Dunai* ECLI:EU:C:2019:207, paras 56 and 65. See also Case C-453/10 *Pereničová and Perenič* ECLI:EU:C:2012:144, para 31; Case C-618/10 *Banco Español de Crédito* ECLI:EU:C:2012:349, para 40; Case C-26/13 *Árpád Kásler and Hajnalka Káslerné Rábai v OTP Jelzálogbank Zrt* ECLI:EU:C:2014:282, para 82.

[99] Treaty on the Functioning of the European Union (consolidated) [2016] OJ C202/1.

[100] European Commission formal notice of 16 June 2016, infringement number INFR(2015)2198. As of 2022, the case was still listed as an active infringement case. The case was closed on 19 April 2023.

The European Central Bank (ECB) issued an opinion on the conversion of Swiss franc loans in Croatia, criticising the retroactivity of the conversion and the financial burdening of credit institutions.[101] Foreign commercial banks initiated several arbitration proceedings before the International Centre for Settlement of Investment Disputes (ICSID) and sought compensation before the national courts. Due to the *Achmea* case and the Member States' Declaration on the fate of bilateral investment treaties (BITs) and investment dispute settlements,[102] most of these claims were withdrawn and settlements were achieved.[103]

However, the legal discourse on the Croatian conversion measure continued, at both national and EU levels. In 2017, the Constitutional Court questioned its legitimacy and found the conversion proportional and necessary for achieving the goals of protecting public policy, social justice and consumer protection in Croatia.[104] The Court dismissed the proposal for evaluation of constitutionality and argued that the conversion was a one-time and extraordinary measure that followed the legitimate goal of 'increasing social protection, and preventing the continuance of credit institutions' unfair commercial practices and deepening of the debt crisis'.[105] The Court pointed to the reciprocal share of conversion costs between banks and consumers, and to the partial retroactivity of some of the amendments.[106]

In March 2020, the Supreme Court issued a legal opinion according to which the conversion was found to follow the legitimate goal of removing unfair commercial practices and mitigate the debt crisis caused by the HRK/CHF and Swiss franc credit agreements.[107] The Supreme Court also addressed the 'converted' credit agreements and stated that these were valid, even if the contract initially contained an unfair variable interest rate or currency clause.[108]

However, this interpretation of the validity of the converted, that is 'transformed', credit contracts is still debated by Croatia's jurists and scholars. There is no uniform case law on the matter, and rulings often annul converted contracts that initially contained disputed unfair contractual terms.[109] Even the Supreme Court has ruled on several other occasions that conversion cannot be a barrier to annulment of a contract that initially contained disputed unfair and invalid contractual terms.[110] Such interpretation seems to be in line with the CJEU case law on unfair contractual terms.

---

[101] ECB Opinion of 18 September 2015 on the conversion of Swiss franc loans in Croatia (CON/2015/32).

[102] Case C-284/16 *Achmea* ECLI:EU:C:2018:15819; Declaration of the Representatives of the Governments of the Member States of 15 January 2019 on the Legal Consequences of the judgment of the Court of Justice in *Achmea* and on Investment Protection in the European Union at https://finance.ec.europa.eu/publications/declaration-member-states-15-january-2019-legal-consequences-achmea-judgment-and-investment_en (accessed 5 February 2023).

[103] M Župan and Ana-Marija Čuljak, 'Croatia' in C Nagy (ed), *Investment Arbitration in Central and Eastern Europe: Law and Practice* (Edward Elgar Publishing, 2019) 68.

[104] Order of the Constitutional Court of the Republic of Croatia of 4 April 2017, U-I-3685/2015 et al.

[105] ibid 87.

[106] ibid 8–11.

[107] Order of Supreme Court of the Republic of Croatia of 4 March 2020, Gos 1/2019-36, 2 and 4.

[108] ibid.

[109] Order of the Supreme Court of the Republic of Croatia of 12 February 2019, Rev-2868/2018-2.

[110] ibid; Order of the Supreme Court of the Republic of Croatia of 26 May 2020, Rev 18/2018-2, 2.

In *Ibercaja Banco*, the CJEU found that the consumer may waive the right to rely on the unfairness of contractual terms by another agreement, 'provided that that waiver is the result of free and informed consent'.[111] However, whether the conversion of contracts offered by the banks was transparent enough for an average consumer, so that they could in fact understand the extent and the meaning of the conversion procedure, is highly questionable. The CJEU concluded that by waiving the right to invoke unfairness, 'the consumer waives the effects that would result from that term being declared to be unfair', provided that the waiver is transparent to the consumer.[112]

The discussion continued before the CJEU, where the Croatian courts sent requests for preliminary rulings under Article 267 TFEU. In one of these cases, the Supreme Court in essence asked if the UCTD was applicable to consumer credit contracts signed before Croatia became a Member State, but which were converted subsequently. The case was removed from the CJEU register for obvious reasons.[113] Not only have the temporal effects of the *acquis* and CJEU competence in such cases been clarified many times before,[114] but also the CJEU is not competent to interpret provisions not related to the *acquis*.

A similar development occurred in *Zagrebačka banka*, where the Municipal Court in Zagreb asked for clarification of the relation between the UCTD and the Conversion Act(s), and whether the conversion contradicts the UCTD and Articles 38 and 47 of the EU Charter.[115] As in the first case, the questions referred concerned national legislation that was not the result of approximation. Therefore, the CJEU concluded that the subject matter of converted credit contracts does not fall within the material scope of the UCTD.[116]

The transformation related to conversion of consumer credit contracts denominated in Swiss francs has had an overall impact on Croatian consumer law. Substantive changes, rendered in the form of amendments to two important acts protecting consumers, namely the CCA and the CIA, triggered a comprehensive transformation of consumer law and B2C relationships. However, unlike other legislative changes, this one transcended the national border due to its far-reaching economic and political effects. Different institutional capacities were engaged and proceedings have been initiated against the measure intended to transform the consequences of a systematic violation of Croatian consumer law.

The main question is therefore not whether this transformation was effected properly – which can of course be discussed – but whether it came too late to protect Croatian consumers. Had the newly introduced consumer law been observed and applied by the authorities and market players during the first phase of transformation, we would most

---

[111] Case C-452/18 *Ibercaja Banco* ECLI:EU:C:2020:536, para 28; Case C-260/18 *Dziubak* ECLI:EU:C:2019:819, para 54.

[112] *Ibercaja Banco* (n 111) para 28.

[113] Request for a preliminary ruling from the Supreme Court of the Republic of Croatia of 30 September 2020, C-474/20, *ID*, removed from the Register by Order of the President of the Court of 18 June 2021, ECLI:EU:C:2021:524.

[114] Case C-630/17 *Milivojević* ECLI:EU:C:2019:123, paras 40–43; Case C-162/0 *Pokrzeptowicz-Meyer* ECLI:EU:C:2002:57, para 50; Case C-256/15 *Nemec* ECLI:EU:C:2016:954.

[115] Request for a preliminary ruling from the Municipal Civil Law Court in Zagreb of 29 October 2020, Case C-567/20 *Zagrebačka banka*. Charter of Fundamental Rights of the European Union [2016] OJ C202/391.

[116] Case C-567/20 *Zagrebačka banka* ECLI:EU:C:2022:352, para 66.

likely not have witnessed the events from the second phase of the transformation of Croatian consumer law. The latter phase brought about an overall change in the attitude towards consumer law, but it also revealed multiple issues and significant weaknesses related to enforcement of consumer law and its effectiveness.

V. Conclusions: Transformation of Croatian Consumer Law, Past, Present and Future

Many lessons are to be learned from the transformation of Croatian consumer law, the main one being that Croatian consumer law can almost be identified with the notion of transformation. Everything was transformed with respect to Croatian consumer law, and this was necessary in order to develop consumer law as a new field of law in Croatia. The temporal aspect of the process reveals three main phases in the transformation of Croatian consumer law: the past, current and future phases.

The first phase was concerned with creation of an entirely new area of law, which had been practically non-existent prior to alignment with the *acquis*. Starting in 2001, first as a candidate and then as an accession country, Croatia transformed its legal order in order to become a Member State. However, with respect to consumer law, this process differed from accession by other Member States and was influenced by Croatia's historical, political, economic and legal background. Historically, Croatia followed the legal tradition of the Austrian Civil Code from the nineteenth century until 1945, when the socialist regime was introduced.[117]

Therefore, Croatia has experienced changes in the form of different political regimes and economic systems, which in turn laid the foundations for future legal development. Regarding consumer law, the foundations were rather weak, in particular due to a shift from the socialist regime to the market economy and because of poor awareness of the consumer's position in society.[118] Consumer law remained neglected for a long time, even after the introduction of consumer law in Croatia, not only by institutions and competent authorities, but also by jurisprudence and indeed consumers themselves.

Significant changes began to occur in the aftermath of the global financial crisis, when tens of thousands of Croatian consumers experienced financial difficulties repaying debts stemming from consumer credit contracts denominated in foreign currency (CHF). This period, which brought about many significant changes and resulted in the development of consumer law, can be identified as the second phase of the transformation. After almost a decade of neglect and poor enforcement of the newly introduced consumer law, consumers entered into the first collective redress proceedings against eight commercial banks, which were using unfair contractual terms in high-risk credit contracts.

---

[117] T Josipović, '200 Jahre der ABGB-Anwendung in Kroatien – 135 Jahre als Gesetz und 65 Jahre als „Rechtsregeln"' in F-Cz Constanze, H Gerhard, Kn Georg and Sch Martin (eds), *Festschrift 200 Jahre ABGB* (Manz Verlag 2011) 157–74.

[118] Development of the market economy began with the proclamation of independence and adoption of the Constitution of the Republic of Croatia, OG Nos 56/90, 135/97, 8/98 (consolidated text), 113/00, 124/00 (consolidated text), 28/01, 41/01 (consolidated text), 55/01 (correction), 76/10, 85/10 (consolidated text), and 5/14, which introduced Art 49 on entrepreneurial and market freedom.

Croatia's legislator, on the other hand, intervened in the substantive dimension of consumer law by introducing amendments increasing transparency in credit contracts, but also by introducing a highly disputable conversion measure. The measure enabled transformation of consumer credit contracts from the moment of their conclusion, namely retroactively, with the intention of transforming high-risk transactions into contracts fulfilling parties' legitimate expectations. As emphasised in one of the Constitutional Court's decisions, the conversion contracts 'could hardly be seen as "regular" private law contracts that form "regular" obligations law relationships'.[119]

These developments had a huge impact on Croatian consumer law and resulted in its further transformation. Especially affected was the procedural dimension and enforcement of consumer law. The difficulties experienced during the collective redress proceedings made the length of the proceedings excessive. These were primarily related to a lack of understanding by the Croatian courts of the main consumer concepts and the courts' reluctance to observe the duty of consistent interpretation and CJEU case law. Although the Constitution and other relevant procedural laws oblige the Croatian courts to 'protect subjective rights based on the European Union *acquis*',[120] the rulings demonstrate a tendency to interpret EU concepts in the light of national civil law. On the other hand, the Constitutional Court invested a great effort and played a crucial role in the evolution of the procedural dimension of consumer law.[121] Despite not being a regular court, the Constitutional Court managed to reverse the outcome of the collective redress proceedings by insisting on observance of the *acquis*.

The lessons learned from the first two phases of the transformation are expected to set the ground for the third phase related to the future development of Croatian consumer law, which should focus on better regulation and more effective enforcement of consumer law. Croatian consumer law still features a high degree of legal fragmentation and disputable quality of consumer regulation, which certainly has an impact on poor enforcement of consumer law.

On the other hand, enforcement can improve and *is* gradually improving. Only recently, the Supreme Court issued a legal opinion demanding *ex officio* assessment of the unfairness of contractual terms in enforcement proceedings.[122] Although this is not a novelty under settled CJEU case law,[123] the Supreme Court provided guidelines with respect to enforcement title documents that did not undergo regular judicial control.[124] A month earlier, the Constitutional Court granted suspension of debt enforcement sought on the grounds of a credit agreement that contained unfair contractual terms.[125] This implies that Croatian consumer law has already entered the third phase of transformation, aimed at strengthening consumer law enforcement.

[119] Decision and order of the Constitutional Court of the Republic of Croatia of 11 October 2015, U-I-2780-2015 et al, 35.

[120] The Constitution of the Republic of Croatia, Art 145(3).

[121] S Barić, 'The Transformative Role of the Constitutional Court of the Republic of Croatia: From the ex-Yu to the EU' Working Paper 6 (2016) Analitika Center for Social Research 1–40.

[122] Supreme Court of the Republic of Croatia, Legal Opinion of 11 March 2022, Posl br Su IV – 87/2022.

[123] E Miscenic, 'The Effectiveness of Judicial Enforcement of the EU Consumer Protection Law' in M Zlatan et al (eds), *Balkan Yearbook of European and International Law* (Springer, 2020) 129.

[124] Supreme Court Opinion (n 122) 1.

[125] Order of the Constitutional Court of the Republic of Croatia of 15 February 2022, U-III-5764/2021. By analogy see Case C-630/17 *Addiko Bank* ECLI:EU:C:2019:537, para 69.

Nonetheless, during this third phase of transformation the courts and competent authorities should recognise that consumer law is not limited to credit contracts and unfairness control alone. So far, there has been a significant lack of case law dealing with other issues, such as non-conformity of goods or unfair commercial practices.[126] While we are still learning about it, EU consumer law is rapidly developing and moving forward in new and more demanding directions, such as digitalisation and sustainability.[127] In order to keep up with these new developments, Croatian consumer law needs to transform once again or it will not catch up with the transformation of EU consumer law taking place today.[128]

---

[126] See the National Consumer Protection Programme from 2021 to 2024, OG No 29/21, with emphasis on better enforcement, protection in digital surrounding, strengthening of institutional capacities and enforcement bodies, as well as better informing of consumers.

[127] E Miscenic, 'The Constant Change of EU Consumer Law: The Real Deal or Just an Illusion?' (2022) *Annals of the Faculty of Law in Belgrade* 679, 679–710; E Miscenic, 'Sustainability, the Circular Economy and Consumer Law in Croatia' (2020) 4 *Journal of European Consumer and Market Law* 172.

[128] See the other chapters in this volume.

12

Slovenia

DAMJAN MOŽINA

I. Introduction: An Overview of the Transformation of Slovene Consumer Law

Before thinking about the next stages of the development of consumer law, such as transformation towards digitalisation and sustainability, it might be useful to see the transformations that consumer law has experienced so far and what the current state of consumer law is. This is particularly so for Slovenia, a small country on the periphery of the European Union (EU),[1] where EU consumer law, although formally transferred before EU accession (2004), needed some time to become at least somewhat established in practice.

The purpose of this chapter is to present the transformation of consumer protection in Slovenia and to discuss the drivers behind the process of transformation. From the Second World War until 1991, Slovenia was a part of Yugoslavia, a socialist country with a rather particular concept of consumer protection. After independence, Slovenia began developing consumer protection based on a market economy, property rights and free economic initiative.

II. The Yugoslav Concept of Consumer Protection

A. The Idea of Consumer Protection within the Concept of Socialist Self-management

In Yugoslavia, two different concepts of consumer protection existed. The first was the concept of consumer protection within the system of socialist self-management and associated labour, which was also the official ideology; and the second comprised

---

[1] See, eg D Kukovec, 'Law and the Periphery' (2015) 21 *European Law Journal* 406, 409; R Mańko, 'Delimiting central Europe as a juridical space: a preliminary exercise in critical legal geography' (2019) 89 *Acta Universitatis Lodziensis Folia Juridica* 63.

the more classic mechanisms of protection in private legal relationships based on the Obligations Act (1978).

The Yugoslav system of 'market socialism' seemed to represent a middle way between capitalism and central planning of the Soviet type. One of its main characteristics was the all-encompassing system of socialist self-management.[2] The 'means of production' (such as pre-revolution businesses) were nationalised and became 'social property', self-managed by the workers but also controlled by the Communist Party; private entrepreneurship was restricted, only state-owned businesses were allowed to exist, with few exceptions.

The basic idea behind the political concept of consumer protection, which was even written into the Yugoslav Constitution (1974), was that 'self-management agreements' were to be negotiated between organisations of producers, traders and consumers. Businesses ('organisations of associated labour') dealing with goods and services for direct consumption were obliged to cooperate and consult with self-managing interest groups, local communities and consumer organisations in 'matters of common interest'.[3] In this sense, the federal Act on Associated Labour (1976) regulated the right of citizens, as consumers of goods and services, to self-organise in local and socio-political communities and to influence the development of production and service activities that satisfied their needs, to prevent monopoly or abuse of a monopoly position and to protect their other interests.[4] Businesses that produced or sold goods or provided services for direct consumption by citizens were obliged to 'create conditions and encourage the organisation of consumers, to research their needs and to coordinate relations between production and consumption on a more permanent basis'.[5] Businesses and consumer organisations should conclude self-management agreements to regulate their rights and obligations regarding the regular and high-quality supply of certain products and services, to determine prices and participation of consumers in income.[6]

These agreements, to which political organisations (local communities) were party, were meant to be a means of integrating producer-seller-consumer interests.[7] It was admitted that the interests of producers, sellers and consumers might conflict but were expected to be 'synchronised' within the system of associated labour by way of collective negotiation.[8]

Consumers were also represented in political organisations at all levels. The 'consumer councils' were a means of collective consumer protection; apart from connecting with

---

[2] See, eg S Estrin, 'Yugoslavia: The Case of Self-Managing Market Socialism' (1991) 5 *Journal of Economic Perspectives* 187, 187–94; MJ Broekmeyer, 'Self-Management in Yugoslavia' (1977) 431 *The Annals of the American Academy of Political and Social Science* 133, 133–40; L Sirc, *The Yugoslav Economy under Self-management* (Palgrave Macmillan, 1979).

[3] See Constitution (1974), Official Gazette of the Socialist Federal Republic of Yugoslavia (SFRY) 9/74, Art 43(4).

[4] See Federal Act on Associated Labour, Official Gazette 53/1976, Art 23.

[5] ibid.

[6] ibid.

[7] See J Vilus, 'Self-Management and Protection of Consumers in Yugoslavia' (1977) 1 *Journal of Consumer Policy* 165, 166.

[8] See M Ilešič, *Pravno varstvo potrošnikov* (English trans: *Legal Protection of Consumers*) (Skupnost slovenskih občin, 1980) 10; Vilus (n 7) 167; I Duda, 'Consumers as Vehicles of Socialism: Consumer Protection in the System of Yugoslav Self-Management and Associated Labour' (2017) 76 *Südost-Forschungen* 1.

businesses (producers and sellers), they were expected to represent consumer interests in local and other political communities, to develop systems of consumer information, but also to react to harm to concrete consumer interests, for instance by taking legal steps.[9]

Among the core substantive consumer rights were the right to freely decide on the purchase of goods or services (that is, with enough information and without pressure), the right to acquire financial means and to pay for goods and services in accordance with socially agreed criteria, as well as the right to purchase goods and services that met contractual or ordinary standards of quality.[10] Methods of consumer protection included legal measures (namely, legislation and the moral principles of socialist society, as well as consumer codes containing standards of quality, price, advertising, claim-handling and the like), but also 'self-control' by businesses (in the sense of adhering to quality standards), development of market competition, self-organisation of consumers, information and education of consumers, and administrative and judicial control.[11] Interestingly, the idea of collective negotiations between businesses or trade organisations and consumer organisations and administrative authorities (on the contents of standard terms, for instance) was also discussed outside Yugoslavia[12] and seems to be practised in some European countries.[13]

However, although many consumer councils were established and consumer codes agreed, the concept of consumer protection within the system of socialist self-management never really functioned as intended. With regard to consumer councils, it was established that they were not effective, as their tasks were too wide-ranging and they had little connection with actual consumers; furthermore, they often existed only formally and did not really meet.[14] The idea of self-management agreements between producers, traders and consumers simply did not work.[15] With regard to consumer codes, it was reported that only around 150 of such codes (self-management agreements containing standards of quality, price, advertising, claim-handling and the like) were adopted between 1970 and 1978, with the conclusion that this kind of regulation 'is still in its initial phase'.[16] Among the reasons stated were lack of initiative on the part of market subjects, as well as that the conclusion of such codes 'requires a great deal of foresight, mutual consideration of the interests of all participants'.[17]

Leaving aside the question whether it was a workable concept at all, two other reasons explain why it never took off in practice: first, because there was little or no control over

---

[9] See Ilešič (n 8) 11; Duda (n 8) 2.

[10] Ilešič (n 8) 10.

[11] See F Pernek, 'Metode varstva potrošnikov' (English trans: 'Methods of consumer protection') (1988) 1–2 *Pravnik* 23, 23–34.

[12] See H-W Micklitz, 'Reforming European Unfair Terms Legislation in Consumer Contracts' (2010) 4 *European Review of Contract Law* 347, 361.

[13] See N Jansen, 'Contents and Effects: Introduction before Art 6:201' in N Jansen and J Zimmermann (eds), *Commentaries on European Contract Law* (Oxford University Press, 2018) 925.

[14] See Government memorandum for the first draft of the Consumer Protection Act (1993), Predlog zakona o varstvu potrošnikov – EPA 457, Poročevalec DZ (Parliamentary report) of 21 December 1993, 34.

[15] ibid.

[16] F Pernek, 'Kodeksi za varstvo potrošnikov pri nas in drugod' (English trans: 'Consumer codes in our country and elsewhere') (1989) 8–9 *Pravnik* 375.

[17] ibid.

its implementation;[18] and, secondly, because there was little time for implementation of the concept as conceived by the Act on Associated Labour (1976), as, only a few years later, Yugoslavia fell into a deep political and economic crisis from which it never recovered. The circumstances of high (even extreme) inflation, high unemployment, falling living standards and political turmoil in the 1980s were far from an ideal environment for the development of consumer protection. It was also claimed that it was the inefficiency of the very system of self-management that contributed to the economic breakdown of the country.[19]

B. Consumer Protection in Individual Legal Relationships

Apart from the system of collective negotiation and political representation of consumers based on the concept of socialist self-management and associated labour, there were also – from the point of view of private law – more traditional means of protection, that is, by claims in individual private legal relationships between autonomous actors with conflicting interests (contract and tort). These were largely based on the Obligations Act (OA), adopted in 1978.[20]

Interestingly, the official ideology of self-management, represented in particular by the Act on Associated Labour (1976), exerted relatively little influence over the OA. With the exception of the introductory provisions reflecting the official ideology of socialist self-management, the OA was a rather classic codification in the sense that it was conceptually based on ideas such as individual (property) rights and freedom of contract – notwithstanding that these were, in fact, severely restricted. With regard to contract law, the single most important source of influence was the Convention on Uniform Sales Law (ULIS, 1964), the predecessor to the UN Convention on Contracts for the International Sale of Goods (CISG, 1980).[21]

Nevertheless, the OA contained a few examples of the approach of socialist self-management to consumer protection, most notably in one of its 'general principles'. According to Article 8 OA, titled 'Obligations towards citizens as consumers and recipients of services', all businesses and 'working people' whose activities aim at 'satisfying the needs of citizens' should conclude and perform contracts in such a way that regular and high-quality satisfaction of citizens' needs is guaranteed, as are the most favourable conditions for meeting those needs. No evidence could be found for the principle of maximum consumer benefit, as derived from Article 8 OA, ever having had any significance in the case law at all.

---

[18] See, eg Vilus (n 7) 165, 170; Duda (n 8) 1, 22.

[19] See, eg, S Estrin, 'Yugoslavia: The Case of Self-Managing Market Socialism' (1991) 5 *Journal of Economic Perspectives* 187, 193.

[20] 'Zakon o obligacijskih razmerjih', Official Gazette of the SFRY, 29/78, 39/85, 45/89, 57/89.

[21] See, eg D Možina, 'Breach of Contract and Remedies in the Yugoslav Obligations Act: 40 Years Later' (2020) *Zeitschrift für Europäisches Privatrecht* 134. For a description of the legislative process, see R Slijepčević, 'Evolucija nastanka Zakona o obligacionim odnosima' (1988) 10–12 *Pravni život* 1429, 1429–48. For the sources of influence on the OA, see I Tot, 'Poredbenopravni utjecaji na Zakon o obveznim odnosima' in I Tot and Z Slakoper (eds), *Hrvatsko obvezno pravo u poredbenopravnom kontekstu: Petnaest godina Zakona o obveznim odnosima* (English trans: *Croatian Law of Obligations in a Comparative Law Context: Fifteen Years of the Obligations Act*) (Ekonomski fakultet Sveučilišta u Zagrebu, 2022) 3.

Additionally, freedom of contract was limited not just by mandatory provisions of the law, but also by the morals of a socialist self-managing society (Article 10 OA). Whether this basic principle played a concrete role in contracts with consumers is unknown.

A further example of the socialist approach to consumer protection was the stipulation that the provisions of 'consumer codes', if such were concluded between the political community, consumer organisations and retail businesses, would automatically and without any reference become a part of all individual contracts concluded by retail businesses for the sale of goods and provision of services.[22] Again, no proof of its application could be found.

The OA also contained several features of protection that, in essence, belong to the core of EU consumer law today, such as judicial control of the fairness of standard contract terms, mandatory buyer protection in sales contracts, the strict liability of the producer (in tort) for the shortcomings of a product as regards its safety, and the right of withdrawal (in instalment sales). However, although consumers were mentioned by Article 8 OA, and the notion of a consumer was defined by the literature,[23] the legal definition of a consumer was lacking and the concept of special legal protection within the B2C relationship was unknown. One author even claimed that the notion of a consumer need not be defined because it is common knowledge.[24] The same protection was granted to everybody. Even businesses could rely on protective mandatory provisions, such as those relating to product liability or buyer protection in sales law. The OA followed the so-called monistic approach and introduced one set of rules for all contracts, with some exceptions for commercial contracts (B2B), but without any particular protection in B2C relationships. Thus the 'consumer' appeared to have been a political rather than a legal category in Yugoslavia.

One of the key areas of legal protection was the law of standard contract terms. In the OA, this is a feature of general contract law. 'Terms prepared in advance by one of the parties' only became part of a contract if the other party was aware or should have been aware of them; they also had to be published 'in the usual way'.[25] The provision on inclusion of general terms was based on the provision from a collection of trade usages ('usances') in commercial contracts of 1954.[26] As mentioned, the OA also contained a rule on the inclusion of general contract terms where these were agreed between the local community, consumer organisations and retail businesses: such terms (the self *ipso facto*) became a part of all contracts concluded by a business.[27] Thus, the legal nature of such general contract terms would be much like that of legislation, that is, they would become part of the contact without party consent. No information exists

---

[22] Art 144 OA.
[23] See, eg Ilešič (n 8) 9, defining the consumer as a natural person, consuming goods and services for his or her own personal or collective personal purposes.
[24] F Pernek, 'Pravna opredelitev pojma potrošnika in njegovega pravnega varstva' (1983) 1–3 *Pravnik* 33, 37.
[25] Art 142(2) and (3) OA.
[26] J Vilus, 'Introduction before art 142' in BT Blagojevic, V Krulj (eds), *Komentar zakona o obligacionim odnosima* (Savremena administracija, 1983) 424. See General Usances for trading with goods, adopted in 1954 by the State Arbitration Tribunal, at that time the supreme authority for commercial disputes, Official Gazette of the FNRY, Nos 40/53, 57/54. For decades, the Usances were the most important source of commercial contract law and were also influential in preparation of the Yugoslav OA.
[27] Art 144 OA.

on application of the provision. The *contra proferentem* rule was a part of general interpretation rules.[28] The essence of protection was the possibility for the court to declare unfair clauses prepared by one of the parties in advance as non-binding (void). Unfairness was understood broadly as a clause contrary to the purpose of the contract, to fair business practices, or otherwise unfair or overly strict towards one of the parties.[29] In the case of unfairness of a clause, general rules on partial invalidity were applicable: the contract continued to exist if its existence was possible without the invalid part, and as long as the invalid part was not of fundamental importance for the parties.[30]

With regard to sales contracts, regular warranty claims by the buyer based on 'material defects' were not mandatory and could be modified (and limited) by agreement, even in contracts between businesses and natural persons.[31] The warranty period was only six months; buyers could bring a claim only if they notified the seller of the defect within a short time after discovery.[32] The buyer could choose freely among remedies (repair and replacement, price reduction, rescission, damages), but could only rescind the contract if the seller was first given a reasonable time to effect repair and replacement.[33] In addition to the warranty system for material defects, there was a system of mandatory buyer protection based on the 'guarantee of proper functioning' for so-called 'technical' goods.[34] If these malfunctioned within a year after delivery, the buyer could claim repair or replacement of the goods, or, if repair or replacement were not completed within a reasonable time, reduce the price, terminate the contract and, in all cases, claim damages.[35] The guarantee-based remedies could be used not only against the seller, but also against the producer of goods.[36] Mandatory one-year guarantee liability was well-established in Yugoslavia, perhaps more so than the parallel system of seller's liability for material defects. The two systems were also connected: the buyer could combine but not cumulate remedies; also, buyer reliance on a guarantee claim was considered to represent notification of a defect by the buyer (a condition for warranty claims).[37] Interestingly, guarantee liability, although not limited to B2C contracts, contained come elements of the seller's mandatory liability later introduced in the EU by Directive 99/44/EC.[38]

The OA survived the dissolution of Yugoslavia and lives on in the law of the independent successor countries with a market economy, seemingly without major

---

[28] Art 100 OA.

[29] Art 143 OA.

[30] Art 105(1) OA.

[31] See Arts 478 et seq OA. See also Možina (n 21) 134, 143.

[32] Art 482 OA.

[33] Art 490(1) OA.

[34] See Yugoslav Obligations Act, Arts 501–507. The list of goods for which the guarantee was mandatory and its duration were prescribed by the Yugoslav Standardisation Act, Official Gazette of SFRY, 38/1977.

[35] On guarantees in Yugoslav and EU law, see D Možina, 'Garancija za ispravno funkcioniranje u jugoslavenskom i europskom pravu' (2011) 1–3 *Pravo i privreda* 29, 29–51.

[36] Furthermore, the content of the guarantee, ie that the goods will function flawlessly for a certain period of time, is similar in substance but not the same as the concept of conformity with the contract. However, fitness for normal use also presupposes that the goods are usable for a certain period of time.

[37] See, eg S Cigoj, *Komentar obligacijskih razmerij* (Uradni List, 1980–1984) 1493.

[38] Directive 1999/44/EC of the European Parliament and of the Council of 25 May 1999 on certain aspects of the sale of consumer goods and associated guarantees [1999] OJ L171/12 (Consumer Sales Directive).

problems. While it is still in force in some of them, such as in Serbia,[39] new codes on the law of obligations were adopted in others, such as Slovenia (2002)[40] and Croatia (2005),[41] but these were largely based on the provisions of the OA. In Slovenia, it was considered that the Yugoslav OA was good legislation and that, paradoxically, the aim of the reform of the Law of Obligations must be the continuity of the OA.[42] Furthermore, preparation of an entirely new obligations statute did not seem realistic.[43]

With regard to consumer protection in Yugoslav times, it should also be mentioned that the Market Inspectorate proved to be a relatively effective (indirect) enforcement mechanism for consumer rights. As such, therefore, it still exists in Slovenia. In particular in consumer matters, the Market Inspectorate – although it did not (and does not) have jurisdiction to resolve disputes (that is, to decide on the rights and obligations of the parties) – could prohibit some practices, such as use of unfair general contract terms, and impose fines for violations of legislation (from 1998, of the Consumer Protection Act (CPA)) and thus exert pressure on businesses.[44] An appeal could be lodged against decisions of the Market Inspectorate, which, in Slovenia today, is decided by the Administrative Court.

III. Slovenia and EU Accession

A. Formal Transposition of EU Consumer Law

After independence (1991), Slovenia continued to use the Yugoslav OA. In 2001 it adopted its own Obligations Code, which, however, is largely based on the Yugoslav OA, only a few minor changes having been made. Among them, the provisions inspired by socialist self-management were deleted, including the principle of maximum consumer benefit (Article 8 OA), as was the provision on the inclusion of 'consumer codes' in non-individually negotiated terms (Article 144 OA).

The transformation of consumer law – or, more precisely, creation of a law that specifically protects consumers – started some years before EU accession.[45] The first draft of new consumer legislation was published in 1992,[46] and the CPA was eventually adopted in 1998.[47] The first Consumer Credit Act was adopted in 2000.[48]

---

[39] See Official Gazette of the SFRY 31/93; and Official Gazette of Serbia and Montenegro 1/2003.
[40] 'Obligacijski zakonik', Official Gazette of Slovenia, 83/01, 28/06, 40/07, 64/16.
[41] 'Zakon o obveznim odnosima', Official Gazette of Croatia, 35/05, 41/08, 125/11, 78/15, 29/18.
[42] See M Ilešič, *Obligacijski zakonik, uvodna pojasnila* (Uradni List 2003) 28.
[43] ibid.
[44] In the area of unfair contract terms, the Market Inspectorate may also impose fines on traders using them but, somewhat contradictorily, cannot annul a clause in an individual contract, see Arts 72 and 77 CPA.
[45] In 1993, a Cooperation Agreement was signed between the EC and Slovenia. In 1996, the EU and Slovenia signed an interim trade agreement, which established a free trade area between the EU Member States and Slovenia. The process of implementing the *acquis* started. In 2002, the consumer *acquis* was largely implemented and the negotiations and an agreement on Slovenia's accession conditions were concluded. On 1 May 2004, Slovenia became a full member of the EU.
[46] See Draft CPA, ESA 695, Publication of the Parliament, Nr 18/1992, 52.
[47] Official Gazette of Slovenia, 20/98.
[48] Official Gazette, 70-3301/2000. Current version: Official Gazette 77/16 and 92/21.

When EU accession was approaching, the bulk of the EU consumer *acquis* was transposed (2002).[49] Already in the first published draft of the CPA of 1992, the legislator aimed at harmonisation with European consumer protection directives. Such was the case with regulation of unfair terms in consumer contracts. However, in 1992, only the draft of the later directive on unfair terms existed.[50] After Directive 93/13/EEC[51] was finally adopted in 1993, in a version rather different from the draft, the Slovene legislator did not adjust the draft, so that the CPA was adopted with provisions on unfair terms still based on the first draft of the Directive.

The general approach with regard to implementation of the European consumer *acquis* was to adopt a separate CPA, while the general law of obligations (Obligations Code, 2002) would remain untouched. The EU consumer *acquis* was simply added to the existing law. Like the Yugoslav OA, the Slovene Obligations Code – although it was being prepared at the same time as implementation of the consumer *acquis* – does not mention 'consumer' at all. Of course, the CPA takes precedence in its sphere of application (*lex specialis*). In the area of product liability, this had the effect that the OA provisions on product liability, which were more favourable to claimants than the Product Liability Directive,[52] could no longer be applied in the area of application of the latter.

The result of poor coordination between the general law of obligations and the transposition of the EU consumer *acquis* into the CPA was that in areas where the (Yugoslav Act on Obligations and) Slovene Obligations Code contained protective measures, such as in the area of unfair terms and consumer sales, two bodies of law regulating the matter in very similar ways now coexisted; one without and the other with the B2C concept. It may be speculated that the confusion created was one of the reasons for slow 'domestication' of EU law by the courts.

There were also shortcomings in the transposition of European directives, which, surprisingly, did not emerge as problematic in case law for a long time. The provision of the CPA on unfair clauses retained the version set out the draft directive of 1990, with a rather different general clause and without the exception regarding core terms from Article 4(2) UCTD. The legislator appears to have been rather careless with regard to transposing the *acquis* regarding unfair terms.[53]

With regard to sales law, transposition of Article 3(3) of the Consumer Sales Directive, containing the hierarchy of the buyer's remedies, was seemingly forgotten, as was transposition of the so-called 'Ikea clause' from Article 2(4).[54] Furthermore, the (one-year) mandatory guarantee of the proper functioning of technical goods was

---

[49] See Amendments to CPA, Official Gazette 110/2002.
[50] See Council, 'Proposal for a Council Directive on unfair terms in consumer contracts' COM (1990) 322.
[51] Council Directive 93/13/EEC of 5 April 1993 on unfair terms in consumer contracts [1993] OJ L95/29 (UCTD).
[52] Council Directive 85/374/EEC of 25 July 1985 on the approximation of the laws, regulations and administrative provisions of the Member States concerning liability for defective products [1985] OJ L210/29.
[53] With regard to implementation of the UCTD, see also M Zgaga, *Meje avtonomije strank v kreditni pogodbi* (English trans: *The Limits of Autonomy of the Parties to a Credit Agreement*) (GV ZALOZBA, 2021) 208. For more examples from the CPA, see D Možina, 'Kaj je narobe z zakonom o varstvu potrošnikov?' (2012) 6–7 *Podjetje in delo* 1437; A Andrić, 'Uveljavitev direktive 93/13/EGS o nepoštenih klavzulah v potrošniških pogodbah v pravnem sistemu RS' (2003) 2 *Pravna praksa* 19.
[54] See also Možina (n 21) 149.

retained.[55] Now, two very similar systems of mandatory protection of the same interest of the buyer co-existed and overlapped.[56]

B. The Quiet Years: 2002–2017

In terms of application of EU consumer law, the first 15 or so years following its formal transposition into Slovene law (2002) were rather quiet. Judging from publicly available case law (Supreme Court, appellate courts), the CPA was applied relatively rarely. In the area of unfair contract terms, only a small number of decisions exist from this time.[57] In those decisions the courts almost never referred to the UCTD, let alone to the case law of the CJEU. Instead, in some cases, the courts applied the general provisions on unfair terms from the Obligations Code, even in B2C contracts.[58] This phenomenon is reported from other countries that emerged from the former Yugoslavia too.[59] For example, in 2011, the High Court of Maribor held that the provisions of the CPA were to be applied only by the Market Inspectorate, not by courts of civil law.[60]

Of course, the small number of judicial decisions in the field of consumer law may also be explained by standard reasons, such as the considerable costs of litigation, the uncertainty of the outcome and the duration of court proceedings, perhaps even by the low level of trust in the judiciary in Slovenia. However, the fact that in more than 15 years since its adoption the law implementing the UCTD was applied in only a small number of cases, and that the case law of the CJEU was never mentioned, is also a result of relatively poor knowledge about (EU) consumer law among Slovene lawyers, particularly judges.

Now (EU) consumer law is taught in universities. But a substantial number of lawyers who studied law before Slovenia's accession to the EU (2004), and even before adoption of the CPA (1998), including judges, appear to have missed out on this education and are not familiar enough with EU directives and the mechanisms for their application. Admittedly, it is difficult for lawyers to change the concepts they learned during their education. But there is no doubt that much more should have been done with regard to training in EU law, particularly for judges.

Another factor to be taken into account is the size of the country. For a long time, little literature on EU consumer law existed in Slovenia. Together with the fact that not all lawyers can use legal literature published in other languages, this might be another cause of the relative under-development of consumer law.

---

[55] See Arts 15b–21 CPA.

[56] For a critical view, see D Možina, 'Obvezna garancija za brezhibno delovanje in varstvo kupca v evropskem pravu' (2011) 1 *Podjetje in delo* 37.

[57] From the time of adoption of the CPA until 2017, commercial case law databases show 14 court decisions assessing the fairness of standard terms and six decisions where the court merely interpreted the contract (without reference to unfairness). A further six decisions by administrative courts upheld or reversed the orders of market inspectors on prohibition of the use of unfair terms.

[58] See, eg Supreme Court, II Ips 27/2011 of 17 April 2014; High Court in Ljubljana, I Cp 3070/2015 of 20 January 2016; High Court in Maribor, I Cp 359/2013 of 14 January 2014; High Court in Koper Cp 1097/2008 of 9 December 2008; High Court in Celje, Cp 697/2014 of 9 April 2015.

[59] See, eg M Karanikić-Mirić, 'Understanding the Enforcement Malfunction of Consumer Legislation in Serbia' (2013) 36 *Journal of Consumer Policy* 231, 232.

[60] See Hight Court of Maribor, I Cp 1902/2010 of 17 March 2011.

A further indication of the country's somewhat frivolous attitude towards EU law is that to this day, the CPA (and, with it, the bulk of the EU consumer *acquis*) is not included on the list of legislation relevant for the national bar exam maintained by the Ministry of Justice.[61] Thus, in Slovenia, one can be admitted to the bar (which is also a condition for becoming a judge) without any knowledge of (EU) consumer law at all. This, too, can serve to explain why EU consumer law has not really come to life in practice for quite a long time.

The consequence is that some key issues in EU consumer contract law simply have not yet been addressed by jurisprudence. Even in a very small legal order such as Slovenia, it is difficult to comprehend that from 1998 – when the CPA governing regulation of unfair terms was adopted – until 2017, the courts never dealt with the question of notion of unfairness in the CPA in relation to Article 3(1) UCTD and whether, in accordance with Article 4(2) UCTD, the core terms of a contract (adequacy of price and remuneration, definition of the main subject matter of the contract) are exempt from judicial review (if transparent) or not. Both issues are highly relevant, as Article 3(1) UCTD was transposed in deviation from the text of the Directive and Article 4(2) was not transposed at all, with no explanation from the legislature.[62]

It is safe to conclude, that, while EU consumer law was formally transposed, it did not become 'domesticated'[63] in Slovenia for some time. The transformation of consumer protection law seems to have been merely formal. In some cases, the courts even continued to apply the general rules of the law of obligations, with which they were well acquainted; it even appears that, for a long time, the very concept of protection within a B2C contract just has not caught on. The state of affairs of consumer law, though dealt with by academic literature, met no response.[64]

C. Domestication Through Mass Claims?

However, things did not remain this way. In the years 2017–18, interest in EU consumer law, and particularly in the UCTD, grew significantly. This was as a result of mass litigation related to Swiss franc loans. Consumer loans indexed in Swiss francs were relatively popular in the times before the worldwide financial and economic crisis that started in 2008. As a consequence of the crisis, the EUR–CHF exchange rate changed, and the obligations of borrowers grew accordingly. In Slovenia, no ad hoc legislation for protecting borrowers was adopted; instead, a great number of individual claims were

---

[61] See list, last updated in March 2021, at https://cip.gov.si/media/2290/seznam-pravnih-virov-in-literature-za-pdi-velja-od-1-3-2021.pdf (accessed 5 December 2022).

[62] As explained, this is due to the fact that the legislator, when adopting the CPA in 1998, followed the text of the draft of the UCTD of 1990 rather than the final text of 1993.

[63] See, eg R Mańko, 'Unfair Terms in Swiss Franc Loans: Overview of European Court of Justice case law' (2021) European Parliamentary Research Service, PE 689.361 at www.europarl.europa.eu/RegData/etudes/BRIE/2021/689361/EPRS_BRI(2021)689361_EN.pdf (accessed 5 December 2022).

[64] See D Možina, 'Kriza slovenskega varstva potrošnikov' (English trans: 'The crisis of consumer protection in Slovenia') in A Vlahek (ed), *Pravo in politika varstva potrošnikov* (GV Založba, 2015) 1330.

filed, aimed at invalidating the foreign currency clause in credit contracts. A lot of the claimants were represented by the same attorney and were very well organised;[65] their representatives appeared in the national media. The attitude of the mainstream media was very favourable towards the claimants. The difficult situation of the borrowers was talked about at the political level too. However, the application of a special law aimed at retroactive conversion of Swiss franc loans into euro loans,[66] which was passed in 2022 (just before the last election), has been annulled by the Constitutional Court due to its retroactivity.[67]

In 2018, claims by consumers reached the Supreme Court, which had to resolve the issues of unfairness and core terms for the first time since adoption of the CPA (1998).[68] The Supreme Court relied on the extensive case law of the CJEU, above all on Case C-186/16 *Andriciuc*.[69] In most claims, the Supreme Court, upon finding that the Swiss franc clause, belonging to the core terms of the contract, was exempt from judicial review, as it deemed that consumers had been sufficiently well informed of its economic significance, rejected the nullity claims. The debate as to whether the Court should have assessed the fairness of core terms, as Article 4(2) UCTD was not expressly transferred into Slovene law, was quite heated. In principle, minimum harmonisation allows for control of terms relating to price or the main subject of the contract. However, the intention of the legislator to include assessment of such terms was not made clear.[70] The Supreme Court held that assessing core terms would interfere with freedom of contract, 'as the main subject of contract is exactly what the parties had in mind when concluding the contract, and they had explicitly agreed to it'.[71] Some claimants nevertheless held that Slovenia purposefully excluded Article 4(2) UCTD in order to ensure a higher level of consumer protection.[72] Some appellate courts even openly rebelled against the Supreme Court, which interpreted the CPA in the sense of Article 4(2) UCTD.[73] The newly adopted CPA expressly provides that a court may assess the fairness of terms relating to price or the main subject of the contract, even if drafted in plain and intelligible language.[74]

Recently, the CJEU gave a judgment based on a preliminary question from Slovenia regarding the meaning of Article 3(1) UCTD, based on a claim regarding a credit contract in Swiss francs.[75] The referring court disagreed with the Supreme Court of Slovenia, which interpreted unfairness in the same way as it is written in Article 3(1)

---

[65] As the 'Swiss-franc society'; in Slovenia this was established as a branch of the Croatian Swiss-franc society (*Udruga franak*) in 2015, see at www.zdruzenje-frank.si/ (accessed 5 December 2022).

[66] Official Gazette, 17/22.

[67] Constitutional Court, U-I-64/22, U-I-65/22 of 17. November 2022.

[68] See Supreme Court, II Ips 201/2017 of 7 May 2018; II Ips 137/2018 of 25 October 2018; II Ips 195/2018 of 25 October 2018; II Ips 197/2018 of 20 December 2018.

[69] Case C-186/16 *Andriciuc and Others v Banca Românească SA* ECLI:EU:C:2017:703.

[70] Art 1(2) UCTD was not transposed either. See Poročevalec DZ (Parliamentary reporter) 81/2002 of 3 September 2002, 10.

[71] See Supreme Court, II Ips 201/2017 of 7 May 2018, Nr 26.

[72] See, eg H Iglič, 'Posledice neprenosa člena 4(2) Direktive 93/13 za varstvo posojilojemalcev' (2019) 27 *Pravna praksa* 11, 11–13.

[73] See, eg High Court of Maribor, VSM I Ip 877/2020 of 15 December 2020, Nr 41.

[74] Consumer Protection Act (CPA-1), Official Gazette 130/2022, Art 23(3).

[75] See Case C-405/21 *FV v Nova Kreditna banka Maribor* ECLI:EU:C:2022:793, para 25.

UCTD, namely, as causing significant imbalance in the rights and obligations under the contract to the detriment of the consumer, contrary to good faith. The referring court seemed to think that consumers would be better off with unfairness being the result of imbalance of contractual rights alone. The CJEU held that although the element of good faith is inherent in the examination of the unfairness of a contractual term, based on Article 3(1) of the Directive, the principle of minimal harmonisation nevertheless allows national legislation to provide for unfairness to be assessed solely with regard to significant imbalance of the rights and obligations and without examining the requirement of 'good faith'.[76] Thus, in the eyes of the CJEU, the interpretation of Slovene law as advocated by the referring court is possible. Whether such an interpretation of national law is reasonable is another question. It would appear that the criteria for assessment of good faith in recital 16 UCTD are the essence of unfairness, namely:

- overall evaluation of the interests of the parties
- the relevance of their relative bargaining strength
- the relevance of whether the consumer's decision to go for the contract was free or 'induced'
- the principles of fairness and equity, taking into consideration the legitimate interests of the consumer
- whether or not the business could reasonably assume that the consumer would have agreed to the term in individual negotiations.[77]

It is these criteria that characterise an imbalance in contractual rights and obligations as unfair. They can hardly be excluded from any assessment of fairness. Be that as it may, it seems that maximum harmonisation of the law of unfair contract terms would save the legislature and courts in Slovenia some of the problems they now face with minimum harmonisation.

In any event, mass litigation has stimulated a lively debate on the law of unfair terms in the literature; several papers have been published.[78] Authors have started to deal in

---

[76] ibid para 37.

[77] See, eg Case C-621/17 *Kiss and CIB Bank* ECLI:EU:C:2019:820, para 50.

[78] See, eg, A Erbežnik, 'Primerjalnopravna analiza sodbe hrvaškega ustavnega sodišča o kreditih v švicarskih frankih' (2022) 14 *Pravna praksa* 12, 12–14; R Preininger, 'Ali je sodna praksa Vrhovnega sodišča RS v zvezi s krediti v švicarskih frankih res enotna, in če ni, ali je skladna s sodno prakso Sodišča Evropske unije' (2020) 3–4 *Podjetje in delo* 637, 637–42; H Iglič, '(Ne)enotna uporaba prava EU?: primerjalni pogled na uporabo meril za presojo preglednosti pogodbenih pogojev' (2020) 5 *Podjetje in delo* 796, 796–814; P Jamšek, 'Evropski pogled na sistemske rešitve problematike kreditov v švicarskih frankih' (2019) 12 *Pravna praksa* 30, 30–31; J Sladič, 'Krediti v švicarskih frankih po ustalitvi sodne prakse pred Vrhovnim sodiščem' (2019) 49–50 *Pravna praksa* II, II–VII; U Ravnikar Šurk, 'Pojasnilna dolžnost pri posojilih v švicarskih frankih' (2019) 19 *Pravna praksa* 30, 30–31; J Sladič, 'Potrošniški krediti v švicarskih frankih v francoski zakonodaji in sodni praksi' (2019) 3 Pravna praksa 12, 12–13; J Sladič, 'Potrošniški krediti, nominirani v švicarskih frankih: na Hrvaškem, v Avstriji, Italiji, Romuniji in Španiji' (2019) 7 *Pravna praksa* II, II–VII; J Sladič and V Trstenjak, 'Pravo EU ter javnopravni in regulatorni vidiki potrošniških kreditov v švicarskih frankih' (2019) 1–2 *Javna uprava* 73, 73–94; B Sedmak, 'Ekonomske pravice potrošnikov in krediti v švicarskih frankih' (2018) 47 *Pravna praska* 11, 11–12; J Hojnik, 'Informiranje o vplivih kreditov v švicarskih frankih na obveznosti potrošnika' (2018) 5 *Bančni vestnik* 6, 6–11; L Varanelli, 'Komentar sodne odločbe o švicarskih frankih: nekaj pomislekov in

detail with issues such as interpretation of the provisions implementing directives, filling gaps in implementation, the concept of minimum harmonisation and the significance of the judgments of the CJEU.

It appears, however, that the much more serious approach of the courts to the application of EU law is not as such the result of mass litigation alone. Of course, the loans and the increase in borrowers' obligations also bear an important social dimension. The claims were also relatively large in comparison with other consumer cases. It is only natural that the law develops with high-profile 'landmark' cases. It also appears that the fact that the courts were under public scrutiny contributed to the development of consumer law. This scrutiny was a result of media pressure in connection with mass claims, exerted by well-organised claimants and supported by the 'entrepreneurial spirit' of their legal representatives. In Slovenia, the general public are rarely informed about the details of application of an EU (consumer law) directive.

As a result of a combination of all these reasons, Slovenia seems to have experienced a kind of substantive transformation, perhaps even some 'domestication' of EU consumer law. For now, this process is limited to the law on unfair terms. The multitude of claims relating to credit contracts in Swiss francs led the courts to become more closely acquainted with the operation of EU directives and with the law on unfair terms. It appears that the main driving forces behind this development were local actors who started to take advantage of consumer protection law.

Currently, the trend continues with collective claims. These are likely to be the drivers behind the further development of EU consumer law in Slovenia, at least as regards the law on unfair terms. While mass litigation regarding credit contracts in Swiss francs comprised a large number of individual claims, many of which were represented by the same attorney, collective claims are the new trend. Since 2018, the new Collective Claims Act is applicable.[79] In 2022, a number of collective claims were filed against banks in connection with the so-called 'interest floor clauses' in credit contracts.[80] Two organisations are competing to represent the borrowers.[81] It appears that the prospects of earnings for the representatives might be the main driving force behind this new development trend too.[82]

---

dilem' (2017) 32 *Pravna praksa* 14, 14–16; J Kristan, 'O švicarskih frankih, kreditih, interventnem zakonu in pravnem mnenju dr B M Zupančiča in dr C Ribičiča' (2017) 41–52 *Pravna praksa* II, II–VIII; B Koritnik, 'Krediti v švicarskih frankih: čigave so težave?' in A Vlahek and M Damjan (eds), *Pravo in politika sodobnega varstva potrošnikov* (Ljubljana, GV Založba, 2015) 407.

[79] See Collective Claims Act, Official Gazette of Slovenia, 55/2017.

[80] According to the claimants, the floor clauses, stipulating the minimum positive interest rate in times of negative values of EURIBOR, are unfair if they do not contain an interest ceiling as well. They are asking for restitution in the amount of the difference.

[81] See, eg, at https://kolektiv99.si/en/ (accessed 5 December 2022) and at www.zps.si/osebne-finance-sp-1406526635/krediti/11434-kolektivna-tozba-proti-banki-sparkasse-kaj-je-dobro-vedeti (accessed 5 December 2022).

[82] While in other claims the maximum allowed contingency fee in Slovenia is 15%, it is 30% in collective claims if the attorneys bear the costs of proceedings, see Collective Claims Act, Art 61.

IV. Conclusions: Slow but Steady Progress on the Long Road Towards Transformation

After this short and somewhat incomplete review, the conclusion has to be that the consumer law of Slovenia has undergone a transformation from the socialist approach to consumer protection in Yugoslavian era to the concept of consumer protection as we know it in the EU.

The Yugoslav approach was twofold: whereas the ideas of self-management agreements between political organisations, businesses (producers and sellers) and consumer organisations, which were supposed to 'align' their interests, and which never really took off in practice, died with the collapse of socialism, nonetheless, at least the private legal approach to protection, based on the provisions of the Obligations Act (1978), survived and became well established among lawyers. The approach to protection was that everyone is equally protected in relation to everyone, as the B2C concept was unknown in Yugoslavia. Slovenia, after having first applied the OA, adopted its own Obligations Code (2002). With regard to consumer protection, it followed the approach of the OA and does not even mention the consumer. The protective measures in B2C relationships were regulated in a separate CPA in 1998.

At the level of practical implementation, there was no real transformation (domestication) of EU consumer law for a long time. For many years, cases involving application of the CPA were rare. In some cases, the courts relied on the provisions of the Obligations Code instead.

Things started to change with the massive litigation regarding loan contracts in Swiss francs from 2015 onwards. Suddenly, interest in consumer law, and in particular EU consumer law, grew noticeably. For the first time since adoption of the CPA (1998), the courts were faced with some of the key issues of the UCTD and its transposition into Slovene law. They applied the CPA in accordance with the Directive and studied the case law of the CJEU in detail. The sheer number of cases and the public scrutiny arising from media pressure by well-organised claimants were the drivers behind this development. At the same time, a lively debate developed in the literature. The level of knowledge of how EU consumer law operates grew significantly. It was a kind of late 'domestication' of EU consumer law, at least in the field of unfair contract terms. Of course, it is only natural that the law develops (and transforms) with high-profile (landmark) cases.

However, at least some doubt remains whether this type of side-effect of private enforcement of EU consumer law is to be expected outside of collective claims, focusing on credit contracts, which are interesting for both lawyers and consumer organisations.

There are also some systemic reasons for the long-lasting 'dead run' of consumer law in Slovenia. The poor quality of legislation, including lack of coordination between the general obligations law and consumer law, could feature among them. However, as is well known, real transformation does not occur through legislation alone, regardless of its quality.

The central problem seems to be lack of familiarity on the part of Slovene lawyers with consumer protection law and EU law. Generations of lawyers who studied before

Slovenia joined the EU (2004) are poorly acquainted with consumer protection law and EU law, and indeed with the B2C concept. Therefore, there can be no doubt that much more can be done in the field of education of lawyers, especially judges. The approach to education, especially at the level of the bar exam (which currently includes neither national nor EU consumer law), needs to be improved too. Only then may it be possible to think about transition to a new development phase of consumer law.

13

Germany: Who Transformed Whom?

PETER ROTT

I. Introduction

In the 1970s, Germany was among the first to engage with the then new discipline of consumer law, together with the Scandinavian countries, the United Kingdom, France and a few other countries. German unfair contract terms legislation dates back to 1976 and was highly influential on the Unfair Contract Terms Directive (UCTD) of 1993.[1] The origins of German consumer credit law even date back to the end of the nineteenth century, when the legislator sought to protect buyers in instalment sales contracts. German unfair commercial practices law was highly protective of consumers, or – put differently – rather restrictive on traders.

In contrast, since the early 2000s at least, Germany has not been a generator of new ideas for the protection of consumers, nor has it voluntarily revolutionised enforcement of consumer law in any way. Its main positive contribution can be seen in advancing the consistency of European Union (EU) consumer law.

While Germany has actively contributed to raising EU consumer law to the level of (previous) German consumer law in areas such as unfair contract terms and unfair commercial practices, it has tried more than once to water down the progress of consumer law at the European level where this would have introduced new elements or concepts, to an extent that other Member States were prepared to outvote Germany.[2] In that sense, EU consumer law has, to some degree, transformed German consumer law, though without being able to change the general attitude of the legislator and the courts.

This chapter takes up these different influences of Germany on EU consumer law and vice versa, starting with the issue of coherence (section II), followed by mutual influence in the areas of substantive law (section III) and enforcement, with a focus

---

[1] Council Directive 93/13/EEC of 5 April 1993 on unfair terms in consumer contracts [1993] OJ L95/29. On the legislative process, see T Pfeiffer, 'Vorbemerkungen vor Art 1' in E Grabitz and M Hilf (eds), *Das Recht der Europäischen Union*, del 13 (CH Beck, 1999) paras 6 et seq.

[2] eg, Germany abstained from adopting Directive (EU) 2019/2161 of the European Parliament and of the Council of 27 November 2019 amending Council Directive 93/13/EEC and Directives 98/6/EC, 2005/29/EC and 2011/83/EU of the European Parliament and of the Council as regards the better enforcement and modernisation of Union consumer protection rules [2019] OJ L328/7, see Council doc 13146/2/19 REV 2 of 23 October 2019.

on collective enforcement (section IV). It does so by using examples, mainly since the early 2000s, and distinguishes between intentional contributions of German legal policy on EU law and involuntary contributions that have arisen out of the incorrect or incomplete implementation of EU consumer law by the German legislator, or out of its incorrect interpretation by German courts that gave the Court of Justice the opportunity to develop EU consumer law.

II. Coherence

A. Intentional Contribution

German law traditionally places much emphasis on coherence of the law and of legal terminology. The German Civil Code is famous for its level of abstraction, regulating general concepts such as conclusion of contracts, mistake, damage and so on, with effect for all parts of private law that are covered by the Civil Code, and even beyond. Legal terminology is usually defined once, with effect for the whole of the Civil Code.

This approach stands in stark contrast to the initial consumer legislation at EU level. One striking illustration was Article 7 of the Doorstep Selling Directive 85/577/EEC,[3] which read in German 'Übt der Verbraucher sein *Rücktrittsrecht* aus, so regeln sich die Rechtsfolgen des *Widerrufs* nach einzelstaatlichem Recht.' Thus, the English term 'renunciation' was translated in two different ways ('*Rücktrittsrecht*' and '*Widerrufsrecht*') in the same provision. In autonomous German law, these two notions described two different legal concepts.

Another phenomenon that attracted criticism in Germany was the fact that the right of withdrawal was regulated differently in different directives.[4] For just one example, the withdrawal period differed between the Doorstep Selling Directive (not less than seven days), the Distance Selling Directive 97/7/EC (at least seven working days), the Timesharing Directive 94/47/EC (10 calendar days) and Directive 2002/65/EC on the distance marketing of financial services (14 calendar days).[5] The same applies to the start of the withdrawal period, to the consequences of withdrawal and so on. German academia therefore often complained about the lack of sophistication of EU consumer law.[6]

---

[3] Council Directive 85/577/EEC of 20 December 1985 to protect the consumer in respect of contracts negotiated away from business premises [1985] OJ L372/31.

[4] See the explanations of the German Government in its draft law for implementation of Directive 97/7/EC of the European Parliament and of the Council of 20 May 1997 on the protection of consumers in respect of distance contracts [1997] OJ L144/19, *Bundestags-Drucksache* 14/2658, 29.

[5] Directive 94/47/EC of the European Parliament and the Council of 26 October 1994 on the protection of purchasers in respect of certain aspects of contracts relating to the purchase of the right to use immovable properties on a timeshare basis [1994] OJ L280/83; Directive 2002/65/EC of the European Parliament and of the Council of 23 September 2002 concerning the distance marketing of consumer financial services and amending Council Directive 90/619/EEC and Directives 97/7/EC and 98/27/EC [2002] OJ L271/16.

[6] See P Schlechtriem, '"Wandlungen des Schuldrechts in Europa" – wozu und wohin' (2002) *Zeitschrift für Europäisches Privatrecht* 213.

Germany first tried to remedy that inconsistency at the national level by harmonising the different rules. For example, in legislation of 2001, Germany abolished the different laws by which it had implemented the Doorstep Selling Directive, the Distance Selling Directive, the Timesharing Directive, the Consumer Credit Directive 87/102/EEC and the Package Travel Directive 90/314/EC,[7] and integrated implemented EU consumer law in the Civil Code. In that process, Germany harmonised the different rights of withdrawal, for example by introducing a uniform withdrawal period of 14 days.[8]

This approach was possible as EU consumer law at the time followed the principle of minimum harmonisation. When the EU legislator turned to fully harmonising areas of consumer law, for example with Directive 2002/65/EC on the distance marketing of financial services and the Consumer Credit Directive 2008/48/EC,[9] autonomous harmonisation at the national level became more difficult, even sometimes impossible.

Germany therefore intensified its efforts at the European level and pushed for coherent legislation at that level. Indeed, one explicit aim of the 2001 reform of the German law of obligations had been to exert influence on the future development of contract law at EU level.[10] German academics were highly influential in the work of the Acquis Group,[11] as well as in the Study Group on a European Civil Code;[12] indeed, critical commentators have remarked that the Common Frame of Reference in its structure and language very much resembled the German Civil Code.[13] Both projects in turn influenced the further work of the EU Commission, notably work on the Consumer Rights Directive 2011/83/EU,[14] which was meant to create a horizontal instrument,[15] a kind of 'general part of EU consumer law'[16] with coherent terminology and coherent rules; a

---

[7] Council Directive 87/102/EEC of 22 December 1986 for the approximation of the laws, regulations and administrative provisions of the Member States concerning consumer credit [1987] OJ L42/48; Council Directive 90/314/EEC of 13 June 1990 on package travel, package holidays and package tours [1990] OJ L158/59.

[8] See, eg, P Rott, 'Widerruf und Rückabwicklung nach der Umsetzung der Fernabsatzrichtlinie und dem Entwurf eines Schuldrechtsmodernisierungsgesetzes' (2001) *Verbraucher und Recht* 78; K von Koppenfels, 'Das Widerrufsrecht bei Verbraucherverträgen im BGB – eine Untersuchung des § 355 Abs 1 BGB-RegE' (2001) *Wertpapier-Mitteilungen* 1360.

[9] Directive 2008/48/EC of the European Parliament and of the Council of 23 April 2008 on credit agreements for consumers and repealing Council Directive 87/102/EEC [2008] OJ L133/66.

[10] See esp former Minister of Justice H Däubler-Gmelin, 'Die Entscheidung für die so genannte Große Lösung bei der Schuldrechtsreform' (2001) *Neue Juristische Wochenschrift* 2281.

[11] Hans Schulte-Nölke was the coordinator of the Acquis Group. On the Acquis Group, see HC Grigoleit and L Tomasic, 'Acquis Principles' in J Basedow, KJ Hopt and R Zimmermann (eds), *Handwörterbuch des Europäischen Privatrechts*, vol I (Mohr Siebeck, 2009) 12, 13.

[12] A prominent German member of the group was Christian von Bar, see M Schmidt-Kessel, 'Study Group on a European Civil Code' in J Basedow, KJ Hopt and R Zimmermann (eds), *Handwörterbuch des Europäischen Privatrechts*, vol II (Mohr Siebeck, 2009) 1453, 1454.

[13] See O Lando, 'The Structure and the Legal Values of the Common Frame of Reference (CFR)' (2007) 3 *European Review of Contract Law* 250.

[14] Directive 2011/83/EU of the European Parliament and of the Council of 25 October 2011 on consumer rights, amending Council Directive 93/13/EEC and Directive 1999/44/EC of the European Parliament and of the Council and repealing Council Directive 85/577/EEC and Directive 97/7/EC of the European Parliament and of the Council [2011] OJ L304/64.

[15] See European Commission, 'Proposal for a Regulation of the European Parliament and of the Council laying down the obligations of operators who place timber and timber products on the market' COM (2008) 644 final 3.

[16] See European Commission, 'Green Paper on the Review of the Consumer Acquis' COM (2006) 744 final 8.

project that was very much in line with German thinking.[17] Overall, it is certainly fair to say that Germany has played an important role in transforming EU consumer law into a (more) coherent legal order.

B. Involuntary Contribution

It should not be overlooked that another player strives for coherence in EU consumer law: the Court of Justice of the European Union ('Court of Justice'), including its Advocates General. Of course, the Court of Justice can only do so when supplied with cases, and in the area of consumer law it was supplied with numerous cases from Germany.

The reasons for this are manifold. First of all, Germany has always relied on litigation to resolve conflicts, whereas other dispute resolution mechanisms have been underdeveloped.[18] In the area of consumer law, this is supported by the fact that many German consumers avail themselves of legal insurance that allows them to challenge traders when they feel they have been treated unlawfully.[19] Second, German consumer organisations are strong (compared to those in many other EU Member States) and every year bring a large number of cases to the courts as well.[20] Third, awareness of EU consumer law is high in German academia as well as among practising lawyers, so that any implementation of EU law is thoroughly scrutinised in academic writing, pointing to potential incorrectness. Thus, national courts dealing with consumer law cases regularly face challenges by lawyers claiming that German law or its interpretation by other courts, including the *Bundesgerichtshof* (Federal Supreme Court, BGH), was not in line with EU consumer law and needed to be (re-)interpreted in the light of EU consumer law. Often, these challenges are well-founded, as will be shown later in this chapter.

In those cases, we often see a clash of legislative cultures. As has been mentioned, German law is highly precise in that it uses the same notions for the same legal concepts, ideally under an explicit definition (*Legaldefinition*), and for distinguishing legal concepts subtly. For the EU legislator, such doctrinal clarity and subtlety is much more difficult to achieve, since EU legislation must be applied in all the Member States with all their different legal backgrounds. As a result, the Court of Justice has, within the limits that the wording allows, resorted to purposive interpretation of EU law as its main method of interpretation,[21] so that the aims and objectives of such legislation as often expressed in the recitals have gained great importance.[22]

---

[17] See also S Wernicke, 'Perspektiven des deutschen Rechts im Wettbewerb der Rechtsordnungen' (2017) *Neue Juristische Wochenschrift* 3038, 3040.

[18] See, eg, E Isermann and C Berlin, 'Außergerichtliche Streitbeilegung in Verbraucherangelegenheiten – Bestandsaufnahme und Maßnahmenpaket der EU für 2014/2015' (2012) *Verbraucher und Recht* 47, 48.

[19] In 2021, 23.4m out of 40.7m households held legal insurance, see Statista, *Bestand an Versicherungsverträgen in der Rechtsschutzversicherung in Deutschland von 1999 bis 2021* at hde.statista.com/statistik/daten/studie/6599/umfrage/vertragsbestand-der-rechtsschutzversicherung-seit-1990 (accessed 11 December 2022).

[20] For 2021, Verbraucherzentrale Bundesverband eV (vzbv) alone listed 145 lawsuits against traders, see vzbv, *Jahresbericht 2021* 12 at www.vzbv.de/sites/default/files/2022-08/VZBV_Jahresbericht_2021_220628_bf.pdf (accessed 11 December 2022).

[21] For the relationship between the wording and the aims and objectives, see SU Pieper, 'Rechtsquellen' in M Dauses and M Ludwigs (eds), *Handbuch des EU-Wirtschaftsrechts*, vol 1 39th del (CH Beck, 2016) B I paras 11 et seq.

[22] ibid para 44.

In implementing EU consumer law directives, the German legislator has in various cases failed to understand the full meaning of EU law, or it has deliberately misunderstood EU law (see section III.B). One reason might be that a German legislator would have expressed provisions differently, and more precisely.[23] Be that as it may, disputes have often reached the Court of Justice and allowed the Court not only to interpret individual terms or provisions of EU law, but also to shape consumer law in a coherent manner where EU legislation was sufficiently open or vague; and the Court has clearly used that opportunity. Notably, the Court has applied general principles, such as the principle of effectiveness, to fill regulatory gaps,[24] but it has also drawn conclusions from comparing different pieces of EU consumer law and tried to establish coherence between them.[25]

Indirectly, Germany has even influenced EU legislation, as decisions of the Court of Justice in German cases have later been codified. For example, the decision in *Quelle*[26] (on which see section III.B.i) is now laid down in Article 14(4) of the Sale of Goods Directive (EU) 2019/771,[27] while the decision in *Pia Messner* stood as a model for Article 14(2) of the Consumer Rights Directive.

III. Substantive Consumer Law

When it comes to the transformation of substantive consumer law, the relationship between EU law and German law may be characterised as difficult.

As already mentioned in the context of coherence (section II), Germany has always tried to transfer German concepts to the European level. At the same time, Germany has always had a tendency to oppose doctrinal concepts of EU consumer law that were in tension with traditional German law. Beyond that doctrinal tension, however, we have also seen a strong alignment between the German Government and business associations in issues of consumer law, in particular during the Merkel era of 2005 to 2021. In legislative procedures at EU level as well as in the implementation phase, the German Government has often adopted the position of business associations and opposed a higher level of consumer protection. As a consequence, we have seen German activity towards regulating consumer law – nationally and at EU level – when it served the interests of German industry, but resistance where it did not.

Finally, the German legislator, German academia and German courts have shown a tendency to see previously adopted German law as already in line with

---

[23] For more examples and illustrative examples, see P Rott, 'Legal Terminology – One Reason for Frictions between German and European Consumer Law' (2012) 20 *European Review of Private Law* 1353.

[24] See Case C-489/07 *Pia Messner v Firma Stefan Krüger* ECLI:EU:C:2009:502, [2009] ECR I-07315.

[25] See, eg Case C-489/07 *Pia Messner v Firma Stefan Krüger* ECLI:EU:C:2009:98, [2009] ECR I-07315, Opinion of AG Trstenjak, making comparisons between the Distance Selling Directive (n 4) and Directive 1999/44/EC of the European Parliament and of the Council of 25 May 1999 on certain aspects of the sale of consumer goods and associated guarantees [1999] OJ L171/12.

[26] Case C-404/06 *Quelle AG v Bundesverband der Verbraucherzentralen und Verbraucherverbände* ECLI:EU:C:2008:231, [2008] ECR I-02685.

[27] Directive (EU) 2019/771 of the European Parliament and of the Council of 20 May 2019 on certain aspects concerning contracts for the sale of goods, amending Regulation (EU) 2017/2394 and Directive 2009/22/EC, and repealing Directive 1999/44/EC [2019] OJ L136/28.

yet-to-be-implemented or newly implemented EU legislation, and more than once they have failed to notice (or have ignored) conceptual differences. This applies, in particular, to the areas of unfair contract terms law and unfair commercial practices law (section III.C).

A. Positive Contributions

With regard to activities in favour of new EU consumer legislation, we can distinguish two types of situation: first, where the level of protection in Germany was higher than in other Member States; and, second, protection against rogue practices.

i. Adjustment to the German Level of Protection

Initially, the legislative activities of the EU in the area of consumer law did not affect German industry, as the minimum standards of early EU directives were usually lower than those in existing German consumer law. This clearly applies to the Misleading Advertising Directive 84/450/EEC[28] and to the Consumer Credit Directive 87/102/EEC.[29] German implementation of the Product Liability Directive 85/374/EEC[30] was not applied in legal practice until the early 2000s, since traditional tort law produced better results for claimants.[31]

A more recent example of the first situation is unfair commercial practices law, where German law has traditionally been more protective of consumers than that of many other EU Member States. This had already led to case law of the Court of Justice in the twentieth century, when the necessity for protective rules or case law was questioned, and thereby its compliance with the fundamental freedoms of the Treaty.[32] Under the principles of private international law,[33] however, all traders had to comply with German standards when operating on the German market.

This changed with the Electronic Commerce Directive 2000/31/EC[34] and the introduction of the country-of-origin principle in online trade. Now, traders from Member States with a more liberal unfair commercial practices law competed with German traders that still had to comply with the restrictive German rules; which in turn led to

---

[28] Council Directive 84/450/EEC of 10 September 1984 relating to the approximation of the laws, regulations and administrative provisions of the Member States concerning misleading advertising [1984] OJ L250/17.

[29] Council Directive 87/102/EEC (n 7).

[30] Council Directive 85/374/EEC of 25 July 1985 on the approximation of the laws, regulations and administrative provisions of the Member States concerning liability for defective products [1985] OJ L210/29.

[31] The turning point was the Second Act Amending Provisions on Damages (*Zweites Gesetz zur Änderung schadensersatzrechtlicher Vorschriften*) of 2002, (2002) I *Bundesgesetzblatt* 2674, which introduced damages for pain and suffering in product liability law that had hitherto only been available in general tort law.

[32] See, eg, Case C-470/93 *Verein gegen Unwesen in Handel und Gewerbe Köln eV v Mars GmbH* ECLI:EU:C:1995:224, [1995] ECR I-01923.

[33] These principles have been codified in Regulation (EC) No 864/2007 of the European Parliament and of the Council of 11 July 2007 on the law applicable to non-contractual obligations (Rome II) [2007] OJ L199/40, Art 7(2).

[34] Directive 2000/31/EC of the European Parliament and of the Council of 8 June 2000 on certain legal aspects of information society services, in particular electronic commerce, in the Internal Market ('Directive on electronic commerce') [2000] OJ L178/1.

pressure on the German Government. As one reaction, certain restrictive laws were abolished, notably the Rebate Act (*Rabattgesetz*) of 1933 and the Regulation on Joint Offers (*Zugabenverordnung*) of 1932. The main goal of the German Government, however, was to achieve the introduction of EU legislation on unfair commercial practices by and large in line with the German Unfair Commercial Practices Act (*Gesetz gegen den unlauteren Wettbewerb* (UWG)). The Government even established a commission whose task was to elaborate not only reform of the UWG but also a new unfair competition law for the EU.[35] In an attempt to influence the EU legislator, the new UWG was adopted in 2004.

Indeed, the Unfair Commercial Practices Directive 2005/29/EC[36] (UCPD) resembles the German model to some extent in that it contains a general clause prohibiting unfair commercial practices, although it is certainly much less restrictive than the old UWG, and Germany had to give up a number of restrictions even after its first and insufficient implementation of that Directive, due to decisions of the Court of Justice.[37]

Notably, the UCPD, like the UCTD before it, has perhaps not 'transformed' EU consumer law, but with its general clause (Article 5(1)), which gives a great deal of interpretative leeway to the courts, it brought some German-style legal technique that was certainly initially an irritant for some (former) EU Member States, such as, arguably, the United Kingdom.[38]

ii. Combatting Fraud

The second area where we can see German influence is in the combatting of fraud (beyond 'mere' breach of consumer law), because combatting fraud does not affect 'regular' business, and fraud may even harm both consumers and regular businesses. One example is the fight against subscription traps, with the introduction of a button or similar function that must be labelled in an easily legible manner with the words 'order with obligation to pay' or a corresponding unambiguous formulation indicating that placing the order entails an obligation to pay the trader (Article 8(2) of the Consumer Rights Directive). This provision was preceded by a provision of German law that was introduced as a solution to a long-standing problem with traders that had hidden an alleged payment obligation in small print at the bottom of the website, only visible after scrolling down.[39]

A new national example of combatting fraudulent behaviour is the introduction of a requirement for electricity and gas supply contracts to be concluded by use of a durable medium.[40] This is a response to practices by some suppliers to claim (falsely)

---

[35] See the Government's explanation of the draft Unfair Commercial Practices Act of 22 August 2003, *Bundestags-Drucksache* 15/1487, 12.

[36] Directive 2005/29/EC of the European Parliament and of the Council of 11 May 2005 concerning unfair business-to-consumer commercial practices in the internal market and amending Council Directive 84/450/EEC, Directives 97/7/EC, 98/27/EC and 2002/65/EC of the European Parliament and of the Council and Regulation (EC) No 2006/2004 of the European Parliament and of the Council ('Unfair Commercial Practices Directive') [2005] OJ L149/22.

[37] On which see section III.C.

[38] On legal irritants, see G Teubner, 'Legal Irritants: Good Faith in British Law or How Unifying Law Ends Up in New Differences' (1998) 61 *MLR* 11.

[39] See B Leier, 'Die Buttonlösung gegen Kostenfallen im Internet' (2012) *Computer und Recht* 378.

[40] Energy Act (*Energiewirtschaftsgesetz* (EnWG)), new § 41b.

that a contract had been concluded over the phone, which was now binding on the consumer.[41]

What is perhaps remarkable with these types of rules is that they seek civil law solutions where other Member States would much more easily resort to public law or criminal law sanctions; the latter are still highly unusual in German consumer law.[42]

B. Resistance

These somewhat rare examples of positive German contributions are outweighed by German resistance against EU consumer legislation that would impose new burdens on businesses. The turning point in the German attitude towards EU consumer law came in the mid-1990s, when EU consumer law began to go beyond German standards. Again, we can distinguish different stages and different players. First is the stage of the legislative process at EU level, where Germany has tried to prevent or water down legislation not only in the Council but also in the European Parliament, through influential members acting as rapporteurs of relevant committees.[43] Then follow the stages of implementation of EU consumer law in national law and its application by the courts.

i. Government and Legislator

At the EU level, we can often see German influence in regulatory options. For example, in Consumer Credit Directive 2008/48/EC, Germany fought in favour of compensation for banks in the event of early repayment;[44] and in the Mortgage Credit Directive 2014/17/EU, Germany insisted on the right to maintain its requirement of the consumer's legitimate interest in early repayment of the mortgage credit.[45] A recent example is the Sale of Goods Directive, where Germany strongly opposed an extended period for reversal of the burden of proof and achieved a reduction of two years, which the Commission had proposed,[46] to one year.[47]

---

[41] In 2020 alone, German consumer centres (*Verbraucherzentralen*) received more than 13,000 complaints relating to alleged contracts that consumers had never concluded, see vzbv (n 20) 21.

[42] Subscription traps, however, have triggered criminal prosecution, after some hesitation by prosecutors. In 2014, the BGH treated them as attempted fraud, see BGH, 5 March 2014 – 2 StR 616/12 (2014) *Neue Juristische Wochenschrift* 2595.

[43] eg, in the legislative proceedings for what became Consumer Credit Directive 2008/48/EC (n 9), the conservative politician Joachim Würmeling (EPP) acted as rapporteur for the committee on Internal Market and Consumer Protection on the first proposal, see EP document A5/2004/224. Later he became director of Sparda banks. Kurt Lechner (EPP) acted as rapporteur on the common position, see EP document A6 0504/2006.

[44] Consumer Credit Directive 2008/48/EC (n 9), Art 16(2). Accordingly, German implementation in § 502 BGB contains none of the optional limitations of Art 16.

[45] Directive 2014/17/EU of the European Parliament and of the Council of 4 February 2014 on credit agreements for consumers relating to residential immovable property and amending Directives 2008/48/EC and 2013/36/EU and Regulation (EU) No 1093/2010 [2014] OJ L60/34, Art 25(5), which corresponds to BGB, pre-existing § 490 para 2.

[46] See European Commission, 'Proposal for a Directive on certain aspects concerning contracts for the online and other distance sales of goods' COM (2015) 635 final, Art 14.

[47] Sale of Goods Directive (n 27), Art 11. For the traders' perspective, see T Stariradeff, 'Vollharmonisierung und Anhebung des Verbraucherschutzniveaus im Online-Kaufrecht' (2016) *MultiMedia und Recht* 715, 717.

In terms of implementing EU consumer law, Germany does not openly refuse implementation but sometimes has chosen less protective implementation in situations where the meaning of a particular provision of EU law was not entirely clear, or when EU legislation could possibly be interpreted so as not to cover a certain legal issue which would then have remained within national competence. For example, during implementation of the Distance Selling Directive 97/7/EC, the trade associations successfully pressed for rules that shifted the risk of dealing with sent goods to the consumer,[48] in breach of Article 6(2) of the Directive, as was later confirmed in the case of *Pia Messner*.[49]

Similarly, the Consumer Sales Directive 1999/44/EC met fierce resistance by German trade associations. For instance, the Directive extended the prescription period from six months under German law to two years, and introduced reversal of the burden of proof in relation to defects that become apparent within the first six months after delivery of goods.[50] The German delegation therefore did its best to make the two-year period independent from discovery of the defect.[51]

Moreover, the German legislator listened to the worries of business and, against the advice of numerous academics,[52] added a provision whereby consumers that asked for replacement of a defective good had to pay compensation for the use they had made of that good up to that time;[53] which the Court of Justice held to be a breach of the Directive in the case of *Quelle*.[54]

Whereas in these cases, the correct implementation of EU law would 'simply' have caused loss of claims by banks or worsened the position of traders, in other situations EU consumer law clashes with fundamental doctrinal approaches of German civil law. The best example is the creditor's duty to assess the consumer's creditworthiness, as enshrined first in Article 8 of the Consumer Credit Directive 2008/48/EC and later in Articles 18 to 20 of the Mortgage Credit Directive. The idea of responsible lending – thus of a bank's responsibility to prevent its contracting partner's uninformed decision that would likely lead to their over-indebtedness – was so alien to mainstream German civil law thinking that academic authors complained about the incapacitation of consumers.[55] The banks of course feared the extra work and damages claims in the event of non-compliance. The legislator helped by making the duty to assess the consumer's creditworthiness a mere public law duty, claiming that it was only meant to protect the stability of the financial market but not individual consumers;[56] which was

---

[48] For in-depth analysis, see Rott (n 8).

[49] *Pia Messner* (n 24).

[50] Concerning the criticism of traders, see W Lehr and H Wendel, 'Die EU-Richtlinie über Verbrauchsgüterkauf und –garantien – Auswirkungen auf Handel und Produzenten' (1999) *Europäisches Wirtschafts- und Steuerrecht* 321, 325.

[51] See D Staudenmayer, 'Die EG-Richtlinie über den Verbrauchsgüterkauf' (1999) *Neue Juristische Wochenschrift* 2393, 2396.

[52] See, eg, W-H Roth, 'Europäischer Verbraucherschutz und BGB' (2001) *Juristenzeitung* 475, 489.

[53] BGB, previous § 439 para 4.

[54] *Quelle AG* (n 26).

[55] See M Rohe, 'Privatautonomie im Verbraucherkreditrecht wohin? – Zum Richtlinienvorschlag zur Harmonisierung der Rechts- und Verwaltungsvorschriften der Mitgliedstaaten über den Verbraucherkredit' (2003) *Zeitschrift für Bank- und Kapitalmarktrecht* 267. Similarly A Danco, 'Die Novellierung der Verbraucherkreditrichtlinie' (2003) *Wertpapier-Mitteilungen* 853, 858.

[56] See the explanations by the German Government in its proposal for legislation to implement the Consumer Credit Directive 2008/48/EC, (2009) *Bundestagsdrucksache* 16/11643, 95 ff.

of course wrong, as the Court of Justice held in *LCL Le Crédit Lyonnais*[57] and even more clearly in *OPR Finance*.[58] Following *LCL Le Crédit Lyonnais*, Germany introduced civil law remedies for breach of that duty.[59]

Tellingly, the last German Government, formed by the CDU and SPD, had agreed to implement EU consumer law 1:1,[60] thus without even thinking about independent gold-plating rules, so as to avoid bureaucratic burdens on business. This became obvious when it came to implementation of the Digital Content and Digital Services Directive (EU) 2019/770,[61] which only focused on the best placement of the new rules within the German Civil Code and rejected any ideas of useful additions.[62]

ii. German Courts

In court, two situations may be distinguished: the situation of uncertainty about the correct interpretation of (the national implementation of) EU consumer law; and the reaction to a decision of the Court of Justice. In both situations, the case law of German courts shows a mixed picture. This even applies to the BGH, which of course consists of a number of different senates and whose judges change from time to time.

While we have seen a vast number of preliminary reference procedures that offered the Court of Justice the opportunity to clarify EU consumer law, there have also been numerous situations in which the BGH has refused to refer cases to the Court of Justice – mainly in recent insurance law and consumer credit law cases – relying on the *acte claire* doctrine of the Court. A telling example is the current discussion on the clarity and conciseness of contractual information that the creditor has to provide under Article 10(2) of Consumer Credit Directive 2008/48/EC and on the compatibility of denying the right of withdrawal due to alleged forfeiture. Against the opinion of lower-instance courts and of academic authors (but backed by academics writing in favour of banks), the BGH has held its consumer-unfriendly interpretation of the law to be 'clear'.[63] In *Kreissparkasse Saarlouis* and *Volkswagen Bank and others*, preliminary proceedings that lower-instance courts – LG Saarbrücken and LG Ravensburg – had initiated, the Court of Justice decided against the BGH.[64] In the same way, the BGH rejected referring to the Court insurance law cases that again turned on forfeiture of the consumer's right of withdrawal.[65] The LG Erfurt had already initiated preliminary proceedings in

---

[57] Case C-565/12 *LCL Le Crédit Lyonnais v Fesih Kalhan*, ECLI:EU:C:2014:190.

[58] Case C-679/18 *OPR-Finance sro v GK*, ECLI:EU:C:2020:167.

[59] BGB, §§ 505a et seq.

[60] See at bundesregierung.de/resource/blob/974430/847984/5b8bc23590d4cb2892b31c987ad672b7/2018-03-14-koalitionsvertrag-data.pdf?download=1 (accessed 11 December 2022).

[61] Directive (EU) 2019/770 of the European Parliament and of the Council of 20 May 2019 on certain aspects concerning contracts for the supply of digital content and digital services [2019] OJ L136/1.

[62] For an appraisal, see P Rott, 'Die Umsetzung der Richtlinien (EU) 2019/770 und 2019/771 in Deutschland' in W Blocher, D Heckmann and H Zech (eds), *DGRI Jahrbuch 2021/2022* (Otto Schmidt Verlag, 2023) forthcoming.

[63] See, eg, BGH, 28 July 2020 – XI ZR 288/19 (2021) *Neue Juristische Wochenschrift* 66, 68.

[64] Case C-66/19 *JC v Kreissparkasse Saarlouis* ECLI:EU:C:2020:242; Joined Cases C-33/20, C-155/20 and C-187/20 *UK v Volkswagen Bank and others* ECLI:EU:C:2021:736.

[65] See M Ebers, 'Krise des Vorabentscheidungsverfahrens im Versicherungsrecht?' (2017) *Verbraucher und Recht* 47; H-P Schwintowski, 'Die Aushöhlung des Widerspruchsrechts nach § 5 a VVG aF durch den Verwirkungseinwand' (2022) *Verbraucher und Recht* 83.

December 2021 to challenge the BGH's approach[66] but had to withdraw its request.[67] The same court launched a new attempt in October 2022;[68] the case is still pending.

At the stage of implementing decisions by the Court of Justice, the BGH has reinterpreted German consumer law in the light of the relevant EU legislation and even against the explicit regulatory intention of the German historic legislator in a number of spectacular decisions. Examples include implementation of the judgments in *Quelle*[69] and in *Weber and Putz*.[70] In contrast, more recently, we have seen cases – again in the area of consumer credit law – where the BGH claimed that a reinterpretation of German law after a decision of the Court of Justice was impossible; an approach that has been objected to in academic writing. It may also be worth mentioning that many consumers have suffered significant detriment from the (incorrect) decisions of the BGH that many lower-instance courts have followed.

C. False Continuity

Another phenomenon may be observed in those areas where German law to some extent stood as a model for EU legislation, namely, unfair contract terms law and unfair commercial practices law. In these areas, the German legislator assumed that there was no substantial difference from previous German law. Thus, the legislator failed to fully adjust German law to the new directives in these areas.

For example, in the area of unfair contract terms law, the German legislator did not implement the transparency requirement of Article 5 UCTD when it first transposed that Directive in 1996. Although the BGH had already developed a transparency principle autonomously before the UCTD was adopted,[71] and continued to apply that principle after the Directive was implemented, the lack of explicit implementation was in breach of EU law.[72] This was only remedied in 2001, when the German law of obligations was generally overhauled in a massive reform.

Even more striking is the legislative history of implementation of the UCPD, which began with the (somewhat delayed) adoption of the First Act Amending the Law against Unfair Competition[73] of 22 December 2008. With this implementation, the legislator tried to keep changes to the UWG to a minimum, which led the European Commission to initiate proceedings against Germany for insufficient implementation of the UCPD,

---

[66] LG Erfurt, 30 December 2021 – 8 O 1519/20 (2021) *Beck-Rechtsprechung* 41768.

[67] See Case C-2/22 *HK v Allianz Lebensversicherungs AG*, ECLI:EU:C:2022:391. German banks and insurance companies often settle, withdraw their application or accept the claimant's claim to avoid a landmark decision.

[68] LG Erfurt, 14 October 2022 – 8 O 1462/20 (2022) *Beck-Rechtsprechung* 30869.

[69] BGH, 26 November 2008 – VIII ZR 200/05 (2009) *Neue Juristische Wochenschrift* 427.

[70] BGH, 21 December 2011 – VIII ZR 70/08 (2012) *Neue Juristische Wochenschrift* 1073.

[71] See only BGH, January 1986 – VIII ZR 318/84 (1986) *Neue Juristische Wochenschrift* 1335; BGH, 11 March 1987 – VIII ZR 203/86 (1987) *Neue Juristische Wochenschrift* 1886.

[72] See Case C-144/99 *Commission v Netherlands*, ECLI:EU:C:2001:257, [2001] ECR I-03541. See also A Staudinger, 'Das Transparenzgebot im AGB-Gesetz: Klar und verständlich?' (1999) *Wertpapier-Mitteilungen* 1546.

[73] *Erstes Gesetz zur Änderung des Gesetzes gegen den unlauteren Wettbewerb*, (2008) *Bundesgesetzblatt* I, 2949.

mainly due to lack of transparency.[74] For example, Germany had failed to expressly implement the criteria for aggressive practices, muddled the provision on misleading omission and had not included relevant definitions. Germany gave in and adjusted the UWG with another amendment of 2 December 2015,[75] by which, amongst other things, the terminology of the UWG was brought into line with the terminology of the UCPD, indicating that differences were not only linguistic but also conceptual. On that occasion, Germany had to abolish certain per se prohibitions, after the Court of Justice had clarified that the black list in the Annex to the UCPD was exclusive.[76] Moreover, provisions relating to consumer protection (stemming from the UCPD) and autonomous rules concerning protection of competitors were separated.

Similarly, some courts show a tendency to seek continuity with old (pre-harmonisation) case law. Rather than trying to grasp the logic of EU private law, they look for common ground between the old law and the new rules, in an attempt to preserve as much as possible. For example, in relation to the then new sales law of the Consumer Sales Directive 1999/44/EC, courts equated the notion of non-conformity of Article 2 of that Directive with the old German concept of defect, not least because the legislator maintained the notion of defect, and they initially interpreted that notion too narrowly. Thus, referring to pre-reform case law by the BGH, the OLG Hamm held that the mere fact that a Renault car was not produced by Renault in France but by Matra in Italy, did not affect its conformity with the contract, although this had an impact on the market value of the car.[77]

D. Summing Up

Without a doubt, EU consumer law has brought new rules and new concepts into German civil law, and these have been widely used by consumer organisations and by law firms to defend consumer rights in court. Has this led to the 'transformation' of German consumer law? Certainly, information obligations as well as the right of withdrawal are now well-established instruments in German law, and they have even been used in areas of law that have not been influenced by EU law, such as in the new provision of § 650l BGB on consumer construction contracts that was introduced with effect from 1 January 2018. The reason may be that these instruments are closest to traditional German doctrine in that they provide for procedural fairness. This may be illustrated with case law of the BGH on breaches of (public law) prohibitions on selling

---

[74] See, eg, A Ohly, 'Nach der Reform ist vor der Reform' (2014) *Gewerblicher Rechtsschutz und Urheberrecht* 1137, 1138; O Sosnitza, 'Vorbemerkungen § 1 UWG Geschichte des Lauterkeitsrechts' in PW Heermann and J Schlingloff (eds), *Münchener Kommentar zum Lauterkeitsrecht*, 3rd edn (CH Beck, 2020) para 33.

[75] *Zweites Gesetz zur Änderung des Gesetzes gegen den unlauteren Wettbewerb*, (2015) *Bundesgesetzblatt* I, 2158.

[76] See, eg, Case C-304/08 *Zentrale zur Bekämpfung unlauteren Wettbewerbs eV v Plus Warenhandelsgesellschaft mbH*, ECLI:EU:C:2010:12, [2010] ECR I-00217.

[77] OLG Hamm, 13 May 2003 – 28 U 150/02 (2003) *Neue Juristische Wochenschrift – Rechtsprechungsreport* 1360. See, in contrast, the judgment by LG Ellwangen, 13 December 2002 – 3 O 219/02 (2003) *Neue Juristische Wochenschrift* 517 on the same issue, where the court held that one of the defects of the Volkswagen car concerned was that it had been manufactured in the Republic of South Africa whereas it was sold as manufactured in the EU.

certain products on the doorstep after Germany had implemented the Doorstep Selling Directive in 1986. Whereas doorstep contracts in such cases had earlier been held to be invalid due to illegality,[78] the BGH then changed its opinion, arguing that the new withdrawal right provided sufficient protection to consumers.[79] Continued resistance rather relates to the sharp consequences of breaches, in particular to the eternal withdrawal right in consumer credit law and insurance law. More welfarist elements of EU consumer law, such as the creditor's duty to assess the consumer's creditworthiness, are still regarded as an ongoing and unpleasant irritant.

There is one other exception, though, that mainstream civil law appears to have endorsed and to which we now turn: the concept of the 'average consumer'.

E. The 'Average Consumer'

One interesting conceptual development is the absorption of the 'average consumer' into German law. Initially, the German consumer image (in unfair commercial practices law) was rather different, and it is usually described by the image of an unobservant consumer who is easily misled.[80] Of course, German courts then had to adapt to the consumer image of the Court of Justice,[81] and the BGH did so with a landmark decision of 1999.[82] Some German courts, however, appear nowadays to take a particularly rigid stance on what an 'average consumer' has to be aware of in the individual case.

A recent example is the above-mentioned BGH case law on information obligations under consumer credit law. Even when it comes to legal information, the BGH regularly refers to the average consumer[83] and argues that an average consumer could not misunderstand a concrete piece of information on a bank's information form, one example being the following sentence in the bank's withdrawal information form:

> The period begins after conclusion of the agreement, but not before the borrower has received all mandatory information referred to in § 492 para 2 BGB (for example, information concerning the type of loan, information relating to the net loan amount, information concerning the contractual term).

The BGH considered this to be 'clear and concise'.[84]

In its request for a preliminary ruling in the case of *Kreissparkasse Saarlouis*, the LG Saarbrücken illustrated that given the contractual information in question, the consumer would not only have to find § 492 paragraph 2 BGB but would then also

---

[78] See K Hopt, 'Die Nichtigkeit von Darlehensverträgen bei Abschluß oder Vermittlung im Reisegewerbe' (1985) *Neue Juristische Wochenschrift* 1665.

[79] BGH, 16 January 1996 – XI ZR 116/95 (1996) *Neue Juristische Wochenschrift* 926.

[80] See, eg, BGH, 21 February 1991 – I ZR 106/89 (1992) *Gewerblicher Rechtsschutz und Urheberrecht* 66, 68.

[81] See only *Verein gegen Unwesen in Handel und Gewerbe Köln eV* (n 32); nowadays enshrined in Art 5(2) with recital 18 UCPD.

[82] BGH, 20 October 1999 – I ZR 167/97 (2000) *Wettbewerb in Recht und Praxis* 517.

[83] See, eg, BGH, 19 March 2019 – XI ZR 44/18 (2019) *Neue Juristische Wochenschrift – Rechtsprechungsreport* 867. For critical appraisal, see C Feldhusen, 'Angabepflichten des Darlehensgebers: Europäisches Verbraucherleitbild als Maßstab?' (2020) *Verbraucher und Recht* 87, 90 ff.

[84] Established case law since BGH, 22 November 2016 – XI ZR 434/15 (2017) *Neue Juristische Wochenschrift* 1306.

have to follow its reference to another provision in another law (Article 247 § 6 of the Introductory Act to the Civil Code (*Einführungsgesetz zum Bürgerlichen Gesetzbuch*)), which the consumer then would have to interpret in order to find out which rules govern the contract.[85]

The BGH's approach was then indeed torn apart by the Court of Justice, which concluded:

> Where an agreement concluded by a consumer refers to certain provisions of national law as regards information which must be provided pursuant to Article 10 of Directive 2008/48, the consumer is not in a position, on the basis of the agreement, to determine the scope of his or her contractual obligations, check whether all the required information, in accordance with that provision, is included in the contract that he or she has concluded, or a fortiori verify whether the period of withdrawal open to him or her has begun.[86]

IV. Enforcement of Consumer Law

In the area of enforcement, Germany has traditionally relied on private law. As early as in 1976, legal standing was introduced for consumer organisations, which could sue for injunctions against traders' abusive standard terms.[87] The consumer organisations that were mainly active in litigation have always been partly financed by the state, which therefore had influence on their budgets, including the budget for litigation.

Thus, the introduction of injunctions by either consumer organisations or public bodies by the Misleading Advertising Directive or the UCTD was perfectly in line with German enforcement tradition. One might also have expected Germany to be happy with the Injunctions Directive 98/27/EC,[88] but in fact it was not, the reason probably being that it extended legal standing for claims against German traders to foreign consumer organisations; mistrust that has become apparent again in the negotiations for the Representative Actions Directive (EU) 2020/1828[89] (see section IV.A).

Injunctions are of course a fairly soft instrument of collective consumer protection, as they do not make good the damage done. In their German version, traders were able to delay their effect by appealing and re-appealing decisions of the first- and second-instance courts, and continued to use unfair terms or harmful practices until a BGH judgment was handed down. In the meantime, claims by individuals who would usually not take action until the legal situation was clarified by the BGH might be time-barred, as indeed they often are.[90] Sometimes, traders would then replace the incriminating

---

[85] LG Saarbrücken, 17 January 2019 – 1 O 164/18 (2019) *Zeitschrift für Bank- und Kapitalmarktrecht* 190.

[86] See *JC v Kreissparkasse Saarlouis* (n 64) para 44. See also P Rott, 'The average consumer is not a lawyer! Case C-66/19 JC v Kreissparkasse Saarlouis' (2020) 27 *Maastricht Journal of European and Comparative Law* 379.

[87] Even earlier, in 1965, injunctions had been introduced in unfair commercial practices law.

[88] Directive 98/27/EC of the European Parliament and of the Council of 19 May 1998 on injunctions for the protection of consumers' interests [1998] OJ L166/51.

[89] Directive (EU) 2020/1828 of the European Parliament and of the Council of 25 November 2020 on representative actions for the protection of the collective interests of consumers and repealing Directive 2009/22/EC [2020] OJ L409/1.

[90] For more detail, see P Rott, 'Rechtsklarheit, Rechtsdurchsetzung und Verbraucherschutz' in H-W Micklitz et al (eds), *Verbraucherrecht 2.0 – Verbraucher in der digitalen Welt* (Nomos, 2017) 221, 238 ff.

clause with a different one, and the game begins again from the start, or the claimant consumer organisation could call upon the court to treat the new clause as a violation of the injunction decision, so that the relevant issue in that new litigation would then be whether or not the new clause was basically the same as the old clause or a different clause.[91] These latter proceedings rarely happen, as the potential sanction, a fine, goes to the state budget rather than to the claimant consumer organisation.[92] Overall, it seems fair to say that the traditional German enforcement system did not hurt traders too much.

However, in the meantime the EU has gone beyond injunctions in two ways: collective redress mechanisms; and public law enforcement.

A. Collective Redress

In the 2000s, the European Commission turned its attention to enforcement issues. Substantive consumer law seemed to be in good shape, but the law in the books did not always correspond with the law in action. The big issue was collective remedies, and in particular group actions; an issue that has proved extremely unpopular with German industry, which has tirelessly warned of a US-style litigation industry[93] (although the plans of the EU Commission differed greatly from the US approach to class actions). The EU Commission is said to have had a proposal for a Directive in its drawer in 2013, but after German intervention it never saw the light of day. Instead, the Commission published a non-binding Recommendation on common principles for injunctive and compensatory collective redress mechanisms in the Member States.[94]

Many years later, the Commission came to realise that the Recommendation had not produced the desired results in terms of voluntary action by Member States,[95] including Germany. Germany had of course noticed the pressure from the EU, but also from German consumer organisations, following the Volkswagen diesel scandal, and in 2019 had established the *Musterfeststellungsklage*, a collective action that only certain consumer organisations can bring and that aims at clarifying certain common issues of law in mass proceedings.[96] The court's decision, however, is only declaratory, which means that individual consumers would have to take action to bring their claims based

[91] See H-W Micklitz and P Rott, '§ 5 UKlaG' in T Rauscher (ed), *Münchener Kommentar zur Zivilprozessordnung*, 6th edn (CH Beck, 2021) para 34.

[92] Injunctions Act (*Unterlassungsklagengesetz* (UKlaG)), § 5, with Civil Procedural Code (*Zivilprozessordnung* (ZPO)), § 890 para 1. See also Micklitz and Rott (n 91) para 22.

[93] eg, BDI, *Prevent risk of abuse through class actions* (2016) at english.bdi.eu/article/news/prevent-risk-of-abuse-through-class-actions (accessed 11 December 2022).

[94] Commission Recommendation of 11 June 2013 on common principles for injunctive and compensatory collective redress mechanisms in the Member States concerning violations of rights granted under Union Law [2013] OJ L201/60.

[95] European Commission, 'Report from the Commission on the implementation of the Commission Recommendation of 11 June 2013 on common principles for injunctive and compensatory collective redress mechanisms in the Member States concerning violations of rights granted under Union law (2013/396/EU)' COM (2018) 40 final.

[96] ZPO, §§ 606 et seq. For details, see H Merkt and J Zimmermann, 'Die neue Musterfeststellungsklage: Eine erste Bewertung' (2018) *Verbraucher und Recht* 363; E Waclawik, 'Die Musterfeststellungsklage' (2018) *Neue Juristische Wochenschrift* 2921.

on the court's declaratory judgment. In German literature, the instrument has been praised by some as being better than nothing,[97] but it has been heavily criticised by many as falling behind as an effective tool for enforcing mass consumer claims.[98]

Be that as it may, the Volkswagen diesel scandal that had illustrated the weaknesses of consumer law enforcement in many Member States of the EU, in particular when compared to the USA, certainly encouraged the European Commission to launch a new attempt to introduce proper collective remedies. Following the Fitness Check of EU Consumer Law – which included an evaluation of the Injunctions Directive 2009/22/EC[99] and confirmed, once again, its lack of teeth[100] – in April 2018 the Commission tabled a proposal for a new directive[101] to turn the Injunctions Directive into a collective redress instrument.

Resistance from Germany against the proposal was fierce. Ironically, Germany could not block the Directive this time, as it was a German company that had caused so much grief to consumers all over the EU, and in addition could not be forced to pay out compensation speedily and on a large scale. Still, during the legislative process of what became the Representative Actions Directive, Germany fought for a number of elements of the new Directive that might allow Member States to create new obstacles to effective enforcement in the future. These include strict requirements for qualified entities that want to engage in cross-border enforcement, considerable leeway to determine strict requirements for qualified entities that act domestically, substantial leeway in determining opt-in requirements for redress procedures and the possibility to prohibit third-party financing.[102]

At the time of writing, implementing legislation is not yet available. However, a draft prepared within the German Ministry of Justice was leaked, and it has already been heavily criticised for making the redress action unnecessarily unattractive to consumers. In particular, consumers would have to opt into a redress action at an early stage, before the beginning of the oral proceedings in court, in order to participate in the action and to benefit from it. This is a stage where the outcome of the action, by which consumers that have opted in are bound, is entirely unclear. Thus, opting in is risky, and it has already been predicted that consumers will turn to alternative enforcement instruments, such as legal tech claims management.[103] Of course, this is a deliberate choice by the Ministry of Justice (led by the business-friendly liberal party); indeed, it was actually

---

[97] See, eg, R Metz, 'Musterfeststellungsklage: Endlich!' (2018) *Verbraucher und Recht* 281.

[98] See, eg A Stadler, 'Musterfeststellungsklagen im deutschen Verbraucherrecht?' (2018) *Verbraucher und Recht* 83.

[99] Directive 2009/22/EC of the European Parliament and of the Council of 23 April 2009 on injunctions for the protection of consumers' interests [2009] OJ L110/30.

[100] See Staff Working Documents SWD(2017) 208 and SWD(2017) 209.

[101] European Commission, 'Proposal for a Directive of the European Parliament and of the Council on representative actions for the protection of the collective interests of consumers, and repealing Directive 2009/22/EC' COM (2018) 184 final; on which see A Halfmeier and P Rott, 'Verbandsklage mit Zähnen?' (2018) *Verbraucher und Recht* 243.

[102] For an overview, see P Rott, 'Nachhaltigkeit durch Verbraucherverbandsklagen' in M Tamm (ed), *Zentrifugalkräfte in Europa und im sozialen Rechtsstaat, Festschrift für Klaus Tonner* (Nomos, 2022) 341.

[103] See I Scherer, 'Abhilfeanspruch gem. Art 9 Abs 1 VerbandsklagenRL / § 1 Abs 1 Nr 1 VDuG-E und Verbraucherschadensersatzanspruch gem § 9 Abs 2 UWG – Kollektivrechtsschutz contra Individualrechtsschutz?' (2022) *Verbraucher und Recht* 443.

proposed in a study commissioned by 14 business associations.[104] In contrast, a study commissioned by the leading German consumer organisation had advocated in favour of the French system,[105] where consumers can opt in after the judgment has been laid down.[106]

B. Public Law Enforcement

Other Member States have had a tradition of enforcing consumer law by public law and/ or criminal law. One example is the United Kingdom,[107] but the Netherlands has also complemented civil law remedies with public law enforcement.[108] In contrast, Germany has traditionally strictly separated private law and public law and the relevant enforcement mechanisms.

While the first pieces of EU consumer law had left it to the Member States whether they entrusted consumer organisations or public authorities with enforcement of EU consumer law, Regulation (EC) No 2006/2004 on cooperation between national authorities responsible for enforcement of consumer protection laws[109] ('CPC Regulation') necessitated establishment of a consumer protection authority. This had not previously existed in Germany, which, however, managed to negotiate that this public authority, the *Bundesamt für Justiz*, was allowed to delegate tasks under the Regulation to private organisations,[110] for which it then determined the *Verbraucherzentrale Bundesverband e V* and the *Zentrale zur Bekämpfung des unlauteren Wettbewerbs e V*. The *Bundesamt für Justiz* itself had only a handful of civil servants for the purposes of the CPC Regulation. With the reform of the CPC Regulation, this has become more difficult, as the new CPC Regulation (EU) No 2017/2394[111] improved the enforcement measures available to the competent authorities, to the extent that they can no longer be placed in the hands of private organisations.

The EU has also introduced the Member States' obligation to set up regulatory bodies in various areas of law, such as energy law. The regulatory agencies have to be

---

[104] A Bruns, *Umsetzung der Verbandsklagerichtlinie in deutsches Recht* (2022) 29 and 47 ff at www.dihk. de/resource/blob/60208/dc65ef7b610a1d1c5c9c769d8782aa1f/gutachten-verbandsklagerichtlinie-data.pdf (accessed 11 December 2022). The same applies to the above-mentioned declaratory action under ZPO (n 96), § 608.

[105] See F Bien, 'Die neue französische Action de groupe der Verbraucherschutzverbände' (2014) *Neue Zeitschrift für Kartellrecht* 507, 508.

[106] See B Gsell and C Meller-Hannich, *Die Umsetzung der neuen EU-Verbandsklagenrichtlinie* (2021) 53 at vzbv.de/sites/default/files/downloads/2021/02/03/21-02-04_vzbv_verbandsklagen-rl_gutachten_gsell_meller-hannich.pdf (accessed 11 December 2022).

[107] See, eg, C Hodges, 'Mass Collective Redress: Consumer ADR and Regulatory Techniques' (2015) 23 *European Review of Private Law* 829.

[108] See P Rott, 'Behördliche Rechtsdurchsetzung in Großbritannien, den Niederlanden und der USA' in H Schulte-Nölke (ed), *Neue Wege zur Durchsetzung des Verbraucherrechts* (Springer, 2017) 31, 56 ff.

[109] Regulation (EC) No 2006/2004 of the European Parliament and of the Council of 27 October 2004 on cooperation between national authorities responsible for the enforcement of consumer protection laws (the Regulation on consumer protection cooperation) [2004] OJ L364/1, as amended.

[110] ibid Art 8(3).

[111] Regulation (EU) 2017/2394 of the European Parliament and of the Council of 12 December 2017 on cooperation between national authorities responsible for the enforcement of consumer protection laws and repealing Regulation (EC) No 2006/2004 [2017] OJ L345/1.

independent and must have sufficient powers and discretion.[112] While the main task of the regulators is to safeguard competition, EU legislation has also recognised the need for those regulatory bodies to play an active role in protecting consumers, and in particular protection of vulnerable consumers.[113]

German regulators have taken on this role with great reluctance. The *Bundesnetzagentur*, responsible, amongst other things, for telecommunications services and energy, has been active in combatting cold calling and fraudulent telephone diallers redirecting customers to high-cost numbers,[114] but it has not made much of an appearance yet in protection of energy consumers.[115] The *Bundesanstalt für Finanzdienstleistungsaufsicht* (BaFin) was given the task of collective consumer protection in 2015,[116] but has only really started to engage with this task since 2021, meeting fierce resistance from traditional civil lawyers who argue that private law should only be enforced through private litigation, certainly not in front of administrative courts.[117] Finally, discussions are under way around the Federal Cartel Office (*Bundeskartellamt*), which would like to obtain comprehensive powers to enforce unfair commercial practices law.[118] This is opposed by, amongst others, consumer organisations that have been highly active in that area until now.

When the prospects of collective redress mechanisms became more concrete, or threatening, industry itself seemed to be positive, for a short while, about the taking on of collective consumer protection by public authorities, hoping that this would harm them less than private law collective redress mechanisms. Indeed, the German Chamber for Industry and Trade (*Deutsche Industrie- und Handelskammer* (DIHK)) advocated establishment of a consumer ombudsman.[119] At least in the case of the banking industry,

---

[112] See, eg, Directive 2009/72/EC of the European Parliament and of the Council of 13 July 2009 concerning common rules for the internal market in electricity and repealing Directive 2003/54/EC [2009] OJ L211/55, Art 35 and recitals 33 and 34.

[113] See, eg, Directive (EU) 2019/944 of the European Parliament and of the Council of 5 June 2019 on common rules for the internal market for electricity and amending Directive 2012/27/EU (recast) [2019] OJ L158/125, Art 58 lit g) and h); also Regulation (EC) No 261/2004 of the European Parliament and of the Council of 11 February 2004 establishing common rules on compensation and assistance to passengers in the event of denied boarding and of cancellation or long delay of flights, and repealing Regulation (EEC) No 295/91 [2004] OJ L46/1, Art 16.

[114] See B Holznagel and C Vierling, 'Instrumente des Verbraucherschutzes in der Netzregulierung' in T Brönneke, A Willburger and S Bietz (eds), *Verbraucherrechtsvollzug* (Nomos, 2020) 75.

[115] For critique, see P Rott, 'Insufficient Prevention of Overindebtedness – Legal and Policy Failures' in F Ferretti (ed), *Comparative Perspectives of Consumer Over-indebtedness – A view from the UK, Germany, Greece, and Italy* (Eleven Publishing, 2016) 189, 200.

[116] See *Finanzdienstleistungsaufsichtsgesetz* (Financial Services Supervision Act (FinDAG)), § 4 para 1a. For a positive view of that provision, see P Rott, 'Thesen zur Durchsetzung des Verbraucherschutzrechts durch die BaFin' (2019) *Wertpapier-Mitteilungen* 1189.

[117] See, eg P Buck-Heeb, 'Missstandsaufsicht durch die BaFin nach § 4 Abs. 1a FinDAG' (2021) *Zeitschrift für Bank- und Kapitalmarktrecht* 141; C Herresthal, 'Keine Informationspflicht des Verwenders bei ergänzender Vertragsauslegung laufender Verträge' (2021) *Zeitschrift für Bank- und Kapitalmarktrecht* 131. For controversial views of the relationship between private enforcement and public enforcement by BaFin, see also VG Frankfurt, 24.6.2021 – 7 K 2237/20.F (2021) *Verbraucher und Recht* 430, with case note by P Rott.

[118] R Podszun, C Busch and F Henning-Bodewig, 'Die Durchsetzung des Verbraucherrechts: Das BKartA als UWG-Behörde?' (2018) *Gewerblicher Rechtsschutz und Urheberrecht* 1004.

[119] See S Wernicke, 'Effektiver kollektiver Rechtsschutz statt amerikanischer Geschäftsmodelle: Ein Plädoyer für eine klageberechtigte Ombudsstelle' in M Schäfer (ed), *Der Gesetzesentwurf zur 'Musterfeststellungsklage'* (2018) 7 at kas.de/documents/252038/253252/7_dokument_dok_pdf_52906_1.pdf/d72519a6-44e2-acd4-2699-5ec851ff e6dc?version=1.0&t=1539647268142 (accessed 11 December 2022). Wernicke is the chief legal officer of DIHK.

this changed completely when BaFin actually started to 'bite'. In the context of failure to honour long-term savings contracts that had promised bank customers interest rates that were now painful to the banks due to the lasting low-interest phase, a BaFin order to the whole banking industry to make reasonable offers to these customers[120] was appealed by more than 1,100 banks.[121]

C. Conclusion on Enforcement

Overall, Germany has not changed its reluctant approach to consumer protection by way of collective redress mechanisms. Rather, we can see a cautious opening up towards public enforcement. One reason might be that businesses hope to fare better with public authorities (with uncertain competences) than with consumer organisations or, even worse, law-firm driven group actions. If public law enforcement were to be strengthened, this would certainly count as a transformation of the German enforcement landscape.

V. Conclusion

Since the early 2000s, German legislators have not been at the forefront of consumer protection, and Germany has been more of a bystander or has even obstructed EU consumer law rather than shaping it. At the same time, EU consumer law has attracted considerable attention in German academia and legal practice, which is why Germany has certainly contributed heavily, through academic writing and court cases, many of which reached the Court of Justice, to the clarification and sophistication of EU consumer law.

Generally speaking, the approach of EU consumer law is more consumer-friendly than German consumer policy, which has been heavily influenced by business organisations since the early 2000s. Of course, Germany had to implement EU consumer law, but it has more than once done so in a way that did not catch the spirit of the new rules, and the Court of Justice has often held German implementing legislation and/or its interpretation by the courts to be in breach of EU law. One reason, beyond political unwillingness, may be found in the differences between Germany and the EU in their respective styles of legislation, and the fact that German civil lawyers are not easily persuaded that anything could trump the German Civil Code. In short, EU consumer law has been endorsed where it fits the traditional concepts of the Civil Code but fiercely rejected where it does not. In that sense, German law has not really been transformed by EU consumer law. The same applies to enforcement of consumer law, where legal instruments beyond individual lawsuits and collective injunction actions are eyed with great distrust.

---

[120] BaFin, 'Allgemeinverfügung bezüglich Zinsanpassungsklauseln bei Prämiensparverträgen' (2021) at bafin.de/SharedDocs/Veroeffentlichungen/DE/Aufsichtsrecht/Verfuegung/vf_210621_allgvfg_Zinsanpassungsklauseln_Praemiensparvertraege.html (accessed 11 December 2022).
[121] See BaFin, 'Prämiensparverträge: BaFin-Anordnung gegenüber Kreditinstituten wegen Rechtsbehelfen vorerst nicht umfassend vollziehbar' (2021) at bafin.de/SharedDocs/Veroeffentlichungen/DE/Meldung/2021/meldung_2021_09_09_Praemiensparvertraege.html (accessed 11 December 2022).

14

Czechia

MARKÉTA SELUCKÁ AND JANA VÁBEK MARKOVÁ

I. Introduction: The Transformation of Czech Consumer Law

In this chapter, we examine how Czech consumer law has been transformed over the first two decades of the new millennium. Like other Central and Eastern European countries joining the European Union (EU) in 2004, Czechia (also known as the Czech Republic) underwent significant political and economic transformation after the fall of communism. Although the role of individuals as consumers was already recognised in Communist-era legislation, consumer law was transformed considerably first in the post-Communist era, and subsequently through the implementation of EU consumer legislation into Czech law.

The objective of this chapter is to trace this transformation in a number of areas. First, we focus on the development of the concept of the consumer and how that concept is understood in the period under review. The ideology that influenced our previous Civil Code will be taken into account. The development of consumer protection in Czechoslovakia and later the Czech Republic will also be discussed. Finally, we consider the impact of EU law on the development and transformation of consumer law.

II. Consumer Protection in the Context of Political Change

Our focus is on the transformation of Czech consumer law from the start of the new millennium, and so we first sketch how Czech consumer law had evolved up to that point. The Czech Republic is a post-communist country in Central Europe with a historical context of civil law and consumer protection strongly marked by Marxist-Leninist ideology, because the Civil Code that was in force in 1989, when social change took place and the totalitarian society became a democratic society, could be characterised as a code that tried to transcend the Soviet model; it could be described as a strongly ideologised code. However, from the perspective of consumer protection, we must paradoxically state that Civil Code no 40/1964 Coll[1] ('CC 1964') (with several amendments that did not have a

[1] Act no 40/1964 Coll, Civil Code, as amended until 31 December 2013, in ASPI [Legal Information System] Wolters Kluwer ČR.

major impact on the ideological concept of the Code and its provisions) was not considered a private law code (Marxism-Leninism fundamentally avoided the term 'private') but rather a code of consumer law. The Civil Code did not contain the traditional private law principles that underlie civil codes in democratic countries but, rather, used the idea that every citizen should fulfil their obligations to the state, and civil law is merely a tool for governing a socialist society. Relations between citizens were perceived as secondary and insignificant, while relations between socialist organisations and the citizen (typically the citizen's rights in the event of a defective product) were a priority. The Civil Code focused on regulation of property relations in so-called civic consumption; from today's perspective, it primarily focused on relations between the entrepreneur (socialist organisations producing goods) and the consumer (citizen). The dispositive nature of legal relations was restricted to the maximum possible limit (only provisions that were so marked in legislation could be considered dispositive) and mandatory legislation strictly protecting the citizen's consumer rights was preferred (the Civil Code of the GDR of 1975 can be described as a similarly consumer-ideological code). For example, the CC 1964 did not mention purchase agreements, liens or leases. However, the reality of actual consumer protection was the opposite; although the citizen had rights in the event of defective performance and the right to protection of those rights, in reality the consumer (citizen) was only protected in the context of the idea that 'a socialist organisation cannot produce defective goods', for example because it is fulfilling the tasks set in its five-year plan.

After the Velvet Revolution[2] and subsequent social changes, the need arose to reintroduce traditional private law principles and ideas into Czech private law. This was done by fundamentally amending the Civil Code: Act no 509/1991 Coll.[3] A new act on consumer protection was also adopted later on (Act no 634/1992 Coll),[4] so consumer protection was divided into two basic instruments: CC 1964 and the Consumer Protection Act (ACP),[5] a dichotomy we still have in our legal system today. While the CC 1964 offered private law protection, the ACP predominantly offered public law protection, although EU law, for example, imposed the obligation for entrepreneurs to inform consumers. We can therefore generally state that the need to protect consumers as the weaker party was present in Czech legislation before the Czech Republic's accession to the EU, and was significantly reflected in both private law (typically, liability for defects) and public law (especially the general obligation for entrepreneurs to provide information,[6] primarily pre-contractual, as well as the prohibition of discrimination against consumers[7] and deception of consumers[8] and so on).

---

[2] The 'Velvet Revolution' is the period of non-violent change of power in the then Czechoslovakia in 1989, heralding the change from the communist system of power to democracy. Apart from the events of 17 November, when demonstrators were attacked by the Public Security Forces, the revolution was not accompanied by violence and not a single life was lost during the coup. Because of its non-violent nature, this revolution is referred to as the 'Velvet Revolution'. Although no violence was used to seize power, the result was a profound social change.

[3] Act no 509/1991 Coll, Act amending, supplementing and regulating the Civil Code, in ASPI Wolters Kluwer ČR.

[4] Act no 634/1992 Coll, on Consumer Protection, as amended, in ASPI Wolters Kluwer ČR.

[5] ibid.

[6] ACP §§9–14.

[7] ACP §6.

[8] ACP §8.

The Czech Republic joined the EU in 2004, so it became necessary to harmonise our legal system with the requirements of EU law in anticipation of accession. Consumer protection in the Czech Republic is not conceived of as a separate constitutionally guaranteed right. The case law[9] of the Constitutional Court assumes that consumers are in an unequal position in their relations with entrepreneurs due to entrepreneurs' professional backgrounds, greater professional experience, better knowledge of the law and easier access to legal services. This inequality is therefore reason to provide an increased level of legal protection for the consumer as the weaker party. Consumer protection is one of the manifestations of the principle of protecting the weaker party, which is part of the constitutional principle of equality according to Article 1 of the Charter of Fundamental Rights and Freedoms,[10] in a substantive conception.[11] Unlike the Czech constitutional order, in EU law consumer protection is an independent fundamental right.

III. Consumer Contract a Contract Concluded with a Consumer

Consumer contracts and their private law regulation were inserted into the CC 1964 by an amendment to Act no 367/2000 Coll.[12] The first transposition of EU consumer protection into Czech private law was unsystematic. The Government prepared transposition without regard to the context of the system of Czech private law. The system of these provisions was therefore somewhat 'chaotic' when the provisions of general consumer law were mixed with regulation of specific consumer relations. General definition provisions (§52) were followed by regulation of specific consumer contracts (distance contracts, distance contracts for financial services) and general provisions (§§55–56), which provide general consumer protection and therefore have a direct relationship to §52. This was followed by regulation of other specific consumer contracts.

In the above context, it is necessary to take into account that some obligations were regulated by the Commercial Code,[13] so there were often questions of application of consumer protection provisions (consumer contracts) for contract types defined in the Commercial Code or contracts named and defined by other laws, as the definition of consumer contracts was based on the idea that they are purchase contracts, contracts for work and contracts referred to in Part Eight CC 1964. There has also been

---

[9] cf Constitutional Court judgment of 24 January 2020, file no II ÚS 78/19; Constitutional Court judgment of 19 January 2017, file no I ÚS 3308/16.

[10] Resolution no 2/1993 Coll, on the promulgation of the Charter of Fundamental Rights and Freedoms as part of the of the constitutional order of the Czech Republic, as amended, in ASPI Wolters Kluwer ČR.

[11] See Constitutional Court judgment of 24 January 2020, file no II ÚS 78/19, para 10.

[12] Amendment to the CC 1964 (n 1), Act no 367/2000 Coll, in ASPI Wolters Kluwer ČR. In this section, we focus on the issue of contracts concluded with consumers. We will follow their definition in the old Civil Code (CC 1964) and their current definition in the new Civil Code (CC 2012) (see n 15). The dualism of Czech legislation will also be outlined: this lies in the fact that before 2012, or since 2014, the Czech Civil Code and the Commercial Code (see n 13) operated in the Czech Republic, which overlapped in some areas.

[13] Act no 513/1991 Coll, Commercial Code, in CODEXIS Atlas consulting.

major controversy over whether it is also possible to apply general consumer protection contained in §51a CC 1964 to unnamed contracts, namely contracts that are not defined and regulated by the CC 1964 or other instruments. The issue of interpreting the term 'consumer contract' was later removed by an amendment to §52 paragraph 1 CC 1964 implemented by Act no 56/2006 Coll,[14] so all contracts concluded between an entrepreneur and a consumer, regardless of whether they are defined in the CC 1964 or not, were considered consumer contracts from the effective date of the amendment. The transformative effect of EU law was therefore initially rather muted, having resulted in confusion more than anything else.

After the turn of the millennium, it was clear that the Czech Republic would move towards integration with the EU. The requirements imposed on the Member States had to be adopted into the Czech legal system. In 2012, the CC 2012[15] was enacted with effect from 2014. The CC 2012 is not just a civil code, as its predecessor was, but is a comprehensive code of private law. The current Code sets out its provisions in a system progressing from the general to the special, as §§1810–1819 CC 2012 contain general consumer protection provisions and form a separate Section 1 of Part 4 (provisions on obligations under consumer contracts), followed by Section 2, which regulates conclusion of distance contracts and obligations under contracts concluded outside business premises (§§1820–1851 CC 2012), while Section 3 of Part 4 contains timeshare legislation (§§1852–1867 CC 2012).

The amendment to the Czech Civil Code at the end of 2022 significantly changed the provisions on consumer protection. The Government prepared transposition of Directives (EU) 2019/771[16] and (EU) 2019/770[17] and drafted a general revision of consumer protection under Czech law. There are changes in the Czech Civil Code, but there are also a number of changes in the ACP. The intention was to clarify consumer protection with the content of EU consumer protection law. The amendment had to respect not only the rules of EU consumer law, but also the case law of the Court of Justice of the European Union (CJEU). It may be said that the result is generally better, but sometimes the new rules lower the standard of consumer protection in the Czech Republic to which the consumer was accustomed. We can say that the changes to consumer protection are more in line with EU consumer law, but also that Czech consumer is losing some of the historically higher levels of consumer protection as a result of the transposition of EU consumer law, and that in some instances, problems with reconciling EU consumer law with existing measures exacerbated that problem.

---

[14] Act no 56/2006 Coll, Act amending Act no 256/2004 Coll, on Capital Market Business, as amended, and other related acts, in CODEXIS Atlas consulting.

[15] Act no 89/2012 Coll., Civil Code, in CODEXIS Atlas consulting.

[16] Directive (EU) 2019/771 of the European Parliament and of the Council of 20 May 2019 on certain aspects concerning contracts for the sale of goods, amending Regulation (EU) 2017/2394 and Directive 2009/22/EC, and repealing Directive 1999/44/EC [2019] OJ L136/28 ('Sale of Goods Directive').

[17] Directive (EU) 2019/770 of the European Parliament and of the Council of 20 May 2019 on certain aspects concerning contracts for the supply of digital content and digital services [2019] OJ L136/1 ('Digital Content Directive').

During discussion of the amendment in the Czech Parliament, it was clear that a transformation of thinking about consumer law and consumer protection is not really taking place in our society. Some lawyers have argued that consumer protection is unreasonable and too threatening to the traditional values of European society. Therefore, despite the addition of EU consumer law to Czech law, there was no noticeable transformation as a result.

IV. The Terms 'Consumer' and 'Supplier'

The term 'consumer'[18] was inserted into the CC 1964 with an amendment to Act no 367/2000 Coll. This term was previously only contained in the ACP, which defined a consumer as a natural person, but only for the purposes of this law, that is, this legal definition could not be used for application of the Civil Code. The CC 1964 was amended in the sense that it labelled both natural and legal persons as consumers, until the amendment to the CC 1964 introduced by Act no 155/2010 Coll,[19] when only natural persons were considered consumers. 'Non-profit' legal entities (civic associations, public benefit companies and the like) therefore lost the status of consumer, which may be described as Euro-conformist in the current conception of consumer protection law in the EU. However, protection of buyers in the sale of goods in commercial trade (transposed Sales of Goods Directive) remained in the legislation for non-profit legal entities as well.[20] Legislators are currently protecting non-business entities with provisions in favour of the weaker party, although the standard of protection is not as high as in the case of consumer protection. The legal definition of the term 'consumer' contained in the CC 1964 has not changed further, and the new CC 2012 kept the Euro-conformist understanding of the term 'consumer' as an exclusively natural person, where §419 defines a consumer as any person who concludes a contract with an entrepreneur or otherwise deals with them outside the scope of their business activity or outside the scope of independent performance of their profession. However, in a broader context it should be noted that other definitions of a consumer are contained in the Electronic Communications Act[21] and the Energy Act,[22] but the term 'consumer' contained in the CC 2012 is understood as a general definition of a consumer not only for private law, but also for the Czech legal system in general. If certain legislation contains a definition of a

---

[18] This section will trace the development of basic terminology in the field. The concepts of consumer and supplier will be examined. The terms will first be defined in the light of the old Civil Code (CC 1964), then in the new Civil Code (CC 2012).

[19] Act no 155/2010 Coll, amending certain acts to improve their application and reduce the administrative burden on entrepreneurs, as originally amended, in CODEXIS Atlas consulting.

[20] See also M Selucká, 'Ochrana spotřebitele: nenápadná změna se zásadními dopady' (English trans: 'Consumer protection: the unobtrusive change with a fundamental impact') (2010) 14 *Právní rozhledy* 513.

[21] Act no 127/2005 Coll, on Electronic Communications and on Amendments to Certain Related Acts, as amended, in ASPI Wolters Kluwer ČR, §2 subpara d).

[22] Act no 458/2000 Coll., on the conditions of business and the exercise of state administration in the energy sector, in ASPI Wolters Kluwer ČR, §2 para 2 subpara a) point 17.

consumer (whether it is identical or relatively different), the rules of *lex specialis derogat legi generali* apply.[23]

Under the CC 1964, the other party to a consumer contract was referred to as a 'supplier' but not as an 'entrepreneur', which resulted in application problems due to the fact that the Czech legal system used the same term, 'supplier', in a different context and in other instruments. The ACP identified the seller as the other party (although the ACP also contained a definition of the term 'supplier', but not in the context of defining a consumer contract),[24] and other labels for the other party could also be found in other instruments and terms in consumer contracts (cf the term 'operator' in §54a paragraph 4 CC 1964: distance contract for financial services).

The current Civil Code (CC 2012) introduced the traditional term 'entrepreneur' and contains two definitions for consumer contracts: one general;[25] the other special and more precise.[26] The concept based on public authority to conduct business has been abandoned and the factual nature of a certain activity has been introduced, that is, it is not important whether the other party is entitled to conduct business or not, but if they are acting as an entrepreneur then the party acting as a consumer will enjoy legal protection as a consumer, regardless of the public authority of the entrepreneur.

The current definitions of 'consumer' and 'supplier' are clearer and remove interpretative problems. The amendment to the Czech Civil Code, adopted at the end of 2022, does not change these definitions, as they are clear and free of interpretation problems. It can be said that transformation of who is a consumer and a supplier in Czech law is thus now unnecessary. After the first transposition of EU consumer law, it was somewhat unclear who a consumer was (for example, was a non-profit organisation also a consumer?), and problems also arose in understanding who a supplier was in the context of Czech doctrine. However, the development of definitions in the law has clarified these issues and we can now observe a transformation of the concepts of 'consumer' and 'supplier'. The evolution of these definitions has also stabilised the understanding of what 'consumer law' is.

---

[23] M Selucká and J Dudová, 'Obecné vymezení některých pojmů a koncepcí' in E Večerková et al, *Společensko-právní aspekty ochrany spotřebitele a jeho zdraví* (English trans: *Socio-Legal Aspects of Consumer Protection and Health*), 1st edn (Masaryk University, 2015) 22.

[24] The term 'supplier' as defined in the ACP corresponded to commercial law terminology (Commercial Code), as a supplier under the Commercial Code was an entrepreneur who supplies products to another entrepreneur.

[25] CC 2012 §420 para 1: 'Anyone who carries out gainful activity on his own account and responsibility, with a trade licence or in a similar manner, with the intention of doing so systematically for the purpose of making a profit shall be considered an entrepreneur with regard to this activity.'

[26] CC 2012 §420 para 2: 'For the purposes of consumer protection and §1963, any person who concludes contracts relating to his own business, production or similar activities or in the independent exercise of his profession, or a person acting on behalf of an entrepreneur, shall be considered an entrepreneur.' §420 defines the basic features of entrepreneurship, ie independence, the performance of gainful activity on one's own account, at one's own entrepreneurial risk, for the purpose of making a profit, on a continuous basis, by means of a trade or other similar method. These characteristics of an entrepreneur must be fulfilled cumulatively in terms of the material definition of an entrepreneur. However, a person who does not fulfil the above-mentioned characteristics of an entrepreneur, but is an entrepreneur because they meet the formal criteria (in particular, registration in the Commercial Register within the meaning of §421 para 1), may also be an entrepreneur.

V. Unfair Contract Terms in Consumer Contracts

Consumer protection against unfair contract terms[27] was also included in the CC 1964, with an amendment made by Act no 367/2000 Coll, §§55 and 56. Both provisions were the result of the Czech legislature's efforts to transpose Directive 93/13/EEC.[28] The Czech Republic introduced a review of unfair contract terms in consumer contracts, whether the contract was negotiated individually or not; protection against unfair arrangements is still based on this, although – in preparation for transposition of Sale of Goods Directive and Digital Content Directive – the draft amendment included a change in the concept of review of unethical consumer contract arrangements exclusively to contracts not negotiated individually.

The original transposition in CC 1964 was made outwith the context of traditional principles of Czech legal doctrine; it therefore caused considerable interpretation problems, as the term 'good faith', which was primarily used in the context of property protection and not contract law, was used. Moreover, the definition of 'unfair contract terms' was considered to be a circular definition, which also did not contribute to the smooth application of §56 paragraph 1 CC 1964. This means that the definition of 'unfair contract terms' has used the same words as the Czech name for the concept of 'unfair contract terms' (something like 'unfair contract terms are unfair terms').

The consequence of a breach of the prohibition on use of unfair contract terms in a consumer contract was based on relative invalidity,[29] that is, the consumer had to be active and invoke the invalidity, and it was only on the basis of that objection that the unethical arrangement was made invalid; the deadline for raising an objection was a general three-year limitation period, which began running from the moment the contract was concluded. After a period of three years, the consumer no longer had the right to object to the invalidity of an unfair contract term, which meant that the entrepreneur could claim that the limitation period had expired. The transposition carried out by the Czech legislature was in direct conflict with EU case law, which explicitly required the authority examining the unreasonable nature of the terms to have the right to *view their unreasonable nature* ex officio.[30] In 2009, the Municipal Court in Brno turned to the Czech Constitutional Court, claiming annulment of part of §40a of Act no 40/1964 Coll, the Civil Code, as amended, namely '§55' in the first sentence of the cited provision, and §55 paragraph 2 of Act no 40/1964 Coll, the Civil Code, as amended.

---

[27] In this section, we will take a closer look at prohibited terms in consumer contracts. This area of regulation in the Czech environment directly reflects EU regulation. The transformation from the CC 1964 to the CC 2012 will be tracked; nowadays, we can see in the CC 2012 the aims of the Directive – or rather its blacklist.

[28] Council Directive 93/13/EEC of 5 April 1993 on unfair terms in consumer contracts [1993] OJ L95/29 (UCTD).

[29] CC 1964 §55 para 2: 'Provisions in consumer contracts under §56 are considered valid if the consumer does not invoke their invalidity (§40a). However, if such a provision directly affects other provisions of the contract, the consumer may invoke the invalidity of the whole contract.'

[30] Joined Cases C-240/98 to C-244/98 *Océano Grupo Editorial SA v Rocío Murciano Quintero* ECLI:EU:C:2000:346, [2000] ECR I-04941; Case C-473/00 *Cofidis SA v Jean-Louis Fredout* ECLI:EU:C:2002:705, [2002] ECR I-10875; Case C-168/05 *Elisa María Mostaza Claro v Centro Móvil Milenium SL* ECLI:EU:C:2006:675, [2006] ECR I-10421.

It stated that in an earlier case conducted by the Municipal Court in Brno,[31] it concluded that the provisions of the legislation to be applied in that case, which concerned the relative invalidity of consumer contracts, were incompatible with the constitutional order, namely the principles of equality, proportionality and legal certainty, and also infringed the obligations of Czechia arising from international agreements under Article 1, paragraphs 1 and 2 of the Constitution of the Czech Republic and Article 1 of the Charter of Fundamental Rights and Freedoms.

However, before the Constitutional Court ruled on the merits, the Czech legislature adopted a 'quick amendment' to the CC 1964, introduced by Act no 155/2010 Coll[32] (effective from 1 August 2010), so the decision on the proposal to annul the relative invalidity of unreasonable arrangements became irrelevant. Moreover, relative invalidity limited by a period of three years and requiring activity on the consumer's part was replaced by absolute invalidity. The amendment of the CC 1964 did not (and could not due to the prohibition of retroactivity) resolve the relative invalidity of unfair contract terms in consumer contracts arising before the amendment came into effect; such arrangements remained only relatively invalid. However, the Constitutional Court ruled in the present case[33] that (although the legislation was changed to impose absolute invalidity instead of relative invalidity) it was not appropriate to claim annulment of the provisions, but that courts of general jurisdiction should proceed in such a way that the

---

[31] File no 37 C 208/2007.

[32] Act no 155/2010 Coll (n 19).

[33] Point 33 Pl 1/2010: 'With reference to the cited judgment of the Constitutional Court, it may be reiterated that, according to the case law of the Court of Justice of the European Communities at the time (hereinafter the 'Court of Justice'), the national court with jurisdiction to apply Community law is required to ensure the full effect of these standards by not applying conflicting provisions of national law, if necessary' [see Case 106/77 *Amministrazione delle Finanze dello Stato v Simmenthal SpA* ECLI:EU:C:1978:49, [1978] ECR 629 ('*Simmenthal II*') 629, paras 21 to 24, cited in accordance with Case C-119/05 *Ministero dell'Industria, del Commercio e dell'Artigianato contro Lucchini SpA* ECLI:EU:C:2007:434, [2007] ECR I-6199, para 61]. The Constitutional Court explicitly endorsed this case law of the Court of Justice in its judgments. In resolution file no Pl ÚS 19/04 of 21 February 2006 (see at https://nalus.usoud.cz/Search/GetRegSignDecisions.aspx?sz=Pl-19-04 (accessed 5 December 2022)) it refused to continue proceedings on a proposal for annulment of a law that had been repealed in the meantime, as would otherwise have been allowed by the doctrine defined by judgment file no Pl ÚS 33/2000 of 10 January 2001 (see at https://nalus.usoud.cz/Search/GetRegSignDecisions.aspx?sz=Pl-33-2000 (accessed 5 December 2022)). According to this doctrine, Art 95 para 2 of the Constitution implicitly obliges the Constitutional Court to provide assistance to the court of general jurisdiction with its decision on the constitutionality or unconstitutionality of the law to be applied, regardless of whether the law was later amended or repealed. According to the legal opinion expressed in the cited resolution file no Pl ÚS 19/04, however, this doctrine must take into account the membership of the Czech Republic in the EU, with the proviso that as of 1 May 2004, every public authority is obliged to apply European Community law in preference to Czech law if Czech law is in conflict with it. As the claimant in the said proceedings argued in its motion that the repealed regulations were primarily in conflict with the law of the European Communities, the Constitutional Court concluded that if it was necessary in the legal opinion of the regional court to apply the repealed laws, it must resolve the matter of the compliance of these regulations with the law of the European Communities itself, without the cooperation of the Constitutional Court. The Constitutional Court concluded that it was not competent to intervene in the assessment of these issues. Point 43 Pl 1/2010 provides: 'The Constitutional Court therefore concluded that if it was not for the situation described above that allows the court of general jurisdiction to keep the challenged and repealed provisions of the Civil Code (which were clearly inconsistent with the law of European Communities), which had not been applied in the particular case (cf para 33), and to decide fairly in accordance with European law, it would be necessary to make a declaratory statement that the provisions in question were also inconsistent with the above-cited articles of the Constitution of the Czech Republic and the Charter of Fundamental Rights and Freedoms.'

conflicting provision of the CC 1964 with reference to EU law would not be applied, that is, the court of general jurisdiction would behave as if this provision did not exist in legislation and would interpret Czech private law and its provisions in such a way as to achieve the meaning and purpose of the transposed directive. The Constitutional Court explicitly referred to the case of *Simmenthal II*, which dealt with the conflict of national public law (veterinary and health inspection fees levied on the import of veal and beef) with EU law. However, it should be noted that this opinion of the Czech Constitutional Court is not currently used and respected by courts of general jurisdiction, although there are several incorrect or directly contradictory transpositions of consumer protection directives in Czech law.

The current Civil Code contains protection against unfair contract terms in consumer contracts in §1813 CC 2012,[34] and introduces the *non negotium* sanction for such legal action (§1815 CC 2012). This means that the consumer does not have to be active in any way if the entrepreneur has used an unfair contract term in a consumer contract, because the court must take that fact into account *ex officio*. In practice, however, courts of general jurisdiction are not noticeably active in dealing with these facts, so if the consumer is not active and does not object to unfair contract terms, then the court itself does not actively assess the arrangements and often applies §1815 CC 2012 formalistically.[35]

In addition to the nullity or invalidity of unfair contract terms in consumer contracts, we also find provisions in Czech private law that prohibit deviations from legal provisions to the detriment of the consumer. The UCTD, as a general directive protecting consumers, did not contain an explicit requirement to prosecute deviations from private law standards if the deviation was to the detriment of the consumer, and the same was true for Directive 2011/83/EU.[36] However, the Czech Civil Code – both the CC 1964[37] and the CC 2012[38] – does contain such a provision. The CC 1964 initially applied relative invalidity to such deviations, but after the amendment introduced by Act no 155/2010 Coll, deviating arrangements that were to the detriment of the consumer were deemed absolutely invalid. The new Civil Code CC 2012 applies the *non negotium* sanction to deviations. However, the difference in the structure of deviations in the different Codes is fundamental, as the CC 1964 prohibited deviations that were to the detriment of the consumer and from dispositive legal provisions of the law, while the CC 2012 prohibits

---

[34] 'Arrangements that, contrary to the requirement of reasonableness, create a significant imbalance in the rights or obligations of the parties to the detriment of the consumer shall be deemed prohibited. This does not apply to arrangements for the subject matter or price, provided that they are presented to the consumer in a clear and comprehensible manner.'

[35] 'An unreasonable arrangement shall not be taken into account unless invoked by the consumer.'

[36] Directive 2011/83/EU of the European Parliament and of the Council of 25 October 2011 on consumer rights, amending Council Directive 93/13/EEC and Directive 1999/44/EC of the European Parliament and of the Council and repealing Council Directive 85/577/EEC and Directive 97/7/EC of the European Parliament and of the Council Text with EEA relevance [2011] OJ L304/64 ('Consumer Rights Directive').

[37] CC 1964 §55 para 1: 'The contractual arrangements of consumer contracts may not deviate from the law to the detriment of the consumer. In particular, the consumer may not waive the rights conferred on him by law or otherwise impair his contractual position.'

[38] CC 2021 §1812 para 2: 'Arrangements deviating from the provisions of the law established for consumer protection shall not be taken into account. This also applies if the consumer waives the special right granted by law.'

deviations from legal provisions that are to the detriment of the consumer only if the legislation is intended to protect the consumer, that is, deviations to the detriment of the consumer are allowed in the case of dispositive provisions. Of course, the cardinal question is what can be considered as legal provisions established for consumer protection, that is, whether they must be explicitly labelled as such, or whether it can be inferred that Czech legislation contains a number of general provisions relevant to consumer protection but applicable to all legal relationships as a general rule; these can be treated as being consumer protection provisions when applied in a consumer context.

In summary, while Czech law contains a prohibition on the use of unfair contractual terms, it also contains a prohibition on deviating from the statutory provisions for consumer protection. We might ask whether this is contrary to EU law, which needs a consumer protection outcome. In order to transpose a directive properly, it is not necessary to insert the provisions from the directive verbatim. Perhaps it was a conflict with EU law when these prohibitive provisions were in the 1964 CC, when any departure from legal provisions to the detriment of the consumer was prohibited, regardless of whether those provisions were for the protection of the consumer or not. However, it is now clear that deviations are only prohibited if they are deviations from consumer protection provisions. The amendment to the Czech Civil Code adopted at the end of 2022 makes this interpretation more precise, as this amendment inserts the words 'to the detriment of the consumer' into §1812. In other words, a deviation in the rights of the consumer is possible, and a deviation to the detriment of the consumer is possible even if the provision from which the deviation is made does not provide for protection of the consumer. We believe that this prohibition is not contrary to EU law, as it is necessary to ascertain the result of this provision. Perhaps we can say that this provision focuses on the outcome of consumer protection in general and sets out and clarifies the general principle of consumer protection that legal protection of consumers cannot be circumvented by contractual freedom. We are able to observe the transformation of unfair contract terms over time. At present, the general consumer protection rules, such as the prohibition on unfair contract terms, are in line with EU law and the case law of the CJEU.

VI.   Sale of Products in a Store

The Sale of Goods Directive was transposed into the Czech Civil Code by an amendment to the CC 1964, namely by Act no 136/2002 Coll.[39] However, the transposition was not fault-free, as the legislator took over the terms used in the Directive but not within the context of Czech private-law theoretical doctrine. For example, Czech private

---

[39] Act no 136/2002 Coll, Act amending Act no 40/1964 Coll., the Civil Code, as amended, and Act no 65/1965 Coll, the Labour Code, as amended. In this section, we focus on legal regulation of sale of goods in a shop. Sale of goods in commerce was framed in the CC 1964. Over time, legislation was influenced by EU law – especially after the turn of the millennium. Several not very successful transpositions of directives will be commented on. Currently, the commercial sale of goods and its regulation are probably the most widely used in the field of consumer contracts.

law distinguishes very strictly between a contract and the obligation arising from it, so that the contract is only the reason why a right or obligation exists at all.

This resulted in a number of inaccuracies and misunderstandings in the legislation. Specifically, two separate classes of rights arising from defective performance were combined, namely:

(a) liability for defects existing during the handover and acceptance of the subject of performance (ie delivery of the goods), that is, conformity with the purchase contract (a term taken from the Directive), on which Sale of Goods Directive is based; and

(b) the traditional Czech quality guarantee, that is, the seller's responsibility for ensuring that the item retains the properties usual for normal use of a purchased item for a certain period.

The six-month statutory quality guarantee was extended to a two-year statutory quality guarantee due to the incorrect transposition of the Directive. Moreover, the Directive was transposed in such a way that it applied to entities that were consumers, as well as to any buyer who concluded a purchase contract under the CC 1964. (Before the CC 2012 entered into force, it was possible to conclude a purchase contract under the CC 1964 or the Commercial Code even if it was not B2B; the Czech Civil Code did not require the other party to the contract to be a entrepreneur for the conclusion of a purchase contract under the CC 1964.) Legislation used the terms 'seller' and 'buyer' strictly, which meant that it could be concluded that if a legal or natural person sold goods as an entrepreneur in the course of business activities, then §§616 et seq CC 1964 were applied regardless of whether or not the other party to the contract was a consumer. A sufficient and defining feature for application of the provisions on sale of goods in a store was the very fact that it was the sale of goods in a store (a purchase contract concluded under the CC 1964), and it did not matter whether it was, or was not, a consumer contract.

When the CC 2012 entered into force in 2014, the two-track legislation was removed. The dualistic system of the Civil and Commercial Codes was unified into a monistic approach; under current Czech law, it is no longer possible to conclude a purchase contract under two legal instruments but only under the CC 2012.

The Sale of Goods Directive was transposed into the CC 2012 in §§2158 et seq, and does not apply only to consumers. Section 2158 CC 2012 states as follows:

> If the seller is an entrepreneur, in addition to the general provisions of the purchase contract, the provisions of this subsection shall also apply to the sale in the course of his business, unless the buyer is also an entrepreneur and it is clear from the circumstances that the purchase also applies to his business.

Although Hubková calls §2158[40] a consumer purchase contract in the commentary, we believe that this label is neither correct nor appropriate. This is specific legislation that takes precedence over the general legislation applying to a purchase contract.[41] We believe buyers are not necessarily always (and will not always be) consumers; the other

---

[40] P Hubková, '§2158 [Consumer Purchase Contract]' in J Petrov et al, *The Civil Code*, 2nd edn (CH Beck, 2022) marg no 13.

[41] cf the conclusions of NS 33 Cdo 4367/2013.

party may also be a non-entrepreneur, typically the weaker party. This means entities directly defined by §433 paragraph 2 CC 2012. These are typically private law corporations, such as an association, a non-profit company, a housing association, a unit owners association or a foundation. The CC 2012 legislation thus basically corresponds to the – previously introduced – standard of broader protection on the sale of goods in a store in the CC 1964.

At the time of writing this chapter, in late 2022, an amendment to the Civil Code was being discussed to take into account the new EU requirements. The two-year statutory guarantee was to be changed by dropping the concept altogether. The rules for publishing user reviews on the Internet are to be tightened. The presumption that goods are defective will also be extended from six months to one year. False discounts are also to end (such as Black Friday and fake sales). Businesses will now have to disclose both the discount given and the lowest price at which they have sold the product in the last 30 days. E-shop owners will also have to tell the consumer that they are committing to payment by pressing a button.

The amendment containing the above was approved by the Senate of Czechia on 3 November 2022. The President signed the amendment at the end of 2022, with its taking effect on 6 January 2023. Czech consumers will thus see another significant step in transformation of the law, which will make consumer law even more pro-consumer.

This big transformation in 2023 may be summarised as taking into account consumer behaviour in the new era. Most purchases of goods are made on the Internet and in e-shops, and there is an increasing need to protect consumers in the digital era.

VII. Package Tours

Legislation on package tour contracts[42] as a legal concept and a separate type of contract, has existed in Czechia only since adoption of the 'new' Civil Code (CC 2012). Previous legislation contained a definition of a travel contract, which was replaced by the new package tour contract in 2014. The previous travel contract was introduced into Czech law with effect from 1 October 2000, when it was inserted into the CC 1964 (§§852a–852k) as a new type of contract by an amendment to the Tourism Act (Act no 159/1999 Coll[43]), by which Directive 90/314/EEC[44] was to be transposed. However, transposition

---

[42] This section examines modification of the tour contract. This is a relatively new type of contract. Under the previous regime, it was very difficult to exit (conditional on an exit clause and bureaucracy). Travel within the then national territory was mostly organised in bulk, eg through the Revolutionary Trade Union (RTU) Movement. The RTU Movement was the monopoly trade union organisation, which was also the most mass social organisation in socialist Czechoslovakia. In many places, in practice, employee membership of the RTU was compulsory and automatic. Nowadays, the field of tour contracts is undergoing constant transformation, mainly due to the strong influence of EU law in this area.

[43] The name was taken from the German world '*Reisevertrag*'. Act no 159/1999 Coll, Act on Certain Conditions of Business in the Field of Tourism and on Amendments to Act no 40/1964 Coll., the Civil Code, as amended, and Act no 455/1991 Coll on Trade Enterprise ('Trade Licensing Act'), as amended, in ASPI.

[44] Council Directive 90/314/EEC of 13 June 1990 on package travel, package holidays and package tours. Repealed and replaced by Directive (EU) 2015/2302 of the European Parliament and of the Council of 25 November 2015 on package travel and linked travel arrangements, amending Regulation (EC) No

of the Directive cannot be considered perfect, as the resulting implementation did not meet all of its requirements.

In the Czech legal community, there was a debate as to whether it was necessary to introduce a new type of contract (travel contract, now package tour contract), or whether it was possible to use other types of contracts and merely transpose the specifics of travel arrangements into legislation. In Czech case law,[45] courts most often refer to §733 CC 1964, which governed contracts for procurement under which the

> procuring entity undertakes to procure a certain thing for the customer. The procuring entity has the right to procure the thing through another person. The customer is obliged to pay the procuring entity a fee for procuring the thing.

It was therefore a contract of mandate.[46]

Since 2014, Czech private law has used the term 'package tour contract', based on the reason for the obligation: the package tour. The appropriateness of renaming this institute is justified by the Explanatory Memorandum to the new Civil Code, which states that the package tour contract is more fitting for the subject matter of the contract, which is not 'travel' as such but rather 'a pre-arranged set of tourism services'.

The new legislation has resulted in increased security for tourists. For example, §2525 CC 2012 introduces the obligation for written confirmation by the organiser of the package deal, which ensures that the passenger will at least receive a document that can serve as proof in the event of a potential dispute. Protection of the customer's good faith has also been strengthened, and greater assistance is guaranteed in the event of trouble. The process of alleging defects in a package tour has been simplified and, last but not least, the ability to claim compensation for non-material damage incurred due to disruption of a holiday, as we know it today, was explicitly introduced.[47]

However, transposition of the Package Tour Directive was not without issues;[48] for example, Article 5 was transposed into §2549 CC 2012, which applies relative invalidity sanctions to all contractual arrangements deviating to the detriment of the customer, requiring the customer to invoke invalidity within a maximum limitation period of three years, although legislators generally declare similar arrangements in consumer contracts void.[49] A possible solution to this problem may be found in EU law, as the CJEU concluded[50] that if more than one directive with similar content can be applied to a given contractual relationship, all of them are to apply unless they explicitly exclude each other.

2006/2004 and Directive 2011/83/EU of the European Parliament and of the Council and repealing Council Directive 90/314/EEC [1990] OJ L158/59 ('Package Travel Directive').

[45] cf 33 Cdo 2549/98 or 25 Cdo 689/99.

[46] See also Judgment of the Regional Court in Pilsen of 31 October 1996, file no 15 Co 625/96.

[47] cf M Selucká, 'Tour deal' (English trans: 'Episode 6') in M Hulmak et al, *The Civil Code: Commentary VI, Law of Obligations: Special Part (§§2055–3014)*, 1st edn (CH Beck, 2014) 934.

[48] M Selucká, 'Die verbraucherrechtlichen Aspekte der Pauschalreise im neuen tschechischen Bürgerlichen Gesetzbuch' in G Saria (ed), *Tourismusrecht* (NWV Neuer Wissenschaftlicher Verlag, 2015) 222.

[49] See CC 2012 §1812 para 2.

[50] Case C-423/97 *Travel Vac SL v Manuel José Antelm Sanchis* ECLI:EU:C:1999:197, [1999] ECR I-02195, para 23.

Package tour legislation has undergone further fundamental changes over the last five years, particularly in CC 2012,[51] in connection with transposition of the Package Travel Directive. First and foremost, it must be stated that transposition was not done in time (most of the legislative process did not take place until 2018, although the transposition measures were to be adopted and published as of 1 January 2018).[52]

A definition of a package tour can currently be found in the Tourism Act. Prior to transposition of the new Directive, the term 'package tour' was defined in both the CC 2012 and the Tourism Act. Adoption of Act no 111/2018 Coll[53] removed the two-track definition in Czech legislation.

Today, a package tour is understood as a set of at least two different types of tourism services, where tourism services include accommodation, transport, motor vehicle rental or other tourism services (the law itself includes the sale of tickets, trips or sports equipment rental). The CC 2012 uses the term 'organiser' and does not include the term 'travel agency', and does so quite deliberately. The CC 2012 thus conveys that the form of the organiser or the existence of public authorisation is not decisive in determining the organiser's obligations.[54] The definition of the term 'organiser' can be found in §2523 CC 2012, which has been amended in recent years; an intermediary is also considered an organiser. An intermediary becomes an organiser under the CC 2012 if it passes on a customer's data to another entrepreneur, or if it make third parties believe that they are providing the package tour at their own risk. Thus, under §2 of the Tourism Act, an intermediary is required to have a concession to operate a travel agency.[55] A customer under the Tourism Act is someone who intends to conclude or concludes a contract with a travel agency for a package tour or related travel services, as well as someone in whose favour these contracts were concluded, or someone to whom the contract was assigned.

VIII. Law Reform

As already mentioned, a legislative process aiming to transpose Directive 2019/2161/EU,[56] the Sale of Goods Directive and the Digital Content Directive into Czech law

---

[51] Of course, there was not just the amendment to the CC 2012. Following the introduction of certain institutes, other amendments had to be made, including the following: Act no 455/1991 Coll, on trade licensing, as amended, and Act no 211/2000 Coll, on the state housing development fund and on the amendment of Act no 171/1991 Coll, concerning the powers of Czech bodies in the transfer of state property to other persons and the National Property Fund of the Czech Republic, as amended. However, the core of transposition of the Directive may be found in the CC 2012 and the Tourism Act.

[52] See generally Document for discussion at sitting 12, Amendment to the Act on Conditions of Business Activities in the Field of Tourism in the EU, Chamber of Deputies of the Parliament of Czechia at www.psp.cz/sqw/text/eudoct.sqw?c=14869&r=12.

[53] Act no 111/2018 Coll, Act amending Act no 159/1999 Coll., on certain conditions of business and on the performance of certain activities in the field of tourism, as amended, and other related acts, in ASPI Wolters Kluwer Č R.

[54] The Package Travel Directive 2015/2302 (n 44) uses the terms uses the terms 'organiser', 'seller' and 'trader'.

[55] cf K Dvořáková, *The Civil Code Commentary*, 2nd edn (C H Beck, 2017) 2685–2686.

[56] Directive (EU) 2019/2161 of the European Parliament and of the Council of 27 November 2019 amending Council Directive 93/13/EEC and Directives 98/6/EC, 2005/29/EC and 2011/83/EU of the European

is currently under way in Czechia.[57] However, the amendment of the CC 2012 and the ACP is much broader and should cover assessment of abusive clauses pursuant to §1813 CC 2012; the blacklist (in §1814 CC 2012) of unfair consumer contract arrangements should also be extended. According to the draft, the deadline for withdrawal from a contract concluded outside business premises will be more than doubled (it is currently 14 days). A maximum deadline for delivery of goods when no specific date has been agreed will be established (this is an issue with which consumers have been dealing recently, when they shop at Chinese or intermediary e-stores with the prospect of better prices only to have to wait weeks or months for their orders to arrive).

IX. Conclusion: Still a Need for Consumer Protection after Transition

Over time, Czechia has undergone significant changes in consumer law, as well as a fundamental change in private law. In general, we can state that Czech consumer protection law has a solid substantive legal basis, not only due to Czechia's membership of the EU and the need to transpose consumer protection directives, but also due to the historical development of society and the rule of law. Consumers are provided with sufficient substantive protection, under both the CC 2012 and the ACP. We can also state that once the Sale of Goods Directive, the Digital Content Directive and the Omnibus Directive are transposed, Czech consumer protection law will have reached an adequate European level.

However, we believe that protection of a consumer's subjective rights is still a fundamental long-term problem, in that although the consumer has sufficient rights to protection, the level of enforceability of protection of consumer rights against the will of entrepreneurs is very low. Czechia is still lacking in protection of the subjective rights of consumers through class actions or a consumer arbitration body (Czechia only has a financial arbitration institution in the consumer protection system, but its competence is closely connected with finance and banking). In short, Czech consumer protection law lacks quick, cheap and effective protection of subjective consumer rights, which is guaranteed by the EU Charter and the Consumer Rights Directive. Czech consumer protection law is at the same level as in other European countries; indeed, in some cases it even offers higher protection than the required uniform standard of consumer protection in the EU.

Overall, in summary, it may be said that Czech law has undergone considerable development over the last 70 years. It has transformed from socialist law, which rather

---

Parliament and of the Council as regards the better enforcement and modernisation of Union consumer protection rules [2019] OJ L328/7 ('Omnibus Directive').

[57] Sněmovní tisk 213/0: Novela z. o ochraně spotřebitele – EU www.psp.cz/sqw/text/tiskt.sqw?O=9&CT=213&CT1=0 accessed 5 December 2022.

degraded the concept of the consumer (as the regime at the time could not produce bad products), to modern consumer protection as it is known today by almost everyone across Europe and, by extension, the EU. After the Velvet Revolution, new avenues opened up and, with EU membership, new freedoms – such as free movement of services and goods, crucial for consumers.

15

How the Romanian Constitutional Court Highjacked Consumer Financial Protection

CĂTĂLIN GABRIEL STĂNESCU*

I. Introduction: Transformation Beyond the Desirable

Like all formerly communist countries of Central and Eastern Europe, Romania suffered a long and difficult transition from the communist to the capitalist political, economic and legal order. Since the country embarked on the path to European Union (EU) accession (ultimately joining in 2007),[1] entire areas of Romanian law have been reshaped to align with Union law. Consumer financial protection was among the areas most significantly affected, leading to substantive, institutional and societal transformations.

From a temporal perspective, several changes in Romanian consumer legislation can be tracked since the turn of the millennium, a period that may be divided into the pre- and post-accession phases (1999–2006 and 2007–present). Each change came with a substantive and institutional element. Regarding the substantive element, the alignment of national law with the EU *acquis*, as well as national legislative projects that ensued to respond to local issues, has changed the scope of consumer law and added to the existing rights and remedies it provides. Regarding the institutional element, the role of national courts and institutions has expanded.

Romanian consumer law has also changed as civil society has grown accustomed to consumer rights and expectations and has become more assertive in requiring compliance with existing standards. This assertiveness is reflected in the number of consumer complaints regarding financial matters addressed to the National Authority for Consumer Protection (NACP), but also to courts and alternative dispute resolution bodies.[2]

* The author would like to thank Hans-Wolfgang Micklitz and Christian Twigg-Flesner for the invitation to be part of this project. Thanks also go to Radu Rizoiu, Maxim Usynin and Liviu Damsa for their feedback on earlier versions of this chapter. Any errors lie entirely with the author.

[1] Ministry of External Affairs, 'Chronology of Romania-EU relations' at www.mae.ro/sites/default/files/file/userfiles/file/pdf/chronology_romania_ue.pdf (accessed 4 November 2022).

[2] According to NACP Letter 5947/04.07.2022, between 2020–22 the consumer authority received 9,279 complaints regarding consumer credit, which represents 12% of all complaints received by the NACP in its 30 years of activity. Moreover, according to NACP's activity reports, during 2018–22 the authority received

The chapter is organised as follows. Section II describes the economic, political and legislative context as a clash between *pro creditor* and *pro debitor* stances that is disputed on constitutional grounds. It also provides a brief overview of the Romanian Constitutional Court (RCC/the Court) and its role and power in light of the Romanian Constitution[3] and the RCC's governing law.[4] Section III summarises the RCC's case law on consumer financial protection since the beginning of the millennium. It evaluates the Court's approach and identifies patterns among its decisions regarding two relevant laws, namely Law 193/2000 on unfair terms in consumer contracts[5] and Government Emergency Ordinance (GEO) 50/2010 on consumer credit[6] contracts.[7] Section IV discusses the RCC's intervention in Law 77/2016 on giving in payment (the *Datio in Solutum* Law).[8] It argues that the RCC assumed a legislative role by altering both the legislator's intent and the law's substantive content, thus overstepping its constitutional powers. It also shows that, through constitutionalisation, the RCC has transformed consumer financial protection law to such a degree that it has ceased to be a protective instrument for consumers. Section V summarises the findings and concludes.

II. A Brief History of the Development of Consumer Law and Finance in Romania

While some elements of consumer-related legislation may be traced to the 1864 Civil Code and the interwar years (1919–39), the first laws specifically addressing the

---

4,788 complaints concerning financial services: 1,608 complaints in 2018, 1,449 complaints in 2019, 1,268 complaints in 2020, and 463 complaints in 2021. At the same time, for its six years of activity the Alternative Banking Dispute Resolution Centre reported an increasing number of complaint applications: 1,335 for the first half of 2022, 2,525 for 2021, 2,498 for 2020, 2,117 for 2019, 1,293 for 2018, 505 for 2017 and 235 for 2016. Unfortunately, Romanian courts do not report how many cases are brought by consumers against banks each year. However, in 2016, the National Bank claimed that more than 10,000 court cases were pending between consumers and financial institutions at that time. See M Banita, 'Păunescu, BNR: Sunt peste 10.000 de litigii cu băncile şi IFN pe rolul instanţelor' (29 March 2016) at www.profit.ro/povesti-cu-profit/financiar/banci/paunescu-bnr-sunt-peste-10-000-de-litigii-cu-bancile-si-ifn-pe-rolul-instantelor-15417503 (accessed 3 November 2022).

[3] The Romanian Constitution at www.presidency.ro/en/the-constitution-of-romania (accessed 3 November 2022).

[4] Law 47/1992 on the organisation and operation of the Constitutional Court, republished in the Official Gazette no 807/3.12.2010.

[5] Law 193/2000 on unfair terms in contracts concluded between traders and consumers, republished in the Official Gazette no 305/2008.

[6] Consumer law usually refers to 'consumer credit agreements', whereas financial institutions use 'loans' when dealing with consumers. For this purpose and to avoid repetition, the terms 'credit' and 'loan' will be used interchangeably throughout this chapter.

[7] Government Emergency Ordinance 50/2010 on consumer credit contracts, published in the Official Gazette no 389/11.10.2010.

[8] Law 77/2016 on giving in payment of certain immovable goods to settle obligations assumed through credits, published in the Official Gazette no 330/2016. Following the RCC's decisions addressed in section III of this chapter, Law 77/2016 was amended by Law 52/2020 for the modification and completion of Law 77/2016 on the giving in payment of certain immovable goods to settle obligations assumed through credits, published in the Official Gazette no 386/2020. This chapter uses Law 77/2016 and the *Datio in Solutum* Law interchangeably.

interests of *consumers* were adopted in 1945 in the aftermath of the Second World War and concerned unfair trading practices.[9]

These practices were criminalised by the communist regime in 1949, and the term *consumer* was replaced by other terminology ('victim'/'buyer').[10] Investigation and enforcement were undertaken by state bodies (prosecutors, police officers, or special operatives of the relevant ministries), an aspect that is reflected in the post-communist consumer protection framework developed in 1992, because the NACP functions as a state agency subordinated to the Government.[11]

The term *consumer* resurfaced sporadically throughout the Ceausescu regime (1965–89). For example, Decree 446/1972 tasked the Ministry for Internal Commerce with 'orienting and influencing the taste and preference of *consumers* towards local products'.[12] This reorientation was coupled with attempts to increase product quality and certify products, work and services;[13] and provide consumers with means of redress.[14] The General State Inspectorate for Product Quality Control,[15] established in 1970, was tasked with controlling domestic consumer products.[16]

The 1960s and 1970s coincided with a rise in Romania's economic development and living standards; the population experienced higher savings potential, diversified consumer goods and better housing conditions.[17] All these factors increased the Party's interest in consumer finance.[18]

Concerning consumer residential credit, the communists maintained and steadily generalised the incentives in former monarchic legislation[19] (cheap state credit and tax exemptions). The foundation was Decision 26/1966, by which the state offered land for construction and granted 15-year loans at a fixed annual interest rate of 1 per cent.[20]

---

[9] Law 351/1945 for the repression of illicit speculation and economic sabotage, republished in the Official Gazette no 126/06.06.1945, Art 1, letter h.

[10] Decree 183/1949 on punishment of economic crimes, published in the Official Gazette no 25/30.04.1949, followed by Decree 202/1953 on amendment of the Criminal Code, published in the Official Gazette no 15/14.05.1953. The term 'consumer' could still be found in Decree 202/1953, Arts 268[17] and 268[23].

[11] Government Ordinance 21/1992 on consumer protection, published in the Official Gazette no 212/28.08.1992, Art 27.

[12] Decree 446/1972 on the organisation and functioning of the Ministry of Internal Trade, published in the Official Gazette no 131/22.11.1972, Art 5 (b) 2nd para (which later became Law 79/1972).

[13] Law 2/1970 on the insurance and control of product quality, published in the Official Gazette no 28/28.03.1970. The law was subsequently replaced by Law 7/1977 on product and service quality, published in the Official Gazette no 63/09.07.1977, which in turn was replaced by Law 4/1989 on the assurance and control of product and service quality, published in the Official Gazette no 24/05.07.1989.

[14] Law 2/1970 (n 13) Art 2; See also Decree 282/1973 on certification of product, work and service quality, published in the Official Gazette no 71/17.05.1973, Art 13 (which became Law 98/1973).

[15] Decree 339/1970 on the establishment and functioning of the General State Inspectorate for Products Quality Control, published in the Official Gazette no 85/17.07.1970 (which became Law 40/1970). This was replaced by Decree 77/1971 on the establishment and functioning of the General State Inspectorate for Products Quality Control, published in the Official Gazette no 31/16.03.1971 (which became Law 35/1971).

[16] Law 2/1970 (n 13) Art 11.

[17] I Stanescu, 'Quality of Life in Romania 1918–2018: An Overview' (2018) XXIX *Calitatea Vietii* 107, 116.

[18] Law 9/1972 on finances, published in the Official Gazette no 9/22.11.1972. The law constituted the legal basis for consumer credit for residential purposes (Art 119).

[19] Law 80/1927 on the encouragement of housing building, published in the Official Gazette, Part I, no 95/03.05.1927, Arts 1, 2, 45 and 49.

[20] Decision 26/1966 on state support for urban citizenry to build their own housing, published in the Official Gazette no 1/12.01.1966, Arts 4 and 11.

Later, Law 4/1973²¹ generalised credit terms and consolidated all previous legislation into a single comprehensive act facilitating housing construction;²² both laws survived the anti-communist Revolution of 1989.

The democratisation of consumer credit in the form of hire-purchase of personal goods began during the post-war economic recovery, although initially such credit was only available to workers.²³ In the late 1960s, consumer credit expanded further to cover more goods²⁴ and types of consumers, such as pensioners.²⁵ The expansion fragmented the legal framework, because each new category of consumers or consumer durables (such as personal vehicles or musical instruments) was governed by its own law. To address this issue, Decision 1319/1972 unified and amended the sale of consumer goods on credit to low-income consumers.²⁶ All these laws were replaced by Decree 205/1981, which survived until 1990.²⁷

After the fall of communism, consumer law emerged relatively quickly with the adoption of Government Ordinance (GO) 21/1992 on consumer protection.²⁸ According to its Statement of Reasons, the GO established the legal framework for safeguarding consumers in their relationship with economic agents that commercialise goods and services for consumption.²⁹ The 2004 Consumer Code was another normative act with general application.³⁰

The transition years led to a re-fragmentation of Romanian residential consumer credit legislation. While Law 50/1991³¹ governed the construction of new dwellings and vacation homes, Decree 61/1990³² and Law 85/1992 addressed the sale of dwellings built from state funds.³³ The two systems ran in parallel until a new residential credit regime was adopted in 1999.

---

²¹ Law 4/1973 on the construction and sale of housing to the population and the construction of personal vacation homes, published in the Official Gazette no 46/31.03.1973.
²² Stanescu (n 17) 126.
²³ Decree 63/1955 supplemented by Decree 123/1955, published in the Official Gazette no 5/11.03.1955, repealed by Decree 296/1959 on the sale and purchase of goods and services with payment by instalments, published in the Official Gazette no 21/12.08.1959. Application norms were adopted later that year through Decision 1087/1059, published in the Official Gazette no 34/21.09.1959.
²⁴ Decision 2628/1967 on sale with payment by instalments of works of fine art, musical instruments, apparatus, accessories and musical works, published in the Official Gazette no 92/26.10.1967; Decision 1379/1971 on sale of radios and televisions with payment by instalments to members of agricultural production cooperatives and individual peasants, published in the Official Gazette no 137/30.10.1971; Decision 1334/1973, published in the Official Gazette no 157/13.10.1973.
²⁵ Decision 1042/1968 on sale of goods and performance of services with payment by instalments by pensioners and for the abrogation of certain provisions of Government Decision 1087/1959 for the application of Decree 296/1959, published in the Official Gazette no 67/20.05.1968.
²⁶ Decision 1319/1972 on sale of goods and performance of services with payment by instalments, published in the Official Gazette no 125/13.11.1972, Art 3.
²⁷ Decree 205/1981 on sale of goods and provision of services with payment by instalments, published in the Official Gazette no 52/20.07.1981, abrogated by Decree 280/1990 on the sale of goods, provision of services and execution of works with payment by instalments, published in the Official Gazette no 46/31.03.1990.
²⁸ Official Gazette no 212/28.08.1992.
²⁹ GO 21/1992, Statement of Reasons 6 (personal archive); see RD Apan, *Protectia juridica a consumatorilor. Creditul destinat consumului si domeniile conexe* (Sfera juridica, 2007) 25.
³⁰ Published in the Official Gazette no 593/01.07.2004.
³¹ Law 50/1991 on authorisation of construction works, published in the Official Gazette no 163/07.08.1991.
³² Official Gazette no 22/08.02.1990.
³³ Official Gazette no 180/29.07.1992.

Consumer credit for durable goods underwent a similar development. Decree 205/1981 was replaced by Government Decision 280/1990.[34] The latter survived until 2004, when it was abrogated as incompatible with 'the new legal order'.[35] Instalment sale legislation was rendered obsolete by the re-fragmentation of consumer credit legislation for personal goods (for instance, the introduction of vehicle-leasing contracts for consumers and businesses[36]), followed by a complete revamping of Romania's legal treatment of security interests in personal property via Law 99/1999[37] and adoption of the EU *acquis*.

In 1993, Romania embarked on the path of legislative harmonisation with the EU *acquis* as a precondition to the country's accession to the EU.[38] The negotiation chapter concerning consumer protection was provisionally concluded in 2001, and the country signed the Joining Treaty on 25 April 2005, thereby committing to further harmonisation efforts.[39]

Several pieces of transposed EU legislation are relevant to consumer protection and consumer credit: Law 58/1998 on banking,[40] Law 193/2000 on abusive terms in consumer contracts,[41] GO 85/2004 on consumer protection in concluding and performing distance contracts for financial services,[42] and Law 289/2004 on the legal regime of credit contracts destined for consumers, natural persons[43] and its Application Norms.[44] Moreover, several additions to the consumer credit regime occurred after accession: Government Emergency Ordinance (GEO) 50/2010 on consumer credit,[45] the 2011 adoption of the New Civil Code (NCC),[46] GEO 52/2016 on credit agreements for immovable property[47] and the debt relief mechanisms of Law 77/2016 on giving immovable property in payment for the discharge of credit agreement obligations.[48]

The year 1999 was defining for another major transformation in Romanian consumer finance. Regarding residential credit, Law 50/1991, which abrogated Law 4/1973, failed to implement any rules for mortgage credit on housing construction, generating a

---

[34] Decision 280/1990 on sale of goods, performance of services and work with payment by instalments, published in the Official Gazette no 46/31.03.1990.

[35] Decision 233/2004 on repealing certain normative acts, published in the Official Gazette no 191/04.03.2004, rectification published in the Official Gazette no 338/19.04.2004, Art 1, Annex 1, c II, 4.

[36] Government Ordinance 51/1997 on leasing operations and leasing companies, published in the Official Gazette no 224/30.08.1997.

[37] Law 99/1999 on certain measures to accelerate economic reform, published in the Official Gazette no 236/27.05.1999.

[38] Law 20/1993 on ratification of the European Agreement of Association between Romania and the European Community and its Member States, published in the Official Gazette no 73/12.04.1993, Title V, Arts 69–71 and Title VI, Art 93.

[39] Apan (n 29) 17–18.

[40] Official Gazette no 121/23.03.1998.

[41] Official Gazette no 560/10.11.2000.

[42] Official Gazette no 796/28.08.2004.

[43] Official Gazette no 611/06.07.2004.

[44] Order 2/2005 of the National Bank and Order 231/2005 of the National Authority for Consumer Protection published in the Official Gazette no 326/20005.

[45] Official Gazette no 389/11.06.2010.

[46] New Civil Code, adopted via Law 71/2011 implementing Law 287/2009 on the Civil Code published in the Official Gazette no 409/10.06.2011.

[47] Official Gazette no 727/20.09.2016.

[48] Official Gazette no 330/28.04.2016.

legislative gap. Law 190/1999 implemented a legal framework for all mortgage loans destined for the construction, purchase, rehabilitation, consolidation and expansion of dwellings,[49] and was coupled with the National Bank's Application Norms 3/2000.[50] The law provided mandatory rules for debtor protection: prior disclosure of contractual terms, a ban on the unilateral modification of terms, the right to early repayment and a limitation of administrative costs. Nevertheless, it opened the door for variable interest rates in consumer contracts, leaving most issues for contractual negotiation. This lack of regulation, coupled with the National Bank's leniency in its role as the supervising authority, enabled financial institutions to dictate terms via adhesion contracts.

Regarding credit for consumer durables, Law 99/1999 caused two key developments. First, it allowed traders other than credit institutions to sell on credit without meeting the banking activity prudential requirements of Law 58/1998.[51] While Law 99/1999 did not reinvent purchases by instalments (which existed before and during communism), it updated and adapted the practice to the new economic reality. Second, Law 99/1999 removed the 1864 Civil Code's restrictions on security interests over movable property and non-possessory security interests, and increased the predictability and enforceability of debts.[52] It also implemented non-possessory pledges and non-judicial mechanisms for recovering collateral, stimulating credit for consumer goods. Because these procedures were deemed too creditor-friendly (especially in consumer relationships), they were later moderated by the 2011 NCC. The NCC re-unified the provisions applicable to security interests in movable and immovable goods[53] and reintroduced judicial safeguards for defaulting debtors, including consumers. Since consumer credit in the late 1990s was mainly handled by commercial banks,[54] prudential rules had to be implemented by their supervisory authority, the National Bank.[55] However, the first norms were adopted only in 2003.[56]

A. The Effects of the Transition from Communism to Capitalism on Consumer Financial Protection

As already illustrated, the transformation of consumer protection and finance law was a sinuous and challenging process for several reasons. First, although some forms of consumer credit existed during communism, such schemes were sponsored by the state or state-owned enterprises and did not seek large profit margins.[57] On the contrary,

---

[49] Official Gazette no 611/14.12.1999.

[50] Official Gazette no 174/24.04.2000.

[51] Law 99/1999 (n 37) Art 100.

[52] V Padurari and AS Burtoiu 'Taking stock of Romanian secured transactions after 15 years of reform: A mapping of past, present and future milestones' in F Dahan (ed), *Research Handbook on Secured Financing in Commercial Transactions* (Edward Elgar, 2015) 403.

[53] ibid 407.

[54] Law 58/1998 (n 39) Art 44.

[55] ibid Art 45.

[56] Apan (n 29) 21–22.

[57] Law 4/1973, Art 29. Interest varied between 2–5% per year, depending on the monthly salary of the consumer.

although they displayed robust mechanisms for mitigating non-payment risk, the terms were consumer-friendly, with fixed, low-interest rates for the entire credit period.[58] As a result, many Romanian consumers who had experienced communist-era consumer credit were unprepared for the financial risks posed by commercial banks' products, which were offered in foreign currency at variable interest rates and with hidden charges. Credit cards and other retail credit products posed similar issues. This reality became apparent in the aftermath of the 2008 financial crisis.

Second, the contractual framework governing consumer financial protection was challenging. Before and after EU accession, consumers were exposed to adhesion contracts by which financial institutions could impose whatever terms they liked. In this context, the transposition and application of the Unfair Contract Terms Directive (UCTD)[59] into national law via Law 193/2000 increased consumer financial protection. However, Law 193/2000 became one of Romania's most disputed issues, especially concerning consumer credit agreements. Not only was the constitutionality of the transposing legislation questioned,[60] but high representatives of Romanian supervisory institutions (such as the National Bank) publicly attacked its provisions and the judges who applied them to the benefit of consumers.[61]

Finally, since Romania was severely impacted by the 2008 financial crisis and in urgent need of credit, the financial lobby influenced governmental policies on consumer financial protection. In 2013, the International Monetary Fund (IMF) publicly denounced consumer protection against abusive contract terms in consumer credit agreements, claiming that it could undermine the entire financial system.[62] Nevertheless, the most egregious example was the Government's 2014 written commitment to the IMF to refrain from enacting personal insolvency legislation or any other mechanism of consumer debt relief that might impact 'payment discipline'.[63]

These developments reveal two antagonistic positions on consumer financial protection legislation. One, adopted by the financial industry and endorsed by the Government and the National Bank, pressed for a limitation on (if not removal of) consumer protection mechanisms. The other, adopted by a handful of Parliament members and consumer activists, advocated for more vigorous enforcement, regulation and debt relief mechanisms to alleviate the effects of the 2008 credit crunch.

Since this antagonism is manifest in the legislature and often leads to opposition between the legislative and executive powers, conflicts over consumer financial protection laws frequently end up on constitutional turf. Thus, the RCC acts as an arbiter in

---

[58] Law 4/1973, Art 22. The minimum down payment and the maximum term for repayment were determined based on the monthly salary or pension at contract signing and varied from 20–30%, depending on the credit term (15–25 years).

[59] Council Directive 93/13/EEC of 5 April 1993 on unfair terms in consumer contracts [1993] OJ L95/29.

[60] See section III.B.

[61] 'Isarescu „abuzeaza" inteligenta clientilor: ai semnat, iti asumi clauzele abuzive!' *Banking News* (8 August 2013) at https://bankingnews.ro/isarescu-clauzele-abuzive.html (accessed 3 November 2022).

[62] 'Isarescu: Intr-un stat de drept, clientii trebuie sa isi asume contractele semnate cu bancile' *Wall-Street* (7 August 2013) at https://www.wall-street.ro/articol/Finante-Banci/152375/isarescu-clauze-abuzive-clienti.html (accessed 3 November 2022).

[63] Romania: Letter of Intent, Memorandum of Economic and Financial Policies, and Technical Memorandum of Understanding (5 March 2014) para 37 at www.imf.org/External/NP/LOI/2014/ROU/030514.pdf (accessed 3 November 2022).

these legislative clashes. Its case law impacts the national private legal order concerning consumer contracts, highlighting the increasing significance of the constitutionalisation of Romanian consumer financial law. Constitutionalisation is generally regarded as a process that improves a legal order (often, one that is biased and driven by neoliberal ideology) by appealing to human and fundamental rights.[64] However, its manifestation in Romania is not entirely 'noble'. On the contrary, the RCC's jurisprudence reveals a somewhat contradictory approach.

At the inception of the new millennium, the RCC adopted a consumer-friendly stance. Indeed, it rejected most pleas against the constitutionality of the transposition of EU consumer protection norms, such as those prescribed by the UCTD or the Consumer Credit Directive (CCD).[65] The Court seems to have rejected the idea of a stronger juristocracy at the expense of democratic policies, despite emphasising the role of ordinary courts in adjudicating consumer financial matters.[66]

This stance shifted in the aftermath of the 2008 financial crisis. Since then, the RCC has repeatedly struck down – either on the merits or on procedural grounds – national legislative projects providing consumers with debt relief mechanisms or increased protection against creditors. The Court has even amended legal provisions to bring them into line with its interpretation of the Constitution, substantively changing the intended mechanisms and altering the legislator's will.

The RCC's overstepping of its constitutional powers involves another peculiar characteristic: it went against the trend among EU Member States of remedying social crises through legislative interventions, instead safeguarding market interests in order to preserve the adjudicatory role of ordinary courts. Put differently, the Court sacrificed consumer financial protection measures that would have mitigated the harm caused by the 2008 financial crisis in order to preserve the primacy of the national judiciary. This approach distinguishes the RCC from other constitutional bodies in Central and Eastern Europe.

B. The Role of the Romanian Constitutional Court

According to the Romanian Constitution, the RCC is an independent authority[67] whose members are politically appointed.[68] It is the guarantor of the supremacy of the Constitution[69] and the sole authority on constitutional jurisdiction in Romania.[70] Its express powers include adjudicating the constitutionality of laws before their promulgation upon notification (*a priori* control)[71] and deciding on objections concerning

---

[64] H Micklitz, 'Introduction' in H Micklitz (ed), *Constitutionalization of European Private Law* (Oxford University Press, 2014) 1.

[65] Directive 2008/48/EC of the European Parliament and of the Council of 23 April 2008 on credit agreements for consumers and repealing Council Directive 87/102/EEC [2008] OJ L133/66.

[66] See section III.C.

[67] Constitution (n 3) Art 145.

[68] ibid Art 142(2)–(3).

[69] ibid Art 142(1) and Law 47/1992 (n 4) Art 1(1).

[70] Law 47/1992 (n 4) Art 1(2).

[71] Constitution (n 3) Art 146 a) and Law 47/1992 (n 4) Art 11(1) A. a).

the unconstitutionality of extant laws and ordinances brought before courts of law or commercial arbitration (*a posteriori* control).[72] Before promulgation, the legal standing of those entitled to challenge constitutionality is limited to public officials or institutions (for example, the Presidency). After promulgation, any party justifying a personal interest can bring an unconstitutionality plea in front of judicial bodies.[73]

The decisions of the RCC are published in the Official Gazette of Romania, after which they are generally binding.[74] If legal provisions are found unconstitutional before promulgation, the Parliament must reconsider them and bring them into line with the RCC's decision.[75] Should extant legal provisions be found unconstitutional, their legal effects are suspended de jure and cease within 45 days of publication if the Parliament or Government cannot bring them into line with the Constitution.[76]

The distinction between laws before promulgation and laws that are in force is relevant because before promulgation, a reference to the RCC's decision implies that the Court could impose directions for the Parliament. In contrast, in the case of laws in force, a reference to the Constitution implies that the Court's role is limited to stating whether the provision in question is constitutional;[77] it can neither instruct the legislator on how to fix it nor fix it of its own accord. In other words, while the RCC is competent to control the constitutionality of statutes in concrete private law cases brought before civil courts, its assessment remains *in abstracto*. This limitation distinguishes the RCC from other Continental European legal systems with written constitutions in which the court can adjudicate on the correct interpretation of the constitution in private law cases.[78]

The powers of the RCC are listed in the Constitution.[79] This enumeration appears exhaustive, even if the final item enables the Court to carry out other duties stipulated by its governing law.[80] However, there is no doubt concerning the interpretation of constitutional provisions: the governing law expressly states that the RCC 'shall not be competent to modify or to supplement the provisions under review'.[81] Thus, the RCC cannot render a decision adding to or amending the provisions of the law under review without overstepping its constitutional powers. Unfortunately, neither the Constitution nor the governing law specifies the outcome of such a breach of constitutional boundaries.

The RCC seldom refers to EU law or to the case law of the Court of Justice of the European Union (CJEU) in its decisions, and it maintains the principle of sovereignty in relation to EU law and institutions with respect to constitutional control. In its

---

[72] Constitution (n 3) Art 146 d) and Law 47/1992 (n 4) Art 11(1) A. d).

[73] 'Settlement of the exception of unconstitutionality' at www.ccr.ro/en/settlement-of-the-exception-of-unconstitutionality/ (accessed 3 November 2022).

[74] Constitution (n 3) Art 147(4) and Law 47/1992 (n 4) Art 11(3).

[75] Constitution (n 3) Art 147(2) and Law 47/1992 (n 4) Art 18(3).

[76] Constitution (n 3) Art 147(1) and Law 47/1992 (n 4) Art 31(3).

[77] Under Law 47/1992 (n 4) Art 31(2), if the unconstitutionality plea is admitted, the Court will also pronounce on the constitutionality of other provisions of the normative act being challenged, from which those mentioned in the referral act cannot obviously and necessarily be dissociated.

[78] A Ciacchi, 'The Constitutionalization of European Contract Law: Judicial Convergence and Social Justice' (2006) 2 *European Review of Contract Law* 169.

[79] Constitution (n 3) Art 146.

[80] ibid Art 146 l).

[81] Law 47/1992 (n 4) Art 2(3).

Decision 623/2016 (which constitutes the core of this chapter),[82] the RCC held that for a European legal provision to be used to assess constitutionality, it must meet two cumulative conditions. First, the provision must either be clear, precise and unequivocal or the CJEU must have clearly and unequivocally established its meaning. Second, the provision must have a certain degree of constitutional relevance such that its normative content supports the idea of an infringement of the Constitution (the only reference norm in constitutional control). In this light, the RCC retains the right to apply CJEU decisions in its assessment of constitutionality or to formulate a preliminary question to the CJEU. However, exercising this option is considered 'an expression of institutional cooperation and judicial dialogue, without acknowledging a hierarchy between the two courts'.[83]

This concept of mere institutional cooperation and judicial dialogue is not new. The RCC developed the doctrine of its sovereignty in a decision regarding a constitutional plea against GEO 50/2008[84] on the introduction of a pollution tax.[85] It held that 'the CJEU has no jurisdiction to rule on the validity or invalidity of national law. The consequence of a given interpretation of the Treaty may be that a provision of national law is incompatible with European law'.[86] It further stated that 'the Constitutional Court is neither a positive legislator nor a court competent to interpret and apply European law in disputes involving the subjective rights of citizens and without reconsidering its case law'.[87] Here, the Court noted that the use of a rule of European law in constitutionality control implies the cumulative conditionality restated in Decision 623/2016. In such a case, the approach of the RCC is distinct from simple application and interpretation of the law, a competence that belongs to the courts and administrative authorities, or from possible issues related to the legislative policy promoted by Parliament or Government, as appropriate.[88]

Through the cumulative conditionality described above, the RCC arrogated the sole discretion to apply CJEU decisions during constitutionality review and to formulate preliminary questions to establish the content of European norms. Moreover, in addition to its claim of a non-hierarchical judicial relationship, the RCC qualified the CJEU's clarification of the European norm in the case at hand within the confines of Article 148(2) of the Constitution: 'the requirements resulting from this judgment are not of constitutional relevance, they are rather related to the obligation of the legislature to enact rules within their meaning or otherwise' (paragraph 13).

To conclude, the Court maintains jurisdictional sovereignty in relation to the CJEU and consistently avoids referring to arguments invoking EU law or case law in its rulings on consumer credit.

---

[82] Decision 623/2016, published in the Official Gazette no 53/18.01.2017.
[83] ibid para 129.
[84] GEO 50/2008 on the introduction of a pollution tax on motor vehicles, published in the Official Gazette no 327/25.04.2008.
[85] Decision 668/2011, published in the Official Gazette no 487/08.07.2011.
[86] ibid para 3.
[87] ibid.
[88] ibid.

III.   The Transformation of Consumer Financial Protection Law Through Constitutional Control

Romanian consumer financial protection law was dramatically transformed at the turn of the millennium when Law 193/2000 transposed the UCTD into national legislation. As a result of the revamping of the banking sector in 1998, the overhaul of credit for residential and personal goods in 1999, the lenient approach of the National Bank and the financial illiteracy of Romanian consumers, most commercial banks and retailers engaged in predatory credit activities. Indeed, most court cases based on Law 193/2000 concerned unfair terms in consumer credit agreements.[89] While such agreements did not necessarily include more unfair terms than other types of contracts, their high financial stakes and long duration increased their impact on consumers' lives. The first public decision on consumer credit was rendered in 2007,[90] coinciding with the first year of Romanian EU membership.

From that moment on, the number of cases alleging the presence of unfair terms in consumer credit agreements rose exponentially. This study employs Mihali-Viorescu's three stages of UCTD-based litigation in consumer credit.[91] The first stage began in 2008–09 with successful court actions initiated by the NACP; it coincided with the first attacks on the constitutionality of transposed EU consumer protection law.

The second stage began in 2010 and was precipitated by (i) implementation of the CCD via GEO 50/2010; (ii) increased public awareness of the possibility to challenge credit agreements in court;[92] and (iii) the social consequences of the 2008 economic crisis, which made most consumers aware of the financial ramifications of their credit agreements. This stage was characterised by numerous disputes, a consolidation of local practice (with some CJEU guidance) and a growing political battle caused by concern in financial circles about the direction of case law.

Finally, the third stage began in late 2013 and early 2014, mainly in connection with foreign currency loans and variable interest clauses. This last stage was slowed by the adoption of Law 77/2016, since most consumer debtors chose to rely on its debt relief mechanism until the RCC's intervention. Each stage involved a degree of transformation of consumer financial protection, either in substance or in approach. As section III.A reveals, one of the leading roles in this transformation was assigned to – and later assumed by – the RCC.

A.   An Overview of RCC Jurisprudence on Consumer Financial Protection

Whether from local initiatives or from transposition of EU law, consumer financial protection legislation has generated a tremendous amount of case law regarding its

---

[89] L Mihali-Viorescu, *Clauzele abuzive in contractele de credit*, 2nd edn (Hamangiu, 2017) 1.
[90] ibid 2.
[91] ibid 2–4.
[92] B Andresan-Grigoriu and M Moraru, 'Country Report Romania' in H Micklitz and I Domurath (eds), *Consumer Debt and Social Exclusion in Europe* (Ashgate, 2015) 117.

constitutionality. The significant areas concern the provisions of or amendments to (i) Law 193/2000 on abusive contract terms in consumer contracts; (ii) GEO 50/2010 on consumer credit agreements; and (iii) Law 77/2016 on *datio in solutum*. In the first instance, especially concerning the constitutionality of Law 193/2000 and GEO 50/2010, RCC jurisprudence displayed the tendency of other European Constitutional Courts towards the constitutionalisation of private law to protect the weaker party, especially in financial matters.[93] The idea behind this phenomenon was to embed new values into private laws to make them more just. The RCC recognised the legislator's exclusive role and afforded a large margin of appreciation for the design of consumer protection rules – even those that may impact economic freedom or property rights.

However, constitutionalisation appears to have had the opposite effect in recent years, especially in relation to Law 77/2016. Indeed, it has disempowered consumers by limiting the legislative advantages they were granted for the sake of social justice, placing the RCC in opposition to its European counterparts. This shift encouraged certain actors to resort to strategic litigation before the RCC to thwart legislative efforts that could alleviate the effects of the 2008 financial crisis through consumer debt relief.

Sections III.B and III.C cover decisions on Law 193/2000 and GEO 50/2010, respectively, while those addressing Law 77/2016 are discussed separately in section IV. The analysis is limited to critical topics since an exhaustive presentation would go beyond the chapter's limits.

B. Case Law Concerning Law 193/2000

The first public Decision of the RCC on Law 193/2000 may be traced back to 2007[94] and coincides with the first case on abusive terms in consumer credit agreements resolved by ordinary courts. Since then, 72 unconstitutionality pleas have been raised against the Law. The RCC has ruled on 67 of them, all of which were rejected. Five more pleas are pending.

The RCC's case law concerning Law 193/2000 is generally consistent and focuses on several areas: the need for enhanced consumer protection, restrictions on economic freedom and rights (including the property right) and the Law's temporal application. The Court's holdings regarding the roles of the legislature and the courts are also discussed.

In the view of the RCC, consumer protection against abusive contract terms stems from the prevalence of adhesion contracts. In these contracts, consumers have only the option to accept or reject the terms imposed on them by professionals.[95]

---

[93] OO Cherednichenko, 'Fundamental Rights' in OO Cherednichenko, *Contract Law and the Protection of the Weaker Party: A Comparative Analysis of the Constitutionalisation of Contract Law, with Emphasis on Risky Financial Transactions* (Sellier, 2007) 4.

[94] Decision 1157/2007, published in the Official Gazette no 5/04.01.2008.

[95] Decision 11/2013, published in the Official Gazette no 110/25.02.2013; Decision 321/2013, published in the Official Gazette no 441/19.07.2013; Decision 779/2020, published in the Official Gazette no 409/19.04.2021, para 7; Decision 245/2016, published in the Official Gazette no 546/20.07.2016, para 44.

The RCC acknowledges that the protection system established by Law 193/2000 is based on the idea that consumers are in a weaker position to sellers or suppliers in terms of both bargaining power and level of information. This leads them to adhere to conditions drawn up in advance without the opportunity to modify their content.[96] For the Court, this imbalance between consumers and professionals justifies legal protection.[97]

According to the RCC, the judge examines an adhesion contract's terms *in abstracto* (that is, whether they are likely to cause a significant economic imbalance between the consumer and trader in general) and assesses them by reference to an ideal balance. It is not essential that the effect of the clause is about to occur or has already occurred; the clause does not have to affect the consumer's assets in order to be deemed unfair.[98]

The sanction against professionals who take advantage of consumers' situation is elimination of unfair terms. This measure also protects debtors who would otherwise be placed in a disproportionately burdensome situation.[99] Moreover, professionals must amend all ongoing adhesion contracts following a finding of unfair terms.[100]

According to the RCC, economic freedom does not mean that there should be no framework to ensure the functioning of a viable market economy in which consumers are protected from abuse by operators in a position of economic strength.[101] Thus, provisions such as those on unfair contract terms merely establish the legal framework for professional activities and ensure a just balance between the interests of professionals and consumers.

The RCC also clarified that the Constitution does not protect or guarantee property rights for monetary gain resulting from unfair terms. On the contrary, the fundamental law obliges the legislator to regulate methods of recovering these amounts (*actio pauliana*, confiscation or action for annulment). The legislator must implement a legislative framework to prevent the creditor from acquiring amounts payable in the future due to unfair terms.[102]

In other words, consumer protection measures do not contradict or infringe on professionals' rights. Any limitations on those individual rights are constitutional given the legislator's intent to protect societal interests, including those of consumers.

Once a court establishes the abusive character of unfair terms, those terms cannot continue to affect ongoing adhesion contracts and must be removed. The professional must also remove unfair terms from pre-formulated contracts still used in the professional's business.[103] However, these effects are not retroactive.

---

[96] Decision 245/2016 (n 95) paras 42 and 46; Decision 214/2017, published in the Official Gazette no 573/18.07.2017, para 21; Decision 779/2020 (n 95) para 6.

[97] Decision 11/2013 (n 95); Decision 214/2017 (n 96) paras 22–23; Decision 455/2017, published in the Official Gazette no 755/21.09.2017, para 22; Decision 525/2018, published in the Official Gazette no 64/25.01.2019, para 15; Decision 468/2019, published in the Official Gazette no 877/31.10.2019, para 20.

[98] Decision 245/2016 (n 95) para 40; Decision 779/2020 (n 95) para 5.

[99] Decision 11/2013 (n 95); Decision 321/2013 (n 95); Decision 245/2016 (n 95) paras 43 and 46; Decision 214/2017 (n 96) para 39.

[100] Decision no 321/2013 (n 95); Decision 245/2016 (n 95) para 55; Decision 602/2016, published in the Official Gazette no 71/27.01.2017, para 33.

[101] Decision 11/2013 (n 95); Decision 214/2017 (n 96) para 37.

[102] Decision 245/2016 (n 95) para 60.

[103] ibid para 66.

In Romania, the non-retroactivity of civil law is a constitutional matter because it can only produce future effects.[104] In other words, the law can only apply to 'new legal situations' that emerge after its entry into force. Unfortunately, there is no clarity regarding what might constitute a new legal situation. However, the RCC does not appear to have concerns regarding the temporal application of Law 193/2000; it has consistently maintained[105] that

> a law is not retroactive when it modifies for the future a previously existing legal situation, nor when it abolishes the future effects of a legal situation created under the old law because in these cases the new law merely regulates the course of action in the period following its entry into force, ie, in its own field of application. It follows that the retroactivity of the law concerns the modification of a situation for the past and not the different regulation of a legal situation for the future.[106]

As this position makes clear, services already provided under the contract cannot be undone. Nevertheless, the professional can no longer benefit from the advantages obtained based on unfair terms. Still, disallowing unfair terms from producing effects does not mean that a judgment rendered under Law 193/2000 applies retroactively.[107] If the professional knows that they may not insert abusive clauses in consumer contracts, the subsequent establishment of a judicial mechanism to ensure compliance with this obligation does not amount to retroactive application of that remedy.[108]

In its jurisprudence on unfair terms in consumer (credit) agreements, the RCC has consistently held that the legislature could implement measures to protect the consumer as the weaker party.[109] It has also acknowledged the legislature's right to adopt more stringent rules to enhance consumer protection.[110]

The limits of these protections – in particular, who qualifies as a consumer – were held to be within the Parliament's exclusive competence as the country's sole legislative power. Since the RCC's competence is limited to evaluating provisions' constitutionality, it could not cure potential omissions of the law since 'amending or supplementing legal rules were the exclusive powers' of the legislature.[111] Thus, the Court rejected the option of a stronger juristocracy that would deny the Parliament its constitutional role as the sole legislative power.

---

[104] Constitution (n 3) Art 15(2).

[105] Decision 784/2010, published in the Official Gazette no 608/27.08.2010.

[106] Decision 245/2016 (n 95) para 49; Decision 602/2016 (n 100) para 23; Decision 214/2017 (n 96) para 26; Decision 779/2020 (n 95) para 22.

[107] Decision 245/2016 (n 95) para 50; Decision 602/2016 (n 100) para 24; Decision 214/2017 (n 96) para 27; Decision 779/2020 (n 95) para 23.

[108] Decision 602/2016 (n 100) para 28.

[109] Decision 11/2013 (n 95); Decision 321/2013 (n 95); Decision 360/2013, published in the Official Gazette no 718/21.11.2013; Decision 245/2016 (n 95) para 44.

[110] Decision 245/2016 (n 96) para 48; Decision 214/2017 (n 96) para 25.

[111] Decision 1157/2007 (n 94); Decision 1129/2008, published in the Official Gazette no 776/19.11.2008; Decision 621/2012, published in the Official Gazette no 487/17.07.2012; Decision 213/2014, published in the Official Gazette no 459/24.06.2014, para 13; Decision 455/2017 (n 97) paras 12–13; Decision 400/2018, published in the Official Gazette no 946/06.11.2018, para 13.

C. Case Law Concerning GEO 50/2010

Further constitutional challenges concerned the provisions and amendments proposed or implemented for GEO 50/2010. The RCC's website lists 35 cases settled via 16 decisions, the latest dating from 2019.[112] Two more pleas were registered in 2022 and are currently pending. In addition, nine pleas were raised against GEO 52/2016 on consumer mortgage agreements,[113] which also modified GEO 50/2010. These were all settled in 2020 by a single decision (Decision 500/2020), referenced in this section.

Unlike the cases regarding Law 193/2000, a division is evident in the Court's position regarding consumer protection measures, especially concerning debt relief mechanisms (*datio in solutum*, currency conversions)[114] or enhanced protection against assignment of debt to professional debt collectors (caps on what debt collectors may recover after purchasing debt portfolios at discounted prices). The RCC also tended to reject any amendment proposed for the transposing instruments of EU consumer legislation that would implement national solutions for national problems.[115]

The starting point in the constitutional assessment of legislation that transposed the CCD is its adoption context – namely, an attempt to limit the effects of the financial crisis on the national economy. The Court referenced the Explanatory Memorandum, which expressly noted the impact of the crisis on individual incomes. In the Court's view, this indicated that GEO 50/2010 constitutes a genuine protective measure for consumers falling within its scope.[116]

In addition to the socio-economic context, the RCC noted two other strong arguments justifying adoption of consumer financial protection measures. First, EU law obliged the national legislator to transpose the CCD or face infringement procedure. Second, failure to transpose legislation on consumer credit agreements deprived consumers of the mobility rights arising from the European normative act, with a direct impact on consumer income (namely, ability to switch to other creditors offering better credit terms and the possibility of repaying contracted amounts without excessive penalties).[117] In the eyes of the Court, these considerations jointly justified the implementation of more robust consumer financial protection.

---

[112] Decision 140/2019, published in the Official Gazette no 377/14.05.2019. All decisions can be consulted on the CCR's website at www.ccr.ro, section 'Jurisprudenta'.

[113] Government Emergency Ordinance 52/2016 on credit agreements offered to consumers for real estate, as well as on amending and supplementing Government Emergency Ordinance no. 50/2010 on credit agreements for consumers, published in the Official Gazette no 727/2016.

[114] Following the RCC's Decision 623/2016 (n 82), all debt relief mechanisms appear to have been circumscribed to the doctrine of unforeseeability developed by the Court; see section IV of this chapter.

[115] L Bercea, 'Riscul valutar, impreviziunea si conversia creditelor in valuta' (2017) 1 *Revista Romana de Drept Privat* 24.

[116] Decision 1446/2011, published in the Official Gazette no 895/16.12.2011; Decision 1540/2011, published in the Official Gazette no 151/07.03.2012; Decision 1541/2011, published in the Official Gazette no 151/07.03.2012; Decision 1622/2011, published in the Official Gazette no 156/08.03.2012; Decision 169/2012, published in the Official Gazette no 271/24.04.2012; Decision 450/2012, published in the Official Gazette no 507/24.07.2012; Decision 1059/2012, published in the Official Gazette no 73/04.02.2013.

[117] Decision 1446/2011 (n 116); Decision 1540/2011 (n 116); Decision 1541/2011 (n 116); Decision 1622/2011 (n 116); Decision 169/2012 (n 116); Decision 450/2012 (n 116); Decision 1059/2012 (n 116); Decision 490/2020, published in the Official Gazette no 968/21.10.2020, para 18.

Here, too, temporal application was a contentious issue. Industry representatives contended that any new consumer legislation could only apply to credit contracts concluded in the future, otherwise the law would have retroactive effect. The matter was first raised in a plea concerning the CCD's transposition via a GEO in 2010. According to the constitutional provisions, any GEO must be subsequently approved by the Parliament. However, the Parliament amended GEO 50/2010's original text via the approving law, affecting some of its effects and temporal application.[118] In particular, an article was introduced to the effect that the ordinance would not apply to pending contracts (but for a few minor exceptions). A majority of the RCC panel found no problem with this amendment, which limited the original application of GEO 50/2010.[119]

Nevertheless, a minority opinion raised strong objections, arguing that the newly inserted provision was discriminatory. In the dissenters' view, consumer credit agreements were contracts with successive performance in time. Each obligation (instalment) already performed produced its effects under the law that governed it, while future obligations would be governed by the law in force at the time. Therefore, they argued, the new law must apply to debtors with pending credit agreements.

The dissenters' concern was that the disputed amendments to GEO 50/2010 disadvantaged only one party: the consumer. They also denounced the financial lobby, given the Government's argument that the European Commission and the IMF had required the changes as a precondition for extending a loan. In their view, the state should protect national interests rather than those of international commercial banks in economic, financial and currency activities.[120]

The RCC also held that a law is not retroactive when it modifies a previously existing legal situation for the future:[121] GEO 50/2010 was constitutional because it only imposed future obligations, obliging creditors to transparently recalculate interest and to eliminate fees charged in the past, as a credit agreement is a contract with successive performance in time.[122]

This approach, which reflects the dissenting opinion expressed in 2010, survived until 2021, when the RCC aligned its position[123] with that of the High Court of Cassation and Justice:

> [B]y its nature, the credit agreement, as a variety of the loan agreement, is a one-time contract, and the fact that the bank assumes an obligation that is performed at once and the other party assumes an obligation of successive repayment does not make it successive in nature, since it cannot be of a dual nature, with one party performing at once and the other party performing successively, the repayment of the loan with interest in monthly instalments being only one

---

[118] Andresan-Grigoriu and Moraru (n 92) 133.
[119] Decision 1656/2010, published in the Official Gazette no 79/31.01.2011.
[120] ibid Dissenting Opinion.
[121] Decision 1446/2011 (n 116); Decision 1540/2011 (n 116); Decision 1541/2011 (n 116); Decision 1622/2011 (n 116); Decision 169/2012 (n 116); Decision 450/2012 (n 116); Decision 1059/2012 (n 116), Decision 140/2019 (n 112) para 66.
[122] Decision 1446/2011 (n 116); Decision 1540/2011 (n 116); Decision 1541/2011 (n 116); Decision 1622/2011 (n 116); Decision 169/2012 (n 116); Decision 450/2012 (n 116); Decision 1059/2012 (n 116); Decision 490/2020 (n 117) para 24.
[123] Decision 623/2019, published in the Official Gazette no 981/05.12.2019.

way of performing the obligation, the repayment obligation being a single one, the successive instalments forming by their nature a single whole.[124]

Consequently, pending consumer agreements remained entirely governed by the law in force at their signing and could not benefit from the amended provisions of GEO 50/2010.

This decision had significant consequences for consumers. In one instance, the amendment to GEO 50/2010 removed the direct executory character of credit agreements assigned to professional debt collectors. This removal made any enforcement action taken by subsequent creditors subject to prior judicial control.[125] The RCC acknowledged the legislator's right to withdraw the agreements' executory character[126] but held that since

> direct enforceability is a characteristic of the claim, being an integral element of its legal regime … a new rule withdrawing the direct enforceability of a credit agreement assigned to a debt recovery entity cannot, objectively speaking, concern credit agreements concluded before it entered into force, but only future agreements concluded from the date of entry into force. Consequently, the temporal scope of the new legislation cannot be extended to credit agreements in progress since such an option – of using the method of performance of the agreement as a criterion for the application of the text in question – is excluded from the legislature's discretion.[127]

Tying direct enforceability to the credit agreement (the old contract) rather than the assignment (the new contract) excluded more agreements from the consumer protection rules instated by GEO 50/2010. Thus, through constitutionalisation, the RCC delayed application of the rules and artificially deprived consumers of their legal protections.

In its jurisprudence on the transposition of consumer credit law, the RCC reasserts the Parliament's exclusive competence as the country's sole legislative power.[128] The Court also maintains and develops its previous holdings that its own competence is limited to assessing constitutionality; it states that to act otherwise would subrogate the legislature's role and violate its governing law. It further adds that it

> can neither rule on provisions de lege ferenda, as it has no power to amend the provisions of the law subject to constitutionality review, nor does it have the power to create new legal norms by supplementing an existing legal text, but only to verify the conformity of existing norms with constitutional requirements and to establish their constitutionality or unconstitutionality.[129]

Despite the above, section IV reveals that the RCC did not follow this approach when assessing constitutionality pleas in connection with the *Datio in Solutum* Law.

---

[124] Decision 500/2020, published in the Official Gazette no 11/06.01.2021, para 37.
[125] ibid paras 40–42.
[126] ibid paras 47–48.
[127] ibid para 49.
[128] Decision 1656/2010 (n 119).
[129] Decision 500/2020 (n 124) para 51.

IV. Transforming Consumer Financial Protection by Overstepping Constitutional Powers

Romania was one of those European countries most affected by the 2008 credit crunch. Its real-estate bubble was based on mortgages financed in foreign currency, mainly euros (EUR) and Swiss francs (CHF). In the aftermath, many Romanians struggled with over-indebtedness[130] and faced eviction from their homes.[131] This profound social crisis urgently required a solution. However, the inadequate regulatory framework for consumer protection related to financial services and debt collection amplified its effects.[132]

The task of addressing and resolving the unfair effects of a broken system was left to the legislators. The solution to the *social force majeure*, as Domurath labelled it,[133] had to be political. A judicial solution based on case-by-case analysis was not feasible in terms of time or resources. Alternative options were considered: (i) a personal insolvency law, or (ii) a debt relief mechanism. Romania opted for the latter. Notwithstanding the chosen solution, it was necessary to address ongoing situations to alleviate the effects of the crisis.

A personal bankruptcy act was adopted in 2015, but its entry into force was postponed until the beginning of 2018 because the institutional framework was still not finalised.[134] Thus, it was surprising that Law 77/2016 on *datio in solutum* came into force despite strong lobbying against it (from the National Bank and the Romanian Presidency). Though imperfect, this solution attempted to deal with a profound social crisis by sharing the responsibility between the contractual parties instead of placing it entirely on consumers.

A. The *Datio in Solutum* Law

Law 77/2016 established a debt relief mechanism that favoured over-indebted consumers engaged in mortgage agreements. It provided them with the right to pay off the entirety of their debts arising from a mortgage contract, at no additional cost, by surrendering the mortgaged property to the creditor in full payment of the debt unless the parties reached another agreement within a certain period.[135] The law applied to 'credit

---

[130] Andresan-Grigoriu and Moraru (n 92) 118–21.

[131] Out of 6.1 million borrowers, about 716,000 were in arrears; Cosmin Pam Matei, 'Câţi debitori pot beneficia de legea "dai casa şi scapi de datorii"' Coditianul.ro (2 December 2015) at www.cotidianul.ro/cati-debitori-pot-beneficia-de-legea-dai-casa-si-scapi-de-datorii-272329/ (accessed 3 November 2015).

[132] C Macovei 'Highlights of the Romanian Perspective of Datio in Solutum for Consumer Borrowers' (2019) 24 *Tilburg Law Review* 89, 89–104.

[133] I Domurath, 'A Map of Responsible Lending and Responsible Borrowing in the EU and Suggestions for a Stronger Legal Framework to Prevent Over-Indebtedness of European Consumers' in Micklitz and Domurath (eds) (n 92) 155.

[134] As per Government Emergency Ordinance 98/2016, Law 151/2015 on the insolvency procedure for natural persons, was supposed to come into force on 1 August 2017. Subsequently, by Government Ordinance 6/2017, the term was extended until 1 January 2018.

[135] Macovei (n 132).

agreements in progress at the time of its entry into force and to contracts concluded after that date.'[136]

The release effect concerned only part of the debt: the difference between the market price of the mortgaged house and the amount of credit. Before the law, once a mortgaged property was repossessed and foreclosed, aggrieved consumers – even after being expelled from their houses – could be pursued for residual payments, putting them in a worse situation than a bankrupt undertaking. Thus, the legislator resorted to an analogy with insolvency law, arguing that relinquishing the property to the lender and wiping out the remaining debt would provide consumer debtors with a clean slate and a fresh start.[137] The legislator further stated that it would be unfair to let the consumer bear all the risk and costs of a mortgage contract in a volatile market such as real estate.[138] As a professional lender, the bank must have known the risks posed by the contract better than the consumer and should have disclosed them.

The Explanatory Memorandum to Law 77/2016 addressed the two-sided issue of inequity and the 'unfair allocation of contractual risk between the creditor and debtor'.[139] The credit institution was equally responsible for issuing credit against an unrealistic value of the mortgaged asset since its experts had valued the property and misinformed consumers.

The Law stirred many reactions both inside and outside Romania. Attorneys and bankers criticised it via both economic and legal arguments.[140] As in Croatia, Hungary and Poland, the financial lobby invoked Bilateral Investment Treaties (BITs) and threatened investor–state arbitration if the Law entered into force,[141] causing the Government to denounce the intra-EU BITs in place at the time.[142] Representatives of the European Commission and financial institutions also spoke against the Law.[143] Meanwhile, consumer protection organisations denounced the hypocrisy of the EU regulatory bodies, which were seen as disregarding consumer interests in favour of the banks.[144]

---

[136] Law 77/2016 (n 8) Art 11.

[137] Explanatory Memorandum of Law 77/2016, para 4 at www.cdep.ro/proiecte/2015/700/40/3/em951.pdf (accessed 3 November 2022).

[138] ibid para 1.

[139] ibid; see also para 4 on contractual risk allocation. Law 77/2016 (n 8), Art 1, para 1, thus states that it is applicable to legal relationships between consumers and credit institutions, non-banking financial institutions or assignees of consumer debt.

[140] A very one-sided approach, signed mainly by the attorneys and representatives of the biggest Romanian banks, is presented in V Stoica (ed), *Legea darii in plata. Argumente si solutii*, 1st edn (Hamangiu, 2016).

[141] D Popa, 'Darea in plata. Raiffeisen a notificat deja Statul roman ca se va adresa instantelor internationale pentru incalcarea tratatelor privind siguranta investitiilor. Ce raspund Finantele?' HotNews.ro (24 August 2016) at economie.hotnews.ro/stiri-finante_banci-21245079-darea-plata-raiffeisen-notificat-statul-roman-adresa-instantelor-internationale-pentru-incalcarea-tratetelor-privind-siguranta-investitiilor-raspund-ministerul-finantelor.htm (accessed 3 November 2022).

[142] ibid. Another reason for denouncing intra-EU BITs was the infringement procedure launched against Romania by the European Commission in 2015, European Commission, 'Press Release: Commission asks Member States to terminate their intra-EU bilateral investment treaties' (18 June 2015) europa.eu/rapid/press-release_IP-15-5198_en.htm accessed 3 November 2022.

[143] 'Comisia Europeana averizeaza: Legea darii in plata si cresterea salariului minim, riscuri pentru Romania' *Mediafax.ro* (3 Mai 2016) www.mediafax.ro/economic/comisia-europeana-avertizeaza-legea-darii-in-plata-si-cresterea-salariului-minim-riscuri-pentru-romania-15280996 accessed 3 November 2022.

[144] D Popa, 'Promulgarea legii darii in plata adanceste fractura dintre clienti si bancheri. Ultimii sunt dezamagiti de Iohannis, in timp ce primii acuza doi comisari europeni ca tin partea bancilor/ Legea a fost publicata in Monitorul Oficial' *HotNew.ro* (28 April 2026) at economie.hotnews.ro/

Despite these criticisms, the enacted version of the Law met most 'best practice' guidelines regarding *datio in solutum*.[145] First, creditors and debtors had to belong to categories mentioned explicitly by the law.[146] Second, a cap on the loaned amount was set at EUR 250,000.[147] Third, the credit must have been either (i) granted for purchasing, extending and renovating a home, or (ii) guaranteed by an immovable used as a home (notwithstanding the purpose of the credit).[148]

The Law was not consumer-friendly in all respects, as it failed to take into account consumers' equity acquired in the mortgaged property via payments already made. In addition, if several assets secured the loan, they all had to be surrendered to the creditor. These provisions dissuaded consumers from surrendering a mortgaged property in which they had invested significant amounts.

However, the choice to use *datio in solutum* belonged entirely to the debtor; it was not conditioned on the commencement of enforcement proceedings by the initial or subsequent creditor(s). This was something the financial industry could not accept, and the industry began a concerted effort to have the Law struck down as unconstitutional. The banks raised no fewer than 700 unconstitutionality pleas.[149] The most relevant outcomes are discussed in section IV.B.

B. The Transformative Impact of RCC Case Law on the *Datio in Solutum* Law: Rewriting Consumer Financial Protection Law

The RCC's case law regarding Law 193/2000 and GEO 50/2010 was largely (though not entirely) consistent in rejecting forms of constitutionalisation that would lead to legislative alterations and strengthen juristocracy. However, the same cannot be said about the jurisprudence concerning the *Datio in Solutum* Law, where the Court assumed the legislator's role and transformed the legislature's intent in order to preserve case-by-case adjudication by ordinary courts.

Perhaps the most impactful decisions on consumer financial protection are Decisions 623/2016[150] and 731/2019,[151] in which the RCC considered the constitutionality of Law 77/2016 on *datio in solutum*. The importance of these decisions stems from two aspects. First, the RCC did not stop at assessing the Law's constitutionality

---

stiri-finante_banci-20964972-promulgarea-legii-darii-plata-adanceste-fractura-dintre-clienti-bancheri-utimii-sunt-dezamagiti-iohannis-timo-primii-acuza-doi-comisari-europeni-tin-partea-bancilor-nu-consumatorilor.htm (accessed 3 November 2022).

[145] London Economics, 'Study on means to protect consumers in financial difficulty: Personal bankruptcy, datio in solutum of mortgages, and restrictions on debt collection abusive practices' (December 2012) Final Report, Contract no MARKT/2011/023/B2/ST/FC 218 at ec.europa.eu/info/sites/default/files/file_import/debt_solutions_report_en_0.pdf (accessed 3 November 2022).

[146] Law 77/2016 (n 8) Art 4, para 1, letter a) corroborated with Art 1, para 1.

[147] ibid Art 4, para 1, letter b).

[148] ibid Art 4, para 1, letter c).

[149] E B, 'CCR admite unele exceptii de neconstitutionalitate la Legea dării in plată' *Revista 22* (25 October 2016) at http://revista22.ro/70257446/ccr-admite-unele-exceptii-de-neconstitutionalitate-la-legea-drii-n-plat.html (accessed 3 November 2022).

[150] Decision 623/2016 (n 82).

[151] Decision 731/2019 published in the Official Gazette no 59/29.01.2020.

but corrected it, thus overstepping its constitutional powers. In Decision 623/2016, it developed a mandatory doctrine of 'unforeseeability' (in Romanian, '*impreviziune*') for national courts to apply in cases concerning *datio in solutum* in consumer mortgage agreements.[152] Second, the RCC expanded this doctrine to all types of contractual obligations by Decision 731/2019, thus removing the consumer protection character intended for Law 77/2016. In this manner, specific legislation establishing a debt relief mechanism for over-indebted consumers was completely transformed by constitutionalisation and deprived of its protective character.

i. Stage I: *The Doctrine of Unforeseeability as a Consumer Protection Mechanism*

It is said that the road to hell is paved with good intentions: Romania's *Datio in Solutum* Law is no exception. Its adversaries objected to the law's so-called 'retroactive' effect (that is, its application to ongoing contracts),[153] and they asked for the Law to be applicable either solely in the future or to be repealed.[154] They also contended that the Law contradicts EU legislation and violates the European Convention on Human Rights (namely, the property right).[155]

However, since the Law was meant to aid debtors affected by the credit crunch by reallocating contractual risks between consumers and creditors, removing ongoing contracts from its scope would have deprived it of its purpose. It would also have created a discriminatory regime depending on when consumers took out mortgages, even where the difference was just one day. Ordinary courts had endorsed this opinion (at least before the RCC rendered its first decisions), holding that

> [t]he legislator adopted this special law to protect those who contracted credits and who were and continue to be in an inferior position in relation to banking institutions, who benefit from relevant information and who can better appreciate with regard to the performance of the contract … The state has a large margin in assessing the necessary measures to address such situations, and the European legislation does not oppose states legislating or adopting measures to protect certain individuals in special situations. One must remember that special situations ask for urgent and special measures which concern not only the bank's profit but also a real protection for debtors.[156]

True to its position on Law 193/2000 and GEO 50/2010, the RCC dismissed[157] the plea regarding the Law's retroactive effect.[158] However, it held that the Law was merely a

---

[152] Decision 623/2016 (n 82) paras 115–120.
[153] On the retroactivity of Law 77/2016 (n 8), see the Government's Objections 3 at www.cdep.ro/proiecte/2015/700/40/3/pvg743.pdf (accessed 3 November 2022); and M Nicolae, 'Despre retroactivitatea aşa-zisei legi de dare în plată' (English trans: 'On the retroactivity of the so-called law for giving in payment') in Stoica (ed) (n 140) 74.
[154] ibid 97.
[155] Decision 917/2016 of Aiud First Instance Court and Decision 230/2017 of Bucharest 5th District Court, reproduced in AM Murgoci-Luca, *Legea darii in plata. Practica judiciara adnotata*, 1st edn (Hamangiu, 2017) 256–65.
[156] ibid 258.
[157] Decision 623/2016 (n 82) paras 115, 130–131.
[158] ibid paras 34–36, 113.

particular application of the unforeseeability doctrine to credit contracts,[159] thereby qualifying *datio in solutum* as the effect of a particular type of impossibility to perform the contract due to unforeseen circumstances. The main effect was to limit the Law's application to situations where judicial control verified all the conditions regarding unforeseeability under the Civil Code and Law 77/2016.[160]

Decision 623/2016 is very lengthy, and a complete analysis of its provisions would go beyond the scope of this chapter. In summary, the relevant points are the following:

- In the absence of an agreement between the parties on *datio in solutum*, ordinary courts are empowered and obliged to apply the unforeseeability doctrine, assuming that all the conditions for its existence are met.[161]

- Law 77/2016 applies only if consumers acting in good faith can no longer fulfil their credit agreement obligations following an external event that they could not have foreseen when concluding the agreement.[162]

- Ordinary courts must apply the unforeseeability doctrine to contracts in progress despite opposition from creditors.[163] Procedurally, ordinary courts will verify fulfilment of the criteria set in Law 77/2016 and those of unforeseeability.

- Ordinary courts – which are independent in their assessment – can apply the unforeseeability doctrine, pronouncing a judgment that orders either adaptation or termination of the contract.[164]

The natural consequence of the Decision was that the legislator could not automatically apply the unforeseeability doctrine to a specific category of contracts, such as consumer mortgages. The Court held that the intervention by the legislator proposed in the *Datio in Solutum* Law would be unconstitutional because it would deprive ordinary courts of their role. In this respect, Decision 623/2016 emphasised that the legislator configured the legal framework represented by Law 77/2016 around an *ope legis* mechanism applicable to all ongoing credit agreements. However, the Law's automatic effect reduced the role of ordinary courts to merely verifying that all legal formalities for *datio in solutum* have been met. In the Court's opinion, this deformed the general conditions for applying unforeseeability, which require assessing the merits of each case. Thus, the only acceptable interpretation under the constitutional framework was that ordinary courts should apply the unforeseeability doctrine only if they found that the consumer proved its general conditions.

---

[159] ibid para 115.

[160] The decision was celebrated by scholars and practitioners for providing the Law with the necessary constitutional coherence and for saving the Law by limiting its sphere. I Popa 'Impreviziunea si creditele oferite consumatorilor. Constituie darea in plata si conversia valutara remedii ale impreviziunii?' *Juridice. ro* (27 February 2017) at www.juridice.ro/496153/impreviziunea-si-creditele-oferite-consumatorilor-constituie-darea-plata-si-conversia-valutara-remedii-ale-impreviziunii.html (accessed 3 November 2022); V Stoica, 'O lectura constitutionala, dincoace si dincolo de Legea darii in plata' Juridice.ro at www.juridice.ro/essentials/836/o-lectura-constitutionala-dincoace-si-dincolo-de-legea-darii-in-plata (accessed 3 November 2022).

[161] Decision 623/2016 (n 82) para 119.

[162] ibid.

[163] ibid para 120.

[164] ibid para 121.

Prima facie, the RCC's reasoning was consistent in its rejection of retroactivity claims and its emphasis on the primary role of ordinary courts in case-by-case assessments. However, the RCC's justifications for this choice are often contradictory or based on incorrect interpretations of civil[165] and consumer law. Indeed, Decision 623/2016 undermines the consistency of the RCC's previous (and ensuing) case law concerning the legislature's exclusive role and the Court's inability to add or correct legislation to align it with its interpretation of the Constitution. Ultimately, the Decision alters the legislator's will and transforms the substance of a consumer debt relief mechanism.

The Romanian legal establishment – which took a heavily pro-creditor approach – was not very critical of the RCC's decision, as it was satisfied with the outcome: a debt relief mechanism without relief. Only a few scholars noted some of the inherent issues.[166] In particular, the Court's reasoning created substantial discretion for the ordinary judge in applying the *Datio in Solutum* Law,[167] considerably reducing its scope. Moreover, aspects such as:

- assessment of consumers' good faith;[168]

- assessment of whether the conditions of unforeseeability in contracts are met;[169] and

- the possibility of applying a remedy other than the statutory *datio in solutum*[170]

are all additions to the Law that the Court implements through constitutional 'interpretation'. The result was a different version of the Law than that published in the Official Gazette, which, as one author noted, cannot be applied without the 'user's manual' provided by the Court's Decision.[171]

Furthermore, the added distinctions are questionable or even wrong from the perspective of civil law.[172] The Court distinguished between good- and bad-faith debtors and between those who can no longer pay and those who no longer wish to,[173] inserting a moral condition for the doctrine. However, no such distinction exists in either Law 77/2016 (*lex specialis*) or the NCC (*lex generalis*). The NCC merely stated that if the contract's performance has become excessively onerous because of an exceptional change in circumstances that would make it manifestly unfair to require the debtor to perform the obligation, then the court may order either adjustment of the contract (to distribute fairly between the parties the losses and benefits arising from the changed circumstances) or its termination.[174] According to the NCC, unforeseeability could be applied only if four cumulative conditions were met: (i) the change in circumstances occurred after conclusion of the contract; (ii) the changes and their extent were not and could not reasonably have been foreseen by the debtor when the contract was concluded; (iii) the debtor did not assume the risk arising from the change

---

[165] Popa (n 152).
[166] ibid.
[167] Decision 623/2016 (n 82) paras 94–103, 115–121.
[168] ibid paras 99, 116.
[169] ibid paras 115–121, 127.
[170] ibid para 121.
[171] Popa (n 152).
[172] ibid.
[173] Decision 623/2016 (n 82) para 116.
[174] NCC (n 46), Art 1271(2).

in circumstances and could not reasonably be considered to have assumed that risk; and (iv) the debtor attempted, within a reasonable time and in good faith, to negotiate a reasonable and fair adjustment of the contract.[175] Evidently, none of the provisions in the NCC distinguishes among debtors in the application of unforeseeability. In other words, the Court not only altered application of the doctrine in line with the law under constitutional scrutiny (Law 77/2016) but also modified the general provisions governing it (Civil Code), even though these were not subject to the Court's review.

In addition, the amendment is problematic because it inserted a subjective element when the general doctrine relied eminently on objective elements. As one author noted, 'a wealthier consumer did not have a greater capacity for foresight than a poor consumer, nor one who can pay more than one who cannot pay'.[176] Therefore, the Court's distinction is incorrect because unforeseeability alleviates an imbalance; it does not indirectly sanction debtors who can perform under much more difficult conditions than they imagined at the time of conclusion of the contract.

Nevertheless, the RCC came to an entirely different conclusion:

> The Court ... reiterates that, in the light of the legal framework existing at the time of the conclusion of the credit agreements, the legal provisions at issue must apply only to borrowers who, although they acted in good faith by Article 57 of the Constitution, are no longer able to fulfil their obligations under the credit agreements as a result of the occurrence of an external event which they could not have foreseen at the time of the conclusion of the credit agreement.[177]

The above shows that the RCC constitutionalised its own *datio in solutum* mechanism and developed its own version of unforeseeability – a tougher version to be applied to consumer contracts. Moreover, it excludes consumer debtors who can pay even if the circumstances have changed, causing a severe imbalance in the original economic equilibrium of the credit agreement. The position also implies that the initiation of *datio in solutum* proceedings by such a consumer would be a manifestation of bad faith. This position is a gross interference in legislative policy and an alteration to the provisions of *lex generalis* (the Civil Code) as identified by the RCC.

Another unjustified addition to the *Datio in Solutum* Law is a hierarchy of unforeseeability remedies. Under the RCC's version of the law, if the elements of unforeseeability are met, the civil judge is bound to apply all remedies of unforeseeability as set in *lex generalis* (the Civil Code). However, the judge is not obliged to apply the only legal remedy provided by *lex specialis* (Law 77/2016) if the parties do not agree or the judge does not consider it appropriate.[178] Following the RCC's decision, application of remedies is left to the judge's discretion, violating the legal principle of *specialia generalibus derogant* (the specific derogates from the general). As one author put it, the legal remedy provided by Law 77/2016 became 'only one of the solutions that the judge in the case may adopt',[179] even though the legislator intended it as the only one. Once

---

[175] ibid Art 1271(3).
[176] Popa (n 160).
[177] Decision 623/2016 (n 82) para 119.
[178] ibid para 121.
[179] Popa (n 160).

again, constitutionalisation has severely altered the legal order and artificially deprived consumers of a debt relief mechanism.

Decision 62/2017[180] expanded the unforeseeability doctrine of Decision 623/2016 to other consumer debt relief mechanisms. The Decision concerned amendments to GEO 50/2010 in order to facilitate conversion of Swiss francs to Romanian Lei (RON) at the exchange rate available on contract signing, which were found unconstitutional.

The possibility of converting credits was included in a law amending GEO 50/2010, which obliged creditors to convert into Romanian Lei the balance of all Swiss franc loans at the currency rate valid on contract signing. Only the unpaid part of the principal would have been subject to conversion, but not the entirety of the loan.[181]

As rightly noted, the proposal's mechanism did not reallocate currency-rate fluctuation risks between parties – it removed them (even if only in part).[182] The payments remained well-performed, while the remaining payments were converted into Romanian Lei. Converting the foreign-currency credit balance into national currency using the exchange rate on concluding the contract changed the obligation's economic value in the consumer's favour and to the bank's detriment (in proportion to the ratio between the 'historical' exchange rate and that at the date of conversion). The new exchange rate amounted to a partial legal waiver of the debt that only benefited borrowers of Swiss franc loans. This led Romanian authors to conclude that 'the mechanism of conversion of the obligation does not represent an adaptation of the contract characteristic of the unforeseeability doctrine' because 'it does not redistribute the losses among parties but transfers them from the debtor to the creditor'.[183]

Nevertheless, in its reasoning, the RCC stated that currency conversion was mere application of the unforeseeability doctrine. As a result, conversion had to follow the conditions of previous case law (Decision 623/2016) and ensure judicial control of factual circumstances on a case-by-case basis. The RCC argued that the possibility for creditors to present the factual situation before a court of law is 'necessary given that the judge must verify the situation so that the … [conversion] should not be a discretionary instrument available to only one party and thus cause imbalance to the contractual relationship'.[184] The principles of equality of arms, the rule of law, the right to a fair trial and the administration of justice were the justifications for removing automatic, collective relief for aggrieved consumers. Consumer financial protection might stem from the law, but the judicial filter could not be avoided.

The Decision raised questions as to its implementation because applying the unforeseeability doctrine to conversion created two types of uncertainty: (i) about the level at which the onerous character of the consumer's obligation becomes excessive; and (ii) about adjustment of parameters to redistribute the effects of unforeseeability.[185] Given the absence of guidelines for judicial intervention, the practical application of unforeseeability in cases involving currency conversions was unclear. Although Romanian

---

[180] Decision 62/2017 published in the Official Gazette no 161/03.03.2017.
[181] L Bercea, 'Protecţia consumatorilor prin conversia creditelor în valută' Juridice.ro at www.juridice.ro/essentials/705/protectia-consumatorilor-prin-conversia-creditelor-in-valuta (accessed 3 November 2022).
[182] ibid.
[183] ibid.
[184] Decision 62/2017 (n 180) paras 49–50.
[185] Bercea (n 181).

doctrine attempted to advance some solutions, the primary position is that the court should never affect the creditor's interests other than by extending the repayment term or reducing credit remuneration.[186] In effect, linking the Swiss franc conversion provision to the unforeseeability doctrine eliminated the debt relief mechanism intended by the legislator.

The 'doctrine of unforeseeability' in consumer agreements was further developed in Decision 93/2017,[187] concerning another plea against the surviving provisions of Law 77/2016 on *datio in solutum*. Credit institutions challenged the automatic suspension of payments by consumer debtors once they had filed a notice for *datio in solutum* with the credit institution. This time, the RCC rejected the plea, returning to its earlier view that since the consumer is the weaker party, the legislator can intervene in credit agreements to pursue legitimate purposes such as consumer protection.

However, the Court maintained that the state's discretion must be assessed according to a multi-stage proportionality test developed by the RCC. First, the Court found that although the creditor holds a protected asset represented by the claim under a consumer credit agreement, the state's intervention pursues a legitimate aim, namely to protect consumers by removing the danger of imminent financial ruin; the exercise of the creditor's rights was not absolute.

Second, the Court examined whether the contested measure was appropriate, necessary and in compliance with a fair relationship of proportionality between general and individual interests. It held that temporary suspension of payments during judicial control could fulfil the legitimate aim identified in stage 1. Subsequently, the Court argued that the criticised legal measure is necessary and that the legislator has full constitutional competence (Articles 15(1), 44(1) and 61(1) of the Constitution) to protect citizens' patrimonial interests when an aspect related to unforeseeability intervenes in the paradigm of a credit agreement's performance.

From the panoply of available measures, the legislator chose temporary suspension of payment under a credit agreement, which limits intrusion on the creditor's property. Moreover, the Court observed that

> the legislative orientation has considered the existing socio-economic realities, an issue on which the legislator had a wide margin of appreciation, as well as the particularities and specifics of the circumstances concerning the imminent initiation or continuation of enforcement proceedings with irreparable effects on the consumer, as well as the professional-consumer relationship, in which the latter is in a situation of economic inferiority.[188]

Third, in the last step of the proportionality test, the Court stated that the contested measure constitutes

> a fair proportionality between general and individual interests in the sense that it balances, on the one hand, the immediate and direct protection of consumers … and, on the other hand, the interest of professionals to see their sums of money resulting from credit agreements performed.[189]

---

[186] ibid.
[187] Decision 93/2017 published in the Official Gazette no 383/22.05.2017.
[188] Decision 93/2017 (n 187) para 45.
[189] ibid para 44.

However, this balance of interest fails to consider that – given the constitutionalisation of the unforeseeability doctrine in Decision 623/2016 – Law 77/2016 was left without practical application and was transformed into a non-functional mechanism.

ii. Stage II: The Doctrine of Unforeseeability as a General Civil Law Instrument

Decision 731/2019 is also relevant to consumer mortgage agreements. It concerns the amendments and expansion of Law 77/2016 that legislators implemented in 2019. The amendments attempted to fix the changes wrought by the unforeseeability doctrine developed in Decision 623/2016 and reintroduced statutory unforeseeability cases, forcing the RCC to respond.

In previous decisions, the RCC had seen the measures of Law 77/2016 as preserving general interests, ensuring consumer financial protection and balancing the interests of both professionals and consumers. Now, however, it expanded the unforeseeability doctrine beyond consumer contracts, thus wholly transforming its substantive character.

The Court held that the debtor's right to invoke unforeseeability is not a consumer protection measure because the creditor can also invoke it.[190] It also found that contractual unpredictability does not concern safety of the debtor as a consumer but legal protection of all contractors, regardless of their consumer or professional status. Thus, it stated that the unforeseeability doctrine is not aimed at consumer protection but merely applies the Civil Code.[191]

The Court ruled that while the legislator is competent to regulate cases and implement criteria for unforeseeability, absolute legal presumptions of unforeseeability that remove the case-by-case judiciary control imposed via Decision 623/2016 cannot be accepted.[192] It added that

> the contractual ruin of the debtor must be analysed from the point of view of the existing contractual relationship between the two parties, in the sense that this assessment does not refer to the evolution/fluctuation of the debtor's financial/material situation, but it is limited, exclusively, to the balance between the contractual benefits of the parties.[193]

The removal of the word 'consumer' from the unforeseeability doctrine precludes the state from interfering with consumer credit under what the RCC had previously called 'a legitimate aim to pursue consumer protection' (based on a power imbalance between consumers and professionals). Thus, after constitutionalisation, Law 77/2016 no longer enables over-indebted consumers to liberate themselves from credit agreements (*lex specialis* concerning consumer credit law), becoming a mere application of general civil law (the Civil Code). This view contradicts the Explanatory Memorandum and Article 1 of Law 77/2016, which stated that the Law applies to legal relationships between consumers and credit institutions, non-banking financial institutions or assignees of financial claims against consumers.

---

[190] Decision 731/2019 (n 151) para 40.
[191] ibid para 42.
[192] ibid paras 56–57.
[193] ibid para 61.

In conclusion, the RCC has wholly modified the legislator's will and the Law's original purpose. Moreover, it inverted the broader legal relationship between *lex specialis* (consumer protection law) and *lex generalis* (the Civil Code) by subordinating *lex specialis* to *lex generalis*. Instead of perceiving Law 77/2016 (with all its flaws) as a special regime applicable to consumer credit contracts, the Court transformed it into a mere application of the Civil Code.

V. A Kafkian Tale: Consumer Protection Denies Consumer Protection

This chapter analysed the transformation of Romanian consumer financial protection law by RCC case law. It highlighted the significant role that the constitutionalisation of consumer financial protection has played in implementing, shaping and enforcing national and EU consumer protection measures. The Court's jurisprudence concerning transposition of EU legislation on abusive terms in consumer credit agreements has consistently found that the legislator enjoys significant freedom when implementing consumer protection rules. This stance was justified by the need to alleviate the effects of the financial crisis or protect the weaker party to a transaction.

However, when evaluating national additions to EU consumer financial protection measures, the RCC has tended not just to assess the legislation's constitutionality but to alter its content – and the legislators' intent – by developing its own rules. This approach places the Court in opposition to European counterparts (such as Croatia) that have used constitutionalisation to reinforce consumer protection laws and debt relief mechanisms intended to alleviate the social effects of the 2008 financial crisis. In contrast, the RCC has changed the substance of such national measures to the point where they can no longer provide relief or act as consumer protection mechanisms.

Using constitutionalisaton to restrict consumer rights is a unique aspect of the Romanian case. The pretext of the RCC was to preserve the role of the ordinary court in granting consumer relief. The broader implications of this approach are twofold – substantive and institutional – and will have long-term effects for consumers. On the one hand, the substantive alterations operated through Decision 623/2016 (and the following) force ordinary courts to adhere to the RCC's guidelines and, for all practical purposes, deny relief. Thus, the RCC did not as much save ordinary courts from applying the arbitrary will of the legislature, but only replaced the will of the legislature with its own. On the other hand, forcing individual assessment of every debt relief request by consumers under Law 77/2016 only has the effect of flooding the courts with even more repeat cases. This increases their administrative burden but lowers their responsiveness to the consumer cause.

Therefore, one can safely conclude that the transformation of consumer law by the RCC's judicial dicta highjacked consumer financial protection and hollowed out consumer rights.

16

United Kingdom: An Incomplete Transformation of Consumer Law

CHRISTIAN TWIGG-FLESNER

I. Introduction

This chapter examines the transformation of consumer law in the United Kingdom (UK) since the turn of the millennium. Its central thesis is that, driven by the growth of consumer law instruments at European Union (EU) level and the obligation on EU Member States to implement those measures into domestic law[1] (prior to the UK's withdrawal from the EU in 2020), two transformative developments occurred in parallel. The first was a willingness to depart from the thereto prevalent approach in UK consumer law of adopting legislation narrowly targeted at specific consumer protection issues to a much more generalised approach with broader coverage, based on general clauses. The second follows from the progressive introduction of legislation on consumer contracts, which has had the effect of gradually separating consumer contract law from the general law of contract developed through the common law. However, neither development is complete: the common law of contract has not been displaced altogether by consumer legislation; at the same time, legislation targeted at specific issues continues to be considered. Nevertheless, there has been a transformation, albeit one that has not yet reached its conclusion. It is unclear, though, whether UK consumer law has reached a pause in its transformation, or whether it has stalled altogether.

The peculiarities of the UK's relationship with the EU explain both why the transformative developments have occurred in the first place, and why the process has ground to a halt. Whilst still a member of the EU, the obligation to implement EU consumer legislation was utilised to modernise swathes of domestic consumer law, taking full advantage of the simplified route for implementing legislation provided under the European Communities Act 1972.[2] One obvious effect of this has been a significant

---

[1] Consolidated version of the Treaty on the Functioning of the European Union [2012] OJ C326/47, Art 288.

[2] This Act provided the main basis within the UK's constitutional structure for both giving effect to directly applicable EU law and for the implementation of EU legislation through secondary legislation, bypassing the full legislative process for primary legislation. See section III.

increase of substantive consumer law in the UK, with a significant proportion of UK consumer law based on EU law. However, this chapter is not concerned with the growth in substantive consumer law per se,[3] but with the wider effects of this for the transformation of UK consumer law.

Withdrawal from the EU ('Brexit') not only halted the 'incoming tide'[4] of EU consumer law, but also removed the relative ease with which consumer law reform could be undertaken through the implementation of EU directives under the simplified procedure offered by the European Communities Act 1972 (see below).[5] During the current decade, there might be a new phase in the transformation of UK consumer law following withdrawal from the EU, although the trajectory of this phase has yet to emerge.

In order to unpack the thesis underpinning this chapter, the discussion will first set out a chronology of the main developments, proceeding thus: the starting point is the state of UK consumer law at the turn of the millennium (section II). This is essential to understand how the influence of EU law has resulted in the transformation explored in this chapter. It will also be necessary to explain the legislative framework governing the interaction between EU and UK law in place at that time (section III). The first and second stages of transformation will then be discussed (sections IV and V). The two factors shaping the transformation of UK consumer law were the adoption of two particular directives at the EU level and the resulting need to implement these into UK law. The two directives in question are, first, the Unfair Commercial Practices Directive (UCPD), adopted in 2005; and second, the process leading up to the adoption of the Consumer Rights Directive (CRD) in 2011.[6] As will be seen, the implementation of the UCPD had a direct and dramatic effect on the landscape of UK consumer law, whereas the CRD's effects were more indirect, although no less significant. This narrative will lead to a discussion of the characteristics of the transformation of UK consumer law, which will flesh out the core thesis of this chapter (section VI). Section VII will look at the likely third transformative development, which is primarily characterised by the rapid weakening of the influence of

---

[3] For a general account of the state of UK Consumer Law, see G Woodroffe, Ch Twigg-Flesner and Ch Willett, *Woodroffe and Lowe's Consumer Law and Practice*, 10th edn (Sweet and Maxwell, 2016).

[4] Lord Denning in *HP Bulmer Ltd v J Bollinger SA* [1974] Ch 401, 418.

[5] For instance, the UK Government has consulted on amending the Consumer Protection from Unfair Trading Regulations 2008 (SI 2008/1277) (which implement Directive 2005/29/EC of the European Parliament and of the Council of 11 May 2005 concerning unfair business-to-consumer commercial practices in the internal market and amending Council Directive 84/450/EEC, Directives 97/7/EC, 98/27/EC and 2002/65/EC of the European Parliament and of the Council and Regulation (EC) No 2006/2004 of the European Parliament and of the Council ('Unfair Commercial Practices Directive') [2005] OJ L149/22 (UCPD)) to add provisions not dissimilar to those introduced by the Directive (EU) 2019/2161 of the European Parliament and of the Council of 27 November 2019 amending Council Directive 93/13/EEC and Directives 98/6/EC, 2005/29/EC and 2011/83/EU of the European Parliament and of the Council as regards the better enforcement and modernisation of Union consumer protection rules [2019] OJ L328/7 (EU's Modernisation Directive). Doing this would require new primary legislation to either make the change directly, or to create a new statutory power, eg for amending the Annex containing prohibited practices by secondary legislation.

[6] UCPD (n 5); Directive 2011/83/EU of the European Parliament and of the Council of 25 October 2011 on consumer rights, amending Council Directive 93/13/EEC and Directive 1999/44/EC of the European Parliament and of the Council and repealing Council Directive 85/577/EEC and Directive 97/7/EC of the European Parliament and of the Council [2011] OJ L 304/64.

EU consumer law following the UK's withdrawal from the EU at the end of January 2020. This has cast UK consumer law adrift, and without the driving force provided by EU consumer law.

II. UK Consumer Law at the Turn of the Millennium

It is necessary to sketch the state of UK consumer law at the turn of the millennium[7] to set the context for the transformation analysed later. Unlike many other European jurisdictions, none of the UK's jurisdictions has a codified private law system, that is, there is no civil code or similar.[8] Instead, private law is overwhelmingly a matter for the common law (ie case law), although legislation has been enacted from time to time to supplement or correct the common law.[9] Contract law, in particular, is well-known for its plethora of cases, dealing with the full range of contracts, from small-scale contracts between private parties to large-scale commercial dealings.[10] The hallmark of (English) contract law is a strong version of freedom of contract, which provides only limited grounds for interfering in a contract once concluded.[11] The common law developed a number of doctrines dealing with situations where the formation of a contract was somehow defective (eg, based on false information provided by one party), such as the doctrines of duress or misrepresentation, as well as the equitable doctrines of undue influence and unconscionability, but these doctrines are 'piecemeal solutions in response to demonstrated problems of unfairness'[12] and do not provide a broad basis for policing contracts. This does not mean that the courts have not been attuned to the specific situation of individual consumers[13] – in applying the common law, some judges have been cognisant of the needs of a consumer party. However, this was a far cry from a dedicated consumer law, and frequently depended on the ideological attitudes of individual judges as to where the balance between the competing interests of consumers and businesses might be struck.[14]

---

[7] For a rich account of the development of consumer law in the UK, see I Ramsay, 'Ordoliberalism and Opportunism? The Making of Consumer Law in the UK' in H-W Micklitz (ed), *The Making of Consumer Law and Policy in Europe* (Hart Publishing, 2021) 235.

[8] Although the Law Commission dabbled with the idea in the 1960s, the idea was abandoned. A 'Contract Code' had been drawn up by Harvey McGregor, which was only published as an academic text in 1993 (H McGregor, *Contract Code drawn up on behalf of the English Law Commission* (Dott A Giuffre Editore, 1993).

[9] In the field of contract law, key examples include the Law Reform (Frustrated Contracts) Act 1943, the Misrepresentation Act 1967, the Unfair Contract Terms Act 1977 and the Contracts (Rights of Third Parties) Act 1999.

[10] See, eg H Beale (ed), *Chitty on Contracts*, 34th edn (Sweet & Maxwell, 2022); E Peel, *Treitel – The Law of Contract*, 15th edn (Sweet & Maxwell, 2020).

[11] See Lord Toulson in *Prime Sight Limited (A company Registered in Gibraltar) (Appellant) v Edgar Charles Lavarello (Official Trustee of Benjamin Marrache a Bankrupt) (Respondent)* [2013] UKPC 22 [47].

[12] Per Bingham LJ (as was) in *Interfoto Picture Library Ltd v Stiletto Visual Programmes Ltd* [1989] QB 433, 439; this general observation was made to contrast English contract law with civil law jurisdictions that recognise a general principle of good faith.

[13] Seminally, of course, see *Carlill v Carbolic Smoke Ball Co* [1893] 1 QB 256 (CA). See AWB Simpson, 'Quackery and Contract Law: The Case of the Carbolic Smoke Ball' (1985) 14 *Journal of Legal Studies* 345.

[14] J Adams and R Brownsword have categorised this as consumer-welfarist reasoning: see J Adams and R Brownsword, *Understanding Contract Law*, 5th edn (Sweet & Maxwell, 2007).

The development of consumer law has therefore been a matter for Parliament. The absence of a civil code or similar codification meant that there was no obvious 'hook' on which to hang legal provisions specifically concerned with consumer protection issues. Instead, new legislation was enacted to deal with specific matters of concern, which sometimes resulted in legislation with a very narrow focus.[15] Over time, Parliament adopted a number of landmark Acts, for example the Trade Descriptions Act 1968, the Fair Trading Act 1973, the Consumer Credit Act 1974, the Consumer Protection Act 1987 or the Timeshare Act 1992. The Trade Descriptions Act 1968 Act, in particular, was a seen as stalwart of UK consumer law, dealing with false or misleading descriptions of goods or services provided by a person in the course of a trade or business. However, the word 'consumer' did not appear anywhere in the Act itself, and consumers were not granted any individual rights under the Act.[16] Rather, the Act made it an offence to apply a false trade description and provided related investigative and enforcement powers. The Act's primary concern was therefore with the conduct of traders and businesses, with an incidental, if significant, effect on consumer protection. The Fair Trading Act 1973 established the now-defunct office of the Director-General of Fair Trading (better known as the Office of Fair Trading, or OFT), established a Consumer Protection Advisory Committee, empowered the OFT to investigate instances of consumer detriment, and generally strengthened the regulation and enforcement dimension of consumer law.

To the extent that there was no specific legislation, the common law was all that consumers could rely on when faced with a problem. In addition, some of the statutes dealing with aspects of commercial and contract law that had been enacted also applied to consumer contracts. Consumer rights in respect of contracts for the supply of goods and services were based on a combination of the common law and the limited legislation relevant to specific contracts. Thus, contracts for the sale of goods[17] fell within the scope of the Sale of Goods Act 1979,[18] and services contracts were covered by the Supply of Goods and Services Act 1982.[19] Neither measure was specifically intended as a consumer law measure, although the Sale of Goods Act had been modified over time to add provisions of particular relevance to consumers. For example, following Law Commission recommendations made in 1997,[20] the main conformity requirement had been changed, in 1994, from the old 'merchantable quality' standard to a 'satisfactory

---

[15] See the Mock Auctions Act 1961 and the Fraudulent Mediums Act 1951 (repealing what remained in force of the Witchcraft Act 1735). Both were repealed by the Consumer Protection from Unfair Trading Regulations 2008.

[16] This was the result of industry lobbying, reflecting the weakness of consumer representation at the time: see Ramsay (n 7) 243.

[17] Defined in Sale of Goods Act 1979, s 2(1) as 'a contract by which the seller transfers or agrees to transfer the property in goods to the buyer for a money consideration, called the price'.

[18] The Sale of Goods Act 1979 is a consolidation of the Sale of Goods Act 1893 and subsequent amendments; the 1893 Act was a partial codification of the increasingly complex case law on contracts for the sale of goods and is a remnant of a brief period of flirtation with codifying some of the common law in the late 19th century.

[19] The 1982 Act also dealt with the supply of goods by way of hire. Contracts for hire-purchase, on the other hand, were covered by the Supply of Goods (Implied Terms) Act 1973. All of these Acts remain in force and continue to apply to non-consumer transactions.

[20] Law Commission, *Sale and Supply of Goods* (Law Com No 160, 1987).

'quality' standard. The Supply of Goods and Services Act had been driven by consumer interests, although it was never confined to consumer contracts.

The UK's consumer law landscape had therefore mostly been shaped by both consumer-specific and general Acts of Parliament, with the common law continuing to provide the foundations on which consumer legislation was built. It was a fragmented picture, but there was nevertheless a good level of consumer law in place even before the EU embarked on, and subsequently accelerated, its legislative programme in this area. Consumer law in the UK was characterised by a strong focus on market regulation, institutionalised in the OFT, and the use of both administrative enforcement powers and the possibility of imposing criminal sanctions.[21]

Although the main transformative push from EU law had yet to occur, by the start of the millennium, a number of EU directives on consumer law had been adopted and implemented into UK Law.[22] As will be discussed more fully in section III, the UK's general approach had been to implement directives through secondary legislation, without any significant effort being expended on maintaining any coherence between these measures and existing consumer laws. The one exception to this is the Consumer Protection Act 1987, which implemented the Product Liability Directive (85/374/EEC),[23] but it also contained separate parts dealing with consumer safety (before the EU adopted its first General Product Safety Directive (92/59/EEC)),[24] as well as provisions on pricing issues. Despite its broad name, the Act only dealt with some areas of consumer protection, though.

This brief sketch demonstrates that, at the turn of the millennium, UK consumer law was an amalgam of the common laws of contract and tort together with legislative additions, Acts of Parliament on a variety of consumer law issues, and secondary legislation implementing the still small number of EU consumer law directives that had been adopted at that point. It was therefore a rather complex picture, with consumer law scattered across a wide number of legislative instruments. The growth of EU activity in

---

[21] P Cartwright, *Consumer Protection and the Criminal Law* (Cambridge University Press, 2007).

[22] These included Council Directive 85/577/EEC of 20 December 1985 to protect the consumer in respect of contracts negotiated away from business premises [1985] OJ L372/31 (Doorstep Selling Directive), Directive 94/47/EC of the European Parliament and the Council of 26 October 1994 on the protection of purchasers in respect of certain aspects of contracts relating to the purchase of the right to use immovable properties on a timeshare basis [1994] OJ L280/83 (the first Timeshare Directive) and Council Directive 93/13/EEC of 5 April 1993 on unfair terms in consumer contracts [1993] OJ L95/29 (Unfair Contract Terms Directive (UCTD)).

[23] Council Directive 85/374/EEC of 25 July 1985 on the approximation of the laws, regulations and administrative provisions of the Member States concerning liability for defective products [1985] OJ L210/29.

[24] Council Directive 92/59/EEC of 29 June 1992 on general product safety [1992] OJ L228/34. See G Howells, *Comparative Product Safety* (Ashgate Publishing, 1998). Directive 92/59/EEC was replaced by Directive 2001/95/EC of the European Parliament and of the Council of 3 December 2001 on general product safety [2001] OJ L11/4. At the time of writing, the EU had just agreed a new Regulation on General Product Safety (Regulation (EU) 2023/XXX of the European Parliament and of the Council on general product safety, amending Regulation (EU) No 1025/2012 of the European Parliament and of the Council, and repealing Council Directive 87/357/EEC and Directive 2001/95/EC of the European Parliament and of the Council (not yet published in the OJ). cf European Commission, 'Proposal for a Regulation of the European Parliament and of the Council on general product safety, amending Regulation (EU) No 1025/2012 of the European Parliament and of the Council, and repealing Council Directive 87/357/EEC and Directive 2001/95/EC of the European Parliament and of the Council' COM (2021) 346 final, whilst the UK is planning its own revisions: Office for Product Safety 7 Standards, *UK Product Safety Review – Call for Evidence Response* (November 2021).

this area resulted in increasing this complexity as further directives were adopted, to be discussed next.

III. The Interaction between UK and EU Consumer Law

One aspect of the thesis put forward in this chapter is that the two key transformative developments that have occurred in UK consumer law since the start of this millennium were driven by the evolution of EU consumer law. Despite its increasing density, EU consumer law did not altogether displace domestic law but relied on an interaction between EU-derived rules and domestic law. Directives dealt with targeted issues only and relied on related areas of private law to function effectively. Prior to the UK's referendum on continued EU membership on 23 June 2016, this deepening interaction was also characteristic of UK consumer law, and thus became the driver behind the transformative developments discussed here.

Generally, the implementation of EU consumer law was dealt with in a rather perfunctory manner. Although the Product Liability Directive had been transposed through primary legislation in part 1 of the Consumer Protection Act 1987, subsequent EU consumer law directives were mostly implemented through secondary legislation adopted under section 2(2) of the European Communities Act (ECA) 1972.[25] The ECA 1972 was the legal basis for giving directly applicable EU law legal effect in UK law, and it supplied the legal basis for the implementation of EU obligations, including directives. Section 2(2) of the 1972 Act empowered the government minister with the relevant portfolio to lay secondary legislation (statutory instruments) before Parliament to give effect to EU obligations, including secondary legislation to implement consumer law directives. This meant that the lengthy parliamentary process for adopting primary legislation (three readings and committee stages in both Houses of Parliament) did not have to be used for implementing EU obligations. Instead, statutory instruments adopted under section 2(2) of the ECA 1972 could follow either the negative resolution procedure (allowing Parliament to pass a measure rejecting the statutory instrument) or the affirmative resolution procedure (requiring Parliament to vote in favour of a statutory instrument before it becomes law).[26] The power granted by section 2(2) was confined to the implementation of 'any EU obligation', so could only be exercised to the extent necessary to implement a directive or other EU obligation.[27] If the Government wanted adopt legislation with a wider scope than that of an EU directive, it had to rely on a different power or enact primary legislation. Thus, the Doorstep Selling Directive was implemented in the Consumer Protection (Contracts Concluded away from Business

---

[25] The one exception to this is Directive 98/6/EC of the European Parliament and of the Council of 16 February 1998 on consumer protection in the indication of the prices of products offered to consumers [1998] OJ L80/27, which was implemented through regulations under the Prices Act 1974: the Price Marking Order 2004 (SI 2004/102).

[26] See ECA 1972, sch 2, para 2(2).

[27] The Legislative and Regulatory Reform Act 2006 provided a procedure to combine secondary legislation with additional changes to remove or reduce burdens, but it is not necessary to go into the detail in this chapter.

Premises) Regulations 1987 (SI 1987/2117). The Directive itself was worded rather sparsely, but the implementing legislation was more elaborate and based on the typical drafting style of domestic legislation. Nevertheless, because of the legal basis for adopting the domestic implementing legislation, the 1987 Regulations did no more than was necessary to give effect to the Directive. When the Government decided to extend the scope of the old doorstep-selling rules beyond 'unsolicited' visits to cover all contracts between a consumer and a trader concluded in a doorstep-selling situation, a separate legislative power had to be included in section 59 of the Consumers, Estate Agents and Redress Act 2007, which became the basis for the Cancellation of Contracts made in a Consumer's Home or Place of Work etc Regulations 2008 (SI 2008/1816).[28]

There was one 'grey area' regarding the scope of section 2(2) of the 1972 Act: many of the earlier consumer law directives were of a minimum harmonisation standard and allowed Member States to retain or adopt more protective legislation, as long as the threshold set by a directive was met. In principle, this allowed for the introduction of stricter rules within the scope of the relevant directive. However, the UK Government took a policy decision regarding the implementation of EU directives to refrain from 'gold plating' whenever possible,[29] that is to do no more than necessary to implement EU legislation and not go any further. This minimalist approach to implementation was also reflected in a much stronger 'copy out' approach, that is a near verbatim implementation of the EU text into domestic legislation. The latter development coincided with the increasingly detailed and precise drafting style at the EU level in its pursuit of more coherent and standardised legal rules.[30] The upshot was that new secondary legislation was simply added to the canon of consumer legislation in such a way as to do little more than to ensure that the UK's obligations under EU law were met.

In the UK, therefore, EU directives were dutifully transposed into domestic law through regulations adopted under the ECA 1972, but usually, little or no regard was had to the possible interaction of implementing legislation with existing domestic legislation. The worst example of this was the implementation of the UCTD through the Unfair Terms in Consumer Contracts Regulations 1994 (SI 1994/3159), later replaced by the 1999 version[31] to correct implementation flaws in the 1994 Regulations. The Unfair Contract Terms Act (UCTA) 1977 already dealt with some contract terms (mostly limitation and exclusion clauses) in both business-to-business and business-to-consumer contracts. It applied a 'reasonableness' test to many of these, as well as rendering some terms ineffective altogether in a consumer contract. The implementing legislation for the UCTD was simply added as a separate statutory instrument, with no changes made to UCTA 1977. The minimum harmonisation approach of the UCTD permitted the retention of more protective provisions, such as the outright prohibition of certain types of exclusion clauses, under the 1977 Act.[32] Inevitably, this state of affairs

---

[28] Subsequently displaced by the Consumer Contracts (Information, Cancellation and Additional Charges Regulations) 2013 (SI 2013/3134) for contracts entered into after 13 June 2014.

[29] Her Majesty's Government, *Transposition Guide: How to implement European directives effectively*, April 2011, para 2.7.

[30] cf Ch Twigg-Flesner, *A Cross-border-only Regulation for Consumer Transactions in the EU* (Springer, 2012) 21.

[31] The Unfair Terms in Consumer Contracts Regulations 1999 (SI 1999/2083).

[32] eg ss 2(1) or 6(2) UCTA pre-2015.

was much criticised,[33] and the Law Commission was asked to prepare proposals for consolidation of the unfair terms regime. Its report in 2005[34] proposed, inter alia, a unified regime for consumer contracts, but despite indicating its intention to act on the report, nothing was done by the Government until plans for a Consumer Rights Act emerged some years later (see section V).

One notable departure[35] from this rather formulaic and technical approach to implementing EU law was the implementation of the first Consumer Sales Directive (99/44/EC).[36] Before the Directive was implemented, consumer sales contracts were covered alongside commercial sales contracts (and private sales) by the Sale of Goods Act 1979. The tension between differing commercial and consumer sales contracts had resulted in some amendments to make specific provision for consumer contracts, including the update to the main conformity requirement that goods supplied in the course of a business have to be of 'satisfactory quality'.[37] But on the whole, consumer sales contracts and non-consumer sales contracts were treated in much the same way. This was particularly so with regard to remedies in respect of non-conforming goods, which were limited to the termination for breach of contract and a claim for damages. The Consumer Sales Directive made repair or replacement of non-conforming goods a primary remedy. It was decided to retain the existing remedies (permitted by the minimum harmonisation nature of the directive), and to add a new part 5A to the Sale of Goods Act 1979 introducing provisions based on the remedial regime from Article 3 of the Directive. The result was a very messy state of affairs[38] – so much so that it was singled out as an example of a particularly bad implementation of EU law.[39]

At the level of legislation, the picture was therefore a rather messy one. The courts, on the other hand, have been more adept at dealing with the impact of EU law on UK consumer law. One good example regarding the accommodation between UK and EU law is the changing attitude towards the fairness test in the UCTD.[40] Initially, the inclusion of 'good faith' in the fairness test was regarded as problematic[41] because of the

---

[33] See R Brownsword and G Howells, 'The implementation of the EC Directive on unfair terms in consumer contracts – some unresolved questions' [1995] *Journal of Business Law* 243.

[34] Law Commission, *Unfair Terms in Contracts* (Law Com No 292, February 2005).

[35] Another example is the implementation of the first Timeshare Directive (n 22), which resulted in some amendments to the Timeshare Act 1992. When Directive 2008/122/EC of the European Parliament and of the Council of 14 January 2009 on the protection of consumers in respect of certain aspects of timeshare, long-term holiday product, resale and exchange contracts (Text with EEA relevance) [2009] OJ L33/10 (the second Timeshare Directive) was implemented, the Timeshare Act was repealed and replaced by the Timeshare, Holiday Products, Resale and Exchange Contracts Regulations 2010 (SI 2010/2960).

[36] Directive 1999/44/EC of the European Parliament and of the Council of 25 May 1999 on certain aspects of the sale of consumer goods and associated guarantees [1999] OJ L171/12. For a detailed analysis of the original implementation of the Directive, see R Bradgate and Ch Twigg-Flesner, *Blackstone's Guide to Consumer Sales and Associated Guarantees* (Oxford University Press, 2003).

[37] Sale of Goods Act 1979, s 14(2) with the amendment made by the Supply of Goods and Services Act 1994, s 1(1).

[38] See Bradgate and Twigg-Flesner (n 36) ch 4.

[39] Davidson Review, *Implementation of EU Legislation – Final Report* (London, TSO, 2006) paras 3.10–3.23.

[40] See, eg *Director-General of Fair Trading v First National Bank* [2001] UKHL 52; *Office of Fair Trading v Abbey National plc* [2009] UKSC 6; *Office of Fair Trading v Foxtons Ltd* [2009] EWCA Civ 288; *ParkingEye v Beavis* [2015] UKSC 67.

[41] Recall Teubner's well-known characterisation of good faith as an 'irritant': G Teubner, 'Legal Irritants: Good Faith in British Law or How Unifying Law Ends Up in New Divergences' (1998) 61 *MLR* 11.

unwillingness, particularly of the English common law, to recognise good faith. The Law Commission had proposed to change the language of the test, but when it was asked to revisit its proposals some years later, it accepted that the courts had shown themselves to be perfectly capable of handling the test.[42] As it had become a familiar aspect of UK consumer law, it would have been more disruptive to make changes, and so the good faith test has been retained (see section V).

IV. Stage 1 of the Transformation: The Implementation of the Unfair Commercial Practices Directive

The first stage arose from the need to implement the UCPD, which produced a transformative effect on both the substance and the legislative approach of UK consumer law. The UCPD emerged from a *Green Paper on EU Consumer Protection*,[43] which had suggested a framework directive on fair commercial practices. In order to inform its negotiating position, the UK Government commissioned an academic study into the implications of adopting something like a duty to trade fairly in consumer law.[44] This was significant for two reasons: first, as a matter of process, the direct involvement of academics in assisting the Government in dealing with the implications of forthcoming EU legislation; and, second, a willingness to engage with the EU's proposal even though the idea of a general clause might have been expected to be rejected summarily.

First, the high profile given to academic work is a noteworthy feature of the transformation process in the UK over both first and second stages. The then Department of Trade and Industry (DTI) established a Consumer Law Academic Advisory Group in 2001, bringing together many of the UK's leading consumer law scholars at the time. The Group met a few times to discuss relevant issues. Over time, the DTI and its successor departments[45] commissioned several academic studies to inform the development of consumer policy and to assist with consumer law reform.[46] Indeed, in the period roughly between 2003 and 2013, there were many opportunities for consumer law academics to discuss reform proposals with civil servants. Eventually, this became less common, possibly because of the retirement and rotation of the civil servants who had been actively involved in these discussions. Although academics can still be involved on an individual basis, the dialogue between the consumer law academic community and civil servant, especially around the time of the reforms made between 2005 and 2015,

---

[42] Although, as Mitchell has pointed out, some courts (including the Supreme Court) have approached the application of consumer law from a non-interventionist perspective, leading to several rulings that are not particularly consumer-friendly: C. Mitchell, *Vanishing Contract Law* (Cambridge University Press, 2022) 67–72.

[43] COM (2001) 531 final, October 2001.

[44] R Bradgate, R Brownsword and Ch Twigg-Flesner, *The Impact of Adopting a Duty to Trade Fairly* (DTI, July 2003).

[45] The DTI morphed in the Department of Business, Enterprise and Regulatory Reform (BERR) in June 2007, then became the Department of Business, Innovation and Skills (June 2009) and, most recently, the Department of Business, Energy and Industrial Strategy (July 2016). It was also known as the Department for Productivity, Energy and Industry for a few days in May 2005. Since February 2023, it has been the Department of Business and Trade.

[46] See studies cited in this section as examples.

has been lost, and academics have been largely relegated to the general pool of consult-ees whenever the Government puts forward new proposals for public consultation.

Second, the idea of introducing general clauses into UK law would be quite a radical step because the UK has traditionally refrained from relying on broad general duties, preferring instead to deal with identified problem areas in a discrete manner. This continues to be the case in the English common law of contract, which has already rejected the idea of a general doctrine of 'inequality of bargaining power'[47] and has continued to resist attempts to introduce a general duty to act in good faith, in both cases favouring discrete doctrines instead.[48] But even statutory consumer law had focused on specific, identified problems rather than introducing broad general obligations of fair conduct on traders. The prospect of introducing a general fairness duty could have been problematic. However, instead of opposing the proposals mooted in the *Green Paper*, the academic report outlined how English law would deal with such a broad duty; in particular, it concluded that courts were more than capable of handling broad general standards. Following several rounds of consultation,[49] the Government did not object to the proposed legislation.

Once the UCPD had commenced its legislative process, the UK Government commissioned further academic research[50] to assist it with understanding how the new Directive would work, in particular with regard to the concepts and terminology the UCPD would introduce. Furthermore, the Government wanted to understand the implications of the UCPD for domestic law, and how domestic law would have to be amended to give effect to the requirements of the Directive. The report identified a large number of domestic measures that would be affected by the UCPD, and explored both the targeted amendment of these measures to ensure they were aligned with the UCPD and, alternatively, the scope for repealing many of these measures in favour of replace-ment by legislation implementing the UCPD.[51]

The report therefore presented the Government with three options: implement the UCPD alongside existing legislation (following the practice in the context of unfair terms); or as a safety-net measure together with amendments to existing legislation necessary to bring this into line with the UCPD requirements; or by replacing existing legislation with a broader measure of general application based on the UCPD's general clauses.

The final decision was in favour of the third option, and the UCPD was eventually implemented through the Consumer Protection from Unfair Trading Regulations 2008. The Regulations repealed around 20 existing measures either in their entirety or to a

---

[47] Championed by Lord Denning (*Lloyds Bank v Bundy* [1975] QB 326), it was firmly rejected by the House of Lords in *National Westminster Bank v Morgan* [1985] AC 686.

[48] See, eg, *Interfoto Library Ltd v Stiletto Visual Programmes Ltd* [1989] QB 433 and *MSC Mediterranean Shipping Company SA v Cottonex Anstalt* [2016] EWCA Civ 789.

[49] See Explanatory Memorandum to the Consumer Protection from Unfair Trading Regulations 2008, 76–77 for a summary of the various consultation rounds prior to the adoption of the 2008 Regulations.

[50] Ch Twigg-Flesner et al, *An analysis of the application and scope of the Unfair Commercial Practices Directive* (DTI, May 2005).

[51] For a shorter discussion, see D Parry and Ch Twigg-Flesner, 'The Challenges Posed by the Implementation of the Directive into Domestic Law – a UK Perspective' in St Weatherill and U Bernitz (eds), *The Regulation of Unfair Commercial Practices under EC Directive 2005/29: New Rules and New Techniques* (Hart Publishing, 2007) 215.

significant extent, and made amendments to many others.[52] As well as ensuring that the UCPD was implemented in full, the 2008 Regulations effected a significant streamlining of UK consumer law by replacing discrete and narrow legislation with the much broader provisions of the Regulations.

It is noteworthy that such far-reaching reform was achieved outside the full legislative procedure in Parliament. Instead, the adoption of the Regulations and the repeal of various primary and secondary measures was all done on the basis of section 2(2) of the ECA 1972. The Explanatory Memorandum noted that the repeal of secondary legislation could also have been achieved on the basis of the enabling powers in other relevant legislation, but this would have required a much more complex legislative process.[53] The section 2(2) route was more straightforward and achieved the same result. This pragmatic approach to saving parliamentary time because of the obligation under EU law to implement the Directive is a distinctive feature of the way in which the UK dealt with its EU obligations under the 1972 Act. This particular instance further demonstrates how the section 2(2) route could be instrumentalised for achieving wide-ranging reforms of domestic law. Through repeals contained in secondary legislation, the landscape of UK consumer law was altered significantly and, arguably, simplified considerably.

V. Stage 2 of the Transformation: Towards the Consumer Rights Act 2015

As explained, the gradual and piecemeal evolution of domestic UK consumer law and the UK's minimalist approach to the implementation of EU Directive had resulted in a fragmented legislative picture. The implementation of the UCPD provided a useful experience of reforming domestic law when implementing an EU Directive, particularly one with as broad a scope as the UCPD. The need to amend domestic law to implement an EU Directive could lead to the streamlining of domestic consumer law. In the case of the UCPD, the regulatory landscape was simplified by replacing a diverse set of discrete legislative measures with a single, broader one. However, when it was enacted, the UCPD focused on the conduct of traders and only provided for enforcement by relevant bodies charged with protecting consumer interests. It did not provide consumer rights that could be enforced directly by individual consumers against recalcitrant traders,[54] at least not until the amendments made to the UCPD by the Modernisation ('New Deal') Directive in 2019.[55]

---

[52] See Consumer Protection from Unfair Trading Regulations 2008, schs 2 and 4. Although much of the Trade Descriptions Act 1968 was repealed, a handful of provisions remain in force.

[53] Explanatory Memorandum to the Consumer Protection from Unfair Trading Regulations 2008, para 3.17.

[54] UCPD (n 5) Art 3(2) stressed that the Directive is 'without prejudice to contract law and, in particular, to the rules on the validity, formation or effect of a contract'. See also recital 9.

[55] Directive (EU) 2019/2161 (n 5). Art 3 of this Directive inserted a new Art 11a into the UCPD (n 5), requiring Member States to provide for a right to redress for consumers harmed by an unfair commercial practice.

After 2008, significant parts of the UK's consumer law landscape had been stream-lined, but there was still a great deal of complexity in the legislation on individual consumer rights, particularly the regulation of consumer contracts. This complexity was partly the result of historical developments, for example the spread of different types of supply of goods transaction across several Acts of Parliament as well as the common law, or the bungled implementation of the UCTD. However, an opportunity for repeating a simplification exercise for consumer contract law soon presented itself when the EU, following its review of the consumer *acquis*,[56] put forward a proposal for a Consumer Rights Directive[57] that would have combined and updated the directives on doorstep selling, distance selling, unfair terms and consumer sales.[58] With the Consumer Rights Directive on the horizon, the Government explored the options for further reforms of aspects of UK consumer law. As with the first stage, academics had a key role in shaping at least some of this process. The potential for extensive reform was explored at a confer-ence hosted by the then DTI on 9 April 2008, at which many consumer law academics spoke,[59] which launched the process towards the Consumer Rights Act 2015.

In 2009, the Department for Business, Innovation and Skills (BIS) published a White Paper[60] outlining plans for a 'Consumer Rights Bill', which would both implement the then forthcoming Consumer Rights Directive and, at the same time, pursue the consoli-dation of other areas of consumer law. Extensive research work was requested to support this objective. The Law Commission was asked to examine several topics for possible legislative action. In particular, it was asked to review its earlier recommendations regarding the consolidation of the unfair terms regime,[61] as well as the consumer reme-dies for faulty goods,[62] and also the possibility of introducing a private right of redress in respect of unfair commercial practices.[63] Furthermore, BIS asked a group of academics to produce a research report examining to what extent consolidation and simplification of UK consumer law was needed and feasible,[64] as well as a separate report on consumer rights in respect of software/digital content.[65] One of the key recommendations of the former report was the consolidation many of the statutory provisions and statutory instruments dealing with consumer rights in one Act of Parliament and, in the process, to enhance the overall coherence and consistency of UK consumer law. The extent of

---

[56] H Schulte-Nölke, Ch Twigg-Flesner and M Ebers, *EC Consumer Law Compendium* (Sellier, 2008); European Commission, 'Green Paper on the review of the consumer acquis' COM (2006) 744 final.

[57] COM (2008) 614 final.

[58] For a discussion of this proposal, see the contributions to G Howells and R Schulze (eds), *Modernising and Harmonising Consumer Contract Law* (Sellier, 2009).

[59] The present author gave a paper on 'Consolidating the Law on the Sale and Supply of Goods and Services', which contributed to setting in motion the process for what eventually became the Consumer Rights Act 2015.

[60] HM Government, *A Better Deal for Consumers – Delivering Real Help Now and Change for the Future* (TSO, 2009).

[61] Its recommendations were published as Law Commission, *Unfair Terms in Consumer Contracts Advice Paper* (Law Com No 292, 2013).

[62] Law Commission, *Consumer Remedies for Faulty Goods* (Law Com No 317, 2009).

[63] Law Commission, *Consumer Redress for Misleading and Aggressive Practices* (Law Com No 332, 2012).

[64] G Howells and Ch Twigg-Flesner (eds), *Consolidation and Simplification of UK Consumer Law* (BIS, 2010).

[65] R Bradgate, *Consumer Rights in Digital Products: A research report prepared for the UK Department for Business, Innovation and Skills* (BIS, 2010).

consolidation recommended in the academic report would have brought together key legal rules on the sale and supply of goods, as well as the supply of services. However, it was beyond the remit of the academic report to examine the case for a comprehensive codification of the entire body of legislative consumer law. A full codification might have entailed not only the consolidation of the many statutory provisions, but also the integration of key elements of the common law. Nevertheless, the case for consolidation was strong, and whilst the arguments in favour were generally accepted, the extent of consolidation (ie which legislation would be included) had not yet been settled.

Following these reports, BIS consulted further on the general approach[66] and on specific proposals.[67] The commitment to law reform had survived a change of government,[68] and a Draft Consumer Rights Bill was presented in June 2013 for parliamentary scrutiny. In the meantime, the CRD had to be implemented by 13 December 2013, and, rather ironically, this was done using the standard route under section 2(2) of the 1972 Act (Consumer Contracts (Information, Cancellation and Additional Charges) Regulations 2013 (SI 2013/3134) (CCR)).[69] At this point, the UK Government could have stopped the reform process that had been set in motion because the obligation to implement the CRD had been fulfilled. However, the problems that had been targeted still needed to be addressed, and so the process continued. The Consumer Rights Bill was introduced into Parliament in January 2014 and completed its parliamentary journey when the Consumer Rights Act (CRA) 2015 received Royal Assent on 26 May 2015.[70] The Act consolidated, and simplified, important aspects of consumer law, although much more could have been done to take full advantage of the CRA 2015.[71] Its main improvements were the consolidation of the law relating to the supply of goods and services, which had previously been spread across three separate Acts of Parliament,[72] as well as the introduction of a new, single regime for unfair terms in consumer contracts. In addition, the UK led the way in introducing a conformity requirement and associated remedies in respect of digital content, and also further enhanced the rules on the enforcement of consumer law.[73] However, the consolidation it achieved was partial, and, rather

---

[66] Department for Business, Innovation and Skills, *Consumer Empowerment Strategy; Better Choices: Better Deals. Consumers Powering Growth* (London, 2011).

[67] Department for Business, Innovation and Skills, *Enhancing Consumer Confidence by Clarifying Consumer Law – Consultation on the Supply of Goods, Services and Digital Content* (London, 2012).

[68] The Labour Government lost its majority in the General Election on 6 May 2010, resulting in a 'hung Parliament'. Eventually, a coalition of the Conservatives and Liberal Democrats assumed office on 12 May 2010. It was not the first time an incoming Conservative Government would pick up consumer law proposals developed under a Labour Government: cf Ramsay (n 7) 270.

[69] Consumer Contracts (Information, Cancellation and Additional Charges) Regulations 2013 (SI 2013/3134). Art 19 CRD had already been implemented early through the Consumer Rights (Payment Surcharges) Regulations 2012 (SI 2012/3110).

[70] This was at the very end of the 2010–15 Parliament, just before the General Election on 30 March 2015.

[71] Generally, J Devenney, 'The legacy of the Cameron-Clegg coalition programme of reform of the law on the supply of goods, digital content and services to consumers' (2018) *Journal of Business Law* 485; Ch Twigg-Flesner, 'Consolidation rather than Codification – or just Complication? The UK's Consumer Rights Act 2015' (2019) *Zeitschrift für Europäisches Privatecht* 170.

[72] The Sale of Goods Act 1979 in respect of contracts of sale, the Supply of Goods (Implied Terms) Act 1973 for hire-purchase contracts, and the Supply of Goods and Services Act 1982 for contracts of hire, barter and the supply of services. All three Acts continue in force in respect of non-consumer contracts.

[73] See P Cartwright, 'Redress compliance and choice: enhanced consumer measures and the retreat from punishment in the Consumer Rights Act 2015' (2016) 75 *Cambridge Law Journal* 271.

ironically, the provisions implementing the CRD have remained in separate secondary legislation instead of being absorbed into the CRA 2015. The 2013 Regulations could have been treated as stop-gap until the 2015 statute had been enacted to comply with EU law obligations. Some provisions were, indeed, moved into the CRA 2015,[74] but the bulk of the 2013 Regulations remained in place.

VI. Unpacking the Transformation after Stages 1 and 2

The preceding two sections have provided a narrative account of the legislative developments that, in two stages, effected a significant transformation of consumer law. It is now time to take a closer look at the elements of this transformation.

The first element is the shift from legislative intervention in response to discrete consumer protection issues to legislation with broad reach and general clauses. This particular shift was most pronounced during the first stage of transformation, when the implementation of the UCPD in the Consumer Protection from Unfair Trading Regulations 2008[75] resulted in the replacement of multiple discrete measures with the much broader prohibition of unfair commercial practices. Admittedly, even with the system of the UCPD (and therefore the 2008 Regulations), there remains scope for targeted interventions, particularly through adding to the Annex of prohibited commercial practices. However, this would still maintain a coherent approach to any new prohibitions instead of resulting in piecemeal legislation on narrow issues.

But even the consolidation in the CRA 2015 has elements of a broader approach. Whilst the conformity elements (correspondence with description, satisfactory quality and fitness for particular purpose) already applied across the different types of supply transactions, their consolidation in one measure simplified what had been a confusing picture (from a consumer perspective at least). There had been much greater variation in the remedies and limitations on their availability under the pre-2015 laws, and the CRA 2015 introduced greater consistency (although some variations between the different types of supply transaction remain).

That said, these important developments do not seem to have heralded a wholesale change of attitude in the way UK consumer law evolves. Not only was the consolidation achieved by the CRA 2015 more limited than originally planned, but the prospect of legislation targeted at specific consumer issues, outside the broad framework established by the 2008 Regulations and the 2015 Act, remains. Moreover, the CRA 2015 itself contains a number of chapters on very specific issues, such as secondary ticketing, which might arguably have already been within the scope of the Consumer Protection from Unfair Trading Regulations 2008 in any case. Invariably, the legislative process provided an opportunity for Parliament to make amendments, but these were not necessarily well-aligned with the rest of the law.

Yet the shift in legislative style, the willingness to explore legislation with general clauses and a broader scope, has also triggered a more significant transformation.

---

[74] Regs 42 and 43 on delivery and passing of risk, which are now in CRA 2015, ss 28 and 29.
[75] See n 5.

The cumulative effect of the progressive introduction of legislation dealing with aspects of consumer contracts, with the CRA 2015 and the CCR 2013 as the cornerstones of this development, has resulted in legislation encroaching further onto the territory of the common law. As explained earlier, legislation dealing with aspects of consumer contracts was generally perceived as only a targeted deviation from the common law rules that otherwise applied to all types of contracts. However, as the density of consumer-specific legislation has increased and its scope extended to cover not only the process of contract formation (withdrawal rights) but also the contents of such contracts, performance and remedies, the common law has effectively been gradually displaced and pushed into a residual role. Now, its function is primarily to govern those aspects that have not (yet?) been addressed in legislation, primarily the fundamental requirements for forming a contract. This remains vital because the existence of a contract between a consumer and a trader is the trigger for much of the legislation specifically focusing on consumer contracts. But many other areas of contract law are barely relevant these days. Even the vitiating factors (misrepresentation, duress and undue influence) now overlap considerably with the provisions of the Consumer Protection from Unfair Trading Regulations 2008, particularly following the introduction of a private right of redress in 2014. If one takes a step back, it becomes clear that much of *consumer* contract law is now statutory, and the common law has a limited role to play. Effectively, consumer and non-consumer contract law have been largely separated. This separation is not just a matter of form (legislation rather than case law), but also with regard to the respective underpinning values.

Legislation on consumer contracts is driven by the distinct regulatory objective of providing a counterbalance to the weaker bargaining position of consumers vis-à-vis traders.[76] In order to achieve this, a variety of instruments have been deployed. Many of these starkly contrast with the fundamental principles of the common law of contract. Indeed, the notion of freedom of contract itself has been significantly curtailed by the extensive unfair contract terms controls now in place. The general rule that there is no duty to disclose information[77] – the *caveat emptor* principle – has been eroded by the many pre-contractual information rules, in both the 2008 Regulations and CCR 2013. Moreover, the basic idea of *pacta sunt servanda* has been circumscribed by the use of rights of withdrawal for many contract types.

There are significant differences between the values of the common law and those inherent in consumer legislation.[78] As consumer legislation expands, as does the reach of these consumer-specific values, and the clash between the common law and statutory consumer contract law becomes more pronounced. It might be arguable that this process remains somehow reconcilable,[79] although the contention here is that it is already too far advanced.

---

[76] eg Case C-92/11 *RWE Vetrieb GmbH v Verbraucherzentrale Nordrhein-Westfalen eV* ECLI:EU:C:2013:180, para 41.

[77] *Smith v Hughes* (1871) LR 6 QB 597.

[78] cf C Willett, 'Re-theorising Consumer Law' (2018) 77 *Cambridge Law Journal* 179.

[79] cf J Paterson and E Bant, 'Contract and the Challenge of Consumer Protection Legislation' in TT Arvind and J Steele (eds), *Contract Law and the Legislature* (Hart Publishing, 2020) 79.

Indeed, Brownsword has argued that 'the regulation of consumer transactions has nothing to do with contract law'.[80] This bold statement reflects the fact that much of the common law of contract has little relevance to consumer contracts (transactions) today. In a similar vein, Beale has pointed out that '[t]o put it simply, English contract law is not for everyone ... [i]t is in effect designed for big business'[81] and therefore not for consumers. Brownsword's view is based on the fundamental difference between classical contract law, as giving effect to a voluntary assumption of obligations on the one hand, and consumer 'transactions', as regulated transactions lacking precisely such voluntary assumption, on the other. Consumers do not usually negotiate the terms of their contract (although the same is true of many commercial contracts) and are generally confined to identifying the supplier(s) that can provide whatever goods or services the consumer requires. Many consumer transactions are entered into online where there is no facility for any form of negotiation, so the choice is essentially limited to deciding whether or not to proceed with a transaction on the terms offered by the trader.

Yet Brownsword argued that the law applicable to consumer transactions should not be seen 'as a discrete body of law, but an element in a regulatory repertoire'.[82] This point reflects his wider exploration of what might be understood by the regulatory environment for transactions, in which (contract) law would be but one element.[83] This would suggest that consumer contract law should not be regarded as a distinct set of rules but rather that the legislation of consumer transactions is an additional tool in the regulatory repertoire alongside the law of contract. However, this chapter argues that the role of the common law of contract in the regulation has been reduced to such an extent that it would now be appropriate to treat consumer contract law as an almost entirely discrete body of law. Retaining contract law within the regulatory repertoire for consumer contracts becomes increasingly difficult because of their different approaches and underlying values. On this view, the strongest transformation of UK consumer law has been the significant separation of consumer contracts from the common law, albeit that this transformation remains incomplete. The very question of whether a contract has been concluded remains firmly within the scope of the common law rules, and much of the consumer-specific legislation presupposes the existence of a contract. Once the common law has recognised a transaction as a 'contract', legislation takes over much of the regulatory work from the common law – but there is no compelling reason why the existence of a contract recognised by the common law has to continue as the trigger.

The consolidation of aspects of consumer law in the CRA 2015 can be criticised for not having gone far enough;[84] indeed, there are still several separate legislative instruments that regulate aspects of consumer contracts. So, whilst it is possible to point to a clear transformational turn in the regulation of consumer contracts, that turn is

---

[80] R Brownsword, 'Regulating Transactions: Good Faith and Fair Dealing' in G Howells and R Schulze (eds), *Modernising and Harmonising Consumer Contract Law* (Sellier, 2009) 87, 88.

[81] H Beale, 'The Impact of the Decisions of the European Courts on English Contract Law: The Limits of Voluntary Harmonization' (2010) 18 *European Review of Private Law* 501, 526.

[82] Brownsword (n 80) 98.

[83] ibid 93–95.

[84] eg Ch Twigg-Flesner and R Canavan, *Atiyah and Adams' Sale of Goods*, 14th edn (Pearson, 2019) 470–71.

incomplete: the common law remains relevant, and the consolidation achieved by the CRA 2015 is partial.

The consolidation efforts of the second transformation phase and the development of a distinctive consumer contract law are connected, although not as intertwined as they could have been. During the preparatory phase leading up to the development of what became the Consumer Rights Bill, there were calls for both more extensive consolidation and, possibly, some form of codification or at least a 'restatement' of both the common law rules that continue to be directly relevant and of all the legislation.[85] The idea of a full codification might seem counter-intuitive to anyone familiar with the common law; yet the particular nature of consumer law would make codification more attainable than any attempt to codify the common law of contract would.[86] There have been repeated calls for the codification of English *commercial* law,[87] and many of the reasons given in this context (eg, improved coherence, corrections to the common law or gap-filling) translate to the field of consumer law.

This transformation towards a distinct consumer contract law remains incomplete, and so the question arises whether this process will continue or whether it will stall and possibly retreat. This chapter has argued that much of this transformation was the result of developments in EU consumer law, but following the UK's withdrawal from the EU, this driver has all but disappeared. The UK is no longer required to implement EU directives and can ignore developments in EU law. However, this is not the only option for the UK post-withdrawal; indeed, there are reasons why it might wish to continue to follow EU developments. The UK's future approach has yet to crystallise, but there are some indications of how the coming years will shape up.

VII. A Third Stage? Post-2016 Stasis, Brexit and Uncoupling of UK Law from EU Law

Since the 2015 General Election, there have been no further significant consumer law reforms, despite a number of landmark developments at the EU level. For instance, the new Consumer Sales Directive (2019/771),[88] the Digital Content/Services Directive (2019/770),[89] the New Deal Modernisation Directive (2019/2161)[90] and the

---

[85] H Beale, 'The Draft Directive on Consumer Rights and UK Consumer Law – Where now?' in G Howells and R Schulze (eds), *Modernising and Harmonising Consumer Contract Law* (Sellier, 2009) 289, 302; Ch Twigg-Flesner, 'Some thoughts on Consumer Law Reform – Consolidation, Codification, or a Restatement?' in L Gullifer and St Vogenauer (eds), *English and European Perspectives on Contract and Commercial Law – Essays in Honour of Hugh Beale* (Hart Publishing, 2014) 67.

[86] The so-called 'McGregor Code' (H McGregor, *Contract Code* (Giuffre, 1993)) had initially been sponsored by the Law Commission but the project was dropped before the Code was published.

[87] M Arden, 'Time for an English Commercial Code?' (1997) *Cambridge Law Journal* 516; R Goode, 'The Codification of Commercial Law' (1988) 14 *Monash Law Review* 135.

[88] Directive (EU) 2019/771 of the European Parliament and of the Council of 20 May 2019 on certain aspects concerning contracts for the sale of goods, amending Regulation (EU) 2017/2394 and Directive 2009/22/EC, and repealing Directive 1999/44/EC [2019] OJ L136/28.

[89] Directive (EU) 2019/770 of the European Parliament and of the Council of 20 May 2019 on certain aspects concerning contracts for the supply of digital content and digital services [2019] OJ L136/1.

[90] See n 5.

Representative Action Directive (2020/1828)[91] have all but been ignored by the UK Government. In addition to the reforms made by those directives, which would have improved consumer law in the UK, there are other aspects of domestic law meriting further reform. One issue, which was identified in the 2010 academic report but remained unaddressed, concerned improvements to the rules on the transfer of ownership in consumer cases. This question was folded into a wider project for the Law Commission on protecting consumer pre-payments. Following its report, the issue of reforming the ownership rules was singled out for further action, and the Law Commission eventually produced a draft Bill on this issue.[92]

The new relationship between the UK and the EU will have a very limited bearing on the development of UK consumer law. Since the expiration of the transition period at the end of 2020, the relationship between the UK and the EU has been governed by the Trade and Cooperation Agreement (TCA). The TCA was agreed at the end of 2020 and took effect from 1 January 2021. The Agreement was ratified by the UK through the European Union (Future Relationship) Act 2020.

The TCA runs to over 2,500 pages,[93] but the word 'consumer' appears only 57 times. Relevant provisions on consumer law in the TCA are few and far between. At a high level, point 7 of the Preamble confirms both the UK's and the EU's 'autonomy and rights to regulate within their territories in order to achieve legitimate public policy objectives such as the protection and promotion of ... consumer protection ... while striving to improve their respective high levels of protection'. This is a rather vague commitment to consumer protection, despite the aspiration to *improve* existing levels. It could be regarded as a twin commitment to maintain and improve existing levels of consumer protection, although it does not mandate that the UK and EU act in unison. It also does not mean that existing consumer law must remain untouched, because the main concern is to maintain and improve the overall level of consumer protection. Furthermore, point 12 of the Preamble states that the TCA should 'contribute to consumer welfare through policies ensuring a high level of consumer protection and economic well-being'.

There is no separate title or chapter on consumer protection in the TCA. Consumer protection is mentioned at various points in the Agreement dealing with specific policy areas. For instance, in Article 123 (Title II, chapter 1 on services and investment), paragraph 2, the TCA reaffirms the regulatory freedom of the EU and UK with regard to, inter alia, consumer protection, but there is nothing more substantial beyond this.[94] One more specific provision can be found in Title III on Digital Trade, Article 208. This relates to consumer protection in the context of electronic commerce transactions only, and largely reflects the broad provisions of the UCPD and the CRD, although there are elements, for example with regard to remedies in respect of unfair commercial

---

[91] Directive (EU) 2020/1828 of the European Parliament and of the Council of 25 November 2020 on representative actions for the protection of the collective interests of consumers and repealing Directive 2009/22/EC [2020] OJ L409/1.

[92] Law Commission, *Consumer Sales Contracts: Transfer of Ownership* (Law Com No 398, 2021).

[93] See at https://assets.publishing.service.gov.uk/government/uploads/system/uploads/attachment_data/file/982648/TS_8.2021_UK_EU_EAEC_Trade_and_Cooperation_Agreement.pdf (accessed 28 September 2021).

[94] See also TCA, Art 198 or Art 302.

practices, that seem to go further.[95] Yet, on the whole, the TCA says very little about consumer protection, and so the UK is not obliged, under the terms of the Agreement, to follow EU consumer law changes in its domestic law.

There is therefore a need for the UK to develop a fresh approach to consumer policy. It is clear from several other contributions to this volume that digitalisation, sustainability and the climate emergency, and crisis resilience also need to be part of current-day consumer policy and law.[96] As at May 2023, there is no clear sense that the UK would recast consumer policy. Were it to do so, such a policy would clearly need to set out the UK's overall approach to consumer policy and law in light of current challenges, but it must also surely say something about the UK's commitments under the TCA, limited as they are, as well as the possible future relevance of EU developments. A first opportunity for the Government to chart the future direction of UK consumer law was a Consultation Paper issued by the Department for Business, Energy and Industrial Strategy (BEIS) in July 2021.[97] The Consultation Paper made a number of specific proposals on matters such as subscription contracts, auto-renewals, introductory offers and the problem of fake reviews. Some of the proposals, for example on fake reviews, mirror what has already been done at EU level through the amendments of Annex to the UCPD by the Modernisation Directive.[98] However, the Consultation Paper did not state that these proposals resembled the EU's reforms, presenting them as arising from research by the Competition and Markets Authority.[99] There were further instances in the Consultation Paper of proposals with an EU equivalent but not identified as such. One might see in this an implicit policy decision to ignore the EU altogether wherever possible. Indeed, the Consultation Paper barely mentioned the EU at all, let alone the relevance of the TCA.[100] Yet this ought to have been the moment for a debate about a future UK consumer policy strategy, including how the UK might take account of developments in EU consumer law. With much of UK consumer law originating in EU measures, the EU's modernisation efforts to address the challenges brought about by digitalisation, as well as the growing focus on sustainability,[101] and resilience (following the Covid 19 pandemic and the cost-of-living crisis), would be a good starting point for the UK when it comes to domestic consumer law initiatives. Perhaps the absence of such a discussion is the result of the ideological position of the government of the day to ignore the EU as much as possible. This is regrettable, because it disregards one important source for informing the future development of UK consumer law. The consequence of withdrawing from the EU, and the impact of the rather vague terms of

---

[95] See S Whittaker, 'Retaining European Union Law in the United Kingdom' (2021) 137 *Law Quarterly Review* 477, 498–501.

[96] See chs 1, 3, 7 and 8 of this volume.

[97] BEIS, *Reforming Competition and Consumer Policy: Driving growth and delivering competitive markets that work for consumers* (CP 488, July 2021).

[98] The EU's Modernisation Directive (n 5) Art 3 inserted points 23b and 23c into Annex I (prohibiting the publication of reviews without checking that consumer reviews are by consumers who have bought or used the product, and prohibiting the submission of, or the commissioning of someone to submit, false consumer reviews).

[99] cf BEIS (n 97) paras 2.32 and 2.43.

[100] It is referred to one on occasion in the context of Competition Law Enforcement, ibid 79, para 1.239.

[101] cf the European Commission, 'Proposal for a Directive on empowering consumers for the green transition through better protection against unfair practices and better information' COM (2022) 143 final.

the TCA with regard to consumer protection, is that the UK has regulatory freedom in the field of consumer law, and is no longer obliged to implement EU legislation. However, there is no reason why this freedom should mean that EU developments are ignored altogether. A debate is needed how the UK will respond to developments in EU consumer law in the future.[102] Surely, it would be right for the UK at least to monitor EU developments and to consult on whether any legislative steps – particularly where these amend and update legislation previously implemented into UK law – should be followed or not, or at least whether such developments should be the starting point for UK reforms. Where EU developments are targeted at novel issues and offer a broadly useful solution, it would seem sensible to follow suit whilst retaining the option to do things differently. After all, EU measures are far from perfect, not least because of the compromises needed in order to seek agreement from both the European Parliament and Member State governments, and the straitjacket of full harmonisation. A discussion on this would be essential if this third transformative stage is maintaining the trajectory of the preceding two stages rather than falling into stasis, possibly leading to retrench-ment and a weakening of UK consumer law.

One glimmer of hope is the Government's follow-up response to the consultation,[103] where it primarily confirmed that it would take some of the proposals forward but not others. Interestingly, it also stated that 'we are now free to take a proportional view on whether to follow the lead of the EU on consumer matters, and where we want to plot our own course to balance the benefits of reforms for consumers with burdens on busi-nesses'.[104] At face value, this might sound like an acknowledgement that EU consumer law developments will not be ignored altogether; however, it is also heavily qualified, and there is no further elaboration of how EU consumer matters will be tracked in order to decide whether to follow its lead or not. The Queen's Speech delivered on 10 May 2022 promised a Draft Digital Markets, Competition and Consumer Bill, which would, inter alia, strengthen consumer rights. The Digital Markets, Competition and Consumer Bill (no longer just a draft bill) was given its first reading in the House of Commons on 25 April 2023. It covers a wide range of aspects on digital markets and competition law, but it also deals with aspects of consumer law. As expected, it includes provisions on subscription contracts, and a basis for enacting provisions on fake reviews at a later point. In addition, the provisions from the Consumer Protection from Unfair Trading Regulations 2008, as well as the Alternative Dispute Resolution for Consumer Disputes (Competent Authorities and Information) Regulations 2015 (SI 2015/542),[105] will be re-enacted, with some adjustments, by the Bill. This is an important develop-ment, because another Bill also before Parliament could have had the potential to seriously deflect any prospect for completing the transformation of UK consumer law: the Retained EU Law (Revocation and Reform) Bill, would, if enacted as intended,

---

[102] Such a debate might well be needed on a broader basis, but these comments are specifically confined to consumer law.

[103] BEIS, *Reforming Competition and Consumer Policy – Government Response to the Consultation* (CP 656, April 2022).

[104] ibid para 0.7.

[105] The Regulations implement Directive 2013/11/EU of the European Parliament and of the Council of 21 May 2013 on alternative dispute resolution for consumer disputes and amending Regulation (EC) No 2006/2004 and Directive 2009/22/EC (Directive on Consumer ADR) [2013] OJ L165/63.

have added a so-called 'sunset clause' into many UK law measures originating in EU law, causing them to expire automatically at the end of a set time period, likely the end of 2023. Notably, this would have applied to domestic legislation originally adopted on the basis of section 2(2) of the ECA 1972, which would have included measures such as the Consumer Contracts Regulations 2013, or indeed the Consumer Protection from Unfair Trading Regulations 2008. For such legislation to continue beyond the sunset date would require a positive step of some kind, and the Digital Markets, Competition and Consumers Bill is a step in that direction.[106] The obvious danger was that other important consumer legislation not due to be re-enacted by the Bill could have lapsed through inadvertence or inertia. The Retained EU Law Act 2023 received Royal Assent on 29 June 2023. Following the change in Prime Minister from Boris Johnson to Rishi Sunak (via the short-lived stint by Liz Truss) over the autumn of 2022, there were efforts to lessen the potential impact of the Retained EU Law Act by limiting the number of measures within the scope of the sunset clause to a defined list in Schedule 1 (which does not include consumer legislation). For now, the risk of losing consumer legislation has been averted.

VIII. Conclusions

This chapter has told a particular story of the transformation of UK consumer law, and has argued that the outcome of this transformation is the crystallisation of consumer law as (mostly) within the legislative domain and therefore all but distinct from the common law.

Among the three main drivers of transformation identified in chapter 1 of this volume, the impact of EU consumer law is (ironically) primarily behind the transformation of UK consumer law. The interaction between UK and EU consumer law has resulted in a distinct legislative style for UK consumer legislation, the substance of which is heavily, albeit not exclusively, based on EU consumer law. However, whilst this transformation has progressed considerably, it remains incomplete. The disconnect between UK and EU consumer law since 2016 may be mostly to blame for this. Had the UK remained a member of the EU, the likelihood of completing this transformation would have been high and EU consumer law would have continued as the key driver behind this transformation. Post-withdrawal, the lack of a clear future direction for UK consumer law and policy has left this transformation in a state of limbo. The case for completing it is strong, but it might not be high on the political agenda, nor might be politically palatable in the post-EU context. One can but hope that as the dust settles, fresh impetus will be given to this transformation.

The transformative effect has manifested both in the substance of UK consumer law and in the way some of the key institutions have responded. In terms of substance, not only has (pre-2016) EU consumer law been absorbed into domestic law, but the

---

[106] The Consumer Contracts Regulations 2013 are not due to be re-enacted in this Bill, but provisions of the Bill would make changes to the Regulations. This would suggest that the Regulations are likely to be kept irrespective of the impact of the Retained EU Law Bill.

UK has at times gone further (eg, the wider scope given to the controls over unfair terms in part 2 of the CRA 2015). Institutionally, both government departments and Parliament did not retreat to a role of merely giving effect to EU law but utilised the opportunities for wider consumer law presented by the obligation to transpose EU law into domestic law.

The transformation of UK consumer law driven for so many years by the EU's influence remains incomplete, and its future is uncertain: EU consumer law has ceased to be the driver of transformation, but it may transpire that the path on which UK consumer law has been set will continue to be followed. The UK's incomplete transformation of consumer law may yet be completed, but it will take some time.

INDEX

Introductory Note

References such as '178–79' indicate (not necessarily continuous) discussion of a topic across a range of pages. Wherever possible in the case of topics with many references, these have either been divided into sub-topics or only the most significant discussions of the topic are listed. Because the entire work is about 'consumer law', the use of this term (and certain others which occur constantly throughout the book) as an entry point has been restricted. Information will be found under the corresponding detailed topics.

Milton Keynes UK
Ingram Content Group UK Ltd.
UKHW030112160224
437848UK00005B/185